Scribal Practices and Approaches
Reflected in the Texts
Found in the Judean Desert

Studies on the Texts of the Desert of Judah

Edited by

Florentino García Martínez

Associate Editors

Peter W. Flint
Eibert J.C. Tigchelaar

VOLUME 54

Scribal Practices and Approaches Reflected in the Texts Found in the Judean Desert

By

Emanuel Tov

BRILL

LEIDEN · BOSTON

2004

This book is printed on acid-free paper.

Acknowledgements for illustrations:
Israel Antiquities Authority for all the PAM photographs.
Israel Museum for illustrations 1, 3, 6, 7, 13, 21.
B. and K. Zuckerman and the Jerusalem West Semitic Project for illustration 18.

Library of Congress Cataloging-in-Publication Data

Tov, Emanuel.
  Scribal practices and approaches reflected in the texts found in the Judean desert / by
Emanuel Tov.
    p. cm. — (Studies on the texts of the desert of Judah, ISSN 0169-9962 ; v. 54)
  Includes bibliographical references and index.
  ISBN 90-04-14001-8 (alk. paper)
  1. Dead Sea scrolls. 2. Manuscripts—Judaea, Wilderness of. 3. Scribes, Jewish. 4.
Hebrew language—Writing. 5. Aramaic language—Writing. 6. Transmission of texts. 7.
Codicology. I. Title. II. Series.

BM487.T6 2004
296.1'55—dc22

2004051834

ISSN   0169–9962
ISBN   90 04 14001 8

PRINTED IN THE NETHERLANDS

DEDICATED TO
THE SCRIBES WHO WROTE THE SCROLLS
AND TO
THE SCHOLARS WHO PUBLISHED THEM

CONTENTS

TEXT EDITIONS

TEXTS FROM THE JUDEAN DESERT

All texts are quoted according to their primary edition, which in most cases is the one included in the *DJD* series (*DJD* I–XXXIX; 1951–2002). Exact references to the volumes in which these texts are published are listed in Tov–Pfann, *Companion Volume* and in E. Tov (ed.), *The Texts from the Judaean Desert: Indices and an Introduction to the* Discoveries in the Judaean Desert *Series* (DJD XXXIX; Oxford 2002). In addition, the following editions are used (see further n. 2 below).

1QIsaᵃ	Parry–Qimron, *Isaiah*; also: Burrows, *The Dead Sea Scrolls*
1QIsaᵇ	Sukenik, *Dead Sea Scrolls*
1QM	Yadin, *War Scroll* and: Sukenik, *Dead Sea Scrolls*
1QHᵃ	Sukenik, *Dead Sea Scrolls* (in parenthesis: column numbers according to Puech, "Quelques aspects")
1QpHab	Burrows, *The Dead Sea Scrolls*, vol. 1; also: Horgan, *Pesharim*
1QapGen	Avigad–Yadin, *Genesis Apocryphon*
1QS	Burrows, *The Dead Sea Scrolls*, vol. 2
4QEnoch	Milik, *Enoch*
11QpaleoLevᵃ	Freedman–Mathews, *Leviticus*
11QTᵃ	Yadin, *Temple Scroll*
Masada texts	*Masada VI*

OTHER TEXTS

MT	*BHS*
LXX	The individual volumes in the Göttingen Septuagint series, when extant. Otherwise the text of LXX is quoted from the edition of Rahlfs, *Septuagint.*
LXXᴹˢ⁽ˢ⁾	The individual volumes in the Göttingen Septuagint series, when extant. Otherwise the text of the manuscript(s) is quoted from the editions of the Cambridge series.
LXXᴸᵘᶜ	The Lucianic tradition of the LXX (mainly ᴍss b,o,c₂,e₂ according to the sigla used in the Cambridge Septuagint), quoted according to the Göttingen and Cambridge editions.
LXX– early papyri	For bibliographical details, see Aland, *Repertorium.*
S	The Leiden edition of the Peshitta: *The Old Testament in Syriac According to the Peshitta Version* (Leiden 1966–98).
Tᶠ	M. L. Klein, *The Fragment-Targums of the Pentateuch According to their Extant Sources*, vols. I–II (AnBib 76; Rome 1980).
Tᴶ	D. Rieder, *Pseudo-Jonathan: Targum Jonathan ben Uzziel on the Pentateuch Copied from the London MS* (Jerusalem 1974).
Tᴺ	A. Díez Macho, *Neophiti I*, vols. I–V (Madrid/Barcelona 1968–78).
Tᴼ	A. Sperber, *The Bible in Aramaic Based on Old Manuscripts and Printed Texts*, vols. I–IVa (Leiden 1959–68).

V	R. Weber, *Biblia Sacra iuxta Vulgatam versionem,* vols. 1–2 (2nd ed.; Stuttgart 1975).
Sam. Pent (SP)	A. Tal, *The Samaritan Pentateuch, Edited According to MS 6 (C) of the Shekhem Synagogue* (Texts and Studies in the Hebrew Language and Related Subjects 8; Tel Aviv 1994).
Mas. Soferim (Sof.)	M. Higger, *Mskt swprym wnlww 'lyh mdrš mskt swprym b'* (New York 1937; repr. Jerusalem 1970). A. Cohen, *The Minor Tractates of the Talmud, Massektoth Ḳeṭannoth,* 1 (London 1965).
Sifre Numbers	H. S. Horowitz, *Sifre de-Ve Rav* (Leipzig 1917).
Sifre Deutero-nomy	H. S. Horowitz and L. Finkelstein, *Sifre 'al Sefer Devarim (Deutero-nomy)* (New York 1969).

PERIODICALS, REFERENCE WORKS, AND SERIES

AASF	Annales academiae scientiarum fennicae
AB	Anchor Bible
ABD	*The Anchor Bible Dictionary*, vols. 1–6 (ed. D. N. Freedman; New York 1992)
AbrN	*Abr-Nahrain*
AHAW	Abhandlungen der Heidelberger Akademie der Wissenschaften
AHDRC	Ancient History Documentary Research Centre (Macquarie University, Sydney)
AnBib	Analecta biblica
ANRW	*Aufstieg und Niedergang der römischen Welt* (Berlin/New York)
AO	*Archiv für Orientforschung*
AOAT	Alter Orient und Altes Testament
AOS	American Oriental Series
ASOR Mon	American Schools of Oriental Research, Monograph Series
ASTI	*Annual of the Swedish Theological Institute*
ATAbh	Alttestamentliche Abhandlungen
BA	*Biblical Archaeologist*
BASOR	*Bulletin of the American Schools of Oriental Research*
BETL	Bibliotheca ephemeridum theologicarum lovaniensium
BHT	Beiträge zur historischen Theologie
Bib	*Biblica*
BibOr	Biblica et orientalia
BIOSCS	*Bulletin of the International Organization for Septuagint and Cognate Studies*
BJPES	*Bulletin of the Jewish Palestine Exploration Society*
BJRL	*Bulletin of the John Rylands University Library of Manchester*
BK	Biblischer Kommentar
BSac	*Bibliotheca sacra*
BT	*The Bible Translator*
BWANT	Beiträge zur Wissenschaft vom Alten und Neuen Testament
BZ	*Biblische Zeitschrift*
BZAW	Beihefte zur Zeitschrift für die alttestamentliche Wissenschaft
CATSS	Computer Assisted Tools for Septuagint Studies
CB	Cambridge Bible for Schools and Colleges
CBQ	*Catholic Biblical Quarterly*
CBQMS	Catholic Biblical Quarterly Monograph Series
ConB	Coniectanea biblica
CRBR	*Critical Review of Books in Religion*
DB	*Dictionnaire de la Bible*
DBSup	*Dictionnaire de la Bible, Supplément*
DSD	*Dead Sea Discoveries*
EBib	*Études bibliques*
EncBib	*Encyclopaedia biblica* (Heb.)
EncBrit	*Encyclopaedia Britannica*

EncJud	*Encyclopaedia Judaica*
ErIsr	*Eretz Israel*
EstBib	*Estudios bíblicos*
ETL	*Ephemerides theologicae lovanienses*
FRLANT	Forschungen zur Religion und Literatur des Alten und Neuen Testaments
HAR	*Hebrew Annual Review*
HAT	Handbuch zum Alten Testament
HSM	Harvard Semitic Monographs
HSS	Harvard Semitic Studies
HTR	*Harvard Theological Review*
HUCA	*Hebrew Union College Annual*
ICC	International Critical Commentary
IDBSup	*The Interpreter's Dictionary of the Bible, Supplementary Volume*
IEJ	*Israel Exploration Journal*
IOMS	The International Organization for Masoretic Studies
JANESCU	*Journal of the Ancient Near Eastern Society of Columbia University*
JAOS	*Journal of the American Oriental Society*
JBL	*Journal of Biblical Literature*
JBR	*Journal of Bible and Religion*
JCS	*Journal of Cuneiform Studies*
JDS	*Judean Desert Studies*
JJS	*Journal of Jewish Studies*
JNES	*Journal of Near Eastern Studies*
JNSL	*Journal of Northwest Semitic Languages*
JQR	*Jewish Quarterly Review*
JQRSup	Jewish Quarterly Review Supplement
JSJ	*Journal for the Study of Judaism in the Persian, Hellenistic, and Roman Period*
JSOT	*Journal for the Study of the Old Testament*
JSOTSup	Journal for the Study of the Old Testament, Supplement Series
JSP	*Journal for the Study of the Pseudepigrapha*
JSPSup	Journal for the Study of the Pseudepigrapha, Supplement Series
JSS	*Journal of Semitic Studies*
JTS	*Journal of Theological Studies*
KeH	Kurzgefasstes exegetisches Handbuch zum Alten Testament
MGWJ	*Monatschrift für Geschichte und Wissenschaft des Judentums*
MSU	Mitteilungen des Septuaginta Unternehmens
NAWG	Nachrichten der Akademie der Wissenschaften in Göttingen
NCB	New Century Bible
NKZ	*Neue kirchliche Zeitschrift*
NTOA	Novum Testamentum et Orbis Antiquus
NTSup	Supplements to Novum Testamentum
NTT	*Nederlands Theologisch Tijdschrift*
OBO	Orbis biblicus et orientalis
OCD	*Oxford Classical Dictionary*
OLA	Orientalia lovaniensia analecta

OLP	*Orientalia lovaniensia periodica*
OLZ	*Orientalische Literaturzeitung*
OTS	*Oudtestamentische Studiën*
PAAJR	*Proceedings of the American Academy of Jewish Research*
PSBA	*Proceedings of the Society of Biblical Archaeology*
PTS	Patristische Texte und Studien
QC	*The Qumran Chronicle*
RB	*Revue biblique*
REJ	*Revue des études juives*
RHR	*Revue de l'histoire des religions*
RevQ	*Revue de Qumran*
SBL	Society of Biblical Literature
SBLDS	Society of Biblical Literature Dissertation Series
SBLMasS	Society of Biblical Literature Masoretic Series
SBS	Stuttgarter Bibelstudien
SBT	Studies in Biblical and Cognate Studies
ScrHier	Scripta hierosolymitana
SCS	Septuagint and Cognate Studies
STDJ	Studies on the Texts of the Desert of Judah
TAPA	*Transactions of the American Philological Association*
ThZ	*Theologische Zeitschrift*
TLZ	*Theologische Literaturzeitung*
TRE	*Theologische Realenzyklopädie*
TRu	*Theologische Rundschau*
TSK	*Theologische Studien und Kritiken*
TU	Texte und Untersuchungen
TynBul	*Tyndale Bulletin*
UF	*Ugarit-Forschungen*
VT	*Vetus Testamentum*
VTSup	Supplements to Vetus Testamentum
WTJ	*Westminster Theological Journal*
ZAW	*Zeitschrift für die alttestamentliche Wissenschaft*
ZDMG	*Zeitschrift der deutschen morgenländischen Gesellschaft*
ZPE	*Zeitschrift für Papyrologie und Epigraphik*

REFERENCES AND SUNDRY ABBREVIATIONS

See § h below	See section/paragraph h below
See ch. *8b*	See chapter 8, section b
See ch. *5a3*	See chapter 5, section a, paragraph '3'
Illustr. 15	Illustration 15 (indicated by shadowed digits) located at the end of this monograph
Figs. 6.1–4	Figures 6.1–4 located at the end of this monograph
TABLE 5	Table 5 in this monograph
2 BCE/CE	Second *century* before the common era/of the common era
4QPs^h 1–2 16	4QPs^h, combined fragments 1–2, line 16 (smaller font)
1QS I 1	1QS col. I, line 1
AMS	Accelerated Mass Spectometry
ch.	chapter
col(s).	column(s)
cr	in APPENDIX 1: single cryptic A letters written in the margin
cross	in APPENDIX 1: crossing out of letters or words with a line
gd	in APPENDIX 1: guide dots/strokes
no-gd	in APPENDIX 1: lack of guide dots/strokes
pal-*el*	in APPENDIX 1: *ʾEl* in paleo-Hebrew characters
(pal-)Tetragr	in APPENDIX 1: paleo-Hebrew Tetragrammaton
par	in APPENDIX 1: parenthesis sign(s)
par (box)	in APPENDIX 1: box-like parenthesis signs
pl(s).	plate(s)
puncta	*Tetrapuncta*
Suk.	Sukenik
v, vv	verse(s)
< >	clarifying addition (in English translations of ancient sources)
LXX	Septuagint
PAM	Palestine Archaeological Museum (referring to photographs)
S	Peshitta
SP	Samaritan Pentateuch
T	Targum
V	Vulgate

DIACRITICAL SYMBOLS

א̊	possible letter
א̣	probable letter
א̇	cancellation dot
°	unreadable letter
א̶א̶א̶	letters crossed out
{א}	erased letter
[א]	reconstructed letter
<א>	modern editor's correction

LIST OF TABLES

Chapter 5

Chapter 6

Chapter 9

Appendix 4

PREFACE

This monograph deals with small details pertaining to scribes. These details are important in their own right for improving our understanding of these scribes and the compositions they copied. They should be added to our storehouse of knowledge relating to the biblical and nonbiblical compositions found in the Judean Desert. At the same time, the various sets of data analyzed in this book can sometimes be combined to form a larger field of information contributing to our understanding of the background of specific Qumran compositions and of the transmission of the biblical text in antiquity. The information gathered here may also be relevant to the study of the transmission of other documents from antiquity, such as ancient Greek literature. I have also looked at parallels in the ancient Near East, but undoubtedly these parallels can be expanded.

This book has been written over the course of twelve years alongside my editorial work for the *Discoveries in the Judaean Desert* series. My mind was always working at two levels; when reviewing text editions and examining photographs for this series, I also jotted down notes for myself concerning matters of special scribal interest. This interest in scribal features goes back to my student days when I wrote a seminar paper on the signs used by the Alexandrian grammarian Aristarchus (*c.* 217–145 BCE) for Prof. B. Lifschitz of the Department of Classical Studies at the Hebrew University.

It is a pleasant task to thank the main libraries used: the Mount Scopus Library and the National and University Library at the Hebrew University, the Andover Divinity Library and the Widener Library at Harvard University, the Bodleian Library and the library of the Semitic Institute in Oxford, and the Theologicum in Tübingen. The photographs used to examine the Judean Desert texts are from the valuable PAM (Palestine Archaeological Museum) series at the Israel Antiquities Authority, Jerusalem. Also used were the newer photographs produced by the Jerusalem West Semitic Project (Claremont, Calif.). All early Greek biblical papyri that could be located in the libraries of the Philologisches Seminar in Tübingen and at Macquarie University in Sydney, Australia (especially in the Ancient History Documentary Research Centre) were consulted.

This book was written over a long period, mainly during brief sabbaticals and research travels. I am grateful to all the institutions that provided hospitality and good conditions for research. In chronological order they were the Oxford Centre for Postgraduate Hebrew Studies (1994–95), Vrije Universiteit, Amsterdam (1999), Sydney University (1999), Harvard Center for Jewish Studies (2000–2001), Tübingen University (2000, 2001), Göttingen University (2002), Uppsala University (2003), and the University of Munich (2003). Thanks are expressed to the Alexander von Humboldt-Stiftung in Germany which, by presenting me with a *Forschungspreis,* enabled my work at German Universities.

Various individuals showed an interest in the topic of this monograph and remarked on my earlier papers which lay at the basis of several sections in the book. At the final stage several colleagues, all of whom are personal friends, were kind enough to read major parts of this book. I am especially indebted to R. A. Kraft from the University of Pennsylvania, an authority in matters papyrological, who saved me from many an imprecision and also made many valuable suggestions. Making good use of his recent retirement, he spent countless hours on my manuscript. I also very much appreciate the insightful remarks of M. Abegg from Trinity Western University in Langley, B.C.,

Canada and A. Lange from the University of North Carolina at Chapel Hill. At an earlier stage, I discussed various issues with J. Strugnell at Harvard.

This book contains thousands of details. Even though it deals with textual criticism, it would be unusual if this book did not leave some mistakes for the connoisseur. All I can say is that I have done my best to eliminate them.

Several previously published segments of this monograph have been integrated here in improved versions, sometimes expanded or shortened. In chronological sequence, they are:

"The Orthography and Language of the Hebrew Scrolls Found at Qumran and the Origin of These Scrolls," *Textus* 13 (1986) 31–57.

"The Textual Base of the Corrections in the Biblical Texts Found at Qumran," in *The Dead Sea Scrolls: Forty Years of Research* (ed. D. Dimant and U. Rappaport; Leiden/New York/Cologne and Jerusalem 1992) 299–314.

"The Qumran Scribal School," in *Studies in Bible and Exegesis, Vol. III, Moshe Goshen-Gottstein: in Memoriam* (ed. M. Bar-Asher et al.; Heb.; Ramat Gan 1993) 135–53.

"Glosses, Interpolations, and Other Types of Scribal Additions in the Text of the Hebrew Bible," in *Language, Theology, and the Bible: Essays in Honour of James Barr* (ed. S. E. Balentine and J. Barton; Oxford: Clarendon, 1994) 40–66. Revised version: *The Greek and Hebrew Bible—Collected Essays on the Septuagint* (VTSup 72; Leiden/ Boston/Cologne 1999) 53–74.

"Letters of the Cryptic A Script and Paleo-Hebrew Letters Used as Scribal Marks in Some Qumran Scrolls," *DSD* 2 (1995) 330–39.

"Scribal Practices Reflected in the Documents from the Judean Desert and in the Rabbinic Literature: A Comparative Study," in *Texts, Temples, and Traditions: A Tribute to Menahem Haran* (ed. M. V. Fox et al.; Winona Lake, Ind. 1996) 383–403.

"Special Layout of Poetical Units in the Texts from the Judean Desert," in *Give Ear to My Words: Psalms and Other Poetry in and around the Hebrew Bible, Essays in Honour of Professor N. A. van Uchelen* (ed. J. Dyk et al.; Amsterdam: Societas Hebraica Amstelodamensis, 1996) 115–28.

"Scribal Practices Reflected in the Paleo-Hebrew Texts from the Judean Desert," *Scripta Classica Israelica* 15 (1996) 268–73.

"Scribal Markings in the Texts from the Judean Desert," in *Current Research and Technological Developments on the Dead Sea Scrolls: Conference on the Texts from the Judean Desert, Jerusalem, 30 April 1995* (ed. D. W. Parry and S. D. Ricks; STDJ 20; Leiden/New York/Cologne 1996) 41–77.

"The Socio-Religious Background of the Paleo-Hebrew Biblical Texts Found at Qumran," in *Geschichte–Tradition–Reflexion, Festschrift für Martin Hengel zum 70. Geburtstag*, I–III (ed. H. Cancik et al.; Tübingen 1996) I.353–74.

"*Tefillin* of Different Origin from Qumran?" in *A Light for Jacob, Studies in the Bible and the Dead Sea Scrolls in Memory of Jacob Shalom Licht* (ed. Y. Hoffman and F. H. Polak; Jerusalem/Tel Aviv: Bialik Institute/Chaim Rosenberg School of Jewish Studies, 1997) 44*–54*.

"The Scribes of the Texts Found in the Judean Desert," in *The Quest for Context and Meaning, Studies in Intertextuality in Honor of James A. Sanders* (ed. C. A. Evans and S. Talmon; Leiden/New York/Cologne 1997) 131–52.

"Scribal Practices and Physical Aspects of the Dead Sea Scrolls," in *The Bible as Book: The Manuscript Tradition* (ed. J. L. Sharpe III and J. Van Kampen; London/New Castle 1998) 9–33.

"The Dimensions of the Qumran Scrolls," *DSD* 5 (1998) 69–91.

"Scribal Practices Reflected in the Texts from the Judean Desert," in *The Dead Sea Scrolls after Fifty Years: A Comprehensive Assessment* (ed. P. W. Flint and J. C. VanderKam; Leiden/Boston/Cologne 1998) 1.403–29.

"Sense Divisions in the Qumran Texts, the Masoretic Text, and Ancient Translations of the Bible," in *Interpretation of the Bible, International Symposium on the Interpretation of the Bible on the Occasion of the Publication of the New Slovanian Translation of the Bible* (ed. J. Krasovec; Ljubljana/Sheffield 1998) 121–46.

"Correction Procedures in the Texts from the Judean Desert," in *The Provo International Conference on the Dead Sea Scrolls: Technological Innovations, New Texts and Reformulated Issues* (ed. D. W. Parry and E. Ulrich; STDJ 40; Leiden/Boston/Cologne 1999) 232–63.

"Paratextual Elements in the Masoretic Manuscripts of the Bible Compared with the Qumran Evidence," in *Antikes Judentum und Frühes Christentum, Festschrift für Hartmut Stegemann zum 65. Geburtstag* (ed. B. Kolbmann et al.; BZNT 97; Berlin/New York 1999) 73–83.

"Opisthographs from the Judaean Desert," in *A Multiform Heritage: Studies on Early Judaism and Christianity in Honor of Robert A. Kraft* (ed. B. G. Wright; Atlanta, Georgia 1999) 11–18.

"The Papyrus Fragments Found in the Judean Desert, " in *Lectures et relectures de la Bible, Festschrift P.-M. Bogaert* (ed. J.-M. Auwers and A. Wénin; Leuven 1999) 247–55.

"A Qumran Origin for the Masada Non-biblical Texts?" *DSD* 7 (2000) 57–73.

"Further Evidence for the Existence of a Qumran Scribal School," in *The Dead Sea Scrolls: Fifty Years After Their Discovery: Proceedings of the Jerusalem Congress, July 20–25, 1997* (ed. L. H. Schiffman et al.; Jerusalem 2000) 199–216.

"The Background of the Sense Divisions in the Biblical Texts," in *Delimitation Criticism: A New Tool in Biblical Scholarship* (ed. M. C. A. Korpel and J. M. Oesch; Pericope 1; Assen 2001) 312–50.

"Scribal Features of Early Witnesses of Greek Scripture," in *The Old Greek Psalter, Studies in Honour of Albert Pietersma* (ed. R. J. V. Hiebert et al.; JSOTSup 332; Sheffield 2001) 125–48.

"Scribal Notations in the Texts from the Judaean Desert," in *The Texts from the Judaean Desert: Indices and an Introduction to the* Discoveries in the Judaean Desert *Series* (ed. E. Tov; DJD XXXIX; Oxford 2002, 323–49.

"The Copying of a Biblical Scroll," *Journal of Religious History* 26 (2002) 189–209.

"The Indication of Small Sense Units (Verses) in Biblical Manuscripts," in *Hamlet on a Hill. Semitic and Greek Studies Presented to Professor T. Muraoka on the Occasion of his Sixty-Fifth Birthday* (ed. M. F. J. Baasten and W. Th. van Peursen; Leuven 2003) 473–86.

"The Corpus of the Qumran Papyri," in *Climate of Creativity: Semitic Papyrology in Context, Papers from a New York University Conference Marking the Retirement of Baruch A. Levine* (ed. L. H. Schiffman; Leiden 2003) 85–103.

"The Text of the Hebrew/Aramaic and Greek Bible Used in the Ancient Synagogues," in *The Ancient Synagogue: From Its Origins until 200 C.E.—Papers Presented at an International Conference at Lund University October 14–17, 2001* (ed. B. Olsson and M. Zetterholm; ConBNT 39; Stockholm 2003) 237–59.

"The *Ketiv-Qere* Variations in Light of the Manuscript Finds in the Judean Desert," *Text, Theology and Translation, Essays in Honour of Jan de Waard* (New York: United Bible Societies, 2004) 183–91, forthcoming.

"The Writing of Biblical Texts with Special Attention to the Dead Sea Scrolls," in *Sefer Moshe: The Moshe Weinfeld Jubilee Volume* (ed. C. Cohen et al.; Winona Lake, Ind. 2004), forthcoming.

"The Special Character of the Texts Found in Qumran Cave 11," in *Things Revealed. Studies in Early Jewish and Christian Literature in Honor of Michael A. Stone* (ed. E. Chazon and D. Satran; Supplements to JSJ; Leiden 2004), forthcoming.

I am ever so grateful to Janice Karnis, who, with her fine feeling for style, form, and format, improved my manuscript wherever needed.

Special thanks are due to F. García Martinez for accepting this monograph in the valuable STDJ series, and to Royal Brill of Leiden, especially to Mr. Hans van der Meij and Mr. Pim Rietbroek for a job well done.

Jerusalem, 1 January 2004

1

INTRODUCTION

a. *Purpose and nature of the description*

The documents from the Judean Desert (often named the 'Dead Sea Scrolls') constitute the largest corpus of texts in non-lapidary scripts providing information regarding scribal habits in early Israel relating to biblical and nonbiblical texts. These practices may be compared with other texts in Hebrew and Aramaic in nonlapidary texts, both those contemporary and earlier, especially the large *corpora* of Elephantine papyri and other Aramaic texts from the fifth and fourth centuries BCE. These two groups of texts are very significant as comparative material for the present analysis; among other things, the analysis in ch. *8b* shows that the texts from the Judean Desert continue the writing tradition of the Aramaic documents from the fifth century BCE in several practices (see SUBJECT INDEX, 'parallels').

The Egyptian Aramaic corpus is significant, as it is extensive and derives from an early period, and provides various relevant parallels. However, the corpus of documents from the Judean Desert is much larger and its scribal habits were far more developed. As such, it constitutes the largest source of information on scribal habits for Hebrew and Aramaic texts from Israel prior to the early Middle Ages, from which time the first documents from the Cairo Genizah derive.

Comparison of these practices with scribal habits of Greek texts from the seventh century BCE onwards is mandatory, and is therefore often invoked in this monograph (see SUBJECT INDEX, 'parallels'). Furthermore, the analysis leads us often to the writing practices of even older cultures such as ancient Egypt, Ugarit, and Mesopotamia. Obviously, one needs to be careful with such comparisons since the texts produced in these areas were written in different languages and often on different materials. Equal care needs to be taken in the comparison with the rabbinic prescriptions, since they are later than the texts from the Judean Desert and pertain only to the writing of Scripture and sacred documents (see SUBJECT INDEX, 'rabbinic literature').

The analysis of scribal practices refers to the following aspects: the copyists and their background (ch. 2 below), writing materials (ch. 3) such as scrolls (3c–d), technical aspects of the writing of scrolls such as ruling, the length of scrolls, sheets, and columns (ch. 4). It also refers to writing practices (ch. 5), such as divisions between words, small sense units (stichs and verses), and larger sense units (sections; *5a*), the special layout of poetical units (*5b*), scribal marks (*5c*), correction procedures (5e–f), the scripts (ch. 6), special scribal characteristics reflected in certain types of texts (ch. 7), and various scribal traditions (ch. 8).

The topics covered in this monograph thus pertain to most aspects of scribal activity, and go a little further, as the production of scrolls is covered as well. Skilled scribes may have been involved in some aspects of this activity, but most probably made use of ready-made writing materials. This study pertains mainly to the *technical* aspects of scribal activity, while the differing scribal approaches are discussed only briefly, for example in ch. *2g* and as background material to the description of most aspects of scribal activity. The analysis covers only some aspects of the textual transmission of compositions (e.g. ch. *2g*), while exegetical approaches and liberties taken by scribes in changing the biblical text are not analyzed at all.

Our description of scribal practices reflected in the documents from the Judean Desert is as complete as possible with the publication of these texts almost completed. Yet, the present survey can only begin to describe the issues at stake. Each of the scribal features to be mentioned below deserves a monographic analysis, and since such coverage is not possible in the present context, treatment of several features is not exhaustive, while that of others is as complete as possible. At the same time, use is made of several helpful partial analyses and descriptions by others, although they are often based on a limited number of texts, namely those known at the time of publication.[1]

The description pertains to several technical aspects of the copying of the texts that are important in their own right, but also have implications for wider areas, such as the provenance and background of the Qumran scrolls, the relation between individual manuscripts of the same composition, the composition and content of the individual texts, and their textual transmission. In due course, when all the relevant data on the scribal practices has been recorded, it may be possible to draw conclusions on such general issues as scribal practices and schools (ch. *8a*) and the background of many of the scrolls found in the Judean Desert. In the meantime, we have to content ourselves with partial conclusions.

For example, the large size of the writing block may be a criterion for the authoritative status of a scroll, possibly in a certain center or period, and not for all scrolls, since small scrolls were equally authoritative (ch. *4e*). Further, on the basis of a study of the intercolumnar margins (ch. *4g*) and the lack of stitching preceding the first column of 4QS^d (4Q258), it appears that the margin before the first column of that scroll is large enough to support the view that this composition (starting with the text which runs parallel to 1QS V 1-21) constituted the beginning of that manuscript, as several scholars believe. According to some scholars, the understanding of the nature of 4QDeut[n]

---

[1] Especially helpful are the following monographs listed in chronological order: C. Kuhl, "Schreibereigentümlichkeiten: Bemerkungen zur Jesaja-rolle (DSIa)," *VT* 2 (1952) 307–33 [henceforth: Kuhl, "Schreibereigentümlichkeiten"]; M. Martin, *The Scribal Character of the Dead Sea Scrolls* I–II (Bibliothèque du Muséon 44, 45; Louvain 1958 [henceforth: Martin, *Scribal Character*])—this extremely detailed study is based only on the major texts from cave 1; H. Stegemann, ΚΥΡΙΟΣ Ο ΘΕΟΣ *und* ΚΥΡΙΟΣ ΙΗΣΟΥΣ: *Aufkommen und Ausbreitung des religiösen Gebrauchs von* ΚΥΡΙΟΣ *und seine Verwendung im Neuen Testament* (Habilitationsschrift, Bonn 1969 [henceforth: Stegemann, ΚΥΡΙΟΣ]); J. P. Siegel, "Final *Mem* in Medial Position and Medial *Mem* in Final Position in 11QPs^a: Some Observations," *RevQ* 7 (1969) 125–30; idem, "The Employment of Palaeo-Hebrew Characters for the Divine Names at Qumran in the Light of Tannaitic Sources," *HUCA* 42 (1971) 159–72; idem, *The Scribes of Qumran. Studies in the Early History of Jewish Scribal Customs, with Special Reference to the Qumran Biblical Scrolls and to the Tannaitic Traditions of Massekheth Soferim*, unpubl. Ph.D. diss., Brandeis University 1971 (University Microfilms, 1972 [henceforth: Siegel, *Scribes of Qumran*]); J. M. Oesch, *Petucha und Setuma, Untersuchungen zu einer überlieferten Gliederung im hebräischen Text des Alten Testament* (OBO 27; Freiburg/Göttingen 1979 [henceforth: Oesch, *Petucha und Setuma*]); idem, "Textgliederung im Alten Testament und in den Qumranhandschriften," *Henoch* 5 (1983) 289–321 [henceforth: Oesch, "Textgliederung"]; various contributions in *Mikra, Compendia Rerum Iudaicarum ad Novum Testamentum*, Section Two, I (ed. M. J. Mulder; Assen–Maastricht/Philadelphia 1988) [henceforth: Mulder, *Mikra*]; A. Steudel, "Assembling and Reconstructing Manuscripts," in Flint–VanderKam, *Fifty Years*, 516–34 [henceforth: Steudel, "Assembling"]; A. D. Crown, "Studies in Samaritan Scribal Practices and Manuscript History, I–V" (1983–87; see bibliography); A. Lemaire, "Writing and Writing Materials," *ABD* 6 (New York 1992) 999–1008; J. Ashton, *The Persistence, Diffusion and Interchangeability of Scribal Habits in the Ancient Near East before the Codex*, unpubl. Ph.D. diss., University of Sydney, 1999 [henceforth: Ashton, *Scribal Habits*]; M. C. A. Korpel and J. M. Oesch, *Delimitation Criticism: A New Tool in Biblical Scholarship* (Pericope I; Assen 2000) [henceforth: Korpel–Oesch, *Delimitation Criticism*]; http://ccat.sas.upenn.edu/rs/rak/jewishpap.html = Kraft, *Jewishpap* (an analysis and images of early Jewish papyri); E. J. C. Tigchelaar, "In Search of the Scribe of 1QS," in Paul, *Emanuel*, 439–52 [henceforth: Tigchelaar, "The Scribe of 1QS"]; P. Alexander, "Literacy among Jews in Second Temple Palestine: Reflections on the Evidence from Qumran," *Hamlet on a Hill. Semitic and Greek Studies Presented to Professor T. Muraoka on the Occasion of his Sixty-Fifth Birthday* (ed. M. F. J. Baasten and W. Th. van Peursen; Leuven 2003) 3–24 [henceforth: Alexander, "Literacy"].

(see illustr. 15) depends to a great extent on the explanation of the following features: the spacing in the middle of the lines in col. IV, on the empty line I 5, on the ruled, uninscribed lines at the bottom of that column, and on the unusual sequence of the text contained in its two surviving sheets (sheet 1 contains Deut 8:5-10, while sheet 2 contains the earlier Deut 5:1–6:1). All these features can be compared with similar phenomena in other texts.

Likewise, the only segment in the texts from the Judean Desert which was subdivided into small sections is Isa 61:10–62:9 in 1QIsaᵃ. In that pericope, small spaces are indicated after each stich (2–5 words) in the running text, but the special meaning of this feature in this particular pericope, probably considered one unit by the scribe, still needs to be analyzed (ch. *5a3*).

Regarding other details, we note that the great majority of the marginal notations in the Qumran scrolls are in the nature of correcting additions and not variant readings (ch. *5f*), that certain small words and particles were often joined to other words (5a1), and that some Qumran writings included markings in the Cryptic A script (5c3). Study of scribal practices is instructive regarding the approaches of scribes to certain types of texts (ch. 7) and about the exegetical aspects of the work of the scribes (*2h*). One of the characteristics of the exegetical dimensions of scribal activity pertains to the marking of sense units within the text (*5a*), while another pertains to scribal signs; more substantial exegetical activity is visible in various forms of scribal intervention in the text itself (*2h*).

b. *Sources*

The analysis pertains to all the texts from the Judean Desert, non-documentary (literary) as well as documentary, with special emphasis on literary texts (in APPENDIX 6 it is suggested that the Masada nonbiblical texts probably derived from Qumran, which if true would confirm our main source of information for this monograph as being the Qumran corpus). The texts discussed were found at the following sites, listed from north to south: Wadi Daliyeh (strictly speaking, beyond the Judean Desert, but published in *DJD*), Ketef Jericho, Qumran (Khirbet Qumran and the Qumran caves), Khirbet Mird, Wadi Murabbaʿat, Wadi Sdeir (= Naḥal David), Naḥal Ḥever (also named 'Seiyal' in the publications), Naḥal Mishmar, Naḥal Ṣeʾelim, and Masada.

The texts found at these locations are quoted here according to their official names and inventory numbers as recorded in the latest lists, especially in *DJD* XXXIX (*The Texts from the Judaean Desert: Indices and an Introduction to the* Discoveries in the Judaean Desert *Series*; ed. E. Tov, Oxford 2002). The texts were examined mainly in photographs, positives as well as the microfiche edition (Tov–Pfann, *Companion Volume*) and sometimes in the originals. They are quoted from the critical editions, mainly *DJD*, but also additional editions relating to the long texts from cave 1,[2] some texts from cave 4,[3] and two texts from cave 11.[4]

---

[2] 1QIsaᵃ   Parry–Qimron, *Isaiah*; Burrows, *The Dead Sea Scrolls*, vol. 1.

1QIsaᵇ   Sukenik, *Dead Sea Scrolls*, together with sections of this manuscript which were published as no. 8 in *DJD* I (Oxford 1955).

1QpHab   Burrows, *The Dead Sea Scrolls*, vol. 1; also: Horgan, *Pesharim*.

1Q19bis (Noah)   J. C. Trever, "Completion of the Publication," *RevQ* 5 (1964–66) 323–44.

1QapGen ar   Avigad–Yadin, *Genesis Apocryphon*.

1QapGen ar I, III–VIII, X, XI, XIII–XVII: M. Morgenstern, E. Qimron, D. Sivan, *AbrN* 33 (1995) 30–54.

1QapGen ar II, IX, XVIII–XXII: Avigad–Yadin, *Genesis Apocryphon*.

1QapGen ar XII   J. Greenfield and E. Qimron, "The Genesis Apocryphon Col. XII," AbrNSup 3 (1992) 70–77.

1QS   Burrows, *The Dead Sea Scrolls*, vol. 2.

Some scribal practices detected in the texts from the Judean Desert were developed *ad hoc*, but more frequently they followed earlier writing traditions in the same language or script or other languages used in the area. For this purpose, other scribal traditions are quoted below for comparison, although direct influence can be established only in some instances. Much older documents are quoted in order to provide background material on individual scribal practices, such as the size and ruling of columns, without assuming direct influence, for example, in the case of documents written in ancient Egypt, Ugarit, and Mesopotamia. Medieval texts, such as manuscripts of MT and SP are also quoted, since these texts meticulously preserved ancient traditions.

The corpora of texts found in the Judean Desert are of a different nature, but their internal differences are less relevant for the present analysis that focuses on scribal practices visible in individual documents. For this analysis, whether or not the Qumranites were Essenes is usually immaterial[5] (in contrast to the analysis of scribal practices in ch. *8a*, where this hypothesis is relevant). Most of the collections are conceived of as deposited by persons who either lived on site for an extended period (Qumran) or a brief time (most other localities). The Qumran text depositories in caves 1, 4, and 11, containing a very large quantity of scrolls (see the lists in *DJD* XXXIX), were primarily meant as secret repositories for the scrolls of the Qumran community.

For most aspects discussed below, it is probably immaterial whether or not the Qumran corpus as a whole or the texts from cave 4 alone should be considered a library, a term used often in the scholarly literature since the influential study by F. M. Cross, Jr., *The Ancient Library of Qumran*, which has dominated scholarship since its first edition (Garden City, New York 1958) and is consulted here in its 3rd edition (Sheffield 1995). Several studies have been written on the basis of the assumption that the Qumran collection, especially that of cave 4, represents a library; e.g. K. G. Pedley, "The Library at Qumran," *RevQ* 2 (1959) 21–41, who went as far as contemplating whether or not there ever existed an inventory of the 'Qumran library' such as that in several ancient libraries. Likewise, the director of the University library in Bonn, V. Burr, devoted a study to the Qumran corpus based on his experience as a librarian: "Marginalien zur Bibliothek von Qumran," *Libri* 15 (1965) 340–52. However, neither the contents of the Qumran corpus nor any external features of the caves or a community building can be adduced as supporting evidence for the assumption that cave 4 housed a library. Several Qumran caves were used as depositories for all the written material owned by the Qumran community, which may have been stored previously in several locations in the Qumran compound itself.[6] Among other things, it is unlikely that *tefillin* and *mezuzot*, scribal exercises, personal notes such as 4QList of False Prophets ar (4Q339) and 4QList of Netinim (4Q340), an inner-Qumran community document

---

	1QM I–XIX	Sukenik, *Dead Sea Scrolls*.
	1QH[a]	Sukenik, *Dead Sea Scrolls* (in parenthesis: column numbers according to Puech, "Quelques aspects").
3	4Q202, 204–206, 210–212. See Milik, *Enoch*.	
4	11QpaleoLev[a]	Freedman–Mathews, *Leviticus*; É. Puech, "Notes en marge de 11QPaléolévitique, le fragment L, des fragments inédits et une jarre de la grotte 11," *RB* 96 (1989) 161–89; E. J. C. Tigchelaar, "Some More Small 11Q1 Fragments," *RevQ* 70 (1998) 325–30.
	11QT[a]	Y. Yadin, *The Temple Scroll*, vols. 1–3 (Jerusalem 1977; Hebrew); *The Temple Scroll*, vols. 1–3 (Jerusalem 1983).
5	Cave 7 contains no sectarian texts at all, while caves 1–6 contain both sectarian and non-sectarian texts. The contents of caves 8–10 are too meager for analysis. It appears that cave 11 contains almost only sectarian texts and texts that were copied by sectarian scribes. See my study "The Special Character of the Texts Found in Qumran Cave 11," *Things Revealed. Studies in Early Jewish and Christian Literature in Honor of Michael A. Stone* (ed. E. Chazon and D. Satran; Supplements to JSJ; Leiden 2004), forthcoming.	
6	For an account as to how these scrolls *may* have reached the caves, see Stegemann, *Library of Qumran*, 67–79.	

such as 4QRebukes Reported by the Overseer (4Q477), and Greek texts, would have been kept in a library of the Qumran community (see APPENDIX 4). It should also be noted that some caves (3, 5, 7, 8, 9, 10) served as temporary dwellings for individuals who left behind their utensils as well as some written material.

The documents studied are fragmentary, and therefore not all the data can be studied satisfactorily. The best-preserved nonbiblical scrolls are 11QT^a (11Q19) and several of the texts from cave 1 (1QM, 1QS, 1QH^a, 1QpHab, 1QapGen ar). As for the biblical scrolls, 1QIsa^a is the only one that has been preserved almost in its entirety containing 54 columns in 17 sheets. Substantial remains of 1QIsa^b, 4QpaleoExod^m, 11QpaleoLev^a, 4QNum^b, 4QSam^a (1–2 Samuel), 4QIsa^c, 4QJer^a, MurXII, 11QPs^a, and 11QtgJob were preserved, while the extant remains of all other scrolls are fragmentary, sometimes very fragmentary. Often a tiny inscribed piece is the only evidence for a biblical scroll identified by its content, and/or script (e.g. in the case of 4QIsa$^{h–r}$).

The Qumran corpus includes a few small groups of texts of a technical nature, namely *tefillin* and *mezuzot*, calendrical texts, and texts written in one of the Cryptic scripts (for all these, see ch. 7). To some extent, each of these groups reflects internally similar scribal habits, but the discrepancies appearing within each group resemble those between other texts in the Qumran corpus.

c. *Background of the documents*

A description of the scribal practices reflected in the documents from the Judean Desert is more encompassing than the name of the geographic area implies. It appears that many, if not most, of the literary texts found in the Judean Desert had been copied elsewhere in Israel. Therefore, the contents and scribal practices reflected in them represent not only the persons who passed through, lived, and wrote in the Judean Desert, but to an even greater extent the culture and scribes of Palestine as a whole.[7] At the present stage of research, the wider scope of the literary documents of the Judean Desert corpora is a mere assumption. However, it may be supported by research into either the content of the texts or their physical components, that is the material (leather and papyrus), the sinews used for sewing the sheets of leather, and the ink.

Some of the letters found in the Judean Desert (Wadi Murabbaʿat and Naḥal Ḥever) mention localities in Judea, and were written either in the area or brought there, but for the Qumran texts, the largest segment of the corpora from the Judean Desert, we have no sound data with regard to the geographic origin of texts written outside Qumran.

Furthermore, with the exception of the dated documents from Murabbaʿat and Naḥal Ḥever, the *dates* of the documents also remain hypothetical, although paleography and AMS (Accelerated Mass Spectometry; carbon-14) analysis provide an ever-increasing probability regarding their dating.[8] The latter procedure, however, has so far only been applied to a very small number of texts (Bonani et al., "Radio-carbon Dating"; for criticisms, see Doudna, "Dating"; idem, *4Q Pesher Nahum*, 675–82; B. Thiering, "The Date and the Order of Scrolls, 40 BCE to 70 CE," in Schiffman, *Jerusalem Congress*, 191–8). The paleographical dates applied to the documents range from the fourth century BCE to the first century CE for the Jericho documents, from 250 BCE to 70 CE for the Qumran texts,[9] from 150 BCE to 70 CE for the Masada texts, and

---

[7] Thus also Wise, *Thunder in Gemini*, 103–57, especially 137: "Thus the most satisfactory explanation for the scribal phenomena of the DSS is to regard them as the product of the wider Hebrew and Aramaic book culture."

[8] See a summary analysis of the procedures involved in VanderKam–Flint, *Meaning DSS*, 20–33.

[9] Some carbon-14 dates fall outside this range. See the evidence discussed by VanderKam–Flint (previous note).

from 75 BCE to 135 CE for the texts from Wadi Murabbaʿat, Naḥal Ḥever, and Naḥal
Ṣeʾelim. However, at least one much older document has been found in the Judean
Desert: the two layers of the palimpsest papyrus Mur 17 (A: papLetter, B: papList of
Personal Names) were dated by J. T. Milik (*DJD* II, 93–100 and pl. XXVIII) to the
eighth century BCE and by F. M. Cross to the second half of the seventh century BCE.[10]

These documents reflect a variety of scribal systems. The languages involved are
primarily Hebrew, secondly Aramaic, and then Greek and Latin, as well as combinations
of these languages, namely Hebrew–Aramaic and Greek–Aramaic in documentary texts.
The scripts involved are the square and paleo-Hebrew scripts for Hebrew documents,
the square script for Aramaic documents, the Greek, Latin, and Nabatean scripts for
texts written in these languages, and three different Cryptic scripts (A, B, and C), which
include paleo-Hebrew and Greek letters, used in a number of sectarian Hebrew
documents.[11] The Copper Scroll (3Q15), written in the square script, contains clusters
of several Greek letters (Lefkovits, *Copper Scroll*, 498–504). The analysis below focuses
on the Qumran documents, written in different places in Israel, but it also treats
documents found at other sites in the Judean Desert. The scribal practices used in the
Nabatean-Aramaic, Greek, and Latin documents from Masada, Naḥal Ḥever, and
Murabbaʿat are covered less fully in this monograph.

At the scribal-practice level, very little distinction was made between the writing and
production of biblical (sacred) and nonbiblical (nonsacred) texts (ch. *7a*), and therefore a
combined discussion of the two types of texts is justified in this monograph. Throughout,
the term 'biblical' refers to the canonical books of Hebrew/Aramaic Scripture. Even
though this usage is anachronistic for the Judean Desert texts, it is made for the sake of
convenience. Special attention is given to noncanonical authoritative writings (Jubilees,
Ben Sira, Enoch, as well as Qumran sectarian writings) if perchance their scribal features
reveal traits in common with the canonical biblical writings. This seems to be the case
with scrolls of very large dimensions (see ch. *4e*). When relevant, the nonbiblical
4QReworked Pentateuch is listed with the biblical texts (e.g. ch. 4, TABLE 10).

Since the documents were written in different periods and localities, they reflect a
variety of scribal practices. For the present purpose, however, these different groups of
documents are described as one large, somewhat artificial, corpus, whose common
practices are described in the main section of this monograph. At the same time, the
analysis in ch. 7 focuses on a few specific groups: (a) biblical texts; (b) texts written in
the paleo-Hebrew script; (c) *tefillin* and *mezuzot*; (d) texts written on papyrus; (e) texts
written in Greek; and (f) *pesharim*.

---

[10] F. M. Cross, "Epigraphic Notes on Hebrew Documents of the Eighth-Sixth Centuries B.C. II. The Murabbaʿat
Papyrus and the Letter Found near Yabneh-Yam," *BASOR* 165 (1962) 34–42.

[11] For an initial analysis of the Cryptic A script (4QHoroscope [4Q186], 4Q249, 4Q298, 4Q317 as well as the more
fragmentary texts 4Q250, 4QMish E [4Q324c], and 4Q313 [unclassified frgs.]), see Pfann, "4Q298" and idem,
"249a–z and 250a–j: Introduction," *DJD* XXXVI, 515–46.

2

SCRIBES

a. *Identity, nature and status*[12]

Copyists, scribes, and soferim

When studying the scribal practices reflected in the texts from the Judean Desert, attention must be given first to the scribes and their background, even though their identities remain anonymous and little is known about them.[13] This interest leads us to examine various issues relating to these scribes, namely, their identity, adherence to tradition, place in society, systems of copying, etc. According to our modern concepts and terminology, this investigation relates to copyists of texts, but when using the term 'copyist,' we probably think more of the writing conditions in the Middle Ages than in antiquity. Although the three terms 'copyist,' 'scribe,' and its Hebrew equivalent, *sofer*, are more or less equivalent, they denote persons who were involved in similar, yet different and sometimes very different activities. All three types of persons were involved in scribal activity, but the nature of that activity differed in each instance.

The term 'copyist' stresses the technical nature of the scribe's work and is based on the assumption that the essence of scribal activity is to transmit as precisely as possible the content of the copyist's text. The assumption underlying the description is based on the realia of the scribes of the Middle Ages who often worked in so-called *scriptoria*. It is uncertain whether scribes of this type existed in antiquity; if so, in the area covered by this study, they would have been employed mainly within the group of the tradents of MT (ch. *8a3*).

In antiquity, the majority of persons involved in the transmission of the biblical and other texts took more liberties than copyists of later periods. As described in § g in

---

[12] For the general background, see H. H. Schaeder, *Esra der Schreiber* (BHT 5; Tübingen 1930) especially 39–59 ("Schreiber und Schriftgelehrter"); A. F. Rainey, "The Scribe at Ugarit: His Position and Influence," *Proceedings of the Israel Academy of Sciences and Humanities* III (Jerusalem 1969) 126–47; E. Lipinski, "Scribes d'Ugarit et de Jérusalem," in *Festschrift J. H. Hospers: Scripta Signa Vocis. Studies about Scripts, Scriptures, Scribes and Languages in the Near East* (ed. H. L. J. Vanstiphout; Groningen 1986) 143–54; H. te Velde, "Scribes and Literacy in Ancient Egypt," ibid., 253–64; A. J. Saldarini, *Pharisees Scribes and Sadducees in Palestinian Society* (Delaware 1988) 241–76 ("The Social Roles of Scribes in Jewish Society"); idem, "Scribes," *ABD* 5 (New York 1992) 1011–16; D. E. Orton, *The Understanding Scribe: Matthew and the Apocalyptic Ideal* (JSNTSup 25; Sheffield 1989); M. Bar-Ilan, "Writing in Ancient Israel and Early Judaism, Part Two: Scribes and Books in the Late Second Commonwealth and Rabbinic Period," in Mulder, *Mikra*, 21–38; idem, "idem, *Swprym wsprym bymy byt sny wbtqwpt hmsnh whtlmwd* (4th ed.; Bar Ilan University, Ramat Gan 1994); D. W. Jamieson-Drake, *Scribes and Schools in Monarchic Judah: A Socio-Archaeological Approach* (Sheffield 1991); Wenke, "Ancient Egypt"; L. E. Pearce, "Statements of Purpose. Why the Scribes Wrote," in *Festschrift W. W. Hallo—The Tablet and the Scroll* (ed. M. E. Cohen; Bethesda, Md. 1993) 185–93; A. Millard, "The Knowledge of Writing in Iron Age Palestine," *Tyndale Bulletin* 46 (1995) 207–17; P. R. Davies, *Scribes and Schools, The Canonization of the Hebrew Scriptures* (Louisville 1998); R. F. Person, Jr., "The Ancient Israelite Scribe as Performer," *JBL* 117 (1998) 601–9; I. M. Young, "Israelite Literacy: Interpreting the Evidence," *VT* 48 (1998) 239–53, 408–22; Schams, *Jewish Scribes*; J. Schaper, "Hebrew and Its Study in the Persian Period," in Horbury, *Hebrew Study*, 13–26; Millard, *Reading and Writing*, 154–84; *Writings and Speech in Israelite and Ancient Near Eastern Prophecy* (ed. E. Ben Zvi and M. H. Floyd; SBL Symposium Series 10; Atlanta, Ga. 2000); Pulikottil, *Transmission*, 32–8; C. Heszer, *Jewish Literacy in Roman Palestine* (Tübingen 2001); Alexander, "Literacy."

[13] By way of exception, the names of two of the scribes of the archive of Babatha are known: Theënas, son of Simeon, who wrote four documents, and Germanos, son of Judah, who wrote eight documents. By the same token, the following two scribes of letters in the archive of Salome Komaïse daughter of Levi are known: Onainos son of Saadallos and Reisha, each of whom wrote one document. See Schams, *Jewish Scribes*, 209–13.

greater detail, many scribes actually took an active role in the shaping of the final form of the text, and therefore the general term 'scribe' is more appropriate for them than 'copyist,' since it covers additional aspects of scribal activity and could easily include creative elements. At the same time, viewed from another angle, the use of the term 'scribe' may create confusion, especially when used in the plural. For the scribes known from rabbinic texts, *soferim*, were scribes of a special type who had a very specific role in the production and perpetuation of the biblical text as well as of other religious documents. Moreover, the *soferim*, especially as known from rabbinic sources and the synoptic gospels (γραμματεῖς), had a special place in society and they appear in the New Testament as a unified group. Since only some of the texts found in the Judean Desert were produced locally, with probably most having been imported from elsewhere, it is very likely that some *tefillin* and biblical texts from the Judean Desert were written by these *soferim* or their precursors. For this reason, *soferim* must be included in our analysis.

Scribes and soferim *in ancient Israel*

Due to its complicated technical nature, the scribal occupation must be considered a profession, rather than an occasional activity.[14] Unnamed as well as identified scribes are mentioned several times in Scripture. Qiryat Sefer, literally 'the city of the book' (*i.a.*, Josh 15:15; the site where an archive was kept?), the earlier name of Debir, may have been the site where many such scribes lived. The explanation of that name as an archive is supported by the LXX translation πόλις (τῶν) γραμμάτων, e.g. in Josh 15:15. On the other hand, the transliteration of the LXX in Judg 1:11 Καριασσωφαρ (MSS Bdfsz; other MSS similarly) reflects an understanding of the name as 'the city of the *sofer*.' It is not impossible that the phrase used in 1 Chr 2:55, 'the families of *soferim* who lived at Jabez,' refers to family-like guilds of scribes. As for individual scribes, 1 Chr 24:6 mentions Shemayah son of Netanel, הסופר מן הלוי, 'the scribe, who was of the Levites.' The best-known scribe in Scripture is Ezra, named סופר מהיר (a skilled scribe) in Ezra 7:6 and, similar to Shemayah, deriving from a priestly family (his direct lineage from Aaron is specified in Ezra 7:1-4). From ancient times onwards, the connection between the function of the scribe and various aspects of public administration is evident. Likewise, in the period to which the texts from the Judean Desert pertain, some scribes functioned as secretaries of towns.

In this period, most scribes occupied themselves with all aspects of scribal activity, that is, the copying of existing documents and literary compositions, as well as the writing of documentary texts (such as found at Wadi Murabbaʿat, Naḥal Ḥever, and elsewhere) and the creative composition of new literary works. In addition, some scribes were involved in various aspects of administrative activity. At the same time, the use of סופר in 11QPsᵃ XXVII 2 is rather unique. In that scroll, David is named a סופר, in the sense of an 'author who is also a scribe' rather than merely a 'scribe,' since the text focuses on his wisdom and compositions and not on his copying of texts. On the other hand, Schams, *Jewish Scribes*, 124–5, 241–3 also considers this use of סופר to mean a 'scribe,' basing herself on the similar characterizing of Moses as a scribe in Targum Neophyti in Num 21:18 and Deut 33:21.

---

[14] For an analysis of professional and occasional writing mentioned in Scripture and Rabbinic literature, see especially Schams, *Jewish Scribes*; see further M. Fishbane, *Biblical Interpretation in Ancient Israel* (Oxford 1985); A. Demsky, "Writing in Ancient Israel and Early Judaism, Part One: The Biblical Period," in Mulder, *Mikra*, 2–20; idem, "Scribe," in *EncJud* 14 (Jerusalem 1971) 1041–3; A. J. Saldarini, "Scribes," *ABD* 5 (New York 1992) 1011–16 provides the most extensive collection of references and analysis.

From rabbinic sources we obtain a narrow picture, since they mainly record the activity of scribes in the religious realm, namely, the copying of religious documents: Scripture, especially Torah scrolls, *tefillin* and marriage and divorce documents (for the latter, cf. *m. Giṭṭ.* 7.2 [גט] אמרו לסופר וכתב). These activities did not involve any creative writing which lay beyond the interest of rabbinic sources. Therefore one should not equate the scribes (*soferim*) mentioned in the Talmud with all the scribes who were active in the period covered by rabbinic literature.

Because of the manifold activities of the scribes, their intimate knowledge of the compositions they copied and the topics on which they wrote, scribes were usually educated and well-read persons. As a result, the connection between scribes and wisdom is stressed in several sources, especially in religious literature. A scribe for whom that connection is described in great detail is that depicted by Ben Sira in the early second century BCE in Sir 38:24–39:11.[15] His wisdom is described in 38:24 as σοφία γραμματέως (= חכמת סופר). That scribe, one might say, the ideal scribe, is portrayed as an expert in all areas of knowledge and administration. His wisdom is divinely inspired, since his main source of knowledge is the 'law of the Most High' which helps him 'to seek out the wisdom of the ancients' and to 'be concerned with prophecies' and 'proverbs' (39:1). That scribe is not only a scholar and teacher, but also an administrator of the highest level (39:4; 38:32–33). Ben Sira himself was probably a scribe of this type, and Enoch is similarly described (Enoch 92:1). At the same time, one should carefully distinguish between the realm of the scribe, which usually is that of a technician, and that of the wise men or intellectuals, as pointed out by Bickerman.[16]

Beyond this general background information on scribes in Palestine, for the period under discussion very few specific details are known regarding the scribes who actually copied the documents found in the Judean Desert, especially since in most cases we do not know where these documents were written. For one thing, the scribes did not record their names in the texts themselves since the custom of writing colophons had not yet been formed in Hebrew and Aramaic manuscripts (an isolated word אמר, possibly indicating the remains of such a colophon, was written three lines below the end of the book of Isaiah in the last column of 1QIsaᵃ). The only information available regarding the many aspects of scribal activity is therefore culled from the texts themselves.[17] These texts allow us to form an opinion on the collaboration between scribes (ch. *2d*), their approach to the texts from which they copied, including the degree of precision (*2g*), the materials used (*3a*), writing practices (ch. *5*), including the use of scribal marks and correction procedures (*5c*), handwriting, mistakes and correction procedures (5c2), scripts (ch. *6*), characteristic scribal features (ch. *7*), the influence of Aramaic (*7f*), etc. On the possible existence of scribal practices and schools, see ch. *8a*.

We know of no official qualifications required of or restrictions placed on persons who wrote literary texts, including religious texts. The only restriction known is that recorded in rabbinic texts stating that religious writings (Torah scrolls, *tefillin*, and *mezuzot*) written by a heretic (מין), pagan (עובד כוכבים), informer (מוסר [against his fellow-Jews to the Roman authorities]), Samaritan (כותי), converted Jew (ישראל מומר), slave, woman,

---

[15] Cf. H. Stadelman, *Ben Sira als Schriftgelehrter* (WUNT 2, 6; Tübingen 1980) especially 216–46; D. J. Harrington, "The Wisdom of the Scribe according to Ben Sira," in *Ideal Figures in Ancient Judaism: Profiles and Paradigms* (ed. G. W. E. Nickelsburg and J. J. Collins; SCS 12; Chico, Calif. 1980) 181–8.

[16] E. Bickerman, *The Jews in the Greek Age* (Cambridge, Mass. 1988) 161–76 ("Scribes and Sages"), especially 163.

[17] More extensive information on scribes and book production is available for a later period covered by the documents from the Cairo Genizah. See especially N. Allony, "Books and Their Manufacture in Mediaeval Palestine," *Shalem* 4 (1984) 1–25 (Heb.). Among other things, Allony writes about the learning of writing skills, about scripts, writing materials, the number of lines in manuscripts, the places of writing, the time needed for writing a Torah scroll (one year), and the prices paid. See also Beit-Arié, *Hebrew Codicology*.

and minor were not acceptable (thus the various opinions in *b. Gitt.* 45b; cf. *b. Menaḥ.* 42b and *Sof.* 1.14). Further, the writing of the divine names in paleo-Hebrew characters in several texts from the Judean Desert, in one instance with different ink, may imply the involvement of special scribes (ch. *5d*) employed especially for sacred purposes.

If many of the Qumran scrolls were written *in situ*, it may be considered unusual that no reference is made in the texts to any scribal activity by the members of that community, other than for administrative purposes. However, an argument of this type referring to the mentioning of writing activities may be less relevant to the present description, and besides, it may be contradicted by the lack of reference in the scrolls to other activities of the Qumranites, such as specific types of manual work, including the date industry discovered by archeologists. The Qumran texts mention the administrative recording of the members of the Qumran community, sometimes by the *mebaqqer* (e.g. 1QS V 23, VI 22; 4QSᵈ [4Q258] 3 ii 3; CD XIII 12), who also wrote down in his private notebook (CD IX 18) the sins committed. 4QRebukes Reported by the Overseer (4Q477) probably contains such personal remarks regarding certain individuals in the Qumran community. In the Qumran texts, the *sofer* is mentioned a few times, such as in 11QPsᵃ XXVII 2 noted above. Further, in the Aramaic Enoch fragments, Enoch is named ספר פרשא, 'a distinguished scribe' (4QEnGiantsᵇ ar [4Q530] 2 ii + 8 14), and in the Ethiopic and Greek fragments of Enoch he is likewise named a 'scribe' (1 Enoch 12:4; 15:1). Finally, the fragmentary 4QNarrative B (4Q461) 2 includes the a word *soferim* without any context. Writing was also an essential part of the warfare depicted in the War Scroll which records in detail the inscriptions inscribed on the standards and engraved on the trumpets and shields to be used in the future war. Writing is mentioned also in 4QJubᵃ (4Q216) IV 6 (Jub 1:27) and 4QMMTᵉ (4Q394) 14–17 ii 2. On the other hand, Scham, *Jewish Scribes*, 259–60 considers the lack of references in the Qumran texts to the copying of scrolls to be intentional since, in her opinion, 'the members of the community did not assign any special importance to the actual writing and copying of scrolls' (p. 260).

Information on scribes and scribal activity in rabbinic sources

Scattered information regarding the writing of Scripture, *tefillin*, *mezuzot*, marriage and divorce documents, as well as about scribes and *soferim*, is found in various places in rabbinic literature. These writing instructions pertaining to very specific details are also combined in a few small compilations dealing with various topics, such as *b. Menaḥ.* 29b–32b, *b. Meg.* passim, *b. Shabb.* 103a–105a, and *b. B. Bat.* 13b–14b. The best organized group of such instructions is probably found in *y. Meg.* 1.71b–72a and in the later compilation *Massekhet Soferim* (see Higger, *Mskt Swprym*). Although this tractate is post-Talmudic (ninth century), it is based on *Massekhet Sefer Torah* (see Higger, *Minor Treatises*) as well as on several early sources, and thus preserves traditions which go back to the Talmudic period. The rabbinic instructions pertain to such matters as writing materials, the preparation of leather, scribes, measurements of sheets, columns, lines, and margins, correction of errors, the writing of divine names, and the storage and reading of scrolls.[18] The data contained in these sources is very valuable as background information for the corpora from the Judean Desert, as long as it is remembered that the rabbinic descriptions and prescriptions refer mainly to the writing of religious texts, at a later period, and in circles which partially overlapped with the circles that produced the

---

[18] The relevant discussions in rabbinic literature were analyzed at length in several valuable monographs: Blau, *Studien*, Krauss, *Talmudische Archäologie*, III.131–98, and Lieberman, *Hellenism*.

texts found in the Judean Desert. Thus, probably only the proto-Masoretic texts from various sites in the Judean Desert (except for Qumran) and some *tefillin* and *mezuzot* (ch. *7c*) derived from the same circles as those described in the Talmudic literature.

Scribes are known from rabbinic sources by various appellations, especially with reference to the writing of Scripture and religious documents:

• סופר, *sofer*. This term, the most frequently used appellation, refers to a person who was basically independent, but who sometimes worked exclusively for a certain Rabbi (e.g. Joḥanan the *sofer* [secretary, more or less] of Rabban Gamliel mentioned in *y. Sanh.* 1.18d and *b. Sanh.* 11b). This term also referred to a scribe working on city affairs (סופר מתא, the scribe of the city [*b. B. Bat.* 21a]).

• כותב (copyist), with the connotation 'calligrapher.'

• לבלר, a loan-word from Greek (λιβελλάριος or λιβλάριος [P.Yad. 15, 17, 18 and 20–22]), itself a loan-word from Latin (*librarius*), e.g. *m. Pe'ah* 2.6; *m. Soṭ.* 9.15; *b. Soṭ.* 20a. According to Blau, *Studien*, 183 the *sofer* and *libellarius* refer to two distinct groups, while according to Krauss, *Talmudische Archäologie*, III.169, the two words denote the same persons, although the loan-word may have carried a somewhat more formal connotation.

• נוטרין = *notarii* (notary).

It stands to reason that literary texts were copied from written *Vorlagen*. There is no reason to assume that scribes who knew their biblical texts well wrote them from memory. Indeed, according to the prescriptions in rabbinic literature, scribes were forbidden to copy Scripture without a text in front of them, even if they knew the whole Bible by heart, in order to secure precision in copying (*b. Meg.* 18b and parallels).

The prescriptions of the rabbis regarding the copying of sacred texts were not followed by all scribes in Israel. In light of this situation, it is not impossible that some scribes wrote from dictation[19] or that mass production (dictating to several scribes at the same time) took place, but there is no evidence supporting this view. Phonetic interchange of letters as evidenced in many Qumran texts does not necessarily prove that they were written by dictation, since any scribe copying from a document could make such mistakes or change the orthography, consciously or not.[20]

The writing of Scripture and *tefillin* was considered so important by the rabbis that scribes of such texts were not supposed to interrupt their work, even for the duty of prayer (*y. Shabb.* 1.3b; *y. Ber.* 1.3b; *y. Bikk.* 3.65c), let alone for less significant occasions or tasks.

In rabbinic literature, there are some references to scribes who produced multiple copies. Thus, according to *b. B. Bat.* 14a, R. Huna wrote seventy Torah scrolls and R. Ami 400 scrolls.

Soferim

The term *soferim* is used in rabbinic literature with two different meanings, the equivalent being the use of either a lower or an upper case letter. The *soferim* were individual copyists, as portrayed in the post-Talmudic tractate bearing that name, but they were also known as a more-or-less organized group of scribes, *Soferim* (henceforth referred to with a lower case letter as *soferim*) with authoritative legal capacities. Scholars are not in agreement on the nature of these *soferim* who carried out legal functions, but only some aspects of this discussion pertain to the present analysis. According to some

---

[19] Thus with regard to 1QIsaᵃ: M. Burrows, "Orthography, Morphology, and Syntax of the St. Mark's Manuscript," *JBL* 68 (1949) 195–211, especially 196; H. M. Orlinsky, "Studies in the St. Mark's Isaiah Manuscript," *JBL* 69 (1950) 149–66, especially 165.

[20] Thus already E. Hammershaimb, reacting to the theories regarding 1QIsaᵃ: "On the Method Applied in the Copying of Manuscripts in Qumran," *VT* 9 (1959) 415–18.

scholars, these *soferim* functioned as pivotal personages in a certain era and at a later stage also constituted a political power.[21]

In rabbinic writings, from the Mishna onwards, these *soferim* are mentioned as authoritative scribes and teachers to whom a number of teachings and *halakhot* are ascribed. As a result, the *soferim* are considered to have been influential figures in Israel from the time of Ezra to the second century CE, both in rabbinic tradition and in modern scholarship. Among other things, they are mentioned in the New Testament as γραμματεῖς and as ἱερογραμματεῖς (Josephus, *Bell. Jud.* VI 5 3 § 292). The latter term shows that these persons dealt mainly with religious writings, and were possibly of priestly descent (indeed, most of the *soferim* whose genealogy is known were priests). The term *soferim* involves the combined activities of the copying of texts, especially of Scripture and other sacred documents, and an intimate knowledge of the documents, and it is often difficult to decide which nuance of the term is intended. This difficulty probably reflects the fact that most *soferim* were skilled in both aspects of their profession.

Various aspects of the *soferim* mentioned in rabbinic literature are of direct relevance to the present analysis. The *soferim* were actively involved in the transmission of Hebrew/Aramaic Scripture, and while, on the one hand, they had a purely passive task in connection with the preservation of the biblical text, they also occasionally made corrections in the text, if the rabbinic traditions are to be trusted. Even if these traditions are incorrect, the very assumption that the *soferim* made corrections (*tiqqunê soferim*) was thus tolerated. It should be admitted that the presumed precision of the *soferim* in the transmission of Scripture cannot be tallied easily with the changes inserted by them, and this argument possibly militates against the assumption of the trustworthiness of the tradition regarding the changes in the text introduced by the *soferim*. The most pervasive group of such changes made by the *soferim* is that of the so-called *tiqqunê soferim*, the 'corrections of the scribes' (*Sifre* Numbers § 84 [on Num 10:35]; *Mek.* Exod 15:7 [*Shirata* § 6]; *Midrash Tanhuma* to Exod 15:7 [*Beshallah* § 16]). These corrections involve a number of changes in MT (eight to eighteen according to different traditions), mainly of euphemistic nature. Other changes ascribed to the *soferim* are the five 'omissions of the *soferim*,' referring to the omission of the *waw* conjunctive. *b. Ned.* 37b also mentions the *miqra' soferim*, 'the reading of the *soferim*,' relating to three words in Scripture. The examples are not explained, but they may indicate the beginning of vocalization, instituted by the *soferim*.[22] For all these groups of changes, see Tov, *TCHB*, 64–7.

---

21 Note the remarks of Ginsburg in his description of the development of the Masorah: "The labors of the Massorites may be regarded as a later development and continuation of the earlier work which was carried on by the Sopherim (סופרים, γραμματεῖς) = the doctors and authorized interpreters of the Law soon after the return of the Jews from the Babylonish captivity (comp. Ezra VII 6; Neh. VIII 1 &c.)." See Ginsburg, *Introduction*, ch. XI; the quote is from p. 287. At a different level, E. Schürer, *A History of the Jewish People in the Time of Jesus Christ*, Second Division (New York 1891) I.306–79 devoted 75 pages to what he called "Scribism." The view that there was a "period of the *soferim*" was suggested for the first time in scholarship by R. Nachman Krochmal in his book *Moreh Nevukhe Ha-zeman* (edited posthumously by L. Zunz and published in 1851; quoted by Urbach, below). Along with others, E. E. Urbach wrote against this view in "The Derasha as a Basis of the Halakha and the Problem of the Soferim," *Tarbiz* 27 (1958) 166–82. For a summary on the views expressed on the *soferim* and for much bibliography, see H. Mantel, "The *Soferim*," in *Society and Religion in the Second Temple Period* (ed. M. Aviyona; Jerusalem/Tel Aviv 1983) 35–8 (Heb.). Among these studies, see especially M. H. Segal, "The Promulgation of the Authoritative Text of the Hebrew Bible," *JBL* 72 (1953) 35–48; M. Greenberg, "The Stabilization of the Text of the Hebrew Bible, Reviewed in the Light of the Biblical Materials from the Judean Desert," *JAOS* 76 (1956) 157–67.

22 At a different level, rabbinic literature mentions several *halakhot*, especially on matters of purity, which are described as דברי סופרים, *dibrê soferim*. These *dibrê soferim* refer only to *halakhot* determined by previous generations, which had already become authoritative by the time of the Mishna (e.g. *m. Kel.* 13.7; *m. Toh.* 4.7; *m. Tebul Yom* 4.6).

b. *Learning scribal skills*

Little is known regarding the training of scribes in the biblical and post-biblical period. The aforementioned family-like guilds of scribes (1 Chr 2:55) possibly underwent some training. Much information about the learning process of scribes comes from other cultures in the ancient Near East,[23] but it is unclear to what extent parallels may be drawn to ancient Israelite practices.

The texts from the Judean Desert reflect different levels of scribal skills, visible not only in the degree of carefulness of the handwriting and its transmission, but also in the knowledge of and adherence to certain scribal conventions. Many, if not most, non-documentary (literary) texts were written by skilled hands, while letters were often written in irregular scripts. The difference between the various levels of scribal skill is reflected *inter alia* in the well-written contracts and letters from Naḥal Ḥever and Wadi Murabbaʿat as opposed to the irregularly written signatures of the writers of the letters and the witnesses. See *i.a.* Mur papLetter from Beit-Mashiko to Yeshua b. Galgula (Mur 42; *DJD* II, 155; illustr. 4 below); XḤev/SeDeed of Sale A ar (XḤev/Se 7, *DJD* XXVII, 19); XḤev/Se papDeed of Sale C ar (XḤev/Se 8a; *DJD* XXVII, 34), 5/6Ḥev 44–46 (*JDS* 3, pls. 76–78).

Some scribes, certainly some of the scribes of the Qumran texts, copied sacred as well as nonsacred texts (ch. *7a*), while others, especially in temple circles, must have specialized in the writing of sacred texts. In rabbinic circles, those specializing in sacred texts copied biblical texts as well as *tefillin*, *mezuzot*, and marriage and divorce documents. Some scribes worked independently, while others were engaged by specific Rabbis, a city, or the Sanhedrin.

Scribes were introduced to their trade during the course of a training period, in which they learned writing and the various scribal procedures connected with it (such as writing at a fixed distance below ruled lines and in columns; the division of a composition into sense units; the treatment of the divine names; the correction of mistakes, etc.). Furthermore, scribes had to master various technical skills relating to the material on which they wrote, the use of writing implements, and the preparation of ink.

The abecedaries (lists of letters of the alphabet) found at Qumran,[24] Murabbaʿat,[25] Masada (Mas ostraca 606, 608), and at many additional sites dating to the First and Second Temple periods[26] probably witness to such a learning process for scribes. Lemaire claimed that such abecedaries deriving from the First Temple period point to the existence of scribal schools, and this argument may be valid also with regard to Qumran.[27]

---

[23] See B. Landsberger, "Scribal Concepts of Education," in *City Invincible* (ed. C. H. Kraeling and R. M. Adams; Chicago 1960) 94–102; W. Hallo, "New Viewpoints on Cuneiform Literature," *IEJ* 12 (1962) 13–26, especially 22–5; R. J. Williams, "Scribal Training in Ancient Egypt," *JAOS* 92 (1972) 214–21; H. Blanck, *Das Buch in der Antike* (Munich 1992) 32–9.

[24] See ostracon 3 from Khirbet Qumran published by E. Eshel in *DJD* XXXVI, pl. XXXIV (see illustr. 5 below). Two additional abecedaries, described as deriving from the first century BCE, are displayed in the Israel Museum as "Qumran ?".

[25] Some of the abecedaries from Murabbaʿat were written on leather (Mur 10B, 11), while others were inscribed on sherds (Mur 73, 78–80), all published in *DJD* II.

[26] See É. Puech, "Abécédaire et liste alphabétique de noms hébreux du début des IIe S. A.D.," *RB* 87 (1980) 118–26; A. Lemaire, *Les écoles et la formation de la Bible dans l'ancien Israël* (OBO 39; Fribourg/Göttingen 1981) 7–32; M. Haran, "On the Diffusion of Literacy and Schools in Ancient Israel," *VTSup* 40 (1988) 81–95; J. Renz and W. Röllig, *Handbuch der althebräischen Epigraphik* 2 (Darmstadt 1995) 22–5; W. Nebe, "Alphabets," *Encyclopedia DSS*, 1.18–20.

[27] Lemaire, *Les écoles*, 7–33. Additional, internal, evidence for the existence of a Qumran scribal practice, referring to scribal traits common to certain documents, is analyzed in ch. *7a*.

A learning process is probably also reflected in such scribal exercises as 4QExercitium Calami A (4Q234), 4QExercitium Calami B (4Q360), and 4QExercitium Calami C (4Q341; see illustr. 2) containing lists of names and other words. Lists of names also served as scribal exercises in other environments; see, e.g. H. Harrauer and P. J. Sijpesteijn, *Neue Texte aus dem antiken Unterricht* (Vienna 1985) items 43–60, 65. 4QExercitium Calami C (4Q341) contains a sequence of proper names starting with the letter *mem*, a series of words, mainly proper names, in alphabetical order, from *bet* to *zayin*, as well as sequences of single letters. A similar mixture of exercises is found in the abecedary published by É. Puech (see n. 26). 4QExercitium Calami A (4Q234) contains words written in three different directions. Similar exercises were listed by Y. Yadin and J. Naveh, *Masada I*, 61–4 ('Writing Exercises and Scribbles'). Similar to 4Q341, Ostraca 608 and 609 from Masada are fragments of two series of personal names in alphabetical order.

Certain Qumran documents, containing very inelegant and irregular handwriting, were considered by some scholars to have been written by apprentice scribes. Thus Milik, *Enoch*, 141 considered 4QEnᵃ ar (4Q201) to be a 'school-exercise copied by a young scribe from the master's dictation.' P. W. Skehan considered 4QPsˣ (4Q98g) to be a 'practice page written from memory.'[28] J. T. Milik suggested that 4QDanSuz? ar (4Q551) was written by an apprentice scribe,[29] and É. Puech surmised that 4QBirth of Noahᵃ ar (4Q534) was written by a child (*DJD* XXXI, 135). Likewise, many of the calendrical texts and *Mishmarot* ('Temple Watches') are poorly inscribed with irregular layout of the lines: 4QMish B (4Q323), 4QMish C (4Q324), 4QMish G (4Q329), 4QMish H (4Q329a), 4QMish I (4Q330), 4QCal Doc D (4Q394 1–2). Furthermore, we cautiously suggest that 4QGenᶠ, containing Gen 48:1–11 and written with an unskilled hand, also constitutes a scribal exercise, as this fragment was written on a single sheet with no signs of sewing on the right side. For a similar type of exercise from Mesopotamia, see W. Hallo, who noted that 'two small tablets from Assur . . . show extracts, not just from two or three compositions, but from ten different series, all of them identifiable as standard books in the neo-Assyrian stream of tradition.'[30] Since the compositions are excerpted in exactly the same order on both clay tablets, Hallo considered them exercise tablets. A large group of such exercises was collected by Harrauer–Sijpesteijn (see previous paragraph).

Other aspects of the training process of members of the Qumran community, especially the study of the Law and of the community rites were described by Lemaire based on descriptions by Josephus and those in the Qumran Rules.[31]

c. *Production of scrolls in the Judean Desert?*

It is difficult to ascertain how many of the texts found in the Judean Desert were actually produced locally, that is, both their physical preparation and the copying of the manuscripts. Undoubtedly, at least some leather scrolls were produced locally (as will be provable in the future by way of DNA analysis of scrolls in comparison with that of local

---

[28] P. W. Skehan, "Gleanings from Psalm Texts from Qumran," in *Mélanges bibliques et orientaux en l'honneur de M. Henri Cazelles* (ed. A. Caquot and M. Delcor; AOAT 212; Neukirchen/Vluyn 1981) 439–52 (439).

[29] J. T. Milik, "Daniel et Susanne à Qumrân?" in *De la Tôrah au Messie* (ed. M. Carrez et al.; Paris 1981) 337–59, especially 355.

[30] W. Hallo, "New Viewpoints," (see n. 23) 13–26; the quote is from pp. 22–3.

[31] Lemaire, "L'enseignement." For parallels in rabbinic literature, see S. Safrai, "Education and the Study of the Torah," in Safrai, *Jewish People*, 945–70; P. Alexander, "How Did the Rabbis Learn Hebrew?" in Horbury, *Hebrew Study*, 71–89, especially 78–82.

animals, both contemporary and present), but at present this assumption cannot be ascertained. Also unascertainable is whether papyrus was produced locally (at Ein Feshkha or elsewhere in Israel) or imported from Egypt (ch. *3a*).

Qumran. If it could be proven that locus 30 at Qumran served as a room in which documents were written (a scriptorium in medieval terminology),[32] the assumption of a Qumran scribal practice would receive welcome support. However, the reliability of the evidence pointing to the existence of such a scriptorium is questionable.[33] Beyond the archeological relevance of locus 30, most scholars now believe, on the basis of the content of the scrolls, that some, many, or all of the documents found at Qumran were copied locally (ch. *8a2*).

Stegemann, *Library of Qumran*, 51–5 holds a maximalistic view on this issue, assuming that most Qumran scrolls were written on site. According to him, one of the main occupations of the Qumran community was the preparation of leather for the writing and mass-production of written texts. These were, in turn, offered for sale to the outside world, and Stegemann pinpoints the places in the community buildings in which the scrolls were manufactured, stored, and offered for sale.[34] Golb, *The DSS* (see n. 33), expressing a minimalist view, claimed that none of the Qumran documents was written locally (Golb did not express himself with regard to other documents from the Judean Desert).

As a result, there is no consensus regarding where the Qumran documents were copied, but since most scholars believe that at least some, if not many, of the texts from Qumran were written locally (see ch. *8a* with regard to the possibility of a Qumran

---

[32] Thus the majority of scholars ever since the description by R. de Vaux, *L'archéologie et les manuscrits de la Mer Morte* (London 1961) 23–6; idem, *Archaeology and the Dead Sea Scrolls* (The Schweich Lectures of the British Academy; London 1973) 29–33; see also R. Reich, "A Note on the Function of Room 30 (the 'Scriptorium') at Khirbet Qumran," *JJS* 46 (1995) 157–60.

[33] In this room, archeologists found a 5-meter-long table, two small 'tables,' a few small benches fixed to the wall, and several inkwells (cf. photograph PAM 42.865), which were situated either in this room or on a second floor which according to some scholars was situated above this room. See Humbert–Chambon, *Fouilles de Khirbet Qumrân*, pls. 114–20; M. Broshi, "Scriptorium," *Encyclopedia DSS*, 2.831. However, doubts were raised with regard to this identification. Several scholars have claimed that the 'table' was too low (70 cm) for writing, or that in that period scribes did not use tables for writing, see B. M. Metzger, "The Furniture of the Scriptorium at Qumran," *RevQ* 1 (1958) 509–15; K. G. Pedley, "The Library at Qumran," *RevQ* 2 (1959) 21–41, especially 35; K. W. Clark, "The Posture of the Ancient Scribe," *BA* 26 (1963) 63–72; Ashton, *Scribal Habits*, 57. This claim was also made by A. Lemaire, "L'enseignement," especially 199, who suggested that this room was the center of the intellectual life of the community members. The most detailed arguments against the assumption of a scriptorium were provided by N. Golb. According to Golb, the fact that no remnants of scrolls were found in the room also proves that it was not used for the purpose of writing: "The Problem of Origin and Identification of the Dead Sea Scrolls," *Proc. Am. Phil. Soc.* 124 (1980) 1–24; "Who Hid the Dead Sea Scrolls?" *BA* 48 (1985) 68–82; "Khirbet Qumran and the Manuscripts of the Judaean Wilderness: Observations on the Logic of Their Investigation," *JNES* 49 (1990) 103–14; idem, *The DSS*. Before Golb, similar doubts, though in less detail, had been voiced by H. E. del Medico, *L'énigme des manuscrits de la Mer Morte* (Paris 1957); K. H. Rengstorf, *Hirbet Qumrân und die Bibliothek vom Toten Meer* (Studia Delitzschiana 5; Stuttgart 1960). Golb's theory was refuted in detail by F. García Martínez and A. S. van der Woude, "A 'Groningen' Hypothesis of Qumran Origins and Early History," *RevQ* 14 (1990) 521–41, but the doubts regarding the relevance of the artifacts found at locus 30 remain. For more recent analyses, see Wise, *Thunder in Gemini*, especially 120; F. Rohrhirsch, *Wissenschaftstheorie und Qumran: die Geltungsbegrundungen von Ausssagen in der Biblischen Archäologie am Beispiel von Chirbet Qumran und En Feschcha* (NTOA 32; Freiburg/Göttingen 1996). The view of P. H. E. Donceel-Voûte, according to whom this room contained couches for reclining, has not been accepted by other scholars: "'Coenaculum': La salle à l'étage du *locus* 30 à Khirbet Qumrân sur la Mer Morte," in *Banquets d'Orient* (ed. R. Gyselen; Res Orientales 4; Bures-sur-Yvette 1992) 61–84. As a result, it is still unknown in which position the writing was executed; most probably scribes were seated either on a bench or on the ground, while holding the sheet on a board on their knees, similar to the writing position of Egyptian scribes.

[34] This theory has been rejected in a detailed analysis by F. Rohrhirsch, *Wissenschaftstheorie* (see previous note), and idem, "Die Geltungsbegründungen der Industrie-Rollen-Theorie zu Chirbet Qumran und En Feschcha auf dem methodologischen Prüfstand: Relativierung und Widerlegung," *DSD* 6 (1999) 267–81.

scribal practice), it remains correct to refer to the texts found at Qumran as the Qumran corpus, as long as the necessary reservations are kept in mind.

Masada. There is no reason to believe that any of the Masada texts were penned at Masada itself, even though the Zealots and presumably also the Essenes remained at Masada long enough to have embarked upon such activity. On the other hand, there is apparently some evidence of tanning of hides at Masada (Netzer, *Masada III*, 634–5) which could imply some scribal activity. Furthermore, some scribal exercises were mentioned in § b above. However, probably none of this evidence is relevant to our evaluation of the literary texts found at Masada which were probably not produced there.

It is probable that the only writing performed at Masada pertains to the Hebrew, Aramaic, and Greek ostraca inscribed before the destruction of the fortress, and to Latin ostraca and some Greek papyri inscribed during the Roman occupation. Other papyrus and leather texts may have been imported (for an analysis, see Cotton and Geiger, *Masada I*, 1–2).

Other sites. A similar type of reasoning applies to the texts found at the other sites in the Judean Desert. Few scholars have claimed that texts were actually written in Wadi Murabbaʿat, Naḥal Ḥever, or Wadi Sdeir.

In short, it appears that the scribes of the Judean Desert texts remain as anonymous today in identity and origin as they were two generations ago. However, while a generation ago the corpus of Qumran documents and their scribes were identified with the Qumran community, this claim is not made today, although undoubtedly a number of texts (one third of the texts found there? [ch. *8a2*]) were copied by that community. By the same token, the documents found at Masada should not be identified with the people who occupied that site. All these documents, including the letters found at Naḥal Ḥever and Wadi Murabbaʿat, reflect the work of scribes from all of Israel, possibly including some local scribes.

d. *Characteristic features of individual scribes*

Because of the lack of external data on the scribes who copied or wrote the documents found in the Judean Desert, our sole source of information regarding them is the scribal activity reflected in the documents themselves. Whether a text under discussion is a copy of an earlier document or an autograph (§ h below), the scribal practices reflected in it do provide information which is relevant to the study of these scribal practices. However, in the analysis of these practices it is often difficult to distinguish between the personal input of the scribes and elements transmitted to them. Thus the division into sense units (sections) and the specific layout of poetical units embedded in the Qumran texts probably derives from the first copies of these compositions (ch. *5a–b*), although in the transmission of these elements scribes displayed a large degree of individuality. The more closely scribes adhered to the scribal practices present in the texts from which they were copying, the less the texts reflected their own initiatives; since the *Vorlagen* of the Qumran manuscripts are unknown, it is obviously difficult to distinguish between the scribe's input and the impact of tradition. In another case, the number of lines per column was determined probably more often by scroll manufacturers than by scribes. Scribes could choose between scrolls of different sizes, and probably ordered a specific size to fit a specific composition. In the case of small-size scrolls, such as the copies of the Five Scrolls (ch. *4c*), it was probably not the individual scribe, but rather tradition, which determined that short compositions were to be written on scrolls of limited dimensions. On the other hand, some practices and approaches were very much exponents of the individuality of scribes, as outlined below.

(1) *Approach toward the content of the base text*

Scribes approached their *Vorlagen* with differing degrees of faithfulness to their *Vorlagen*; some scribes felt more freedom than others to insert, omit, and change details. This approach has been discussed at length for biblical manuscripts, and to a lesser extent for nonbiblical texts (§ g below).

(2) *Handwriting*

The size of the letters written by individual scribes differed greatly. Petite letters (sometimes less than 0.1 cm) were used in *tefillin*, while other documents were written in regular or even large characters. Note, for example, fragments on pl. XV of *DJD* III inscribed with regular-sized letters next to fragments written in a smaller handwriting (2QJub[a] [2Q19], 2QJub[b] [2Q20], and 2QapocrDavid [2Q22]). On pl. XXVI in the same volume, fragments written in regular handwriting appear next to the smaller handwriting of 6QApocr ar (6Q14) and the larger handwriting of 6QPriestly Prophecy (6Q13). Differences in spacing and sizes of letters are visible in four calendrical texts presented in pl. VII of *DJD* XXI, with letters ranging in size from petite with an interlinear space of 0.4 cm (4QMish I [4Q330]), to medium-size letters with 0.4 cm (4QMish H [4Q329a]) or 0.1–0.2 cm space between the lines (4QCal Doc D; 4Q394 1–2; illustr. 16), and medium-size letters with 0.8 cm between the lines (4QCal Doc E? [4Q337]). Different sizes of letters are also visible on pl. XXXVIII in *DJD* XVI: compare the regular-sized letters of 4QChr (0.2–0.3 cm) with the petite letters of 4QEzra (0.1–0.15 cm) and the large letters of 4QDan[e] (0.4–0.5 cm). Another way of comparing the different script sizes is to compare the differing heights of scrolls containing the same number of lines. Thus 4QGen[e], MurGen-Num, 4Q[Gen-]Exod[b] containing *c.* 50 lines measure approximately 50 cm in height, while 4QShirShabb[d] (4Q403) written with minute letters, had a height of merely 18 cm (ch. *4*, TABLE 15).

When two or more scribes wrote segments of the same manuscript, such differences are sometimes clearly visible. Thus, scribe C of 1QH[a] used much larger characters than scribe A (see the data in TABLE 1 below). Different scribal hands are probably also behind the writing of והשמר לכה (followed by writing in petite letters) in much larger characters than the following lines in 4QInstr[g] (4Q423) 5 1a. The writing on that first line, in the top margin itself, was probably added after the column had been completed.

When a scribe realized upon approaching the end of the line that the available space was insufficient for him to write a long word before the left vertical of the column, he could either leave the space uninscribed, or attempt to crowd the letters into the available space (ch. *4f*). In rare cases, one or more letters of the incomplete word were written above or beneath it.

Also in documents written in the same style, occasionally the size of letters differs unintentionally. Note, e.g. the large *kaph* in כול וכול in 1QS XI 11 and מות compared with the context in 4QRP[e] (4Q367) 3 4. The large *ʾaleph* of אלהיך in 4QDeut[g] 6–9 13 (Deut 26:4), probably written by a later hand and with thicker strokes than the other letters, may be in the nature of a correction. The size of the letters in 4QTQahat ar (4Q542) 1 is very irregular; e.g. 1 i 12 has very large letters at the end of the line. 4QJosh^a col. V 14 was written with different ink and in larger characters than the preceding lines.

Similarly large letters in the medieval text of MT, which were probably originally unintentional, have become part and parcel of the transmission of MT: e.g. Gen 30:42 ובהעטיף; Num 27:5 משפטן; Deut 29:27 וישלכם.[35] See ch. *5c9*.

On the other hand, the top part of what resembles a very large *lamed* in 4QM^a (4Q491) 11 i (4Q491c), next to lines 19–22, served a very specific purpose, which is however, unclear. It is unlikely that this letter contained the single dedicatory *lamed*, followed in the next line by the reconstructed מלך, as suggested by M. O. Wise, "מי כמוני באלים, A Study of 4Q491c, 4Q471b, 4Q427 7 and 1QH^a 25:35–26:10," *DSD* 7 (2000) 173–219 (182, 191–3) as such a practice is not paralleled elsewhere (the parallel of the *waw*s in open spaces [ch. *5c1*] is invalid, as these were written in spaces between sections, in the paleo-Hebrew script). Equally unclear is the nature of the top part of what resembles a large *lamed* in photograph PAM 44.102 (*DJD* XXXIII, pl. XLI) frg. 22. Further examples of large letters in the margins are 4QCant^b IV (frg. 3) 14 (large *mem*) and 4QVisions of Amram^d ar (4Q546) frg. 9 (large *mem*), in the latter case possibly designating מ[ו]שה (thus É. Puech, *DJD* XXXI, 346). Skehan–Ulrich recognize a large *lamed* in 4QIsa^m 4–5 5, but the evidence is unclear.

(3) *Frequency of errors*

Scribes approached their *Vorlagen* differently, as described in § g. By the same token, they also displayed differing degrees of precision. The errors extant in the texts from the Judean Desert reflect those found in any other text of that period. Some scribes erred more than others in specific types of mistakes, such as haplography. Thus scribe B of 1QIsa^a left out several relatively long sections which were added subsequently in that scroll, see TABLE 1.

As for interchanges of letters, in the period covered by the Judean Desert texts, the two graphically closest letters are *yod* and *waw*, and consequently the largest number of mistakes is made with these letters. In several scrolls, such as 11QPs^a, there is almost no distinction between these two letters; furthermore, in that scroll ligatures of *ʿayin–waw* (e.g. col. XXVIII 4 עוגב), *ʿayin–zayin* (XVI 14 ועזות), and *ʿayin–yod* (XXVIII 3 וצעיר) are not distinguishable (besides, all three combinations resemble a *sin/shin*). In other scrolls, a combination *ʿayin–pe* could be very similar.

Interchanges of graphically or phonetically similar letters are often mentioned in rabbinic literature, e.g. in *Sifre* Deuteronomy § 36 1 on Deut 6:9 (similarly *b. Shabb.* 103b):

---

[35] At the same time, other large letters in MT do convey a certain message. Large or upper case letters were indicated in most manuscripts and many editions in order to emphasize certain details. In this way, the first letter of a book (Genesis [בראשית], Proverbs, Canticles, Chronicles) or section (סוף Qoh 12:13), the middle letter in the Torah (נחון Lev 11:42), and the middle verse in the Torah (התגלח Lev 13:33) were emphasized. Cf. *b. Qidd.* 30a: 'The ancients were called *soferim* because they counted every letter in the Torah. They said that the *waw* in נחון (Lev 11:42) is the middle consonant in the Torah, דרש דרש (Lev 10:16) the middle word and התגלח (Lev 13:33) the middle verse.' Cf. F. I. Andersen and A. D. Forbes, "What *Did* the Scribes Count?" in D. N. Freedman et al., *Studies in Hebrew and Aramaic Orthography* (Winona Lake, Ind. 1992) 297–318.

The Masorah, *b. Qidd.* 66b, and *Sof.* 9.1–7 also indicated a few imperfectly written letters, such as Num 25:12 שלום, written with a 'broken *waw*,' that is, a *waw* with a horizontal gap halfway down the vertical stroke. There are countless such letters in the Qumran texts and these do not reflect any special message. Broken letters (אותיות . . . מקורעות) are also mentioned in *b. Meg.* 18b.

At least some of the special letters (for lists see Elias Levita, *Massoreth Ha-Massoreth* [Venice 1538] 230–33 in the edition of C. D. Ginsburg [London 1867]) were already written in this way in ancient texts and were mentioned in the Talmud. Thus in *b. Menah.* 29b בה'בראם ('when they <the heaven and earth> were created,' Gen 2:4) was exegetically explained as representing two words, בה, 'with the letter *he*,' and בראם, 'He created them.'

If one has written an ʿ*ayin* instead of an ʾ*aleph*, an ʾ*aleph* instead of an ʿ*ayin*, a *kaph* instead of a *bet*, a *bet* instead of a *kaph*, a *ṣade* instead of a *gimel*, a *gimel* instead of a *ṣade*, a *resh* instead of a *dalet*, a *dalet* instead of a *resh*, a *ḥeth* instead of a *he*, a *he* instead of a *ḥeth*, a *yod* instead of a *waw*, a *waw* instead of a *yod*, a *nun* instead of a *zayin*, a *zayin* instead of a *nun*, a *pe* instead of a *ṭet*, a *ṭet* instead of a *pe* . . . a *samekh* instead of a *mem*, a *mem* instead of a *samekh* . . . , such scrolls should be stored away <and are invalid>.

(4) *Correction procedures and the degree of scribal intervention*

The procedures used in correcting mistakes and the frequency of such intervention reflect to a great extent the personal preferences of scribes. See ch. *5e*.

(5) *The indication of sense units (sections)*

The analysis in ch. *5a* shows that it was often the personal taste of scribes that determined the indication or non-indication of the text division with open and closed sections, as well as the decision whether or not to indent the beginning of a new section. At the same time, it is almost impossible for us to decide which elements reflect the personal input of scribes and which reflect traditions passed on to them. That there were different scribal approaches in this regard is shown by the differences between parallel manuscripts of the same biblical book. Thus some texts, such as 4QSam^c, indicated content divisions infrequently or not at all.

(6) *Scribal signs*

The texts from the Judean Desert, especially from Qumran, contain various scribal markings, some of which recur in several texts. These markings, analyzed in detail in ch. *5c*, indicate the content division of the text as well as various types of scribal intervention, such as the correction of errors. The very use of scribal signs is somehow connected to the scribal context from which the copies derive, since they occur especially in those written according to the Qumran scribal practice, such as 1QIsa^a (illustrations 1, 6) and 1QS–1QSa–1QSb (these three compositions were written by the same scribe who also inserted some corrections in 1QIsa^a), 4QCant^b (illustr. 8a), 4Qpap pIsa^c (4Q163), and 4Q502–511. However, since many scribal signs may have been inserted by readers, they are not necessarily characteristic of the scribes.

(7) *Use of final and nonfinal letters*

Most scribes indicated final letters at the ends of words, while some scribes were less systematic in this regard. Some scribes also used final letters in the middle of the word, especially in penultimate position. See ch. *5g*.

(8) *Adherence to horizontal and vertical ruling*

Scribes usually adhered to the ruled lines under which they hung the letters, while a very few wrote on the lines or disregarded the dry rulings altogether and wrote through the lines (ch. *4f*). Virtually all scribes adhered to the right vertical ruling indicating the beginning of the column, while more precise scribes also adhered to the vertical lines at the left margin.

(9) *Special layout*

In the Judean Desert texts, a special arrangement of poetical units is known almost exclusively for biblical texts (including Ben Sira [2QSir and MasSir]) with only a few such layouts occurring in the nonbiblical poetical compositions. Thirty texts were written completely or partially in a special layout, while twenty-seven other scrolls of the same biblical books were written without a stichographic arrangement; for details, see ch. *5b*. It is difficult to ascertain whether the use or non-use of a special layout follows a pattern, and to what extent the choice was a result of the personal preference of the scribe.

By the same token, different layouts are recognized for the writing of calendrical texts (see the beginning of ch. *5b*).

(10) *Orthography*

While orthography was determined to a large extent by tradition and the guidance of scribal schools, at least within the scribal school that was active at Qumran and other places personal preferences of scribes are clearly visible when the practices of specific scrolls and scribes are compared. Thus the differences in orthography between scribes A and B of 1QIsa[a] and A and C of 1QH[a] are clearly recognizable (see TABLE 1).

(11) *Employment of number signs*

Several documentary and literary texts present numerals with the Aramaic numeral signs. In parallel copies of the same text, the individuality of the scribes (or different scribal habits?) can easily be seen. Some scribes use number signs, while others write the numbers in full. See ch. *5c9*.

(12) *Writing of the Tetragrammaton*

While most scribes of the Qumran texts presented the Tetragrammaton in the square script, twenty-eight (twenty-nine?) texts written in the Qumran scribal practice used the paleo-Hebrew script for this purpose. Differing practices were in vogue even within that scribal environment as thirty-five texts written in the Qumran scribal practice employed the square script (contrast the data in ch. 6 TABLE 1 with TABLE 2).

e. *Identification of scribal hands*

With the aid of paleographical analysis different scribal hands can be identified within the same documents, although scholars often disagree on key issues (see below on 1QIsa[a]). For example, the identification of scribal hands is also crucial in the case of three fragments ascribed to different scrolls in Tov, "The Jeremiah Scrolls from Qumran," *RevQ* 14 (1989) 189–206, and now named 4QJer[b], 4QJer[d], and 4QJer[e]. These fragments had previously been assigned to the same scroll (then named 4QJer[b]).

Several Judean Desert scrolls were written by more than one scribe. Seven of the nine examples of Hebrew scrolls written by more than one scribe which are mentioned in TABLE 1 pertain to texts written in the Qumran scribal practice, a fact which may further strengthen the idea of a Qumran scribal practice (ch. *8a*).

For long scrolls especially, it is difficult to ascertain how many were written by more than one scribe. The usual procedure was probably that each scroll, long or short, was written by a single scribe, with the involvement of more than one scribe being the exception rather than the rule. 1QIsaᵃ, a long scroll, was written by two scribes, as was 4QApocryphal Psalm and Prayer (4Q448; illustr. 11), a very small scroll. Changes of hand in the middle of the text are recognizable in several documents (TABLE 1), but the background of these changes is often not evident. In one case, each scribe wrote half of the scroll (1QIsaᵃ), while in other cases one of the scribes wrote very little (1QpHab scribe B, 1QHᵃ scribes B–C, 1QS scribe B, 11QTᵃ [11Q19] scribe A), which seems to imply that the involvement of more than one scribe was not planned from the outset. In the case of 11QTᵃ (11Q19), the first sheet may have been a repair sheet (see TABLE 1 and p. 125 below). In any event, the writing of a scroll by more than one scribe is not necessarily connected to the practice known as bisection (the writing of a composition in more than one scroll), for which see ch. *4c*.

TABLE 1: *Changes of Hands in Qumran Manuscripts*

• 1QIsaᵃ: Scribe A left three lines empty at the end of the last sheet written by him (at the end of col. XXVII). Scribe B started at the beginning of the next sheet with col. XXVIII (Isa 34:1–36:2; illustr. 6).[36] It is unlikely that the two scribes worked concurrently, since a calculation of the number of columns and sheets needed for the first scribe's assignment could not be easily made. This is also the main argument against the assumption that a single scribe copied the two sections of the scroll from different *Vorlagen*. The assumption of different scribes was accepted by several scholars, while others maintained that the two segments of that scroll were written by the same scribe.[37] However, the assumption of different scribes seems to be defensible not only at the paleographical level, but also at other levels. Scribe B inserted fewer corrections in guttural letters than scribe A (Giese, "Further Evidence"), used different scribal marks (unless some of them were inserted by later readers), and left out more sections than scribe A, which were filled in subsequently by himself or a different hand, in small letters, between the lines and in the margin: cols. XXVIII 18 (Isa 34:17b–35:2); XXX 11–12 (Isa 37:4b–7); XXXII 14 (Isa 38:21); XXXIII 7 (Isa 40:7); XXXIII 15–16 (Isa 40:14a–16; illustr. 1). Scribe B also adopted a fuller orthography than scribe A. Note, for example, the preponderance of the short form of the second person singular masculine suffix in the first part of the scroll as against the longer form (כה–) in the second part, as described in detail by M. Martin, "The Use of the Second Person Singular Suffixes in 1QIsaᵃ," *Le Muséon* 70 (1957) 127–44. Furthermore, scribe B consistently wrote כיא *plene*, but scribe A did so only in 20 percent of the instances. Scribe A consistently wrote כה defectively, while scribe B wrote כוה. These differences are also felt in morphology: Scribe A consistently used the forms הוא and היא, while scribe B used the longer הואה and היאה. Scribe A employed forms of the type *qᵉṭaltem*, while scribe B used *qᵉṭaltemah*. For further examples, see Cook, "Dichotomy" (see n. 36).

• 1QpHab: Towards the end of the composition, in the middle of col. XII 13, scribe B started to write using larger characters, limiting his activity to the end of that column and the four lines of the next column, until the end of the composition (illustr. 3). See Martin, *Scribal Hands*, I.78–81.

• 1QHᵃ: The transitions from one scribe to another in this scroll are clearly visible in col. XI in Sukenik's edition where a first scribe copied the text to the middle of line 22, a second one took over for a very short stretch of text (lines 23–26), and a third one copied lines 27–35 and at least col. XII (illustr. 7). However, the exact division between the three scribes is not clearly visible in Sukenik's edition, since the fragments and columns are arranged in the wrong order. An alternative fragment order was indicated by Martin, *Scribal Hands*, I.59–64 and perfected by Puech, "Quelques aspects." In the new arrangement, scribe A copied the text until (the new) col. XIX 22, scribe B copied lines 23–26 of that column, and scribe C penned

---

[36] For an analysis of the features of the two scribal hands of Isaiah, see M. Noth, "Eine Bemerkung zur Jesajarolle vom Toten Meer," *VT* 1 (1951) 224–6; Kuhl, "Schreibereigentümlichkeiten," especially 332–3; W. H. Brownlee, "The Literary Significance of the Bisection of Isaiah in the Ancient Scroll of Isaiah from Qumran," *Proceedings of the 25th Congress of Orientalists* (Moscow 1962–63) 431–7; K. H. Richards, "A Note on the Bisection of Isaiah," *RevQ* 5 (1965) 257–8; Giese, "Further Evidence"; J. Cook, "The Dichotomy of 1QIsaᵃ," in *Intertestamental Essays in Honour of Józef Tadeusz Milik* (ed. Z. J. Kapera; Qumranica Mogilanensia 6; Kraków 1992) I.7–24; M. Abegg, "1QIsaᵃ and 1QIsaᵇ: A Rematch," in Herbert–Tov, *The Bible as Book*, 221–8 (statistics of different orthographic systems); Pulikottil, *Transmission*, 18–20.

[37] Martin, *Scribal Character*, I.65–73; Kutscher, *Language*, 564–6; J Cook, "Orthographical Peculiarities in the Dead Sea Biblical Scrolls," *RevQ* 14 (1989) 293–305, especially 303–4.

the remainder of the column (lines 27–35) and those following. The letters at the end of col. XI (Suk. = Puech XIX) and in col. XII (Suk. = Puech XX) are larger, different, and less regular than the hand in the first part of that column. The division between the two hands is clearly visible in the spelling systems, as scribe C adopted a fuller orthography than scribe A. Scribe A wrote לא almost exclusively without *waw*, while scribe C wrote the same word almost exclusively *plene*. Scribe A preferred כי, while scribe C preferred the *plene* spelling כיא. By the same token, scribe A wrote almost exclusively the pronominal suffix of the second person masculine singular as –*k* (except for his last two columns), while scribe C used *plene* forms, e.g. מלככה, *mlkkh*, etc.

• 1QS VII 1: In the running text, או לכול דבר אשר לו was written by scribe B, followed by a five-letter word, now erased, while the cancellation dots above and below were left. In line 21 scribe B likewise wrote several words in the running text. The work of scribes A and B in 1QS VII–VIII was described in detail by Martin, *Scribal Hands*, I.43–56 and Metso, *Community Rule*, 95–105. According to Martin, I.55–56, this cooperation continued in 1QSa–1QSb.

• 4QTanḥ (4Q176): For the details regarding the distinction between the two hands, see Strugnell, "Notes," 229 and pl. II.

• 4QJubᵃ (4Q216): The change of hands between scribes A and B is clearly visible in frg. 12 which forms the dividing line between the segments written by the two scribes. This fragment consists of the last column of a sheet written by scribe A and the first column of a sheet by scribe B, stitched together by a thread. According to J. VanderKam and J. T. Milik, who published this text in *DJD* XIII, the beginning of the scroll written by scribe A represents a repair sheet, but it seems equally possible that the scroll was written by two different scribes.

• 4QCommunal Confession (4Q393): Frgs. 1–2 i–ii are composed of segments of two sheets sewn together, although they are of a different nature: the handwriting on the two sheets differs as does the number of lines (the right hand sheet has one line more than the left hand sheet). The relation between the content of the two sheets is unclear.

• 4QApocryphal Psalm and Prayer (4Q448); illustr. 11): This small document was written by scribes A (col. I) and B (cols. II and III).

• 11QTᵃ (11Q19): This scroll was written by scribes A (cols. I–V) and B (cols. VI–LXVII). Yadin, *Temple Scroll*, I.11–12 believes that sheet 1 (cols. I–V) was a repair sheet replacing the original sheet (ch. *4i*). Scribe A left excessively large spaces between the words.

• 8ḤevXIIgr: Scribe B started in the middle of Zechariah. For a description of the differences between the two hands relating to material, letters, and scribal practices, see Tov, *DJD* VIII, 13.

Whether in these cases the change of hands indicates a collaboration of some kind between scribes, possibly within the framework of a scribal school (cf. ch. *8a*), is difficult to ascertain. Sometimes (4QJubᵃ [4Q216]) the second hand may reflect a corrective passage or a repair sheet. The situation becomes even more difficult to understand when the hand of a scribe B or C is recognized not only in independently written segments, but also in the corrections of the work of a scribe A. Thus, according to Martin, *Scribal Character*, I.63, scribe C of 1QHᵃ corrected the work of scribe A, while scribe B corrected that of both scribes A and C.

When scribes recorded their own names, as in several of the documentary texts, identity can easily be established. Thus Matat son of Simeon, who wrote XḤev/Se 13, also wrote 5/6Ḥev 47b and XḤev/Se 7 (A. Yardeni, *DJD* XXVII, 65). However, this procedure reflects the exception rather than the rule, and in literary texts no names were indicated.

It is difficult to identify scribal hands by an analysis of handwriting and other scribal features, partly because of the formal character of the handwriting of many texts. However, if this uncertainty is taken into consideration, one notes that among the Qumran manuscripts very few individual scribes can be identified as having copied more than one manuscript. It stands to reason that several of the preserved manuscripts were written by the same scribe, but we are not able easily to detect such links between individual manuscripts, partly because of the fragmentary status of the evidence and partly because of the often formal character of the handwriting. For possible identifications, see TABLE 2. Further research may lead to more scribal identifications than are known today. In the meantime we are unable to perform comparative studies of scrolls written by the same scribe, such as that carried out by W. A. Johnson (*The Literary Papyrus Roll*) for the Oxyrhynchus Greek papyri from the second to fourth century CE.

TABLE 2: *Scribes of Qumran Manuscripts Writing More Than One Manuscript?*

• One individual apparently copied the nonbiblical texts 1QS, 1QSa, 1QSb, and the biblical text 4QSam[c], and his hand is also visible in several corrections in another biblical text, 1QIsa[a] (Ulrich, "4QSam[c]" and Tigchelaar, "The Scribe of 1QS"). In addition, 1QS (to the right of V 1, VII bottom margin, and IX 3) and 1QIsa[a] (VI 22 in the margin to the right of Isa 7:8) share three unusual marginal signs that were probably inserted by this scribe (ch. *5c4*), although they could also have been inserted by a reader. Indeed, AMS analysis yielded similar dates for 4QSam[c] and 1QS (Doudna, "Dating," 451), usually ascribed to 100–75 BCE.[38] 1QS, 1QSa, 1QSb, and 4QSam[c] share the same orthography and morphology (see APPENDIX 9). According to Allegro, *DJD* V, 58, this scribe, or more precisely, the one who copied 1QS, also copied 4QTest (4Q175), both of them using *Tetrapuncta* (ch. 5, TABLE 19). According to Larson–Schiffman (*DJD* XXII, 311), 4QNarrative G (4Q481b) was copied by the same scribe, while Martin, *Scribal Character*, II.710 tentatively identified the final hand of 1QS with hand B of 1QpHab. J. Strugnell ascribed 4QTQahat ar (4Q542)[39] to the same hand as 4QSam[c] and he further ascribed 4QIndividual Thanksgiving A (4Q441), 4QPersonal Prayer (4Q443),[40] and 4QEschatological Hymn (4Q457b)[41] to the same hand as 1QS. It is noteworthy that compositions that presumably were written by the same scribe were found in two different caves. For a detailed study of the idiosyncrasies of this scribe, see Tigchelaar, "The Scribe of 1QS."

• J. R. Davila, *DJD* XII, 57: 4QGen[f] and 4QGen[g] were probably written by the same scribe.

• Strugnell, "Notes," 199, 201, 204: 4QpHos[a] (4Q166), 4QpHos[b] (4Q167), and 4QpMic? (4Q168) were copied by the same hand.

• J. T. Milik, *Enoch*, 5 suggested that 4QEn[f] ar (4Q207) and 4QLevi[d] ar (4Q214) were written by the same scribe.

• Alexander–Vermes, *DJD* XXVI, 150: One scribe wrote both 4QS[e] (4Q259) and 4QOtot (4Q319), which were probably included in the same scroll; 4QOtot (4Q319) would have started a few lines after the end of 4QS[e] (4Q259) col. IV, after line 8. This assumption was also accepted in J. Ben-Dov's edition of 4QOtot, *DJD* XXI, 200. However, the evidence is unclear, and it is possible that 4Qs[e] and 4QOtot belonged to the same composition, or alternatively that 4QOtot was not included in the same scroll.

• Steudel, "Assembling," 519, n. 14: 1QH[a] and 4QD[a] (4Q266) were written by the same scribe.

• J. T. Milik, "Milkî-ṣedeq et Milkî-reša[c] dans les anciens écrits juifs et chrétiens," *JJS* 23 (1972) 95–144 (129) suggested that the following compositions were written by the same scribe: 4QCurses (4Q280), 5QRule (5Q13), and possibly 5QS (5Q11) and 4QapocrJer C[e] (4Q390).

• D. Falk, *DJD* XXIX, 23–4: Scribe A of 4QCommunal Confession (4Q393) also copied 4QWorks of God (4Q392). According to this scholar, this scribe also copied 4QpsEzek[d] (4Q388) and 4QapocrJer C[c] (4Q388a).

• J. P. M. van der Ploeg: One scribe copied both 11QT[b] (11Q20) and 1QpHab.[42]

• García Martínez–Tigchelaar–van der Woude: 11QT[c]? (11Q21) and 11QJub (11Q12 + XQText A) were written by the same hand (*DJD* XXIII, 411).

---

[38] See F. M. Cross, *Scrolls from Qumran Cave I. The Great Isaiah Scroll, The Order of the Community, The Pesher to Habakkuk from Photographs by John C. Trever* (Jerusalem 1972) 4, note 8.

[39] See Bonani et al., "Radiocarbon Dating," 28. G. L. Doudna, "Calibrated Radiocarbon Dates from Tucson and Zurich on Dead Sea Texts and Linen," paper delivered to the SBL conference, Philadelphia, Nov. 20, 1995, p. 6, disagrees with this assumption, referring to both radiocarbon analysis and paleographical considerations.

[40] For 4Q441 and 4Q443, see S. A. Reed and M. J. Lundberg, *The Dead Sea Scrolls Catalogue. Documents, Photographs and Museum Inventory Numbers* (Atlanta, Ga. 1994) 114. I owe this information to Tigchelaar, "The Scribe of 1QS," 439, n. 5.

[41] See E. Chazon, *DJD* XXIX, 410.

[42] J. P. M. van der Ploeg, "Les manuscrits de la grotte XI de Qumrân," *RevQ* 12 (1985–87) 9; idem, "Une *halakha* inédite de Qumran," in *Qumrân: sa piété, sa théologie et son milieu* (ed. M. Delcor; BETL 46; Paris/Leuven 1978) 107–13. In this publication, van der Ploeg commented on the identity of the scribe of the two documents, but he did not identify the cave 11 document as 11QT[b] (11Q20).

• A. Yardeni, *DJD* XXVII, 65: XḤev/Se 7 and 13 as well as 5/6Ḥev 47b were written by the same scribe, whose name is mentioned in XḤev/Se 13 12.

If indeed the Qumran scrolls were written by a large number of different scribes, it is apparent that only a very small proportion of their work is known to us, since many of the scribes were professionals who must have produced many scrolls. On the other hand, according to E. G. Turner, only a limited number of scribes was involved in the writing of Greek literature as known from Oxyrhynchus.[43]

The identification of the scribal hand visible in 1QS, 1QSa, 1QSb, and the biblical text 4QSam^c, as well as in some corrections in 1QIsa^a shows that at least in this case same scribe copied texts that we know as biblical, along with other texts that we know as nonbiblical. By the same token, there is no indication that *tefillin* were copied by a separate group of scribes, and therefore the category of scribes specializing in sacred writings probably developed only in rabbinic circles.

f. Background of scribal traditions

The scribal practices embedded in the documents from the Judean Desert reflect the writing of the period under review. However, at the same time they also reflect writing styles continuing from earlier periods when scribal practices for literary and documentary texts on papyrus and leather, as well as for inscriptions on other types of material, were developed. Several practices shared by the Judean Desert texts and Aramaic documents of the fifth century BCE (ch. *8b*) lead us to believe that many texts from the Judean Desert continue earlier traditions of writing in the square script. To a lesser degree, scribes were influenced by the Alexandrian Hellenistic scribal traditions (as reflected especially in some correction procedures analyzed in ch. *8c*). At the same time, it is unclear whether certain scribal practices had developed at an earlier stage of the writing of Hebrew in square characters, or were influenced by contemporary customs in neighboring countries (see, for example, the discussion of the use of the *paragraphos* in ch. *5c1*).

g. Approaches of scribes to their Vorlagen

The approach of scribes to literary texts changed over the course of the centuries; with regard to the biblical text it also differed from one milieu to another, and above all from person to person. For the period preceding the earliest Qumran documents (deriving from the mid-third century BCE), and also, to a great extent, the period under review, the term 'scribe' is somewhat misleading. The function of the scribe was less technical and subordinate than is implied by the medieval and modern understanding of the word. The earlier scribes were involved not only in the copying of texts, but to a limited extent also in the creative shaping of the last stage of their content. Expressed differently, at one time scribes often took the liberty of changing the content, adding and omitting elements, sometimes on a small scale, but often substantially.[44] In this context, one is reminded of the aforementioned use of *sofer* as an author in 11QPs^a XXVII 2 (referring to David). The nature of this creative scribal activity requires us to conceive of the persons involved

---

[43] E. G. Turner, "Scribes and Scholars of Oxyrhynchus," *Act. der VIII Int. Kongr. Papyrolog.* (Vienna 1956) 141–6, especially 143, 145–6. See also K. McNamee, "Greek Literary Papyri Revised by Two or More Hands," *Proceedings of the XVI Int. Congr. of Papyrology* (Chico, Calif. 1981) 79–91.

[44] On the other hand, A. R. Millard, "In Praise of Ancient Scribes," *BA* (1982) 143–53 opined that scribes in the ancient Near East meticulously represented their *Vorlagen*, allowing only for minor orthographic variations. However, that description does not address the whole spectrum of the reality in antiquity. In the present context, this topic cannot be treated satisfactorily. For some data and analyses, see Tov, *TCHB*, chapters 3 and 4.

as scribes-editors, who were not only active in the transmission of texts, but also in the final stage of their creative edition. This applies to most compositions found at Qumran, but not for all milieus, since in the texts belonging to the Masoretic family this freedom was not sanctioned in the period under consideration.

Some scribes acted with more precision than others with regard to their *Vorlagen* and the manuscripts they created. Three different aspects seem to be involved in the definition of scribal precision:

• *Precision in copying.* Common to all scribes was the unconscious creation of scribal mistakes (minuses, pluses, changes, and differences in sequence). The fewer mistakes made, the more careful the scribe must have been. Some scribes were more prone to making mistakes than others, and in principle, a scribe who otherwise remained close to his *Vorlage* could nevertheless have erred as much as others. Accordingly, careful and careless scribes can be identified anywhere in the Qumran corpus.

• *The approach to the Vorlage.* It would be simplistic to say that a scribe either did or did not follow his *Vorlage* closely. What is at stake is not just the faithfulness of scribes to the text from which they copied, but their general philosophy regarding their role in the transmission process. In the last century BCE and the first centuries CE, scribes were involved *mainly* in the transmission process, but prior to that most (except for the proto-Masoretic (proto-rabbinic) family, evidenced from 250 BCE onwards) often considered themselves also to be petty collaborators in the creation of the books. This is the only possible explanation for the early differences between the texts and groups of texts. See, for example, the differences between the parallel nonbiblical texts listed below. In the biblical realm, 4QSam[a], which is basically a precisely transmitted scroll, nevertheless incorporated some rewriting in small and large details (inserted by either the scribe or his source).

Accordingly, from the point of view of later developments, early scribes were often considered imprecise, but such a characterization would be anachronistic, since the concept of an exact transmission had yet to be created. We do not know when that concept came into being. One could say that it was conceived together with the creation of MT, but the *Vorlage* of the LXX was probably also a precise text. Also the pre-Samaritan 4QpaleoExod[m] was a careful copy. Different types of approaches are also visible among nonbiblical texts, but in this category precision had no religious significance, although this may not necessarily be true for the Qumran sectarian writings. The main copy of the Temple Scroll (11QT[a] [11Q19]) was executed carefully, as were certain copies of H, M, S, etc.

The modernizing of the orthography and morphology must have been permitted throughout the transmission of the biblical text, since the 9th–7th century practices are not reflected in the later copies. By the same token, the script was changed, final letters were inserted (see ch. *5g*), and possibly word-division was added as well (see ch. *5a1*). From a certain period onward, however, such modernizing was no longer permitted in certain textual traditions, definitely not in the circles that carefully transmitted MT. Other scribes allowed for continued modernization in orthography and morphology, as visible in the texts written in the Qumran scribal practice (ch. *8a2*), the Torah copy of Rabbi Meir (Tov, *TCHB*, 123), and to a lesser extent in the SP.

• *External shape.* Precision in copying is usually accompanied by elegant external features in the handwriting and the scroll (high-quality leather, adherence to margins, consistently sized columns and margins, high-quality handwriting). It is unknown whether this scribal precision was matched by such external elegance by the fifth-fourth centuries BCE, but this definitely is the case for the late copies among the Judean Desert scrolls (first century BCE, first century CE). The most elegant among them were probably luxury scrolls (see ch. *4j*), mainly evidenced for Scripture scrolls. Such manuscripts were found mainly outside Qumran, and were probably copied from master copies in the temple court.

The rabbinic sources are well aware of the differing levels of scribal skills and precision, as evidenced by the praise expressed for careful scribes. The following terms are used in that literature for careful scribes (cf. Krauss, *Talmudische Archäologie,* III.135–6): אומן לבלר, 'a skilled scribe' (*b. Shabb.* 133b); כותבנים אומנים, 'skilled copyists' (*y. Meg.* 1.71d), pertaining to the scribes of the Hagira family; ספרי דווקני, ספרא דווקנא, '(an) accurate scribe(s)' (*b. Ab. Zar.* 10a; *b. Menah.* 29b); כתבן טב מובחר, 'an exceedingly skilful copyist' (Qoh. Rabb. 2:18).

In the case of the scribes copying biblical texts, precision is a *conditio sine qua non* according to rabbinic sources. This precision is reflected in the dictum in *b. Qidd.* 30a: 'The ancients were called *soferim* because they counted (*saferu*) every letter in the Torah.' The meticulous care in the transmission of MT is also reflected in the words of R. Ishmael: 'My son, be careful, because your work is the work of heaven; should you omit (even) one letter or add (even) one letter, the whole world would be destroyed' (*b. Sot.* 20a). This precision even pertained to matters of orthography, since various *halakhot,* 'religious instructions,' were, as it were, fixed on the basis of the exact spelling of words. For example, the number of the walls of the *sukkah* (four) is determined by the number of letters in the spelling סֻכֹּת (*b. Sukk.* 6b), rather than that in the full spelling סוכות, with five letters. Some of the examples of this type actually were formulated at a later period. The mentioned precision is reflected in the biblical texts from all sites in the Judean Desert other than Qumran, and slightly less so in the proto-Masoretic texts from Qumran (ch. *4j*). The so-called Masoretic *corrections of the scribes* (*tiqqunê soferim*) also reflect a greater degree of liberty than one would connect with the term scribe (see above § a).

Small and extensive changes introduced in the course of the creative reshaping of the biblical text were illustrated by Talmon[45] and in Tov, *TCHB,* 258–84, while the collecting of such changes for the nonbiblical texts has just begun. Much material relating to layers of editorial changes is reflected in the differences between the overlapping segments of several of the Qumran compositions transmitted in multiple copies, for which see TABLE 3 (for a more extensive list of these overlaps, see E. J. C. Tigchelaar, "Annotated Lists of Internal Overlaps and Parallels in the Non-biblical Texts from Qumran and Masada," *DJD* XXXIX, 285–322).

TABLE 3: *Major Overlaps of Qumran Compositions*

Community Rule	One well-preserved copy (1QS); further: 4QSᵃ⁻ʲ (*DJD* XXVI), 5QS (5Q11).
Instruction	1QInstr (1Q26); 4QInstrᵃ⁻ᵍ (*DJD* XXXIV).
War Scroll	One well-preserved copy (1QM); further: 4QMᵃ⁻ᶠ (*DJD* VII).
Hodayot	One well-preserved copy (1QHᵃ); also: 1QHᵇ (1Q35), 4QHᵃ⁻ᶠ (*DJD* XXIX).
Damascus Document	Two well-preserved copies found in the Cairo Genizah (CD, manuscripts A and B); further: 4QDᵃ⁻ʰ (*DJD* XVIII).
Miqṣat Maʿaśe ha-Torah	4QMMTᵃ⁻ᶠ (*DJD* X); possibly also 4QcryptA Miqṣat Maʿaśe ha-Torahᵍ? (4Q313; *DJD* XXXVI).
4QMishmarot/Cal. Docs.	4Q320–330 (*DJD* XXI).
4QDibre Hameʾorot	4Q504–506 (*DJD* VII).
4QNarrative and Poetic Composition	4Q371–373 (*DJD* XXVIII).
Temple Scroll	One well-preserved copy (11QTᵃ [11Q19]); further: 4QTᵃ? (4Q365a), 4QTᵇ (4Q524), 11QTᵇ,ᶜ? (11Q20, 11Q21); cf. Qimron, *Temple Scroll*

---

[45] S. Talmon, "The Textual Study of the Bible: A New Outlook," in Cross–Talmon, *QHBT,* 321–400, especially 332 ff. ("Biblical Stylistics and the Textual Study of the Bible").

The differences among the parallel texts were a result of differing scribal-editorial treatment of the texts. Thus, in his analysis of the types of differences among the parallel nonbiblical texts from Qumran, G. Vermes remarked that they resemble those among different manuscripts of the biblical text.[46] However, the overlapping segments in these texts have not been analyzed extensively from this perspective, neither in a comparative analysis of individual compositions, nor in an overall analysis of all the nonbiblical compositions. Study of the parallel texts would involve an examination of the differences in small and large details regarding the wording and content, the relation between corrections in one text and the parallel texts, and the division into sense units (sections).

The data collected in the apparatuses in the various editions nevertheless allow us a glance at the main types of differences between parallel texts: the Damascus Document and CD (J. Baumgarten, *DJD* XVIII, especially pp. 3–5), Serekh ha-Yaḥad (Alexander–Vermes, *DJD* XXVI, especially pp. 9–12; Charlesworth, *Rule of the Community*, 41; Metso, *Community Rule*; P. Garnet, "Cave 4 MS Parallels to 1QS 5.1–7: Towards a *Serek* Text History," *JSP* 15 [1997] 67–78), 1–4QHodayot (E. Schuller, *DJD* XXIX, 69–75 and *eadem*, "Some Contributions of the Cave Four Manuscripts (4Q427–432) to the Study of the Hodayot," *DSD* 8 [2001] 278–87, especially 284), 4QMMT (Qimron–Strugnell, *DJD* X), 4QInstr (Strugnell–Harrington, *DJD* XXXIV). Small differences between all the parallel Qumran texts have been tabulated in great detail by P. Muchowski, *Hebrajski Qumrański jako język mówiony* (Poznán 2001). For partial analyses, see the following studies:

• J. Duhaime pointed out that 4QMᵃ (4Q491) and 1QM do not relate to one another as a source and its revision, but that both reworked an earlier source, now lost.[47] Thus, 1QM insisted more on purity than 4QMᵃ (4Q491), and the former often has a longer text than the latter. At the same time, several scholars suggested that 1QM is a *later* revision of the cave 4 copies of the War Scroll.[48]

• 4QSᵇ (4Q256) and 4QSᵈ (4Q258) present shorter versions of the Community Rule than 1QS. Abbreviating took place in individual words, short phrases, and sentences, as indicated in the notes in the edition of Charlesworth, *Rule of the Community*. Thus also P. S. Alexander, "The Redaction History of Serekh-Ha-Yaḥad: A Proposal," *RevQ* 17 (1996) 437–56. The exact relation between the various manuscripts of the Serekh ha-Yaḥad was outlined by Alexander–Vermes, *DJD* XXVI, 9–12. These scholars distinguish between 'at least four recensions of S': 1QS, 4QSᵇ (4Q256) and 4QSᵈ (4Q258), 4QSᵉ (4Q259), 4QSᵍ (4Q261). One also notices that in contradistinction to all other texts of the Community Rule, which reflect the so-called Qumran orthography and morphology (ch. *8a*), 4QSᵈ (4Q258) and 4QSʲ (4Q264) reflect a system of orthography and morphology which resembles that of MT. While the shorter texts of S from cave 4, 4QSᵇ (4Q256) and 4QSᵈ (4Q258), probably abbreviated a text such as 1QS, it is very difficult to decide in which details these texts represent shorter formulations or, alternatively, textual mishaps. The fact that the phrase 'sons of Zadok the priests who keep the covenant' is found in 1QS V 2, 9, but is lacking in both 4QSᵇ and 4QSᵈ, seems to indicate that the omission or addition is intentional. The same problems obtain with regard to 1QS V 9 ולרוב אנשי בריתם which lacks יחד when compared with עצת אנשי היחד of 4QSᵇ (4Q256) IX 8 and 4QSᵈ (4Q258) I 7. On the other hand, in the same col. V of 1QS there are seven occurrences of יחד, the community's self-appellation, which are lacking in the parallel sections in 4QSᵇ (4Q256) and 4QSᵈ (4Q258). In the case of 4QSᵉ (4Q259), Metso, *Community Rule*, 69–74 believes that the shorter text of that manuscript is more original than the longer text of 1QS. On the other hand, Doudna,

---

[46] G. Vermes, *The Dead Sea Scrolls Forty Years On: The Fourteenth Sacks Lecture Delivered on 20th May 1987* (Oxford Centre for Postgraduate Hebrew Studies, 1987) 10–15.

[47] J. Duhaime, "Dualistic Reworking in the Scrolls from Qumran," *CBQ* 49 (1987) 32–56; idem, "Étude comparative de *4QMᵃ Fgg. 1–3* et *1QM*," *RevQ* 14 (1990) 459–72. For the sources, see the editions of 1QM (Y. Yadin; Oxford 1962) and 4QM (M. Baillet, *DJD* VII); *The Dead Sea Scrolls: Hebrew, Aramaic, and Greek Texts with English Translations, 2, Damascus Document, War Scroll, and Related Documents* (ed. J. H. Charlesworth; Tübingen/Louisville 1995). For a more elaborate reconstruction, see P. Alexander, "The Evil Empire: The Qumran Eschatological War Cycle and the Origins of Jewish Opposition to Rome," in Paul, *Emanuel*, 17–31, especially 22.

[48] F. García Martínez, "Estudios Qumranicos 1975–1985: Panorama crítico," *EstBib* 46 (1988) 351–4; B. Nitzan, "Processes of Growth of Sectarian Texts in Qumran," *Beth Miqra* 40 (1995) 232–48 (Heb.); E. and H. Eshel, "Recensions of the War Scroll," in Schiffman, *Jerusalem Congress*, 351–63.

4Q Pesher Nahum, 707–10 believes that the differences between the various copies of S reflect 'free variants—expansions, paraphrases, glosses added for clarity' (p. 707).

• The following corrections in 1QH[a] may have been based on 4QH[c] (4Q429) and 4QpapH[f] (4Q432):

4QH[c] (4Q429) 1 ii 1 [הבגירכה] בי	1QH[a] XIII (Suk. = Puech V) 17 בי supralinear
4QH[c] (4Q429) 1 ii 5 סערה [ת]	1QH[a] XIII 20 סערה נֹפֹשׁ תשׁיב
4QH[c] (4Q429) 1 iv 2 ויהמו בכנור ריבי	1QH[a] XIII 32 original text (?) corrected to בכנור
4QH[c] (4Q429) 1 iv 5 והודי	1QH[a] XIII 34 original text (?) corrected to והודי
4QpapH[f] (4Q432) 3 2 ומכיחי צדק	1QH[a] II 4 צדק in original text ומ[וכיחי צדק was marked with cancellation dots, and אמה was added interlinearly

h. *Autographs*?

Many of the documents from the Judean Desert were original compositions rather than copies of earlier sources. This pertains mainly to letters and documentary texts such as the archives of Babatha and Salome Komaïse daughter of Levi from Naḥal Ḥever,[49] in which the names of four scribes are mentioned (see n. 13). However, it is possible that some literary texts, especially sectarian compositions, also represented autographs, even though solid criteria are lacking for distinguishing between autographs and copies. One could argue that if a composition is preserved in a single copy it *could* represent an autograph, but there is no reason to believe this is the case, for example, for the *pesharim*,[50] even though they are attested only in single copies. Furthermore, the following arguments suggest that specific Qumran texts reflect copies rather than autographs:

    • A change of hands within a manuscript, attested relatively frequently in Qumran scrolls (§ e above), attests to a manuscript's status as a copy rather than an autograph. Note, for example, the unusual change of hands toward the end of 1QpHab, in col. XII 13. See illustr. 3.

    • The erroneous copying of the scribal sign X as a single ʾaleph in 1QpHab II 5 (end of the line), where it serves no purpose, shows that this scroll was a copy of another one in which the X served as a line-filler (ch. 5c6). This ʾaleph is written in exactly the same position as the X-signs, slightly to the right of the left vertical ruler.

    • 1QS X 4 למפתח נ   ואות נ : The unusual space after the *nun* may indicate that the scribe could not read his *Vorlage*.

    • Instances of vertical dittography show that the manuscript was based on an earlier copy, such as in the case of 4QTob[e] (4Q200) 6 2 ותְמהִים (cf. next line); 4QJub[f] (4Q221) 1 6 ומכול תועבתם וש[מור] (cf. line 5); see further the examples on p. 203. The dittography in 4QM[a] (4Q491) לש[מֹחֹת (cf. next line) shows that this manuscript was copied from a source that had equally long lines.

    • The uninscribed segment in 4QCommGen A (4Q252) II 4–5, with no scribal sign, probably reflects copying of a faulty copy.[51] The unusual text shown here was not corrected by any subsequent scribe or reader.

תמימה לימים שלוש מאות ששים וארבעה באחד בשבת בשבעה	3
אחת ושש נח מן התבה למעוד שנה	4
תמימה ויקץ נח מיינו וידע אֵת אשר עשה	5

---

[49] For the Babatha archive, see Beyer, *Ergänzungsband*, 166–84; B. Isaac, "The Babatha Archive: A Review Article," *IEJ* 42 (1992) 62–75; Y. Yadin, J. C. Greenfield, and A. Yardeni, "Babatha's *Ketubba*," *IEJ* 44 (1994) 75–101; Schams, *Jewish Scribes*, 209–13. On the archive of Salome Komaïse daughter of Levi, see H. M. Cotton, *DJD* XXVII, 158 ff.

[50] This line of argument is followed by E. Hammershaimb, "On the Method," and Wise, *Thunder in Gemini*, 103–57 ("Accidents and accidence: A scribal view of linguistic dating of the Aramaic scrolls from Qumran"), especially 121.

[51] Thus T. Lim, "The Chronology of the Flood Story in a Qumran Text (4Q252)," *JJS* 43 (1992) 288–98, especially 294; E. Qimron, "The Riddle of the Missing Text in the Damascus Document," in *Fifty Years of Dead Sea Scrolls Research—Studies in Memory of Jacob Licht* (ed. G. Brin and B. Nitzan [Heb.]; Jerusalem 2001) 244–50 (244).

These spaces can easily be filled in with the contextually correct text (the present text is not intelligible; note line 4 אחת ושש).

• The scribe of 4QCal Doc C (4Q326) erred with regard to the use of number signs: in the first line of the text he represented the numeral with regular words, באחד ברביעֹי, and he likewise started the numeral of the second line with regular letters בא, probably for בא]חד עשר[, but continued the word with a symbol: בו שֹבֹֹת באר without erasing the *'aleph*. This mistake probably implies that this scribe was accustomed to writing the number signs, but was copying from a text that did not use such signs.

• In ch. *5g* it is suggested that the appearance of final letters in penultimate position such as 4QDeutʲ X 2 (Exod 12:48) אתכמה usually implies that the scribe first wrote the standard short pronominal suffix, possibly as extant in his *Vorlage*, but subsequently remembered that he should have written the long one.

• Scribal mistakes which are clearly based on a written *Vorlage* show that a specific scroll was a copy rather than an autograph. Thus, the supralinear addition ואוהבי יהוה כיקר כורים פשרו על בחירו[in 4QpPsᵃ (4Q171) III 5 by the original scribe of this manuscript was written after the completion of the text. See ch. *7f*.

Correction of mistakes cannot serve as a criterion for a document's status as a copy since these corrections could have been inserted by a reader of the text.

i. *Identification of the* Vorlagen *of Qumran texts?*

It is difficult to ascertain which specific copies of Qumran texts were actually used within the community. For example, it would be beneficial if we could pinpoint the actual exemplar from which 1QIsaᵃ was copied. Only very limited evidence is available:

• Among the large number of texts found at Qumran, only one has been identified from which another text may have been copied (4QDanᵇ possibly copied from 4QDanᵃ).[52]

• 4QShirShabbᵃ (4Q400) 2 1–2: The limited context is identical to 4QShirShabbᵇ (4Q401) 14 i 7–8.

• 4QTest (4Q175) 14–20: The quotation from Deut 33:8-11 is based either on 4QDeutʰ as shown by several unique agreements between the two scrolls (J. A. Duncan, *DJD* XIV, 68–70; Tov, *Greek and Hebrew Bible*, 297) or a closely related scroll.

• 4QLevᵈ: According to E. Eshel, "4QLevᵈ: A Possible Source for the Temple Scroll and *Miqsat Maʿaśe ha-Torah*," *DSD* 2 (1995) 1–13, both 11QTᵃ (11Q19) and 4QMMT used 4QLevᵈ.

Since little is known regarding the *Vorlagen* of the Qumran texts, no conclusions can be drawn regarding whether or not scribes followed the layouts contained therein. That is, in principle, a scribe could have imitated the column layout of his *Vorlage* in such a way that the words in the copy would occur in exactly the same position as in the original. From the outset, however, such an assumption is unlikely because of the lack of agreement in dimensions between most leather copies of the same composition (ch. *4e*); even if the dimensions are similar, the columns differ within the individual sheets and between one sheet and another. The uniformity that is visible in many papyri found in Egypt was possible because papyrus sheets were taken from large rolls of identical dimensions. This situation allowed W. A. Johnson, *The Literary Papyrus Roll* to determine which papyrus scrolls of the first centuries CE followed the dimensions of their *Vorlagen* and which did not. Likewise, many medieval manuscripts of MT have identical dimensions.

In some cases, internal differences between segments of a scroll, especially in orthography, suggest that a scribe used different *Vorlagen* for its various parts:

• The first four columns of 4QDeutʲ differ from those following in orthography and morphology. See n. 340.

• The 'Apostrophe to Zion' (col. XXII) differs from the remainder of 11QPsᵃ in the writing of the second person singular pronominal suffix. See n. 392.

• Some scholars suggested that the differences between scribes A and B of 1QIsaᵃ (see TABLE 1 above) are best explained by the assumption of different *Vorlagen*.

---

[52] Thus Ulrich, *The Dead Sea Scrolls*, 148–62. The two texts share only a few readings, but the assumption of a direct relation between them is mainly suggested by the identical layout of the columns.

· The first biblical quotation in 4QTest (4Q175) which combines Deut 5:28-29 and 18:18-19 is close to SP and 4QRP^a (4Q158, of a pre-Samaritan character), while the third one, from Deut 33:8-11, is very close to 4QDeut^h, and may have been based on that scroll or a similar one.[53] These two quotations show that the author of 4QTest used at least two biblical scrolls of a different character, that is a pre-Samaritan text and 4QDeut^h, a textually independent text.

---

[53] See E. Tov, "The Contribution of the Qumran Scrolls to the Understanding of the LXX," *Septuagint, Scrolls and Cognate Writings: Papers Presented to the International Symposium on the Septuagint and Its Relations to the Dead Sea Scrolls and Other Writings (Manchester, 1990)* (ed. G. J. Brooke and B. Lindars; SCS 33; Atlanta, Ga. 1992) 11–47 (31–5); J. A. Duncan, "New Readings for the 'Blessing of Moses' from Qumran," *JBL* 114 (1995) 273–90.

3

WRITING AND WRITING MATERIALS

The texts from the Judean Desert were written mainly on leather and papyrus, on individual sheets or in scrolls. There are no codices from this area and, indeed, the codex only came into common use in a period later than that covered by the present monograph.[54]

The great majority of the documents from the Judean Desert were written on leather and papyrus (the latter comprise some 14% or 131 texts of the 930 Qumran texts; see § 3e below). In addition, a large number of ostraca were found, especially at Masada, but also at Murabbaʿat (Mur 72–87, 165–168), Naḥal Ḥever (8Ḥev 5–6), Naḥal Mishmar (1Mish 4–8), as well as at Khirbet Qumran (KhQ Ostraca 1–3) and Qumran cave 10 (10QOstracon). Only the Copper Scrolls from cave 3 were inscribed on that material, according to Lefkovits, *Copper Scroll*, 463 in order to solve 'the problem of ritual impurity.' Two texts were inscribed on wooden tablets: 5/6Ḥev 54 (P.Yadin 54)[55] and Mas 743 from 73 or 74 CE (*Masada II*, 90).[56] For additional writing materials used in this and earlier periods, see A. Lemaire (n. 57).

The use of different materials at the various sites in the Judean Desert reflects the differences in genre among the documents found at these locations. The great majority of the literary texts as included in the corpora found at Qumran and Masada were written on leather, while papyrus, was used for most of the documentary texts, such as letters and various administrative texts, found at Naḥal Ḥever, Naḥal Ṣeʾelim, Wadi Murabbaʿat, and the other sites. At the same time, in ancient Egypt and the Graeco-Roman world, papyrus was the preferred material for texts of any kind, and writing on various forms of leather was far less frequent (see also Gamble, *Books and Readers*, 45–6).

There is no direct evidence regarding the main writing material for *long* texts used in ancient Israel before the period attested by the Judean Desert documents. Both leather and papyrus were in use in Egypt at a very early period (see § b below), but it is not impossible that leather was preferred in ancient Israel because it was more readily available than papyrus which had to be imported from far-away Egypt. Thus R. Lansing Hicks, "*Delet* and M*e*gillah: A Fresh Approach to Jeremiah XXXVI," *VT* 33 (1983) 46–66, believed that leather was used for the writing of ancient biblical scrolls. One of the arguments used by Lansing Hicks (p. 61) is that a knife was used by Jehoiakim to cut the columns of Baruch's scroll exactly at the sutures since the text mentions that after each three or four columns Yehudi cut the scroll (Jer 36:23). On the other hand, according to Haran, "Book-Scrolls," a few allusions in Scripture suggest

---

[54] On the transition from scroll to codex, see C. H. Roberts and T. C. Skeat, *The Birth of the Codex* (London 1983); *Les débuts du codex* (ed. A. Blanchard; Bibliologia elementa ad librorum studia pertinentia 9; Turnout 1989); I. M. Resnick, "The Codex in Early Jewish and Christian Communities," *JRH* 17 (1992) 1–17; Gamble, *Books and Readers*, 49–66; E. J. Epp, "The Codex and Literacy in Early Christianity and at Oxyrhynchus: Issues Raised by Harry Y. Gamble's *Books and Readers in the Early Church*," *CRBR* 10 (1997) 15–37.

[55] For a detailed description of these slates or tablets, one of which contains one of the Bar Kochba letters, see M. Haran, "Codex, *Pinax* and Writing Slate," *Scripta Classica Israelica* 15 (1996) 212–22 (Hebrew version in *Tarbiz* 57 [1988] 151–64).

[56] For the use of wood as writing material in the ancient Near East, see K. Galling, "Tafel, Buch und Blatt," in *Near Eastern Studies in Honor of William Foxwell Albright* (ed. H. Goedicke; Baltimore/London 1971) 207–23.

that papyrus served as the main writing material during the First Temple period, even though no biblical papyrus texts have been preserved from that era[57] and the Qumran corpus contains very few biblical papyrus copies.

a. *Papyrus*

Although literary works from the Judean Desert were mainly written on leather, many papyrus copies of these compositions are also known, albeit probably without any distinctive features at the content level (below, § e). Papyrus probably was considered less durable than leather, and the papyri from the Judean Desert made a less professional impression (lines were less straight and no neat column structure can be observed). On the other hand, it was easier for scribes to remove letters from an inscribed papyrus than from leather. Papyrus may therefore have been preferred by certain scribes, but it was probably the availability of the writing material that determined the choice of either papyrus or leather; in the case of the biblical texts, additional factors must have played a role (see below). It is not impossible that papyrus was the preferred medium for private copies of literary compositions (thus Wise, *Thunder in Gemini*, 125 ff.), at Qumran involving mainly nonbiblical compositions, especially sectarian.[58] On the other hand, Alexander, "Literacy," 7 surmised that during the early stages of their residence at Qumran, the members of the Qumran community may have found it easier to obtain papyrus scrolls from external sources than to produce leather scrolls themselves.

For a complete list of the papyrus texts from the Judean Desert, see APPENDIX 2. See further: J. Maier, *Die Qumran-Essener: Die Texte vom Toten Meer* (Munich/Basel 1996) III.8; Tov–Pfann, *Companion Volume*, 20–72; Wise, *Thunder in Gemini*, 131 ff.; S. Talmon, *Masada VI*, 26–9. For circumstantial evidence for the existence of papyri (impressions of the papyrus fibers on clay bullae) in Jerusalem and Lakhish, see Y. Shiloh, "A Hoard of Hebrew Bullae from the City of David," *ErIsr* 18 (Heb.; Jerusalem 1985) 73–87 (especially 78); H. Torczyner et al., *Lachish I, The Lachish Letters* (Oxford 1938) 106–9. For an example of a closed documentary papyrus tied with a string, see Jer papSale of Date Crop (Jer 7) in *DJD* XXXVIII, pl. XII.

The writing of Scripture on papyrus was forbidden by rabbinic literature, see *m. Meg.* 2.2 (at the same time, early Christian writings were written on that material):

הייתה כתובה בסם ובסקרא ובקומוס ובקנקנתום על הניר ועל הדפתרא לא יצא, עד שתהא כתובה אשורית על הספר ובדיו

If it was written with caustic, red dye, gum, or copperas, or on paper <i.e. papyrus>, or *diftera*, he has not fulfilled his obligation; but only if it was written in Assyrian writing, in a <leather> scroll and with ink.

cf. *y. Meg.* 1.71d

הלכה למשה מסיני שיהו כותבין בעורות

It is an oral prescription delivered to Moses at Sinai that one would write on skins.

It therefore stands to reason that the few Qumran biblical texts written on papyrus did not derive from a milieu that was influenced by the aforementioned rabbinic instructions.

---

[57] Jer 51:63 mentions the binding of a stone to a scroll so that it would sink in the Euphrates River. According to Haran, this scroll was made of papyrus, since a leather scroll would have sunk even without a stone. In support of this assumption Haran mentions the Egyptian influence on Canaan in this period which would have included the use of papyrus, the low price of papyrus in contrast to leather, and the biblical use of the root מח"ה, a verb signifying erasure of a written text with water. According to Haran, at the beginning of the Second Temple period scribes started to use leather when the need was felt for the use of materials capable of containing longer texts. However, in Egypt, this need was not felt, as papyrus was used for very long texts, too; see ch. *4c*. See further the discussion by A. Lemaire, "Writing and Writing Materials," 999–1008.

[58] A similar suggestion was made for early papyrus copies of the Qur'an, described as 'popular' texts intended for private study by G. Khan, "Standardisation and Variation in the Orthography of Hebrew Bible and Arabic Qur'an Manuscripts," *Manuscripts of the Middle East* 5 (1990–91) 53–8, especially 57.

The rabbinic instructions were formulated at a later period than the writing of the Qumran papyrus scrolls, but it may be assumed that the Talmudic traditions reflected earlier customs that would have been already followed during the time of Qumran occupancy. In view of this situation, an examination of the textual character of the biblical papyrus fragments is in order. While several of the fragments are too small to determine their character, the larger fragments 6QpapKgs, and possibly also 6QpapDan, are non-Masoretic and are more specifically classified as being independent, possibly meaning that they did not derive from Pharisaic circles.[59] See further below, § e ('Texts written on papyrus').

In this context it is noteworthy that all the texts from Qumran written in the paleo-Hebrew script are inscribed on leather rather than papyrus.

On the production of papyrus, papyrus sheets, and scrolls see, among others, Hall, *Companion*, ch. I; N. Lewis, *L'industrie du papyrus dans l'Égypte Gréco-Romaine* (Paris 1934); idem, *Papyrus*; idem, "Papyrus and Ancient Writing," *Archaeology* 36 (1983) 31–3. On the use of papyrus at the time of the First and Second Temples, see the bibliography in Tov, *TCHB*, 201 as well as Galling, "Tafel, Buch und Blatt" (see n. 56); Ashton, *Scribal Habits*, ch. 2. For an extensive commentary on the *locus classicus* of the production of papyrus in antiquity, Pliny, *Natural History*, XIII.74–82, see Lewis, *Papyrus*, 34–69. So far, the papyrus fragments from the Judean Desert have not revealed any new technical details regarding writing on this substance. Papyrus could have grown in such places as Ein Feshkha or the Ḥuleh marshes, and indeed there is ancient evidence for the growth of papyrus at various locations in Israel (Lewis, *Papyrus*, 6), but further investigation is warranted regarding whether the fragments found at Qumran and the other sites were written on local or non-local papyrus. The plant itself (גמא) was known in Israel (see Isa 35:7 and Job 8:11), but as there is no evidence for the local production of papyrus from the plant, the material used for writing may have been imported from Egypt.

The papyri found at Qumran were written during the period of settlement of the Qumran community as well as by several generations prior to that time. At the same time, one of the texts from Wadi Murabbaʿat, viz. the two layers of the palimpsest papyrus Mur 17 (A: papLetter, B: papList of Personal Names), is much earlier as its two scripts have been dated to the eighth or seventh century BCE (ch. *1b*).

b. *Leather*

The oldest known leather documents written in any language are described by Driver, *Aramaic Documents*, 1; Diringer, *The Book*, 172–4; Millard, *Reading and Writing*, 26, referring among other things to an ancient Egyptian text written more than 2000 years BCE. As for the leather texts from the Judean Desert, various technical examinations need to be completed before the full picture will be known. Additional research is needed to determine from which animal skins the various texts from the Judean Desert were prepared. In the meantime, partial evidence is available regarding calves, fine-wooled sheep, medium-wooled sheep, wild and domestic goats, gazelles, and ibexes.[60]

• According to examinations made in 1958 and the early 1960s by M. L. Ryder and J. Poole & R. Reed,[61] the leather fragments found at Qumran were made mainly from skins of sheep and goats.[62] A

---

[59] It is unlikely that the use of papyrus indicated the non-canonical status of the aforementioned biblical books, as suggested by D. Barthélemy, *DJD* I, 150 with regard to 6QpapDan. If Daniel were the only text written on papyrus, the case would have been more convincing.

[60] The knowledge from which section of the animal a particular piece of skin derives could at times improve the reconstruction. T. Elgvin, "4Q413—A Hymn *and* a Wisdom Instruction," in Paul, *Emanuel*, 205–21 (especially 207, 211) uses this information as a basis for the separation of 4Q413 and 4Q413a.

[61] M. L. Ryder, "Follicle Arrangement in Skin from Wild Sheep, Primitive Domestic Sheep and in Parchment," *Nature* 182 (1958) 1–6; J. Poole and R. Reed, "The Preparation of Leather and Parchment by the Dead Sea Scrolls Community," *Technology and Culture* 3 (1962) 1–26; idem and idem, "A Study of Some Dead Sea Scroll and

more detailed study mentioned the following four species: calf, fine-wooled sheep, medium-wooled sheep, and a hairy animal that was either a sheep or a goat.[63]

• The material of 4QSam[c] was described by E. Ulrich, *DJD* XVII, as 'cream-coloured sheep or goat skin.'

• A report published by Freedman–Mathews, *Leviticus*, 3 ascribes the material of 11QpaleoLev[a] to a kid (young goat) rather than a hairy sheep, but the latter is not excluded.

• The material of the *tefillin* described by Y. Frankl in Yadin, *Tefillin*, 43–4 is that of 'kidskin.'

• DNA examination of 11QT[a] (11Q19) determined the material of some fragments of this scroll as being goatskin and ibex.[64] A later study mentions eleven unidentified fragments probably deriving from wild and domestic goats (seven pieces) and gazelle or ibex.[65]

The sole detail mentioned in rabbinic sources is

‏. . . שכותבין על עורות בהמה טהורה ועל עורות חיה טהורה‏

. . . That one should write on the skins of pure domestic and wild animals (*Sof.* 1.1 = *Massekhet Sefer Torah* 1.1).

M. Bar-Ilan, "Writing Materials," *Encyclopedia DSS*, 2.996 described the preparation process as follows: 'The hide was removed from the carcass and then soaked in a solution of salt and other agents in order to remove any remaining particles of hair and fat, then stretched, dried, smoothed with a rock, and treated with a tanning solution. This improved its appearance, and perhaps made it easier for the leather to absorb the ink. Next, the hide was cut into the longest possible rectangular sheet to serve as a scroll.' When referring to material of this kind found in the Judean Desert, scholars use different terms for the animal skins prepared for writing: skin, hide, parchment, and leather. We use the last term.

There is no firm knowledge regarding the preparation stages, locally and elsewhere, of the leather and papyrus fragments found in the Judean Desert. It is not impossible that the skins from which some Qumran leather documents were prepared were immersed in basins at Ein Fashkha.[66] According to Stegemann, *Library of Qumran*, 51–5 the process of refining these skins took place at Qumran, but there is no solid evidence in support of this assumption.[67] There is also some evidence for the existence of a tannery at Masada, see E. Netzer, *Masada III*, 634–5. The tanning techniques applied to the manuscripts found at Qumran were discussed by M. Haran, who considered the Qumran scrolls to be 'basically parchments, but with moderately tanned surfaces to facilitate writing.'[68]

Rabbinic descriptions distinguish among three types of leather (see the description by M. Glatzer, "The Book of Books—From Scroll to Codex and into Print," in *Jerusalem Crown, The Bible of the Hebrew University of Jerusalem;* ed. M. Glatzer; Jerusalem: N. Ben-Zvi Printing Enterprises, 2002, 61–101, especially 63–4): G[e]vil, the thick leather

---

[63] M. L. Ryder, "Remains Derived from Skin," *Microscopic Studies of Ancient Skins* (Oxford 1965).

[64] S. R. Woodward et al., "Analysis of Parchment Fragments from the Judean Desert Using DNA Techniques," in Parry–Ricks, *Current Research*, 215–38, especially 228.

[65] D. W. Parry, D. V. Arnold, D. G. Long, S. R. Woodward, "New Technological Advances: DNA, Electronic Databases, Imaging Radar," in Flint–VanderKam, *Fifty Years*, 496–515, especially 505–6.

[66] Thus R. de Vaux, "Fouilles de Feshkha," *RB* 66 (1959) 225–55, especially 230–37. This view was contradicted by J. B. Poole and R. Reed, "The 'Tannery' of ʿAin Feshkha," *PEQ* 93 (1961) 114–23 and F. Rohrhirsch (see n. 33 above), mainly because no remnants of the chemical components needed for the tanning were found there. For the data, see Humbert–Chambon, *Fouilles de Khirbet Qumrân*, 251 ff. and photographs PAM 42.538–543.

[67] According to K. G. Pedley, the table, of which remnants were found at locus 30 in Qumran (see n. 33), served for all the activities in connection with the scrolls for which a long surface was needed, such as the sewing together of the sheets of which the scrolls were composed, treating them with oil, rolling them out, but there is no supporting evidence for his view. See K. G. Pedley, "Library," 21–41, especially 35–6.

[68] M. Haran, "Bible Scrolls in Eastern and Western Jewish Communities from Qumran to the High Middle Ages," *HUCA* 56 (1985) 21–62 (the quote is from p. 38); idem, "Technological Heritage in the Preparation of Skins for Biblical Texts in Medieval Oriental Jewry," in P. Rück, *Pergament–Geschichte, Struktur, Restaurierung, Herstellung* (Historische Hilfswissenschaften 2; Sigmaringen 1991) 35–43.

inscribed on the hairy side, $k^e laph$, and *dukhsustos*. The latter two are different layers of the same leather that are split apart and prepared differently; $k^e laph$ is inscribed on the flesh side and *dukhsustos* on the hairy side. A detailed study of the material of the Qumran scrolls is still required, but Glatzer, ibid., believes that most of them are relatively thick, of the $g^e vil$ type, inscribed[69] on the hairy side. Such is also the instruction in rabbinic literature for Torah scrolls (*Sof.* 1.8 and *y. Meg.* 1.71d: 'One writes on the hairy side of the skin' (cf. *Massekhet Sefer Torah* 1.4). On the other hand, the very thin scroll 11QT^a (11Q19), of the $k^e laph$ type, was inscribed on the inside of the skin (the flesh side).

It stands to reason that the approximate *length of the composition* was calculated before the writing was commenced; with this information, the required number of sheets could be ordered from a manufacturer or prepared to fit the size of the composition. Subsequently, the individual sheets were ruled and inscribed and only afterwards stitched together. The fact that some ruled sheets were used as uninscribed handle sheets (e.g. the final sheets of 11QT^a and 11QShirShabb [ch. *4g*]) and that some uninscribed top margins were ruled (the second sheet of 1QpHab [see below]) shows that the ruling was executed as part of a separate process from the writing. The numbering of a few sheets (ch. *5c8*) probably indicates that they were inscribed individually, to be joined subsequently based on the numerical sequence (however, the great majority of the sheets were not numbered). On the other hand, some sheets must have been joined before being inscribed (§ c below).

A further indication of the separate preparation of the individual sheets is the different nature of the two surviving sheets of 1QpHab. The first sheet (cols. I–VII) contained regular top margins of 2.0–3.0 cm, while the top margins of the second sheet (VIII–XIII) measuring 1.6–2.0 cm contain one, two, or three uninscribed ruled lines (illustr. 3). Since ruled lines are visible in the top margin of the second sheet, while all other sheets from Qumran compositions have unruled top margins, it is evident that the manufacturer of this scroll used an existing ruled sheet of larger specifications than needed for the second sheet of this scroll; when preparing this scroll, he cut the sheet to the size required for the present purpose, cutting off the unruled top margin of that sheet, and using the ruled area as top margin. A similar procedure was followed for the first sheet of 4QDeut^n (illustr. 15) which was cut to the size of the second sheet. Additional relevant material is recorded in § d below listing the juxtaposition of unrelated sheets that must have been prepared separately.

There is evidence for the existence of rolls of blank papyrus sheets at Elephantine[70] and possibly also in Murabbaʿat.[71] These rolls consisted of sheets that had been glued together, from which the required smaller pieces were then cut off.

---

[69] It is usually assumed that the skins and papyri were inscribed soon after their preparation, but Thiering refers to the possibility that the leather remained unused for a very long period (100–200 years): B. Thiering, "Use of Radiocarbon Dating in Assessing Christian Connections to the Dead Sea Scrolls," *Radiocarbon* 41 (1999) 169–82, especially 175.

[70] Cf. the description of the Elephantine papyri in Porten–Yardeni, *TAD* 3.xiii: 'Fresh, rectangular papyrus sheets were not stored in a pile but were glued together along their length to make a scroll. In writing a document, the scribe detached from the scroll a piece of required size.' A similar remark with regard to the papyrus production in Egypt was made by S. Emmel, "The Christian Book in Egypt: Innovation in the Coptic Tradition," in *The Bible as Book—The Manuscript Tradition* (ed. J. L. Sharpe III and K. Van Kampen; London and New Castle, Del. 1998) 35–43. Emmel remarked that many of the single-sheet documents from Egypt include a seam, where two originally separate sheets were overlapped and glued together. In other examples from the classical world, some single papyrus sheets had stitches on both sides.

[71] Lewis, *Bar Kochba*, 10: 'Papyrus was shipped from the factories in rolls formed by gluing together the overlapping edges of consecutive sheets. A standard roll contained twenty sheets.'

The calculation of the number of sheets needed for copying a composition could never be precise, as evidenced by the ruled column often left uninscribed following the final inscribed column of a sheet (ch. *4g*).

c. *Sheets*

Documents were written either on single pieces of leather or papyrus (a sheet or a scrap of leather) or on scrolls composed of several sheets.

Short documents were written on single sheets and in rare cases on scraps of leather. For example, letters and other documentary texts written on papyrus and 4QTest (4Q175) written on leather were inscribed on single sheets. Likewise, P.Nash of the Decalogue probably consisted of only a single sheet (thus Peters, *Nash*, 5). The shape of some documents is irregular (neither rectangular nor square, with uneven borders); it is probable that they were inscribed on remnants left after large rectangular sheets had been cut from the hides for regular scrolls. Thus, the irregular shape of 4QExercitium Calami C (4Q341) made it necessary for the scribe to shorten the last lines in accordance with the slanting bottom margin (illustr. 2). Likewise, most *tefillin* and *mezuzot* were written on small pieces of irregularly shaped leather, which were probably remnants of skin left after rectangular sheets had been cut out. Thus in 4QPhyl J (illustr. 9) the unusual shape of the leather necessitated the writing of long lines at the beginning of the text and very short lines at the end.

Likewise, 4QList of False Prophets ar (4Q339) and 4QList of Netinim (4Q340) were written on very small pieces of leather of irregular shape. The original measurements of 4Q339 were probably 8.5 x 6.0 cm including margins on all sides. In addition, 4QPrayer of Nabonidus ar (4Q242; large, straight, margin of 2.5 cm before frg. 1) probably constituted a separate sheet of leather.

Scrolls consisted of sheets of leather or papyrus prepared by one or more scroll manufacturers, not necessarily in the same way. In addition, the sheets could have been ruled by different persons for one of several purposes. These differences account for the variations in the number of ruled lines on the individual sheets (see the analysis of 1QpHab and 11QT^a in § b above) and in the practice of the guide rules (ch. *4a*).

Sheets were ruled before being sewn together (§ b above; thus also Crown, *Samaritan Scribes*, 76), and after being joined, the scribe or manufacturer must have made an effort to align the rulings on the different sheets in order to achieve a uniform appearance throughout the scroll; see, for example, most of the fifty-four columns in 1QIsa^a. However, when the columns were positioned at slightly different heights in adjacent sheets, the lines in these sheets were often not continuous. This practice explains the differences in height between the columns in the adjacent sheets of the following scrolls:

- 1QS
- 4QDeut^n sheets 1 (col. I) and 2 (II–VI); in this portion, the bottoms of the two sheets were cut evenly after the two sheets were combined.
- 4QToh A (4Q274) 3 i and ii
- 4QCal Doc/Mish A (4Q320) 4 iii–vi (differences may be due to shrinkage)
- 11QtgJob VIIB and VIII, XVII and XVIII, XXXI–XXXII, XXXV–XXXVI; however, the writing on either side of the join, at cols. XIX–XX is at the same level.
- 11QT^a; e.g. XLVIII–IL; LX–LXI
- 11QpaleoLev^a
- MasSir I–V as opposed to VI–VII

Within the sheets themselves, the writing was almost always (not exclusively) at the same level, due to the continuous ruling. One exception occurs in 4QInstruction-like Composition A (4Q419) frg. 8 where cols. i and ii are written on a different level, and further the ink of col. i is darker than that of col. ii.

Sheets were ruled with lines from beginning to end, often with the help of guide dots. These lines were usually not spaced evenly, resulting in the same pattern of spacing throughout the sheet. See below, ch. *4a.*

It was convenient to inscribe sheets before they were stitched together or, in the case of papyri, glued together (see below), and as a rule sufficient space was left for the stitching. However, in some cases, the sheets of some scrolls must have been inscribed after being joined.

 • 4QXII[a]: The writing in col. III at the end of the sheet is so close to the stitching that it is hard to imagine that the sheets were stitched after being inscribed.

 • 4QLevi[a] ar (4Q213): This scroll was inscribed to the very edge of the leather, and in one instance (1 7) also beyond the edge, rendering it likely that these sheets had already been joined.

 • 4QLevi[b] ar (4Q213a): It is difficult to ascertain whether the sheets were joined before or after the writing.

 • 4QCal Doc/Mish A (4Q320): The stitches are very close to the writing of the text between cols. 4 iii and iv. The sheets in this document are extremely narrow (ch. *4*, TABLE 14), and undoubtedly were stitched together before being inscribed.

 • 1QIsa[a]: The line added in this scroll between lines 11 and 13 of col. XXX and vertically in the margin of the next sheet shows that the correction was made after the sheets had been joined. Since this is a correction, this example differs from the other ones in this group.

Longer scrolls were composed of sheets of leather sewn or, in the case of papyrus, glued together (see below). The stitching was usually executed in such a way that the two sheets butted up against one another (without any overlap) and that they were joined by threads inserted through holes. The holes left by these stitches as well as the threads used for stitching are visible in many fragments (see illustrations 1, 6, 14, 15); codices are unattested in these materials and were not yet in general use in this period.

Some sheets were not stitched to the very top and bottom edges of the leather but somewhat below the top or above the bottom edges of the following columns: 4QNum[b] XV; 4QSapiential Work (4Q185); 11QT[a] (11Q19) XLIX, LIII, LVII, LXI, LXIV, LXVII (further research is needed in this area). This practice resembles the later rabbinic instruction for texts of Scripture:

צריך שיהא משייר מלמעלן ומלמטן כדי שלא יקרע

An area should be left <unstitched> at the top and at the bottom <of the sheets> in order

that the scroll be not torn <in use> (*Sof.* 2.18; cf. *b. Meg.* 19b and *y. Meg.* 1.71d).

On the other hand, in most preserved scrolls, the stitching extended to the top and/or bottom edges of the leather, for example

1QIsa[a] I (bottom), III–IV, XV–XVI, XIX–XX (all: top and bottom), etc. See illustr. 6.
1QapGen ar XXII–XXIII (bottom)
1QS III–IV, V–VI, VII–VIII, X–XI (all: top)
1QSa II (top)
4QpaleoExod[m] XXVII–XXVIII (top)
4QDeut[c] frg. 53 (bottom)
4QDeut[n] I–II (top and bottom)
4QDeut[q] 5 i–ii (bottom)
4QIsa[g] (top)
4QXII[c] 18 (top)
4QLevi[a] ar (4Q213) 1 i–ii (top)
4QToh A (4Q274) 1 (top and bottom)
4QcryptA Words of the Maskil (4Q298; top and bottom)

4QCommunal Confession (4Q393) 1 (bottom)
4QRitPur A (4Q414) 7 (top)
4QH^b (4Q428) 10 (bottom)
4QapocrLam B (4Q501; top and bottom)
11QPs^a XXIV–XXV (top)
MurXII IX–X (bottom)

Only one document is known in which three tiny fragments of leather (each of four lines) were stitched together one above the other (rather than adjacent to each other horizontally), namely 4QIncantation (4Q444; see illustr. 10 and *DJD* XXIX, pl. XXVI).

Papyrus sheets (*kollemata*, sg. κόλλημα) were glued together with an adhesive (Lewis, *Papyrus*, 12–13, 38–41, 47–9, 64–9). The glued joins between two sheets of papyrus are described in *DJD* XIII, 363 for 4Qpap paraKings et al. (4Q382) frg. 10; in *DJD* VIII for 8ḤevXIIgr cols. XVII–XVIII (leather); and in *DJD* IX, 223 for 4Qpap paraExod gr (4Q127).

According to rabbinic prescriptions, scroll sheets are to be joined with sinews of the same ritually clean cattle or wild animals from which the scroll itself was prepared. Cf. *b. Menaḥ.* 31b בנידין אבל בגרדין לא ('only with sinews, but not with thread') and *Sof.* 1.1 (see further *y. Meg.* 1.71d):

והלכה למשה מסיני שכותבין על עורות בהמה טהורה ועל עורות חיה טהורה ותופרין בגידן

It is also an oral prescription delivered to Moses at Sinai that <scrolls> shall be written on the skins of ritually clean cattle or ritually clean wild animals, and be sewn together with their sinews.

The evidence suggests that most of the stitching material used in the scrolls from Qumran indeed consists of sinews. However, further investigation should be able to determine which threads were made of animal sinews and which of flax, in the latter case contrary to rabbinic custom. In their 1962 research, Poole–Reed[72] claimed that the stitching material which they examined was of vegetable origin and most probably derived from flax. It is not known, however, which specific scrolls were examined for this purpose.

• 1QIsa^a: The stitching material was described by Burrows, *The Dead Sea Scrolls*, I.xiv as 'linen thread.'

• 4QNum^b: N. Jastram, *DJD* XII, 217 concluded that the unraveling of the thread preceding col. XV (frg. 22b) suggested that it consisted of flax rather than sinews.

• 4QcryptA Words of the Maskil (4Q298): S. J. Pfann, *DJD* XX, 2 describes the stitching material as flax.

• 4QApocryphal Pentateuch A (4Q368) frg. 4: The stitching material is probably flax.

The two biblical scrolls quoted as deviating from the rabbinic custom (4QNum^b [pre-Samaritan, Qumran scribal practice] and 1QIsa^a [Qumran scribal practice]) are non-Masoretic.

It is not impossible that a damaged inscribed sheet was on occasion replaced with a repair sheet:

• According to VanderKam–Milik, the beginning of 4QJub^a (4Q216) written by scribe A contains a repair sheet. The change of hands between scribes A and B of 4QJub^a (4Q216) is clearly visible in frg. 12.

• According to J. Strugnell, the first sheet of 4QDeut^n (illustr. 15), containing Deut 8:5-10 in a single column and followed by a sheet containing 5:1–6:1, may have been a wrongly positioned repair sheet. See the analysis by S. A. White (Crawford), quoted in n. 167 and for a different view, see below ch. *4a*.

Tefillin were folded in a special way, for which see Yadin, *Tefillin*, 15–21. According to Broshi–Yardeni, *DJD* XIX, 77, the tiny fragment 4QList of False Prophets ar (4Q339) was folded twice and held together by a string passed through

---

[72] Poole–Reed, "The Preparation of Leather" (n. 61). The quote is from p. 22.

holes still visible on the fragment. This fragment was named a 'card' by Steudel, "Assembling," n. 3.

See further ch. *4d* regarding the dimensions of the sheets.

d. *Scrolls*

Documents comprising more than one column were contained in scrolls (rolls)[73] composed of sheets of leather or papyrus.[74] Each such scroll from the Judean Desert contained but a single unit (composition, document),[75] although some exceptions are recognized when different, possibly related, compositions may have been written by the same scribe or two others in the same scroll:

• 4QMeditation on Creation C (4Q305): According to T. Lim, *DJD* XX, 157, the two columns of this text represent two different compositions written in the same scroll, separated by an intercolumnar margin of 2.0 cm, with the right column starting one line above the level of the left column.

• 4QOtot (4Q319) and 4QS[e] (4Q259): See ch. *2*, TABLE 2.

• 4QWorks of God (4Q392) and 4QCommunal Confession (4Q393): It is not clear how the fragments of these works relate to one another, but it is evident in 4Q393 1 that the right-hand sheet was joined to the left sheet, even though the two were inscribed by different hands with a different line layout (D. Falk, *DJD* XXIX, 23–4 and pl. II).

• 4QInstruction-like Composition A (4Q419) frg. 8: Cols. i and ii of this composition are written on a different level, and further the ink of col. i is darker than that in col. ii. The text of both columns is fragmentary, and they may well represent two different compositions.

• 4QApocryphal Psalm and Prayer (4Q448): The different components in this scroll (cols. I and II–III) are not necessarily related to one another. See illustr. 11.

• Mur papFarming Contracts (Mur 24) contains a long series of different contracts, but they are related since they all deal with farming (for a similar combination of texts, see the Greek P.Oxy. 2.274).

In biblical and rabbinic Hebrew, a scroll is named מגילה (e.g. Jer 36:28; Ezek 3:1), מגילת ספר (Jer 36:2, 4, 6; Ezek 2:9; Ps 40:8), or just ספר (see Isa 34:4); according to A. Hurvitz, מגילה, both when used absolutely and in the pleonastic phrase מגילת ספר, derived from Aramaic and reflects a late linguistic layer in the Bible.[76] In the Qumran scrolls, this phrase occurs in 4QWays of Righteousness[b] (4Q421) 8 2 (מגי]לת ספר]), while מגלה alone occurs in 4QprEsth[b] ar (4Q550a) 5. *Sifre* Deuteronomy § 160[77] explains ספר in Deut 17:18, used in reference to the 'book of the king,' as a מגילה (scroll), portraying every ספר in Scripture as a מגילה of leather. Indeed, to the best of our knowledge, scrolls were used from very early times onwards for Scripture, and it appears that the original

---

[73] The words 'scroll' and 'roll' are apparently synonymous. Scroll is described as follows in J. A. Simpson and E. S. C. Weiner, *The Oxford English Dictionary* (Oxford 1989) XIV.746: 'A roll of paper or parchment, usually one with writing upon it.' The list of early appearances of this word shows that it was used especially with regard to scrolls mentioned in Hebrew and Greek Scripture, as early as Tyndale's translation of Rev 6:14 in 1526. The term is used also especially for the Jewish 'Scroll of the Law' (*sefer ha-Torah*) with the earliest occurrences listed in the *Dictionary* dating from 1887.

[74] Very little is known about papyrus scrolls deposited in the Judean Desert, as no complete scrolls have been preserved (see below § e concerning fragmentary papyrus scrolls). Egyptian papyrus scrolls were strengthened with a reinforcement strip at the beginning and/or end.

[75] Conversely, each ancient text was once written in a single scroll (although longer documents would have been written in more than one scroll). This applies to the individual books of the Bible, even to the books of the Minor Prophets, which at a later stage were combined into a single unit (scroll). See M. Haran, "The Size of Books in the Bible and the Division of the Pentateuch and the Deuteronomistic Work," *Tarbiz* 53 (1984) 329–52 (Heb. with Eng. summ.). At a later period, however, when larger scrolls were in use, several units were combined into one scroll (the Minor Prophets, the Torah, Former Prophets). For a discussion of the relevant Qumran evidence, see ch. 4, TABLE 11 and the discussion there.

[76] A. Hurvitz, "The Origins and Development of the Expression מגילת ספר: A Study in the History of Writing-Related Terminology in Biblical Times," in *Texts, Temples, and Traditions: A Tribute to Menahem Haran* (ed. M. V. Fox et al.; Winona Lake, Ind. 1996) 37–46.

[77] Ed. Finkelstein (New York/Jerusalem 1993) 211.

copies of all Scripture books were written on scrolls, there probably being no alternative for the writing of portable copies.[78] Therefore the insistence in Jewish tradition on this as the earliest form of the *Torah* is probably realistic.

Scrolls of all dimensions (ch. *4c*) could be unrolled (גלל, e.g. *m. Yom.* 7.1; *m. Soṭ.* 7.7; πτύσσω Luke 4:17) easily and rolled back to the beginning (ἀναπτύσσω Luke 4:20)[79] upon completion of the reading, thus ensuring that the first sheet of the scroll or its uninscribed handle sheet (ch. *4g*) remained the external layer. By the same token, when a reader had reached the middle section of a scroll or any sheet thereafter, upon completing the reading it was easier for him/her to roll the scroll until the end, so that upon reopening the scroll he/she could roll it back. See, further, ch. *4g* where the evidence for the beginnings and ends of the scrolls is scrutinized.

Scrolls were usually rolled up tightly in order to aid preservation and to economize on space. For examples, see the following photographs:

- Yadin, *Temple Scroll*, pl. 6.
- Van der Ploeg–van der Woude, *Targum Job,* 105.
- 11QPsᵃ as in *DJD* IV, pl. I.
- 11QapocrPs (11Q11), 11QShirShabb (11Q17), and 11QNJ ar (11Q18), as in *DJD* XXIII, pl. LIII.
- *JDS* 3, plates 1–10.

Due to the tightness of the rolling, sometimes a segment of the scroll left a mirror-image imprint on the back of the previous layer, which occasionally extended onto the front of that layer:

- 4QXIIᵍ: R. E. Fuller: *DJD* XVI, 275 (the term 'verso' in that edition refers to 'mirror-image').
- 4QCommGen A (4Q252) frg. 1: G. Brooke, *DJD* XXII, 186.
- 4QApocryphal Pentateuch B (4Q377) 1 and 2: J. VanderKam, *DJD* XXVIII, 205.
- 4QParaGen-Exod (4Q422): Elgvin–Tov, *DJD* XIII, 417.
- 11QTᵃ: Yadin, *Temple Scroll*, pls. 5–12. With the aid of these mirror-image imprints the readings of two columns were improved by J. H. Charlesworth, "The *Temple* Scrollᵃ [11Q19, 11QTᵃ (11Q19)]. Columns 16 and 17: More Consonants Revealed," in Paul, *Emanuel,* 71–83.

It is possible that some evidence that is explained as pointing to a palimpsest may actually also reflect this phenomenon (ch. *4b*).

Sometimes the stitching left a very clear imprint on the face of the next layer. See 11QTᵃ (11Q19) cols. XXVI (pl. 13*), XXXVI, LVI and illustr. 13 below.

Leather scrolls were *closed or fastened* in one of three ways:

(1) Many scrolls were fastened by tying thongs (inserted in reinforcing tabs) or strings around them. In the words of J. Carswell, "Fastenings on the Qumran Manuscripts," *DJD* VI, 23–8, 'The fastening of each scroll appears to have consisted of two elements, a reinforcing tab of leather folded over the leading edge of the scroll and a leather thong slotted through it, one end of which encircled the scroll and was tied to the exterior' (p. 23). A tool such as KhQ 2393 (*DJD* VI, 25) may have been used for this purpose. Different systems of tying were used (see the diagrams of Carswell). The thong was connected to a reinforcing tab attached to the scroll itself (only at its beginning), in such a way that the thong was tied either straight or diagonally around the scroll (thus 4QDᵃ [4Q266]). In the latter case, the one preserved specimen of this type has uninscribed areas of 3.5–4.3 cm preceding the first column and 9.0 cm following the final column, both folded for further strengthening before the thong was tied around the

---

[78] The writing of all of the Torah (or Deuteronomy) on stones, as prescribed in Deut 27:3, 8 may never have been done, although Josh 8:32 records that Joshua wrote the complete Torah on altar stones.

[79] However, according to Snyder, Luke refers to a codex, as πτύχες is the basic word for 'writing tables.' See H. G. Snyder, *Teachers and Texts in the Ancient World, Philosophers, Jews and Christians* (London/New York 2000) 281.

scroll (*DJD* VI, pl. IV; *DJD* XVIII, pls. I, XIV). The fact that the uninscribed area at the beginning of some forty scrolls has been preserved (ch. *4g*) while only two tabs survive in place (see below) may or may not be significant, as the methods used for attaching the tabs to the scrolls may not have been identical.

Many detached reinforcing tabs made of coarse leather, differing from the prepared leather of the inscribed scrolls, were found in the Qumran caves; see Carswell, 'Fastenings,' *DJD* VI, 23–8 and pl. V and Sussmann–Peled, *Scrolls*, 114–5. In cave 8, archeologists discovered sixty-eight such reinforcing tabs, usually of coarse leather, together with remains of only five manuscripts. Since each reinforcing tab was once attached to a scroll, this cave probably contained a leather workshop or depository, unless it originally contained an equal number of scrolls and reinforcing tabs and many of the former subsequently disintegrated. In only two cases have scrolls with attached reinforcement tabs been preserved, namely, 4QApocryphal Psalm and Prayer (4Q448; see illustr. 11) and 4QD^a (4Q266; see *DJD* VI, pls. IVa–IVb and *DJD* XVIII, pls. I, XIV).

Although only two thongs have been found attached to scrolls, there is still much evidence of their use through the imprint of thongs or strings on the leather itself, which created a horizontal fold in the middle of most columns of 1QpHab, 1QS, 1QSa, 1QSb, 1QIsa^a, 4QTest (4Q175), and 4QcryptA Words of the Maskil (4Q298; see S. J. Pfann, *DJD* XX, 5). According to G. Brooke, *DJD* XXII, 190, there is also the imprint of a reinforcement tab in the margin preceding the first column of 4QCommGen A (4Q252).

A similar method of binding scrolls was referred to by Catullus 22.7, who mentioned a 'lora rubra,' a red thong tied around the scroll (quoted by Birt, *Buchwesen*, 68).

In the case of the Qumran scrolls, it is unclear whether the reinforcement tabs were attached to the scrolls before or after inscription. Most scrolls in which an uninscribed area has been preserved at the beginning had room for such a tab. In the case of 4QApocryphal Psalm and Prayer (4Q448; illustr. 11), it appears that the large uninscribed area at the beginning of col. I enabled the attachment of the tab; the bottom part of the scroll (col. II) could then be inscribed closer to the edge of the leather. The remains of this scroll create the impression that it contained a special arrangement of three columns, but this layout probably resulted from the space left for the tab.

Scrolls could also be tied by single strings or thongs not connected to a reinforcement tab; some of these strings could have been passed through holes in the leather of the scroll or a cover sheet. According to Broshi–Yardeni, *DJD* XIX, 77, the tiny fragment 4QList of False Prophets ar (4Q339) was folded and held together by a string passed through holes still visible on the fragment.

Contracts were rolled up, while the string around them was strengthened with a seal. For illustrations, see Schubart, *Das Buch*, 55. The systems for tying the *tefillin* were described in detail by Yadin, *Tefillin*.

(2) Several scrolls were protected by linen wrappings. For a general description of such wrappings without detailed proof relating to archeological evidence, see M. Bélis, "Les étoffes de lin pour protéger les manuscrits," *Le monde de la Bible* 107 (1997) 32. Remnants of wrappings detached from the scrolls were found in caves 1 and 11 (for the former, see Sukenik, *Mgylwt gnwzwt*, illustrations 2 and 3; for the latter, see *DJD* XXIII, 431). One section of a scroll was found in cave 1 still enclosed in its wrapper with the leather stuck to a broken jar sherd (*DJD* I, pl. I, 8–10). According to the description by G. Lankester Harding, *DJD* I, 8, upon opening the wrapping, the scroll material corroded to a solid black mass. Some of the linen fragments found in the same

cave probably derived from such wrappings.[80] 1QIsa[a] was also once covered with a linen wrapping (see the evidence quoted by G. M. Crowfoot, *DJD* I, 18–19). Reportedly, the wrapper of 11QT[a] is now in the Schøyen collection in Oslo, Norway.

The linen fragments from cave 1 are both non-dyed and dyed, in the latter case sometimes with rectangular patterns. The use of linen wrappings for scrolls is referred to in *m. Kil.* 9.3 and *m. Kel.* 28.4 (both: מטפחות (ה)ספרים, 'wrappers for scrolls') and in *y. Meg.* 1.71d (מפה, 'cover'), for which G. M. Crowfoot mentioned some parallels from the classical world (see further Safrai, *Jewish People*, 940). Josephus, *Ant.* XII 11 § 90 likewise states with regard to the Torah scroll sent to Egypt from Jerusalem: "and when they had taken off the covers (ἐνειλήματα) wherein they were wrapt up ... ." The linen fragments from cave 1 displaying rectangular patterns and blue elements may be similar to the wrappers described in the Talmudic literature with figures 'portrayed on them' (מצוירות).

(3) In a combination of the two aforementioned systems, some scrolls were both enclosed in linen wrappings and tied with a leather thong. One of the linen fragments from cave 4 (Israel Museum photograph X94.920) was attached to such a leather thong and must have enveloped a scroll together with the leather thong. This system is not otherwise known from the literature.[81] If the evidence mentioned under systems *1* and *2* for 1QIsa[a] is correct, that scroll was also tied in two ways.

Literary scrolls were not sealed as were most documentary texts that were tied up as scrolls. Many such seal impressions (bullae) were found among the Wadi Daliyeh Samaritan texts, and in a few cases the seals were still attached to the tied-up documents (*DJD* XXIV, pl. XXII). See further *JDS* 3, pl. 14.

Little is known with certainty regarding the *storage* of scrolls at Qumran, but several details may be inferred from archeological remains. Caves 1 and 3 at Qumran held large numbers of cylindrical jars, several of which were probably used for storing scrolls (for an early parallel, see Jer 32:14), while a smaller number of remains were found in other caves and in Khirbet Qumran.[82] These jars may have been sealed with pieces of linen, as suggested by G. M. Crowfoot, *DJD* I, 19, 24, but they were also closed with lids such as have been found. Although it is not known which scrolls were stored in the jars, those found in cave 1 that remained in a relatively good state of preservation, namely, 1QIsa[a], 1QM, 1QpHab, 1QS, 1QapGen ar, and 1QH[a] were probably stored in this manner. According to Pfann, "*Kelei Dema*ᶜ," damage patterns on some of the scrolls show which scrolls were stored in jars.[83]

No scroll was actually found in a jar by archeologists, and the evidence is therefore circumstantial. Surviving from antiquity are descriptions by Origen (185–254 CE) concerning the finding of a Greek scroll in a jar in the vicinity of Jericho (Eusebius [260–340 CE], *Ecclesiastical History* 6.16 1–3) and by Epiphanius concerning finds of Greek and Hebrew scrolls in the same area (Migne, *Patrologia Graeca* 43, 265–68). Furthermore, *Assumptio Moses* (*The Testament of Moses*) 1:16 refers to the depositing

---

[80] See the description of this material by G. M. Crowfoot, *DJD* I, 18–38, especially 24–8 ('The Linen Textiles'). See p. 24 ibid.: "It seems probable that all the cloths were made for one of two purposes, either as scroll wrappers or as jar covers."

[81] The linen fragment was dated to 160–41 BCE in the radiocarbon analysis performed by Jull et al., "Radiocarbon Dating," that is, the period of the scrolls themselves. The quoted article also presents a photograph of the linen fragment with the attached thong.

[82] For a thorough description and analysis, see Pfann, "*Kelei Dema*ᶜ."

[83] In Pfann's words, 'The wavy patterns along the bottom or upper edges of these scrolls reveal the pressure points where the rolled document, which stood at a tilt, touched the bottom and side of the jar, leaving damage on one point on the bottom edge and one point on the top edge.' (p. 169, n. 23). According to Pfann, such patterns are visible in scrolls from caves 1 and 11.

of writings in 'earthenware jars.' From modern times, we have the witness of Muhammed ed-Dhib, the shepherd who found the first scrolls in cave 1, who reported that one of the jars in that cave contained three scrolls, two of them wrapped in linen.[84] In addition, in cave 1 excavators found a decomposed scroll fragment in its linen wrapper stuck to a jar neck (*DJD* I, 7 and pl. I.8-10). The numerous cylindrical scroll jars found at Qumran, Ein Feshkha, Jericho and other sites in the Judaean Desert (see Pfann, "*Kelei Dema*ᶜ," 167) are only known from this region; they were used for general storage, reportedly including that of scrolls. However, according to Doudna, the known specimens are much too large for this purpose (average height: 60 cm; see *DJD* I, 14–17), and this scholar claims that food was probably stored in them rather than the scrolls, which were kept in shorter jars.[85] According to Pfann, "*Kelei Dema*ᶜ," scrolls were stored in the large jars, but he concludes that these jars were not intended originally as 'scroll jars' but for the storing of tithes.[86] Noting that the jars ranged between 46.5 and 75.5 cm in interior height, while the cave 1 scrolls averaged no more than 30.0 cm, Pfann realized that they were stored rather loosely. Several scrolls could be stored in a single Qumran jar, which must have been the case in the cave 1 jars.

For a similar type of stationary storage, note the storage of Egyptian papyrus scrolls in either wooden containers (boxes) or jars (Černy, *Paper*, 30; for a photograph of a box, see Posener-Kriéger, "Old Kingdom Papyri," pl. 1). J. T. Milik, "Le giarre dei manoscritti della grotta del Mar Morto e dell'Egitto Tolemaic," *Bib* 31 (1950) 304–8, pl. III compares the Qumran jars with the ones found at Deir el-Medineh. In ancient Greece, scrolls were stored in a bookcase; see the depiction by the 'Eretria painter' in the interior of a red-figured cup (Louvre G 457 [*c.* 430 BCE]), reproduced in Lewis, *Papyrus*, pl. 8.

The scrolls in cave 4 probably were stored on wooden shelves attached to the walls, for which there is some archeological evidence.[87] On these shelves, the long side of the scroll was probably facing the user as suggested by the evidence of the name tags (ch. *4h*). On the other hand, according to Alexander, "Literacy," 11, scrolls were stored vertically: "This would explain the remarkable fact that so many of them are better preserved at the top than at the bottom. The bottom of the scroll was exposed to damp seeping up from the ground and so decayed more quickly."

That scrolls were stored in the synagogue, first in an adjacent room and later in a special niche or in an ʾaron ha-qodesh, is established by Luke 4:16-21. According to these verses, Jesus entered the synagogue in Nazareth and was handed a scroll of Isaiah. He unrolled it, read the text, and then rerolled the scroll after use.[88] Storage of such scrolls in the synagogue is also mentioned in rabbinic literature[89] and is established for several synagogues starting with that of Dura-Europos in the mid-second century CE and including that of Khirbet Shema in the mid-third century.[90]

---

[84] See J. T. Milik, *Ten Years of Discovery in the Wilderness of Judaea* (London 1959) 12.

[85] G. L. Doudna, *Redating the Dead Sea Scrolls Found at Qumran: The Case for 63 BCE* (QC 8; Kraków 1999) 52–7; idem, *4Q Pesher Nahum*, 711–5.

[86] "... these jars were indeed originally intended at Qumran to be used by the Levites as tithe jars to gather and transport tithed produce ..." (ibid., 178).

[87] Scholars mention holes in the walls of cave 4a, but to the best of my knowledge, detailed archeological evidence has not been presented. I am grateful to H. Eshel, who mentioned cave C north of the aqueduct as a parallel. In that cave, excavated by him and M. Broshi, such holes indicated the presence of shelves in a closet-like structure (personal communication, June 2003).

[88] It is also evident from several ancient sources that some synagogues contained a collection of Scripture scrolls; see Safrai, *Jewish People*, 940 for references to rabbinic sources. Likewise, the implication of Acts 17:10-11 is that Scripture scrolls were stored in the synagogue. *y. Meg.* 3.73d specifically mentions the keeping of separate scrolls of the Torah, Prophets, and Hagiographa in synagogues.

[89] See Safrai, *Jewish People*, especially 927–33, 940.

[90] For the evidence and an analysis, see E. M. Meyers, "The Torah Shrine in the Ancient Synagogue," in *Jews, Christians, and Polytheists*, 201–23.

e. *Texts written on papyrus*

The number of papyrus fragments found at the various sites in the Judean Desert does not reflect the number of papyri deposited there. However, for the sake of convenience we assume that the material has decayed at the same rate at all sites, thus presenting us with a reliable impression of the relation between the different corpora of papyri from each site as they were left *in situ*. Papyrus was often more susceptible to decay than leather, and one notes that the Qumran papyri are not at all well preserved: none of the Qumran literary papyri has preserved beginnings and endings (only very few documentary papyri have been found at Qumran [see below]). In no instance has a complete column of a literary papyrus been preserved together with its top and bottom margins, while partial data is available for 4QpapTob^a ar (4Q196) 2, 17, 18 (on the other hand, such information is available for some documentary texts from other sites, among them Mur 19, 30, 42, 44; 5/6Hev 3, 13, 16–18 [*JDS* 3]).

Because of the fragmentary condition of the papyrus and leather fragments, the total number of compositions preserved will never be known, and the assessment of the relation between the numbers of the preserved papyri and leather fragments remains difficult. The figures in TABLE 1 are based on the judgments of the scholars who published the texts. In the case of the Qumran papyri, some scholars combined many or possibly too many fragments as one item, while others designated almost every individual fragment as a separate composition. Thus, such single inventory items as 1Q69 and 1Q70, both named '1QpapUnclassified fragments,' may represent many more texts than these two numbers suggest while, conversely, many minute fragments written in the cryptA script were presented by S. J. Pfann in *DJD* XXXVI as thirty-six individual texts (4Q249, 249a–z, 250, 250a–j).

The figures in TABLE 1 relate to the total number of papyri from the Judean Desert and their nature. The two sides of opisthographs (ch. *4b*) are counted as a single item even if they contain two separate compositions,[91] while the number in parenthesis, which counts each side of the opisthograph as a separate item, is not taken into consideration in the statistics.

TABLE 1: *Hebrew, Aramaic, Greek, Latin, and Nabatean-Aramaic Papyri from the Judean Desert*
(Listed from North to South)

Site	Total Papyri	Non-documentary Papyri No.	Non-documentary Papyri Percentage of Total	Documentary Papyri No.	Documentary Papyri Percentage of Total
Jericho	23+	0	0	23+	100
Qumran	131 (138)	121 (128)	92	10	8
Nar	3+	0	0	3+	100
Wadi Ghweir	1	0	0	1	100
Murabbaʿat	101+	5	5	96+	95
Sdeir	1	0	0	1	100
Hever/Seiyal	166+	0	0	166+	100
Mishmar	3	0	0	3	100
Seʾelim	3	0	0	3	100
Masada	31 (34)	3 (5)	7	28 (29)	93

---

[91] In this regard we follow the inventories, which in turn are based on the publications of these texts.

TABLE 1 reveals that the situation at Qumran differs totally from that at the other sites in the Judean Desert. While in almost all the other sites in the Judean Desert documentary papyri form the majority among the papyrus texts, in Qumran almost all papyri are non-documentary (literary). Non-documentary papyri are found at only two other sites, Murabbaᶜat and Masada, where they form a small minority.

TABLE 2 compares the papyrus texts with the leather texts found at these sites:

TABLE 2: *Comparison of Hebrew, Aramaic, Greek, Latin, and Nabatean-Aramaic Papyri and Leather Texts from the Judean Desert (Listed from North to South)*

		Papyri		Leather Texts	
Site	*Total Papyri and Leather Texts*	*No.*	*Percentage of Total*	*No.*	*Percentage of Total*
Jericho	23+	23+	100	0	0
Qumran	930	131 (138)	14.0	800	86
Nar	3+	3+	100	0	0
Wadi Ghweir	1	1	100	0	0
Murabbaᶜat	151+	101+	67	50	3 3
Sdeir	4	1	25	3	75
Ḥever/Seiyal	179	166+	93	13	7
Mishmar	3	3	100	0	0
Ṣeᵓelim	3	0	0	3	100
Masada	45	31 (34)	70	14	30

As in TABLE 1, TABLE 2 shows that the situation at Qumran differs from that at the other sites in the Judean Desert. At Qumran (and Masada [see below]), the papyri form a minority of the texts found there (14%), while at all other sites excluding Sdeir they form a majority. This points to a very basic difference between the Qumran corpus and that of the other sites. The Qumran corpus contains almost exclusively non-documentary texts bearing witness to literary activity, while the other sites evidence the daily life experienced at these places, though with some literary activity recorded as well (only a small number of non-documentary leather texts has been found at these sites). The leather texts from Qumran do not reflect any daily activity, with the exception of 4QRebukes Reported by the Overseer (4Q477) and the Greek 4QAccount gr (4Q350) written on the back of frg. 9 of the Hebrew 4QNarrative Work and Prayer (4Q460). When the papyri found at Masada are separated into two groups consisting of (1) the Hebrew papyri deposited there prior to the siege (2 [3]) and (2) the Latin and Greek documentary papyri and other material left there by the Roman army (28 [30]),[92] a similar situation to that at Qumran is recognized. If the Masada fragments are separated in this fashion, we note that only a few papyri were left by the Jewish inhabitants (2 [3]) as opposed to fourteen Hebrew leather texts (one of which may have been written in Aramaic).

It is difficult to ascertain how many valid parallels to the almost exclusively literary corpus of Qumran are known from antiquity. Many collections of Greek papyri from Egypt contain more documentary than non-documentary texts, but the following corpora are valid parallels to the Qumran corpus: the philosophical corpus found in the "villa of the papyri" at Herculaneum (*terminus ante quem* 79 CE), a segment of the Oxyrhynchus corpus if the literary texts from that site came from a specific part of the city, and some 60% of the Antinoopolis corpus. However, the most valid parallels are probably the libraries which were lost, that is, the collections stored in Alexandria, Pergamon, and Ephesus from the Hellenistic

---

[92] Including Mas 721 r + v containing one or two lines of Virgil on the recto and one or two lines of an Unidentified Poetical Text on the verso (see APPENDIX 6).

period, Roman libraries from later periods, and Christian libraries from the fourth century CE in Jerusalem, Alexandria, and Caesarea, all discussed by Gamble, *Books and Readers*, 154–70, 176–96 and Millard, *Reading and Writing*, 17–22. The Nag Hammadi literary corpus derives from a slightly later period. While it remains unknown what would have been included in any Jerusalem temple library, we can assume that it would have contained at least all the Scripture scrolls on leather.[93]

Beyond these statistics, even though the number of papyri found at Qumran is a mere 14.0 percent of the total number of texts found there, the 131 mainly non-documentary papyri is nevertheless an impressive number. These texts were written on single sheets as well as in papyrus scrolls. Complete scrolls have not been preserved in Qumran, but the dimensions of some may be reconstructed from the preserved fragments.

For descriptions of Aramaic, Greek, and Egyptian papyrus scrolls found elsewhere and for analyses of the production of papyrus, see E. M. Thompson, *An Introduction to Greek and Latin Palaeography* (Oxford 1912) 44–51; Černy, *Paper*; Kenyon, *Books and Readers*, 40–74; Kraeling, *Aramaic Papyri*, 127; Porten–Yardeni, *TAD* 3, especially p. xiii; T. C. Skeat, "Early Christian Book Production: Papyri and Manuscripts," in *The Cambridge History of the Bible* (ed. G. W. H. Lampe; Cambridge 1969) 2.54–79; Wenke, "Ancient Egypt"; Posener-Kriéger, "Old Kingdom Papyri"; Caminos, "Reuse of Papyrus"; W. A. Johnson, *The Literary Papyrus Roll*; Talmon, *Masada VI*, 26–9; Ashton, *Scribal Habits*, ch. 2; Gamble, *Books and Readers*, 44–54. An attempt at a detailed technical analysis of writing on papyrus is provided by S. J. Pfann, *DJD* XXXVI, 515–22 in the introduction to 4Q249–250 written in the Cryptic A script.

The majority of the Qumran papyri were written in Hebrew (in the square and Cryptic A scripts, not in the paleo-Hebrew script), while some were written in Aramaic. Because of their fragmentary status, it is sometimes hard to distinguish between these two languages in badly preserved texts. Twenty-two Greek texts have also been preserved. On the whole, it is impossible to assess the exact number of papyrus texts discovered in the caves, since many texts are very fragmentary, and it is often hard to distinguish between the different handwritings on these fragments. TABLE 3 records the papyrus fragments found in six Qumran caves.

TABLE 3: *Papyrus Fragments Found in the Qumran Caves*

Cave	No. of Papyri
1	3
4	86 (of which 7 are opisthographs)
6	21
7	19 (all in Greek)
9	1
11	1

A special case is 4Q51a (4QpapUnclassified frags.), consisting of two inscribed papyrus fragments which, together with other uninscribed fragments, were applied to the back of several columns of the biblical leather scroll 4QSamᵃ for strengthening (*DJD* XVII, pl.

---

[93] Note, for example, *m. Yom.* 1.5 according to which the elders of the court read to the High Priest from Job, Ezra, Chronicles, and Daniel on the day before the Day of Atonement. These books, together with the master copy of the Torah, were probably part of a temple library. The founding of such a library by Nehemiah was mentioned in 2 Macc 2:13-15 ('books concerning kings, prophets, David, and royal letters'). Josephus mentions the temple library on various occasions (e.g. *Ant.* III 38; IV 303; V 61), once also with regard to the copy of the Jewish Law which was taken by Titus (*Bell. Jud.* VII 150, 162). For further references to such a library and an analysis, see A. F. J. Klijn, "A Library of Scriptures in Jerusalem?," *TU* 124 (1977) 265–72. The mentioning of the finding of a Torah scroll in the temple in 2 Kgs 22:8 does not necessarily prove the existence of a library in the seventh century BCE, *pace* A. Lemaire, "Writing and Writing Materials," 999–1008 (1005). See further S. Safrai in Safrai, *Jewish People*, 908–44, especially 940.

XXIII). Frg. a contains remains of six lines, but neither this fragment nor frg. b can be deciphered.

It is difficult to ascertain whether the preserved papyrus fragments from Qumran represent a proportionate and coherent picture of the papyri left behind in the caves, but a few observations should be made:

• Most of the texts from cave 6 are Hebrew papyri (21 papyri, a few biblical, out of a total of 31 items). This collection of texts must have derived from a special source, different from that of the main depository of texts in cave 4.

• Cave 7 contained only Greek papyrus fragments (19 items), probably mainly biblical texts (see below).

• The proportion of Hebrew biblical papyrus fragments is much smaller than the proportion of Bible fragments among the Qumran scrolls in general, viz., merely two, three, or four biblical papyrus texts from cave 6 and one, two, or three papyri from cave 4 as opposed to some 200 biblical texts written on leather within the corpus of 930 Qumran texts. In other words, while the nonbiblical papyri constitute 14% of the Qumran corpus, biblical papyri constitute less than 1%. For the Greek fragments, the proportion of biblical papyri is greater than for Hebrew (APPENDIX 4), but no exact calculations can be made because of the lack of clarity regarding the texts from cave 7 which probably contain the LXX, but which were identified by others as Enoch or parts of the New Testament.[94]

• The great majority of Qumran papyri contain literary texts. There are also ten documentary texts from caves 4 and 6 (TABLE 4), but it is possible that they did not derive from Qumran.

TABLE 4: *Documentary Papyri from Qumran (?)*

4Q347	4QpapDeed F ar, part of XHev/Se 32, and hence probably not deriving from Qumran (*DJD* XXVII, 106–7)[95]
4Q352	4QpapAccount of Cereal B ar or heb
4Q352a	4QpapAccount A ar or heb
4Q353	4QpapAccount of Cereal or Liquid ar or heb
4Q358	4QpapAccount F? ar or heb
4Q359	4QpapDeed C? ar or heb; cf. XHev/Se 7
4Q360a	4QpapUnidentified Fragments B ar
4Q361	4QpapUnidentified Fragment gr
6Q26	6QpapAccount or Contract
6Q29	6QpapCursive Unclassified Fragment (containing figures)

Cf. also a Greek documentary text on leather, 4QAccount gr (4Q350), written on the back of the Hebrew 4QNarrative Work and Prayer (4Q460) frg. 9 (cf. n. 124).

The case for a non-Qumranic origin for the two documentary texts from cave 6 cannot be made conclusively, but various arguments may be adduced for an origin beyond Qumran for some of the cave 4 documentary texts, if not all of them (see n. 124).

• TABLE 5 records the nonbiblical Hebrew and Aramaic papyri that are paralleled by copies of the same composition on leather.

---

[94] For references, see my paper "The Nature of the Greek Texts from the Judean Desert," *NovT* 43 (2001) 1–11.

[95] J. Strugnell (personal communication, February 2000) records his reservations regarding this conclusion, since the assumed Ḥever fragment did not come from the same type of controlled excavations as the Ḥever papyri found by Yadin (5/6Ḥever), published in *JDS* 3. See further n. 124.

TABLE 5: *Nonbiblical Hebrew and Aramaic Papyri from Qumran Paralleled by Copies on Leather*

Papyri	Additional Copies on Leather
4Qpap pIsa[c] (4Q163)	4 copies of the same work or cycle: 4Q161, 4Q162, 4Q164, 4Q165
4QpapTob[a] ar (4Q196)	4 copies: 4Q197–200
4QpapJub[b?,h] (4Q217, 4Q223–224), 4QpapJub[i]? (4Q482), 4QpapGen[o] or 4QpapJub[j]? (4Q483)	9 copies: 1Q17–18, 4Q216, 4Q218–222, 11Q12 + XQText A
4QpapS[a,c] (4Q255, 4Q257)	10 copies: 1Q28, 4Q256, 4Q258–264, 5Q11
4QpapD[h] (4Q273)	9 copies: 4Q266–272, 5Q12, 6Q15
4QpapCal Doc A? (4Q324b), 6QpapCal Doc (6Q17)	5 or 6 copies: 4Q324g, 4Q324h, 4Q313c, 4Q326, 4Q337, 4Q394 frgs. 1–2 (if these fragments represent a separate composition)
4Qpap apocrJer B? (4Q384)	7 copies of the same composition or cycle: 4Q383, 4Q385a, 4Q387, 4Q387a, 4Q388a, 4Q389, 4Q390
4Qpap psEzek[e] (4Q391)	5 copies of the same work or cycle: 4Q385, 4Q385b, 4Q385c, 4Q386, 4Q388
4QpapMMT[e] (4Q398)	5 or 6 copies: 4Q394–397, 4Q399 as well as possibly 4QcryptA Miqṣat Ma‘aśe ha-Torah[g]? (4Q313)
4QpapH[f] (4Q432)	7 copies: 1QH[a], 1Q35, 4Q427–431
4QpapM[f] (4Q496)	6 copies: 1Q33, 4Q491–495
4QpapDibHam[b,c] (4Q505, 4Q506)	1 copy: 4Q504
4QpapPrFêtes[c] (4Q509)	2 copies: 4Q507–508
6QpapGiants ar (6Q8)	9 copies of EnGiants: 1Q23–24, 2Q26, 4Q203, 4Q206 2–3, 4Q530–533
4Qpap cryptA Serekh ha-‘Edah[a–i] (if these are *separate* copies)	1 copy: 1Q28a

While the survival of Qumran texts is to a great extent due to happenstance, it cannot be coincidental that the aforementioned literary compositions are, as a rule, represented by four/five, sometimes seven/eight, copies on leather and one (and in some cases, two or three) on papyrus. This numerical relationship indicates that the material used for the literary documents left behind by the Qumran community was predominantly leather, supplemented by a number of papyrus scrolls. Whether these two groups of texts derived from different sources is unknown. However, a case can be made that the Greek biblical fragments from cave 7 and the collection of papyri from cave 6 came from a source different from that of the large collections of texts in caves 1, 4, and 11.

The information concerning the relation between papyrus and leather texts of the same composition is supplemented by that concerning Qumran compositions that are well represented on leather, but not at all on papyrus (TABLE 6). Thus, not included among the papyrus scrolls, possibly coincidentally, are the following nonbiblical compositions, several copies of which were found at Qumran on leather. These compositions are singled out due to their relatively large number of extant copies.

TABLE 6: *Well-represented Nonbiblical Compositions from Qumran Not Extant on Papyrus*

Text	Cave No.; No. of Copies
Mysteries	Cave 4: 3; Cave 1: 1
Instruction	Cave 4: 7; Cave 1: 1
Tohorot	Cave 4: 4
Berakhot	Cave 4: 5
Narrative and Poetic Composition (4Q371–373)	Cave 4: 3

Shirot ʿOlat ha-Shabbat	Cave 4: 8; Cave 11: 1; Masada: 1
Mishmarot ('Temple Watches')	Cave 4: 9
Barkhi Nafshi	Cave 4: 5
Ordinances	Cave 4: 3
Temple	Cave 4: 1 or 2; Cave 11: 3
Reworked Pentateuch	Cave 4: 5
Enoch ar	Cave 4: 7
Enastr ar	Cave 4: 4
Levi ar	Cave 4: 6; Cave 1: 1? (4Q21)
psDaniel ar	Cave 4: 3
New Jerusalem ar	Cave 4: 2; Caves 1, 2, 5, 11: 1 each
Visions of Amram ar	Cave 4: 7
prEsth ar	Cave 4: 6

• The list of nonbiblical Hebrew and Aramaic papyri which are paralleled by several copies of the same composition on leather (TABLE 5) leads to some further thoughts regarding the nature of the complete corpus of Qumran papyri. The majority of the papyri are sectarian or of interest to the Qumran community (Jubilees and Giants). These sectarian texts include several literary genres of the community's writing: Rules, *halakhot*, liturgical works, poetical compositions, *pesharim*, and sapiential works. Only a small number of papyri are non-sectarian (Aramaic texts, Hebrew and Greek biblical texts). For the Hebrew papyri from Qumran, these data suggest a close connection between the writing on papyrus and the Qumran community:

α. Sectarian compositions (twenty-two texts *together* with papyri [below, β] written in the Cryptic A script) are indicated by a number in bold face in APPENDIX 2. The sectarian nature of these compositions, including the liturgical texts 4QpapPrQuot (4Q503), 4QpapDibHam^{b,c} (4Q505–4Q506), and 4QpapPrFêtes^c (4Q509), is accepted by most scholars. Our analysis of their sectarian character usually follows Dimant, "Qumran Manuscripts."

β. Texts written in the Cryptic A script (see also ch. 7g) were probably written by the Qumran community. This group is rather sizeable (according to S. J. Pfann, thirty-six papyri from cave 4, two of which are opisthographs containing different texts), but may represent a far smaller number of texts. According to S. J. Pfann, the writing in the Cryptic A ('esoteric') script reflects authorship by the Qumran community,[96] but a strong case cannot be made for all compositions regarding their sectarian background. This script is described by S. J. Pfann, "4Q298" as a development from the Late Phoenician scripts. It is used for several texts of a Qumran sectarian nature as well as for other texts which must have had a special meaning for the Qumran community (see also his article, "The Writings in Esoteric Script from Qumran," in Schiffman,

---

[96] The main compositions are:
  4Qpap cryptA Midrash Sefer Moshe (4Q249)
  4QcryptA Words of the Maskil (4Q298)
  4QcryptA Lunisolar Calendar (4Q317)
  Several more fragmentary groups of inscribed remains are only tentatively identified:
  4Qpap cryptA Serekh ha-ʿEdah^{a–i} (4Q249a–i)
  4Q249j–z: sundry small papyrus fragments
  4Qpap cryptA Text Concerning Cultic Service A, B? (4Q250, 4Q250a)
  4Q250b–j: sundry small papyrus fragments
  4QcryptA Miqṣat Maʿaśe Ha-Torah^g? (4Q313)
  4QcryptA Unidentified Texts P, Q (4Q313a, b)
  4QcryptA Cal Doc B (4Q313c)
  11QcryptA Unidentified Text (11Q23)

Jerusalem Congress, 177–90). According to Milik and Pfann, this script was used especially by the Maskil; see especially 4QcryptA Words of the Maskil to All Sons of Dawn (4Q298). If this composition indeed contains the instructions of the *Maskil* to the Qumran novices, it is understandable that it was written in a special script, and this case can be made also for 4QcryptA Lunisolar Calendar (4Q317) and possibly for 4Qpap cryptA Midrash Sefer Moshe (4Q249).

A number of papyrus fragments in the list are irrelevant to the question under discussion: unclassified and unidentified fragments (21), texts in Greek (21) and Aramaic (8), and biblical texts (2–6). If these groups are disregarded, the majority of the texts are sectarian (63) or of special interest to the sect (Jubilees [2] and Giants [1]). At the same time, ten fragmentary papyri are of undetermined nature (TABLE 7).

TABLE 7: *Fragmentary Papyri of Undetermined Nature*

Text No.	Name	Sectarian	Qumran Scribal Practice
4Q331	4QpapHistorical Text C	no data	no data
4Q391	4Qpap psEzek^e	no data	no data
4Q465	4QpapText Mentioning Samson?	no data	no data
4Q478	4QpapFragment Mentioning Festivals	no data	no data
4Q484	4QpapTJud? (4QpapJub^k?)		no data
4Q485	4QpapProphetical/Sapiential Text		no data
4Q486	4QpapSap A?		no data
4Q487	4QpapSap B?		no data
6Q10	6QpapProphecy		no data

• While many of the literary papyri are paralleled by leather copies of the same composition (TABLE 5), other papyri present the only evidence of the composition contained in them (TABLE 8).

TABLE 8: *Compositions Known Only from Papyrus Fragments*

4QpapAdmonitory Parable (4Q302)
4QpapHistorical Text C (4Q331)
4Qpap paraKings et al. (4Q382)
4QpapHodayot-like Text B (4Q433a)
4QpapText Mentioning Samson? (4Q465)
4QpapFragment Mentioning Festivals (4Q478)
4QpapTJud? (4QpapJub^k?; 4Q484)
4QpapProphetical/Sapiential Text (4Q485)
4QpapSap A? (4Q486)
4QpapSap B? (4Q487)
4QpapApocryphon ar (4Q488)
4QpapApocalypse ar (4Q489)
4QpapWar Scroll-like Text A (4Q497)
4QpapSap/Hymn (4Q498)
4QpapHymns/Prayers (4Q499)
4QpapBenedictions (4Q500)
4QpapRitMar (4Q502)
4QpapPrQuot (4Q503)
4QpapRitPur B (4Q512)
6Qpap apocrSam-Kgs (6Q9)
6QpapProphecy (6Q10)

6QpapBened (6Q16)
6QpapHymn (6Q18), possibly a copy of ShirShabb? (thus J. Strugnell,
    personal communication, February 2000)
6QpapUnclassified frags. ar (Words of Michael?; 6Q23)

• The Qumran papyri consist of a negligible number of biblical texts (2–6), mainly from cave 6 (TABLE 9).

TABLE 9: *Biblical Texts on Papyrus*

4QpapIsa^p (4Q76)
4QpapGen^o or 4QpapJub^j? (4Q483)
6QpapDeut? (6Q3)
6QpapKgs (6Q4)
6QpapPs? (6Q5)
6QpapDan (6Q7)

While the evidence for the cave 4 biblical papyri is very scanty and does not necessarily indicate the existence of complete biblical scrolls (note that the biblical text 4QpapIsa^p contains only a few words, and could therefore have represented a *pesher* such as 4Qpap pIsa^c (4Q163), the group of cave 6 biblical scrolls is slightly more significant.

From the point of view of their content, it is difficult to characterize the corpus of the Qumran papyri which contains almost exclusively non-documentary texts (TABLE 1). The non-documentary papyrus texts represent several, if not most, genres of texts represented in the Qumran corpus. The papyri listed in TABLE 5 reflect these genres, but in the main these texts are sectarian, as is further underlined by the copies of non-sectarian texts written in the Qumran scribal practice listed in APPENDIX 2 and analyzed beneath TABLE 6. At the same time, the long list of texts that are represented frequently among the leather manuscripts of Qumran (TABLE 6) shows that not all genres of Qumran texts are represented among the papyri. Notably absent from the corpus of Qumran papyri are eschatological writings and biblical papyri, of which only a very small minority were found at Qumran (TABLE 9).

We suggest that the collection of Qumran papyri is mainly sectarian and liturgical, and usually nonbiblical. Most papyri may reflect personal copies owned by members of the Qumran community, while some may have been imported from other sources.

As far as we can ascertain, the corpus of the Qumran non-documentary papyri does not reflect any specific content features. Thus, for example, the content of 4QpapMMT^e (4Q398) does not display any features that set it aside from the copies of MMT written on leather.

Notably absent from the Qumran corpus of papyri are texts written in the paleo-Hebrew script. This probably is no coincidence, since in the Qumran corpus this script was used mainly for the writing of Scripture texts on leather (Torah and Job). On the other hand, one papyrus from Murabba'at (Mur 17) was written in the ancient Hebrew script and one papyrus from Masada (Mas 1o) was written in the paleo-Hebrew script.

The scribal practices reflected in the Qumran papyri can be examined best in a few texts that were relatively well preserved:

4Qpap pIsa^c (4Q163)
4QpapTob^a ar (4Q196)
4QpapS^c (4Q257)
4QpapAdmonitory Parable (4Q302)

4Qpap paraKings et al. (4Q382)
4QpapMMT^e (4Q398)
4QpapH^f (4Q432), see E. Schuller, *DJD* XXIX, pls. XIII–XIV and foldout pl. III

With some exceptions, the scribal conventions used in writing on papyrus are similar to those used for writing on the leather texts from the Judean Desert, insofar as they relate to the spelling systems, the use of final letters (ch. *5g*), word division (ch. *5a1*), paragraphing (ch. *5a3*), writing in columns, use of margins, occasional writing on two sides, etc. Furthermore, *paragraphos* signs (ch. *5c1*) are evidenced in some papyri, e.g. 4Qpap paraExod gr (4Q127) 17 2–3. The fishhook sign is evidenced in 4QpapM^f (4Q496) 10 iii 13; 4QpapSap/Hymn (4Q498) 15; 4QpapRitMar (4Q502) 19 5, 142, 318; 4QpapPrQuot (4Q503) III 1, 6, 12, 18, 23, IV 6, VIII 2, 22; XI 1, 6, 4QpapPrFêtes^c (4Q509) 10 ii–11 8 (according to Baillet) 49, 225, 265; 4QpapRitPur B (4Q512) 13, 15 ii (both col. IX), XII 7, 48–50 5. Scribal signs (ch. *5c2*), such as those known from the leather texts, are also found in a few papyri, notably 4Qpap pIsa^c (4Q163) II, which uniquely displays several scribal signs not known from other texts. Because of the fragmentary state of the papyri, little is known regarding the dimensions of the Qumran papyri or of their individual columns or sheets.

The main differences in scribal habits between texts written on leather and those on papyrus result from the material used: the lack of ruling on papyri (ch. *4a*), and therefore also the absence of guide dots (horizontal fibers must have provided some form of guidance); the crossing out of letters or words with a line (scribes of papyri preferred to use other systems of erasing, mainly washing out letters or words, such as in 4QpapPrQuot [4Q503] 11 4; see further ch. *5f*, x); and probably also: the absence of cancellation dots (ch. *5c2*).

The only cases of a paleo-Hebrew divine name (ch. *5d*) written on papyrus are in 6QpapHymn (6Q18) 6 5, 8 1, 10 3 (in all: אל). Otherwise, *Tetrapuncta* are found in three papyri: 4Qpap paraKings et al. (4Q382) 9 5; 4QpapTob^a ar (4Q196) 17 i 5, 18 15; 4Qpap psEzek^e (4Q391) 36, 55, 58, 65. However, the distribution of the writing of divine names in papyri cannot be examined well, as no instances have been preserved of the Tetragrammaton written in square characters, excluding 4QpapAdmonitory Parable (4Q302) 1 i 8 (יי).

The great majority of the *papyrus* texts found in the Judean Desert outside Qumran are documentary, excluding

Mas 1o recto (Mas pap paleoText of Sam. Origin)
Mas 1o verso (Mas pap paleoUnidentified Text)
Mas papVirgil lat (Mas 721 recto)
Mas papUnidentified Poetic Text lat (Mas 721 verso)
Mas papLiterary Text? gr (Mas 739)
Mur 108–112[97]

The following Judean Desert papyri are documentary:

Jericho: 7+ in Hebrew, 6+ in Aramaic, and 10+ in Greek.
Qumran: 17 documents in Hebrew, Aramaic, and Greek from cave 4 and two from cave 6 (see n. 124).
Wadi Nar: 3+ in Greek and Hebrew/Aramaic.
Wadi Ghweir: one in Greek.
Wadi Murabba'at: 60+ in Greek, thirteen in Aramaic, and twenty-three in Hebrew.

---

[97] One of these, Mur papPhilosophical Text gr (Mur 108) is a poetical text, possibly in iambic trimeters. This text may reflect a tragedy, see J. Strugnell, *The Antiquaries Journal* 43 (1963) 304; C. Austin, *Comicorum graecorum fragmenta in papyris reperta* (Berlin 1973) no. 360; C. P. Thiede, *The Dead Sea Scrolls and the Jewish Origins of Christianity* (Oxford 2000) 78–9 (Ezekiel the Tragedian).

Sdeir: one in Aramaic.

All the texts found at Naḥal Ḥever: from cave 5/6 derive thirty-one papyri in Greek, nine in Nabatean Aramaic, sixteen in Aramaic, and seven in Hebrew; one in Greek from cave 8 as well as small fragments in Hebrew. From 'XḤev/Se' derive fourteen and many unidentified fragments in Greek, and from the same site also 36–46 fragments in Aramaic (mainly) and Hebrew (note also many unidentified fragments from 'Ḥev/Se?').

Naḥal Mishmar: one in Greek and two in Hebrew.

Naḥal Ṣeʾelim: two in Greek and one in Aramaic.

Masada: probably eleven texts in Greek and twenty in Latin.

All the aforementioned numbers are approximate due to the fragmentary state of the material.

f. *Ink*

To date, insufficient research has been conducted regarding the ink used in the documents from the Judean Desert, which were almost exclusively written with black ink, while in a few texts red ink was also used. For a general study of the types of ink used in antiquity and the Middle Ages, see Diringer, *The Book*, 544–53 and Ashton, *Scribal Habits*, ch. 3. Scholars suggested and partly identified the existence of two types of black ink in antiquity, but the pattern of their distribution in the scrolls is unknown:

• Carbon ink, based on lampblack or soot, described by Vitruvius, *De Architectura*, VII.10 2 and Dioscorides, *De Materia Medica*, V.162.

• Iron-gall ink, consisting of copperas (green vitriol), treated with a decoction of oak-nut galls.[98]

In *m. Shabb.* 12.4, various types of writing liquids are mentioned, partly coinciding with the components of the inks assumed for the Qumran texts: סם (arsenic [caustic]), סקרא (red chalk), קומוס (gum), and קנקנתום (sulphate of copper [copperas]).[99] Further, in *m. Shabb.* 12.5, additional liquids and materials are mentioned which disappear after the writing: unspecified liquids, fruit-juice, dust of the roads, and writer's sand.

On the basis of examinations carried out on several fragments from caves 1 and 4 in 1995, Nir-El–Broshi, "Black Ink" concluded that no metal ink was used in writing the Qumran scrolls.[100] These scholars assumed that the copper elements in the ink used for the papyrus and leather fragments derived from copper inkwells used by scribes, and that the ink used was carbon-based. A similar suggestion was made earlier by H. J. Plenderleith, *DJD* I, 39 for the texts from cave 1, by S. H. Steckoll 1968 (see n. 98), and by Haran, "Workmanship," 81–4 on the basis of theoretical observations. On the other hand, according to the editors of 4QpaleoExod^m in *DJD* IX, 18, the ink used in that manuscript contained iron. However, according to Haran, metal-based ink was used only from the second century CE onwards.

That different types of black ink were used is clear from the differing states of its preservation. While in most cases, the ink has been preserved very well, on some scrolls it has corroded and eaten through the leather, often creating the impression of a photographic negative. This is the case with 1QapGen ar, 4QpaleoExod^m, 4QExod-

---

[98] The description is by Nir-El–Broshi, "Black Ink." For earlier literature, see S. H. Steckoll, "Investigations of the Inks Used in Writing the Dead Sea Scrolls," *Nature* 220 (1968) 91–2.

[99] The English translations are by H. Albeck, משה סדרי משנה, סדר מועד (Jerusalem/Tel Aviv 1958) 48. Alternative translations in brackets are by H. Danby, *The Mishnah* (Oxford 1964).

[100] See further Y. Nir-El, "mqwrw sl ḥsbʿn bdyw shwrh bktybt sprym, tpylyn wmzwzwt," *Sinai* 57 (1993–94) 261–8. For a different type of evidence, see Milne–Skeat, *Scribes*, 79–80 who remarked on the ink of codex S: ' . . . the ink was in the main an iron compound, and not the old carbon-and-gum ink which is found almost universally on papyri . . . a carbon ink would not stick to the surface of the vellum, whereas a chemical ink held, often only too well.')

Lev^f, 4QLev^d, 4QDan^d, 4QShirShabb^g (4Q406). According to F. M. Cross, *DJD* XII, 133, the ink has etched the leather 'presumably because of some residual acid in the ink from its storage in a metal inkwell.' On the other hand, according to Nir-El–Broshi, "Black Ink," this deterioration was caused by the binding agents of the carbon-based ink, namely 'vegetable gum, animal size, oil or honey.'

Red ink is used in four compositions, apparently mainly for new units:

> 2QPs: The first two lines of Psalm 103.
> 4QNum^b: The first line(s) or verse(s) of new sections; see the analysis in ch. *5a3*.
> 4QD^e (4Q270) 3 i 19: Heading of a new section; see ch. *5a3*.
> 4Q481d, a composition of undetermined nature (named '4QFragments with Red Ink' by E. Larson, *DJD* XXII): Unclear circumstances.

For the use of red ink to indicate new units, cf. Egyptian literary texts from the eighteenth dynasty onwards in which a raised dot (often in red ink) indicated the end of a section; see Janzen, *Hiërogliefen*, 45; A. F. Robertson, *Word Dividers*; J. Assmann, "Die Rubren in der Überlieferung der Sinuhe-Erzählung," in *Fontes atque pontes: Eine Festgabe für H. Brunner* (ed. M. Görg; Ägypten und Altes Testament 5; Wiesbaden 1983) 18–41. In these texts, red ink was also used to mark headings and main divisions. Cf. also the Aramaic inscription from Deir ʿAllah (eighth century BCE),[101] which used red ink for titles and new sections.[102] For references to Talmudic parallels, see the discussion of 2QPs by M. Baillet, *DJD* III, 70 and of 4QNum^b by N. Jastram, *DJD* XII, 221–2. Note also the red ornaments in the titles of the books in codices A and S of the LXX, as well as the titles and some subscriptions of the Psalms in these codices. For a parallel in a later source see the manifold headers in codex Ambrosianus of the Peshitta. Drawings of Egyptian scribes often depict them as holding two pens in the same hand, one for writing with black ink, and the other one for writing with red ink. Y. Nir-El and M. Broshi, "The Red Ink of the Dead Sea Scrolls," *Archaeometry* 38 (1996) 97–102, suggested that the red ink is composed of mercury sulphide (cinnabar), brought to Palestine from Spain through Rome.

Although not specifically mentioned, the use of red ink as appearing in the biblical scrolls 2QPs and 4QNum^b probably would be forbidden by rabbinic sources, just as the use of purple ink is forbidden according to *Sof.* 1.8. However, Jerome, *Prefatio S. Hieronymi in librum Job, PL* 28.1142 refers to the existence of such early manuscripts. See, among other things, the Vienna Genesis (4–6 CE) written on purple leather with silver letters.

The copy of the Hebrew Torah that was sent from Jerusalem to Alexandria according to the *Epistle of Aristeas* § 176 for the purpose of translation into Greek was written with letters of gold. No such copies are known to have existed, and such writing was explicitly forbidden by *Sof.* 1.8. However, that treatise mentions an Alexandrian Torah scroll in which the divine names were written in gold letters, so there may be some truth to the story. (Alternatively, does the reference in *Soferim* depend on the *Epistle of Aristeas*?). On the other hand, if the copy of the Torah from which Greek Scripture was translated derived from Jerusalem, as most scholars believe, it is unlikely to have contained any gold writing (see the later prohibition in *Sof.* 1.8). In that case, the writing in gold may have been one of the literary embellishments of the *Epistle of Aristeas*.

Two *inkwells* were found by R. de Vaux in locus 30 of Qumran, the so-called scriptorium, one made of ceramic material and one of bronze (in 1997 both were exhibited in the Jordan Archaeological Museum in Amman).[103] A third inkwell, of

---

[101] For the date, cf. J. Hoftijzer and G. van der Kooij, *The Balaam Text from Deir ʿAllah Re-evaluated. Proceedings of the International Symposium Held at Leiden 21–24 August 1989* (Leiden 1991). On p. 237 in that volume, É. Puech mentions the first part of the 8th century BCE and on p. 257 G. van der Kooij speaks of the period between 800 and 720 BCE.

[102] J. Hoftijzer and G. van der Kooij, *Aramaic Texts from Deir ʿAlla* (Leiden 1976) 184.

[103] See S. Goranson, "Qumran: A Hub of Scribal Activity," *BAR* 20 (1994) 36–9; idem, "An Inkwell from Qumran," *Michmanim* 6 (1992) 37–40 (Heb.). See further n. 33 above.

ceramic material, also found by de Vaux, came from locus 31,[104] a fourth one, found by Steckoll, came from an unspecified place at Qumran,[105] and a possible fifth one is mentioned by Goranson, "Inkwell." Dried ink remains are present in two of these inkwells. See further M. Broshi, "Inkwells," *Encyclopedia DSS*, 1.375.

g. *Writing implements*

Little is known regarding the *pens* used for writing the Judean Desert texts, as these have not been preserved. The pens used were probably of the *calamus* (κάλαμος, קולמוס) type, made from reed (קנה, κάννα, κάννη, *canna*). See Haran, "Workmanship," especially 76; Diringer, *The Book*, 553–63. For a detailed description of scribal implements in the ancient Near East, see Ashton, *Scribal Habits*, ch. 3. Pfann, *DJD* XXXVI, 520 notes with regard to the pens used for the texts written in the Cryptic A script: 'For the most part a reed pen tip, that had been carefully honed to have a rectangular cut tip, was used, which allowed the scribe to produce strokes with shading (normally vertical or slightly diagonal) depending upon the direction of the stroke. At other times another more or less round or square-tipped pen was used, which produced strokes with little or no shading (cf. 4Q249y 1–2 and 4Q249z 41). A change of pen (and/or scribe) can be discerned in the lower lines of 4Q249 1.'

---

[104]R. de Vaux, "Fouilles au Khirbet Qumran: Rapport préliminaire sur la dernière campagne," *RB* 61 (1954) 206–33, especially 212 and pls. 5, 6, and 10b. For further information on inkwells found in ancient Israel, see Goranson, "Inkwell," 38.

[105]S. H. Steckoll, "Marginal Notes on the Qumran Excavations," *RevQ* 7 (1969) 33–40, especially 35.

4

TECHNICAL ASPECTS OF SCROLL WRITING

Some technical aspects of the writing of scrolls have been studied in monographs as well as in the introductory paragraphs of the *DJD* editions in vols. VIII ff., but most aspects still need to be studied in greater detail. A start has been made in the monographic studies[106] to be mentioned below as well as in this book, but these do not exhaust the subject.

a. *Ruling, guide dots/strokes* (illustrations 2a, 3, 12, 13, 15)

Almost all Qumran and Masada texts written on leather had ruled horizontal lines in accordance with the practice for most literary texts written on leather in Semitic languages and in Greek.[107] Early parallels of different types allow us to assume that also the earliest biblical scrolls must have been ruled.

Ruling is evidenced in earlier times on cuneiform clay tablets (Driver, *Semitic Writing*, 39–40), in lapidary inscriptions, and in some papyrus and leather documents in various Semitic languages (Ashton, *Scribal Habits*, ch. 6). The ruling of the Deir ʿAllah inscription from the eighth century BCE was described by A. R. Millard, "Epigraphic Notes, Aramaic and Hebrew," *PEQ* 110 (1978) 23–6 (especially 24). In some inscriptions, these lines were not clearly visible, while in others they were very distinct, almost ornamental, especially in the Samaritan inscriptions of later periods. See also some early Aramaic inscriptions and the ossuary of Simon 'builder of the temple' written in the paleo-Hebrew script in the first century CE.[108] For the ruling on leather texts, as in those from Qumran, no earlier evidence is available. For early documents, see the ruling of Akkadian clay tablets that usually ceases to be visible after inscription.[109] For the later evidence for ruling, see most medieval scrolls and codices of MT (Sirat, *Ha-ketav*, 33–6) and SP.[110]

In contrast, Judean Desert texts written on papyrus were not ruled (for Qumran, see, e.g. 4QpapMMTᵉ [4Q398], 4QpapJubʰ [4Q223–224], and the Greek texts 4QpapLXXLevᵇ and 4Qpap paraExod gr [4Q127]). The horizontal and vertical fibers probably provided some form of guide for the writing, although the horizontal fibers were not precisely horizontal (Alexander, "Literacy," 9). Most Egyptian papyri, like those from the Judean Desert, were not ruled (for exceptions see Ashton, *Scribal Habits*, 106, 111). On the other hand, Turner, *Greek Manuscripts*, 6 (with references to ancient sources) suggests that a lead instrument was used in the writing of papyri leaving a mark on the papyrus which has now disappeared. At the same time, possibly ink guide marks were used and subsequently erased.

---

[106]For an initial analysis of several valuable technical data on the scrolls, see H. Stegemann, "Methods for the Reconstruction of Scrolls from Scattered Fragments," in *Archaeology and History in the Dead Sea Scrolls: The New York University Conference in Memory of Yigael Yadin* (ed. L. H. Schiffman; JSOT/ASOR Mon 2; Sheffield 1990) 189–220; see further the studies mentioned in n. 1 above.

[107]For a general introduction, see J. Leroy, *Les types de reglure des manuscrits grecs* (Paris 1976). Turner, *Greek Manuscripts*, 4–5.

[108]For a discussion of the evidence, see J. Naveh, "An Aramaic Tomb Inscription Written in Paleo-Hebrew Script," *IEJ* 23 (1973) 82–91, especially 89.

[109]Oral communication, Z. Abusch.

[110]For a description, see especially J. Fraser, *The History of the Defter of the Samaritan Liturgy* (unpubl. diss. University of Melbourne, 1970) 60 ff.; further: Crown, *Samaritan Scribes*, 73–7; Robertson, *Catalogue*, 2; S. Talmon, "Some Unrecorded Fragments of the Hebrew Pentateuch in the Samaritan Version," *Textus* 3 (1963) 63; T. Anderson, *Studies in Samaritan Manuscripts and Artifacts: The Chamberlain–Warren Collection* (ASOR Mon 1; Cambridge, Mass. 1978) 16.

Tefillin, also, were not ruled; see those from the Judean Desert and the prescriptions in *b. Menaḥ.* 32b; *b. Meg.* 18b.

Most scribes writing on any material needed some form of graphical guide for their writing. This was provided by horizontal ruling (scoring) for the individual lines, as well as vertical ruling for the beginning and/or end of the columns (illustr. 13). The ruling was sometimes applied with the aid of guide dots/strokes, or with a grid-like device (see below on 4QpsEzek^c [4Q385b] and 11QT^a), while in other instances no aid was used.

The technique of ruling, prescribed by Talmudic sources for sacred scrolls, is named שרטוט (*b. Shabb.* 75b; *b. Meg.* 18b). In Palestinian texts, it is referred to as מסרגלין בקנה, 'one rules with a reed' (*y. Meg.* 1.71d; *Sof.* 1.1).

The first step in the preparation of the scrolls for writing was that of the ruling (scoring) meant to enable writing in straight lines. The so-called blind or dry-point ruling was usually performed with a pointed instrument (such instruments have not been preserved), probably a bone, which made a sharp crease in the leather, causing the leather to be easily split in two and even broken off (e.g. 1QapGen ar XXI–XXII; 1QIsa^a XXXVIII, XLVI11; 11QT^a [11Q19] XVIII, XXII). It is unclear why some sheets in the mentioned scrolls are split more than others; it is not impossible that differences in material, ways of preparing the skin, or force used with these rulings may account for the variations.

TABLE 1 records the few manuscripts that were ruled with *diluted* ink. The large proportion of D and S texts among these documents should be noticed. Alexander–Vermes, *DJD* XXVI, 6, n. 7 assert that the use of diluted ink for ruling may have been more widespread than evidenced by the preserved manuscripts, since the examination of ink is complicated by possible fading.

TABLE 1: *Manuscripts Ruled with Diluted Ink*

4QDan^d: S. Pfann, "4QDaniel^d (4Q115): A Preliminary Edition with Critical Notes," *RevQ* 17 (1996) 37–71, especially 39 ('very diluted ink).
4QS^b (4Q256) and possibly also 4QS^f (4Q260): Alexander–Vermes, *DJD* XXVI, 6.
4QD^{b,c,d,e,f}: S. Pfann, *DJD* XVIII, 95, 115, 123, 137, 169.
4QUnid. Frags. C, c (4Q468c).
11QShirShabb (11Q17): García Martínez–Tigchelaar–van der Woude, *DJD* XXIII, 260, 304. On p. 304, this ink is described as 'red.'
Unidentified fragment PAM 43.692, 81 (letters written *on* the line): *DJD* XXXIII, pl. XXXI.

Usually, the horizontal ruling on the sheets was continuous for each of the sheets within the scroll, starting to the right of the vertical line indicating the beginning of the first column of the sheet, and continuing as far as the left border of the sheet beyond the left vertical line of the final column; for good examples, see 11QT^a (11Q19), e.g. XXVI–XXVIII; 11QtgJob XVII–XVIII. In all these cases, the ruling was continued in the blank interlinear spaces. Usually, vertical ruling was also continuous, extending beyond the written text into the top and bottom margins as far as the edges of the leather (see, e.g. 1QIsa^a II–IV; 1QIsa^b VIII; 1QM VII; 4QGen^c 1 ii; 4QDan^a frg. 3; 4QD^e frg. 7 representing the end of the scroll [4Q270; illustr. 12]; 11QT^a [11Q19], e.g. XXVII).

In the few Qumran documents that were *not* ruled, the distance between the lines is irregular and the writing is not straight. The absence of vertical ruling meant that the beginnings of the lines were also not straight (e.g. 4QToh A [4Q274] 1 i). Some of the Egyptian leather texts were ruled, while others were not (Ashton, *Scribal Habits*, 112).

Several demotic literary papyri from the 2nd and 3rd centuries CE had horizontal ruled lines on which the text was standing (Tait, "Guidelines"). The Aramaic documents from the fifth century BCE published by Driver, *Aramaic Documents*, were not ruled.

For examples of unruled literary texts, see 4QJer^c (illustr. 20), 4QCant^b (illustr. 8a), 4QFlor (4Q174), 4QLevi^a ar (4Q213 [however, guide dots are attested in frg. 2]), 4QLevi^b ar (4Q213a), 4QJub^e (4Q220), 4QPrayer of Nabonidus ar (4Q242), 4QM^c (4Q493), 4QapocrLam B (4Q501), 4QDibHam^a (4Q504), 4QTQahat ar (4Q542), 5QDeut, 5QLam^a, 5QLam^b. Likewise, two small lists, 4QList of False Prophets ar (4Q339) and 4QList of Netinim (4Q340), whose original form was probably not much larger than their present fragmentary shape, were not ruled.

It is unclear what these unruled texts have in common otherwise, apart from possibly a less professional preparation method. 4QJer^c is a somewhat carelessly produced text in which damaged sections were stitched both before and after the writing (illustr. 20), and 4QCant^b is in all aspects an unusual and imprecise copy. This pertains also to 4QLevi^a ar (4Q213) which does not have straight right or left margins and has been inscribed until the very edge of the leather, and in one instance (1 7) even beyond. Because of the lack of ruling, the words in 4QJub^e (4Q220) are written irregularly, sometimes above and sometimes below the imaginary line.

For an example of a text that was only vertically ruled (left margin only), see 4QTest (4Q175; single column composition). 4QNum^b was only ruled on the right side of the column (double vertical ruling).

The most frequently used system of *vertical ruling* was employed at both the beginning (right side) and end (left side) of the column. The horizontal margin line at the end of a column and the vertical line to the right of the following column indicate the structure of the columns and the intercolumnar margin. For some examples, see 1QIsa^a, 1QIsa^b, 1QS, 1QapGen ar, 1QH^a, 1QM, 1QpHab, 1QMyst (1Q27), 3QpIsa (3Q4), 4QpaleoGen-Exod^l, 4QpaleoExod^m, 4QNum^b, 4QSam^a, 4QQoh^a, 4QpIsa^b (4Q162), 4QpHos^a (4Q166), 4QpNah (4Q169), 4QS^d (4Q258), 4QExposition on the Patriarchs (4Q464) 3 i–ii, 4QOrd^b (4Q513), 6QCant, 11QpaleoLev^a, MasPs^a, and MasSir. Usually the vertical lines are more or less perpendicular to the horizontal lines, creating a rectangular shape. In rare cases, the left line is redrawn. In texts written in the paleo-Hebrew script where words could be split between two lines, scribes were more consistent in not exceeding the left margin; see below § f.

Vertical ruling as a means of separating between columns of writing is also evidenced in Egyptian and Etruscan sources; see Ashton, *Scribal Habits*, 114–5.

In a few cases, a *double vertical ruling* was applied to the right of the column, especially at the beginning of the first column of a sheet (TABLE 2). Such ruling was performed with two dry lines, spaced a few millimeters apart, while the writing started after the second vertical line. The technique may have been used for purposes of neatness (Martin, *Scribal Character*, I.99), and in the case of the ruling on the left side it would have ensured that the scribe observed the left margin. A somewhat similar practice is known from demotic literary papyri from the 2nd and 3rd centuries CE in which double vertical lines as well as horizontal lines surrounded each column, drawn in ink with a ruler or freehand (for a discussion and examples, see Tait, "Guidelines"). TABLE 2 records some Qumran texts in which double vertical ruling is applied.

TABLE 2: *Double Vertical Ruling in Qumran Documents*

1QH[a]	Before col. IX (Suk. = Puech XVII): irregular occurrence at the beginning of a sheet (with an interval of 1.0 cm) and to the left of cols. X–XII (Suk. = Puech XVIII–XIX; interval of 0.2 cm) within the sheet until the final column, both in the segment written by scribe A.
4QNum[b]	Before cols. I, X, XV: to the right of the columns, only at the beginnings of sheets (with an interval of 0.3 cm).
4QDan[d]	Between cols. 2 i and 2 ii (interval of 0.7 cm; one extra line). However, according to E. Ulrich, *DJD* XVI, 279 there were two lines between the two columns.
4QS[f] (4Q260)	Frg. 1 (PAM 43.265) in the middle of a sheet: right-hand side of the column (interval of 0.3 cm); the other columns (frgs. 2a, 5) have no vertical lines at all.
4QRP[c] (4Q365)	Frg. 23: right margin (interval of 0.25 cm), but not in the other columns, which were marked with a single vertical, or not at all.
4QMMT[f] (4Q399)	Between cols. ii and iii (uninscribed), but not before col. ii; interval of 0.9 cm.
4QCreation? (4Q457a)	Two vertical lines (0.8 cm apart) to the right of the text in frg. 1. See ch. *4b*.
4QOrd[b] (4Q513)	Frg. 2 i: left margin (interval of 0.2 cm); no further margins preserved.
11QtgJob	Before col. XXIV in the middle of a sheet (frg. 21; with an interval of 0.6 cm), but not elsewhere in the scroll.

Double vertical ruling is also found occasionally in some Egyptian papyri written in page form (Ashton, *Scribal Habits*, 106). Some manuscripts of SP also have double vertical rulings at the left edge of the column; see the ends of cols. V, XVII, XIX–XXIV in *Sefer Abisha* (Pérez Castro, *Séfer Abiša*),[111] and MS Topkapi G i 101 (Crown, *Dated Samaritan MSS*). The purpose of the vertical ruling in SP differs from that in the Qumran scrolls, as it sets apart the last letter or two letters of the text, and does not denote the margin itself.

The ruling may have been executed by the scribes themselves, but more likely it was applied—often with the aid of guide dots/strokes (see below)—by the scroll manufacturers. They had no precise knowledge of the text to be inscribed as indicated by discrepancies between the inscribed text and the ruled lines:

• After the final inscribed column, several compositions have one or more ruled columns (§ g).

• Some uninscribed handle sheets at the end of scrolls were ruled (§ g).

• Above the writing block of the second sheet of 1QpHab, containing cols. VIII–XIII, there are one, two, or three uninscribed horizontal lines, that are not indicated on the sheet containing the previous columns (I–VII). See ch. *3b*.

• The first sheet of 4QDeut[n] (illustr. 15), representing a single column (col. I), contains a block of eight horizontal ruled and inscribed lines (line 5 in the middle of the text is empty), and in addition one ruled line above and six below the text, totaling fifteen ruled lines. This sheet was prepared originally for a larger scroll, and was subsequently adapted to the needs of 4QDeut[n]. Likewise, in the second sheet, the first column (col. II) but not those following, has twelve inscribed but fourteen ruled horizontal lines, two of which appear in what is now the bottom margin. For a different view, see ch. *3c* above.

• 4QCal Doc/Mish D (4Q325): An irregularly ruled horizontal line between lines 5 and 6 was disregarded by the scribe.

• 4QBarkhi Nafshi[c] (4Q436) frg. 1 has eleven ruled, but ten inscribed lines.

• 4QRP[c] (4Q365) 7 i–ii has three uninscribed dry lines at the bottom of both columns in the middle of the composition.

• 4QMMT[f] (4Q399) has twelve ruled, but only eleven inscribed lines as well as an uninscribed ruled final column.

• Disregarding the existing ruling, the scribe of 11QT[a] (11Q19) often wrote two lines instead of one between the horizontal rulings in the last two columns, in order to squeeze in the remaining text and finish the writing at the bottom of that column (see col. LXVI 7–8, 11–12, 14–15 in illustr. 13). However, upon reaching the penultimate ruled line, he realized that he had erred in his calculation and had surplus space

---

[111]See the description by Talmon, "Some Unrecorded Fragments," 63.

left. He therefore left most of this line open (his line 16) and also left space within the final line (line 17), towards the end.

On the *distance* between the ruled lines, see below, § f.

The writing in all the scrolls from the Judean Desert was executed in such a way that the letters were hanging from the lines; see § f.

In fifty-six or fifty-seven Qumran texts (TABLES 3 and 4) written on leather in the square and paleo-Hebrew scripts, single *guide dots* ('points jalons') or sometimes *strokes* were indicated with the purpose of guiding the drawing of dry lines (for examples, see illustrations 2a, 10a, and 15).[112] These dots or strokes were indicated in the space between the right edge of the sheet and the beginning of the first column as in 4QDeut^n (illustr. 15) or between the left edge of the final column in a sheet and the end of the sheet, as in 4QT^a? (4Q365a), usually at a distance of 0.5–1.0 cm from the edge of the sheet (TABLE 7). In a few instances they appear at a considerable distance from the edge of the sheet: 4QUnid. Frags. C, c [4Q468c]; 3.0 cm), MasSir V (2.5 cm), 2QpaleoLev (1.5 cm), 4QRP^e (4Q367; 1.5 cm).

In 4–6 manuscripts, the dots appear in the intercolumnar margin in the middle of a sheet serving as a vertical line:

- 4QpHos^a (4Q166) to the right of the column
- 4QRP^c (4Q365) 12a to the left of the column
- 4QShirShabb^f (4Q405) 17–19a, 20 i, and 23 i to the left of the column on a fold in the leather
- 4QNarrative A (4Q458) to the left of the column on a fold in the leather
- 4QVisions of Amram^e ar (4Q547) 4 (probably)
- 4QDan^d 2 4, 5 (to the left of col. 2 i), only in these two lines and not in the previous ones.

The first three texts were copied in the Qumran scribal practice.

The guide dots/strokes were intended to guide the drawing of dry lines and were therefore inserted by the persons who manufactured the scrolls, rather than the scribes themselves. Just as scribes often wrote beyond the left vertical line (§ f below), they also wrote very close to these dots, on and even beyond them (e.g. 4QGen-Exod^a 19 ii; 4QIsa^a 11 ii). As a result, the space between the dots/strokes and the left edge of the writing differs from scroll to scroll, also within the scroll, and even between the lines in individual columns. In contrast, within a manuscript, dots indicated to the right of the column always appear at the same distance from the right edge (see TABLE 7).

The dots/strokes at one of the two extremities of the column appear at different distances from the vertical line. In some manuscripts, they were indicated 1–2 millimeters before the line: 1QMyst (1Q27), 4QXII^c 18, 4QRP^a (4Q158) 1, 4QShirShabb^f (4Q405) 17, 20 i, 23 i, 4QIndividual Thanksgiving A (4Q441), 4QNarrative A (4Q458); and sometimes slightly after the line: 4QpaleoExod^m col. I, 4QT^a? (4Q365a) 1.

The employment of guide dots/strokes reveals some details regarding the preparation of sheets although not of their provenance. The use of guide dots/strokes is limited to a minority of scrolls from Qumran and Masada (MasSir only). One notes that none of the large Qumran scrolls had guide dots/strokes. In the case of Qumran, a special pattern is noticeable. Among the documents containing guide dots/strokes, the majority of nonbiblical texts, that is, nineteen of the twenty-six identified texts written in Hebrew, reflect the characteristics of the Qumran scribal practice. A connection between this system of preparing scrolls and the Qumran scribal practice is therefore likely, at least during a certain period. At the same time, another forty-three texts written according to the Qumran scribal practice do not seem to have guide dots/strokes (TABLE 6). Such a situation shows that scribes writing in what we label the Qumran scribal practice either

---

[112]For other uses of dots in manuscripts, see SUBJECT INDEX, 'dot.'

used skins prepared elsewhere using a different convention or themselves employed differing manufacturing procedures over the course of several generations.

A further point of interest:

• 4QLevi[a] ar (4Q213) and 4QLevi[b] ar (4Q213a) are prepared with the same type of dots, appearing very close to the edge of the sheet.

Usually all sheets containing a particular composition were prepared in the same way, and accordingly if guide dots/strokes were present, they appeared in the same position in all sheets. However, several compositions consisted of sheets prepared by different persons resulting in variations, with some sheets having no guide dots/strokes. Some scrolls have guide dots only in either the right or left margin. For details, see TABLES 3 and 4 and the list below.

The guide dots/strokes usually appear level with the top of the letters, coinciding with the ruled lines. In a few cases, they appear level with the middle or bottom of the letters, see TABLE 7. The explanation for the latter position seems to be that the scribe intended to indicate the letter size: 4QIsa[g] 1–8; 4QWork Containing Prayers B (4Q292) 2; 4QShirShabb[f] (4Q405) 20 i; 4QNarrative A (4Q458) 2 i.

The guide dots/strokes aided the manufacturer in ruling the lines from the beginning of the sheet to its end, while excluding the right and left edges of the sheet beyond the guide dots. In some cases, the ruling extended beyond the dots/strokes to the edge of the sheet: 2QDeut[c], 4QIsa[f], 4QIsa[g], 1QMyst (1Q27), 4QRP[a] (4Q158) 1, 4QShirShabb[f] (4Q405) 17, 4QUnid. Frags. C, c (4Q468c).

Each sheet was ruled separately, usually without reference to the preceding and following sheets; compare e.g. 11QtgJob col. XXXI (last column of sheet 11) with the following column, XXXII (first column of sheet 12) and 11QT[a] (11Q19) XLVIII (last column in a sheet) with col. XLIX (first column of a sheet). However, in some scrolls (*de luxe* editions? [§ j]), a grid-like device ensuring fixed spacing in the columns in each sheet must have been used for one or more sheets. Within each column, often no fixed spaces were left between the lines. For details, see § f below.

As a rule, the guide dots/strokes aided the scribes in the drawing of lines. Occasionally, however, there is no physical evidence of ruling. In such cases, either the dots themselves guided the writing as in 4QLevi[a] ar (4Q213) 2 (left margin), or the ruling, once present, is no longer visible. In yet other cases in which a grid was presumably used, as in 11QT[a], there was no need for guide dots.

Turner, *Greek Manuscripts*, 4 mentions several instances of guide dots in Greek papyrus scrolls, placed in different positions, at mid-line or preceding each or every few lines. From a much earlier period, the Old Kingdom Egyptian papyri from Gebelein and Abu Sir contain similar dots (Ashton, *Scribal Habits*, 103).

Guide dots or strokes occur at the beginnings and/or ends of sheets in nineteen or twenty biblical scrolls, as illustrated in TABLE 3.

TABLE 3: *Guide Dots/Strokes Indicated in Biblical Scrolls*

4QGen[k]	frg. 1: right margin (probable).
4QGen-Exod[a]	frg. 19 ii: left margin; frg. 22 ii: right margin (MT).
4QpaleoExod[m]	oblique strokes in the left margin of col. I and the right margin of col. II; not in the right margins of cols. XXVII, XXXVIII, XLV (pre-Samaritan).
2QpaleoLev	left margin; oblique strokes (character unclear).
4QLev-Num[a]	frgs. 6, 27: right margins; frgs. 54, 69: left margins (not easily visible on the plates, but see the description in *DJD* XII, 153; MT/SP).
4QLev[b]	frg. 2: right margin; dots, diagonal strokes (MT/SP).

4QNum^b	XIX and XXIV: left margins, but not the right margin of col. I (pre-Samaritan/ LXX; Qumran scribal practice).
1QDeut^a	frg. 12: left margin (Qumran scribal practice).
2QDeut^c	right margin (Qumran scribal practice).
4QDeut^n	sheet 2: right margin (some lines, with strokes in other lines), but not in the single-column sheet 1 (independent); illustr. 15.
4QDeut^o	frgs. 3, 14: right margins, but not in the left margin of frg. 2 (MT/SP).
4QIsa^a	frg. 9: right margin (?); frg. 11 ii: left margin (MT/LXX).
4QIsa^f	frg. 27: right and left margins (MT/LXX).
4QIsa^g	frgs. 1–8: right margin (MT/LXX).
4QIsa^i	right margin (character unclear).
4QJer^d	left margin (close to the LXX).
4QEzek^a	frg. 4: right margin (independent).
4QXII^c	frg. 18: left margin (independent, Qumran scribal practice).
4QPs^b	I, XX: right margins (independent); illustr. 19.
4QPs^f	frg. 11 iii (col. X): left margin (independent).

While the majority of biblical Qumran texts reflect MT, only two of the aforementioned texts in which guide dots are found belong to this group. As a result, this practice must have been followed in particular by scribes who produced texts other than the proto-rabbinic Scripture texts.

Guide dots or strokes are also found in nineteen nonbiblical texts written according to the Qumran scribal practice as well as in eight additional Hebrew texts, six Aramaic texts, and nine or ten unidentified fragments.

TABLE 4: *Guide Dots/Strokes Indicated in Nonbiblical Scrolls*[113]

Texts Written in the Qumran Scribal Practice

1QMyst (1Q27)	frg. 1: right margin.
1QHymns (1Q36)	frg. 24: right and left margins.
4QRP^a (4Q158)	frg. 1: right margin (dots, horiz. strokes); frgs. 3 and 5: left margins.
4QpHos^a (4Q166)	middle of sheet, to the right of col. i.
4QTNaph (4Q215)	horizontal strokes in the right margin, starting above the writing surface in the top margin.
4QPsJub^c? (4Q227)	frg. 2: left margin.
4QD^f (4Q271)	frg. 3: left margin.
4QBer^a (4Q286)	frg. 20a: left margin.
4QBer^b (4Q287)	frg. 2b: left margin (combination of dots and a stroke).
4QWork Cont. Prayers B (4Q292)	frg. 2: left margin.
4QCal Doc/Mish C (4Q321a)	frg. 5: right margin.
4QCal Doc C (4Q326)	right margin.
4QRP^b (4Q364)	frg. 14: right margin, strokes.
4QRP^c (4Q365)	frgs. 6b (illustr. 2a), 8a, 36: right margin; frg. 12a: middle of sheet, left margin; frgs. 12b iii, 30, 33b: left margin, usually in a combination of dots and strokes.
4QT^a? (4Q365a)	frg. 1: left margin, strokes.
4QShirShabb^f (4Q405)	frgs. 9, 11b, 17: left margins; frgs. 17–19a, 20 i, and 23 i to the left of the column on a fold in the leather in the middle of the sheet.
4QSapiential Hymn (4Q411)	right margin.
4QInstr^d (4Q418)	frg. 81: right margin, frg. 190: left margin; not in frg. 7b (left margin), frgs. 9, 204, and 207 (right margins).
4QM^e (4Q495)	frg. 2: right margin.

[113]Strokes are specified in this table. All other references pertain to dots.

2QSir	frg. 2: left margin.
4QRP[d] (4Q366)	frg. 1: left margin.
4QRP[e] (4Q367)	frg. 3: left margin.
4QapocrJer A (4Q383)	frg. 6: right margin; strokes (orthographic practice unclear).
4QIndiv. Thanksgiving A (4Q441)	right margin (orthographic practice unclear).
4QNarrative A (4Q458)	frg. 2 i: left margin in the middle of the sheet; dots, strokes (orthographic practice unclear).
4QUnid. Frags. C, c (4Q468c)	right margin (orthographic practice unclear).
4QHymnic Text A (4Q468h)	right margin.

Aramaic Texts

1QNJ ar (1Q32)	frg. 21: left margin.
4QEnastr[c] ar (4Q210)	frg. 1 ii: left margin.
4QLevi[a] ar (4Q213)	frg. 2: left margin, not in the right margin of frg. 1 ii.
4QLevi[b] ar (4Q213a)	right margin, not in the left margin of frg. 1.
4QVisions of Amram[d] ar (4Q546)	frg. 14: right margin.
4QVisions of Amram[e] ar (4Q547)	frg. 4: middle of sheet (probably).

Unidentified Texts

PAM 43.663, frg. 46 (*DJD* XXXIII, pl. IV)	right margin (strokes).
PAM 43.666, frg. 58 (*DJD* XXXIII, pl. VII)	left margin.
PAM 43.672, frg. 63 (*DJD* XXXIII, pl. XIII)	left margin.
PAM 43.675, frg. 60 (*DJD* XXXIII, pl. XVI)	right margin; the strokes resemble scribal marks in 4Qpap pIsa[c] (4Q163) 4–7 ii.
PAM 43.682, frg. 32 (*DJD* XXXIII, pl. XXII)	right margin (strokes).
PAM 43.686, frg. 41 (*DJD* XXXIII, pl. XXVI)	right margin (strokes).
PAM 43.689, frg. 88 (*DJD* XXXIII, pl. XXVIII)	left margin.
PAM 43.694, frg. 44 (*DJD* XXXIII, pl. XXXIII)	left margin, strokes; a paleo-Hebrew unidentified fragment.
PAM 43.697, frg. 61 (*DJD* XXXIII, pl. XXXVI)	left margin.
PAM 44.102, frg. 14? (*DJD* XXXIII, pl. XLI)	right margin.

Masada

MasSir	left margin of col. V; not right margin of col. VI.

Greek Text

4Qpap paraExod gr (4Q127)	frgs. 14 and 31 (Skehan–Ulrich–Sanderson, *DJD* IX, 223).

The evidence for the use of small diagonal and horizontal strokes in Qumran texts is summarized in TABLE 5. These texts may have derived from certain manufacturers and may have other features in common.

TABLE 5: *Strokes Indicated in the Margins of Qumran Scrolls*

2QpaleoLev	diagonal
4QpaleoExod[m]	diagonal
4QLev[b]	dots, diagonal strokes
4QDeut[n]	dots, horizontal strokes

4QRP[a] (4Q158) 1	dots, horizontal strokes
4QTNaph (4Q215)	horizontal
4QBer[b] (4Q287) 2b	dots and a horizontal stroke
4QRP[b] (4Q364)	horizontal
4QRP[c] (4Q365)	diagonal, horizontal strokes with dots
4QT[a]? (4Q365a)	horizontal
4QapocrJer A (4Q383) 6	diagonal
4QNarrative A (4Q458)	dots, horizontal strokes
PAM 43.663, frg. 46	horizontal
PAM 43.675, frg. 60	horizontal strokes resembling scribal marks in 4Qpap pIsa[c] (4Q163) 4–7 ii
PAM 43.682, frg. 32	horizontal
PAM 43.686, frg. 41	horizontal
PAM 43.694, frg. 44 (paleo-Hebrew)	horizontal

The system of indicating guide dots or strokes resembles that of pinpricking in manuscript codices of later periods. Compare, for example, the elaborate pricking system of codex S of the LXX (Milne–Skeat, *Scribes*, 73–4). For investigations on this system, see the detailed bibliography on New Testament manuscripts listed by B. M. Metzger.[114] For still later sources, see the description of the pricking in medieval Hebrew manuscripts by M. Beit Arié and M. Glatzer.[115]

Within the present analysis, it is also relevant to list the forty-three Qumran texts written in the Qumran scribal practice which do *not* have guide dots at the beginnings or ends of sheets:

TABLE 6: *Qumran Scrolls Written according to the Qumran Scribal Practice Which Do* Not *Give Evidence of Guide Dots/Strokes*

Biblical Scrolls

1QIsa[a] (scribes A and B)
2QJer
4QDeut[j]
4QIsa[c]
4QLam
11QPs[a]

Nonbiblical Scrolls

1QS, 1QSa (right and left margins), 1QSb (right margin)
1QpHab
1QH[a,b]
1QM
1QapGen ar
4QTest (4Q175)
4QCatena A (4Q177)
4QHoroscope (4Q186)
4QJub[f] (4Q221)
4QCommGen A (4Q252)
4QMiscellaneous Rules (4Q265) 6 (right margin)
4QD[a] (4Q266)

---

[114]B. M. Metzger, *The Text of the New Testament* (Oxford 1964) 8, n. 1.

[115]M. Beit Arié, "Some Technical Practices Employed in Hebrew Dated Medieval Manuscripts," in *Litterae textuales, Codicologica 2, Éléments pour une codicologie comparée* (Leiden 1978) 72–92, especially 84–90; idem, *Hebrew Codicology*, 69–72; M. Glatzer, "The Aleppo Codex: Codicological and Paleographical Aspects," *Sefunot* 4 (1989) 210–15 (Heb. with Eng. summ.).

4QD^b (4Q267)
4QD^d (4Q269)
4QToh A (4Q274) 1 (right margin)
4QCommunal Confession (4Q393) 1 (right and left margins)
4QMMT^a (4Q394)
4QShirShabb^b (4Q401)
4QShirShabb^d (4Q403)
4QVision and Interpretation (4Q410) 1 (left margin)
4QRitPur A (4Q414; right margin)
4QInstr^a (4Q415) 9 and 10 (right and left margins)
4QInstr^b (4Q416 1; right margin)
4QInstr^c (4Q417 1, 2; right margins)
4QInstruction-like Composition A (4Q419)
4QH^b (4Q428) 1 (right margin)
4QBarkhi Nafshi^b (4Q435)
4QHodayot-like Text C (4Q440) 3 (left margin)
4QIndividual Thanksgiving A (4Q441)
4QNarrative C (4Q462)
4QapocrLam B (4Q501)
4QDibHam^a (4Q504)
5QCommunity Rule (5Q11)
11QapocrPs (11Q11)
11QT^a (11Q19)
11QT^b (11Q20; frgs. 2 [col. I]; 8 [col. IV]; 13 [col. VII]; 28 [col. XIV])

TABLE 7 summarizes the position of guide dots in the manuscripts. In this table, texts that presumably were written in the Qumran scribal practice are printed in boldface.

TABLE 7: *The Position of Guide Dots/Strokes in the Judean Desert Scrolls*

Name	Position	Strokes[116]	Distance from Edge of Text (cm)	Position Relative to Letters in Text and Distance from Edge of Sheets
			BIBLICAL TEXTS	
1QDeut^a	left		0.5	level with top of letters
2QpaleoLev	left	diagonal	0.0–0.2	0.2 cm above top of letters; 1.5 cm
2QDeut^c	right		1.2	top; 0.5 cm
4QGen-Exod^a 19ii	left		0.0–0.2	middle; 0.7 cm
4QGen^k	right?		0.1	top; 1.8 cm
4QpaleoExod^m I	left, right (col. II not well visible)	diagonal	0.0–0.1	just beyond the vertical rule, middle to top; 1.1 cm
4QLev-Num^a	right, left		0.3	top; 0.5 cm
4QLev^b	right	dots, diagonal strokes	0.1	top; 1.3 cm
4QNum^b	left		0.0–0.1	top; 1.1 cm
4QDeut^n	right	dots, horizontal strokes	0.1 cm above first letters in the col.	top; 1.0 cm
4QDeut^o	right		0.3–0.7	top
4QIsa^a 11 ii	left		0.0	top; *c.* 2.0 cm

---

[116]Strokes are indicated, while dots are not indicated.

4QIsa^f	right, left		0.3	top; 0.5 cm
4QIsa^g	right		0.1	middle or bottom
4QIsa^i	right		0.4	top; 0.7 cm
4QJer^d	left		0.0–0.1	top and middle; 1.0 cm
4QEzek^a	right		0.2	top; 1.2 cm
4QXII^c	left		0.3	top; 0.7 cm
4QPs^b	right		0.4	top; 0.7 cm; illustr. 19
4QPs^f	left		0.0–0.1	on the vertical lines in the margin; top; 0.8–1.2 cm

NONBIBLICAL TEXTS

1QMyst (**1Q27**)	right		0.2	on the vert. lines, sometimes coinciding with tops of letters; 1.0 cm
1QHymns (**1Q36**)	right, left		1.0	no data
2QSir (2Q18)	left		0.6–1.0	top; 0.5 cm from edge
4QRP^a (**4Q158**) 1	right	horizontal	0.2	top; 0.7 cm
4QRP^a (**4Q158**) 5	left	dots, hor. strokes	0.0–0.5	top; 0.7 cm
4QpHos^a (**4Q166**)	right (middle of sheet)		0.2	1.1 cm from the following column; irregular layout
4QEnastr^c ar (**4Q210**)	left		no data	0.3 cm
4QLevi^a ar (**4Q213**)	left		0.2–0.4	top, middle, and bottom; 0.1 cm
4QLevi^b ar (**4Q213a**)	right		1.3	top; 0.1 cm
4QTNaph (**4Q215**)	right	horizontal	0.0	top; 0.7 cm
4QPsJub^c? (4Q227)	left		0.1–0.8	top; 0.3 cm
4QD^f (**4Q271**)	left		0.1–0.8	top; 0.3 cm
4QBer^b (**4Q287**)	left	dots, hor. stroke	0.1	top; 0.3 cm
4QWork Cont. Pray. B (**4Q292**)	left		0.4	bottom; 2.0 cm
4QCal Doc/Mish C (**4Q321a**)	right		1.2	top
4QCal Doc C (**4Q326**)	right		0.4	top of letters and between letters; 2.0 cm
4QRP^b (**4Q364**) 14	right	horizontal	0.2	between letters; 1.0 cm
4QRP^c (**4Q365**) 6b	left		0.2	top; 0.7 cm
4QRP^c (**4Q365**) 8a	right		0.2	top; 0.6 cm
4QRP^c (**4Q365**) 12a	left (middle of sheet)		0.3	1.3 cm from the following column
4QRP^c (**4Q365**) 12b iii	left	horizontal strokes, dots	1.0	top; 1.2 cm
4QRP^c (**4Q365**) 33b	left		0.0–0.5	top; 0.8 cm
4QRP^c (**4Q365**) 36	right	one diagonal stroke, dots	0.2	top; 1.0 cm
4QT^a? (**4Q365a**) 1	left	horizontal strokes, dots	0.5	top; left of the vertical rule; 0.7+ cm
4QRP^e (**4Q367**)	left		0.0–0.9	top; 1.5 cm
4QapocrJer A (**4Q383**)	right	diagonal	0.3	top; 1.0 cm
4QShirShabb^f (**4Q405**) 11b	left		0.3–1.0	top; 0.5 cm

4QShirShabb^f (4Q405) 17	left (middle of sheet)		0.1–0.5	top; on the vertical line; 1.0 cm to following col.
4QShirShabb^f (4Q405) 20 i	left (middle of sheet)		0.0–0.2	bottom; on the vert. line; 1.5 cm to following col.
4QShirShabb^f (4Q405) 23 i	right (middle of sheet)		0.6	top; on the vertical line; 1.3 cm to following col.
4QSapiential Hymn (4Q411)	right		0.2	0.1 cm above top of letters; 0.7 cm
4QInstr^d (4Q418) 9	right		1.1	0.1 cm above top; 0.2 cm
4QInstr^d (4Q418) 81	right		0.3	top; 0.3 cm
4QInstr^d (4Q418) 190	left		1.2	top; 0.2 cm
4QInd. Thanksgiving A (4Q441)	right		1.7	top; 1.0 cm; on the vertical rule
4QNarrative A (4Q458)	left (middle of sheet)	dots, horizontal strokes	0.0–0.3	bottom; on the vertical rule
4QUnid. Frags. C, c (4Q468c)	right		0.2	top; 3.0 cm
4QM^e (4Q495)	right		0.0–0.1	0.3 cm above top; 1.8 cm
4QVisions of Amram^d ar (4Q546)	right		0.4	top; 1.5 cm
11QNJ ar (11Q18)	left		0.2	top; 1.5 cm

MasSir			1.2 average	top; 1.5 cm

PAM 43.694 (paleo-Hebrew)	left	horizontal	0.3	top; 1.0 cm
PAM 43.675 frg.60	right	horizontal	0.1	top; 0.5+ cm

b. *Opisthographs and palimpsests*

(1) *Opisthographs*

(α) *Background*

The great majority of literary compositions from the Judean Desert contain single texts written on one side of the material.[117] This section deals with texts inscribed on both sides.

In papyri, the inscribed side, on which the fibers run horizontally, is named the recto; the verso, usually uninscribed, is the side on which the fibers run vertically. However, sometimes it is difficult to differentiate between the recto and verso,[118] and sometimes only the verso is inscribed (thus the Aramaic texts published by Kraeling, *Aramaic Papyri*; see p. 127 there). In documents written on leather (skin), the term recto represents the hairy, usually inscribed, side, while the verso indicates the

---

[117]In several instances different though related literary compositions were written by the same or two different scribes in the same scroll (see ch. *3d*).

[118]Thus 4QpapS^a (4Q255) is described in *DJD* XXVI, 28 by Alexander–Vermes as the verso, and 4QpapHodayot-like Text B (4Q433a) as the recto, while E. Schuller, *DJD* XXIX, 237 describes them as recto and verso respectively. Schuller bases herself on the view of J. T. Milik as reflected in the *Preliminary Concordance* and on the paleographical dating of 4QpapHodayot-like Text B (4Q433a) as being later than the text on the other side (75 BCE).

uninscribed flesh side. Here also the distinction is sometimes hard to make, and some scholars call any inscribed surface 'recto,' even if it happens to be the flesh side.

In the documents from the Judean Desert, the reverse side of the papyrus or leather was used relatively infrequently for writing. Likewise, the Aramaic documents written on leather and papyrus from the fifth and fourth centuries BCE published by Kraeling, *Aramaic Papyri* and Driver, *Aramaic Documents* were usually inscribed on one side only. On the other hand, Porten–Yardeni, *TAD* 3.xiii, note that the Egyptian papyrus letters published in *TAD* were usually written on the recto and verso, while contracts were only rarely written on both sides. More in general, Egyptian papyri of *all* periods were often inscribed on both sides, especially when the scribe had no more papyrus available. Egyptian letters were also written on both sides (Diringer, *The Book*, 138; Černy, *Paper*, 18).

From a technical point of view, there were no major impediments to the writing on both sides of the material from the Judean Desert. Yet, the flesh side of the leather probably had to be prepared in a special way for this purpose—most leather documents were inscribed only on the hairy side of the leather. Papyrus was vulnerable to damage and even more so when inscribed on both sides. In spite of these complications, writing on both sides of the material was introduced at an early stage due to the scarcity and high cost of the writing materials (note the very early Egyptian papyri mentioned above). In some cases the writing on two sides was planned from the outset (§ γ), in other cases the original text lost its earlier importance. Ezek 2:10 mentions an early scroll, probably papyrus, that was 'inscribed on both the front and back' (כתובה פנים ואחור).[119] Further sources mentioning opisthographs are Rev 5:1 (a βιβλίον inscribed on both sides and sealed with seven seals) and such classical sources as Lucian, *Vitarum Auctio* 9 and Pliny, *Epistol.* III.5.17 (*opisthographi*).[120]

Only a relatively small number of texts found at Qumran were inscribed on both sides (ὀπισθόγραφον, *opisthograph*); see a list of such texts from the Judean Desert in APPENDIX 3 and an earlier, less complete, list in Wise, *Thunder in Gemini*, 133. Most Qumran opisthographs are papyri, but the corpus also contains six opisthographs on leather.[121] Half of the texts are literary, while the other half are documentary. The exact number of Qumran opisthographs cannot be determined, among other things because the collections of fragments named 1Q70, 4Q249–250, and 4Q518 display several scribal hands. Mas 1o (Mas pap paleoText of Sam. Origin [recto] and Mas pap paleoUnidentified Text [verso]) is also inscribed on both sides, in two different handwritings. In Murabbaʿat, three opisthographs were found: Mur papLiterary Text gr (Mur 109 recto) and Mur papLiterary Text gr (Mur 110 verso); Mur papLiterary

---

[119]It is unclear from the context whether this inscribing on both sides was the rule or the exception in the prophet's eyes. According to W. Zimmerli, *Ezekiel 1* (Hermeneia; Philadelphia 1969) 135, it was exceptional for the prophet to be confronted with such a scroll, but the arguments presented are not convincing. Possibly many ancient scrolls were written in this way.

[120]A mural painting from the synagogue in Dura-Europos (dedicated 244–5 CE) is probably less relevant in this regard (see N. de Lange, *The Illustrated History of the Jewish People* [London 1997] 52). This mural depicts a scribe holding a leather scroll inscribed on the outside, probably representing the public reading from the Torah. The drawing infers that the inside of the scroll was also inscribed. Such Torah scrolls have not been found, and the artist probably merely wanted to visualize the fact that this scroll was inscribed (by depicting the inscribed external side of the scroll, the scribe implied that the inside was inscribed as well). The written surface of the column depicted was at least 50 cm long, a fact which further underlines the unrealistic nature of this scroll.

[121]The claim of Haran, "Book-Scrolls," 172 that 'writing on both sides of a skin . . . was unknown before the beginning of the Christian era' is not supported by the dating of the Qumran leather opisthographs, some of which are ascribed to the late Hasmonean era (4QNarrative Work and Prayer [4Q460]: 75–1 BCE; 4QMish C [4Q324]: 50–25 BCE).

Text gr (Mur 112 recto) and Mur papProceedings of Lawsuit gr (Mur 113 verso); Mur papExtracts from Official Ordinances gr (Mur 117 recto and verso).

All the Qumran opisthographs are poorly preserved, rendering our information on them defective. More data is known regarding opisthographs from the classical world; see Diringer, *The Book*, 138; M. Manfredi, "Opistografo," *Parola del Passato* 38 (1983) 44–54; Haran, "Book-Scrolls," 171–2.

Beyond rare cases of Qumran literary texts inscribed on both sides and the documentary papyri for which this practice is more frequent, there is one group of texts that were often inscribed on both sides, viz., *tefillin* (J. T. Milik, *DJD* VI and the description there, p. 36). The inscribing of *tefillin* on both sides was not prescribed in the Torah; this tradition must have developed subsequently as a space-saver.

In two groups of texts, the verso was inscribed with a few words; these texts are not considered opisthographs proper:

• On the verso of a few texts, readers or scribes wrote the title of the composition in such a way that it would be visible when the scroll was rolled up (ch. *4h*).

• In many Hebrew, Aramaic, Greek, and Nabatean-Aramaic documentary texts, signatures (as many as seven) were written on the back, e.g. in 4QDeed A ar or heb (4Q345); XḤev/Se papMarriage Contract? ar (XḤev/Se 11); XḤev/Se papUnclassified Frag. A ar (XḤev/Se 9a); Mur 18, 19, 21, 22, 29, 30; 5/6Ḥev papMarriage Contract gr and ar (P.Yadin 18). In 'simple deeds,' the signatures were written on the recto, and in 'double deeds' ('tied documents') on the back, beside the strings (A. Yardeni, *DJD* XXVII, 11 and Millard, *Reading and Writing*, 94). Likewise, the name of the addressee in pap. XIII in Kraeling, *Aramaic Papyri*, is written on the verso.

(β) *Systems employed*

In the writing of opisthographs, three systems were used for the writing of the *second* text.

• In leather documents, with the exclusion of most *tefillin*, the verso was usually inscribed upside-down vis-à-vis the text written on the recto (e.g. 1Q70/1Q70a; 4Q201/4Q338; 4Q414/4Q415). This pertains also to some papyrus texts: Mas pap paleoSam. Text (recto)/Mas pap paleoUnidentified Text (verso); 4Q433a/4Q255; 4Q509, 4Q505, 4Q509 (*sic*; recto)/4Q496, 4Q506 (verso).

• In documentary papyri, the writing of signatures on the verso is usually perpendicular to that on the front, in both cases in accord with the fibers that were horizontal on the recto and vertical on the verso. This pertains to the signatures written, for example, on 4QDeed A ar or heb (4Q345); XḤev/Se papMarriage Contract? ar (XḤev/Se 11); XḤev/Se papUnclassified Frag. A ar (XḤev/Se 9a); XḤev/Se papDeed of Gift gr (XḤev/Se 64); XḤev/Se papCancelled Marriage Contract gr (XḤev/Se 69); MasLoan on Hypothec (P.Yadin 11). It also pertains to Mur papLiterary Text gr (recto: Mur 112) and Mur papProceedings of Lawsuit gr (verso: Mur 113); Jer papList of Loans ar (Jer 1) and Jer papDeed of Sale ar (Jer 3). The same system is used for some texts written on leather, e.g. 4QLetter nab (4Q343) and 4Q460 frg. 9 (Hebrew)/4Q350 (Greek), and various *tefillin* (*DJD* VI). In the case of *tefillin*, the writing on the verso is often performed in two different directions (see the description of 4QPhyl J by J. T. Milik, *DJD* VI, 36 and in illustr. 9 below, and see further 4QPhyl K and M).

• In some instances, the text on the verso was written on the flip side of the document, that is, upon turning the material 180 degrees. This system is evidenced for 4QpapHymns/Prayers (4Q499)/4QpapWar Scroll-like Text A (4Q497); 4QpapPrQuot (4Q503)/4QpapRitPur B (4Q512); 4QNarrative Work and Prayer (4Q460) frg. 9/4QAccount gr (4Q350).

The dimensions of the texts inscribed on each side were different. The intercolumnar margins and the top/bottom margins of 4Q414/4Q415 were of different sizes. Likewise, in 4Q324/4Q355, the spaces between the lines differed on both sides of the leather and the arrangement of columns in 4QpapM^f (4Q496) (verso) differed from that on the recto (M. Baillet, *DJD* VII, 57). P.Scheide of the LXX of Ezekiel (codex) has 52–57 lines on the recto and 49–53 lines on the verso.

(γ) *Relation between the texts on the recto and verso*

Writing on both sides of the material sometimes implies that the texts on the recto and verso are somehow related with regard to their content or external features. For example

• The recto and verso are closely related when the verso continued the text of the recto, as probably was the case in 4QLetter nab (4Q343). In short texts containing a single column, the verso would immediately continue the text written on the recto, but few such texts have been preserved.

• The recto and verso of the fragments of 4Qpap cryptA Text Concerning Cultic Service B? (4Q250a) are both written in the Cryptic A script. The relation between the content of the two sides is unclear.

• 4QEnᵃ ar (4Q201) I–III containing the first chapters of Enoch, which ultimately go back to Gen 5:18-24, has on its verso 4QGenealogical List? (4Q338). Little is known regarding this text, but one reads הוליד and הו[ליד on two different lines, and its subject matter (a genealogical list of the patriarchs?) may therefore be connected to the recto.

• In many opisthographs, both the recto and verso were written in the Qumran scribal practice (see below).

• The nature of Mas 1o is unclear. The two sides of this papyrus fragment (Mas pap paleoText of Sam. Origin [recto] and Mas pap paleoUnidentified Text [verso]), written in paleo-Hebrew in two different handwritings, probably represent two different compositions.[122] At the same time, the link between the two sides is not only the writing in the paleo-Hebrew script, but also the use of little triangles as word dividers (elsewhere one finds dots or, more rarely, strokes).

• The relation between Mas papVirgil lat (Mas 721 recto) and Mas papUnidentified Poetic Text lat (Mas 721 verso) is unclear. See APPENDIX 6.

More frequently, the content of the two sides is not related, as in several Egyptian, Greek, and Aramaic opisthographs[123] in which the verso is used for a completely unrelated text simply because writing material was scarce. Two opisthographs from Qumran and many Greek papyri from Egypt are of this type, with a literary text on the recto and a documentary text on the verso. Thus, one fragment of the Hebrew 4QNarrative Work and Prayer (4Q460 frg. 9) has on its verso a documentary text in Greek, viz., 4QAccount gr (4Q350) and 4QMish C (4Q324) has on the verso 4QAccount C ar or heb (4Q355). Mur 112 (Mur papLiterary Text gr) has on its verso Mur papProceedings of Lawsuit gr (Mur 113).

In a similar vein, a large collection of different compositions and two different copies of the same composition may be found on the two sides of a papyrus: a single papyrus, as reconstructed by M. Baillet, *DJD* VII, contains on the recto 4QpapPrFêtesᶜ (4Q509), 4QpapDibHamᵇ (4Q505), and again 4QpapPrFêtesᶜ, while 4QpapMᶠ (4Q496) and 4QpapDibHamᶜ (4Q506) appear on the verso. Other opisthographs of this type are:

recto	4Q433a	4QpapHodayot-like Text B
verso	4Q255	4QpapSᵃ (4Q255)

---

[122]The two sides were published by S. Talmon as representing a single text in *Masada VI*, 138–47. Talmon suggests (*Masada VI*, 142–47) that this fragment is of Samaritan origin, based especially on the continuous writing of הרריים, which is indeed customary in Samaritan sources, although not exclusively so. Talmon considers the two sides of the document to contain a 'Samaritan prayer or hymn of adoration directed to holy Mount Garizim' (p. 142). However, the two sides seem to have been written by different hands, with a different ductus, in different letter-sizes, and involving a few differently shaped letters. Whether or not the two sides reflect two different texts remains difficult to determine, and even the connection with the Samaritans is debatable. Pummer and Eshel stress the problematical aspects of this assumption, emphasizing the occurrence of the continuous writing of הרריים in non-Samaritan sources, such as once in Josephus, *Bell. Jud.* I 63, the Old Latin translation of 2 Macc 5:23; 6:2; Pliny, *Natural History* V.14.68, Pap. Giessen 13, 19, 22, 26 of Greek Scripture (if these texts are not taken as representing a Samaritan-Greek translation), as well as various Church Fathers from the fifth century CE onwards: R. Pummer, "ΑΡΓΑΡΙΖΙΝ: A Criterion for Samaritan Provenance?" *JSJ* 18 (1987) 18–25; H. Eshel, "The Prayer of Joseph, A Papyrus from Masada and the Samaritan Temple on ΑΡΓΑΡΙΖΙΝ," *Zion* 66 (1991) 125–36 (Heb.).

[123]See Černy, *Paper*, 22 for the Egyptian parallels; Gallo, *Papyrology*, 10; Kenyon, *Books and Readers*, 63–4 for the Greek parallels; and Porten–Yardeni, *TAD* 3, xiii for the Aramaic texts from Egypt. Occasionally, even a biblical text was reused; the Greek P.Leipzig 39 of Psalms (4 CE) has a list on the reverse. Likewise, P.Alex. 240 (PSI 921) of Psalm 77 LXX (3 CE) is written on the verso of a fiscal document.

recto	4Q499	4QpapHymns/Prayers
verso	4Q497	4QpapWar Scroll-like Text A
recto	4Q503	4QpapPrQuot
verso	4Q512	4QpapRitPur B

The theory that many Qumran documents were copied by a scribal school that was active and Qumran and other places is supported by the fact that several texts written according to the school's practices were reused for other purposes at Qumran itself, possibly by the Qumran covenanters; see TABLE 8.

TABLE 8: *Opisthographs in Which the Two Sides Were Written According to the Qumran Scribal Practice*

	No.	Title	Sectarian	Qumran Scrib. Practice
recto	4Q250a	4Qpap cryptA Text Concerning Cultic Service B?	y	no data
verso	4Q250a	4Qpap cryptA Text Concerning Cultic Service B?	y	no data
recto	4Q433a	4QpapHodayot-like Text B	y	no data
verso	4Q255	4QpapSᵃ	y	no data
recto	4Q415	4QInstrᵃ	y?	y
verso	4Q414	4QRitPur A	no data	y
recto	4Q460 9	4QNarr. Work and Prayer (Hebrew)	no data	y
verso	4Q350	4QAccount gr (see below)	—	
recto	4Q499	4QpapHymns/Prayers	y	y?
verso	4Q497	4QpapWar Scroll-like Text A	y	no data
recto	4Q503	4QpapPrQuot	y	y
verso	4Q512	4QpapRitPur B	y	y
recto	4Q505	4QpapDibHamᵇ	y	y?
verso	4Q506	4QpapDibHamᶜ	y	y
recto	4Q509	4QpapPrFêtesᶜ	y	y
verso	4Q496	4QpapMᶠ	y	y

If the understanding of 'recto' and 'verso' is correct in the texts recorded in this table, the sectarian use of the material is both primary and secondary. In other words, sectarian scrolls of various natures were subsequently reused by others, among them sectarian scribes. The fragment on which the Hebrew 4QNarrative Work and Prayer (4Q460 9) appears on the recto, and 4QAccount gr (4Q350; both: *DJD* XXXVI) on the verso is probably irrelevant to this analysis.[124]

[124]According to our analysis, the recto (4Q460 9) was copied (not necessarily authored) in Hebrew by a sectarian scribe, while its verso contains a text of a completely different nature inscribed in Greek. Parallels to the Greek document are found in Mur 90, 91, 96, 97. According to Tov, "Greek Texts," Greek was not in active use among the Qumranites, as no documentary Greek texts were found at Qumran, but this document is an exception, and the implications are unclear. If it were certain that all documentary Hebrew/Aramaic and Nabatean-Aramaic texts and the one Greek text labeled 'Qumran' were indeed found there, it would seem that they are part of a probably larger depository of administrative documents. However, serious doubts regarding the Qumranic origin of 4Q342–360 were raised by A. Yardeni, *DJD* XXVII, 283–317. In some instances, Yardeni points to joins with texts which definitely derived from Naḥal Ḥever (note especially 4QpapDeed F ar [= XḤev/Se 32] which forms, together with 4Q347, one document). Radiocarbon analysis of the documentary leather texts 4QLetter? ar r + v (4Q342) and 4QDebt Acknowledgment ar (4Q344), viz., late first and early second century CE indeed points to a late date which

It should be noticed that *both* copies of 4QRitPur (A [4Q414]; B [4Q512]) were written on the verso of other texts.

(2) *Palimpsests*

A palimpsest is a piece of material (papyrus or leather) which has been used a second time by writing over the original text, after it had been partially or mostly erased or washed off (in the case of papyri). Thus, the long Ahiqar papyrus from Elephantine (fifth century BCE) was partly written on sheets of papyrus which had contained a customs account and which were subsequently washed off (Porten–Yardeni, *TAD* 3.23). Among the Egyptian Aramaic papyri, several such palimpsests were detected (Porten–Yardeni, *TAD* 3.xiii). For other Egyptian parallels, see Černy, *Paper*, 23 and in greater detail Caminos, "Reuse of Papyrus."

The texts from the Judean Desert contain very few *palimpsests* (see TABLE 9 in which the strongest evidence pertains to papyri). According to a variant in *Sof.* 1.5, the writing on נייר מחוק, 'erased papyrus,' is forbidden, but the correct reading is probably נייר ('papyrus') without מחוק ('erased'). The late tractate *Soferim* refers to sacred texts, but among the texts from the Judean Desert only a certain percentage was considered sacred.

TABLE 9: *Palimpsests from the Judean Desert*

- Mur 10: Account (10A) and Abecedary (10B).
- Mur 17: papLetter (17A) and papList of Personal Names (17B). Both layers of this papyrus were dated by the editor (J. T. Milik, *DJD* II, 93) to the eighth century BCE and by F. M. Cross to the second half of the seventh century BCE (see n. 10 above).
- 4Qpap cryptA Midrash Sefer Moshe (4Q249): the possibility that this text is a palimpsest is raised by S. Pfann, *DJD* XXXV, 6.
- 4QRenewed Earth (4Q475): This is a palimpsest according to T. Elgvin, *DJD* XXXVI, 464 who, with the aid of a microscope, discerned traces of an earlier layer of writing which was erased when the scroll was used for the second time.
- 4Q457a and 4Q457b (two layers of a single document?) display clusters of letters which are less distinct than the main text of the fragment, in the form of very narrow columns above the beginning of most lines and in the margin to the right of the column. These letters do not belong to the main text of the fragment, and may represent an earlier layer of writing (thus E. Chazon, *DJD* XXIX, 409): 4Q457a (4QCreation?) and 4Q457b (4QEschatological Hymn). One notes that two vertical lines (0.8 cm apart) were drawn to the right of the text in frg. 1, before the supposed first and second layers of the text. The left line more or less indicates the beginning of the original layer of the text (4Q457a). These lines, which are not known to appear in the wide margin at the beginning of other documents, resemble intercolumnar lines seen in other texts. On the basis of this explanation, it appears that this fragment reflects a secondary use of the leather in which a scribe or manufacturer attempted to recycle a fragment that was located in the middle of another scroll, but did not completely succeed in removing the first layer. Another possible explanation would be to regard the letter remains as the imprint of a layer placed on top of the fragment, in which the ink has presumably bled through the leather, as in the case of 4QParaGen-Exod (4Q422); for a description, see Elgvin–Tov, *DJD* XIII, 430.
- 4QHistorical Text F (4Q468e): M. Broshi (*DJD* XXXVI, 406) described this text as a palimpsest, whose first layer is still visible in places.

---

would suit that site. Some of these texts may have derived from other sites. For a detailed analysis, see the end of APPENDIX 4 below. A different view on the contested Qumran texts is expressed by H. Eshel, who believes, on the basis of a new reading and analysis, that three Hebrew documentary texts did derive from Qumran: H. Eshel, "4Q348, 4Q343 and 4Q345: Three Economic Documents from Qumran Cave 4?" *JJS* 52 (2001) 132–5; idem, "The Hebrew in Economic Documents from the Judean Desert," *Leshonenu* 63 (2000–2001) 41–52 (Heb.). Each text must be judged separately, and indeed 4Q343 (Nabatean), 4Q345, and 4Q348 would be too early for Naḥal Ḥever. See further H. Cotton and E. Larson, "4Q460/4Q350 and Tampering with Qumran Texts in Antiquity," in Paul, *Emanuel*, 113–25.

c. *Length and contents of scrolls*

A comparative analysis of the size of the Judean Desert scrolls adds a welcome dimension to their discussion, since it provides data not only on specific scrolls, but also on the compositions contained in them. In this regard, the tradition of copying and transmitting is at times rather uniform, but more frequently diverse. The data analyzed refer to the length and contents of individual scrolls, the sizes of columns and writing blocks, and further the varying sizes of scrolls containing the same composition. This comparative information is important for the reconstruction of individual columns, sheets, and scrolls. The scope of scrolls and columns in antiquity no longer needs to be inferred from the post-Talmudic tractate *Massekhet Soferim*, often vague inferences in rabbinic literature, or even medieval codices or modern editions (thus Blau, *Studien*, 70–84). Now, the ancient sources themselves can be examined, even if the corpora of texts from the Judean Desert are not necessarily representative for all of Israel.

The great majority of Qumran fragments constitute parts of scrolls of leather or papyrus. Some scrolls found at Qumran were probably prepared locally, but others, especially those copied in the third or early second century BCE, must have been copied elsewhere. With regard to the details discussed below, no major differences between the two groups are visible. Nor is it known whether the differences between the various scrolls disprove the existence of any scribal school, as it is unclear whether a scribal school would use only scrolls or measures of the same parameters. Insufficient data is available on the length of these scrolls, since very few have been preserved intact, but some partly reconstructed data are mentioned below.[125]

A few compositions written on one-column sheets were found at Qumran: 4QTest (4Q175), 4QList of False Prophets ar (4Q339), 4QList of Netinim (4Q340), 4QExercitium Calami C (4Q341 [illustr. 2]). The latter text was written on a scrap of leather, while 4Q339 and 4Q340 were written on regularly shaped albeit very small pieces of leather. Several additional texts which are only partially known, such as 4QSelf-Glorification Hymn (4Q471b) and 4QText Mentioning Descendants of David (4Q479), may also have been written on single sheets. While 4QTest (4Q175) is preserved well on a neatly cut sheet of leather, most other one-column fragments are only partially preserved.

Most documentary papyrus texts from sites other than Qumran (Wadi Murabbaʿat, Naḥal Ḥever, and Naḥal Ṣeʾelim) were written on single sheets.

The length of the scrolls is directly related to the column size (§ e below and TABLE 11): the longer the column, the larger the scroll. Small leather scrolls measured up to 1.5 meters. Some scrolls must have been even smaller, such as possibly 4QApocryphal Psalm and Prayer (4Q448; illustr. 11) and some of the calendrical texts (note 4QCal Doc/Mish C [4Q321a] with 0.80 m). 4QDeut^n (illustr. 15) was probably a similarly small scroll. Likewise, according to T. Elgvin, *DJD* XIII, 418, the length of 4QPara-Gen-Exod (4Q422) was a mere 0.70 m.

Examples of medium-sized scrolls are 1QS (1.87 or 3.00 m), 1QM (2.7 m), and 4QD^a (4Q266; 4.23 m or more).

---

[125]For an attempt to measure the length of fragmentarily preserved Qumran scrolls, see D. Stoll, "Die Schriftrollen vom Toten Meer: mathematisch oder Wie kann man einer Rekonstruktion Gestalt verleihen?" in *Qumranstudien* (ed. H.-J. Fabry et al.; Schriften des Institutum Judaicum Delitzschianum 4; Göttingen 1996) 205–18.

Long texts naturally required longer scrolls, recognizable by their length and column height. TABLE 11 contains reconstructed evidence for scrolls measuring as much as 25 meters in length. It is unclear what the maximum length of scrolls was when those found at Qumran were written. At a later period, *b. B. Bat.* 13b makes reference to large scrolls containing all the books of the Torah,[126] Prophets, *or* Writings, or even a scroll containing them all (מדובקין, 'bound up'), but the Qumran evidence neither supports nor contradicts the existence of such large scrolls. TABLE 10 records possible manuscript evidence from the Judean Desert for a complete Torah scroll (Mur 1: Genesis-Exodus and possibly Numbers), as well as for some combinations of books of the Torah in six copies referring to Genesis-Exodus, Exodus-Leviticus, and Leviticus-Numbers. As the joins between several of these pairs of books have not been preserved, the evidence for the juxtaposition of two or more books is often hypothetical.

TABLE 10: *Two or More Biblical Books Contained in the Same Scroll*

4QGen-Exod^a	The join between the two books has not been preserved.
4QpaleoGen-Exod^l	The preserved part of the column starting with the last word of Genesis, followed by three empty lines, and continuing with Exodus is preceded by at least one sheet of written text.
4QExod^b = 4Q[Gen-]Exod^b	Exodus is preceded by two mid-column blank lines indicating that the book was probably preceded by Genesis (cf. *DJD* XII, pl. XIV).
4QExod-Lev^f	The join between the two books has not been preserved.
4QLev-Num^a	The join between the two books has not been preserved.
Mur 1 (Genesis, Exodus, and Numbers?)	This scroll contained Genesis, Exodus, and possibly Numbers (*DJD* II, 75–8 and pls. XIX–XXI). These fragments, written in the same handwriting, probably belong to the same scroll, but the join between the books has not been preserved.
4QRP^c (4Q365) (Leviticus-Numbers?)	In frg. 26a–b, the first verse of Numbers is preceded by what is probably a paraphrastic version of the last verse of Leviticus, followed by an empty line.
4QLam (a scroll containing several *Megillot*?)	This scroll may have contained all five *Megillot* or at least more than Lamentations alone. The first preserved column of 4QLam starts at the top with Lam 1:1b, and since the column length of the scroll is known (10–11 lines), the preceding column would have contained at least the first line of the book, a few empty lines, and the end of the book preceding Lamentations.
MurXII, 4QXII^b, and 4QXII^g, 8HevXIIgr (*Greek*) (Minor Prophets)	A space of three lines was left between various books in MurXII, as evidenced by the transitions Jonah/Micah, Micah/Nahum, and Zephaniah/Haggai (*DJD* III, 182, 192, 197, 200, 202, 205 and pls. LXI, LXVI, LXIX, LXXI, LXXII). This practice follows the tradition also known from *b. B. Bat.* 13b for combining these books as one unit. In 4QXII^b 3 5, one line is left between Zephaniah/Haggai and in 4QXII^g 70–75, one-and-a-half lines were left between Amos/Obadiah. In 8HevXIIgr (*Greek*) at least six lines were left between Jonah/Micah.

The large column size in several of these scrolls confirms the assumption that they contained two or more books since a large number of lines often implies that the scroll was long: 4QGen-Exod^a (36 lines; evidence unclear), 4QpaleoGen-Exod^l (55–60 lines), 4QExod^b (= 4Q[Gen-]Exod^b; *c.* 50 lines), and possibly also 4QExod-Lev^f (*c.* 60 lines), 4QLev-Num^a (43), and Mur 1 (*c.* 60). On the basis of the large parameters of these

---

[126] A possible allusion to the combining of books of the Torah or Psalter is found in 1QLiturgical Text A? (1Q30) 1 4]ο חומשים פרים[ס. This phrase, without any context, was translated by the editor, J. T. Milik, as 'li]vres du Pentateuque/du Psautier.' The phrase may refer to the individual parts of the Torah, but the use of חומשים for the parts of the Torah has not been attested prior to the rabbinic literature that is a few centuries later.

scrolls, it may be presumed that other Torah scrolls likewise contained two or more books: 4QGen[e] (*c.* 50 lines), 4QExod[e] (*c.* 43), MasDeut (42), SdeirGen (*c.* 40), 4QGen[b] (40; illustr. 18).

It is likely that several scrolls found at Qumran contained more than one book of the Torah, and possibly all of the Torah, in which case they would have measured 25–30 meters. According to *Sof.* 3.4, two books of the Torah should not be combined if there was no intention to add the other three books to them. If this rule was followed in the case of the scrolls found at Qumran, all the instances of two attached books of the Torah mentioned in TABLE 10 would have belonged to longer Torah scrolls. However, it is unknown whether this rule was followed in the scrolls from the Judean Desert. M. Haran, while not referring to the Qumran evidence, and basing himself on rabbinic and other references, believes that no scrolls combining all five books of the Torah were in existence in this early period.[127]

The only solid evidence for long scrolls pertains to 1QIsa[a] and 11QT[a] (11Q19). TABLE 11 records the data known or reconstructed for the scrolls from the Judean Desert in descending order of size.

TABLE 11: *Reconstructed Length of Some Scrolls from the Judean Desert (Meters)*

4QRP[a–e]	22.5–27.5 (E. Tov, *DJD* XIII, 192)
4QJer[c]	16.30–17.60 (E. Tov, *DJD* XV, 180)
1QapGen ar	More than 11.83 (the missing part at the beginning is reconstructed as 9m by M. Morgenstern, "A New Clue to the Original Length of the Genesis Apocryphon," *JJS* 47 (1996) 345–7, while the part published by Avigad–Yadin, *Genesis Apocryphon* is 2.83m.
8ḤevXIIgr	9.64–10.07 (91–95 cols.; E. Tov, *DJD* VIII, 9) *Greek*
2QJer	9.50 (68 cols.; M. Baillet, *DJD* III, 62)
4QH[b] (4Q428)	9.50 (68 cols.; E. Schuller, *DJD* XXIX, 127–8)
11QT[a] (11Q19)	8.75 (67 cols.; slightly reconstructed; Yadin, *Temple Scroll* [*Hebrew*] 8; preserved: 8.148 [62 cols.])
4QpaleoExod[m]	7.82–9.66 (average: 8.74) + handle sheet? (57 cols.; reconstructed on the basis of the data provided by Skehan–Ulrich–Sanderson, *DJD* IX, 56–7)
4QJer[a]	7.90–8.50 (54–58 cols.; E. Tov, *DJD* XV, 148)
1QIsa[a]	7.34 (54 cols.) + handle sheet before col. I (Burrows, *The Dead Sea Scrolls*, I.xiv)
11QtgJob	7.00 (68 cols.) + handle sheets (García Martínez–Tigchelaar–van der Woude, *DJD* XXIII, 86)
4QNum[b]	6.80 (12 sheets; N. Jastram, *DJD* XII, 207)
4QKgs	6.25 (50 cols.; J. Trebolle Barrera, *DJD* XIV, 179). If this scroll had contained Joshua–Samuel and Kings, it would have been 20 meters long; see ibid., p. 182.
4QLev-Num[a]	6.00 (*c.* 51 cols.; E. Ulrich, *DJD* XII, 154, 175)
MasEzek	5.74–6.15 (*c.* 60 cols.; Talmon, *Masada VI*, 61)
MasLev[b]	5.40–5.60 (48–50 cols.; Talmon, *Masada VI*, 50)
11QEzek	5.00–5.50 (44 cols.; E. D. Herbert, *DJD* XXIII, 19–20)
MurXII	5.00 (40 cols. + two handle sheets; J. T. Milik, *DJD* II, 182)
4QD[a] (4Q266)	4.23 or more (31 cols. or more; S. Pfann, *DJD* XVIII, 24)
11QPs[a]	4.11 preserved (J. A. Sanders, *DJD* IV, 5); 5.0 reconstructed (36 cols.; Flint, *Psalms Scrolls*, 40)
MasDeut	4.00 (38 cols.; Talmon, *Masada VI*, 58)
4QD[f] (4Q271)	3.70 or more (29 or more cols.; S. Pfann, *DJD* XVIII, 169)
4QH[a] (4Q427)	3.70 (E. Schuller, *DJD* XXIX, 86)
4QD[e] (4Q270)	3.55 minimal length (30 or more cols.; S. Pfann, *DJD* XVIII, 137)

---

[127]M. Haran, "Torah and Bible Scrolls in the First Centuries of the Christian Era," *Shnaton* 10 (1986–89) 93–106 (Heb. with Eng. summ.).

4QInstr[d] (4Q418)	3.2–3.5 (25–27 cols.; Elgvin, *Analysis*, 24)
11QShirShabb (11Q17)	3.00 + handle sheets (García Martínez–Tigchelaar–van der Woude, *DJD* XXIII, 261)
6QCant	2.90 (27 cols.; M. Baillet, *DJD* III, 113)
1QM	2.70 (Sukenik, *Dead Sea Scrolls*)
4QS[b] (4Q256)	2.73 (23 cols.; *DJD* XXVI, 41)
4QInstr[b] (4Q416)	2.57–3.00 (Elgvin, *Analysis*, 19)
4QInstr[c] (4Q417)	2.31–2.86 (17–20 cols.; Elgvin, *Analysis*, 19)
4QapocrJer C[a] (4Q385a)	2.50 (24 cols.; D. Dimant, *DJD* XXX, 131)
4QpapS[c] (4Q257)	2.25 (Metso, *Community Rule*, 33)
4QPs[g]	2.08 (Skehan–Ulrich–Flint, *DJD* XVI, 107). This scroll probably contained only Psalm 119.
1QS	1.87 or 3.00 with the inclusion of 1QSa and 1QSb. Although the dimensions of 1QSa differ slightly from those of 1QS, they probably belonged to the same scroll. The arguments in favor of the assumption that the three scrolls were once joined, possibly by stitching, are provided by J. T. Milik, *DJD* I, 107. The most cogent argument is probably the destruction pattern of the bottom line of the final column of 1QS and the cols. of 1QSa, but the details are not convincing.
4QS[d] (4Q258)	1.30 (Alexander–Vermes, *DJD* XXVI, 86) or 2.70 (Metso, *Community Rule*, 39)
4QCal Doc/Mish C (4Q321a)	0.80 (S. Talmon, *DJD* XXI, 82)
4QParaGen-Exod (4Q422)	0.70 (T. Elgvin, *DJD* XIII, 418)

The single longest reconstructed scroll from the Judean Desert would probably be the combined scroll MurGen-Exod-(Lev)-Num, if indeed all four books were contained in the same scroll (thus J. T. Milik, *DJD* II, 75).

On the basis of this list, the (reconstructed) data for the different scrolls of the same composition are compared in TABLE 12. For two compositions these data are rather similar, while in one instance they differ greatly.

TABLE 12: *Reconstructed Length of Different Qumran Scrolls of the Same Composition (Meters)*

4QS[b] (4Q256)	2.73 (*DJD* XXVI, 37)
4QpapS[c] (4Q257)	2.25 (Metso, *Community Rule*, 33)
1QS	1.87, or 3.00 with the inclusion of 1QSa and 1QSb.
4QS[d] (4Q258)	1.30 (Alexander–Vermes, *DJD* XXVI, 86) or 2.70 (Metso, *Community Rule*, 39)
4QJer[c]	16.30–17.60 (88–95 cols.; E. Tov, *DJD* XV, 180)
2QJer	9.50 (68 cols.; M. Baillet, *DJD* III, 62)
4QJer[a]	7.90–8.50 (54–58 cols.; E. Tov, *DJD* XV, 148)
4QD[a] (4Q266)	4.23+ (31+ cols.; S. Pfann, *DJD* XVIII, 24)
4QD[f] (4Q271)	3.70+ (29+ cols.; S. Pfann, *DJD* XVIII, 169)
4QD[e] (4Q270)	3.55+ (30+ cols.; S. Pfann, *DJD* XVIII, 137)
4QInstr[b] (4Q416)	2.57–3.00 (Elgvin, *Analysis*, 21)
4QInstr[c] (4Q417)	2.31–2.86 (17–20 cols.; Elgvin, *Analysis*, 21)
4QInstr[d] (4Q418)	3.20–3.50 (25–27 cols.; Elgvin, *Analysis*, 32)

On the sizes of *papyrus* scrolls and sheets from the Judean Desert, see below § d.

Unlike the far older papyri from Egypt which were often placed in boxes (containers) and jars, the Qumran papyri were not afforded any special protection, since most of them did not possess the same level of sanctity as the Qumran leather scrolls (see p. 252 below). Therefore, in no single case has the full size of a papyrus column been preserved with its top and bottom margins.

It is difficult to compare the aforementioned data relating to scrolls composed of leather sheets with the data from the classical world, since most Greek and Latin scrolls were written on papyrus. For detailed data on such scrolls, see Birt, *Buchwesen*, 256–73, 288–341; Černy, *Paper*, 9; Schubart, *Das Buch*, 55–63; Ashton, *Scribal Habits*, 65.

Much data regarding the size (length) of leather scrolls is derived from the scope of individual columns, since there was a direct correlation between the size of the leather and columns and the length of the scroll: large columns imply long scrolls and small columns imply small scrolls. In *b. B. Bat.* 14a, this proportion is laid down as a rule for Torah scrolls:

ספר תורה לא ארכו יותר על היפקו ולא היפקו יותר על ארכו

Our Rabbis taught: A scroll of the Torah should be such that its length does not exceed its circumference, nor its circumference its length (thus also *Sof.* 2.9).

In other words, the circumference of the Torah scroll when rolled in two separate rollers (see the continued discussion in *b. B. Bat.* 14b) should not exceed the column height. This rule applied only to the rabbinic rules for the writing of Torah scrolls, but evidence from Qumran shows that it also pertained to other scrolls.

Because of the close relationship between the length of scrolls and their column sizes, some general remarks on small and large scrolls are included in § e below. Furthermore, the data included in TABLE 11 above may be supplemented by the data in TABLE 15 below regarding the column sizes of all categories of scrolls (small, medium-size, large, and very large).

There is evidence for long scrolls in ancient Egypt as well as Greece,[128] but it is unclear to what extent this evidence is relevant to Hebrew Scripture, as the Egyptian scrolls were ceremonial and not meant for reading which would have been made difficult by their length. However, it may also be possible that some Torah scrolls were ceremonial. In fact, all views about the length of the *earliest* biblical scrolls are hypothetical, the only evidence being the description of a scroll containing the prophecies of Jeremiah (Jeremiah 36), but its scope is unknown. Zech 5:2 mentions a scroll of ten meters in length (twenty cubits), but as its height is mentioned as five meters (ten cubits), these measures should not be taken at face value (they probably imitate the measures of the אולם, 'porch,' before the temple as described in 1 Kgs 6:3).

Haran, "Size of Books" (n. 75) tackled the issue of the scroll size from another angle; see also idem, "Bible Scrolls in the Early Second Temple Period: The Transition from Papyrus to Skins," *ErIsr* 16 (1982) 86–92 (Heb.). Taking the length of individual biblical books such as those of the Torah or the prophetic books as his point of departure, Haran claimed that the following three compositions could *not* have been contained in single scrolls at the time of their composition: the Torah, the historiographical cycles Joshua-Judges-Samuel-Kings, and Chronicles-Ezra-Nehemiah. The Qumran evidence is too late for Haran's hypothesis and actual data for earlier periods, almost certainly involving papyrus scrolls, are lacking.

Contents of Qumran scrolls. The length of scrolls is closely connected to that of their contents. Scripture scrolls feature frequently in the list of long scrolls, and statistically they form the majority among the longer Qumran scrolls. However, these statistics are

---

[128]Much evidence pertaining to Egyptian papyrus scrolls ranging between 17 and 44 meters in length is provided by Diringer, *The Book*, 129–33; Černy, *Paper*, 9; Kenyon, *Books and Readers*, 50 ff. Thus the 'large' Harris papyrus of 'The Book of the Dead' from the eleventh century BCE is 41 meters long (see Kenyon, ibid., 53 and Millard, *Reading and Writing*, 61). Greek papyrus scrolls of 12 meters and less were mentioned by Kenyon, *Books and Readers*, 54, while Gamble, *Books and Readers*, 47 refers to the average Greek papyrus scroll as measuring 7–10 meters.

misleading since the contents of Scripture scrolls are known, and therefore scholars have indulged in more speculation regarding their length than for other scrolls.

To the best of our knowledge, each Qumran scroll contained only a single literary composition, and very few scrolls are known that contain a compilation of different literary works on one side of the writing surface; for possible examples, see the list in the beginning of ch. *3d*. When scrolls were inscribed on both sides (opisthographs), often different compositions were inscribed on the two sides of the leather or papyrus (§ b above).

If two or more biblical books were contained in a single scroll, these books were part of a larger unit. However, evidence for scrolls containing such a larger unit is scanty (TABLE 10), while there is evidence for single books within those larger units that were demonstrably *not* part of such larger units. Of course, scrolls starting with Genesis (4QGen^{b,g,k}), Joshua (XJosh), Kings (5QKgs), Isaiah (1QIsa^a and MurIsa), or the Minor Prophets (4QXII^d), preceded by a handle sheet or a large uninscribed area should cause no surprise. Nor should it be surprising that MasDeut, MasPs^b, and 11QPs^a ended with a final handle sheet or an uninscribed area. At the same time, there is some evidence for scrolls which contain a single biblical book and are not part of a larger unit:

• 11QpaleoLev^a, ending with a ruled uninscribed area of 15.6 cm—covering a complete column—as well as with a separate handle sheet, was not followed by Numbers.

• 4QLev^c and 4QDeut^h, both beginning at the top of a column, probably started a new scroll, although they also could have followed the previous biblical books, which ended somewhere on the previous column.

• 6QDeut? (6Q20), starting with an initial uninscribed area of 5.0+ cm, was not part of a larger scroll of the Torah.

• 1QIsa^a, not followed by an additional book (no sheet was stitched unto it), formed a single scroll probably preceded by an uninscribed handle page.

• Most extant Qumran copies of the Five Scrolls were probably contained in separate scrolls (note their small dimensions recorded in TABLE 18; see also the analysis there).

There is no evidence that large compositions found in the Judean Desert were written on more than one scroll, with the exception of the books of the Torah. 1QIsa^a was written by two scribes (ch. *2e* and TABLE 1 there), but the sheets written by these scribes were sewn together. Hence, the custom to subdivide large compositions into different scrolls (bisection) may derive from either different circles or later (earlier?) times. Thus, while 4QSam^a contains the text of both 1 and 2 Samuel, later manuscripts divided the book into two segments.

It is difficult to date the bisection of 2 Samuel, Jeremiah, and Ezekiel in the LXX scrolls, but it could have occurred around the turn of the era (E. Tov, *The Septuagint Translation of Jeremiah and Baruch: A Discussion of an Early Revision of Jeremiah 29–52 and Baruch 1:1–3:8* [HSM 8; Missoula, Mont. 1976] 161 ff.). Also in the classical world, large compositions were subdivided into independent units (scrolls), often regardless of their content. See Birt, *Buchwesen*, 131–40; Hall, *Companion*, 7–8; F. G. Kenyon, "Book Divisions in Greek and Latin Literature," in *William Warner Bishop: A Tribute* (ed. H. M. Lydenberg and A. Keogh; New Haven 1941) 63–76 (especially 73–4); idem, *Books and Readers*, 64–70; J. van Sickle, "The Book-Roll and Some Conventions of the Poetic Books," *Arethusa* 13 (1980) 5–42; Gamble, *Books and Readers*, 42–66.

d. *Dimensions of Sheets*

At Qumran, the length of most sheets of leather varied between 21 and 90 cm. The natural limitations of the sizes of animal hides determined the different lengths of these sheets within each scroll, which varied more in some scrolls than in others. In two instances (MurXII, 11QpaleoLev^a), the preserved sheets are more or less of the same length. Some examples of the sheet sizes in well-preserved scrolls are listed in TABLE 13 in ascending order of size. 4QCal Doc/Mish A (4Q320) 4 iii (4.7 cm) and iv–v (9.8 cm) are extremely narrow sheets. In this case, the scroll manufacturer may have had access to these small pieces only.

The dimensions of papyrus sheets were more uniform than those of leather. In Egypt, the most frequent width of papyrus sheets was 48–96 cm in the Old Kingdom, 38–54 cm in the Middle Kingdom, and 16–20 cm in the New Kingdom, all measured between the joins of sheets (Černy, *Paper*, 9, 14–16; for a detailed analysis, see Ashton, *Scribal Habits*, 65–6). On the sizes of single papyrus sheets from the Judean Desert and elsewhere, see Lewis, *Bar Kochba*, 11–12 and Kenyon, *Books and Readers*, 50 ff. Kraeling, *Aramaic Papyri*, 127 notes that Egyptian papyri were manufactured in 40 cm-long sheets, while Wenke, "Ancient Egypt" speaks of sheets of 16–42 cm in length. No comparable data are available for columns or sheets of Qumran papyrus texts.

TABLE 13: *Length of Sheets (cm)*

4QCal Doc/Mish A (4Q320) 4 iii, iv–v	4.7; 9.8
11QtgJob	21–45
1QIsa[b]	26–45
1QIsa[a]	25–62.8
11QT[a] (11Q19)	37–61 (Yadin, *Temple Scroll*, 1.10)
4QDan[c]	*c.* 38
1QapGen ar	45–82
1QM	47–89
4QNum[b]	56 (N. Jastram, *DJD* XII, 207)
4QCommGen A	60
MurXII	62
1QpHab	62–79
11QpaleoLev[a]	63
11QapocrPs (11Q11)	64
11QPs[a]	72–87

The *number* of sheets per scroll depends on the scope of the composition and the length of individual sheets. This information can be calculated only for the scrolls in which both the beginning and end have been preserved. Thus 1QIsa[a] consists of seventeen sheets (ten sheets measuring 35–47.7 cm, five 48.7–62.8 cm, and two 25.2–26.9 cm). 11QT[a] is composed of nineteen sheets (eight measuring 37–43 cm, ten 47–61 cm, and the final sheet measuring 20 cm). Precise details regarding the dimensions of sheets in well-preserved scrolls were listed for 1QIsa[a] by J. C. Trever in Burrows, *The Dead Sea Scrolls*, I.xvii–xviii; for 11QpaleoLev[a] by Freedman–Mathews, *Leviticus*, 7; for 11QT[a] (11Q19) by Yadin, *Temple Scroll (Hebrew)*, 11–12; and in most *DJD* editions of long texts.

Data for Aramaic papyrus scrolls were summarized by Porten–Yardeni, *TAD*, 3.xiii. Černy, *Paper*, 9 notes that papyrus scrolls in Egypt and Rome usually contained twenty sheets (cf. Pliny, *Natural History*, XXIII.77). On the whole, however, comparative material for scrolls is not as easily available as it is for early codices recorded by E. G. Turner, *The Typology of the Early Codex* (Philadelphia 1977).

In accordance with their differing sizes, sheets contain varying *numbers of columns* of written text, typically three or four (e.g. 1QIsa[a] and 11QT[a]).[129] The seven columns appearing in both 1QapGen ar and 1QpHab and the single columns of the first sheet of

---

[129]A scroll containing three or four columns per sheet is also mentioned in Jer 36:23. See the analysis by Lansing Hicks, "*Delet* and M[e]*gillah*," 46–66 (see p. 31 above), especially 61.

4QDeut[n] (with stitching on both sides), the final sheets of 1QS and 4QDeut[q], and the first and last columns of 4QD[a] (4Q266) are exceptions. 4QCal Doc/Mish A (4Q320) 4 iii–v presents an unicum: with one sheet of 4.7 cm (col. iii) and one of 9.8 cm (cols. iv–v) this document presents the narrowest sheets in any Qumran document. There is no uniformity in the number of columns, as shown by the data in TABLE 14.

T ABLE 14: *Number of Columns per Sheet*

4QDeut[n]	**1** (first sheet), **6+** (second sheet); S. W. Crawford, *DJD* XIV, pl. XXVIII.
4QDeut[q]	**1** (last sheet; insufficient data); Skehan–Ulrich, *DJD* XIV, pl. XXXI.
4QCal Doc/Mish A (4Q320) 4 iii–v	**1** (col. iii; 4.7 cm) and **2** (cols. iv–v; 9.8 cm); see the description above and S. Talmon, *DJD* XXI, pl. II, and p. 38.
4QD[a] (4Q266)	**1–3** cols. in 13 sheets. The exact number of columns per sheet is unclear; the first and the last sheets have one column only, the latter followed by an uninscribed handling area of 9.0 cm; S. Pfann, *DJD* XVIII, 24.
1QSa	**2**; D. Barthélemy, *DJD* I, pls. XXII–XXIV.
11QtgJob	**2** (2x), **3** (7x), **4** (3x), **5** (1 x); *DJD* XXIII, 83.
11QpaleoLev[a]	**3+**, **4** (end of scroll); Freedman–Mathews, *Leviticus*, 5.
1QIsa[a]	**3** (10x), **4** (5x), **2** (2x; XXVI–XXVII, LIII–LIV); Burrows, *The Dead Sea Scrolls*, I.xvii; altogether 54 cols. in 17 sheets.
11QT[a] (11Q19)	**3** (7x), **4** (10x), **5** (1x?), **1** (1x), but mainly **3**, **4**; Yadin, *Temple Scroll*, 9, 11; altogether 19 sheets.
1QS	**3** (I–III), **2** (IV–V), **2** (VI–VII), **3** (VIII–X), **1** (XI; final sheet); altogether 11 cols. in 5 sheets.
4QDan[c]	**3** (I–III); E. Ulrich, *DJD* XVI.
1QM	**4**, **6**, **5**, **3**, and a remnant of one column on a fifth sheet; Sukenik, *Dead Sea Scrolls*, fig. 26 (5 sheets, 19 cols.).
11QapocrPs (11Q11)	**4** (II–V); *DJD* XXIII, pls. XXII–XXV.
1QH[a]	**4**, **4**, **4** cols.; Sukenik, *Dead Sea Scrolls*, 37.
11QPs[a]	**4?**, **6**, **6**, **5**, **4**; J. A. Sanders, *DJD* IV, 4.
1QapGen ar	**4**, **5**, **7**, **6**; Avigad–Yadin, *Genesis Apocryphon*, 14–15.
4QNum[b]	**5**, **4**, **5**, **5**, **3**, **2**, **4**, **4**; altogether 8 sheets with 32 cols.; N. Jastram, *DJD* XII, 207.
MasSir	**5+** (I–V, possibly preceded by other cols.), **2+**; Yadin, *Masada VI*, pl. 8.
4QDibHam[a] (4Q504)	**5+** (III–VII); M. Baillet, *DJD* VII, pl. XLIX.
4QD[e] (4Q270)	**5+** cols. (frg. 6); J. Baumgarten, *DJD* XVIII, 137.
4QCommGen A (4Q252)	**6**; G. Brooke, *DJD* XXII, 186.
1QpHab	**7**, **7** (the final column of the second sheet was uninscribed).

Sheets containing merely one or two columns are forbidden for biblical scrolls in *b. Menah.* 30a, *y. Meg.* 1.71c–d, and *Sof.* 2.10, according to which one should not write less than three columns of Scripture or more than eight. The one-column first sheet of 4QDeut[n], probably preceded by another sheet, would therefore not be permitted according to the Rabbis. 4QDeut[q] is a special case since that scroll probably ended with the last preserved sheet, containing the end of Deuteronomy 32. It was followed by an uninscribed area and not the last two chapters of the book (the rule of *b. Menah.* 30a, which states that single sheets are acceptable for the last sheets of scrolls, may not have been applicable to this scroll as it probably contained merely a small portion of the book of Deuteronomy).

The great majority of scrolls containing five, six, or seven columns per sheet are nonbiblical: 1QapGen ar, 1QpHab, 1QM, 4QCommGen A (4Q252), 4QD[e] (4Q270), 4QDibHam[a] (4Q504), 11QPs[a], 11QtgJob, MasSir. Two such scrolls are biblical,

4QNum[b] and 4QDeut[n], but the latter is probably a liturgical scroll (rather than a regular biblical text) and the evidence for the former is unclear.

e. *Writing blocks, columns, and margins*

The idea of arranging the inscribed text in columns of more or less uniform dimension was reflected already in cuneiform clay tablets, where the text was subdivided by horizontal and vertical lines, and in ancient Egyptian papyrus scrolls. The great majority of Judean Desert texts were likewise arranged in writing blocks that cover the greater part of the surface, leaving margins on all sides of the inscribed surface. The rationale of these margins was to enable the orderly arrangement of the writing blocks in geometric shapes, even when the edges of the leather were not straight. The margins also enabled the handling of the scroll without touching the inscribed area. For this purpose the margins at the bottom were usually larger than those at the top.

Columns

The inscribed surface was usually, and always in the case of literary compositions, organized in the form of a column (דלת in Lachish ostracon 4 3–4 and Jer 36:23 [σελίς in the LXX][130] or דף in rabbinic literature, e.g. *y. Meg.* 1.71c), and in texts consisting of more than one, these columns always follow one another horizontally. In one document, 4QIncantation (4Q444; illustr. 10), three tiny fragments of leather (each with four lines of inscription) followed each other vertically, one atop the other. Each group of four lines constituted a single column, stitched to the next column *under* the writing block. In the case of 4QApocryphal Psalm and Prayer (4Q448; illustr. 11), the different column arrangement probably derived from the adhesion of a reinforcement tab which necessitated a large margin at the beginning of the scroll (col. I). See ch. *5b*.

There is a positive correlation between the height and width of columns: the higher the column, the wider the lines, and the longer the scroll.

While it is in order to measure the width of columns according to the number of letters or letter-spaces (that is, a space occupied by either a letter or a blank space between words) for purposes of reconstruction, for an overall understanding of the scroll it is more useful to calculate according to the column width. Since individual sheets contained columns of varying width, one should always be careful when attempting to link a certain column-width with a specific scroll.

The *column* sizes differ in accordance with the number of columns per sheet, the measurements of the sheets (§ d), and the conventions developed by the scroll manufacturers. The different parameters of the columns pertain to their width and height as well as to the size of the top, bottom, and intercolumnar margins.

In some Qumran scrolls, the height and width of columns are fairly consistent, while in most scrolls these parameters vary from sheet to sheet as well as within each sheet, in accordance with the size of sheets. Thus, the width of some columns in 1QM and 4QLam differs by as much as fifty percent from other columns in the same scrolls. Considerable differences among the widths of columns are visible in 11QT[a] (11Q19) and 8ḤevXIIgr, while even larger differences are evident in 1QIsa[a] (cf. col. XLIX [16.3

---

[130]According to J. P. Hyatt, "The Writing of an Old Testament Book," *BA* 6 (1943) 71–80 (74); repr. with additions in G. E. Wright and D. N. Freedman, *The Biblical Archaeologist Reader* (Garden City, N.Y. 1961) 22–31, this term is based on the wooden tablets used for writing in an earlier period (26). Many parallels for this terminology from the ancient Near East were listed by R. Lansing Hicks (see p. 31). According to H. Eshel, "Two Epigraphic Notes," *Zeitschrift für Althebraistik* 13 (2000) 181–7 (especially 185–7), the term occurs also in Prov 8:34.

cm] with LII [8.8 cm]) in the same section written by scribe B, 1QS (cf. I [9.7 cm] and II [11.5 cm] with other columns measuring 16, 18 and 19 cm) and 4QLam (col. III is almost twice as wide as cols. I and II). The width of the columns of 4QSam^a differs noticeably from one column to the next, ranging from 8.5 cm in col. III to 13.5 cm (reconstructed for frgs. 164–165). At the same time, a certain regularity in column size is noticeable. In many cases, the available space in a sheet was evenly divided between the columns, but the differing sizes of sheets often did not always permit such uniformity. Columns that are unusually wide or narrow are generally found at the beginning or end of sheets.

The average column-width in 1QM is 15.0 cm, 13.0 cm in 1QH^a, and 9.5–15.5 cm in 1QS.

An example of a scroll with very wide columns measuring 21–24 cm is 4QJer^b (115–130 letter-spaces; reconstructed).

The narrowest columns measuring 1.7–2.0 cm (illustr. 16) are found in 4QMMT^a (4Q394) 1–2 cols. i–v, probably reflecting a separate composition, 4QCal Doc/Mish D (thus S. Talmon, *DJD* XXI, 157–66). If, indeed, frgs. 1–2 belong to the same scroll as frgs 3–9, as the editors of *DJD* X (Qimron–Strugnell) believe, the difference in column-widths would be striking, as the columns in frgs. 3–9 are 10–11 cm wide. The scribe of 4Q394 presented the information in a narrow format in order to record only one piece of information per line, either a number or a date; there are some exceptions, including when the word בו appears and when compound numerals are written on either one or two lines. Another example is col. II of 4QApocryphal Psalm and Prayer (4Q448) with nine lines of 1–3 words (*c.* 2.7 cm). In another calendrical text, 4QCal Doc/Mish A (4Q320), the internal differences are striking: in frg. 4 ii the widest line is 2.0 cm, while in cols. iii and v the width of the lines is 4.0 cm. Furthermore, all the poetical compositions that present the text stichographically with hemistichs (system *1a* in ch. *5b*), such as in most columns of 4QPs^b written in hemistichs measuring *c.* 3.7–4.5 cm, present narrow columns (illustr. 19).

Greek papyrus scrolls containing prose were written usually in narrow columns (5.0–7.0 cm [Kenyon, *Books and Readers*, 56]), while poetry texts could be as wide as 10–14 cm.

According to *Sof.* 2.15, half the length of a column in a Torah scroll must not exceed its breadth nor must the breadth exceed half its height (cf. Blau, *Studien*, 126). However, since the columns in the Qumran scrolls are usually of variable width while their length is usually identical, they could never have been written according to this rule. Thus, in 1QIsa^a neither the narrow columns (e.g. col. LII) nor the wide columns (e.g. col. LI) follow these parameters. In general, this rule is neither followed for short nor long columns in the extant Qumran scrolls.

According to *y. Meg.* 1.71c, the minimum line-length is nine letters in Scripture texts. In the nonbiblical texts described above, the columns are sometimes narrower.

The wider columns often occur at the beginning of sheets; compare, for example, the first column of the second sheet of 1QIsa^a measuring 12.3 cm (col. IV) with the following columns (11.5, 11.9, and 11.4 cm). The person who made the grid for these columns probably did not pay close attention to the exact size of the sheet, and began with too wide a column. Likewise, wider columns often appeared at the end (cf., e.g. col. XLIX of 1QIsa^a measuring 16.3 cm with the preceding two columns of 14.2 and 14.8 cm), to fill out the uninscribed area.

By the same token, narrow columns often were positioned at the ends of sheets (compare, e.g. col. XLIII of 1QIsa^a measuring 12.9 cm with the preceding two columns of 15.7 and 16.3 cm, and col. LII measuring 8.8 cm with the preceding two columns of 13.3 and 14.0 cm). A similar situation pertains also in 1QM and 11QPs^a XIV–XIX, where the first four columns are of similar length (between 13.2 and 13.6 cm), while the last two columns are both narrower at 12.0 cm each. This observation was made by G. Brooke, *DJD* XXII, 190 who assumed a similar situation for 4QCommGen A (4Q252). These diminishing dimensions reveal that the person who ruled the columns had to reduce the size of the later columns after realizing that the earlier ones were too large. Likewise, narrow columns are often drawn at the beginning of sheets in an attempt to conserve space.

The *average number of lines* per column in Qumran scrolls is probably twenty, with a height of approximately 14–15 cm (including the top and bottom margins). Larger scrolls contained columns with from 25 to as many as 60 lines. Scrolls of the smallest dimensions contained merely 5–13 lines and their height was similarly small.

Greek literary papyrus scrolls of less than twenty-five lines are rare (Kenyon, *Books and Readers*, 59). The dimensions of the Qumran papyrus scrolls are not known as no complete columns have been preserved together with their top and bottom margins. In Egyptian papyrus scrolls, beyond those of full size for which the dimensions are recorded in § d, half-size scrolls are also known (10–12 cm high in the Old Kingdom), created by cutting the papyrus in two halves (Posener-Kriéger, "Old Kingdom Papyri," 25).

The data in TABLE 15 relating to the *number of lines and the height of the leather* is meant to be exhaustive for the well-preserved and/or easily reconstructable scrolls from the Judean Desert. The items are listed in ascending order of the number of lines per column, and within each group of texts with the same number of lines, the scrolls are arranged in ascending order of the absolute height of the leather, including the top and bottom margins when this information is available. Usually, the number of lines is indicative of the size of the scroll. However, when the line-spacing is unusually wide (e.g. 4QDan[a] compared with 4QJer[c] [illustr. 20], both 18 lines) or narrow (e.g. 4QGen[e], MurGen-Num, 4Q[Gen-]Exod[b] containing 50 lines with a height of approximately 50 cm compared with the minute script of 4QShirShabb[d] [4Q403], with a height of 18.0 cm), the height of the scroll is not necessarily indicated. The definition of the four writing-block sizes (small [4–14 lines], medium-sized [15–24], large [25–34], and very large [35–60]) is impressionistic, and is made mainly for the sake of convenience. However, in the case of the 'very large scrolls', this definition is meaningful since virtually all such scrolls contain Scripture texts.

TABLE 15: *Number of Lines per Column and Leather Height*

Leather Scrolls with a Small Writing Block

4QIncantation (4Q444)	**4** (the three fragments of four lines each contained a consecutive text). Frg. 1: 2.4+ cm, frg. 4: 3.2 cm, and frg. 5: 2.6 cm; illustr. 10 and E. Chazon, *DJD* XXIX, 368.
5QCurses (5Q14)	**5** (4.5+ cm); J. T. Milik, *DJD* III, 183.
4QBirth of Noah[b] ar (4Q535)	**6** (6.5 cm); É. Puech, *DJD* XXXI, pl. X.
5QLam[a]	**7** (6.2–7.2 cm); J. T. Milik, *DJD* III, 174–5, pls. XXXVII–XXXVIII: I and II (7.0+ cm), III (6.5+ cm), IV (6.2+ cm), V (7.0+ cm).
4QprEsth[b] ar (4Q550a)	**7** (6.5 cm).
4QCal Doc/Mish D (4Q325)	**7** (7.0 cm, slightly reconstructed); S. Talmon, *DJD* XXI, pl. VII.
6QCant	**7** (7.8 cm); M. Baillet, *DJD* III, pl. XXVIII.
4QprEsth[a] ar (4Q550)	**7, 8** (5.8 cm).
4QprEsth[d] ar (4Q550c)	**7, 8** (6.0 cm).

4QHalakha B (4Q264a)	**8** (6.5 cm); J. Baumgarten, *DJD* XXXV, pl. V.
4QDanSuz? ar (4Q551)	8 (6.6 cm).
2QRuth^a	8 (7.6+ cm); M. Baillet, *DJD* III, pl. XIV.
4QPs^g	8 (8.1 cm); illustr. 17a and Skehan–Ulrich–Flint, *DJD* XVI, pl. XIV.
4QExod^e	8 (8.2 cm); J. E. Sanderson, *DJD* XII, 129.
4QCal Doc/Mish B (4Q321)	8, 9 (7.7–8.5 cm); S. Talmon, *DJD* XXI, pls. III–IV.
4QToh A (4Q274) 1–2	**9** frg. 1: 5.5 cm, frg. 2: 5.2 cm; J. Baumgarten, *DJD* XXXV, 99, and pl. VIII.
4QapocrLam B (4Q501)	9 (5.8 cm); M. Baillet, *DJD* VII, pl. XXVIII.
4QapocrMos^a (4Q375)	9 (7.0 cm); J. Strugnell, *DJD* XIX, 111.
XHev/SeEschat Hymn (XHev/Se 6)	9 (7.5 cm); M. Morgenstern, *DJD* XXXVIII, pl. XXXI.
4QList of False Prophets ar (4Q339)	9 (8.5 cm); Broshi–Yardeni, *DJD* XIX, 77 and pl. XI.
4QapocrDan ar (4Q246)	9 (8.5–8.8 cm); É. Puech, *DJD* XXII, 165.
4QZodiology and Brontology (4Q318)	9 (10.1 cm); M. Sokoloff, *DJD* XXXVI, pls. XV–XVI.
4QShir^a (4Q510)	9 (10.5 cm); M. Baillet, *DJD* VII, pl. LV.
4QDan^e	9 (6.1 cm + margins); E. Ulrich, *DJD* XVI, 287.
4QApocryphal Psalm and Prayer (4Q448)	9 (cols. II–III), 10 (col. I; 9.5 cm); illustr. 11 and E. Eshel, *DJD* XI, 403–4.
4QS^j (4Q264)	**10** (4.4 cm); Alexander–Vermes, *DJD* XXVI, 201.
4QS^f (4Q260)	10 (7.6 cm). Slightly reconstructed by Alexander–Vermes, *DJD* XXVI, 5, 153.
4QcryptA Words of the Maskil (4Q298)	10 (8.4 cm); S. Pfann, *DJD* XX, pls. I–II.
4QAges of Creation A (4Q180)	10 (10.5 cm); J. Allegro, *DJD* V, pl. XXVII.
4QpIsa^b (4Q162)	10 (11.0 cm); J. Allegro, *DJD* V, pl. VI.
4QAdmonition Based on the Flood (4Q370)	10 (12.0 cm); C. Newsom, *DJD* XIX, pl. XII.
Mas apocrJosh	10 (12.5 cm); Talmon, *Masada VI*, 105–6.
4QLam	10, 11 (11.8 cm); F. M. Cross, *DJD* XVI, pl. XXIX.
4QMMT^c (4Q396)	**11** (9.0 cm); Qimron–Strugnell, *DJD* X, 15.
4QBarkhi Nafshi^c (4Q436)	11 (9.7 cm); Weinfeld–Seely, *DJD* XXIX, 295.
4QGen^d	11 (10.8 cm); J. R. Davila, *DJD* XII, 43.
4QDeut^q	11 (11.4 cm); Skehan–Ulrich, *DJD* XIV, 137.
4QEzek^b	11 (11.4 cm); J. E. Sanderson, *DJD* XV, 216.
4QRuth^b	11 (6.2–8.2 cm + margins); Ulrich–Murphy, *DJD* XVI, 192.
4QDeutⁿ II–V	**12** (7.1 cm); S. W. Crawford, *DJD* XIV, 117.
4QMMT^f (4Q399)	12 (11 inscribed; 7.5 cm); Qimron–Strugnell, *DJD* X, pl. VIII.
4QH^c (4Q429)	12 (10.3 cm reconstructed); E. Schuller, *DJD* XXIX, pls. XI–XII.
4QpNah (4Q169)	12 (12.5 cm); J. Allegro, *DJD* V, pl. XII.
4QEnGiants^c ar (4Q531) 22	12 lines? É. Puech, *DJD* XXXI, pls. III–IV.
4QBer^b (4Q287)	**13** (8.2 cm); B. Nitzan, *DJD* XI, 49.
4QS^d (4Q258)	13 (8.4 cm, slightly reconstructed); Alexander–Vermes, *DJD* XXVI, 85 and pl. XII.
4QTQahat ar (4Q542)	13 (9.5 cm); É. Puech, *DJD* XXXI, pl. XV.
4QBirth of Noah^c ar (4Q536)	13 (11.0 cm); É. Puech, *DJD* XXXI, pl. X.
4QS^b (4Q256)	13 (12.5 cm); Alexander–Vermes, *DJD* XXVI, pl. XIII.
4QSefer ha-Milḥamah (4Q285)	*c.* 13; Alexander–Vermes, *DJD* XXXVI, 229.
4QapocrLam A (4Q179)	13, 15 (8.2 cm); J. Allegro, *DJD* V, pl. XXVI.

4QM^c (4Q493)

14 (9.1+ cm; slightly reconstructed); M. Baillet, *DJD* VII, pl. VIII.

4QCant^a

14 (9.3 cm); E. Tov, *DJD* XVI, pl. XXVI.

4QPsJub^a (4Q225)

14 (10.0 cm, slightly reconstructed); *DJD* XIII, pl. X.

4QGen^g

14 (11.4 cm; reconstructed); *DJD* XII, pl. XII.

4QDeut^j

14 (12.2–12.5 cm, slightly reconstructed); J. Duncan, *DJD* XIV, 75 and pl. XXI.

4QCal Doc/Mish A (4Q320)

14 (14.0 cm, slightly reconstructed); S. Talmon, *DJD* XXI, pls. I–II.

4QCant^b

14, 15 (9.9 cm); E. Tov, *DJD* XVI, pl. XXVII.

Leather Scrolls with a Medium-sized Writing Block

5QDeut

15 (12.6 cm; slightly reconstructed); J. T. Milik, *DJD* III, pl. XXXVI.

4QSapiential Work (4Q185)

15 (12.6 cm); J. Allegro, *DJD* V, pl. XXIX.

4QPs^l

15 (15.4 cm); Skehan–Ulrich–Flint, *DJD* XVI, 127.

4QMessianic Apocalypse (4Q521)

15/16 (11.4–11.5 cm; slightly reconstructed); É. Puech, *DJD* XXV, 2–3 and pl. II.

4QtgJob

15–18 (14.0 cm); García Martínez–Tigchelaar–van der Woude, *DJD* XXIII, 85.

4QCal Doc D (4Q394 1–2)

16 (9.0 cm; reconstructed by S. Talmon, *DJD* XXI, 160–61; Qimron–Strugnell, *DJD* X, 3 and edition: 20 or 15–18 lines).

4QJob^a

16 (10.0 cm; reconstructed by Ulrich–Metso, *DJD* XVI, 171).

4QCatena A (4Q177)

16 (11.2 cm); J. Allegro, *DJD* V, pl. XXIV.

4QJosh^b

16 (12.0–12.5 cm); E. Tov, *DJD* XIV, 153.

4QBarkhi Nafshi^d (4Q437)

16 (15.0–15.4+ cm); Weinfeld–Seely, *DJD* XXIX, pl. XXII.

4QDan^c

16, 17; E. Ulrich, *DJD* XVI, 269.

4QPs^b

16, 18 (14.0 cm); illustr. 19 and Skehan–Ulrich–Flint, *DJD* XVI, pls. IV–VI.

4QGen^f

17 (13.5 cm); J. R. Davila, *DJD* XII, pl. XI.

4QWiles of the Wicked Woman (4Q184)

17 (13.5 cm); J. Allegro, *DJD* V, pl. XXVIII.

4QJub^a (4Q216)

17 (14.5 cm); VanderKam–Milik, *DJD* XIII, 1.

1QpHab

17 (15.0 cm; slightly reconstructed); Burrows, *The Dead Sea Scrolls.*

4QDan^a

18 (14.8 cm); E. Ulrich, *DJD* XVI pls. XXX–XXXII.

4QJer^c

18 (25.3–26.3 cm); illustr. 20 and E. Tov, *DJD* XV, 178–9.

4QapocrJer C^b (4Q387)

18; D. Dimant, *DJD* XXX, 173.

4QS^e (4Q259)

19 (14.2 cm); Alexander–Vermes, *DJD* XXVI, 130–31.

5QNJ ar (5Q15)

19 (16.0 cm); J. T. Milik, *DJD* III, pls. XL–XLI.

4QVisions of Amram^c ar (4Q545)

19 (16.3 cm); É. Puech, *DJD* XXXI, pl. XIX.

4QpHos^a (4Q166)

19 (16.8 cm); J. Allegro, *DJD* V, pl. X.

4QFlor (4Q174; 4QMidrEschat^a)

19 (18.0 cm); J. Allegro, *DJD* V, pls. XIX–XX.

4QPs^d

19 (13.8 cm + margins); Skehan–Ulrich–Flint, *DJD* XVI, 63.

4QD^g (4Q272)

20 (13.5 cm); J. Baumgarten, *DJD* XVIII, 188, pl. XL.

4QQoh^a

20 (14.9 cm; slightly reconstructed); E. Ulrich, *DJD* XVI, pl. XXVIII.

4QMMT^a (4Q394)

20 (16.6 cm); Qimron–Strugnell, *DJD* X, 3.

4QXII^a

20 (18.6 cm); R. Fuller, *DJD* XV, 221.

1QM

20 (reconstructed by Yadin, *War Scroll*, 248) or 23–25.

4QShirShabb[a] (4Q400)	**21** (12.7 cm); C. Newsom, *DJD* XI, 173.
4QD[e] (4Q270)	21 (13.5 cm); J. Baumgarten, *DJD* XVIII, 136.
4QD[f] (4Q271)	21 (14.0 cm, slightly reconstructed); J. Baumgarten, *DJD* XVIII, 169 and pl. XXXIX.
4QPs[h]	21 (15.0 cm); Skehan–Ulrich–Flint, *DJD* XVI, 113.
4QInstr[b] (4Q416)	21, 22 (16.5 cm); Strugnell–Harrington, *DJD* XXXIV, 73.
4QEn[e] ar (4Q206)	21; Milik, *Enoch*, 227.
4QCommGen A (4Q252)	**22** (13.0 cm); G. Brooke, *DJD* XXII, 186, 190.
2QJer	22 (15.6 cm); M. Baillet, *DJD* III, 62.
4QDan[b]	22 (20.8+ cm); E. Ulrich, *DJD* XVI, 255.
4QDeut[e]	*c.* 22 (16.5 cm); J. A. Duncan, *DJD* XIV, 39; pl. XI.
11QT[a] (11Q19)	22 (almost all cols.) and 28 (XLIX–LX)[131] or according to the calculation of Qimron, *Temple Scroll*, 7: 22 (almost all cols.), 25/26 (XLV–XLVIII), 28 (many cols., no details), 29 (LXV).
4QSam[c]	**23**, 25 (21 cm); E. Ulrich, *DJD* XVII
4QPs[f]	23–25; Skehan–Ulrich–Flint, *DJD* XVI, 85.
4QIsa[d]	**24** (18.0 cm); Skehan–Ulrich, *DJD* XV, 75.
4QEnGiants[b] ar (4Q530)	24; É. Puech, *DJD* XXXI, pls. I–II.
4QGen[j]	*c.* 24; J. R. Davila, *DJD* XII, 63, 65.
4QD[a] (4Q266)	24, 25 (18.4–19.2 cm); S. Pfann, *DJD* XVIII, 24.

Leather Scrolls with a Large Writing Block

11QMelch (11Q13)	**25** (14.9 cm); García Martínez–Tigchelaar–van der Woude, *DJD* XXIII, 221.
MasSir	25 (17.0 cm); Yadin, *Masada VI*, pl. 8.
MasLev[b]	25 (18.0 cm); Talmon, *Masada VI*, 49.
4QpPs[a] (4Q171)	25 (20.5 cm); J. Allegro, *DJD* V, 45.
4QGen[c]	*c.* 25 (14.2+ cm); J. R. Davila, *DJD* XII, 39; pl. IX.
4QEn[g] ar (4Q212)	25–26 (19.0 cm); Milik, *Enoch*, 247.
11QPs[a]	25, 26; J. A. Sanders, *DJD* V, 5, 28.
4QPs[e] 15, 20	25, 26; Skehan–Ulrich–Flint, *DJD* XVI, 73.
4QDeut[b]	*c.* **26** (*c.* 18.0 cm); J. A. Duncan, *DJD* XIV, 9.
MasShirShabb	26 (21 cm); C. Newsom, *DJD* XI, 239.
11QT[b] (11Q20)	26 (26.9–27.9cm + margins); García Martínez–Tigchelaar–van der Woude, *DJD* XXIII, 361.
1QS	26, 27 (24.5 cm); same scroll as 1QSa (different dimensions; see below)?
4QJosh[a]	**27**[132] or 27–30 (E. Ulrich, *DJD* XIV, 144).
4QEn[a] ar (4Q201)	27 (23 cm); Milik, *Enoch*, 140.
XJosh	27 (24 cm); J. Charlesworth, *DJD* XXXVIII, 236.
4QDeut[c]	*c.* 27; S. W. Crawford, *DJD* XIV, 14.
4QDeut[d]	*c.* 27 (16.9+ cm); S. W. Crawford, *DJD* XIV, 35.
4QInstr[c] (4Q417)	27, 28 (20.0–21.5 cm); Strugnell–Harrington, *DJD* XXXIV, pls. VIII–XI.
4QLXXLev[a]	**28** (20 cm); P. W. Skehan, *DJD* IX, 161 (*Greek*).
1QIsa[a]	28–32 (24.5–27 cm).

---

[131]According to Yadin, *Temple Scroll*, I.15, the scribe increased the number of lines in cols. XLIX–LX in order to not increase the size of the scroll, but he decreased the number of lines upon realization that he would not succeed in doing so. It is, however, more likely that he simply used sheets of leather of identical size, but with a different number of ruled lines.

[132]Reconstructed by M. van der Meer, *Formation and Reformulation—The Redaction of the Book of Joshua in the Light of the Oldest Textual Witnesses* (Leiden 2001) 382–93.

4QEn[b] ar (4Q202)   28, 29 (30 cm); Milik, *Enoch*, 164.

MurIsa   **29** (19.5 cm); J. T. Milik, *DJD* II, 79.
1QSa   29 (23.5 cm); same scroll as 1QS (different dimen-
                                     sions)?

MasPs[a]   29 (25.5 cm); Talmon, *Masada VI*, 76–90 and illustr.
                                     5 a below.

4QPs[q]   29 (23.6 cm); Skehan–Ulrich–Flint, *DJD* XVI, 145.
4QInstr[d] (4Q418)   *c.* 29 (Strugnell–Harrington, *DJD* XXXIV, 214) or 28
                                     (E. J. C. Tigchelaar, *RevQ* 18 [1998] 593).

4QTest (4Q175)   **30** (23 cm); J. Allegro, *DJD* V, 58 and pl. XXI.
4QEn[c] ar (4Q204)   30 (24 cm); Milik, *Enoch*, 182.
4QDeut[h]   *c.* 30; J. A. Duncan, *DJD* XIV, 61.
4QJer[a]   30–32 (28.6–30.2 cm); E. Tov, *DJD* XV, 147.
4QNum[b]   30–32 (30 cm); N. Jastram, *DJD* XII, 208.
4QKgs   30–32; J. Trebolle Barrera, *DJD* XIV, 172.

11QEzek   **31**, 32 (21.5 cm); E. D. Herbert, *DJD* XXIII, 20–21.

4QpaleoDeut[r]   *c.* **32** (33 cm); Skehan–Ulrich–Sanderson, *DJD* IX,
                                     131.

4QpaleoExod[m]   32, 33 (35+ cm); Skehan–Ulrich–Sanderson, *DJD* IX,
                                     56–7.

11QPs[d]   32–34; García Martínez–Tigchelaar–van der Woude,
                                     DJD XXIII, 63.

4QNarrative and Poetic Composition[b]   32+ (18.0+ cm); Schuller–Bernstein, *DJD* XXVIII,
    (4Q372) 1   165.

4QPs[c]   **33** (*c.* 26 cm); Skehan–Ulrich–Flint, *DJD* XVI, 49.

1QapGen ar   **34** (30.5–31.0 cm); Avigad–Yadin, *Genesis Apocryphon*,
                                     15.

<u>Leather Scrolls with a Very Large Writing Block</u>

1QIsa[b]   **35** (23 cm; slightly reconstructed).
4QIsa[a]   35 (31 cm); Skehan–Ulrich, *DJD* XV, 7.
4QPs[a]   35; Skehan–Ulrich–Flint, *DJD* XVI, 7.
4QIsa[e]   35–40; Skehan–Ulrich, *DJD* XV, 89.

4QProv[a]   **36** (*c.* 32+ cm); Ulrich–Metso, *DJD* XVI, 181.
11QPs[c]   36 (*c.* 28 cm); García Martínez–Tigchelaar–van der
                                     Woude, *DJD* XXIII, 49–50.

4QGen-Exod[a]   *c.* 36; J. R. Davila, *DJD* XII, 8; 22 lines preserved,
                                     unclear evidence regarding the reconstructed length.

4QJub[d] (4Q219)   **38**; VanderKam–Milik, *DJD* XIII, 39.

MurXII   **39** (35.5 cm); J. T. Milik, *DJD* II, 182.
4QDeut[i]   *c.* 39; S. W. Crawford, *DJD* XIV, 71.
XḤev/SeDeut   *c.* 39 (*c.* 28 cm; P. Flint, *DJD* XXXVIII, 179).
4QRP[b] (4Q364)   39–41 (35.6–37.2 cm); E. Tov, *DJD* XIII, 198.

4QGen[b]   **40** (35 cm), reconstructed by J. R. Davila, *DJD* XII, 31
                                     on the basis of two adjacent columns; 30 lines
                                     preserved; illustr. 18.

4QIsa[g]   40 (35 cm); Skehan–Ulrich, *DJD* XV, 113.
SdeirGen   *c.* 40 (27.6–33.4 cm; reconstructed by C. Murphy, *DJD*
                                     XXXVIII, 118 on the basis of two adjacent columns;
                                     8 lines preserved).

4QIsa[c]   *c.* 40 (30 cm); Skehan–Ulrich, *DJD* XV, 45.

4QEnastr^b ar (4Q209)	*c.* 40 (reconstructed by Milik, *Enoch*, 274); 38–43 lines (reconstructed by Tigchelaar–García Martínez, *DJD* XXXVI, 133).
4QLev^b	**41** (36.1–36.7 cm); E. Ulrich, *DJD* XII, 177.
1QH^a	41, 42 (32 cm).
11QpaleoLev^a	**42** (26–27+ cm); Freedman–Mathews, *Leviticus*, 8.
4QPs^s	42 (29 cm); Skehan–Ulrich–Flint, *DJD* XVI, 153.
MasEzek	42 (29.5 cm); Talmon, *Masada VI*, 61.
4QEzek^a	42 (32 cm); J. E. Sanderson, *DJD* XV, 209.
MasDeut	42 (40 cm; reconstructed by Talmon, *Masada VI*, 57 on the basis of two adjacent cols.; 9 lines preserved).
4QSam^a	42–44 (30.1 cm); F. M. Cross and D. W. Parry, *DJD* XVII
8ḤevXIIgr	42–45 (35.2 cm); E. Tov, *DJD* VIII, 2. *Greek*
4QLev-Num^a	*c.* **43** (35.2–37.2 cm; reconstructed by E. Ulrich, *DJD* XII, 153 on the basis of two adjacent columns; 17 lines preserved).
4QExod^c	*c.* 43 (38 cm; reconstructed by J. E. Sanderson, *DJD* XII, 97 on the basis of two adjacent top margins; 38 lines preserved).
4QRP^c (4Q365)	43–47 (34.1–36.2 cm); E. Tov, *DJD* XIII, 256.
XḤev/SeNum^b	**44** (*c.* 39.5 cm); P. W. Flint, *DJD* XXXVIII, 173.
MasPs^b	44 or 45 (25–26 cm; reconstructed by Talmon, *Masada VI*, 96–7 on the basis of adjacent columns).
4QIsa^b	**45** (29 cm; reconstructed by Skehan–Ulrich, *DJD* XV, 19 [42 lines extant]).
4QShirShabb^d (4Q403)	**50** (18.0 cm); C. Newsom, *DJD* XI, 278.
4QGen^e	*c.* 50 (reconstructed by J. R. Davila, *DJD* XII, 47; two adjacent columns of 14–15 lines preserved).
MurGen–Num	*c.* 50 (46.5 cm; reconstructed by J. T. Milik, *DJD* II, 75 on the basis of pairs of 6–8 lines in adjacent columns of MurGen and MurExod).
4Q[Gen–]Exod^b	*c.* 50 (*c.* 51 cm + margins; reconstructed by F. M. Cross, *DJD* XII, 80 on the basis of two adjacent columns; 23 lines preserved).
4QpaleoGen-Exod^l	**55–60** (38 cm; reconstructed by Skehan–Ulrich–Sanderson, *DJD* IX, 19; two adjacent columns preserved, one with 30 lines).
4QExod-Lev^f	*c.* **60** (30 cm; reconstructed by F. M. Cross, *DJD* XII, 134; 31 lines and two adjacent bottom margins preserved).
4QPs^r	60+ (33+ cm) reconstructed by Skehan–Ulrich–Flint, *DJD* XVI, 151 on the basis of the assumption that all Psalms between Psalms 27 and 30 were included. Six lines and adjacent bottom margins are extant.

Papyrus Scrolls

4QpapS^a (4Q255)	**12** (reconstructed by Metso, *Community Rule*, 20).
4QpapTob^a ar (4Q196)	**13** (frg. 2: 17.0 cm), 16 (frgs. 17 ii, 18: 18.7 cm); same scroll? See J. Fitzmyer, *DJD* XIX, 7.
4QpapH^f (4Q432)	**17** (19.0 cm + margins); E. Schuller, *DJD* XXIX, 209.

4QpapS^c (4Q257)	**20**, 21 (Metso, *Community Rule*, 33) or 24 (20.1 cm; Alexander–Vermes, *DJD* XXVI, 66).
4QpapJub^h (4Q223–224)	**54**; VanderKam–Milik, *DJD* XIII, 96.

Conclusions regarding the correlation between the data in the above list and the *content* and *nature* of the compositions are tentative due to the fragmentary nature of the evidence. The data below refer solely to leather scrolls, as the evidence for papyrus scrolls is very limited. Since the column size is directly related to the length of the scroll (§ c above), small and large column blocks indicate their inclusion in equally small and large scrolls.

Small scrolls include[133]

• All known copies of the Five Scrolls (with the exception of 4QQoh^a [Qumran scribal practice] with 20 lines): 2QRuth^a (8), 4QRuth^b (11), 4QLam (10, 11), 5QLam^a (7), 4QCant^a (14), 4QCant^b (14, 15), 6QCant (7).

• A few excerpted biblical books of various types that were probably intended for liturgical purposes: 4QDeut^n (12) probably containing selections of Deuteronomy, 4QDeut^q (11) probably comprising only Deuteronomy 32, and 4QPs^g (8) containing only Psalm 119. 4QExod^e (8) and 4QDan^e (9) probably belong to the same category.

• Other small liturgical compositions: 4QIncantation (4Q444; 4 lines); 4QShir^a (4Q510 [9]); 5QCurses (5Q14 [5]); XHev/SeEschat Hymn (XHev/Se 6 [8]).

• Further small compositions (up to 10 lines): 4QapocrDan ar (4Q246 [9]); 4QHalakha B (4Q264a [8]); 4QToh A (4Q274 [9]); 4QZodiology and Brontology (4Q318 [9]); 4QCal Doc/Mish B (4Q321 [8, 9]); 4QCal Doc/Mish D (4Q325 [7]; 4QapocrMos^a (4Q375 [9]); 4QApocryphal Psalm and Prayer (4Q448 [9, 10]); 4QapocrLam B (4Q501 [9]); 4QBirth of Noah^b ar (4Q535 [6]); 4QprEsth^{a,b,d} ar (4Q550 [7–8]); 4QDanSuz? ar (4Q551 [8]); and 4QOrdo (4Q334) according to U. Glessmer, *DJD* XXI, 168 (13–14 [10.0 cm high] or 8–9 [7.0 cm]).

In his discussion of excerpting in classical antiquity, Birt noted that some classical compositions were excerpted due to their excessive length and stated that travelers preferred to carry smaller editions.[134] In this regard, for the period between 1 BCE to 2 CE Turner, *Greek Manuscripts*, 19 notes that 'rolls of relatively small height were in fashion for books of poetry.'

J. T. Milik, *RevQ* 15 (1992) 363–4 linked the short length of certain scrolls to their literary character ('narratives in Aramaic; Hebrew commentaries, prayers, lamentations, and the Community Rule'). Milik's suggestion certainly explains some data satisfactorily, but since his analysis is based on less than half of the scrolls of small size, his description is not complete. We notice a relatively large number of small liturgical scrolls; possibly the small copies of the Five Scrolls fit into this category.

Long scrolls contained long compositions,[135] especially Scripture. Among the scrolls with a large writing block, Scripture scrolls constitute 60 percent, or more, if noncanonical authoritative scrolls are included (Sirach and Enoch).[136] Among the scrolls

---

[133] For earlier lists of small Qumran scrolls, see A. Rofé, "The Composition of Deuteronomy 31," *Shnaton* 3 (1979) 59–76 (Heb.), especially 64–6; E. Eshel, *HUCA* 62 (1991) 150; S. J. Pfann, *DJD* XX, 5, n. 15; J. T. Milik in his discussion of 4QprEsth ar (4Q550), "Les modèles araméens du livre d'Esther dans la grotte 4 de Qumrân," *RevQ* 15 (1992) 321–406, especially 363–4.

[134] T. Birt, *Kritik und Hermeneutik nebst Abriss des Antiken Buchwesens* (Munich 1913) 349.

[135] For an initial list of scrolls of larger dimensions, see M. O. Wise, *A Critical Study of the Temple Scroll from Qumran Cave 11* (SAOC 49; Chicago 1990) 55 (some details in this list differ from the data adduced here).

[136] These statistics may be considered misleading since the contents of the biblical scrolls are known, and therefore scholars have indulged in more speculation regarding their length than for other scrolls. However, this argument is probably invalid because under the circumstances a larger number of nonbiblical scrolls would still be expected

with a *very* large writing block (35–60 lines), virtually all thirty-nine contain Scripture, and if other authoritative scrolls are included (Jubilees, Enoch, 4QRP [possibly Scripture itself?]), the coverage approaches 100 percent. In fact, the only non-Scripture scrolls among the very large scrolls are 4QShirot ʿOlat ha-Shabbat and 1QHᵃ, which may also have been considered authoritative. One explanation for the preponderance of biblical scrolls in this group is that these compositions, together with a few nonbiblical scrolls, were the only ones that contained a long text for which a large writing block was needed. Another explanation which comes to mind is that the large format was used mainly or only for authoritative texts, since this distinctive format gave the scroll prestige, as in the case of the luxury scrolls (TABLE 27 below). These *de luxe* scrolls are recognized especially by their large top and bottom margins (ch. *4j*), but the size of the writing block is also of importance. If indeed the large size of a scroll was an indication of its authoritative status, this assumption would have to be linked with a certain center or period, since many small scrolls contained equally authoritative texts.

The following noncanonical texts are included among the scrolls with large or very large writing blocks:

> 11QMelch (11Q13) (25 lines)
> MasSir (25)
> 4QEnᵍ ar (4Q212) (25–26)
> MasShirShabb (26)
> 11QTᵇ (11Q20) (26)
> 1QS (26–27)
> 4QEnᵃ ar (4Q201) (27)
> 4QInstrᶜ (4Q417) (27, 28)
> 4QEnᵇ ar (4Q202) (28)
> 1QSa (29)
> 4QInstrᵈ (4Q418) (*c.* 29)
> 4QTest (4Q175) (30)
> 4QEnᶜ ar (4Q204) (30)
> 4QNarrative and Poetic Compositionᵇ (4Q372) 1 (32+)
> 1QapGen ar (34)
>
> 4QJubᵈ (4Q219) (38)
> 4QRPᵇ (4Q364) (39–41)
> 4QEnastrᵇ ar (4Q209) (*c.* 40)
> 1QHᵃ (41, 42)
> 4QRPᶜ (4Q365) (43–47)
> 4QShirShabbᵈ (4Q403) (50)

With regard, in particular, to the six noncanonical scrolls included among the scrolls with a very large writing block, it is possible that the large format indicated that these scrolls were considered authoritative outside and within the Qumran community.[137]

Among the scrolls with a large writing block, one finds many texts from Qumran, as well as *all* the scrolls from Masada, Naḥal Ḥever, Sdeir, and Murabbaʿat which can be measured. The latter group of sites contains scrolls which are usually somewhat later than those found at Qumran. The *terminus ad quem* for the Masada texts is more or less identical to that of Qumran, yet the finds of Qumran include earlier texts. The texts

---

among the long scrolls. After all, the nonbiblical manuscripts are three times as frequent as biblical scrolls; yet there are almost none found among the long Qumran scrolls.

[137]For an analysis of the texts considered authoritative by this community, see J. C. VanderKam, *The Dead Sea Scrolls Today* (Grand Rapids, Mich. 1994) 150–57. VanderKam mentions Jubilees, Enoch, and the Temple Scroll. RP can easily be added to this group, if this text is considered Scripture. In a later publication, VanderKam–Flint, *Meaning DSS,* 178–79 these authors list the following writings as authoritative: RP, Jubilees, Temple Scroll, 1 Enoch.

from Naḥal Ḥever, Sdeir, and Murabbaᶜat have as their *terminus ad quem* the Second Jewish Revolt. The manuscript evidence from these sites thus may attest to a later, or at least a different, practice:

MurIsa	29 lines
MurXII	39
SdeirGen	*c.* 40
8HevXIIgr	42–45 (*Greek*)
XHev/SeNum[b]	44
MurGen-Num	*c.* 50

as well as *all* the Masada texts for which such evidence is known:

MasSir	25
MasLev[b]	25
MasShirShabb	26
MasEzek	42
MasDeut	42
MasPs[b]	44 or 45

In fact, no scrolls with a small writing block are known from these sites (the evidence for the reconstruction of a block of ten lines for Mas apocrJosh, as suggested by Talmon, *Masada VI*, 105–6 is unclear). The evidence suggests that the scribal traditions at these sites reflect writing on larger scrolls than the average size found at Qumran. This situation may be connected to specific manufacturing procedures, but more likely the data reflect the finding of *de luxe* editions at these sites, most of which were of a large format (§ j below).

Since the scrolls from sites other than Qumran are mainly of large format, it may seem that this feature is an exclusive sign of a late production date. However, most *Qumran* scrolls containing a large writing block are ascribed to the first century BCE, and two are even earlier. The dates given are quoted from the *DJD* editions:

4QGen[b]	40 lines	50–68 BCE
4QLev[b]	41	middle of 1 BCE
4QLev-Num[a]	*c.* 43	middle or end of 2 BCE
4QRP[c] (4Q365)	43–47	late Hasmonean–early Herodian
4QIsa[b]	45	3rd quarter of 1 BCE
4QShirShabb[d] (4Q403)	50	early Herodian
4QGen[e]	*c.* 50	third quarter of 1 BCE
4QpapJub[h] (4Q223–224)	54	75–50 BCE
4QpaleoGen-Exod[l]	55–60	first half of 1 BCE
4QExod-Lev[f]	*c.* 60	middle of 3 BCE

It is difficult to know whether scroll manufacturers had in mind certain *standard* measures of the number of lines. It appears that the persons who prepared the leather had a more or less fixed concept regarding the sizes of margins and that they determined the number of columns and lines according to the space that was left after the margins were taken into consideration. Accordingly, scrolls of any number of lines were prepared, e.g. 13, 14, 15, 16, 17, 18, 19, 20, 21, 22, 23, 24, 25, lines etc.

The only *fixed* number of lines used in large scrolls seems to be *42*, appearing in an impressively large number of instances (including reconstructed columns and scrolls for which 40–45 lines were reconstructed [= 'r.']):

TABLE 16: *Scrolls Containing 40–45 (Reconstructed) Lines*

4QGen[b]	40 (r.)
4QIsa[g]	40 (r.)

4QIsa^c	*c.* 40 (r.)
SdeirGen	*c.* 40 (r.)
4QEnastr^b ar (4Q209)	*c.* 40 (r.)
4QLev^b	41 (r.)
1QH^a	41, 42
11QpaleoLev^a	42 (r.)
MasDeut	42 (r.)
4QEzek^a	42 (r.)
MasEzek	42 (r.)
4QPs^s	42 (r.)
4QSam^a	42–44 (r.)
8ḤevXIIgr	42–45
4QExod^c	*c.* 43 (r.)
4QLev-Num^a	*c.* 43 (r.)
4QRP^c (4Q365)	43–47 (r.)
XḤev/SeNum^b	44 (r.)
MasPs^b	44 or 45
4QIsa^b	45
cf. 8QMez	42

On the basis of these data, it stands to reason that several texts with 40–45 reconstructed lines may also have to be reconstructed as 42. It is noteworthy that almost all texts of 41–45 (reconstructed) lines contain Scripture, and it may well be that this was one of the traditionally fixed numbers, also known later from *Sof.* 2.11, and subsequently followed in the medieval tradition, from the *geonim* onwards (see the discussion by Barthélemy, *Critique textuelle 1992*, lx, ccxxxviii ff.).[138] As a rule, most medieval codices of MT indeed have 42 lines. Note further that codex Vaticanus (B) of the LXX also has 42 lines in most pages (pp. 335–534, 555–1536; the other pages have 44 or 40 lines), while codex S(inaiticus) has 48 lines per page.

For comparison, the numbers of lines per column mentioned in *Sof.* 2.6 (42, 60, 72, and 98) are very sizeable when compared with the earlier Qumran evidence.

For SP, the following numbers of lines are known, listed by Anderson, *Studies*, 15–44:

CW 2478b	12–13	(15.5 cm)
CW 10311	23	(21 cm)
CW 2483	24	(17.5 cm)
CW 2484	33	(26 cm)
CW 2473	34	(28 cm)
CW 2482	36	(10.9 cm)
CW 2481	38	(31.6 cm)
CW 2478a	41	(28 cm)

Consistency in the height of columns (number of lines). Usually scrolls were written with the same number of lines per column throughout a sheet and generally throughout all the sheets, but TABLE 17 shows that some scrolls display slight variations. For bibliographical details, see TABLE 15. In some cases, it is unclear whether the columns had a different number of lines.

---

[138]Against this assumption, one could argue that there may have been an equally large number of nonbiblical texts with 40 or 42 lines, but that such texts are not easily identified as their reconstruction is difficult due to their unknown content. Nevertheless, the content of several nonbiblical texts is known, partly through parallel texts. More importantly, it cannot be denied that the great majority of the known texts of large dimensions are biblical (canonical). Thus, if we take the random number of 38 lines as our point of departure, 28 of the 32 texts of 38 lines or more are biblical (see TABLE 15).

TABLE 17: *Inconsistency in the Number of Lines*

4QprEsth[a] ar (4Q550)	7, 8 (5.8 cm)
4QprEsth[d] ar (4Q550c)	7, 8 (6.0 cm)
4QCal Doc/Mish B (4Q321)	8, 9 (7.7–8.5 cm)
4QApocr. Psalm and Prayer (4Q448)	9, 10 (9.5 cm)
4QLam	10, 11 (11.8 cm)
4QapocrLam A (4Q179)	13, 15 (8.2 cm)
4QpapTob[a] ar (4Q196)	13 (frg. 2: 17.0 cm), 16 (frgs. 17 ii, 18: 18.7 cm); same scroll?
4QCant[b]	14, 15 (9.9 cm)
4QDan[c]	16, 17
4QPs[b]	16, 18 (14.0 cm)
4QInstr[b] (4Q416)	21, 22 (16.5 cm)
11QT[a] (11Q19)	See TABLE 15
4QSam[c]	23, 25 (21 cm)
4QPs[f]	23–25
4QD[a] (4Q266)	24, 25 (18.4–19.2 cm)
4QEn[g] ar (4Q212)	25–26 (19.0 cm)
11QPs[a]	25, 26 (25–26 cm; reconstructed)
4QPs[e] 15, 20	25, 26
1QS	26, 27 (24.5 cm)
4QInstr[c] (4Q417)	27, 28 (20.0–21.5 cm)
1QIsa[a]	28–32 (24.5–27 cm)
4QNum[b]	30–32 (30 cm; both reconstructed)
4QJer[a]	30–32 (28.6–30.2 cm)
4QKgs	30–32
11QEzek	31, 32 (21.5 cm)
4QpaleoExod[m]	32, 33 (35 cm)
11QPs[d]	32–34
4QRP[b] (4Q364)	39–41 (*c.* 35.6–37.2 cm)
1QH[a]	41, 42 (32 cm)
4QSam[a]	42–44 (30.1 cm)
8ḤevXIIgr	42–45 (35.2 cm)
4QRP[c] (4Q365)	43–47 (34.1–36.2 cm)
4QpaleoGen-Exod[l]	55–60 (38 cm)

The details in TABLE 17 show that adjacent sheets may contain different numbers of lines even though the dimensions of the leather are identical. In these cases the line-spacing or the size of the lower margins is different in the two sheets.

• 11QT[a] (11Q19) XLVIII (25, 26 lines) at the end of the sheet compared with col. LIX (28 lines) on the following sheet.

• 1QIsa[a] XXVII (29 lines) at the end of the last sheet written by scribe A compared with col. XXVIII (31 lines) on the following sheet (illustr. 6) inscribed by scribe B.

• 4QToh A (4Q274) written in columns of 9 lines until the end of the first sheet (frgs. 1, 2, 3 i), compared with the following sheet, frg. 3 ii with a densely written column (12 lines extant, 14 lines reconstructed; J. Baumgarten, *DJD* XXXV, 99 reconstructs 12 lines).

• 4QInstr[d] (4Q418) 103 i has one line more than col. ii.

• 4QCal Doc/Mish B (4Q321) has 8 lines in cols. I–III but 9 lines in cols. IV–VI.

Similar differences between columns are visible in classical compositions. Schubart, *Das Buch*, 62 noted that classical compositions frequently differ in column height with differences of up to 5–8 lines. Among other things, Schubart refers to a papyrus roll of the Ilias in which the longest column contains 63 lines, while the shortest one has 42 lines. Černy, *Paper*, 20 notes similar variations in Egyptian papyrus scrolls, in one instance as much as 8 to 14 lines in a 16 cm-high papyrus (P.Berlin 3023 ['Eloquent Peasant']).

The recto and verso of a scroll could be inscribed with compositions of different dimensions. See ch. *4b1*.

Most columns *start* at the same level, while some have a larger or smaller number of lines than those adjacent. There are hardly any known compositions in which a column starts one or more lines above the level of the others on the same sheet. However, the barely legible first column of 4QMeditation on Creation B (4Q304) seems to start one line higher than col. ii, but this line probably served as a superscription.

Different manuscripts of the same composition were often written on scrolls of differing sizes, although in some cases a certain regularity is visible. Since these data are only available for some compositions (TABLE 18), conclusions made on the basis of the following list must be tentative. The measurements listed below refer to the column height expressed by the number of lines ruled and usually inscribed, and not to its width which may vary considerably. The items in TABLE 18 are arranged in ascending order of line numbers. *Fuller data* on the reconstructions are provided in TABLE 15.

TABLE 18: *Number of Lines in Different Manuscripts of the Same Composition*

<u>Biblical Scrolls</u>

4QGen[d]	11 (10.8 cm)
4QGen[g]	14 (11.4 cm; slightly reconstructed)
4QGen[f]	17 (13.5 cm)
4QGen[j]	*c.* 24
4QGen[c]	*c.* 25 (14.2+ cm)
4QGen-Exod[a]	*c.* 36
4QGen[b]	40 (28 cm)
SdeirGen	*c.* 40 (27.6–33.4 cm)
4QGen[e]	*c.* 50 (J. R. Davila, *DJD* XII, 47)
MurGen-Num	*c.* 50 (46.5 cm)
4Q[Gen-]Exod[b]	*c.* 50 (*c.* 51 cm + margins)
4QExod[e]	8 (8.2 cm)
4QpaleoExod[m]	32, 33 (35 cm)
4QExod[c]	*c.* 43 (38 cm)
MurGen-Num	*c.* 50 (46.5 cm); see under *Genesis*.
4Q[Gen-]Exod[b]	*c.* 50 (*c.* 51 cm + margins)
4QpaleoGen-Exod[l]	55–60 (38 cm)
4QExod-Lev[f]	*c.* 60 (30 cm)
MasLev[b]	25 (18.0 cm)
4QLev[b]	41 (36.1–36.7 cm)
11QpaleoLev[a]	42 (26–27+ cm)
4QLev-Num[a]	*c.* 43 (35.2–37.2 cm)
MurGen-Num	*c.* 50 (46.5 cm); see under *Genesis*.
4QNum[b]	30–32 (30 cm)
4QLev-Num[a]	*c.* 43 (35.2–37.2 cm)
XḤev/SeNum[b]	44 (*c.* 39.5 cm)
MurGen-Num	*c.* 50 (46.5 cm); see under *Genesis*.
5QDeut	15 (12.6 cm)
4QDeut[e]	*c.* 22 (16.5 cm)
4QDeut[b]	*c.* 26 (*c.* 18.0 cm)
4QDeut[c]	*c.* 27
4QDeut[d]	*c.* 27 (16.9+ cm)

4QDeut[h]	*c.* 30
4QpaleoDeut[r]	*c.* 32 (33 cm)
4QDeut[i]	*c.* 39
XḤev/SeDeut	*c.* 39 (*c.* 28 cm)
MasDeut	42 (40 cm)

The following three texts are not regular biblical texts, but probably contained liturgical excerpts:

4QDeut[q]	11 (11.4 cm)
4QDeut[n] II–V	12 (7.1 cm)
4QDeut[j]	14 (12.2–12.5 cm)
4QJosh[b]	16 (12.0–12.5 cm)
4QJosh[a]	27 or 27–30
XJosh	27 (24 cm)
4QIsa[d]	24 (18.0 cm)
1QIsa[a]	28–32 (24.5–27 cm)
MurIsa	29 (19.5 cm)
1QIsa[b]	35 (23 cm)
4QIsa[a]	35 (31 cm)
4QIsa[e]	35–40
4QIsa[g]	40 (35 cm)
4QIsa[c]	*c.* 40 (30 cm)
4QIsa[b]	45 (29 cm)
4QJer[c]	18 (25.3–26.3 cm)
2QJer	22 (15.6 cm)
4QJer[a]	30–32 (28.6–30.2 cm)
4QEzek[b]	11 (11.4 cm)
11QEzek	31, 32 (21.5 cm)
MasEzek	42 (29.5 cm)
4QEzek[a]	42 (32 cm)
4QPs[g]	8 (8.1 cm); Psalm 119 only.
4QPs[l]	15 (15.4 cm)
4QPs[b]	16, 18 (14.0 cm)
4QPs[d]	19 (13.8 cm + margins)
4QPs[h]	21 (15.0 cm)
4QPs[f]	23–25
11QPs[a]	25, 26
4QPs[e] 15, 20	25–26
MasPs[a]	29 (25.5 cm)
4QPs[q]	29 (23.6 cm)
11QPs[d]	32–34
4QPs[c]	33 (*c.* 26 cm)
4QPs[a]	35
11QPs[c]	36 (*c.* 28 cm)
4QPs[s]	42 (29 cm)
MasPs[b]	44 or 45 (25–26 cm)
4QPs[r]	60+ (33+ cm)
5QLam[a]	7 (6.2–7.2 cm)
4QLam	10, 11 (11.8 cm)
6QCant	7 (7.8 cm)
4QCant[a]	14 (9.3 cm)
4QCant[b]	14, 15 (9.9 cm)

2QRuth[a]	8 (7.6+ cm)
4QRuth[b]	11 (6.2–8.2 cm + margins)
4QDan[e]	9 (6.1 cm + margins)
4QDan[c]	16, 17
4QDan[a]	18 (14.8 cm)
4QDan[b]	22 (20.8 cm)

Nonbiblical Scrolls

4QEn[e] ar (4Q206)	21
4QEn[g] ar (4Q212)	25–26 (19.0 cm)
4QEn[a] ar (4Q201)	27 (23 cm)
4QEn[b] ar (4Q202)	28, 29 (30 cm)
4QEn[c] ar (4Q204)	30 (24 cm)
4QJub[a] (4Q216)	17 (14.5 cm)
4QJub[d] (4Q219)	38
4QpapJub[h] (4Q223–224)	54
4QS[j] (4Q264)	10 (4.4 cm)
4QS[f] (4Q260)	10 (7.6 cm)
4QpapS[a] (4Q255)	12
4QS[d] (4Q258)	13 (8.4 cm)
4QS[b] (4Q256)	13 (12.5 cm)
4QS[e] (4Q259)	19 (14.2 cm)
4QpapS[c] (4Q257)	20–21 or 24 (20.1 cm)
1QS	26, 27 (24.5 cm), same scroll as 1QSa?
1QSa	29 (23.5 cm), same scroll as 1QS?
4QD[g] (4Q272)	20 (13.5 cm)
4QD[e] (4Q270)	21 (13.5 cm)
4QD[f] (4Q271)	21 (14.0 cm)
4QD[a] (4Q266)	24, 25 (18.4–19.2 cm)
4QRP[b] (4Q364)	39–41 (*c.* 35.6-37.2 cm)
4QRP[c] (4Q365)	43–47 (34.1–36.2 cm)
4QMMT[c] (4Q396)	11 (9.0 cm)
4QMMT[f] (4Q399)	12 (11 inscribed; 7.5 cm)
4QMMT[a] (4Q394)	20 (16.6 cm)
4QShirShabb[a] (4Q400)	21 (12.7 cm)
MasShirShabb	26 (21 cm)
4QShirShabb[d] (4Q403)	50 (18 cm)
4QInstr[b] (4Q416)	21, 22 (16.5 cm)
4QInstr[c] (4Q417)	27, 28 (20.0–21.5 cm)
4QInstr[d] (4Q418)	*c.* 29 or 28
4QH[c] (4Q429)	12 (10.3 cm)
4QpapH[f] (4Q432)	17 (19.0 cm + margins)
1QH[a]	41, 42 (32 cm)
4QBarkhi Nafshi[c] (4Q436)	11 (9.7 cm)
4QBarkhi Nafshi[d] (4Q437)	16 (15.0–15.4+ cm)

4QprEstha ar (4Q550)	7, 8 (5.8 cm)
4QprEsthd ar (4Q550c)	7, 8 (6.0 cm)
4QprEsthb ar (4Q550a)	7 (6.5 cm)
11QTa (11Q19)	22, 28 *or* 22, 25/26, 28, 29
11QTb (11Q20)	26 (26.9–27.9 cm + margins)
4QCal Doc/Mish D (4Q325)	7 (7.0 cm, slightly reconstructed).
4QCal Doc/Mish B (4Q321)	8, 9 (7.7–8.5 cm)
4QCal Doc/Mish A (4Q320)	14 (14.0 cm, slightly reconstructed)
4QCal Doc D (4Q394 1–2)	16 (9.0 cm)

In the formulation of some general conclusions on the scope of compositions written in leather scrolls, many details remain uncertain, especially since some biblical scrolls probably contained only selections. With some exceptions, biblical and nonbiblical compositions are contained in scrolls of similar dimensions, while in some of them, a remarkable degree of consistency is recognizable (the Five Scrolls, 4QprEsth ar, 4QD). It should be remembered that as a rule the number of lines is indicative of the size of the scroll: the higher the column, the wider the lines, and the longer the scroll.

Biblical Scrolls

Torah: The average scroll of a single book of the Torah probably contained 20–30 lines per column. Scrolls of a smaller size would not have contained the complete books, and the longer ones (40–60 lines) could have contained two or more books. Thus in Genesis five long copies (4QGenb,e, SdeirGen, MurGen-Num, 4QExodb [= 4Q[Gen-]Exodb]) contain 40–50 lines, while the smaller ones, 4QGend,g,f, contain 11, 14, and 17 lines. Medium-length copies contain 24 and 25 lines. 4QGend, with merely 11 lines and 4QExode with 8 lines definitely did not contain the complete books. 4QDeutj,n,q probably contained liturgical excerpts.

Major Prophets: Average copies of a single scroll contained 30–40 lines in the cases of Isaiah and Ezekiel and 20–30 lines in the case of Jeremiah. 4QEzekb with 11 lines is an exception, and according to J. E. Sanderson, *DJD* XV, 216 it is unlikely that this scroll contained the entire text of Ezekiel as it would have been an improbable 32 meters long with 280 columns. A single scroll of Isaiah is also mentioned in Luke 4:16-21. Prior to reading, Jesus unrolled this scroll and then rerolled it (πτύσσω and ἀναπτύσσω in vv 17 and 20) once he had finished.

Psalms: The smaller scrolls were of a limited size, containing only Psalm 119 (1QPsa, 4QPsg [illustr. 17a], 4QPsh, 5QPs [for the latter two and 1QPsa, no measurements can be made]), Psalm 104 (4QPsl), or a small anthology of psalms, while the longer ones contained all or most biblical Psalms. At the same time, we lack specific data on the contents of many of the Psalms scrolls that are known in a variety of sizes, from 8 to 60+ lines.

Five Scrolls: All known copies of the Five Scrolls (with the exception of 4QQoha) are small; see the analysis in TABLE 15. With the exception of 4QLam, which probably was preceded by another book, probably all preserved specimens of the Five Scrolls contained a single book only.

Daniel: 4QDana,b,c contained 16–22 lines, while 4QDane was smaller (9 lines). According to E. Ulrich, *DJD* XVI, 287, the latter scroll probably contained only a segment of the book, as 120 columns would have been needed to contain the complete book.

Nonbiblical Scrolls

H: 4QHc (4Q429) with 12 lines (cf. 4QpapHf [4Q432]) is much smaller than 1QHa (41, 42 lines).

S: 10–27 lines, while 1QS has larger dimensions.

4QMMT: 11–20 lines.

D: 20–25 lines.

4QShirShabb: 4QShirShabba (4Q400) and MasShirShabb contain 21 and 26 lines respectively as opposed to 50 lines in 4QShirShabbd (4Q403).

4QInstr: 21–29 lines.

4QprEsth ar (4Q550): 7, 8 lines.

Since the number of lines differs in these scrolls containing the same compositions, it is to be expected that they were written in different layouts, and that the words appearing at the beginning of each line differed from copy to copy. This discrepancy also entailed differences in the indication of open and closed sections in such parallel manuscripts (ch. *5a3* and TABLE 4). Exceptions are the pairs 4QDan[a]/4QDan[b] and 4QShirShabb[a] (4Q400) 2 1–2/4QShirShabb[b] (4Q401) 14 i 7–8 as described in ch. *2i* and further:

4QD[a] (4Q266) 1a–b 22 אֻׄבֻׄ. The scribe wrongly wrote a word which should be written at the beginning of the following line. This mistake probably indicates that the column of the scribe's *Vorlage* had the same width as the present copy.

4QD[a] (4Q266) 11 15 ואשר ידרוש שלומו וׄהׄמׄשׄתׄלׄהׄ ואשר יֵאות עמו. The scribe wrongly copied this word from the same position in the previous line, continuing the correct text upon crossing out the word. This mistake probably indicates that the column of the scribe's *Vorlage* had the same width as the present copy.

Margins

All texts written in scrolls and on single sheets were copied with clearly indicated margins on all sides, with the exception of *tefillin* that used all the available space for writing. This pertains also to small scraps such as 4Q339 (4QList of False Prophets ar), which has clearly recognizable margins (top, bottom, left).

In *b. Shabb.* 116a, any margin (top, bottom, and intercolumnar margins, as well as uninscribed spaces at the beginning and end of the scroll) is named גליון.

Top and bottom margins. The margins in the Qumran scrolls are usually of the same size within each sheet, although they may differ between sheets due to slight differences in the size of the leather. In the Qumran leather and papyrus texts, the bottom margins are usually larger than the top margins (TABLE 19). This is also the case with the SP manuscripts (Crown, *Samaritan Scribes*, 74–5 and idem, "Samaritan Scribal Habits," 175–7). In some Qumran scrolls the two margins are identical and in others, a larger top margin is made. No rule can be defined for content differences between the scrolls reflecting the two types of margins; different conventions must have been followed by scroll manufacturers. Large bottom margins enabled easy handling of the scroll, and as such, they were prescribed for Scripture by rabbinic sources, see *b. Menaḥ.* 30a (cf. *Massekhet Sefer Torah* 2.4):

שיעור גליון מלמטה טפח מלמעלה ג' אצבעות ובין דף לדף כמלא ריוח רוחב שתי אצבעות ובחומשין מלמטה שלש

אצבעות מלמעלה שתי אצבעות ובין דף לדף כמלא ריוח רוחב גודל

The width of the bottom margin shall be one handbreadth <7.62 cm>, of the top margin three fingerbreadths <4.56 cm>, and of the intercolumnar margin two fingerbreadths <3.04 cm> <in all the books of Scripture>. In the books of the Torah the bottom margin shall be three fingerbreadths <4.56 cm>, the top margin two fingerbreadths <3.04 cm>, and the intercolumnar margin a thumb-breadth <2.0 cm>.[139]

Likewise, *y. Meg.* 1.71d and *Sof.* 2.5 prescribe two fingerbreadths <3.04 cm> above the text and three below <4.56 cm> for all the books of Scripture, except the Torah. The discussion in these places also mentions the view of Rabbi prescribing for the Torah three fingerbreadths above the text and a handbreadth below the text.

In the Qumran scrolls, the top margins are usually 1.0–2.0 cm, and the bottom margins are 1.5–2.0 cm, while larger margins, especially in late texts from sites other than Qumran, are commonly a sign of a *de luxe* format (§ j below). These large margins, especially in biblical texts, conform to the pattern that was later spelled out in rabbinic literature. Greek *de luxe* editions of literary papyri also often have large margins, such as in the Thucydides papyri P.Oxy. 61.4103–4112 with margins of

---

[139]The calculations are quoted from Yadin, *Temple Scroll*, I.16.

4.0–8.0 cm (four texts of 2 CE). Small columns did not necessitate smaller margins. The data in TABLE 19 record the sizes of the top and bottom margins, measured from the bottom line of the letters (excluding the long final letters such as *nun*) of the last line to the bottom edge of the leather, and from the top line (ceiling) of the letters of the first line (excluding *lamed*) to the edge of the leather. See further Yadin, *Temple Scroll*, I.13–14, García Martínez–Tigchelaar–van der Woude, *DJD* XXIII, 81–2 (11QtgJob) as well as most *DJD* volumes published after 1990. According to Yadin's calculations, the dimensions of 11QT[a] (11Q19) usually agree with the prescriptions of the Talmud (see above). Further details on other scrolls were provided by Fields.[140]

TABLE 19: *Sizes of Top and Bottom Margins (cm)*

a. LARGER BOTTOM MARGINS IN LEATHER SCROLLS

Name	Top margin	Bottom margin
1QIsa[a]	2.0–2.8	2.5–3.3
1QS	1.5	2.2
1QSb	1.7+	2.4
4QGen[d]	1.3	1.7–1.9
4QGen[f]	1.1	1.5
4QpaleoExod[m]	3.0–3.5	4.3–4.5
4QLev-Num[a]	1.8	2.2
4QNum[b]	1.9	2.6
4QDeut[e]	1.5–1.7	1.8–2.0
4QDeut[h]	2.0	2.3
4QDeut[j]	1.5–1.7	1.7–1.8
4QDeut[n]	0.6	1.0
4QDeut[q]	0.7	2.5
4QSam[a]	2.2–2.6	2.9–3.1
4QIsa[d]	1.8	2.2
4QIsa[e]	2.0	2.6
4QJer[a]	2.2	2.8
4QDan[a]	1.1–1.3	1.9
4QPs[b]	1.5	2.0
4QPs[c]	1.5+	3.2+
4QpIsa[e] (4Q165)	1.8	2.5
4QpNah (4Q169)	1.5	2.3
4QTest (4Q175)	1.4	1.7
4QCatena A (4Q177)	1.0	1.5
4QapocrLam A (4Q179)	0.5	1.3
4QWiles of the Wicked Woman (4Q184)	1.3+	1.8–2.5
4QSapiential Work (4Q185)	1.5	2.0
4QJub[a] (4Q216)	1.3	1.6
4QapocrDan ar (4Q246)	0.9	1.9–2.1
4QCommGen A (4Q252)	1.3	1.6
4QD[e] (4Q270)	1.8	2.6
4QcryptA Words of the Maskil (4Q298)	0.7	1.1
4QCal Doc/Mish B (4Q321)	1.8	2.0
4QapocrMos[a] (4Q375)	0.8	1.5
4QMMT[a] (4Q394)	1.1	2.1
4QMMT[f] (4Q399)	1.0	1.5

---

[140]W. Fields, "Qumran Scribal Practices and the Size of the Column Block in the Scrolls from the Judean Desert," seminar paper, Hebrew University (Jerusalem 1987).

4QShirShabb[a] (4Q400)	1.0–1.3	1.3
4QShirShabb[b] (4Q401)	1.3	1.6
4QInstr[d] (4Q418)	1.0–1.6	1.1–2.9
4QH[c] (4Q429)	0.9	1.3–1.6
4QBarkhi Nafshi[c] (4Q436)	1.25	2.0
4QapocrLevi[b]? ar (4Q541)	1.1–1.9+	3.0
4QTQahat ar (4Q542)	0.4–0.5	0.6–0.9
4QprEsth[d] ar (4Q550c)	0.9–1.1	1.1–1.4
11QMelch (11Q13)	0.8	1.6
11QT[b] (11Q20)	1.8	2.8
XḤev/SeEschat Hymn (XḤev/Se 6)	0.5	1.0
MurXII	2.6–4.0	4.5–5.0
MasLev[b]	1.8	2.7
MasPs[a]	2.4	3.0
Mas apocrJosh	1.2+	1.8+
MasSir	1.7–1.9	2.0–2.2

b. IDENTICAL TOP AND BOTTOM MARGINS IN LEATHER SCROLLS

1QSa	1.2–1.7	1.7+
1QapGen ar	2.2–3.1	2.6–3.0
4QExod-Lev[f]	1.3	1.2+
4QXII[a]	1.2	1.2
4QDan[b]	2.2	2.2
4QpHos[a] (4Q166)	2.0	2.0
4QpPs[a] (4Q171)	1.7	1.7
4QFlor (4Q174)	2.7	2.7
4QAges of Creation A (4Q180)	2.0–2.3	2.0–2.3
4QLevi[a] ar (4Q213)	1.6	1.6
4QBer[b] (4Q287)	0.9	0.8–1.0
4QZodiology and Brontology ar (4Q318)	0.8	0.8
4QRP[c] (4Q365)	2.0	1.4–2.2
4QAdmonition Based on the Flood (4Q370)	2.6	2.0+
4QM[a] (4Q491)	1.5	1.5
4QVisions of Amram[b] ar (4Q544)	1.5	1.5
5QLam[a]	1.5	1.5
6QCant	1.5	1.5

c. LARGER TOP MARGINS IN LEATHER SCROLLS

4QExod[c]	4.0–4.4 (frgs. 30,32)	3.1 (frg. 33)
4QExod[e]	1.5	1.2
4QPs[g]	2.1	1.3
4QQoh[a]	1.55	1.35
4QHoroscope (4Q186)	2.0	1.5
4QMyst[c]? (4Q301)	1.3	1.0
4QRP[d] (4Q366) 1	2.9	2.5
4QapocrLam B (4Q501)	0.9	0.3–0.5
8ḤevXIIgr (*Greek*)	4.2–4.5	3.8

d. COMPARATIVE MATERIAL FOR NONDOCUMENTARY PAPYRUS SCROLLS

4QpapTob[a] ar (4Q196)	1.7	2.5
4QpapJub[b]? (4Q217)	1.3	
4QpapS[a] (4Q255)	2.0–2.3	
4QpapS[c] (4Q257)	2.0	
4QpapHistorical Text C (4Q331)	3.0	
4Qpap paraKings et al. (4Q382)	1.7 (3.5? [frg. 110])	2.0

4QpapH^f (4Q432)	1.8–2.2+	
4QpapHodayot-like Text B (4Q433a)	2.3+	
4QpapBenedictions (4Q500) 1	2.1	
4QpapPrQuot (4Q503)	1.0–1.2	2.9
4QpapPrFêtes^c (4Q509) 13	2.1	
4QpapRitPur B (4Q512)	3.0	
6QpapHymn (6Q18)	1.7	

Large top and/or bottom margins are recorded in descending order of size in TABLE 20 referring to margins of 7.5 to 2.3 cm, mainly for leather scrolls (sample of texts). See further TABLE 27 below.

TABLE 20: *Large Top and Bottom Margins (cm)*

MurNum 6	7.5 (bottom; J. T. Milik, *DJD* II, 75 and pl. XXI [wrong scale])
XHev/SeNum^b	7.2–7.5 (bottom)
4QDeut^g 11	5.7+ (bottom)
2QNum^a	5.7+ (bottom)
4QJudg^b 3	5.3 (bottom)
MurGen 1	5.2 (top)
MurXII	2.6–4.0 and 4.5–5.0
34ṢeNum	5.0 (top)
8HevXIIgr (*Greek*)	4.2–4.5 and 3.8
4QpaleoExod^m	3.0–3.5 and 4.3–4.5
4QJer^c	2.5–4.5 (bottom)
4QExod^c 33, 40, 42	4.0–4.4 and 3.1
4QpaleoGen-Exod^l 35	4.0+ (bottom)
XJosh	4.0 (bottom)
4QCommGen C (4Q254) 16	3.8 (bottom)
11QT^a (11Q19)	2.8–3.6 (bottom)
MasDeut	3.4 (top)
1QIsa^a	2.0–2.8 and 2.5–3.3
4QcryptA Lunisolar Calendar (4Q317)	2.9–3.1 (bottom)
4QPs^c	1.5+ and 3.2+
4QGen^b	3.2 (top); illustr. 18
4QDeut^{k1}	3.2+ (bottom)
11QSefer ha-Milḥamah (11Q14)	3.2+ (bottom)
1QM	2.7–3.5 (top)
4QEzek^a	3.0+ (top)
MasEzek	3.0 (top)
MurIsa	3.0+ (bottom)
MasPs^a	2.4 and 3.0
4QapocrLevi^b? ar (4Q541)	1.1–1.9+ and 3.0
4QpapHistorical Text C (4Q331)	3.0 (bottom)
4QpapRitPur B (4Q512)	3.0 (bottom)
1QapGen ar	2.2–3.1 and 2.6–3.0
4QSam^a	2.2–2.6 and 2.9–3.1
4QInstr^d (4Q418)	1.0–1.6 and 1.1–2.9
4QRP^d (4Q366) 1	2.9 and 2.5
4QT^a? (4Q365a) 3	2.9 (top)
4QpapPrQuot (4Q503)	1.0–1.2 and 2.9
4QTime of Righteousness (4Q215a) 2, 3	2.8 (top)
4QEnastr^b ar (4Q209)	2.8 (bottom)
4QJer^a	2.2 and 2.8

MasLev[b]	1.8 and 2.7
4QIsa[a]	2.7 (top)
4QPrFêtes[b] (4Q507)	2.7 (bottom)
4QFlor (4Q174)	2.7 and 2.7
4QPs[f]	2.7 (bottom)
4QPs[e] frgs. 15, 20	2.7 (top)
4QD[e] (4Q270)	1.8 and 2.0
4QIsa[e]	2.0 and 2.6
4QNum[b]	1.9 and 2.6
4QShir[b] (4Q511)	2.4–2.6 (bottom)
4QWiles of the Wicked Woman (4Q184)	1.3+ and 1.8–2.5
1QHymns (1Q36) 25	2.5 (bottom)
4QM[b] (4Q492)	2.5 (top)
4QpIsa[e] (4Q165)	1.8 and 2.5
4QDeut[q]	0.7 and 2.5
4QpapTob[a] ar (4Q196)	1.7 and 2.5
1QapGen ar	2.5 (top)
4QLev[b]	1.8–2.5 (top)
1QSb	1.7+ and 2.4
4QapocrLam A (4Q179)	2.4 (top)
4QPs[a]	2.4 (bottom)
4QIsa[f]	2.4 (bottom)
4QInstr[g] (4Q423)	2.4 (top)
4QpNah (4Q169)	1.5+ and 2.3
4QpapHodayot-like Text B (4Q433a)	2.3 (bottom)
4QAges of Creation A (4Q180)	2.0–2.3 and 2.0–2.3
4QpapS[a] (4Q255)	2.0–2.3 (top)

Intercolumnar margins. Columns are separated by intercolumnar margins which are best visible when at least the left ends of the writing block are indicated by vertical lines (§ a above) and when scribes adhered to these ruled margins. The right margin of the column (where the writing commenced) was almost always straight (an exception is 4QTest [4Q175]). However, in the absence of a left margin indication (ruled line), when scribes adhered to a 'notional' margin (thus Herbert, *A New Method*, 21–4, 63–76; see § f below), the intercolumnar left margin is still visible and can be used as a base for calculations. When a scribe paid little attention to the left margin, thus creating a rather ragged separation line between the columns (e.g. 4QapocrDan ar [4Q246] 1 ii 3, 6, 9), he nevertheless left an impression of his notional margin which can be used for measurements. In calculating the intercolumnar margins, the space between the vertical lines or the notional margins is measured, while words falling short or exceeding these lines are disregarded.

The scroll manufacturer decided upon the width of the intercolumnar margins in multi-column sheets. Such margins are usually 1.0–1.5 cm; see, for example, 4QSam[a], 4QIsa[b,c], 4QJer[a], and 4QpapAdmonitory Parable (4Q302), 4QRP[b] (4Q364; see *DJD* XIII, 200), 4QRP[c] (4Q365; see *DJD* XIII, 258). The margins in 4QCommGen A (4Q252) are between 0.58 and 1.5 cm. The margins in 4QEnGiants[b] ar (4Q530; 1.5–2.5 cm), 4QIsa[d] (1.5–2.0 cm), 4QJer[c] (1.3–1.9 cm), 11QtgJob (1.2–1.9 cm) are slightly larger. A rather wide margin of 2.0–2.2 cm is found in 4QInstr[d] (4Q418) 45 and in 4QcryptA Lunisolar Calendar (4Q317; 2.2 cm). In *y. Meg.* 1.71d, the size of the intercolumnar margin is described as a 'full thumb' (מלוא גודל) and likewise in *b. Menaḥ.* 30a as מלא ריוח רוחב גודל.

An exceptionally small right margin appears at the beginning of the first sheet in 4QWords of Michael ar (4Q529) 1 (0.2–0.5 cm), preceded by stitching (and a handle sheet). However, this is a special case as there were no earlier sheets for the scribe to take into consideration.

Detailed data on the intercolumnar margins are recorded in most *DJD* editions as well as in Yadin, *Temple Scroll*, I.13–14.

f. *The written text vis-à-vis horizontal and vertical ruling*

Most literary texts from the Judean Desert were ruled (§ a), and in the great majority of these texts, the letters (except for the *lamed*) were suspended from below horizontal lines in such a way that their tops were written flush with these lines or just under them.

In earlier times, this procedure was used on cuneiform clay tablets from the Ur III period onwards (Ashton, *Scribal Habits*, 110, 113). In some Egyptian demotic texts and in Greek papyri, a similar procedure was followed; for the latter, cf. some early papyri of the New Testament.[141] In later periods, letters were suspended also in Samaritan manuscripts (Robertson, *Catalogue*, xix: 'The bodies of the letters thus appear to hang free in the interlinear space, like clothes pegged to a clothes-line.'). According to some scholars, this custom was adopted from the Elamite cuneiform script by the Jewish scribes who began to use the Aramaic script during the Exile.[142]

According to Ulrich, *DJD* IX, 161, 195 a similar practice was followed in 4QLXXLev[a] and 4QLXXDeut, and according to Kraft[143] this was also the case with P.Rylands Greek 458 of Deuteronomy (2 BCE) and 8HevXIIgr scribe B (end of 1 BCE). Even though no ruling is visible on the plates, and possibly was not applied to the texts, these scribes worked with at least an imaginary continuous line indicating the position of the tops and bottoms of letters, since the writing of these texts, as all Greek texts from the Judean Desert, is extremely regular.

In a few Qumran texts, many of the letters are written slightly below the ruled lines; see, for example, 11QT[a] (11Q19) cols. XLV–XLVIII (0.1 cm below the line), 4QXII[g] (0.1 cm), and 4QHodayot-like Text C (4Q440; 0.2 cm). In some other texts, scribes disregarded the guidance of ruled lines altogether.

• 1QMyst (1Q27): The words are more frequently written on the lines than below them. Words are also written between the lines.

• 3QpIsa (3Q4): Most words are written through the line.

• 4QSam[a]: Words are sometimes written through the line (*DJD* XVII, pl. XII and frg. 26).

• 4QText with a Citation of Jubilees (4Q228) 1: The letters were written irregularly between the lines, at some distance from them, and they were also written through the lines.

• 4QCal Doc/Mish D (4Q325): An irregularly ruled line between lines 5 and 6 was disregarded by the scribe.

• 4QapocrMos[a] (4Q375): The words are more frequently written on the lines than below them. Words are also written between the lines.

• 4QProphecy of Joshua (4Q522), especially frgs. 9–10 and 22–24: The letters were written irregularly between the lines, on the lines, and often also through them (illustr. 17). Among other things, the scribe squeezed two lines of writing between two ruled lines (frgs. 9 i–10 13–14).

• An unidentified Qumran fragment: PAM 43.684, frg. 97 (*DJD* XXXIII, pl. XXIV).

• An unidentified Qumran fragment: PAM 43.692, frg. 81 (*DJD* XXXIII, pl. XXXI).

• Mas apocrJosh: The scribe of this manuscript, possibly reflecting the same composition as 4QProphecy of Joshua (4Q522), but written in a different script, wrote words through the line (A 4–5).

• MasSir IV: This column is often written through the lines, as is evident from a comparison of that column with the adjacent col. V written neatly below the lines. The two columns are juxtaposed in Yadin, *Ben Sira*, and idem, *Ben Sira* 1999, pl. 5.

The *regularity* of the line-spacing depends on the nature of the ruling, which varies from document to document, and sometimes from sheet to sheet:

---

[141]See Metzger, *Text of the New Testament*, 12.

[142]R. D. Barnett, "A Legacy of the Captivity: A Note on the Paleo-Hebrew and Neo-Hebrew Scripts," *ErIsr* 16 (1982) 1–5; Ashton, *Scribal Habits*, 121. In that script, Barnett noticed a 'top-line consciousness' (p. 4).

[143]http://ccat.sas.upenn.edu/rs/rak/lxxjewpap/style1.jpg.

• 1QIsaᵃ: Differing line-levels are visible in some adjacent columns in the same sheet, e.g. col. XIII compared with XII and XIV.

• 1QpHab: Irregular spacing is noticeable in the individual columns.

• 4QpaleoExodᵐ: 'The vertical distance between the lines of script ranges from 0.65 cm to 1.0 cm. Fluctuation occurs both between columns and within columns. Contrast, for example, cols. IX and X, averaging 0.8–0.9 cm, with I and II, averaging 0.7–0.8 cm; and contrast within col. XVII the distance between lines 32–33, which measures 1.0 cm, with that between lines 5–6 and 17–18, which measures only 0.7 cm.' (Skehan–Ulrich–Sanderson, *DJD* IX, 57).

Such line-spacing was often guided by a grid-like device sometimes leaving unequal spaces between the lines.

• 4QpsEzekᶜ (4Q385b) 1 i–iii: The distance between lines 2 and 3 in all three adjacent columns is larger than that between the other lines.

• 11QTᵃ (11Q19): Three sheets containing cols. XLV–LX were ruled with the same grid, while two subsequent sheets (cols. LXI–LXVI) were ruled with a different one, leaving more space between the lines. Within each column and sheet, no fixed spaces were left between the lines. The ruling was performed for the sheet as a whole, so that the slight deviations always recur at the same place in each column within a sheet or in several sheets. Thus in cols. XLV–LX, the space between the second and third preserved lines is consistently slightly narrower than in the remainder of the column. For details, see Yadin, *Temple Scroll (Hebrew)* I.11–12.

Many *DJD* editions record data regarding line-spacing (in cm); for an example, see vol. XV:

4QIsaᵃ	0.55–0.9
4QIsaᵇ	0.45–0.75
4QIsaᶜ	0.45–0.8
4QIsaᵈ	0.5–0.7
4QIsaᵉ	0.65–0.8
4QIsaᶠ	0.6–0.9
4QJerᶜ	0.6–1.5

The distances in cm between the lines fluctuate as follows in other well-preserved compositions:

1QpHab	0.5–0.9
1QIsaᵇ	0.4–0.7
1QM	0.6–0.9
1QHᵃ	0.6–1.0
1QapGen ar	0.6–0.8
4QShirShabbᵈ (4Q403)	0.3–0.5
4QInstrᵃ (4Q415)	0.5–0.8
4QInstrᵇ (4Q416)	0.5–0.8
4QInstrᶜ (4Q417)	0.5–0.8
11QPsᵃ	0.7–0.9
11QapocrPs (11Q11)	0.5–0.9
11QtgJob	0.5–1.1
11QTᵃ	0.6–1.0

Exceedingly large spaces (4.0–4.25 cm) are found between the lines of 4QcryptB Unclassified Text (4Q363).

y. Meg. 1.71d and *b. Menaḥ.* 30a contain an instruction that the space between two inscribed lines should be identical to the height of an inscribed line, but this rule is rarely adhered to in the known Qumran texts. In principle, such a format can be observed only in documents written in large letters, such as 11QPsᵃ and MasPsᵃ (illustr. 5a) which almost conform to the rabbinic rule.

In texts written in the *paleo-Hebrew script* it was relatively easy to adhere to the left border, since in these texts inscription was ceased at the end of a line and words were completed on the next line (i.e., split between lines). For example, in 11QpaleoLevᵃ col.

III, the following words are split at the ends of lines: א/תו, א/ל, ב/נ, יש/ראל, יהו/ה. As a result of this splitting of words, virtually straight left margins were obtained, e.g. in 4QpaleoExod[m] I, VI, IX, in all the columns of 11QpaleoLev[a] (cf. Freedman–Mathews, *Leviticus*, 9), and 4QpaleoDeut[s]. A similar system was used in the medieval manuscripts of SP (see below).

In texts written in the square script, scribes were also not very strict in the observance of the left margin when there was no special reason to economize in space. Frankly, it would have been difficult to be so, as it required an exact planning of every word in the line, something that is possible only when copying from a *Vorlage*. While there are some exceptions that display careful adherence to the left margin (see below), usually that margin was adhered to only in a general sense. Only in the medieval traditions of MT did scribes adhere strictly to a left margin.

A special case is 4QHoroscope (4Q186), the text of which was written in reverse direction in different scripts. Here, the left margin is straight and unusual indentations appear in the right margin which marks the ends of lines and not the beginnings.

The degree of margin observance in the scrolls from Qumran cave 1 was described in detail by Martin, *Scribal Character*, I.109–17 and additional texts were described by Herbert, *A New Method*, 21–4; 63–76. In any event, the (different) prescriptions of *b. Menaḥ.* 30b and *Sof.* 2.3 for the number of letters which could be written beyond the vertical left margin in Scripture scrolls were not adhered to in most scrolls that are written with square characters.

נזדמנה לו תיבה בת חמש אותיות לא יכתוב שתים בתוך הדף ושלש חוץ לדף אלא שלש בתוך הדף ושתים חוץ לדף

נזדמנה לו תיבה בת שתי אותיות לא יורקנה לבין הדפין אלא חוזר וכותב בתחילת השיטה

If <when almost at the end of a line> one has to write a word of five letters, one must not write two letters in the column and three outside <in the intercolumnar space>, but three in the column and two outside. If <when one has come to the end of the line> one has to write a word of two letters, one may not insert it in the intercolumnar space, but must write the word at the beginning of the following line (*b. Menaḥ.* 30a–b).

מניחים בין דף לדף שם בן ארבע אותיות לא יכתוב שתים בסוף הדף ושתים בין דף לדף אבל לא משם קטן ואם היה

שם קטן בפני עצמו של שלוש אותיות אסור

It is permitted to insert in the intercolumnar space <part of> a word of four letters. One may not write two letters within the column and two beyond <the column>; but this is not the case with a short word. If <the part of a longer word forms> a short word of three letters on its own, it is forbidden <to insert it in the intercolumnar space> (*Sof.* 2.3).

Whereas Martin, *Scribal Character*, I.112–3 stressed the scribal disregard for the ruled margin, Herbert, *A New Method*, 21–4, 63–76 suggested that scribes often did not necessarily adhere to the ruled margin, but rather to a 'notional' margin, that is, a margin which they had in mind. This margin could be either to the left (1QIsa[a], 1QS) or to the right (1QpHab) of the ruled margin; e.g. 0.375 cm to the left of the ruled margin in cols. I–XXVII of 1QIsa[a], and 0.525 cm to the left in cols. XXVIII–LIV of that scroll (Herbert, ibid., 39–41).

Systems for maintaining a straight left margin. In those instances in which scribes wished to obtain a straight left margin on the writing block, but found difficulty in doing so because of the constraints of the text, other means were sometimes devised:

(1) Leaving extra spaces between words toward the end of the line (*proportional spacing*, as in printed texts and computer editing), so that the end would be flush with the left marginal line.

1QH[a] I (Suk. = Puech IX) 8–17

4QGen[c] 1 ii 9–18

4QGen[f] 1 11–17

4QpaleoExod^m I 3–5; XIX 11; XXXVIII

4QNum^b, a scroll which has left vertical rules, cf. I 9, 13; XII 26; XVIII 27; XIX 29;
  XXXI 12, 14, 15. This practice probably was the rule for this scroll (XVI 14 is an exception).

4QDeut^h 1 5–7; 4 3

4QEn^c ar (4Q204) 1 v 5,8; xii 25–29; 5 i 23; see Milik, *Enoch*, 179

4QCommGen B (4Q253) 4 i 1–3

4QCommGen D (4Q254a) 3 1

4QH^e (4Q431) passim

11QPs^c 4 2

This practice is known from various ancient sources. J. T. Milik, *RB* 65 (1958) 70, n. 1 and *Recherches d'épigraphie proche-orientale* I (Paris 1972) 79–80 listed several references to inscriptions in Greek, Latin, Palmyrene, and Samaritan scripts. It is also known from Akkadian clay tablets (oral communication, Z. Abusch) and, in a more developed way, from medieval biblical manuscripts of MT (Beit-Arié, *Hebrew Codicology*, 87–8; idem and N. Pasternak, "Comfort of Reading, Comfort of Writing," *Gazette du livre médiéval* 31 (1997) 9–21, especially 10), among them SP. It is therefore probably no coincidence that the aforementioned 4QNum^b is closely related to SP. In the manuscripts of SP, the last letters of the line were similarly pressed against the vertical left rules, at the expense of leaving elegant spaces elsewhere in the line, both between words and within words. It is, however, somewhat inappropriate to compare SP with other manuscripts, since texts written in the paleo-Hebrew script (like SP) allowed for the splitting of words. Examples of the layouts of SP manuscripts can be viewed in Crown, *Dated Samaritan MSS*.

(2) *Cramming* letters in the ends of the lines or writing them in a smaller size in the line itself (illustr. 5a).

  1QIsa^a: Almost no space was left between the last two words at the ends of lines in col. XV 30 (Isa 19:22); XXIV 4 (Isa 29:23); XXVII 26 (Isa 33:22), all written by scribe A.
  4QCommGen A (4Q252) I 5 end of the line: על is written in smaller letters beyond the vertical line.
  4QapocrJer C^e (4Q390) 2 i 10
  MasPs^a II 11, 22, 26, 27; III 28, 29 (illustr. 5a and Talmon, *Masada VI*, 21)

For further examples, see Kuhl, "Schreibereigentümlichkeiten," 309, n. 2. For similar practices in Greek manuscripts, see Turner, *Greek Manuscripts*, 17 and codex A of the LXX; for parallels in medieval Hebrew manuscripts, see Sirat, *Ha-ketav*, 37 and illustr. 20; Beit-Arié, *Hebrew Codicology*, 89.

(3) Writing of parts of words *at the end of the line*, to be repeated in full on the following line (illustr. 4). When the scribe realized in the middle of the word that his writing would extend too far beyond the vertical line, he discontinued writing that word, and represented the complete word on the following line. The unfinished word on the previous line was sometimes erased, and at other times left untouched. For an analysis and further examples, see O. Eissfeldt, "Zeilenfüllung," *VT* 2 (1952) 87–92 (especially 88–9); for similar practices in medieval manuscripts, see Sirat, *Ha-ketav*, 38 and illustrations 21–22; Beit-Arié, *Hebrew Codicology*, 88–9.

• 1QIsa^a II 11 (Isa 2:4): The scribe wrote הו in small characters before realizing that the complete word, והוכיח, would exceed the left margin. He then rewrote the complete word on the following line even though there would have been sufficient room for it on the leather by extending into the margin. He left the two letters, and the ink to the left of the *he* indicates that he may have inserted a cancellation dot. In the same scroll, see further: VII 19–20; XL 29 (erased); XLI 10–11.

• 4QD^a (4Q266) 11 16: The scribe wrote י at the end of the line, but upon realizing that the complete word would exceed the notional left edge of the column, even though there was space for it in the margin, he crossed out these two letters (יֹ) and wrote the complete word (יושבי) on the following line.

• 4QapocrJer C^b (4Q387) 2 ii 9: מישראל was divided into מישר on the line, and אל below the line. The scribe created a straight left margin for most of the lines of that column, and although there was actually space for אל in the margin, he did not write in that area. In line 5 המחזקים is beyond the left margin, probably because the word was initially overlooked. The scribe divided that word into two parts at the end of the line, המח on the line, and זקים below the line.

• 4QMMT^c (4Q396) 1–2 iii 9: The scribe commenced a word beginning with a *ḥet* at the end of the line, but then realized that the complete word, החטא, would exceed the left margin. Even though there was room on the leather for the whole word, he dotted the letter (ח֗), and wrote the complete word on the following line.

• Mur papLetter from Beit-Mashiko to Yeshua b. Galgula (Mur 42) 5 (not erased as transcribed in *DJD* II, 156). See illustr. 4 below.

(4) Writing of symbols or letters as *line-fillers*, especially in the papyri from Naḥal Ḥever (ch. *5c6*), in order to create a straight left edge to the column.

(5) Splitting of words between lines in texts written in paleo-Hebrew characters (see above), resulting in straighter margins than those of texts written in square characters in which words were not split between lines.

(6) Supralinear and infralinear writing at the end of the line, inserted in order not to exceed the left margin of the column, creating a straight left margin.

> 1QIsa^a III 19 (Isa 3:19) בבתי֯כ֯. For additional examples relating to this scroll, see O. Eissfeldt, "Zeilenfüllung," *VT* 2 (1952) 87–92 (especially 87–8).
>
> 4QPs^x: See the description by P. W. Skehan (see n. 28) of the ends of the lines.
>
> 4QPhyl A, B, G–I, J–K, L–N, S: In writing the supralinear and infralinear additions in these scrolls, scribes had almost no choice since the ragged shape of *tefillin* did not enable the completion of words at the edges.
>
> 4QD^a (4Q266) 10 i 6 והשופטי֯ם
>
> 4QCal Doc/Mish A (4Q320) 3 i 12: There was room for the *mem* in the line itself, but the letter was written below the line in order to preserve a straight column structure: שׁני֯ם.
>
> 4QapocrJer C^e (4Q390) 2 i 7 במועל֯
>
> MasSir VI 19 (Sir 43:24): The scribe had room to complete נשמתם on the line, yet wrote the last letter below the line so as not to exceed the left vertical: נשמת֯ם

The expansion (dilatation) of letters, as in medieval manuscripts of MT (Sirat, *Haketav*, 38 and illustrations 26–27; Beit-Arié, *Hebrew Codicology*, 87), is not known among the Judean Desert texts.

g. Conventions used at the beginnings and ends of scrolls

The partially preserved beginnings and/or ends of some eighty scrolls from the Judean Desert provide us with valuable information on the content of these scrolls and the conventions employed at their beginnings and ends. In some cases, the extremities of these scrolls are recognizable because of conventions practiced by scroll manufacturers and scribes (uninscribed areas, handle sheets, etc.), while in other cases segments of the first or last columns have been preserved without such external features. At the same time, in the absence of data regarding external features or content, it is sometimes unclear whether a specific column represents the beginning or end of a scroll.

It is unclear why some scrolls are better preserved than others. Coincidence must have played a role, as well as the enhanced protection provided by certain places or layers within the caves, or by jars, as in the case of several scrolls stored in cave 1 (and possibly cave 11; thus Pfann, "*Kelei Dema*^c" 169, n. 23). In all cases, the innermost section of the scroll should have had a better chance of survival than its external layers, since it was protected not only by the jar or by the natural shelter of a cave, but also by the outer layers. In the usual situation, the scroll would be rolled up with its beginning on the outside, in which case the final columns would have had a better chance of survival. However, the evidence presented below seems to indicate that more scrolls were rolled up with their beginning on the inside. This would have occurred when a reader had reached any sheet after the middle section; after finishing his reading, it would have been easier for him to continue rolling the scroll to the end, so that upon reopening, the scroll could be rolled back to the required column. According to this explanation, the rolling up of a scroll which exposed its end probably shows that the scroll was in active use. The fact that more beginnings than ends of scrolls survived (see below) may indicate that the group of scrolls with preserved beginnings were in active use when they were stored. The survival of these scrolls as compared with the scrolls whose ends have been preserved displays no specific pattern. The only noteworthy feature is that of the eight known copies of 4QD, the extremities of four have been preserved, either their beginning (4QDᵇ [4Q267]) or end (4QDᵈ [4Q269], 4QDᵉ [4Q270]), and in the case of 4QDᵃ (4Q266) both its beginning and end.

The beginnings, or parts thereof, of a number of texts from Qumran (fifty-one or 5.5% of all the preserved scrolls) and the other sites in the Judean Desert (two scrolls) have been preserved, while the ends of a smaller number of scrolls have been preserved (twenty-nine from Qumran [3.1% of the total scrolls from that site] and two from Masada). It is probably no coincidence that for a large percentage of the texts from cave 11 (six of the twenty-one texts from that cave, disregarding the small unidentified fragments), one of the two extremities has been preserved, in this case always the ending. Similarly meaningful data for cave 11 are recorded after TABLE 25 relating to final handle sheets. These features imply relatively favorable storage conditions in that cave.

The data in the following lists regarding the beginnings and ends of scrolls pertains to scrolls found in any cave.[144] In three cases, both the beginning and end of a scroll have been preserved: 1QIsaᵃ, 4QIsaᵇ, and 4QDᵃ (4Q266). This situation indicates favorable conditions of storage, in the case of 1QIsaᵃ probably in a jar. For 1QS, the beginning and probably also the end have been preserved (see below). In a fifth case, 4QSamᵃ, sections near the beginning of 1 Samuel and the end of 2 Samuel have been preserved.

TABLE 21 records fifty-one biblical and nonbiblical scrolls as well as two unidentified fragments among the Judean Desert texts with partially preserved *beginnings*. The second column in the table refers to the survival of a title appearing in the first words in the running text in fifteen *nonbiblical* texts. In most other nonbiblical texts (thirteen texts), the first words have not been preserved. Since in only very few texts (five of the texts listed here) did the first words *not* contain a title, it may be surmised that scrolls usually began with a title of some kind. For an analysis of the titles, see § h.

The table contains seventeen (8.5%) of the 200 biblical texts from Qumran and two from other sites, as well as thirty-two (4.4%) of the 730 nonbiblical texts from Qumran, and two from other sites.[145]

---

[144]The statement by Stegemann, *Library of Qumran*, 62, that only in caves 1 and 4 were scrolls found which had the end of the composition on the outside when they were found (1QDM [1Q22], 1QMyst [1Q27], 1QHᵃ, 1QM, 1QS, 4QGenᵇ, 4QFlor [4Q174], 4QShirShabbᵇ [4Q401]) is problematic, since for almost all of these texts the endings have not been preserved.

[145]One could add to this list all the one-page compositions from Qumran: 4QTest (4Q175), 4QList of False Prophets ar (4Q339), 4QList of Netinim (4Q340), 4QExercitium Calami C (4Q341). 4QDibHamᵃ (4Q504) should not be added to the list. The uninscribed area at the end of this composition, which in reality is much larger than represented in *DJD* VII, pl. XLIX, represents the verso of this opisthograph, and is therefore an *unicum* when compared with the other scrolls.

TABLE 21: *Scrolls with Partially Preserved Beginnings*

Name	Title	Remarks
a. BIBLICAL TEXTS		
1QIsaᵃ		*initial handle sheet*
4QGenᵇ		see illustr. 18
4QGenᵍ		*initial handle sheet*
4QGenᵏ		*initial handle sheet*
4QLevᶜ		
4QDeutʰ		
4QIsaᵃ		
4QIsaᵇ		
4QIsaʲ		
4QPsʰ		probably contained only Ps 119
4QPsˡ		probably contained only Ps 104
4QXIIᵈ		
4QRuthᵃ		
4QRuthᵇ		
5QKgs		
6QDeut? (6Q20)		
6QCant		
MurIsa		
XJosh		
b. NONBIBLICAL TEXTS[146]		
1QM	title	
1QMyst (1Q27)	—	*initial handle sheet*
1QS[147]	title	*initial and final (?) handle sheets*
1QSa	title	*initial handle sheet*
1QSb	title	
3QpIsa (3Q4)	the beginning words of Isaiah	
4QAges of Creation B (4Q181) 2 (probably the beginning)	—	
4QEnᵃ ar (4Q201)	—	
4QPrayer of Nabonidus ar (4Q242)	title	
4QCommGen A (4Q252)	no title	*initial handle sheet*
4QpapSᵃ (4Q255)	title	
4QpapSᶜ (4Q257)	—	
4QSᵈ (4Q258)	title	
4QDᵃ (4Q266)	title	
4QDᵇ (4Q267)	—	
4QcryptA Words of the Maskil(4Q298)	title	
4QShirShabbᵃ (4Q400)	—	
4QShirShabbᵇ (4Q401) (probably the beginning)	title?[148]	
4QInstrᵇ (4Q416)	no title	*initial handle sheet*
4QBarkhi Nafshiᵃ (4Q434; cf. 4Q435)	title?	
4QBarkhi Nafshiᵇ (4Q435)	—	*initial handle sheet*
4QLament by a Leader (4Q439) (probably the beginning)	—	

---

[146]'‿' indicates that the first words of the scroll have not been preserved.

[147]1QS, 1QSa, and 1QSb are usually conceived of as a single composition, mainly because of the reconstructed title of 1QS which may have referred to 1QSa and 1QSb as well (‏[ספר סר]ך היחד ומן‏). However, 1QSa and 1QSb also began with a title, and 1QSa could not have been stitched after 1QS (see n. 149).

[148]Frgs. 1 and 2 of this scroll were probably reconstructed as the first fragments because of their wide initial margin. They contain the *fourth* Sabbath Song (and not the first one), so that the other manuscripts of this composition must have been arranged differently.

4QApocryphal Psalm and Prayer (4Q448; see illustr. 11)	title	
4QUnid. Frags. C, c (4Q468c)	no title	
4QSelf-Glorification Hymn (4Q471b) (probably the beginning)	—	
4QText Mentioning Descendants of David (4Q479) 1, 3	—	
4QWords of Michael ar (4Q529) 1	title	*initial handle sheet*
4QBirth of Noah[a] ar (4Q534) (probably the beginning)	no title	
4QVisions of Amram[a] ar (4Q543)	title	*initial handle sheet*
4QVisions of Amram[c] ar (4Q545)	title	
4QExorcism ar (4Q560)	—	
XHev/SeEschat Hymn (XHev/Se 6)	probably no title	

c. UNIDENTIFIED TEXTS

PAM 43.682, frg. 31 (*DJD*XXXIII, 161–74)	—	
PAM 43.695, frg. 9 (*DJD* XXXIII, 257–60)	—	

Another twenty-eight texts preserve sections *near* the beginning of the book, indicating that at one point the beginning, rather than the end, had a better chance of survival: 1QGen, 1QpaleoNum, 1QDeut[a], 1QDeut[b], 1QDan[a], 2QExod[a], 2QDeut[a], 3QPs, 3QLam, 4QGen[d], 4QGen[h1], 4QGen[h2], 4QGen[k], 4QLev[b], 4QDeut[h], 4QpaleoDeut[r], 4QSam[a], 4QIsa[f], 4QEzek[b], 4QProv[a], 4QQoh[b], 4QLam, 4QDan[a], 4QBarkhi Nafshi[c] (4Q436; cf. 4QBarkhi Nafshi[a,b]), 4QInstr[d] (4Q418), 5QAmos, 11QDeut, 11QPs[c].

The *ends* of twenty-nine scrolls from Qumran (3.1% of all the scrolls) and two from Masada have been preserved; see TABLE 22. Among these texts, the ends of seven biblical texts from Qumran (3.5% of all the biblical texts) and two from other sites have been preserved. In addition, according to E. Schuller, *DJD* XI, 121, the uninscribed fragment 32 of 4QNon-Canonical Psalms B (4Q381) may have been part of the final uninscribed sheet.

TABLE 22: *Scrolls Whose Ends Have Been Preserved in Part*

Name	Remarks
BIBLICAL TEXTS	
1QIsa[a]	*initial handle sheet*
1QIsa[b]	
4QDeut[q]	ending with Deut 32:43
4QJudg[b]	
4QIsa[b]	
4QIsa[c]	
11QpaleoLev[a]	*final handle sheet*
MasDeut	*final handle sheet*
MasPs[b]	
NONBIBLICAL TEXTS	
1QS[149]	*initial and final handle sheets*

[149] 1QS, 1QSa, and 1QSb were probably rolled up together (see J. T. Milik, *DJD* I, 107). 1QSa was not stitched after 1QS (disproved by the physical evidence): The stitching holes in 1QSa parallel to lines 1–8 in that scroll have no counterparts in the well-preserved end of the last sheet of 1QS, and therefore the two texts cannot have been stitched together. However, 1QSb could have been stitched after 1QSa. The sheet that was stitched onto the end of 1QSa probably was not an empty handle sheet, but rather contained the first sheet of 1QSb, as a single letter or

1QSa	*initial and final handle sheets*
1QSb	
1QpHab	
1QH[b] (1Q35) 2	*final handle sheet?*
4QText with a Citation of Jubilees (4Q228) 1[150]	
4QpsDan[c] ar (4Q245)	
4QD[a] (4Q266)	
4QD[d] (4Q269) 16 (H. Stegemann, *DJD* XXXVI, 201)	*final handle sheet*
4QD[e] (4Q270) 7	
4QCal Doc/Mish B (4Q321)	
4QMish H (4Q329a)[151]	
4QOrdo (4Q334) 7 (probably the end)[152]	
4QMMT[f] (4Q399)	
4QHodayot-like Text C (4Q440) 3	
4QShir[b] (4Q511)	
4QapocrLevi[b]? ar (4Q541)	
11QPs[a]	
11QtgJob	
11QapocrPs (11Q11)	*final handle sheet*
11QShirShabb (11Q17)	*final handle sheet*
11QT[a] (11Q19)	*final handle sheet*

Other texts preserve sections *near* the end of the book: 1QpaleoLev, 1QpaleoNum, 1QDeut[b], 2QRuth[a], 4QpaleoGen-Exod[l], 4QNum[b], 4QDeut[l], 4QpaleoDeut[r], 4QSam[a] (2 Samuel), 5QLam[a], 6QpapKgs, MurNum.

The second column in the table shows that handle sheets were often attached at the two extremities of the scrolls in order to prevent the handling of inscribed areas by users and to protect the scroll. Not all scrolls with preserved beginnings or ends are mentioned below, since in several scrolls the area adjacent to the first or last letters in the column has not been preserved. Lack of evidence does not allow us to state which system was the most frequently used:

SYSTEMS USED AT THE BEGINNINGS OF SCROLLS

(1) *Uninscribed area to the right of the first inscribed column* (illustr. 18)

At the beginning of the first sheet, the scribe often left an uninscribed area (see, e.g. 4QGen[b] in illustr. 18) which was always larger than the intercolumnar margin (usually 1.0–1.5 cm), and sometimes as extensive as a whole column; this custom was already practiced in Egyptian papyrus scrolls in which the blank area at the beginning of the scroll was often strengthened by a protective strip of one or two layers (Černy, *Paper*, 19). This blank area at the beginning of the scroll was generally unruled, although in nine instances the surface was ruled up to the right edge (TABLE 24). In the literature,

---

sign (*paragraphos?*), not recorded in the editions, is visible on the strip preserved level with line 20 of 1QSa. The preserved fragments of the first column of 1QSb would have belonged to this sheet. On the other hand, according to Metso, *Community Rule*, 13 the three sections were part of the same scroll. See further the analysis in Martin, *Scribal Hands*, I.43–56.

[150]This fragment was not indicated as the end of 4Q228 by J. T. Milik and J. VanderKam, *DJD* XIII, 177.

[151]Upon realizing that there was no room for an additional line at the end of the final column of the sheet, the scribe wrote the last line vertically in the left margin starting at the lower left corner. Had there been an additional sheet, the scribe probably would not have written the last line of the column in the left margin.

[152]The space of 2.2 cm to the left of this fragment probably indicates the end of the scroll rather than an intercolumnar space (thus U. Glessmer, *DJD* XXI, 173).

this uninscribed area is often called *page de garde* (e.g. J. T. Milik, *DJD* III, 171 regarding 5QKgs), but it is probably best to reserve that term for a separate sheet.

This system was imitated in the Copper Scroll (3Q15), in which the first column was preceded by a handling area of 6.0 cm.

(a) *Large unruled margin*

The data for a relatively large unruled margin are tabulated in TABLE 23. Whenever the relevant data is available, the width of the uninscribed leather preceding the first column is contrasted with the smaller intercolumnar margins. The vertical right edge is often described as 'unstitched,' implying the absence of a handle sheet. In other instances no relevant information is available, and in those cases the existence of a handle sheet cannot be excluded. Note that the scrolls in group *3* below had both an uninscribed area at the beginning of the first inscribed sheet and a separate handle sheet.

TABLE 23: *Unruled Wide Margins at the Beginnings of Scrolls*

Name	Initial Margin (cm)	Intercolumnar Margin (cm)	Attachment of Handle Sheet?
1QM	7.1+	2.0	unstitched
1QSa (see n. 147)	2.1	1.2	*initial handle sheet*
4QGen[b]; see illustr. 18 and *DJD* XII, pl. VI, but not pl. VII	10.8+	1.1	no evidence
4QPs[h] (probably contains only Psalm 119)	2.7+	—	no evidence
4QPs[l] (probably contains only Psalm 104)	2.4+	—	no evidence
4QAges of Creation B (4Q181) 2 (probably the beginning)	2.7+	0.8	no evidence
4QPrayer of Nabonidus ar (4Q242)	2.5	—	unstitched
4QCommGen A (4Q252)	2.6	0.6	*initial handle sheet*
4QpapS[a] (4Q255)	1.7	—	unstitched
4QInstr[b] (4Q416)	3.2	1.1–1.5	*initial handle sheet*
4QVisions of Amram[c] ar (4Q545)	2.5+	—	no evidence
4QExorcism ar (4Q560)	9.0	—	no evidence
5QKgs	7.0	—	unstitched
6QCant	2.5+	—	no evidence
MurIsa	10.2	—	no evidence
XHev/SeEschat Hymn (XHev/Se 6)	3.5	—	unstitched
XJosh	5.7+	—	no evidence
PAM 43.682, frg. 31 (unidentified text)	5.0	—	unstitched

The beginnings of documentary texts are not included in TABLE 23. For an example of such a text, see XHev/Se papDeed of Sale C ar (XHev/Se 8a) with an initial margin of 5.0 cm.

(b) *Ruled margin*

The data for relatively large ruled margins are tabulated in TABLE 24.

TABLE 24: *Ruled Wide Margins at the Beginnings of Scrolls*

Name	Initial Margin (cm)	Intercolumnar Margin (cm)	Attachment of Handle Sheet?
1QS	2.8–3.0	1.0–1.5	*initial handle sheet*
3QpIsa (3Q4)	4.0+	—	no evidence
4QIsa[j]	1.8+	—	no evidence
4QXII[d]	4.4	—	unstitched
4QS[d] (4Q258); beginning runs parallel to 1QS V 1–21	2.1 cm before col. I	0.9–1.2	unstitched
4QLament by a Leader (4Q439) 2, probably the beginning	2.8+	1.5	no evidence
4QUnid. Frags. C, c (4Q468c)	2.6	—	unstitched
4QBirth of Noah[a] ar (4Q534)1 probably the beginning	1.7+	—	unstitched
6QDeut? (6Q20)	5.0+	—	no evidence

(2) *Initial handle sheet*

A separate uninscribed handle sheet (protective sheet, *page de garde*) was often stitched before the first inscribed sheet; it is unclear whether, in such cases, a handle sheet was also attached to the last inscribed sheet. This was not the case in 1QIsa[a], while for 1QS and 1QSa such evidence is extant at both extremities. Remnants of an *attached* initial handle sheet have been preserved only for 4QBarkhi Nafshi[b] (4Q435); in all other instances the evidence is indirect, indicated by stitch holes at the right edge of the leather of the first inscribed sheet.

Similar beginning sheets were also known from the tradition of ancient Greek and Latin manuscripts as a *protocollon* (πρωτόκολλον), which is the initial glued sheet of a scroll, whether inscribed or not. Evidence for a beginning handle sheet has been preserved for the following texts, all of which contain initial margins of a regular size, unlike those recorded in TABLES 23 and 24:

• 1QIsa[a]: initial margin of 1.3 cm preceded by a handle sheet (stitch holes). The handle sheet was seen apparently by Metropolitan Samuel when it was still connected to the scroll (thus J. C. Trever in Burrows, *The Dead Sea Scrolls*, I.xiii). Fragments of this handle sheet are preserved in the Schøyen collection in Oslo, Norway (*DJD* XXXII, in preparation).

• 1QMyst (1Q27): initial margin of 1.4 cm preceded by a handle sheet (stitch holes); see photograph PAM 40.523 (not *DJD* I, pl. XXI, where the stitch holes were cropped off).

• 4QGen[g]: initial margin of 1.1–1.3 cm preceded by a handle sheet (stitch holes).

• 4QGen[k]: initial margin of 1.7–1.9 cm preceded by a handle sheet (stitch holes).

• 4QBarkhi Nafshi[b] (4Q435): initial margin of 0.8 cm preceded by a handle sheet, of which 1.2 cm has been preserved. *DJD* XXIX, 287 and pl. XX.

• 4QWords of Michael ar (4Q529) 1: a minute initial margin of 0.2–0.5 cm preceded by a handle sheet (stitch holes).

• 4QVisions of Amram[a] ar (4Q543): initial margin of 1.7 cm preceded by a handle sheet (stitch holes).

Note further:

• 4QGen[h-title] (4Q8c). A little fragment on the 'recto' bearing the title (ברשית) of a manuscript, now detached from that scroll, constituted, according to J. Davila, *DJD* XII, 63 a remnant of a handle sheet.

This assumption is suggested by the stitch holes on the left edge indicating the existence of a subsequent sheet, presumably the first inscribed sheet of the book. See further below, § h2.

(3) *Uninscribed area preceded by a handle sheet*

In a combination of both systems, the first inscribed column was (probably rarely) preceded by a large uninscribed area as well as by a handle sheet. The texts in this category are also mentioned in group *1*.

• 1QS: initial margin (ruled) of 2.8–3.0 cm preceded by a handle sheet (stitch holes). A section of this handle sheet, with the title on the verso, has been preserved (1Q28).

• 1QSa: initial margin of 2.1 cm preceded by a handle sheet (stitch holes). See n. 147.

• 4QCommGen A (4Q252): initial margin of 2.6 cm, contrasted with an intercolumnar margin of 0.6 cm, preceded by a handle sheet (stitch holes at the bottom).

• 4QInstr[b] (4Q416): initial margin of 3.2 cm preceded by a handle sheet (see stitch holes and minute remains of the sheet).

• 1QM: initial margin of 7.1+ cm. According to Sukenik, *Dead Sea Scrolls*, 35 the scroll began with an uninscribed handle sheet, now detached, of which 35.5 cm are preserved. However, this assumption is unlikely, as the first sheet shows no evidence of stitch holes.

(4) *No indication*

In one case, the beginning of a scroll was not indicated by any external system.

• 4QBarkhi Nafshi[a] (4Q434). That frg. 1 contains the beginning of this composition can be shown by the parallel 4Q435 which also contains the beginning of the work. In 4Q434, the first column is preceded by a small initial margin of 1.3 cm and an unstitched edge, not preceded by a handle sheet. The fact that this scroll contains the only such specimen casts some doubts on the interpretation of frg. 1 presented here.

SYSTEMS USED AT THE ENDS OF SCROLLS

The final column was usually ruled beyond the last inscribed line as far as the end of the column, e.g. 1QpHab, 1QIsa[a], 4QText with a Citation of Jubilees (4Q228), 4QCal Doc/Mish B (4Q321), 11QtgJob, 11QPs[a]. Beyond the last inscribed column, the end of the scroll was indicated by one of the following systems:

(1) *Uninscribed area*

The final column was often followed by an uninscribed area (with no handle sheet attached), which was either unruled or ruled, often as much as the width of a complete column: 1QpHab; 4QMMT[f] (4Q399 [probably]); 11QpaleoLev[a]; 11QPs[a]; 11QtgJob. Often the unstitched vertical edge of the scroll has been preserved, but in other cases such evidence is lacking; in those cases the uninscribed area is indicated in TABLE 25 as, e.g. 'uninscribed area of 5.8+ cm.' In such cases, a handle sheet could have been attached, but no scrolls with a large uninscribed area at the end have been preserved together with an *attached* handle sheet. The fact that a scribe left such a large ruled area uninscribed indicates that the precise surface needed for writing could not be calculated when the scroll was prepared. For details, see TABLE 25.

For parallels to an unruled blank area at the end of a composition in a Greek papyrus, see P.Oxy. 31.2536 (*Hypomnema* of Theon on Pindar, *Pythians* [8.5 cm]) and Turner, *Greek Manuscripts*, document 61; P.Oxy. 5.843 (Plato, *Symposium*); in the latter case the name of the composition is written in the uninscribed area (7.0 cm). The existence of a marginal area (גליון) at the end of a Scripture scroll was mentioned in *m. Yad.* 3.4 (according to the majority view, this area had the same degree of sanctity as the inscribed surface, while according to R. Yehudah it did not, unless it be attached to a wooden bar) and *b. Shabb.* 116a. Uninscribed areas at both ends of the scroll for the convenience of rolling the scroll around an

עמוד ('roller') or עמודים are mentioned in *b. B. Bat.* 13b–14a. Cf. further the instruction of *Sof.* 2.7–8 (cf. 1.12) which refers to either an uninscribed area or a handle sheet:

> If one finished <writing nearly> all the book and one column of text remained, one need not hesitate to make a small sheet of it. [8]At the conclusion of the <last> column <sufficient parchment> must be left to wind <round the scroll>.

TABLE 25: *Uninscribed Area at the End of Scrolls*

Name	Uninscribed Area (cm)	Ruled	Unstitched
1QpHab	8.5+	x (= yes)	—
4QDeut[q]	4.5	—	x (= yes)
4QJudg[b]	4.0 (partly reconstructed)	—	x
4QpsDan[c] ar (4Q245)	5.8+	x	—
4QD[a] (4Q266)	9.0	—	x
4QD[e] (4Q270) 7	7.6	x	x?
4QMish H (4Q329a), see n. 151	1.0	—	x
4QOrdo (4Q334) 7 (probable end)	2.2+	—	x[153]
4QMMT[f] (4Q399)	5.2+ [154]	x	—
4QHod.-like Text C (4Q440) 3	[155]	x	—
4QShir[b] (4Q511) 63	4.1	x	x?
11QtgJob	10.0	x	x
11QPs[a]	13.0	x	x
MasPs[b]	2.0	x	x

(2) *Final handle sheet*

A separate (ruled or unruled) uninscribed handle sheet (protective sheet, ἐσχατοκόλλιον) was often stitched after the last inscribed sheet, especially in the sectarian texts from cave 11 (note that cave 4 preserved twenty times more texts than cave 11). In several instances, the handle sheet is still attached (see below).

• 1QS: final margin of 0.0–1.0 cm (unruled) followed by a handle sheet, of which minute parts have been preserved. See n. 149.

• 1QSa: minute final margin (unruled) followed by a handle sheet, of which an area of 0.7 cm has been preserved. See n. 149.

• 4QD[d] (4Q269) 16: minute final margin (unruled) followed by stitch holes (probably); see H. Stegemann, *DJD* XXXVI, 201.

• 11QpaleoLev[a]: final margin of 1.5 cm (unruled) followed by a handle sheet as indicated by the stitch holes. The large uninscribed area of 15.0 cm, vertically and horizontally ruled, following the last inscribed column, preserves the bottom part of the last column of which the major part, not preserved, was inscribed (Lev 27:20-34).

• 11QapocrPs (11Q11): a final handle sheet of 7.0 cm (unruled) together with a wooden bar are still attached at the end of the scroll. This is the only case of the presence of such wooden bars known from later periods for sacred scrolls (see below).

• 11QShirShabb (11Q17): the remnants of a ruled final section (11.0+ cm) are presented in *DJD* XXIII, pl. XXXIII. Although there is no evidence that these four fragments present remnants of a separate

---

[153]Thus U. Glessmer, *DJD* XXI, 175.

[154]The area has the size of a ruled column, for which the right vertical line and the beginnings of horizontal lines have been preserved.

[155]Since the width of col. ii is unknown, it is unclear how much of the ruled final margin has been preserved. The extent of the ruled surface beyond the inscribed area on photograph PAM 44.101 may be misleading, as it also covers the uninscribed part of frg. 3 ii.

handle sheet, rather than an uninscribed area continuing the last inscribed column as in 11QPs[a], the width of the preserved fragments suggests that this may have been a separate handle sheet.

  • 11QT[a] (11Q19): this scroll presents a beautiful example of a handle sheet of 19.6 cm (ruled), still attached. See Yadin, *Temple Scroll (Hebrew)* 3, pl. 82.

  • MasDeut: final handle sheet of 9.0 cm, still attached, with an unstitched left edge (unruled).

The high frequency of texts from cave 11 in this group is striking (similar data are recorded in TABLE 22 relating to scrolls whose endings have been preserved). With the exception of 11QpaleoLev[a], all the Qumran texts preserving a final handle-sheet are sectarian and were copied according to the Qumran scribal practice. The preservation of a large number of scroll ends reveals favorable storage conditions in cave 11, while the preponderance of handle sheets among the cave 11 scrolls reflects a specific type of preparation of the scrolls, in this case sectarian scrolls. The existence of such separate uninscribed end-sheets is paralleled by sheets at the beginning of scrolls, although only in the case of 1QS and 1QSa has actual evidence for such handle sheets been preserved at both ends. All the examples of final handle sheets pertain to leather scrolls, and not to papyri.

(3) *Uninscribed area and final handle sheet?*

In one instance, the two systems were combined, a final uninscribed area followed by a handle sheet:

  • 1QH[b] (1Q35) 2: uninscribed area of 3.0+ cm followed by a handle sheet as indicated by a small fragment attached to the left of this area (J. T. Milik, *DJD* I, 137). The evidence is unclear.

(4) *No indication*

Probably only very few manuscripts had no external system for indicating the end of the scroll. One such case is 1QIsa[a] in which the unstitched vertical edge following the last column is inscribed almost to the end of the sheet rendering it necessary for users of this scroll to hold it by the inscribed areas. This resulted in the ends of lines 1–10 of the last column having to be re-inked (ch. *4i*).

Summarizing the data for biblical scrolls, evidence for initial handle sheets has been preserved for two copies of the Torah (4QGen[g], 4QGen[k]) and one of Isaiah (1QIsa[a]), and there is indirect evidence for a final handle sheet for 11QpaleoLev[a] and MasDeut. This evidence is in agreement with *Sof.* 1.8 according to which such handle sheets should be attached to both sides of the Torah scrolls and only at the beginning of the scrolls of the Prophets (note that 1QIsa[a] did not have such a handle sheet at its end). In twelve other biblical scrolls evidence for handle sheets is either negative or absent.

It is unclear why in a few cases the beginnings and ends were not indicated in a special way, while in other instances two different procedures were followed. These different procedures probably reflected the preferences of manufacturers and/or 'librarians,' and were probably unrelated to the contents of scrolls (see the last columns in TABLES 23 and 25). Various systems were used in manuscripts of the same work due to the fact that scrolls were manufactured by different persons at different times. Thus 4QBarkhi Nafshi[b] (4Q435) was preceded by a handle sheet, while 4QBarkhi Nafshi[a] (4Q434) was not. In the case of the latter scroll, there was almost no uninscribed area for handling when reading the scroll.

The only evidence for the existence of *wooden bars, rollers* (עמודים, *ʿamudim*) for handling the scrolls pertains to 11QapocrPs (11Q11, ascribed to 50–70 CE), described as follows by García Martínez–Tigchelaar–van der Woude: 'The handle with which the scroll was rolled has been preserved. It has the appearance of a stick and is now somewhat curved . . . the stick has been attached to it with pieces of string on the upper and lower part' (*DJD* XXIII, p. 183 and pl. XXII). This scroll was rolled around a single bar, while the main evidence for the use of single and double wooden bars for synagogue scrolls derives from a later period. See, *inter alia m. Yad.* 3.4; *b. B. Bat.* 14a; *y. Meg.* 1.71d; *Sof.* 2.5, all referring to a single bar attached to the end of a regular scroll and two bars for the Torah scrolls, each attached to one of the extremities (*y. Meg.* 1.71d). Such bars (wooden or bone sticks) are also known from the classical world, where they were named ὀμφαλοί or *umbilici*. According to M. Haran, "Torah and Bible Scrolls," 101 (see n. 127), these bars were invented in the Roman world. In the synagogue, ʿamudim became integral components of sacred scrolls.

h. *Titles of compositions and headers of sections*

Since the beginnings and ends of most scrolls were lost, only partial data is available on the existence of titles or name tags denoting the content of compositions. Full or partial data for the beginnings of fifty-three compositions from the Judean Desert (fifty-one from Qumran) are available, thus presenting us with a good impression of the recording of titles in these scrolls. The evidence for titles pertains only to nonbiblical scrolls, with one doubtful case of a biblical scroll (4QGen[h-title] [4Q8c]).

There seems to be sufficient evidence for establishing two different titling practices which also *may* have been used concurrently since they served two different purposes: (1) the first words in the running text, identifying the scroll for the user; and (2) on the outside, for users and 'librarians' when the scroll was stored. 1QS preserves evidence for both systems; this pertains also to 4QpapS[c] (4Q257), which could have had a title in addition to the inscription on the verso.[156]

A further system, the use of name tags glued to the outside of scrolls, is not evidenced for the Qumran collection. In the classical world, titles often were written on small labels attached to the rolled scroll (σίλλυβοι). They were easily visible when the scroll was stored; cf. Hall, *Companion*, 14; Kenyon, *Books and Readers*, 62; Turner, *Greek Manuscripts*, 13, 34 and documents 6–8; R. P. Oliver, "The First Medicean MS of Tacitus and the Titulature of Ancient Books," *TAPA* 82 (1951) 232–61; T. Dorandi, "Sillyboi," *Scrittura e civiltà* 7 (1983) 185–99. These titles were written in a different hand from that of the main text of the scroll, probably by 'librarians' or owners. The fact that such name tags are lacking in the Qumran collection implies not only a different convention for indicating names; it also shows that a different storage method was employed for scrolls found in the Qumran caves (mainly: cave 4) than that used for scrolls with name tags. The data do not suffice for persuasive conclusions, but the little evidence available (ch. *3d*) shows that the scrolls found at Qumran were probably stored on shelves in such a way that the full *length* of the scroll was visible, as evidenced also for five texts from Hellenistic and Roman Egypt. This convention may have a bearing on the storage conditions in cave 4 and/or at an earlier stage in the community buildings. The system used in the classical world of labeling scrolls with name tags suggests they were stored either in a *capsa* (container, box) or on shelves in such a way that the *ends* were visible.

A further system for indicating names, that of writing the title at the end of the composition, evidenced in Greek papyri and codices (Turner, *Greek Manuscripts*, 13 and documents 17, 18, 61; Oliver, "The First Medicean MS," [cited in the previous paragraph] 243), is not evidenced for the Judean Desert texts. In Greek sources, such titles were initially placed mainly at the end, and only later were they also written at the beginnings of compositions.

---

[156]Another system for indicating the name of a composition was cautiously suggested by Ulrich–Murphy in their edition of 4QRuth[a] (*DJD* XVI), where dark spots in the top margin above the *bet* of באיך were explained as possibly reflecting the title of the book ספר רוּֿﬣ which would have appeared above the first column of the scroll. Since this would be the only occurrence of this system, it is unlikely that this interpretation is correct.

(1) *The first words in the running text*

In nonbiblical scrolls, the title of a composition was usually included among the first words of the running text, without any special layout, as also occurs in most biblical Psalms (ch. *5b*) and previously in Ugaritic texts, e.g. KTU.1.161 (RS 34.126) צלם ספר דבח. Fifteen such titles have been preserved, a rather large percentage for the twenty nonbiblical texts of which the first words are extant. Accordingly, as far as the preserved evidence may be trusted, the first words of most nonbiblical texts denoted the contents of the composition as a whole, and only in five of the twenty texts was such a title lacking, while in eleven texts the first words have not been preserved.

Usually the title defined the literary genre:[157]

serekh: 1QM, 1QS,[158] 1QSa, 4QpapSª (4Q255)
benediction: 1QSb
prayer: 4QPrayer of Nabonidus ar (4Q242), also indicating attribution
authorship/attribution: 4QcryptA Words of the Maskil (4Q298), 4QWords of Michael ar (4Q529),
  4QVisions of Amramª ar (4Q543), 4QVisions of Amramᶜ ar (4Q545)[159]
midrash: 4QSᵈ (4Q258), 4Qpap cryptA Midrash Sefer Moshe (4Q249), possibly 4QDª (4Q266)
'psalm': 4QApocryphal Psalm and Prayer (4Q448)
repeated opening phrase for individual units: 4QShirShabbᵇ (4Q401), 4QBarkhi Nafshiª (4Q434),
  probably 1–4QH (not preserved).

TABLE 26: *Titles*

Names of Compositions

1QM	למ[שכיל סרך] המלחמה - For the In[structor the Rule] of the war
1QS, toward the end of the first line	ספר סר]ך היחד [?] – [The book ? of the Ru]le of the community
1QSa	וזה הסרך לכול עדת ישראל – This is the Rule for all the congregation of Israel
1QSb	דברי ברכ[ה] למשכיל – Words of blessi[ng] for the Instructor
4QPrayer of Nabonidus ar (4Q242)	מלי צ[ל]תא די צלי נבני – The words of the pr[ay]er uttered by Nabunai
4QpapSª (4Q255), end of first line	ספר סרכ היחד – The book of the Rule of the community
4QSᵈ (4Q258)	מדרש למשכיל על אנשי התורה המתנדבים (= 4QSᵇ [4Q256] 5 1) – Teaching for the Instructor concerning the men of the Torah who have freely pledged themselves
4QDª (4Q266)	פרוש המשפטים למשכיל לב]נ[י אור thus J. Baumgarten, *DJD* XVIII, 31 or:
	מדרש התורה האחרון לב]נ[י אור thus H. Stegemann, *DJD* XXXVI, 218–9; cf. 4QDᵉ (4Q270) 7 ii 15
4QcryptA Words of the Maskil (4Q298)	דבר]יᵐ משכיל אשר דבר לכול בני שחר], in the square script.[160] [The word]s of the Instructor to all sons of dawn
4QApocryphal Psalm and Prayer (4Q448)	הללויה מזמ[ור] שי[ר] (extrapolated in the margin) – Praise the Lord, a Psal[m], a song of
4QWords of Michael ar (4Q529)	מלי כתבא די אמר מיכאל Words of the book authored by Michael
4QVisions of Amramª ar (4Q543)	פרשגן כתב מלי חזות עמרם - Copy of the book of the words of the vision of Amram
4QVisions of Amramᶜ ar (4Q545)	פרשג]ן כתב מלי חזו[ו]ת עמרם – Cop[y of the book of the words of the visi]on of Amram

Opening Phrase for Individual Units

4QShirShabbᵇ (4Q401)	למשכיל – For the Instructor

---

[157] Cf. the biblical משלי שלמה and שיר השירים.
[158] If a new composition starts with 1QS V 1, that composition, too, begins with the term *serekh*.
[159] If 1QS V 13–IV 26 contains a separate composition (thus, for example, A. Lange, *DJD* XXXIX, 132), that composition contains a title (למשכיל).
[160] The scroll itself was written in the Cryptic A script. Also the title of 4Qpap cryptA Midrash Sefer Moshe (4Q249) 1 verso was written in the square script, while the composition itself was written in the Cryptic A script. See below.

4QBarkhi Nafshi[a] (4Q434)   ברכי נפשי את אדני – Bless, my soul, the Lord

Parts of Books[161]

1QapGen ar V 29 after an empty line   כתב מלי נֹחֹ[162] – Book of the words of Noah
4QEn[c] ar (4Q204) VI 9 after an indentation   ספר מלי קושט]א (= 1 En 14:1) - Book of the words of trut[h]

Likewise, the title of a small collection starting with Jer 23:9 is now part of the running text: '*Concerning the prophets*. My heart is crushed within me . . . '

See further the evidence below and in ch. *5b* relating to the special layout of headers in poetical units, mainly Psalms.

(2) *Inscription on the verso or recto of the rolled scroll* (illustr. 11a)

In five instances, the title was written on the back of the first inscribed sheet (4Qpap cryptA Midrash Sefer Moshe [4Q249]; 4QDibHam[a] [4Q504]) or of the handle sheet (1QS, 4QGen[h-title] [4Q8c]) in order for it to be visible when the scroll was unrolled with its beginning as the outermost layer, or possibly when it was stored on shelves. In 4QpapS[c] (4Q257), the title was written on the back of the second sheet, a custom which is paralleled in Greek secular papyri (see below). Since the beginnings of fifty-one scrolls have been preserved, in full or in part, it can be said safely that this practice was not implemented often.

The practice described here is also known from five Greek literary papyrus scrolls from Egypt from 2 BCE to 2 CE as described by W. Luppe, "Rückenseitentitel auf Papyrusrollen," *ZPE* 27 (1977) 89–99 and Turner, *Greek Manuscripts*, 14. That only five such scrolls were known to Luppe and Turner shows that the system was used very infrequently in Egypt, since the corpus examined by these scholars is more extensive than that from Qumran. In two cases, the titles were inscribed perpendicular to the direction of writing of the scroll (P.Rylands 19 of Theopompus of 2 CE; P.Oxy. 23.2358 of Alkaios of 2 CE), while in three instances the title was written parallel to the direction of the writing of the scroll itself (P.Würzburg of Sosylos of 1–2 CE, P.Oxy. 2803 of Stesichoros of 1 BCE, P.Oxy. 35.2741 of a commentary on Eupolis, *Marikas*, of 2–3 CE); in all instances the titles were written on the back of the first or second column rather than that of the handle sheet.

While the writing of titles as the first words of the text was performed by scribes, the inscribing of the name on the back, in different handwriting, could also have been executed for the convenience of users in any environment in which more than one scroll was kept. These names could have been inscribed on the scrolls by owners or users, and also by persons administering a scroll collection ('librarians' in our terminology), either in a community building at Qumran or in their earlier locations before being brought to Qumran.

That the titles were sometimes added for the convenience of users is also evidenced by the fact that the title of 4Qpap cryptA Midrash Sefer Moshe (4Q249) was written on the back in the square script, while the scroll itself was written in the Cryptic A script.

• 1QS, verso of the handle sheet: סרך] היחד ומן, published separately as 1Q28 in *DJD* I, 107 and pl. XXII. The handle sheet was stitched to the following sheet, which can be identified as the first sheet of 1QS based on the matching stitch holes. The title was written perpendicular to the writing of the manuscript. In this title, ומן may have referred to other compositions, probably 1QSa and 1QSb, which may have been rolled together with 1QS, but not stitched together (see n. 149).

• 4QGen[h-title] (4Q8c) verso of the handle sheet: בראשית. This single fragment is now detached from the manuscript of Genesis to which it may have belonged. J. R. Davila, *DJD* XII, 63 suggests that the fragment (which is inscribed on what he names the 'recto' or hairy side) is a remnant of a handle sheet

---

[161]These titles are not included in the statistics.
[162]See R. C. Steiner, "The Heading of the *Book of the Words of Noah* on a Fragment of the Genesis Apocryphon: New Light on a 'Lost' Work," *DSD* 2 (1995) 66–71.

which was attached to the first inscribed sheet. The word appears in the middle of the piece of leather (6.4 x 3.3 cm) with space on all sides and no signs of additional writing. The exact orientation of the fragment vis-à-vis the first sheet (perpendicular or parallel) is unclear. Although this tag would be the only specimen bearing the name of a biblical book, there seems to be no alternative explanation of its nature. This would be the earliest reference to a biblical book indicated by its first word. The unusual spelling of the name of the book is not inconsistent with some spellings in 1QIsaᵃ (cf. Isa 36:16 חנתו [= תאנתו MT]; 65:25 זב [= זאב MT]) and other scrolls.

• 4Qpap cryptA Midrash Sefer Moshe (4Q249) 1 verso: מדרש ספר מֹשה in the square script. The title was written perpendicular to the writing of the manuscript (S. J. Pfann, *DJD* XXXV, 7 and pl. II).

• 4QDibHamᵃ (4Q504) 8 v (the recto probably contained the beginning of the composition): דברי המֿאֿוֹרֹת. See M. Baillet, *DJD* VII, 138 and pls. XLIX and LIII (illustr. 11a below). The title was written perpendicular to the writing of the scroll, towards the right edge of the first inscribed sheet. Since only part of the column has been preserved, there is no data regarding possible stitching.

A fifth item is less certain:

• 4QpapSᶜ (4Q257) frg. 1a verso: ‎°[　　　]°ס° לוֹס °° כיבֹו according to Alexander–Vermes, *DJD* XXVI, 69 and pl. VI (explained as a title or the name of the scroll owner [unparalleled in the texts from the Judean Desert], now undecipherable), or סרכ הֿיֹ|חד[ל°°°[according to S. J. Pfann, *DJD* XXXV, 1, n. 2, or ספר°°° לים in the *Preliminary Concordance*. The inscribed words are found 12.4 cm from the right edge of the papyrus written in the same direction as the text itself. It is questionable whether these letters reflect the title since they may not have been visible when the scroll was rolled up: (1) The inscribed words are written at least 15 cm from the right edge on the second sheet and would have been visible only if the scroll had an equally large circumference; (2) unlike the other four instances, the inscription is written parallel to the text. However, these problematical aspects are paralleled by procedures followed in Greek sources. In the previously mentioned Sosylus papyrus, the inscription is also remote from the beginning (16.2 cm), appearing on the first sheet but on the verso of the second column, written in the same direction as the writing of the scroll. Luppe, "Rückenseitentitel" (see above) makes a similar suggestion for the Stesichoros papyrus. As a result, the inscription on the back of 4QpapSᶜ (4Q257) may well have included the title.

The evidence shows that in five instances the title was written on the verso of either the handle sheet or the first or second sheet in such a way that the name would be visible when the scroll was stored on a shelf. The titles were inscribed perpendicular to the direction of the writing, a practice that probably reflected a form of storage on shelves which rendered the long side of the rolled scroll visible to the user. When the scrolls were stored, the user could easily review their contents, especially if they were stacked one above the other in such a way that their names were visible. The closer the inscription was to the edge of the scroll, the more clearly visible it would be. In 1QS and 4QDibHamᵃ (4Q504), the positioning of that inscription close to the edge of the first sheet (the bottom third when viewed from the verso) rendered the inscription clearly visible. The title in 4Qpap cryptA Midrash Sefer Moshe (4Q249) was a little higher, but would still have been visible. For 4QpapSᶜ (4Q257), a large scroll circumference must be assumed for the inscription to have been visible when rolled up.

It is noteworthy that all four texts for which these titles were secured have a sectarian content. The fifth title, that of Genesis, may have been attached to any Genesis scroll, preserved or not, among them one written according to the Qumran scribal practice, such as 4QGenᵏ. The fact that the specific spelling of the tag lacks the quiescent *aleph* may point to the Qumran community. The names may have been written on the back of the scrolls when they were stored in cave 4, but it is more likely that these names were attached when the scrolls were stored in one of the community buildings before being transferred to that cave.

Likewise, documentary texts sometimes contained an identifying inscription on their external layer, see Babatha's *ketubbah* (cf. n. 49) and Porten–Yardeni, *TAD*, B2.1–11 (the Mibtahiah archive from 471–460 BCE); B3.1–13 (the Anani archive from 456–402 BCE).

For headers of sections, see ch. *5b*.

i. *Uneven surface, damage, repair stitching, and patching*

Uneven surface (illustr. 15). At their time of preparation, some scrolls were of high quality, while the surface of others was sometimes uneven, often showing scar tissue.

In both biblical and nonbiblical scrolls, patches of poor tanning, scar tissue, and stitching forced the scribes to leave these areas uninscribed. Beyond the examples mentioned by Kuhl, "Schreibereigentümlichkeiten," 313, see the following instances:

- 1QIsaᵃ XIX 1: The fold required the scribe to write the first letter of אמלל below the line.
- 1QM: Several segments were left uninscribed.[163]
- 1QS after VII 7: Three lines were left uninscribed, probably due to a defect in the leather (Metso, *Community Rule*, 15).
- 4QGenᵍ: The scribe left an interval of eight letter-spaces between the first and second word of Gen 1:5 due to uneven surface.
- 4QDeutⁿ: The scribe avoided writing on many lines (III 9 and IV 1–4, 7–8; probably also I 5). The intervals in col. IV 1, 7–8 could have been part of the intended format, but those in III 9 and IV 2–4 were left for some other reason. The surface of the leather is poor in all these lines (illustr. 15).
- 4QMiscellaneous Rules (4Q265) 6 4, 5: The curious arrangement is probably due to an uneven surface:

ביום *vac* השבת *vac* אל יו[צא אי]ש מאהלו כלי ומאכל

ביום *vac* השבת *vac* אל יעל איש בהמה אשר תפול

- 4QDᵃ (4Q266) 2 ii 9–12: Bad surface necessitated that the scribe not inscribe parts of these lines. Among other things, stitches appear in the leather in the middle of the text, evidently inserted prior to the writing since the scribe left spaces in the text.
- 4QRPᵇ (4Q364) 9a–b 5–7: These lines are indented since the first part of the column could not be inscribed.
- 4QRPᵉ (4Q367) 3 5–14: A large portion of the middle section of these lines was left uninscribed due to surface problems.
- 4QInstrᵇ (4Q416) 2 ii 19–21: A major segment at the beginnings of these lines was left uninscribed, probably due to a defect in the leather.
- 4QInstrᵇ (4Q416) 2 iii 5 ושם חה: A space was left in the middle of a word due to the poor surface.
- 11QpaleoLevᵃ: The scribe avoided writing in frg. H 6 and col. 3 6.
- 11QPsᵃ: Several segments were left uninscribed: J. A. Sanders, *DJD* IV, 14.

Damage. It has been suggested that damage was inflicted on certain scrolls in antiquity, mainly by Roman soldiers' swords,[164] even though there is no solid evidence for this assumption either in the historical descriptions or in the accounts of the scrolls themselves. Furthermore, it remains difficult to understand the realia of this situation: if these fragments were torn by subsequent occupants of the site after the Qumran community, this would imply that they had access to the hidden treasures of one or more caves and chose not to burn the contents, but rather damage only a few scrolls. Realizing these difficulties, this assumption was nevertheless suggested cautiously by H. Cotton and E. Larson, "4Q460/4Q350" (see n. 124), and "Tampering with Qumran Texts in Antiquity," in Paul, *Emanuel*, 113–25, especially 123–5.

- 4QGen-Exodᵃ 19 i: This fragment 'has suffered an ancient tear (or sword cut?)' (J. R. Davila, *DJD* XII, 7).
- 4QPsᶠ: 'The scroll seems to have been slashed horizontally by a knife, sword, or other sharp instrument, probably by Roman soldiers who were ravaging the Qumran site in 68 CE' (Flint, *Psalms Scrolls*, 35).
- 4QRPᶜ (4Q365) 12b iii and 23: Note the diagonal creases.

---

[163]Y. Yadin, *The Scroll of the War of the Sons of Light against the Sons of Darkness* (Oxford 1962) 249–51 and fig. 18, group A, frg. 19.

[164]H. del Medico, "L'état des manuscrits de Qumran, I," *VT* 7 (1957) 127–38; de Vaux, *Archaeology* (see n. 32) 100, n. 3; idem, *DJD* VI (1977) 21; J. Allegro, *The Dead Sea Scrolls: A Reappraisal* (Harmondsworth 1964) 56.

• 4QLiturgical Work B (4Q476): According to T. Elgvin, *DJD* XXIX, 437, all three fragments of this composition were torn by a human hand.

• 11QT[a]: According to H. Stegemann: 'Yadin's Temple Scroll was in part already damaged by its former readers in antiquity, mainly at its beginning and end, but also in the bottom parts of some other columns. Repairs dating to the first half of the first century CE are clearly visible [reference is made to the stitching of damaged surface]. The first and last sheet of the scroll with about four columns each were cut off and replaced by new sheets.'[165]

• XḤev/SeDeed of Sale A ar (XḤev/Se 7): This document is described by A. Yardeni, *DJD* XXVII, 19 as having been cut with a knife.

• MasShirShabb: 'The left-hand edge of the fragment seems to have been deliberately cut or torn away.' (C. Newsom and Y. Yadin, *Masada VI*, 120). On the basis of earlier notes by Yadin, Talmon, *Masada VI*, 36 makes a similar suggestion regarding MasLev[a].

Any damage caused to scrolls by frequent handling necessitated discontinuation of their use for cult service and their storage in a special area (גניזה, *genizah*). According to *y. Meg.* 1.71c, damaged letters are not permitted in scrolls of Scripture. There is no evidence for such *genizot* at Qumran, even though during the first generation of scroll research the Qumran caves were often described as such storage places for discarded scrolls. In a similar vein, in modern Hebrew the Qumran scrolls often continue to be named המגילות הגנוזות. At Masada, there is, however, ample evidence for this custom, since a scroll of Deuteronomy and a scroll of Ezekiel were buried under the synagogue floor, in two separate *genizot*. It is not impossible that the final sheet or sheets of MasDeut had become damaged due to excessive use, and hence was/were placed in storage without the remainder of the book. See APPENDIX 6 ('The Hebrew texts from Masada').

Repair stitching (illustrations 8a, 15). When a scroll was torn before or after being inscribed, it was often stitched. Stitching applied prior to the inscribing of a scroll made it necessary for the scribe to leave blank segments in the middle of the text, which were frequently as extensive as two complete lines. Stitching that was executed after the writing necessarily rendered some words illegible (e.g. 4QJer[c] col. XXIII). Accordingly, when stitching appears in the middle of an inscribed area it can usually be determined whether it was executed before or after the writing. When the stitching appears in the uninscribed margins, as in most instances, it cannot be determined when the scroll was stitched.

• 4QGen[g]: Stitches in the middle of the text before Gen 1:20 prior to the writing.

• 4QLev[c] 5: Stitches in the bottom margins with the preservation of segments of thread.

• 1QIsa[a]: Several tears were stitched both before (e.g. col. XVII 4 from bottom) and after the leather was inscribed (e.g. cols. XVI and XII, in the latter case with stitches over the full column height).

• 4QJer[c]: Tears were stitched both before the writing (cols. IV, XXI [illustr. 20], and XXIII) and afterwards (e.g. col. XXIII). In col. XXI, the scribe had to leave spaces in lines 4 and 5 in the middle of the sentence. It is difficult to ascertain when the stitches in col. XVI were inserted.

• 4QPs[k]: The two fragments of this manuscript were stitched together in antiquity by way of repair.

• 4QCant[b] 1: Stitches in the bottom margins with the preservation of parts of thread (illustr. 8a).

• 4QD[a] (4Q266) 2 ii: Bad surface necessitated the scribe to leave parts of lines 9–12 uninscribed. An area in the middle of the text was stitched prior to the writing.

• 4QInstruction-like Composition B (4Q424) 1 7–10: Bad surface required the scribe to leave sections of 1–3 spaces uninscribed on the right side of the column, in one instance in the middle of a word: משפט ך (line 10).

• PAM 43.662 (*DJD* XXXIII, pl. III), frg. 94: The nature of the stitching on the bottom and left side of the fragment is unclear.

---

[165]H. Stegemann, "The Literary Composition of the Temple Scroll and its Status at Qumran," in *Temple Scroll Studies* (ed. G. J. Brooke; JSPSup 7; Sheffield 1989) 123–48; the quote is from p. 124.

According to *b. Menaḥ.* 31b, stitching of an already inscribed scroll was permitted only when the damage was of a limited size:

אמר רב זעירא אמר רב חננאל אמר רב קרע הבא בשני שיטין יתפור. בשלש אל יתפור

R. Zeira said in the name of R. Hananel who said it in the name of Rab. If a tear <in a scroll of the Law> extended into two lines it may be sewn together; but if into three lines it may not be sewn together.[166]

See also *Sof.* 2.17 (majority opinion; for the view of R. Simeon, see below):

אין דובקין בדבק ולא כותבין על גבי המטלית ולא תופרין במקום הכתב

<A tear in a leather sheet of a Torah scroll> may not be joined with glue, nor is it permitted to write on a patch, nor may <the sheets> be sewn together on the written side.

Since the rabbinic texts refer to the Torah scroll as an existing unit, and not to the sheets prior to being joined, stitching that occurred before the writing may have been permitted, while there were limitations placed on stitching occurring after the writing.

Patching (illustr. 14). Wear and tear in both inscribed and uninscribed areas of scrolls in antiquity was sometimes mended with a patch stitched onto the scroll. Most of these patches were not inscribed (e.g. the back of 11QTᵃ [11Q19] XXIII–XXIV [Yadin, *Temple Scroll*, pl. 12*] and the front of col. XXVII), while there is very limited evidence for inscribed patches.

• The only known inscribed patch from Qumran was once attached to col. VIII of 4QpaleoExodᵐ (see *DJD* IX, 84–5 and pl. XI as well as illustr. 14 below). This patch displays a script and orthography different from those of the remainder of the scroll (אהרן is spelled defectively on the patch, but *plene* in the main text of the scroll; furthermore, in the patch the paleo-Hebrew *waw* was followed by text written after the space, while in the other instances the space continues until the end of the line, see ch. 5c1). The patch was sewn on from the back of the manuscript, as is clear from the partially written words on the patch written within the stitching and blank rims of the patch (illustr. 14). These partially written words were continued in the main text of the manuscript that has not been preserved. The patch shares its line-length with the main manuscript, and also the distinctive use of the *waw* in closed sections (fig. 5.1) when the following word would have started with a conversive *waw*. The results of AMS analysis (Jull and others, "Radiocarbon Dating") *may* confirm a slightly later date for the patch (between 98 BCE and 13 CE) than for the scroll itself (between 159 BCE and 16 CE).

• There may be indirect evidence for another patch. On 5/6ḤevPs 9, P. W. Flint notes in *DJD* XXXVIII, 141 (pl. XXVII): 'On frg. 9 there is a circular impression with several holes around its perimeter, which is clearly visible on the museum plate. It is difficult to account for this impression, which may be due to a patch or a hard object that was once placed on the leather.'

The writing on attached patches was not acceptable according to the majority view expressed in *Sof.* 2.17:

. . . ולא כותבין על גבי המטלית

. . . nor is it permitted to write on a patch

but the patching and writing were acceptable according to R. Simeon ben Eleazar (ibid.) and *y. Meg.* 1.71d:

אמר ר' שמעון בן אלעזר משום ר' מאיר שדובקין בדבק וכותבין על גבי המטלית אבל אין תופרין במקום הכתב מבפנים
ותופרין הכתב מבחוץ

R. Simeon b. Eleazar said in the name of R. Meir: <A torn sheet> may be joined with glue and it is permitted to write on the patch. It is forbidden, however, to do the sewing on the written side, but it must be done on the outside.

---

[166]In the continuation, the Talmud mentions certain circumstances regarding the preserved texts: 'Rabbah the younger said to R. Ashi: Thus said R. Jeremiah of Difti in the name of Raba: The rule that we have laid down, namely, that if it extended into three lines it may be sewn together, applies only to old scrolls; but in the case of new scrolls it would not matter. <that is, it may always be sewn together.> Moreover 'old' does not mean actually old, nor 'new' actually new, but the one means prepared with gall-nut juice and the other means not so prepared.'

It is therefore relevant to note that the one text in which an inscribed patch has been identified does not belong to the MT family, viz. 4QpaleoExod[m] (pre-Samaritan). Similar inscribed patches are known from the scribal tradition of SP (Anderson, *Studies*, 24).

Replacement of a sheet. The evidence is unclear as to whether complete sheets were replaced when damaged beyond repair, but the first sheets of three different scrolls have been explained in this way. This assumption is invoked by J. Strugnell for the first sheet of 4QDeut[n] (illustr. 15) which, according to him, was a replacement sheet erroneously sewn to the right of what now constitutes the second sheet.[167] Likewise, in their edition of 4QJub[a] (4Q216), VanderKam–Milik suggested that the first sheet of that scroll, written by a different scribe than that of the following sheet, was worn and replaced with a new one. See ch. *2e* above. Yadin, *Temple Scroll*, I.11–12 suggested that sheet 1 (cols. I–V) of 11QT[a] (11Q19) was a repair sheet replacing the original sheet. It was written by a different scribe (A) than the one who wrote the remainder of the scroll (cols. VI–LXVII written by scribe B). The end of sheet 1 written by scribe A partly overlapped with col. VI indicating that scribe A either copied the text from a different original or duplicated a section so as not to leave an uninscribed area. No samples have been found of sheets presenting new material which have been added to scrolls.

Repair. Inscribed (4QUnclassified fragments [4Q51a]) and uninscribed papyrus strips were attached in antiquity to the back of the leather of 4QSam[a] for support. Likewise, J. C. Trever, "Preliminary Observations on the Jerusalem Scrolls," *BASOR* 111 (1948) 3–16 (especially 5), who was the first to study several scrolls in 1948, writes on 1QS: 'A fairly large piece of this white leather (or parchment?) was glued to the back of columns 16 and 17, and another along the top back edge of column 19. The bottom edge had a similar treatment in several places where needed (cols. 3, 4, 7, and 12, where dark brown leather was used; and cols. 47 and 48, where a very light leather was used).' The same scholar noted in Burrows, *The Dead Sea Scrolls*, xiv that 'a thin strip of somewhat darker leather about 1 1/2 inches wide [was] placed along the top back edge' of the first four and a half columns 'to keep it from breaking away.' He notes that similar strips were attached to several places in this scroll.

Re-inking. It is unclear how many words in the Judean Desert texts were re-inked in antiquity when the ink had become faint. Some examples are listed by Martin, *Scribal Character*, II.424, but it is difficult to evaluate their validity. The final column of 1QIsa[a] was probably damaged in antiquity, possibly since it did not have a handle sheet or an uninscribed section for handling; as a result, the ends of lines 1–4, 6, 7, 9, 10 were re-inked.

Similarly, *b. Meg.* 18b mentions broken letters (מקורעות . . . אותיות) and letters which have become faint (מטושטשות).

j. De luxe *editions* (illustr. 5a)

Large *de luxe* editions, in scrolls from 50 BCE onwards, including a number of scrolls from the first century CE, seem to have been used especially for Scripture scrolls, mainly reflecting the proto-rabbinic text (§ γ below). The assumption of such *de luxe* editions among the Judean Desert texts is based on the following data:

---

[167]See p. 38 above. This view was quoted and discussed by S. A. White (Crawford), "4QDt[n]: Biblical Manuscript or Excerpted Text?" in *Of Scribes and Scrolls, Studies on the Hebrew Bible, Intertestamental Judaism, and Christian Origins Presented to John Strugnell* (ed. H. W. Attridge et al.; College Theology Society Resources in Religion 5; Lanham, Md. 1990) 193–206.

a. A large *de luxe* format was used especially for biblical scrolls (TABLE 27), and also for a few nonbiblical texts. Some manuscripts are of better quality than others with regard to their replication (precision in copying) and external shape (regularity of the ruling, quality of leather, aesthetics of layout, and adherence to a neat column structure), e.g. 1QM, 1QIsa[b], 11QPs[a], 11QT[a] (11Q19), 11QT[b] (11Q20), MasEzek, MasPs[a] (illustr. 5a). However, it appears that the use of large top, and bottom margins is the major criterion for establishing that a scroll was prepared as a *de luxe* edition (as in similar Alexandrian Greek scrolls, see below), together with a large writing block, fine calligraphy, the proto-rabbinic text form of Scripture, and only a limited amount of scribal intervention. MasPs[a] probably serves as the best sample of such a choice text.

TABLE 27 presents *all* the Judean Desert texts with large-sized top and bottom margins (more than 3.0 cm). The purpose of the table is to establish that these parameters were used especially for *de luxe* editions of biblical texts. Other data are also recorded for these texts (number of lines, height, date, textual character for the biblical texts, and the number of lines between corrections in the text). In this table, 'r' signifies 'reconstructed.' In other cases ('—'), the relevant evidence is lacking. Since top and bottom margins usually measure 1.0–2.0 cm in the texts from the Judean Desert, margins such as MurNum (7.5 cm), 2QNum[a] (5.7+ cm), 4QDeut[g] (5.7+ cm), XHev/SeNum[b] (7.2–7.5 cm) are quite unusual. The dates listed below are quoted from Webster, "Chronological Index."

TABLE 27: *Hebrew/Aramaic de Luxe Editions among the Texts from the Judean Desert (Main Criterion: Large Top/Bottom Margins)*

a. BIBLICAL TEXTS

Name	Top Margin (cm)	Bottom Margin (cm)	No. of Lines	Height (cm)	Date of MS	Textual Character	No. of Lines between Corrections
2QNum[a]	—	5.7+	—	—	30–68 CE	—	17+
4QGen[b]	3.2	—	40 r	35 r	30–100 CE	MT	62
4QExod[c]	4.0–4.4	3.1	*c.* 43 r	38 r	50–25 BCE	MT	17
4QpaleoGen-Exod[l]	—	4.0	55–60 r	38 r	100–25 BCE	MT	105
4QpaleoExod[m]	3.0–3.5	4.3–4.5	32, 33	35+	100–25 BCE	SP	197
4QDeut[g] 11	—	5.7+	—	—	1–25 CE	MT/SP	43
4QDeut[k1]	—	3.2+	—	—	30–1 BCE	Q-ortho; independent	12
4QJudg[b] 3	—	5.3	—	—	30–1 BCE	MT	8
4QSam[a]	2.2–2.6	2.9–3.1	42–44 r	30.1	50–25 BCE	ind./LXX	110
4QJer[c]	—	2.5–4.5	18	25.3–26.3	30–1 BCE	MT	25
4QEzek[a]	3.0+	—	42 r	29.5 r	50–25 BCE	independent	50
4QPs[c]	1.5+	3.2+	3 3	*c.* 26	1–50 CE	MT	52
MurGen 1	5.2	—	50 r	46.5 r	*c.* 115 CE	MT	23+
MurNum 6	—	7.5	50 r	46.5 r	*c.* 115 CE	MT	—
MurIsa	—	3.0+	—	—	20–84 CE	MT	—
MurXII	2.6–4.0	4.5–5.0	39	35.5	*c.* 115 CE	MT	75
XHev/SeNum[b]	—	7.2–7.5	44 r	39.5 r	50–68 CE	MT	28+
34ṢeNum	5.0	—	—	—	—	—	—
MasDeut	3.4	—	42	3 3	50–1 BCE	MT	17
MasEzek	3.0	—	42	29.5	50–1 BCE	MT	18
MasPs[a]	2.4	3.0	29	25.5	25–1 BCE	MT	74+
XJosh	—	4.0	27	*c.* 24	40–68 CE	MT	—

b. NONBIBLICAL TEXTS

Name	Top Margin (cm)	Bottom Margin (cm)	No. of Lines	Height (cm)	Date of MS		No. of Lines between Corrections
1QM	2.7–3.5	—	20 or 23–25 r	—	30–1 BCE		17
1QapGen ar	2.2–3.1	2.6–3.0	34	30.5–31	30 BCE–68 CE		17
4QCommGen C (4Q254) 16	—	3.8	—	—	25–1 BCE		40
4QcryptA Lunisolar Cal. (4Q317)	—	2.9–3.1	22	—	—		—
4QpapHistorical Text C (4Q331)	3.0	—	—	—	*c.* 50 BCE		—
4QpapRitPur B (4Q512)	3.0	—	—	—	*c.* 85 BCE		32
4QapocrLevi[b]? ar (4Q541)	1.1+	3.0	—	—	*c.* 100 BCE		35
11QT[a] (11Q19)	—	2.8–3.6	22–29 r	—	1–30 CE		16

The number of biblical texts among the scrolls with wide top and bottom margins is very large. Among this group of thirty texts, twenty-two (or 73.3%) are biblical, which implies that large-format inscription was used especially for the books of Hebrew Scripture. Since among the 930 Qumran texts, only 200 (or 21.5%) are biblical, the percentage of biblical scrolls among the large-format scrolls is striking.

Wide top and bottom margins are possibly connected to any large scroll, not only those containing biblical text, since such margins would be more appropriate aesthetically for any large writing surface. However, among the Qumran scrolls, there are more nonbiblical tall scrolls than the eight scrolls appearing in the table. It therefore remains correct to say that wide margins were used especially in biblical *de luxe* scrolls.

In most cases, the combined size of the top and bottom margins equals some twenty percent of the total height of the leather, while in the case of MurXII these margins amount to twenty-five percent. These proportions conform with the Herculaneum Greek papyri as described by G. Cavallo, *Libri scritture scribi a Ercolano* ([Naples]: Macchiaroli, 1983) 18, 48.

According to W. A. Johnson, *The Literary Papyrus Roll*, 230–33, the major criterion for recognizing *de luxe* editions among the Oxyrhynchus papyri is the margin size, such as in the case of the Thucydides papyri P.Oxy. 61.4103–4112 with margins of 4.0–8.0 cm (four texts from of 2 CE) as well as various Herculaneum papyri with margins of 5.0–6.0 cm (Cavallo, *Libri scritture*). See further the observations on Greek *de luxe* papyrus rolls by Turner, *Greek Manuscripts*, 7.

β. In the above examples of *de luxe* editions, large margins usually appear together with a large or very large writing block (as recorded in TABLE 15 above). On the other hand, in other tall scrolls of 30–50 lines (even 60 lines), no such large margins are found.

γ. The great majority of scrolls written in *de luxe* format reflect the medieval text of MT, in an exact form in the ten texts from sites other than Qumran, and slightly less so in the nine texts from Qumran, with two scrolls deviating a little more from MT. On the other hand, 4QpaleoExod[m] resembles the Sam. Pent., 4QDeut[k1] was written in the Qumran scribal practice, and 4QSam[a] and 4QEzek[a] are independent. Since the *de luxe* format was used mainly for the scrolls of the Masoretic family, we assume that many *de luxe* scrolls were produced in the spiritual center of Judaism (see below), the center which subsequently was to formulate the rules for writing which were transmitted in the Talmud and *Massekhet Soferim*.

Among the texts found in the Judean Desert, luxury editions are recognized especially among the biblical texts found at sites other than Qumran. It is not impossible that these scrolls are the 'corrected copies' mentioned in rabbinic literature, *inter alia* in *b. Pes.* 112a: 'When you teach your son, teach him from a corrected copy (ספר מוגה).' These precise scrolls were corrected according to a central text found in the temple court and then used anywhere in ancient Israel. In any event, it is remarkable that the large size of these margins conforms more or less with the instructions in rabbinic literature (§ e above). This fact is rather important for the argument that these scrolls belong to the inner circle of proto-rabbinic scrolls.[168]

δ. As a rule, *de luxe* scrolls are characterized by their low level of scribal intervention, as may be expected among predominantly carefully written manuscripts, since the fewer mistakes that are made, the fewer the corrections needed. However, scribal intervention pertains not only to the correction of mistakes, but also to the insertion of scribal changes in the text. We measure this scribal intervention by referring to the average number of lines between two instances of scribal intervention (supralinear corrections, deletions, erasures, reshaping of letters, linear and supralinear scribal signs), listed in the last column of the table. The lower the number, the higher the rate of scribal intervention. This number merely provides an indication of the extent of scribal intervention since partially surviving lines are counted as being complete (for the full data, see APPENDIX 1). Much scribal intervention is evidenced, for example, in a scroll such as 1QIsaᵃ that is far from being a *de luxe* edition (with an average of one correction in every four lines) and is therefore not included in TABLE 27. One correction per twenty or more lines should probably be considered a low degree of scribal correction, but most scrolls in the table have (far) fewer corrections: 4QGenᵇ, 4QpaleoGen-Exodˡ, 4QpaleoExodᵐ, XHev/SeNumᵇ, 4QDeutᵍ, 4QJerᶜ, 4QEzekᵃ, MurXII, MasPsᵃ. For a fuller analysis of scribal intervention in these and other texts, see ch. 7a. A relatively high level of scribal intervention is evidenced in 4QExodᶜ and 4QDeutᵏˡ. Other proto-Masoretic scrolls from Qumran which were not written in *de luxe* format sometimes also reflect little scribal intervention, while scrolls beyond the Masoretic family display more such activity.

The implication of this analysis is that we should posit a group of *de luxe* Bible editions, especially among the later scrolls, characterized by large top and bottom margins, a large number of lines, a high degree of proximity to or even identity with MT, and a low incidence of scribal intervention. In fact, *all* the scrolls from Naḥal Ḥever, Murabbaʿat, and Masada, for which the margins are known,[169] are of this type, while MasLevᵃ (2.8 cm), MasLevᵇ (2.7 cm), and 5/6HevPs (2.5–2.7 cm) come very close. At the same time, some *de luxe* editions are of a different textual nature, as is shown by 4QpaleoExodᵐ and 4QSamᵃ.

Other scrolls of large or very large vertical dimensions (tall scrolls of 28 lines or more) listed in TABLE 28 had no exceptionally wide margins, but usually they are larger

---

[168]The argument is developed in my study "The Text of the Hebrew/Aramaic and Greek Bible Used in the Ancient Synagogue," in *The Ancient Synagogue: From the Beginning to about 200 CE. Papers Presented at the International Conference Held at Lund University Oct. 14–17, 2001* (ed. B. Olsson and M. Zetterholm; ConBNT 39; Stockholm 2003) 239–62.

[169]All the biblical scrolls found at these sites attest to the medieval text of MT.

than average, and often approach 3.0 cm, which has been used as the cut-off measure for TABLE 27. For further details on these texts, see TABLE 15. Some of these texts may also have been intended as *de luxe* editions.

TABLE 28: *Hebrew/Aramaic Scrolls of Large Dimensions That May Have Been* de Luxe *Editions*

Name	No. of Lines	Height (cm)	Top/Bottom Margins (cm)
4QEn[b] ar (4Q202)	28, 29	30	—
4QInstr[d] (4Q418)	*c.* 29	—	—
1QSa	29	23.5	1.2–1.7 and 1.7+
4QPs[q]	29	23.6	top 2.0
MurIsa	29	19.5	bottom 2.7+
4QEn[c] ar (4Q204)	30	24	bottom 2.3
4QDeut[h]	*c.* 30	—	bottom 2.0
4QTest (4Q175)	30	23	1.4 and 1.7
4QJer[a]	30–32	28.6–30.2	2.2 and 2.8
4QNum[b]	30–32	30	1.9 and 2.6
11QPs[d]	32–34	—	top 1.8+
4QNarrative and Poetic Comp[b] (4Q372) 1	32+	18.0+	bottom 1.0
1QIsa[b]	35	23	top 1.7
4QIsa[a]	35	31	top 2.7
4QIsa[e]	35–40	—	2.0 and 2.6
4QGen-Exod[a]	*c.* 36	—	top 1.7+
4QProv[a]	36	*c.* 32+	bottom 2.2
4QJub[d] (4Q219)	38 (reconstructed)		bottom 1.7
4QRP[b] (4Q364)	39–41	35.6–37.2	bottom 2.1
4QIsa[c]	*c.* 40	30	bottom 2.1
4QIsa[g]	40	35	top 1.6
4QEnastr[b] ar (4Q209)	40 or 38–43	—	bottom 2.7
11QpaleoLev[a]	42	26–27+	bottom 2.0+
4QPs[s]	42	29	bottom 1.9
4QLev-Num[a]	*c.* 43	35.2–37.2	1.8 and 2.2
4QRP[c] (4Q365)	43–47	34.1–36.2	2.0 and 1.4–2.2
4QIsa[b]	45	29	top 2.3
4QShirShabb[d] (4Q403)	50	18.0	top 1.0
4QExod-Lev[f]	*c.* 60	30	1.3 and 1.2+

5

WRITING PRACTICES

The writing practices reflected in the various texts from the Judean Desert differ internally in many details. They often show a common idiosyncratic heritage, while other practices sometimes coincide with writing conventions known from other cultures.

Both sacred and nonsacred texts were written in the same scripts and with identical orthographic practices, with the employment of the same systems of sense division, scribal marks, correction, etc. (below, ch. *7a*). Also, there are virtually no differences between the scribal systems used for the writing in the square script and the paleo-Hebrew script excluding the details mentioned in ch. *7b*.

a. *Divisions between words, small sense units (stichs and verses), sections, poetical units, and books*

Divisions in the text, whether between words, stichs, verses, sections, larger units, and books are indicated in a variety of ways in the Judean Desert texts.

(1) *Word division*

The various languages and corpora of texts from the ancient Middle East employed different systems of word division, while some had no such division at all. For an overall analysis, see Ashton, *Scribal Habits*, ch. 7; A. F. Robertson, *Word Dividers*; Gordon, *Ugaritic Textbook*, 24 (vertical wedge); idem, "Non-Word Divider Use of the Small Vertical Wedge in Yarih and Nikkal and in an Akkadian Text Written in Alphabetic Cuneiform," in *Ki Baruch Hu, Ancient Near Eastern, Biblical, and Judaic Studies in Honor of Baruch A. Levin* (ed. R. Chazan et al.; Winona Lake, Indiana 1999) 89–109; W. Horowitz, *Graphemic Representation of Word Boundary: The Small Vertical Wedge in Ugaritic*, unpubl. Ph.D. diss., Yale 1971; Tov, *TCHB*, 208–9; A. R. Millard, "'Scriptio Continua' in Early Hebrew—Ancient Practice or Modern Surmise?" *JSS* 15 (1970) 2–15; idem, "Were Words Separated in Ancient Hebrew Writing?" *Bible Review* VIII, 3 (1992) 44–47; J. Naveh, "Word Division in West Semitic Writing," *IEJ* 23 (1973) 206–8. P. Saenger, *Space between Words, The Origins of Silent Reading* (Stanford, Calif. 1997) provides an in-depth analysis, but mainly of practices in European languages and literatures.

Scriptio continua

The overwhelming majority of the Judean Desert texts use one of two systems for separating words in Hebrew and Aramaic, employing either word-dividers of some kind (mainly dots) in texts written in the paleo-Hebrew script, or spacing between words in the texts written in the square script. Words in most Greek texts from that area are separated by spacing. Continuous writing (*scriptio/scriptura continua*) or that with very few breaks is attested only in some texts or groups of texts, probably with the purpose of economizing on space, since the texts use final Hebrew letters, or for aesthetic reasons:

• All the *tefillin* and *mezuzot*; *see* illustr. 9.
• The Copper Scroll (3Q15).
• MurGen, MurExod, and MurNum (same manuscript?), written almost continuously, with minute spaces between the words.
• MurIsa.

• The *Greek* Qumran texts of the Pentateuch (*DJD* IX), as well as hand A of 8HevXIIgr (hand B used spacing).

In the early Aramaic, Hebrew, and Moabite texts, *scriptio continua* is used only sparingly (Ashton, *Scribal Habits*, 131). Usually words were separated by dots or very short vertical lines: the Tell Fekheriyeh inscription from the ninth century BCE (occasionally), early inscriptions in the Hebrew script such as the Moabite Mesha Stone, the Tell Dan inscription from the eighth or ninth century BCE, other Hebrew inscriptions (Siloam, Ekron, and Ophel) and a few Phoenician inscriptions such as the plaque from Sarepta. On the basis of this evidence, it seems likely that word division of some kind (dots or lines?) was also used in the earliest biblical scrolls (so Millard and Naveh in the studies mentioned above). The custom of systematically separating words with spacing developed later. If this opinion is correct, the word division in the earliest sources reflected the views of the biblical authors, editors, or first scribes.

On the other hand, several scholars claim that the earliest biblical scrolls were written without any word division in the *scriptio continua,* as already suggested by Nachmanides in his introduction to the Torah.[170] This assumption is supported both by some Phoenician inscriptions, which do not contain word division, and by indirect evidence, viz., many variants in biblical manuscripts and the ancient versions that reflect differences in word division (see Tov, *TCHB*, 252–3). These variants, representing different views on the content of the text, may indeed have been created with the introduction of word division. However, they could also have been created only in those cases in which the indication of word division was unclear in the ancient scrolls.

Dots, strokes, and triangles in paleo-Hebrew texts (illustrations 14 and 14a)

In the Judean Desert texts written in the paleo-Hebrew script, most words were separated by dots, while sometimes similar graphic dividers were used (for the background of this practice, see Tov, *TCHB*, 208–9).[171] The practice of separating words with dots in papyri is evidenced as early as the eighth-seventh century BCE, the date assigned to the papyrus palimpsest Mur 17 (A: papLetter; B: papList of Personal Names). These dots were written on the line from which the letters were suspended (see 4QpaleoExodᵐ and 11QpaleoLevᵃ), at the same level as the tops of letters. This practice is reflected also in the only text employing the Cryptic C script, 4QcryptC Unclassified Religious Text (4Q363a). This text is written mainly in paleo-Hebrew letters, intermingled with some cryptic signs.

W. J. Horwitz, "The Ugaritic Scribe," *UF* 11 (1979) 389–94 showed that scribes in Ugarit divided words with small vertical strokes. See further D. Sivan, "The Glosses in the Akkadian Texts from Ugarit," *Shnaton* 11 (1997) 222–36 (Heb.). In cuneiform texts, originally there was no word division, but at a later stage a sign was inserted between the words (Driver, *Semitic Writing*, 42). Dots are employed as word dividers in early inscriptions written in the Hebrew script. viz., the Moabite Mesha Stone, and the Siloam, Dan, Ekron, and Ophel inscriptions. Likewise, the words in all manuscripts of SP are separated by dots (Crown, *Samaritan Scribes*, 80). These dots were written level with the tops of the letters, although sometimes they were written at the mid-letter level, see MS Nablus 8 (Crown, *Dated Samaritan MSS*). Words were separated by spaces with dots in the middle in most Latin inscriptions. See J. C. Egbert, *Introduction to the Study of Latin Inscriptions* (New York/Cincinnati/Chicago 1896).

The word-dividers in 2QpaleoLev, 4QpaleoDeutˢ, and 6QpaleoGen are shaped like small oblique strokes (which may be compared with vertical line dividers in many early lapidary texts), while in Mas 1o (Mas pap paleoText of Sam. Origin [recto] and Mas pap paleoUnidentified Text [verso]) the word-dividers resemble small triangles. In 4QpaleoJobᶜ, the words were separated either by dots or small strokes. Several scribes forgot to insert some word-dividers within the line. At the ends of lines they were usually omitted (4QpaleoGen-Exodˡ, 4QpaleoExodᵐ, 4QpaleoDeutˢ, and 11QpaleoLevᵃ), and this practice was continued in SP manuscripts prior to the sixteenth century (Crown,

---

[170]Pp. 6–7 in the edition of C. B. Chavel, *Commentary on the Torah by Moshe Ben Nachman (Nachmanides)*, vol. 1 (Jerusalem 1959).

[171]For other uses of dots in manuscripts, see SUBJECT INDEX, 'dot.'

Samaritan Scribes, 80 and Robertson, *Catalogue*, xxvi). The scribe of 2QpaleoLev placed both the dots serving as word-dividers and short oblique lines guiding the drawing of horizontal lines at the end of the lines.

The only known paleo-Hebrew text in which words were not separated by signs, but rather by spacing, is 4QpaleoDeut[r].

Spacing

In most Qumran texts written in the square script, as well as in 4QpaleoDeut[r], words were separated by single spaces, although in some cases this practice was not carried out consistently. Thus 4QTob[a] ar (4Q196) has only minimal spaces between words, even at the beginning of what constitutes a new chapter in the later division (2 9 [Tob 2:1]). Likewise, 5/6ḤevPs and MasPs[a] (illustr. 5a) as well as the aforementioned Mur 1 and 3 often left almost no spaces between the words. 4QTQahat ar (4Q542) is extremely inconsistent with regard to the size of word-spaces as well as of letters. As a rule, however, the space between words equals the size of a single letter (thus also *y. Meg.* 1.71d). On the other hand, in 11QT[a] II–V written by scribe A, unusually large spaces were left between words, amounting to 0.7–0.9 cm in cols. IV–V.

Word division by spacing is attested in early Aramaic lapidary texts from the seventh century BCE onwards (Ashton, *Scribal Habits*, 128). Likewise, according to *b. Menaḥ.* 30a and *y. Meg.* 1.71d, in Torah scrolls a space the size of a small letter ought to be left between words. According to *b. Menaḥ.* 29a, letters ought not to touch one another ('any letter which is not surrounded by *gevil* on its four sides is unacceptable'). In *Sof.* 2.1 (cf. *Massekhet Sefer Torah* 2.1) this custom is laid down as follows:

מניחים בין שם לשם כדי שיהא ניכרים ובאותיות כדי שלא יהא מעורבין

One leaves a space between words, so that they are separated, as well as between letters, so that they are not joined.

In some Qumran texts, exceptions were made for small words that were joined to that following. This pertains in particular to the following types of words, illustrated by Qimron, *Grammar*, 121–5 and Kuhl, "Schreibereigentümlichkeiten" (1QIsa[a]), and exemplified here by a few select examples. Qimron distinguishes between the juxtaposition of two short words (e.g. כיאם), of a short word and a long word (e.g. אתמנשה), and a long word and a short word (e.g. 1QS II 9 יהיהלכה). In the following examples, the plates rather than the transcriptions should be consulted.

1. The *nota accusativi* את

4QGen[c] 1 ii 15 (Gen 41:8) אתכל
1QSa I 4 אתכול
1QIsa[a] IX 12 (Isa 9:20) אתמנשה, אתאפרים; XI 2 (Isa 11:13) אתיהודה; XXII 18 (Isa 27:15) אתמות.
4QGen[g] 1 1 (Gen 1:1) אתהשמים and ואתהארץ, 3 (Gen 1:4) אתהאור; other occurrences of את in this scroll were separated by spaces (Gen 1:7, 21).
4QLev[c] 2 8 (Lev 4:4) אתידו
4QTest (4Q175) 6, 13 אתכול
4QCommGen A (4Q252) IV 2 אתזכר
4QText Mentioning Temple (4Q307) 1 7 אתישראל

2. Prepositions

על

1QIsa[a] I 6 (Isa 1:5) עלמה; IX 11 (Isa 9:19) ועלשמאול; XI 16 (Isa 13:7) עלכן, 20 (Isa 13:11) עלתבל; the space between the two words is smaller than that between the other words.
4QAdmonition Based on the Flood (4Q370) 6 עלכן
MasUnidentified Text heb or ar (Mas 1p) 2 אלכן (possibly); cf. P.Nash line 15 עלכן

אל

1QIsa^a XXXI 12 (Isa 27:33) אלמלך⸗אשור
4QNum^b X 11 (Num 19:1) אלמושה ואל אהרון
4QJosh^a V 14 (Josh 8:18?) אלהעי
4QWays of Righteousness^b (4Q421) 13 1 כי אם אלפ]ני[המה

עד

1QIsa^a XXIX 26 (Isa 36:17) עדבואי; L 11 (Isa 62:1) עדיצא
1QS X 21 עדתום

עם

1QIsa^a XX 11 (Isa 25:12) עמארבות; XXIII 11 (Isa 29:6) מעמיהוה

לפי

1QS III 23 לפירזי

מן

4QNum^b X 8 (Num 18:8) מזהיקב
4QPs^x 3 (Ps 89:21) מושמן

3. Conjunctions and adverbs

1QIsa^a I 23 (Isa 1:20) אמתמאנו; XI 10 (Isa 12:5) כינאות; XVI 29 (Isa 22:12) אמתבעון; XXXIX 22 (Isa 47:3) גמתראה
1QSa I 10 כיאם
4QGen^g 1 3, 12; 2 8 (Gen 1:4, 10, 18) כיטוב
4QJer^a VII 3 (Jer 12:4) כ]יאמרו[

4. Interrogatives

1QIsa^a IX 16 (Isa 10:3) ומהתעשו; XVII 23 (Isa 22:16) מהלך

5. ל(ו)ס

1QIsa^a I 6 (Isa 1:5) כולראוש; XXIII 16 (Isa 29:8) כולהגואים
4QAdmonition Based on the Flood (4Q370) 1 כלנפש
4QNarrative and Poetic Composition^b (4Q372) 9 3 כלהגוים

6. אל and בל

1QIsa^a XXXVII 8 (Isa 44:2) אלתירא; XXXIV 13 (Isa 41:10) אלתשמע; XXXIV 17 (Isa 41:14) אלתיראי
4QS^f (4Q260) 5 5 אלתהספר
4QD^f (4Q271) 5 I: While many occurrences of אל are followed by spaces (lines 5, 6), and others by half-spaces, in some instances there is no spacing at all: אליתערב (line 1) אלימר (line 7).
4QInstr^c (4Q417) 2 i 7 אלתחשוב
4QParaGen-Exod (4Q422) 10 9 בלירא]ה[
11QpaleoLev^a I 9 אלתפנו

7. Closely connected words, especially short words[172]

1QIsa^a XXXI 12 (Isa 27:33) אלמלך⸗אשור; XXIII 22 (Isa 29:13) העמהזה; XXIX 30 (Isa 63:20) אלוהיהארצות; XXXVI 8 (Isa 42:25) ותבערֿבֿו
1QS X 4, 7 זהלזה; 1QS XI 7 עממעון
4QNum^b XII 15 (Num 20:17) י[מיןושמא]ול; XIX 14 (Num 26:15) ובניגד, but cf. v 20 ibid. בני יהודה
4QDeutⁿ IV 3 (Deut 5:15) ובזרוענטויה
4QQoh^a II 17 (Qoh 7:3) י]ןטבלב
4QTest (4Q175) 9 בנבעור; 13 בנישית
4QList of False Prophets ar (4Q339) 3 ה]זֿקן מביתאל

---

[172]Cf. the Masoretic tradition which is divided regarding the writing of several compound names as one or two words (e.g. עמיאל). See the list in *y. Meg.* 1.72a.

4QapocrJosh[b] (4Q379) 22 i 6 אלדעות;22 ii 9 יציבדלתיה
4QRP[b] (4Q364) 26b,e ii 3 פסל לכה = פסלכה
4QNarrative Work and Prayer (4Q460) 7 5 להיותלי
11QPs[a] XXVI 12 אזראו
Mas pap paleoText of Sam. Origin (Mas 1o recto) הרגרי[ז]ו[ם], as in SP (passim)

By the same token, some short words were not separated by dots in 11QpaleoLev[a] (although there were spaces between the words) in the following instances: B 4 כלהעדה; C 7 מכלכלי; I 9 אלחפנו; col. 5 5 אתחית; col. 5 9 בידאיב. Conversely, a few words that were written too close to one another were subsequently separated by a dot (§ c7).

Cf. further the Tell Dan inscription dating from the eighth or ninth century BCE that has dots between all words, except for ביתדוד in line 9. There also is no dot in lines 2–3 מלכ יש[ר]אל, but there is sufficient space between these two words to indicate that a separation was intended. Likewise, in the Lakhish and Arad ostraca dating to the end of the First Temple period two words are often combined, e.g. Arad 2 6 אלהאחר. The Edomite ostracon from Hirbet Uzzah likewise reads in line 5 [בח?]עלמז.

Closely connected to the lack of space between certain words is the orthographic convention of 1QIsa[a] to represent monosyllabic words with a nonfinal rather than a final *mem*. See § g.

Words were *not split* between lines in texts written in the square script. The splitting of words between two lines is evidenced only in the following forms of writing:

• The paleo-Hebrew script, but not the related Samaritan script.

• The writing in the *scriptio continua* in the *tefillin* and *mezuzot* as well as in the Copper Scroll (e.g. III 1–2, 5–6, 12–13).

• Greek papyri and manuscripts (Turner, *Greek Manuscripts*, 17), including those found in the Judean Desert.

(2) *Indication of small sense units (stichs and verses) in biblical manuscripts*

Among all the Hebrew and Aramaic texts from antiquity and more particularly from the Judean Desert, the division into smaller units than the larger section divisions (open and closed sections), though not the smallest units possible, is evidenced only in Hebrew Scripture. The earliest biblical manuscripts must have contained either a single type of sense division, that of open and closed sections (thus § 3η below), or none at all. Over the course of generations, as exegetical traditions developed, smaller units began to be indicated, at first orally and later in a written form.

It remains a matter of speculation as to why among the early texts the text division into small units developed only for the biblical texts (except for the Mesha stone that used small vertical lines); the issue is not often discussed in the scholarly literature. In particular, it remains difficult to know where and in which period the tradition of verse division developed. It is suggested here that the division into small sense units originated in conjunction with the public reading of Scripture (in the synagogue service).[173] That reading had to be interrupted at intervals smaller than open or closed sections, for the sake of the reader and listeners, and at a later stage also for the *meturgeman*. After the verse division had come into existence, that system was of practical use, as it could be

---

[173]Although the reading from the Torah is mentioned in Neh 8:8, it is difficult to know when the organized oral reading of the Torah in the synagogue service started, but there seems to be stable evidence for such reading from the middle of the second century BCE onwards. See, in much detail, C. Perrot, "The Reading of the Bible in the Ancient Synagogue," in Mulder, *Mikra*, 137–59. A similar point may be made for select readings from the Prophets and Hagiographa. *B. Qidd.* 30a attributes the counting of the verses, and therefore probably also the verse division, to the period of the *Soferim*.

invoked in order to determine the length of units to be read liturgically.[174] Only the Torah and some additional segments of Scripture were read in public service, but the existence of versification in these books and segments must have influenced the creation of such a system also in the remainder of the biblical books.

Thus, while the system of subdividing the text into open and closed sections reflects a writing tradition, similar to other writing traditions (§ 3 below), the division into verses has its origin in the oral tradition of Scripture reading.

The scribes of the Hebrew/Aramaic biblical texts from the Judean Desert did not indicate small sense units (verses), not because such a procedure had yet to be developed, but because that practice was initially only oral. At the same time, the beginnings of verse divisions may be visible in one or two Hebrew/Aramaic Qumran texts (see below), while fully developed evidence is known only for early manuscripts of LXX and T. The indication of these sense divisions in the translations partly followed the oral traditions for the Hebrew text,[175] and partly the syntax of the translations and the scribal practices used in the languages of the translations.

The indication of small text units developed differently for texts written in prose and poetry. Some poetical units in the Bible were written stichographically, though in different systems, in thirty texts from the Judean Desert, mainly from Qumran (ch. *5b*). The details of this layout, especially the extent of stichs and hemistichs, are necessarily based on an exegetical tradition or *ad hoc* exegesis, which often differs from that of the Masoretes and/or the early versions.

Only in Isa 61:10–62:9 in 1QIsa[a] have such stichs—consisting of 2–5 words—been indicated in the running text by the inclusion of small spaces after each stich. The section as a whole is separated from the context by beginning and closing open section marks as well as by *paragraphoi*.[176] It is unclear why only this segment of 1QIsa[a] among the Judean Desert texts was singled out for the notation of stichs, which differ in a few details from the Masoretic division into units (note the differences in 61:10 and 62:6).

Units larger than stichs, but still smaller than sections, were initially indicated in antiquity in both poetry and prose segments of biblical texts, in the sources mentioned below. These small units are known in modern parlance as 'verses.'

Oral traditions. The main tradition of verse division was oral (as mentioned by *b. Ned.* 37b with reference to the accent system), invoked for the reading of Scripture. The fact that the earliest available evidence from the Judean Desert and elsewhere for the division into verses (see below) is found only in early witnesses of two ancient translations (LXX, T) and not in Hebrew manuscripts from the same period, with the possible exception of two late Qumran texts, cannot be coincidental. Accordingly, the earliest manuscripts (the 'original' manuscripts) of the LXX and T probably already indicated what we now name 'verse divisions' (thus also Oesch, *Petucha und Setuma*, 341). At the same time, for the Hebrew manuscripts, the evidence suggests that from an early period onwards verse division was part and parcel of the oral rather than the

---

[174]Thus *m. Meg.* 4.4 'He who reads in the Torah may not read less than three verses; he may not read to the interpreter more than one verse' <because otherwise the interpreter may forget the contents when translating Scripture into Aramaic>.

[175]This assumption requires a further assumption, namely that the translators who rendered Scripture into Greek and Aramaic were aware of the details of the Hebrew oral tradition.

[176]This phenomenon was first recognized by Bardke, "Die Parascheneinteilung," 72. The details were subsequently analyzed by J. C. de Moor, "Structure and Redaction: Isaiah 60,1–63,6," in *Studies in the Book of Isaiah, Festschrift Willem A. M. Beuken* (ed. J. van Ruiten and M. Vervenne; BETL CXXXII; Leuven 1997) 325–46. The special layout was not marked in Burrows, *The Dead Sea Scrolls*, but was indicated in Parry–Qimron, *Isaiah*.

written tradition. Indeed, at a later stage the use of verse indication in Torah scrolls was explicitly forbidden (*Sof.* 3.7):

ספר שפסקו [177] ראשי הפסוקים שבו אל יקרא בו

If a Torah scroll has spaces <to mark> the beginning of verses, it may not be used for the lections.

The oral division of Scripture into verses is mentioned often in rabbinic literature which stringently preserves the details of this tradition, conceived of as going back to Moses (cf. *b. Meg.* 22a 'Rab said . . . Any verse which Moses had not divided, we do not divide'). In that tradition, such a small unit was known as a פסוק, *pasuq*, that is, a unit after which one interrupts (פסק) the reading and leaves a pause, and which subsequently was indicated with a *silluq* accent. The indication of this accent, usually combined with a dicolon, at the end of a verse indicated the original oral division into verses and was therefore the end product of an exegetical procedure, rather than its beginning.

What exactly constituted a verse in prose sections has not been determined and further research is needed for the different books of the Bible, especially the prose books.[178] The boundaries of the verses are not a matter of fact. Some long verses may be separated into two short ones, while some short verses may be combined into longer ones. Direct speech introduced by לאמר usually follows in the same verse, if the section quoted is not too long, but sometimes it forms a separate verse. Nevertheless, the division into verses probably followed certain principles. Usually, the boundaries of verses are fixed by syntactical considerations, but sometimes the end point of the verse in MT is artificial.[179] At the same time, it is unlikely that the length of verses was determined by the memory limitations of *meturgemanim* (thus Barthélemy, "Les traditions anciennes" [see n. 190] 31), since the sizes of verses differ greatly and different customs were in vogue at different times (according to *m. Meg.* 4.4, the *meturgeman* offered his translation after each verse in the Torah and after three verses in the Prophets). The main issue at stake is therefore the exegetical traditions which determined the limits of verses. For example, on the basis of content exegesis in MT and other ancient traditions, the first verse in the Torah ends after הארץ ('earth') reading the second word as *bara'* ('created') rather than *b^ero'* ('[began] to create') as it was understood by Rashi, several modern commentators, and the NJPST translation.[180] The latter understanding would involve a larger unit (vv 1-3 of MT) for the first verse of the Torah.

Written evidence

a. *Hebrew/Aramaic biblical texts.* In the great majority of the Hebrew/Aramaic biblical texts (and by implication, all nonbiblical texts) from the Judean Desert, small units (verses or 'Kleinstspatien' in the terminology of Oesch, *Petucha und Setuma*) were *not* indicated, while larger sense units (sections) were indicated by a system of 'open' and 'closed' sections, as described in § 3 below. On the other hand, there is possible evidence for the indication of some form of a division into *verses* in one or two biblical

---

[177]Some manuscripts add או שנקרו or או שעקרו (see Higger, *Mskt Swprym*).

[178]Thus, the phrase . . . ויהי ערב ויהי בקר יום is part of a small verse in Gen 1:5, 8, 31, while in vv 13, 19, 23 the same phrase constitutes a separate verse, probably in order to avoid an overly long verse together with the preceding sentence. Similar differences between traditions are quoted in *b. Qidd.* 30a with an example from Exod 19:9 to be quoted below.

[179]For example, Gen 36:3 contains a mere six words of which two are connected with a *maqqeph*, and the verse has no *'etnachta*.

[180]*Tanakh* תנ״ך. *A New Translation of THE HOLY SCRIPTURES According to the Traditional Hebrew Text* (Philadelphia/New York/Jerusalem: The Jewish Publication Society, 1985).

scrolls. While early written evidence for verse division in Hebrew sources is very scarce or perhaps non-existent, it does exist for ancient witnesses of the Aramaic and Greek translations (see below and APPENDIX 5A), the earliest of which are contemporary with the witnesses of Hebrew Scripture from the Judean Desert. Such evidence also exists for the medieval witnesses of SP and the Peshitta, both with a dicolon.[181] In addition, the ancient oral tradition of verse division is reflected in the accent system of MT, sometimes mentioned in the earlier rabbinic literature.

Although it has been suggested that a few Qumran manuscripts reflect verse division, it appears that there is insufficient evidence for such a claim, with the possible exception of the first two sources mentioned below. Partial evidence is not regarded as the beginning of a system of indicating verse division: we presume that traditions of oral division already existed at the time, and in view of the rabbinic prohibition of written indication (see above), such division was either indicated in all or almost all instances in a given scroll or not at all.

• 4QDan[a]: This manuscript indicates spaces after six verses (2:24, 26, 28, 33, 48; 5:16; the space after 1:17 may have been created by the flaking away of the leather), but not in *fifteen* other instances (1:19; 2:19, 21, 34, 40, 42; 3:1; 7:25, 26, 27; 8:2, 4; 10:18, 19; 11:15). Further, the preserved fragments contain one closed section (Dan 2:45) and two open sections (2:49; 7:28). Some spaces after verses in this manuscript (2:24, 26; 5:16) as well as in 4QDan[d] (Dan 3:24; 4:5) occur before or after verbs of speaking, which may well reflect a special feature of these Daniel manuscripts, also known for SP and some Greek documents (see below). The scribe of this manuscript may have indicated a few small section divisions, such as in 4QEn[a] ar (4Q201), for a smaller degree of division (also indicated in three places which do not coincide with verse endings), but the evidence is insufficient for establishing that the manuscript reflects verse division.

• 4QDan[d]: While S. Pfann and E. Ulrich suggested that small spaces in this manuscript represent verse division,[182] the evidence (after Dan 3:24; 4:5, 12; 7:18) is insufficient and may well reflect section indications.

• 4QIsa[d]: According to Skehan–Ulrich, *DJD* XV, 77, some spaces in this manuscript coincide with the ends of verses, but the evidence is inconclusive, and in other instances verse endings were not indicated in this manuscript.

• 1QIsa[a]: Crown, "Studies. III," 376 suggested that this manuscript indicated some verse divisions (Isa 43:23 ff. [XXXVII 17]; 45:17 [XXXVIII 24]). Furthermore, the small space before col. XXI 4 in that scroll coincides with the beginning of Isa 26:21. However, even though col. XXI seems to provide a sizeable number of instances in which ends of verses were indicated by spacing, the great majority of the ends of verses in this scroll are not indicated in this manner. Korpel–Oesch, *Delimitation Criticism*, 13 mention spaces between verses in Isa 50:1-11 (XLI 29–XLII 13), where indeed a larger number of spaces than usual are found between verses (after vv 2, 4, 5, 6, 7, 8, 9 [the end of v 10 occurs at the end of a line]), while the ends of vv 3 and 11 coincide with open sections. Two closed sections are indicated in the middle of v 2. The reason for the conglomeration of section breaks in this pericope is unclear, but since this practice pertains to a very small part of 1QIsa[a], it cannot be taken as proof for the indication of verses in this scroll.

• 1QIsa[b]: This manuscript displays a few small spaces after verses and in the middle of a verse (for the evidence, see Oesch, *Petucha und Setuma*, 249), but these instances do not reflect a system of verse division, since no spaces are indicated after the great majority of verses.

• 1QpaleoExod and 1QpaleoLev: According to Oesch, *Petucha und Setuma*, 356, n. 13 these scrolls indicated some verses ('Kleinstspatien'), but the evidence for the first scroll is incorrect, and that for the second is partly incorrect and partly pertains to section divisions.

b. *Targumim.* 4QtgLev (4Q156), one of the two Qumran manuscripts of the Targum from cave 4 ascribed by J. T. Milik, *DJD* VI, 86–9 to the second-first centuries

---

[181]The relatively late indication of verses in the manuscripts of S (*pasoqa*) has not been analyzed for this study. For the data and bibliographic references, see Korpel–de Moor, *Structure*, 6–9 and passim.

[182]S. Pfann, "The Aramaic Text and Language of Daniel and Ezra in the Light of Some Manuscripts from Qumran," *Textus* 16 (1991) 127–37, especially 136; idem, "4QDaniel[d] (4Q115): A Preliminary Edition with Critical Notes," *RevQ* 17 (1996) 37–71, especially 49–52; E. Ulrich, *DJD* XVI, 239–40.

BCE, systematically indicates the ends of verses and of some half-verses (Lev 16:12, 14a, 14b, 18a, 18b, 20, 21a) with a dicolon (:). This notation is in accord with the writing tradition in that language and script.[183] The evidence for 4QtgJob (one space after Job 5:1) is unclear, while 11QtgJob has no verse divisions at all (the spaces after Job 28:26 [XIII 8] and 29:12 [XIV 7] are probably coincidental). The medieval codex Neophyti of the Targum likewise indicated dicola at the ends of verses.

c. *Greek translations.* The earliest Greek evidence for verse division from the second century BCE onwards (texts from Qumran and Naḥal Ḥever, Egyptian papyri) shows that verses were indicated by spacing, rendering stable the evidence for the early division into verses of this version. At a later stage, these spaces were filled in with graphic indicators in accord with the Greek writing tradition, namely the dicolon and dot (high, median, and low).[184] The evidence regarding the indication of verses in these early Greek sources (spacing, dicolon, dot), presented in detail in APPENDIX 5A, thus refers to both verses and groups of words within verses (half-verses). At the same time, several Greek manuscripts of 2 CE onwards have no verse division at all, probably reflecting a secondary development.

A comparison of the verse division details in the ancient Greek biblical manuscripts and the Masoretic tradition is hampered by the fact that the transmission of the Greek biblical manuscripts, certainly in Christian copies, moved away from the original translation. The original understanding of the verse divisions cannot be reconstructed easily, but there are indications of differences in details between the Hebrew and Greek traditions. Some details in the Greek sources may reflect early traditions, or even the original translation itself, while others may have been inserted secondarily, such as the indication of a pause after groups of words, especially in the middle of the verse, but also in other positions; see the third column in the TABLE in APPENDIX 5 (for the details regarding 8ḤevXIIgr, see Tov, *DJD* VIII, 11–12). These mid-verse divisions probably reflect pauses that were natural for a scribe or early reader. A relatively late source such as P.Oxy. 11.1352 (leather) of Psalms 82–83 LXX (early 4 CE), presenting dicola in spaces after groups of words, shows how unnatural this tradition (often against MT may have been. The spacing in P.Oxy. 4.656 of Genesis 14–27 (2 or 3 CE) separating the verbs of speaking from the direct speech in 15:7a, 9a and in P.Chester Beatty VIII of Jeremiah 4–5 (2–3 CE) before speech in Jer 4:31 are paralleled by 4QDan[a] mentioned above and SP to be mentioned below. See also the high dots preceding or following personal names in accordance with the Greek writing system (cf. Threatte, *Attic Inscriptions*, 82, 85) in P.Fouad 266a–c (942, 848, 847) of Genesis and Deuteronomy (1 BCE), P.Berlin 11766 of Exodus 5–7 (4 CE) as well as the spaces in these places in 4QpapLXXLev[b] (1 BCE) and 4Qpap paraExod gr (4Q127).

d. *Sam. Pent.* In most medieval manuscripts of SP, the ends of verses were indicated with a straight (:) or oblique (:) dicolon (*afsaq*), while larger sense units (sections) were indicated by the *qiṣṣah* sign in combination with a completely empty line (see the analysis in § 3t). Direct speech within a verse would start with two dots level with the tops of the letters (··), e.g. Gen 3:12, 17. Although all the SP manuscripts derive from the Middle Ages, the scribal traditions recorded in them probably reflect ancient practices.[185] The SP

---

[183]For parallels in the cuneiform Uruk inscription in Aramean, see C. H. Gordon, "The Aramaic Incantation in Cuneiform," *AO* 12 (1938) 105–17; B. Landsberger, "Zu den aramäischen Beschwörungen in Keilschrift," ibid., 247–57; Beyer, *Ergänzungsband*, 132.

[184]For other uses of dots in manuscripts, see SUBJECT INDEX, 'dot.'

[185]Thus Anderson, *Studies*; Crown, "Studies. III"; E. J. Revell, "Biblical Punctuation and Chant in the Second Temple Period," *JSJ* 7 (1976) 181–98; Robertson, *Catalogue*, xxi–xxii, xxv–xxvi, 3. See also Crown, *Samaritan Scribes*, 80.

differs often from the other textual witnesses with regard to the indication of subdivisions of verses, but these sources may nevertheless be based on a common exegetical tradition (thus Oesch, *Petucha und Setuma*, 313). Usually, units ending with an *afsaq* in SP equal verses of MT, but sometimes they are larger than the Masoretic verses. On the other hand, examples of larger verse units as recorded in Tal's edition (see p. x above) based on MS 6 (C) of the Shekhem synagogue are Gen 2:16b-17; 3:1b-4; 8:6-7; 10:13-14; 19:12-13a. Sometimes, the divisions of verses in SP equal half-verses of MT as in Gen 1:29a, b; 3:1a, 1b; 3:5a, b.

e. *Masoretic accents.* Various early written traditions concerning the division of the text into small units (verses) have come down to us as described above. All these texts are based probably on an ancient reading tradition that initially was oral. Such an oral reading tradition was put into writing at a later stage, and integrated into the recording of the accents of MT. Within this tradition, each unit ending with a *silluq* is considered a verse.[186] According to Revell, an additional, parallel, system for verse division was once operative, visible now only in the so-called pausal forms, occurring not only at the ends and in the middle of the Masoretic verses, but also in other positions.[187] When the verse division was still being developed orally, there must have been some lack of clarity in individual instances. This is alluded to by the rabbinic tradition regarding the five verses in the Torah 'of undecided syntactical adhesion' (שאין להן הכרע) concerning the type of relation between a word and that preceding or following. These doubts pertain to the divisions at the end and in the middle of these Masoretic verses.[188]

f. *Different verse divisions in the biblical text quoted in the* pesharim? The *pesharim* from caves 1 and 4 at Qumran often differ from the Masoretic tradition regarding the scope of the biblical text quoted in the lemmas. Thus, while the lemmas quoting the biblical text in the exposition in 1QpHab sometimes conform to what is now a verse in the Masoretic tradition of Habakkuk (1:5, 11, 12, 17; 2:14, 15, 16, 18), more frequently they comprise half-verses or even smaller segments (1:3a, 3b, 4bα, 1:4bβ, 6a, 6b, 10a, 10b, 1:13aα, 13b; 2:3a, 3b, 4a, 4b, 8b, 17a, 17b), one-and-a-half verses (1:1-2a; 1:6bβ-7; 1:12b-13a; 2:7-8a), or stretches of two (2:1-2, 5-6, 12-13, 19-20), or three (1:14-16; 2:9-11) verses. Similar deviations from the scope of the verses of MT are reflected in the lemmas of 1QpMic (1Q14), 4Qpap pIsaᶜ (4Q163), 4QpIsaᵈ (4Q164), and 4QpNah (4Q169), and to a lesser degree 4QpHosᵃ (4Q166) and 4QpPsᵃ (4Q171). The lemmas in 4QpIsaᵃ (4Q161), (4Q162), (4Q165) present the biblical text mainly in clusters of two or more verses. For details, see APPENDIX 7.1. These different types of quotation are inherent in the quotation systems of the *pesharim* in which the subject matter sometimes requires the mentioning of a unit larger or smaller than a verse in MT. Therefore the segmentation of the biblical text in the *pesharim* probably does not reflect any tradition differing from that of MT.

That the divisions into sections (below, § 3) and verses derived from different origins is evident, if only because the former was part of the early written tradition for the biblical texts, and the latter was not. The fact that rabbinic instructions pertain only to the divisions into closed and open sections (see *b. Shabb.* 103b and *Sof.* 1.15, both as quoted in § 3γ), and disallowed the indication of verses provides sufficient evidence of their different development histories.[189] Accordingly, what on a formal level appears to be a subdivision of a section in the biblical text into verses (that is, a unit starting and ending with a closed or open section), may not historically represent such a subdivision, if, as seems likely, the two systems of sense division had different origins. The indication

---

[186]These verses were not numbered until a system of chapter division was introduced in the copies of the Vulgate in the thirteenth century by Archbishop Stephen Langton (d. 1228). From the Vulgate, that numbering system was introduced into editions of the Hebrew Bible as well as in manuscripts and editions of the other ancient versions. For the differences between the Hebrew editions, see J. S. Penkower, "Verse Divisions in the Hebrew Bible," *VT* 50 (2000) 379–93.

[187]E. J. Revell, "Pausal Forms in Biblical Hebrew: Their Function, Origin and Significance," *JSS* 25 (1980) 165–79.

[188]See the discussion in S. Kogut, *Correlations between Biblical Accentuation and Traditional Jewish Exegesis: Linguistic and Contextual Studies* (Jerusalem 1994) 33–8 (Heb.); T. Jansma, "Vijf teksten in de Tora met een dubieuze constructie," *NTT* 12 (1957–58) 161–79; M. Breuer, "Biblical Verses of Undecided Syntactical Adhesion," *Leshonenu* 58 (1994–5) 189–99 (Heb.).

[189]Therefore the two types of divisions should not be treated together as in Oesch, *Petucha und Setuma*, passim, e.g. 342, even though several segments are indicated in some sources as a verse or half-verse, while in other sources as sections.

of open and closed sections almost necessarily coincided with the beginning and/or end of some verses, but occasionally the two systems collided when a new section began in the middle of a verse. Such a case is traditionally named a *pisqah beʾemṣaʿ pasuq*, a section division occurring in the middle of a verse (below § 3ζ). The very existence of such a category further accentuates the different origin of the two systems, especially in Samuel where such instances abound.

In the analysis of verse divisions, two issues are at stake: the different systems used for the indication of small sense units and the exegesis behind each individual pause after a content unit. The latter aspect is not treated here.

In several early sources, no verse divisions were indicated at all (most early witnesses of the Hebrew/Aramaic Bible; 11QtgJob; several Greek manuscripts of 2 CE onwards, probably reflecting a secondary development). The systems for the indication of verses are either spacing (two Hebrew/Aramaic Qumran manuscripts of Daniel analyzed above [insufficient evidence], early sources of Greek Scripture from 2 CE onwards), or various graphic systems (dicola in 4QtgLev of the second-first centuries BCE, Medieval Masoretic manuscripts, and Targum Neophyti; high, median, and low dots or dicola in later Greek sources; various graphic indicators in the medieval sources of the SP, Targumim, and Peshitta). For the Greek sources, see APPENDIX 5A.

The verse division of all sources mentioned above differs in many details, in regard to both the main pause at the end of the verse and minor pauses in the middle of the verse which were indicated in MT, SP, Peshitta, and Greek Scripture texts, in the latter case with the same type of indicator as the major pause at the end of the verse (indicated in APPENDIX 5A as a 'group of words'). The internal differences among these sources were listed in the edition of the HUBP and *BHS* (less frequently), and in greater detail in the studies by members of the so-called Kampen school of 'delimitation criticism' as represented by Korpel–de Moor, *Structure* and Korpel–Oesch, *Delimitation Criticism*. At the same time, no overall conclusions on the characteristics of the different witnesses were drawn in these two sources.

The different traditions of the division of the text into verses differ from one another since verse division represents exegesis; while the Masoretic system presents the best-known tradition, it does not necessarily reflect the earlier division in the best way possible. Since the beginning of verse division was oral and therefore possibly reflected secondary developments following the writing of the original copies of the biblical books, it is probable that no authentic verse division ever existed, and all attempts to arrive at the 'original' verse division are therefore hypothetical.

Differences in verse division are also attested in later periods in the manuscripts of MT, not only in manuscripts of the same books, but also between parallel passages in MT which probably go back to earlier periods. Some of these differences were created by the early authors, for example, when the author of Chronicles structured his text according to slightly different principles than the earlier texts, by adding or omitting elements which would or could involve a different verse structure. Other differences may be based on early deviating exegetical traditions. Such differences are easily visible in the graphic representation of parallel texts in A. Bendavid, *Parallels in the Bible* (Jerusalem 1972), while other examples were listed by Sperber, *Grammar*, 511–14. TABLE 1 exemplifies some such differences. However, beyond these and similar differences, the extent of unity in the verse division of parallel passages in MT is remarkable.

TABLE 1: *Internal Differences within MT Concerning the Scope of Verses in Parallel Passages*

Source 1	Number of Verses	Source 2	Number of Verses
Gen 10:22-23	2	1 Chr 1:17	1 (shorter version of Gen)
Gen 25:14-15a	1,5	1 Chr 1:30	1 (different verse division continues in v 31)
Gen 36:23-24a	1,5	1 Chr 1:40	1
Gen 36:27-28	2	1 Chr 1:42	1 (slightly shorter version)
Gen 36:31-32	2	1 Chr 1:43	1 (slightly shorter version)

Gen 38:7	1	1 Chr 2:3c	0,5 (different content)
Josh 21:13-14	2	1 Chr 6:42	1 (slightly shorter version)
2 Sam 24:13	1	1 Chr 21:11a-12	1,5
1 Kgs 8:65	1	2 Chr 7:8-9b	1,5 (longer version)
Ps 96:8-9a	1,5	1 Chr 16:29	1 (difference in verse division continues in v 30)

The remarkable agreement between Masoretic and non-Masoretic traditions (probably in 80–90 percent of the instances) may point to one common source for verse division (among other things, this would imply that the Greek translators were influenced by that source).

The verse division underlying biblical quotations in the Talmud and the counting of verses[190] basically agrees with the tradition of the Masoretic accents; e.g. Exod 15:1 quoted in *m. Soṭ.* 5.4 and Deut 8:8 in *b. Ber.* 41a; see further Blau, "Masoretic Studies III," 135–8. On the other hand, there are some quotations of verses whose scope may differ from that of MT, see Blau, ibid., 138–41, but the evidence is unclear.[191] If, for example, Ps 82:5b is quoted for Scripture reading in *b. Soṭ.* 55a, this does not necessarily imply a tradition of a verse starting with v 5b. At the same time, the term *pasuq* also refers to a unit larger than that of a verse. The most convincing example of verses whose scope differs from MT given by Blau is probably the quotation of Deut 4:30-31 in *y. Sanh.* 10:28c and the *Pesiqta* (ed. Buber 162b 2) as הפסוק הזה, 'this *pasuq.*'

b. Qidd. 30a contains a statement concerning differences between Babylon and Palestine regarding verse division, exemplified by the traditions for Exod 19:9: 'When R. Aḥa b. Adda came <from Palestine to Babylon> he said: "In the west [scil. Palestine] the one verse (Exod 19:9) is divided into three verses".' This statement follows an earlier dictum that 'in the division of verses we are no experts either' (נמי לא בקיאינן בפסוקי).

What exactly constituted a verse in the prose sections of the Bible has not been determined. The division into verses, that is rather uniform in the various textual witnesses, had its origin in the oral tradition of Bible reading, as opposed to the written division into sections. The earliest sound evidence for such a division is found in Qumran scrolls of two Bible translations (LXX, Targum); later evidence is contained in the SP and Masoretic accents.

---

[190]The rabbinic literature mentions the total number of verses of some of the books, implying that these verses formed distinct units, e.g. *b. Qidd.* 30a; *b. Taʿan.* 27b; *b. Ned.* 37a. For example, the details given in *b. Taʿan.* 27b agree with the number of verses in MT for Genesis 1. At the same time, it is sometimes unclear what exactly was meant by these פסוקים. For example,

תנו רבנן חמשת אלפים ושמונה מאות ושמונים ושמונה פסוקים הוו פסוקי ס"ח. יתר עליו תהלים שמונה. חסר ממנו דברי הימים שמונה
Our rabbis taught: There are 5888 verses in the Torah; the Psalms exceed the Torah by eight, while <Daniel and?> Chronicles are less by eight (*b. Qidd.* 30a).

Exactly how the tradition arrived at these numbers remains unclear, but it appears that they are based on a different understanding of the concept of a verse in the various books. Thus, while the number of verses quoted for the Torah approaches the number of these verses in the Masoretic manuscripts (5845), the numbers given for the other books greatly exceed the known data for Psalms (2527) and Chronicles (1765). Therefore, in the latter two books, a different counting system of the verses must have been used on the basis of smaller units. The count was probably based on stichs or hemistichs, such as graphically indicated in several Qumran manuscripts (see § *b* below). If the arrangement of the Psalms in hemistichs, as in system 2 in § *b*, is made the basis for a calculation of the book of Psalms, it comes close to the number mentioned in *b. Qidd.* 30a. To this larger number one should also compare the Greek stichometry, based on stichs, for the book of Psalms counting 5000–5500 verses and the stichometry of the Peshitta counting 5630 verses. For details, see L. Blau, "Massoretic Studies, IV. The Division into Verses," *JQR* 9 (1897) 476. For a general study on the differences between the traditions, see D. Barthélemy, "Les traditions anciennes de division du texte biblique de la Torah," in *KATA TOUS O': "Selon les Septante,"* *Trente études sur la Bible grecque des Septante en hommage à Marguerite Harl* (ed. G. Dorival and O. Munnich; Paris 1995) 27–51. (On the other hand, J. Penkower [see n. 186 above] 380, n. 7 prefers the reading 8888 of some manuscripts of the Talmud).

[191]For an analysis of the use of *pasuq* in rabbinic literature, see also A. Samely, "Scripture's Segments and Topicality in Rabbinic Discourse and the Pentateuch Targum," *Journal for the Aramaic Bible* 1 (1999) 87–123, especially 111–15.

(3) *Division between large sense units (sections)*

a. *Background*

In the great majority of biblical and nonbiblical texts from the Judean Desert (not in the documentary texts, for which see *DJD* II, XXVII, XXXVIII), as in most Greek texts from the Hellenistic period (again not in documentary texts; see, e.g. Lewis, *Bar Kochba*), and in earlier Aramaic texts from the fifth and fourth centuries BCE, the text was subdivided into meaningful units that were separated from one another by means of spacing. This system was imitated in the Copper Scroll (3Q15).

In addition to the primary sources from antiquity, such as the Judean Desert texts, the system of sense divisions can also be analyzed in such secondary sources as the ancient translations of the Bible. These translations were made from texts such as those found in the Judean Desert, and at least some translators transferred the sense divisions from the Hebrew manuscripts to their translations. However, over the course of the transmission of these translations, the original sense divisions were often obliterated (§ ι).

The system of subdividing a text into larger sense units by means of spacing was used for the transmission of many texts in antiquity, sacred and nonsacred, in Hebrew, Aramaic, and Greek. Prior to the discovery of the Qumran texts, this system was often wrongly considered to be characteristic of the transmission of only Hebrew Scripture, where the sections thus indicated were named *parashiyyot*. The widespread use of such divisions was recognized long before the discovery of the Qumran scrolls by L. Blau.[192] Unsurprisingly, in Qumran texts of all types, this system of sense division was the rule rather than the exception.

Because the system of division into section units in the Judean Desert texts is so widespread, any description of its nature should not be based on a single source (in the past the system of 1QIsa^a [illustrations 1 and 21] was often considered to be representative for all the Qumran texts) or isolated remarks in rabbinic literature, but an attempt should be made to discover the guiding principles behind the system as a whole. These principles were discussed in great detail by Oesch, *Petucha und Setuma*, 198–248; idem, "Textgliederung"; Steck, *Jesajarolle*; idem, "Abschnittgliederung"; Olley, "Structure"; Korpel–de Moor, *Structure*; the various studies included in Korpel–Oesch, *Delimitation Criticism*, especially M. C. A. Korpel, "Introduction to the Series Pericope" (pp. 1–50) and J. Oesch, "Skizze einer synchronen und diachronen Gliederungskritik im Rahmen der alttestamentlichen Textkritik" (pp. 197–229). See also earlier studies by Bardke, "Die Parascheneinteilung"; Perrot, "*Petuhot et setumot*"; and Siegel, *Scribes of Qumran*, 46–79.

β. *Technique of denoting section units*

Section units are indicated anywhere in the column, including the first and last lines, although naturally there would be a reticence to start a major section on the last line of the column (cf. the modern avoidance of 'widow' lines). At least one instance is known, 8HevXIIgr, where contents of the last line in col. XVIII (line 42) were erased and rewritten in the following column in order that the first verse of the new section (Hab 3:1) would appear at the top of a new column (which has not been preserved).

---

[192]L. Blau, *Papyri und Talmud in gegenseitiger Beleuchtung* (Leipzig 1913) 15.

It is not easy to reduce the manifold scribal practices to a small number of systems pertaining to all the texts, since each scribe was to some extent individualistic in denoting sense units; nevertheless two major systems can be discerned in the Judean Desert texts. In these texts, the content is divided into small and larger units (illustrations 1, 3, 8, 15, and 21). A certain hierarchical relation between these two systems may often be assumed; that is, according to the modern way of thinking we would probably say that larger sense units are often subdivided into smaller units. It is, however, unclear whether this hierarchical relation should always be assumed, and in some cases it can be demonstrated that such a relation did not exist when the two systems of sense division were of equal value, distinguished merely by their place on the line (1QpHab; see below). The idea of consistently subdividing a larger unit into smaller ones may well be a western concept, even though such subdivision can often be demonstrated.[193] It is probably safer to assume that scribes often directed their attention to the type of relation between the unit they had just copied and that they were about to copy, without forming an opinion on the adjacent units. It also stands to reason to assume, with Jenner, that the closed section often referred back to a previous unit of a larger order, namely an open section, while the marking of an open section itself often introduces a completely new theme, and hence refers to what will follow.[194]

To a great extent, the division into section units by scribes was impressionistic, as we shall see below. After all, in order to ascertain the exact relation between the various section units, a scribe would have to carry out a close reading of the context and be involved in literary analysis of several adjacent section units. Since we do not believe that scribes were so actively involved in content analysis, it appears that scribal decisions on the type of relation between section units should often, but definitely not always, be considered *ad hoc*, made upon completion of one unit and before embarking on the next. To some extent, this explains the differences between manuscripts of the same composition, as scribes often took a different approach to the relation between two units.

No rule exists regarding the length of a section that is separated from the context by preceding and following section units. This parameter depends on the nature of the literary composition and on the understanding of the scribe. The two extremes can be seen: there are manuscripts with virtually no section divisions, such as several units in medieval manuscripts of MT undoubtedly continuing earlier traditions. The book of Ruth in MT contains only one section division, after 4:17. Other divisions are called for, but they were simply not included in this text. There are also other books in MT containing very few section divisions; for a discussion, see § ε. At the other extreme are small sections separated from the context as illustrated in TABLE 2.

TABLE 2: *Small Section Units in the Qumran Texts*

Reference	Description
1QIsaᵃ XXI (Isa 26:19–28:2)	A sequence of successive small section units (open and closed sections), containing seven open and four closed sections, and one indentation. The column contains 31 narrow lines of text.
4QpaleoExodᵐ I, 5 (Exod 6:27)	הוא משה ואהרון, separated from the context by closed sections.

---

[193]Therefore, the criticisms against invoking western thinking are not always relevant. For such criticisms in Korpel–Oesch, *Delimitation Criticism*, see M. C. A. Korpel (p. 10) and J. M. Oesch (p. 207).

[194]K. D. Jenner, "Petucha and Setuma: Tools for Interpretation or Simply a Matter of Layout?" in *Studies in Isaiah 24–27: The Isaiah Workshop, De Jesaja Werkplaats* (ed. H. J. Bosman; OTS 43; Leiden 2000) 81–117, especially 87–8.

4QJub^d (4Q219) II 34	ויצא מאתוה שמח, preceded by a closed section and followed by an open one coinciding with the end of ch. 21 of Jubilees.
4QBer^a (4Q286) 5 8; 7 i 7; 7 ii 1, 6	After each אמן statement indicating the conclusion of a
4QBer^b (4Q287) 4 6; 6 6; 7 2	blessing or curse considerable space was left in the middle or end of the line (B. Nitzan, *DJD* XI, 4).
4QInstruction-like Composition B (4Q424) e.g. 3 7–9	Brief sapiential statements are separated by closed sections.
4QWisdom Text with Beatitudes (4Q525) 2–3 ii	Each brief אשרי saying ended with a closed section.

The following two main systems are recognized in texts written in the paleo-Hebrew and square scripts:

(a) A space in the middle of the line ('closed section' in the Masoretic tradition) usually denotes a segmentation of a larger unit (such as described in *b*) into one or more smaller units (illustrations 1 and 21):

```
xxxxxxxxxxxxxxxxxx          xxxxxxxxxxxxxxxxxxxxxxxx
xxxxxxxxxxxxxxxxxxxxxxxxxxxxxxxxxxxxxxxxxxxxxxxxxxx
```

In principle, a closed section is 'thematically related to what immediately precedes it' (thus Siegel, *Scribes of Qumran*, 73), but the vagueness of this definition leads to differences of opinion with regard to the interpretation of this relation. If this thematic relation was not recognized, scribes usually denoted the new section as an 'open section.' According to Perrot's definition, "*Petuhot et setumot*," 81, a closed section denotes a 'pause à l'intérieur d'un paragraphe,' that is, a subdivision of a larger unit, and an open section denotes the beginning of a 'long paragraph' (probably to be defined as the end of a 'long paragraph').

It is unclear whether the *differently sized* spaces in the middle of the line in the same scroll were meant to indicate different degrees of contextual subdivision, that is, small spaces for small subdivisions and larger spaces for a larger difference between units of contextual relevance. It appears that the differing space-sizes were often merely a result of inconsistency or were determined by the space available in the line. Thus in 1QIsa^a, the spacing within the line corresponds to 2, 3, 4, or 7 letter-spaces, but these internal differences probably do not indicate different degrees of ceasing (illustr. 1). Likewise, the different space-sizes in the middle of the lines in 11QT^a (11Q19) were probably not intentional (cols. XLIX 19: 4.7 cm; L 16: 4.0 cm; LI 6, 7: 1.5 cm). On the other hand, the scribe of 4QEn^a ar (4Q201) probably did make a distinction between small and large subdivisions in content, indicated by spaces of 2–3, 4–6, and 10–18 letters, as well as a half line. Thus Milik, *Enoch*, 179, who also relates this understanding to 1QS, 1QM, and 1QIsa^a. In 11QPs^a and 1QapGen ar, these closed sections are often very wide (25–30 letter-spaces in the latter text).

Some scholars believe that the indentations in 1QIsa^a, as well as the *paragraphos* signs (§ c1 below) used in connection with the section divisions, reflect a further refinement (thus Oesch, *Petucha und Setuma*, 227). However, the *paragraphos* signs should be excluded from this discussion since some, and perhaps all, were inserted in the manuscripts by later scribes and users and they were used very inconsistently (§c1). Indentations were limited to very specific conditions.

The indication of closed sections is evidenced in all texts written in the square script as well as in the paleo-Hebrew script; for the latter, see the evidence relating to 4QpaleoExod^m in *DJD* IX, 60 (TABLE 5). In this scroll as well as in 11QpaleoLev^a, a *waw* is often written in the interval when the word after the section division would have started with that letter (below § c1).

(b) A space extending from the last word in the line to the end of the line (illustrations 1, 3, 8, 15, and 21) indicates a major division (an 'open section' in the Masoretic tradition), that is, a section which is 'thematically distinct from the section which immediately precedes it' (as defined by Siegel, *Scribes of Qumran*, 73; cf. also *b*.

Menaḥ. 31b–32a where according to R. Meir an open section should be used in *mezuzot* for a major content break).

xxxxxxxxxxxxxxxxxxxxxxxxxxxxxxxxxxxxxxxxxxxxx
xxxxxxxxxxxxxxxxxxxxxxxxxxxxxxxxxxxxxxx
xxxxxxxxxxxxxxxxxxxxxxxxxxxxxxxxxxxxxxxxxxxxx

In most scrolls, this system reflects the largest degree of separation between sections. This system is evidenced in all texts written in the square script as well as in the paleo-Hebrew script; for the latter see, for example, the evidence relating to 4QpaleoExod[m] in *DJD* IX, 59 (TABLE 4).

Not all spaces left by scribes reflect section divisions. Poor surface often necessitated that scribes leave a segment uninscribed (ch. *4i*), and it is sometimes unclear whether the spaces reflect bad surface or a sense division. Thus, it is unclear why after ואחרי כן in 4QGen[j] 9–10 4 (Gen 45:15) the remainder of the line was left empty (part of the leather has peeled off in this line, but the remaining section would not have created a surface problem for the copyist).

When the writing concluded near the end of the line, there was insufficient room remaining to leave a long enough space to indicate the new unit, and in such cases one of two different solutions were invoked:

(i) An indentation at the beginning of the line indicates that the previous line should have ended with a space (illustrations 3 and 21).

xxxxxxxxxxxxxxxxxxxxxxxxxxxxxxxxxxxxxxxxxxxxxxx
xxxxxxxxxxxxxxxxxxxxxxxxxxxxxxxxxxxxxxxxxxxxx
xxxxxxxxxxxxxxxxxxxxxxxxxxxxxxxxxxxxxxxxxxxxxx

This system is evidenced in several texts written in the square script (illustrations 3 and 21), but not in the paleo-Hebrew script; therefore, the indentation reconstructed for 4QpaleoExod[m] IX 31 (*DJD* IX, 61) is unlikely.

Hebrew manuscripts only employed indentations and did not use enlarged letters protruding into the margin (*ekthesis*), such as used in several Greek manuscripts, e.g. 8ḤevXIIgr XIX 39 (Hab 3:14); for a discussion, see APPENDIX 5.

χ[ηλου] σελε
Διετρη[σα]ς εν ραβδοις αυτου κεφαλην
ατει[χισ]των αυτου σεισθ[η]σονται του

The frequent indentations in 1QIsa[a] were often marked with a paragraph sign above the indentation: e.g. VII 10; X 14, 18; XIII 31; XVI 30; XXXVII 2 (scribes A and B). As in the case of the spacing in the middle of the line, the different-sized indentations were probably not intentional; accordingly, the large indentations in XXXVIII 15 and XLIV 16 probably carried the same meaning as smaller ones elsewhere.

MurXII contains eight such indentations (e.g. VII 11 [Amos .7:10]; XIX 4 [Hab 3:1]; XX 16 [Zeph 2:5]). 4QapocrDan ar has an indentation in col. ii 4. In 1QapGen ar XXI, XXII and 1QH[a] II, III, VII (Suk. = Puech X, XI, XV) these indentations were often very extensive (15–20 [2.5–3.0 cm] and 20–30 letter-spaces [5.0–6.5 cm] respectively). 4QInstr[d] (4Q418) likewise has large indentations at the beginnings of new sections (e.g. 69 ii 10; 126 ii 11; 148 ii 4). In 1QH[a] col. VII (Suk. = Puech XV), the indentation is half-a-line wide and in 4QBarkhi Nafshi[a] (4Q434) 1 i 12, 5.5 cm in a column of 13.5 cm wide; in 4QEn[c] ar (4Q204) 1 vi 4.0 cm. 4QVisions of Amram[g] ar (4Q549) 2 7 has an indentation of 3.4 cm. Usually, however, these indentations are small. In 11QPs[a] they occupy sometimes merely four letter-spaces (e.g. XVI 8; XX 3, 8), in other cases some twenty letter-spaces (e.g. XXVI 4; XXVII 12), and sometimes as much as half a line (e.g. III 7; XXV 6).

The unusually large indentation extending over three lines in 11QPs[a] XXVII 2–4 probably does not indicate the beginning of a prose section (lines 2–11) toward the end of this scroll which is almost exclusively written in poetry; rather, the indentation is due to scar tissue in the scroll (thus J. A. Sanders, *DJD* IV, 93).

(ii) A completely empty line indicated a regular section division, illustrations 17a, 18 (differing from system *c* below which probably denotes a greater hierarchy of division).

xxx

xxx

This system is represented in several texts written in the square script, and only in 4QpaleoGen-Exod[l] among those written in the paleo-Hebrew script. MurXII contains no less than 32 empty lines indicating new sections (e.g. VII 15 [Amos 7:11]; XI 17 [Jonah 3:3]). The procedure followed is well exemplified in the layout of Genesis 1 in 4QGen[b] in which the account of each day ends with an open section (illustr. 18). However, in frg. 1 i 27, the end of the account of the fifth day (Gen 1:23) reaches the end of the line, leaving no room to indicate an open section, and accordingly the scribe left the following line completely empty. The same layout of this pericope was followed in 4QJub[a] (4Q216) and 4QGen[g], but in the latter text there was enough room to indicate the open sections at the end of the account of each day of the creation.

Empty lines are found in many additional biblical and nonbiblical scrolls, e.g. 1QM (e.g. V 14–15; VI 6–7); 4QpaleoGen-Exod[l] (e.g. 3–4 7 after Exod 2:25; 7 ii 13 after Exod 11:10); 4QNum[b] (e.g. VI 20 after Num 16:7; XXXI 13 after Num 35:21); 11QT[a] (e.g. XIX 10; XXI 11); 4QCant[a] II 7 after Cant 3:11; 11QtgJob (e.g. III 2 before ch. 20; X 7 before ch. 27); MasSir VII 23.

This system was also used for the indication of stanzas within 4QPs[g] (illustr. 17a) and 11QPs[a], both in Psalm 119, and of individual Psalms (see § 4 below).

Most scribes of ancient documents did not present a text division into units of a higher hierarchy than that of open sections, such as that initiated in the Middle Ages with the division of the text into chapters. On the other hand, one of the scribal marks added to 1QIsa[a] by a later scribe or user, a slightly curved horizontal *paragraphos* line with a semi-circle on top (fig. 1.6; see § c1), possibly denotes just such a section unit, similar to that of the chapter division of the Middle Ages. According to modern logic it would have been helpful, for example, to mark a group of sections ending with open spaces in a special way, such as the biblical story of the creation, the Table of the Nations in Genesis 10, the Decalogue, or other groups of laws, but such a system was not devised in antiquity (the practical division of the text into units for the reading of the Torah in a triennial or annual cycle does not pertain to this issue, and in any event, it was not indicated in the early manuscripts). The medieval division of Scripture into chapters by Stephen Langton (see n. 186) tried to address a practical need, and according to our modern understanding the chapter division facilitates the reading, even though that system, too, is often flawed and some chapter divisions are inappropriate.[195]

Even though the scrolls denote no consistent higher hierarchy beyond open sections, some scribes inconsistently used two types of marking that were intended to indicate such a hierarchy:

(c) The greatest section division, at least according to some scribes, was a space extending from the last word in the line to the end of the line (open section) followed by a completely empty line; illustr. 1 (differing from system *b ii* above).

xxxxxxxxxxxxxxxxxxxxxxxxxxxxxxxxxxxxxxxxxxxx
xxxxxxxxxxxxxxxxxxxxxxxxxxxxxxx

xxxxxxxxxxxxxxxxxxxxxxxxxxxxxxxxxxxxxxxxxxxxx

• Various individual Psalms, see § 4 below.

---

[195]See Tov, *TCHB*, 52–3 and J. Penkower, "The Chapter Divisions in the 1525 Rabbinic Bible," *VT* 48 (1998) 350–74.

• 1QIsa^{a} after XXXIV 15 (Isa 41:11) in the segment written by scribe B. This scribe may have left such a space in places in which he realized that a section had to be supplemented. In this particular case, segments of Isa 41:11, 12 were not represented in the scroll and not supplemented by a later hand. In three other places, however, similar lines were left empty by the first scribe, and two or more lines of writing were subsequently added in regular or smaller characters in the space: XXVIII 18 (Isa 34:17b–35:2); XXX 11–12 (Isa 37:4b-7); XXXIII 15–16 (Isa 40:14b-16; illustr. 1).

• 1QIsa^{b} III 9–10 before a major break (Isa 39:1).

• 1QH^{a} V, VII, VIII, IX etc. (Suk. = Puech XIII, XV, XVI, XVII) before new hymns.

• 1QM II 15; III 12 before new sections.

• 4QJer^{a} V, part 1 5 after Jer 10:11, the sole Aramaic verse in that book.

• 4QpIsa^{a} (4Q161) 2–6 ii 20 between the *pesher* and the lemma (APPENDIX 7.2).

• 4Qpap pIsa^{c} (4Q163) 6–7 ii 9 between the *pesher* and the lemma (APPENDIX 7.2).

• 4QpPs^{a} (4Q171) 1–10 ii 5 between the *pesher* and the lemma (APPENDIX 7.2).

(d) A similarly major section division is a space at the end of the line followed by an indentation at the beginning of the following line.

xxxxxxxxxxxxxxxxxxxxxxxxxxxxxxxxxxxxxxxxxxxxxx
               xxxxxxxxxxxxxxxxxxxxxxxxxxxxxxxx
xxxxxxxxxxxxxxxxxxxxxxxxxxxxxxxxxxxxxxxxxx
xxxxxxxxxxxxxxxxxxxxxxxxxxxxxxxxxxxxxxxxxxxxxx

• 1QH^{a} VII (Suk. = Puech XV) 6, 26.

• 4QCant^{b} 2 ii 6–7, indicating a major content division and move from Cant 4:1-3 to vv 8-11.

• 4QTest (4Q175): The fourth section (lines 21–30) is separated in this way from the preceding sections in order to indicate a larger content division. This section adduces a nonbiblical text (known from 4QapocrJosh^{b} [4Q379] 22 ii), and not a biblical text, as the first three sections.

• 4QBarkhi Nafshi^{a} (4Q434) 1 i 12.

In addition to the use of spaces as an indication of division of section units, several texts used two additional devices to indicate new sections:

• *Paragraphos signs*. Several texts contain one of the variations of the *paragraphos* sign, used in addition to a spacing system (§ c1):

xxxxxxxxxxxxxxxxxxxxxxxxxxxxxxxxxxxxxxxxxxxxxxxxxx
xxxxxxxxxxxxxxxxxxxxxxxxxxxxxxxxxxxxxxxxxx
xxxxxxxxxxxxxxxxxxxxxxxxxxxxxxxxxxxxxxxxxxxxxxx

These signs were inserted infrequently and inconsistently in the Judean Desert texts as indications of divisions (see, for example, 1QM, 1QapGen ar, 11QT^{a}, probably not by the original scribes, but by later scribes or users, especially in order to draw attention to certain sections and topics. A number of persons were involved in the indication of these signs as shown by their differing shapes within a single scroll.

• *Red ink*. In 2QPs and 4QNum^{b}, red ink was used at the beginning of new units, while in 4QD^{e} (4Q270) it indicated a heading.[196] For parallels in Egyptian and other sources, see ch. *3f*.

2QPs: The first two lines of Psalm 103.

4QNum^{b}: The beginnings of ten new sections. The scribe either wrote the first verse of the new section in red (that is, the first line and its continuation on the next line; see XII 21–22 [Num 20:22-23]) or, more frequently, the first line of the new section (e.g. XIII 27 [Num 21:21]; XXVI 25 [Num 31:37, 38]; XXVII 3 [Num 31:48]; XXVIII 6 [Num 32:25]; XXVIII 23 [Num 33:1]), continuing the remainder of the verse on the next line in black ink. See N. Jastram, *DJD* XII, 210–11 and pl. XLIX. The red and black ink were

[196]The function of the red ink in the fragmentary 4Q481d ("Fragments with Red Ink" [*DJD* XXII]) is unclear (in one instance two consecutive lines were written in red ink).

used by the same scribe who alternated pens, while adhering to the same scribal practices (proportional spacing at the end of the line in order to finish the line flush with the left vertical marginal line; see ch. *4f* and XII 21 [Num 20:21] written with red ink). In all the mentioned instances, the writing with red ink denoted a sense division, usually after an open section, extant or reconstructed, and in one instance after a reconstructed indentation (XIV 16 [Num 22:21]).[197]

4QD[e] (4Q270) 3 i 19: the heading for a new section (J. Baumgarten, *RevQ* 19 [1999] 217–25 and idem, *DJD* XVIII, 147).

(γ) *Background and meaning of the section units in Hebrew manuscripts*

All systems of dividing the text are necessarily subjective and impressionistic (§ θ), and even more so is the hierarchical relation between such units often indicated by the employment of either open or closed sections. That is, a unit that was denoted as an open section by one scribe could be denoted as a closed one by the scribe of another manuscript of the same composition. This situation explains the many differences between parallel manuscripts, both in the Qumran corpus and within the medieval Masoretic family. In the course of that comparison, one realizes that the Qumran manuscripts were usually subdivided into more clearly demarcated units than the Masoretic manuscripts. They often have open sections where the Masoretic manuscripts have closed ones, and section divisions were often inserted where the Masoretic manuscripts have none. For a comparison between parallel sources, see § δ below.

The subjective nature of the division into either open or closed sections is also mentioned in rabbinic literature with regard to the writing of *mezuzot*. See ch. *7c*.

The contextual relevance of the spacing comes to light especially in the *pesharim* in which the scribes usually marked a separation between the lemma (the biblical text) and the *pesher*, before the *pesher*, after the *pesher*, or in both places. For a detailed presentation and parallels with scribal practices in Greek manuscripts, see ch. *5a2, 7f*.

A similar contextual importance is attached to the spacing in 4QWisdom Text with Beatitudes (4Q525) 2–3 ii, where each אשרי saying ended with a space in the middle of the line.

When the archetype of the Masoretic Text became sanctified, all the constituent elements, such as the notation of section units, became part of the transmitted text. Thus the system of indicating a specific type of section was considered obligatory by *b. Shabb.* 103b:

פרשה פתוחה לא יעשנה סתומה. סתומה לא יעשנה פתוחה

An open section may not be written closed, nor a closed section open.

Likewise *Sof.* 1.15:

פתוחה שעשאה סתומה. סתומה שעשאה פתוחה. הרי זה יגנז

If an open section was written as closed or a closed section as open, the scroll must be stored away (see further *Sifre* Deuteronomy § 36.1 on Deut 6:9).

The fact that scrolls were considered unfit for use if the indication of the sections was imprecise may have been unrealistic, even in Second Temple times, since all known texts, such as those of the proto-Masoretic family, differ internally. Therefore, the quoted traditions give the impression of reflecting a comparison of manuscripts with a master scroll, whose divisions were considered authoritative.

---

[197]It is unclear why the beginnings of some new sections were written with red ink, while others were not. Thus, in the following instances, 4QNum[b] denoted the new section by a system of spacing, writing the first line, like those surrounding, with black ink: I 6 (Num 12:1); XVIII 15 (Num 25:7); XVIII 25 (Num 25:16). Jastram's explanation (ibid., 211) that these rubrics indicate liturgical divisions (*sedarim*) is unsupported.

(δ) *Differences in section divisions between parallel manuscripts of the same composition*

As a rule, scribes copied the divisions between section units from their *Vorlagen*, but they sometimes deviated from them, and it is difficult to determine under which conditions they did so. Some discrepancies were caused by differences in column dimensions between the scribe's *Vorlage* and the manuscript he created, as a result of which scribes often were not able to recreate the division which they found before them. Beyond this description, scribes must have felt free to change the section divisions of their *Vorlage* and to add new ones in accord with their understanding of the context. They must have made their decisions *ad hoc*, guided mainly by their general understanding of the content.

Because of this situation, there are many differences between parallel manuscripts of the same composition with regard to section units, both in antiquity and in the Middle Ages. So far, most attention has been directed to internal differences between the biblical manuscripts, but similar ones also exist between nonbiblical manuscripts.

Differences between medieval biblical manuscripts were recorded by Perrot, "*Petuhot et setumot*" and Oesch, *Petucha und Setuma*. Differences between Qumran manuscripts and MT were recorded in the various *DJD* volumes, sometimes in a special apparatus below the text and often in separate tables (see, for example, the evidence regarding 4QJer[a,c] in E. Tov, *DJD* XV, 148–50, 181–2; the analysis of 4QNum[b] by N. Jastram, *DJD* XII, 208–10; and the analysis of 4QSam[a] by Herbert, *A New Method*, 85–7) as well as in Oesch, *Petucha und Setuma* (incomplete data). The differences in section units between the manuscripts of Isaiah were tabulated by Oesch, *Petucha und Setuma*, 198–248; idem, "Textgliederung"; Y. Maori, "The Tradition of Pisqaʾot in Ancient Hebrew MSS: The Isaiah Texts and Commentaries from Qumran," *Textus* 10 (1982) ‎א–‎א (Heb. with Eng. summ.); Olley, "Structure." The different systems used in these manuscripts are analyzed by Steck, "Abschnittgliederung," 60–82; e.g. differences between 1QIsa[a] and 4QIsa[c] are mentioned on p. 64.

The comparison between the divisions (without distinguishing between open and closed sections) in ancient biblical manuscripts and the medieval manuscripts shows different tendencies. In some cases, the ancient scroll has fewer section units than the medieval counterpart. Thus, 1QIsa[a] and 4QSam[a] present only 70–80 percent of the section units of the medieval manuscripts of MT, and 1QIsa[b] only 56% of the sections of MT. In other cases, the ancient scroll has more sections than the medieval texts; for example, 4QpaleoExod[m] and 4QNum[b] have more sections than MT, also in the middle of verses, in the latter case 20 percent more. The overall number of differences between 1QIsa[a] and 1QIsa[b] is tabulated by Olley, "Structure," 24–5 and analyzed by Steck, "Abschnittgliederung," 71–2. Olley notes that indentations are far more frequent in 1QIsa[a] than in 1QIsa[b]. In yet other texts, the numbers of the different types of divisions are more or less identical in MT and the ancient witnesses. It is impossible to find any pattern in these relations, for example, the assumption that certain groups of texts would display either more or less intervals than MT. Apparently the decision whether or not to indicate a new section is very subjective, and is unrelated to the textual character of the manuscripts.

Also *within* MT, differences in the indication of sections between parallel texts are visible between 1–2 Chronicles and the parallel passages in Samuel-Kings, which can be reviewed in the graphical representation (not always precise) in A. Bendavid, *Parallels in the Bible* (Jerusalem 1972).

For differences among the various *pesharim* in the spacing of the units of the biblical lemmas and the *pesharim*, see APPENDIX 7.2 (data and analysis).

TABLES 3 and 4 list a few examples of divisions in parallel biblical and nonbiblical manuscripts. The tables record the presence or absence of sections, sometimes reconstructed, regardless of their type.

TABLE 3: *Section Units in Parallel Manuscripts of Biblical Books*

a. AGREEMENT IN THE INDICATION OF A SECTION

Passage 1 (after the biblical verse)	Section	Passage 2	Section
1QIsa[a] II 13 (Isa 2:4)	open	4QIsa[b] 2 3	open
1QIsa[a] III 21 (Isa 3:15)	open	4QIsa[b] 3 i 10	open
1QIsa[a] V 2 (Isa 5:17)	open	4QIsa[b] 3 ii 3	open
1QIsa[a] X 25 (Isa 11:9)	open	4QIsa[c] 6 9	indentation
1QIsa[a] XVIII 21 (Isa 23:14)	closed	4QIsa[c] 9–12 20	empty line
1QIsa[a] XVIII 27 (Isa 23:18)	open	4QIsa[c] 9–12 27	closed
1QIsa[a] XX 12 (Isa 25:12)	open	4QIsa[c] 12–15 26	open
1QIsa[a] XLV 25 (Isa 55:5)	open	4QIsa[c] 44–47 17	empty line

b. DIFFERENCE IN THE INDICATION OF A SECTION

1QIsa[a] XIII 28 (Isa 16:10)	none	1QIsa[b] 3 5	open
1QIsa[a] XX 14 (Isa 26:2)	none	4QIsa[c] 12–15 28	open
1QIsa[a] XL 1 (Isa 47:11)	none	1QIsa[b] V 26	open/closed
1QIsa[a] XLV 2 (Isa 54:5)	none	1QIsa[b] X 33	[closed]
4QJer[a] XIV 17 (Jer 22:5)	[none]	4QJer[c] XI 5	open

TABLE 4: *Section Units in Parallel Manuscripts of Nonbiblical Compositions*

a. AGREEMENT IN THE INDICATION OF A SECTION

Passage 1	Section	Passage 2	Section
1QM XVI 8	empty line	4QM[a] (4Q491) 11 ii 8	closed
1QS III 12	open	4QpapS[a] (4Q255) 2 9	open
1QS VIII 12	closed	4QS[d] (4Q258) 2 6	closed
1QS IX 21	closed	4QS[d] (4Q258) 3 ii 5	closed
4QTest (4Q175) 23	closed (small)	4QapocrJosh[b] (4Q379) 22 ii 9	closed[198]
4QS[b] (4Q256) 6a i–6b 4	closed	4QS[d] (4Q258) VIII 5	closed
4QD[a] (4Q266) 2 i 6	closed	4QD[c] (4Q268) 1 8	closed
4QD[a] (4Q266) 5 i 12	closed	4QD[b] (4Q267) 5 ii 5	closed
11QT[a] (11Q19) XX 14	closed	11QT[b] (11Q20) 7 2	open

b. DIFFERENCE IN THE INDICATION OF A SECTION

1QS VIII 8	open	4QS[d] (4Q258) 2 2	none
4QS[f] (4Q260) 3 5	closed	1QS X 23	none
4QShirShabb[f] (4Q405) 3a ii b 12	empty line	4QShirShabb[d] (4Q403) 1 i 20–21	none
4QH[a] (4Q427) 6 2	none	4QpapH[f] (4Q432) 7 4	closed
4QH[a] (4Q427) 7 ii 7	closed	1QH[a] XXVI (Suk) 29; 4QH[e] (4Q431) 2 9	none
4QH[a] (4Q427) 7 ii 7	closed	4QH[e] (4Q431) 2 6	none
11QT[a] (11Q19) XLI 7	closed	4QT[a]? (4Q365a) 2 ii 2	none

---

[198]Most scholars believe that 4QTest (4Q175) quoted from 4QapocrJosh[b] (4Q379), so that the author of the former text probably followed the layout of the latter. However, according to H. Eshel, the dependence is reversed: "The Historical Background of 4QTest in the Light of Archaeological Discoveries," *Zion* 55 (1990) 141–50 (Heb.); idem, "The Historical Background of the Pesher Interpreting Joshua's Curse on the Rebuilder of Jericho," *RevQ* 15 (1992) 413–19.

(ε) *Personal preference of scribes in the indication of section units*

The many differences between the individual manuscripts accentuate the subjective and impressionistic nature of the indication of section units, visible among other things within the MT family (TABLES 3 and 4 above). Manuscripts differ with regard to the indication of divisions and their type. Although it is unclear at which stage section divisions were added in the manuscripts, lack of any division probably reflects the preference of the original author. The analysis of some biblical and nonbiblical manuscripts suggests that the personal preference of scribes may often be at work in the indication of sections.

• 1QpHab: The different spacing methods do not reflect a hierarchy of content divisions, but were determined rather by where in the line the quotation of the biblical text ended, necessitating the insertion of a content division, and where the following *pesher* began. See APPENDIX 7.1 for the data as well as an analysis of 1QpHab and the other *pesharim*.

• 4QpaleoGen-Exod[l]: This manuscript only rarely indicated division into closed sections (in 23 5, 9, 12 and in a few reconstructed verses), while more frequently it indicated open sections as the main division (e.g. 22 3; 30 8, 10 [for the complete data, see *DJD* IX, 20]). In many of these instances, the open section was followed by a completely empty line (above, system *c*), also when enough space was left in the previous line to indicate the open section (e.g. 16 3–4; 19 5–6). From the content point of view, there seems to be no reason for indicating these verses with a high degree of division, showing that this scribe probably did not follow a clear and consistent system of content divisions.

• 4QDeut[n]: This manuscript has a large number of section breaks in a very small pericope (8:5-10): after 8:6 (open section), 8 (empty line, possibly due to uneven surface), 9 (closed section), 10 (open section). This pericope has no section breaks at all in the medieval manuscripts.

• 4QSam[c]: The preserved fragments lack all the divisions found in the medieval manuscripts: 2 Sam [14:7]; 14:9; [14:17]; [14:20]; [14:23]; 14:24; [14:27]; 14:30; [14:33]; [15:6, 9].

• 4QRP[a–e] (4Q158, 4Q364–367): As a rule, the preserved fragments of these manuscripts have more section breaks than the parallel biblical manuscripts, for which see the tables in *DJD* XIII, 201, 259–60. Usually, exegetical additions are separated from the running biblical text by spacing of some kind. Open sections are indicated or reconstructed in 4QRP[b] (4Q364) 3 ii 6 before Gen 28:6; 4b–e ii 20 after Gen 30:36; 14 2 before Exod 24:12; 23a–b i 4 after Num 20:18 and before Deut 2:8; 27 2 before Deut 10:6; 4QRP[c] (4Q365) 6a i 9–10 in the middle of Exod 14:19: the addition is separated from the running text by a closed section; 6a ii and c 7, before Exod 15:22; 26a–b 2 before Num 1:1; 28 4 between Num 4:49 and 7:1. On the other hand, in this manuscript there is no separation between Num 27:11 and 36:1 which are juxtaposed in frag. 36 3. In 4QRP[e] (4Q367) 2b 4, a closed section appears between Lev 19:4 and 19:9.

• MurXII: This manuscript contains only three closed sections (VII 11 [Amos 7:10], XIX 4 [Hab 3:1], XX 16 [Zeph 2:5]) in addition to 32 empty lines and 10 open sections. The Masoretic manuscripts of the Minor Prophets diverge greatly, and usually have more open sections than closed ones, but nowhere is the proportion so clearly in favor of open sections as in MurXII.

• The medieval MT manuscripts of Genesis: see the analysis after TABLE 5.

• The medieval MT manuscripts of Numbers did not indicate the narrative sections and poetical units between Num 22:2 and 25:1, as opposed to the manuscripts of SP.

In spite of these and other differences between parallel manuscripts of the same composition, there usually seems to be a relative stability in the transmission of section units, perhaps reflecting the very first manuscript of the composition.

The internal differences in the notation of section units are most clearly visible in the Medieval Masoretic manuscripts of the different books of Hebrew Scripture, which, though representing different types of literature, and consisting of manuscripts of a different character, are nevertheless a good source for investigation. TABLE 5 summarizes the sections of MS L, calculated with the aid of the Accordance computer program (version 5.3: 2002). This table records the number of closed and open sections in each book, but because of the different book-sizes, meaningful statistical information can only be extracted from the data by comparing the total number of section units with the number of verses in each book. This information is statistically expressed as the average number of verses occurring between any two sections. The smaller the number of verses, the more sections the book contains. The larger the number, the fewer sections the book contains.

TABLE 5: *Frequency of Section Units in Codex L*

Biblical Book	Closed Sections	Open Sections	Total of Sections	Total of Verses	Average No. of Verses Occurring Between Any Two Sections
Genesis	50	40	90	1534	17.04
Exodus	94	70	164	1207	7.35
Leviticus	48	55	103	859	8.33
Numbers	63	94	159	1288	8.10
Deuteronomy	135	32	167	955	5.71
Joshua	42	52	94	656	6.97
Judges	27	64	91	618	6.79
1–2 Samuel	211	106	317	1506	4.90
1–2 Kings	81	110	191	1536	8.04
Isaiah	167	41	208	1272	6.11
Jeremiah	245	58	302	1365	4.51
Ezekiel	112	71	183	1273	6.95
Hosea	13	6	19	197	10.36
Joel	4	2	6	73	12.16
Amos	15	15	30	146	4.86
Obadiah	0	0	0	21	0
Jonah	2	1	3	48	16.0
Micah	7	9	16	105	6.56
Nahum	2	1	3	47	15.66
Habakkuk	5	4	9	57	6.33
Zephaniah	5	0	5	53	10.60
Haggai	3	4	7	37	5.28
Zechariah	27	10	37	211	5.70
Malachi	4	3	7	55	7.85
Psalms	0	0	0	2527	0 (see below)
Proverbs	1	46	47	915	19.46
Job	13	25	38	1070	28.15
Canticles	19	1	20	117	5.85
Ruth	0	1	1	85	43.00
Lamentations	84	5	89	154	1.73
Qohelet	2	1	3	222	74.00
Esther	12	11	23	167	7.26
Daniel	8	22	30	357	11.90
Ezra–Nehemiah	186	66	252	685	2.71
1 Chronicles	184	72	256	943	3.68
2 Chronicles	93	74	167	822	4.92
Whole Bible	*1962*	*1172*	*3136*	*(23173)*	*11.61*

The personal taste of the scribes of the manuscripts included in the archetype of MT is clearly visible in several instances. While most books in MT average one section unit per 7–10 verses (the average of 11.61 for the whole Bible is higher due to such small books as Ruth and Qohelet), some books stand out having a substantially lower or higher percentage.

• The story of Ruth has virtually no section units, although they are called for at several points in the story, especially after 1:22 and 3:18. The only place in which a division is indicated in MT is after 4:17 (closed section), separating the main story from the genealogy of David in 4:18-22. 2QRuth[a,b] and 4QRuth[a,b] have no content divisions either, but these manuscripts are fragmentary. The locations in ch. 3 in which such divisions *could* have been indicated are shown by M. C. A. Korpel, "Unit Division in the Book of Ruth: With Examples from Ruth 3," in Korpel–Oesch, *Delimitation Criticism*, 130–48 referring to divisions indicated in manuscripts of the ancient versions and by modern interpreters.

• Genesis, containing mainly narratives, has far fewer sections than the other narrative books (one section per 17.04 verses). That this book has very few section divisions is illustrated by a comparison with the rewritten story of Genesis 14 in 1QapGen ar. There are no divisions at all in this chapter in MT, while the parallel pericope 1QapGen ar has two closed sections in XXI 23 ff., one indented section, and one open section. Since 1QapGen ar is fragmentary, the complete text could have contained more divisions. Likewise, the medieval manuscripts of Genesis have no sense divisions between Gen 28:10 and 32:14, nor between 41:1 and 44:18. In these narrative chapters, *BHS* inserted many section units; the Qumran manuscripts are too fragmentary a source for information, while in one instance 4QGen[e] has an open section after 43:10.

• Among the books of the Minor Prophets, Nahum and Jonah stand out having very few section units: one division after an average of 15.66 and 16.0 verses respectively. Likewise, very few sections are found in Proverbs (one per 19.46 verses) and Job (one per 28.15 verses). In Job, these divisions usually occur at the ends of what later became chapters.

• Very frequent sections are found in Lamentations (a closed section after an average of 1.73 verses), Ezra-Nehemiah (after an average of 2.71 verses), and 1–2 Chronicles (after an average of 4.3 verses).

• The situation in Psalms differs from that of the other books. There are no open or closed sections in the Masoretic manuscripts within the Psalms, but many manuscripts indicate spaces between hemistichs.

• Qohelet has very few content divisions. 2QQoh[a,b] have no content divisions at all, but these manuscripts are fragmentary.

(ζ) *The division of the text into sections and verses*

As expected, the great majority of the section units in Scripture coincide with the beginnings of verses. That the tradition of the division into sections was separate from that of the division into verses is shown by the instances of a so-called *pisqah beʾemṣaʿ pasuq*, that is, 'a section in the *middle* of a verse' transmitted in the *Masorah parva* and *magna*. These section divisions were determined at an early stage, and when subsequently the verses were indicated, first orally, and later in a written form, in the Masoretic tradition by a *silluq* accent, some differences between the two systems came to light. These disagreements between the two practices are a necessary result of their different background, that of the section divisions as a writing practice, and that of the verse indication as an oral tradition (§ 2 above). When the divisions into larger sections and into the smaller verse units were integrated, it became apparent that some beginnings of sections were actually not located at the end of verses, but in their middle.[199] Thus the *Masorah parva* to Gen 4:8 notes 28 instances of a *pisqah beʾemṣaʿ pasuq* in the Bible, while the *Masorah parva* to Gen 35:22 lists 35 such instances (e.g. Gen 4:8, 35:22; 1 Sam 16:2), indicated in some or all of the manuscripts and editions by a space the size of either an open or closed section. See Gen 35:22:

> While Israel stayed in that land, Reuben went and lay with Bilhah, his father's concubine; and Israel found out.   Now the sons of Jacob were twelve in number.

---

[199]See R. Kasher, "The Relation between the *pisqah beʾemṣaʿ pasuq* and the Division into Verses in the Light of the Hebrew MSS of Samuel," *Textus* 12 (1985) נה–לב (Heb. with Eng. summ.); P. Sandler, "lḥqr hpysqʾ bʾmṣʿ hpswq," *Sefer Neiger* (Jerusalem 1959) 222–49; S. Talmon, "Pisqah bᵉʾemṣaʿ pasuq and 11QPsª," *Textus* 5 (1966) 11–21.

By the same token, the section division in some Qumran texts occurred in the middle of what later became verses in MT. For example

- 11QpaleoLevᵃ: Lev 23:8, closed section.
- 1QIsaᵃ XXXVII 8: Isa 44:2 (MT: *ʾetnachta*), closed section.
- 1QIsaᵃ XLII 2–3: Isa 50:2 (MT: *segolta* and *ʾetnachta*), two closed sections.

Likewise, the segmentation of the biblical text in the *pesharim* often reflects a half-verse or one-and-a-half verses which would have been denoted as a *pisqah bᵉʾemṣaʿ pasuq* if these manuscripts were Masoretic. For details, see § a2 above and APPENDIX 7.1.

(η) *Origin of the division into sections in Hebrew Scripture*

It is unclear when the use of spaces indicating new sections was first used in Hebrew Scripture scrolls. The spacing system, which represents a logical procedure of subdividing the text into sections, does not present the only procedure that could have been chosen. Texts also could have been divided by a system of graphic dividers (see below) or written without any division system. However, in the wake of ancient parallels, it stands to reason that some kind of sense division was already embedded in the earliest biblical scrolls, probably spacing.

Several nonbiblical documents preceding our earliest biblical manuscripts already reflected a division into section units. For a brief list of such sources, see M. C. A. Korpel in Korpel–Oesch, *Delimitation Criticism*, 25–6 and H. Bardke, "Die Parascheneinteilung," 34–5, the latter starting with the Mesha Stone(small vertical lines), even though that inscription indicated the equivalents of verses, not sections. Some of the Ugaritic texts often used horizontal lines to separate sense units (W. J. Horwitz, "The Ugaritic Scribe," *UF* 11 [1979] 389–94 and D. Sivan, *A Grammar of the Ugaritic Language* [Leiden 1997] 11–12). Also the two segments of the Kilamuwa inscription (ninth century BCE; *KAI*, 24) were separated by a double horizontal line. In many cuneiform texts, sections were separated by a line or lines drawn across the clay tablet ('section lines'), e.g. the Hammurabi Code and the Middle-Assyrian laws (Driver, *Semitic Writing*, 43–5; A. F. Robertson, *Word Dividers*). In addition, in these laws, the first sign of each section is indented, and sometimes lines were left open. In Egyptian literary texts from the eighteenth dynasty onwards, a raised dot (often in red ink) indicated the end of a section (Janzen, *Hiёrogliefen*, 45; Černy, *Paper*, 25; A. F. Robertson, *Word Dividers*). In other Egyptian texts, vertical lines were used (Ashton, *Scribal Habits*, 113–14).

Many of the Aramaic texts from the fifth century BCE recorded in Porten–Yardeni, *TAD*, such as the Elephantine papyri, displayed open and closed sections (for open sections, see, e.g. Ahiqar, lines 80, 86, 103, 106; for closed sections, see, e.g. lines 88, 90, 105). Several of these papyri also used the same horizontal *paragraphos* signs (§ 5c2 below) as found in the later documents from the Judean Desert (Porten–Yardeni, *TAD* 2, e.g. B3.3, 3.6, 8.3, 8.4, 8.7). Similar to the scribal tradition of several texts from the Judean Desert (cf. § 5c2), some early Aramaic texts also contained scribal signs written in 'closed sections' indicating new sections (also once in the Ahiqar text in an open section [below, ch. *5c*], and once in the middle of a blank line in court record B8.5 of 431 BCE in Porten–Yardeni, *TAD* 2; see figs. 3a–b). Greek texts from all periods also display open and closed sections. For secular texts, see Schubart, *Griechische Palaeographie*, 173; Turner, *Greek Manuscripts*, 8 and index.

On the other hand, in the case of the New Testament, it was suggested by Gächter, "Zur Textabteilung," especially 319–20, that the earliest manuscripts contained no text divisions at all since P.45 and P.46 (in the Chester Beatty collection) lacked such divisions.

In the wake of these parallels, it stands to reason that the earliest Scripture scrolls already indicated section division, as suggested by Oesch, *Petucha und Setuma* (especially pp. 343, 364) and before him by H. Hupfeld, *Ausführliche Hebräische Grammatik* (Cassel 1841) and idem, "Beleuchtung dunkler Stellen der alttestamentlichen Textgeschichte," *TSK* 10 (1837) 830–61. Likewise, Langlamet, "Samuel" (especially p. 518) believes that these divisions were found already in the manuscripts of Samuel used by the final editors. According to him, these divisions were adopted by the final editors, who integrated them in the version created by them. If this opinion is correct, the original sense division reflected the views of the biblical authors (editors), while subsequently variations in sense division were created during the textual transmission.

(θ) *The rationale of the division into sections*

The indication of a section division is very subjective, whether inserted by the first transcriber or subsequent copyists of the text. If the original authors or scribes embedded a hierarchical subdivision in the text, that division necessarily reflected their exegesis, and this understanding was often changed by later scribes, sometimes in a minor way, and sometimes in a major way.

Leaving aside the question of who first inserted the large sense divisions (the original authors/transcribers or subsequent scribes), it is important to know when and why such divisions were indicated in the text. Since these divisions are subjective, there are no *a priori* rules for them. The logic of the section divisions in one source (1QIsa^a) was studied in detail by Steck, *Jesajarolle*; idem, "Abschnittgliederung"; idem, "Bemerkungen"; idem, "Sachliche Akzenten"; Olley, "Structure," and previously Bardke, "Die Parascheneinteilung." Likewise, the MT of the Torah was examined by Perrot and Langlamet (see below). According to Steck, the system of section divisions and *paragraphoi* in 1QIsa^a is internally consistent (e.g. "Abschnittgliederung," 53; "Sachliche Akzenten," 150), a conclusion which is highly debatable. Both Steck and Olley list the phrases occurring at the beginnings of new sections, such as כ(ו)ה אמר יהוה appearing after a closed or open section (e.g. VI 21 [Isa 7:7]). However, not all such phrases start new sections, and conversely not all new prophecies or units start with an easily recognizable phrase. One therefore wonders about the validity of such a listing. It would seem preferable to argue in general terms that content analysis made the scribe realize that a new section (prophecy) started at a particular point, and that certain phrases may have aided him in reaching his decision. The divisions also could have been fixed by scribes without paying attention to any phrases. Besides, if the content divisions were already inserted in the very first manuscript of Isaiah—a possibility mentioned above—no listing of criteria is necessary at all, since the author or editor knew where to denote his sense divisions. Against the lists of criteria, it should also be argued that since the sections in 1QIsa^a differ from those in the other manuscripts, among them the Medieval Masoretic texts, each source may have followed different principles.

The assumption of Perrot, "*Petuhot et setumot*," 84–9 that there is a connection between the sense divisions and the liturgical readings in the Torah may be correct, since such readings would logically start with new sections, but this connection was probably made after the divisions already existed. Both Bardke, "Die Parascheneinteilung" and Perrot, "*Petuhot et setumot*" examined the section divisions in 1QIsa^a with special attention to the theological exegesis of the Qumranites and their interest in certain topics, but this approach is very questionable. Furthermore, in other biblical books that are likewise written with section markings no such theological tendencies can be detected.

Since these types of interpretation may be less relevant, different explanations come to mind for section divisions in individual units. It appears that we are often faced with practices, not systems, of individual scribes, and that there is no overall explanation for the whole corpus or for Hebrew Scripture. The original authors and/or scribes made their contextual decisions while writing or copying and not as part of an overall scheme.

Undoubtedly some divisions can be explained in different ways, and often another type of division may be proposed which appears to be more appealing to our understanding (hence the frequent differences between codex L and *BHS* on which also below, TABLE 7). Among other things, it should be noted that the notion of 'original sense divisions,' which some scholars try to establish, is as difficult as that of establishing the original text of Hebrew Scripture. We should therefore content ourselves with a few observations on the rationale of some of the section divisions.

1. *Schematically* written descriptions and lists were usually separated by open sections, e.g. the segments in the census in Numbers 1–4 in MT and 4QLev-Num[a]. However, there are differences in details.

4QGen[b,g] as well as the medieval Masoretic texts of Genesis 1 end the description of each day of the creation with an open section. Usually there are no subdivisions within the narration of what was created on each day, but in 4QGen[g] there is a closed section after v 10, between the creation of the dry land (1:9-10) and of the vegetation (1:11-12).

Likewise, the different offerings in Leviticus are separated by open or closed sections; in the medieval manuscripts of MT they are indicated by alternating closed and open sections, and in the Qumran texts mainly by open sections, but TABLE 6 shows that the evidence is more complicated. Thus 4QLev[b] (Lev 1:11–3:1; 3:8-14) contains only open sections. One wonders to what extent the alternation of open and closed sections in the medieval texts of MT is intentional. A new unit starts in Lev 1:14 with burnt offerings of birds, and when in 2:1 the text continues with a meal offering, it would be logical that this verse would start after an open section, but unlike in 4QLev[b], this is not the case in MT. This verse is separated from the previous one with a closed section, as, in fact, are all other instances of meal offerings in this chapter (after vv 4, 5, 7, 14). On the other hand, these laws are separated by open sections in the Qumran scroll (vv 4, 14), but not in vv 5, 7. In the medieval texts, there are thus more instances of division than in 4QLev[b]. Further, MT has closed sections where 4QLev[b] has open sections.

TABLE 6: *Section Units in Lev 1:14–2:12*

Before Verse	Topic of New Section	Section in MT	Section in 4QLev[b]
1:14	burnt offerings of birds	open	open
2:1	meal offering	closed	open
2:4	cereal offering	closed	open
2:5	cereal offering (baked)	closed	none
2:7	cereal offering (cooked)	closed	none
2:14	cereal offering (first fruits)	closed	open

2. When determining new section units during the course of the writing, without any overall plan, scribes would have been influenced by external factors, such as the occurrence of certain words or phrases that in their mind would be appropriate beginnings of new units.

Scribes may have been influenced by the fact that in the Torah many of the new sections coincide with the beginning of divine speech. 123 of the 290 open sections (not of the closed ones) listed in the traditional list of Maimonides, *Code*, book II, *Ahabah*, *Hilkhot Sefer Torah*, VIII 4, start with either וידבר or ויאמר. Although Perrot and

Langlamet[200] attached much importance to this fact (Perrot suggested that this situation reflected the public reading of the Law), it was only to be expected that many new sections in the Torah would begin with divine speech. By the same token, many new section units in 1QIsa[a] start with phrases of divine speech (Olley, "Structure," 29). Furthermore, Langlamet, "Samuel" suggested that certain phrases at the beginning of new units in the book of Samuel, such as ויהי, verbs of moving, etc. triggered the indication of a new unit.

3. The *impressionistic* nature of the section divisions may be illustrated by two examples:

• While 11QT[a] (11Q19) indicated many section divisions, according to the logic of its scribe, other divisions should also have been indicated in col. LVII in order to separate the different topics:

Lines 1–5	Organization of the army and officers.
5–11	The bodyguard (topic changes in the middle of line 5 without a sense division).
11–15	The judicial council (topic changes in the middle of line 11 without a sense division).
15–19	Ban on polygamy (closed section in the middle of line 15).
19–21	Duties of the king toward his people (topic changes in the middle of line 19 without a sense division).

Likewise, in col. LII 8–21 in a section in which 11QT[a] juxtaposed various laws deriving from different chapters in Deuteronomy, which in the scribe's mind were connected, no divisions were indicated. All these laws were presented in 11QT[a] (11Q19) as one running text without sense divisions:

> The firstborn (Deut 15:19-23)
>
> Muzzling of the ox (Deut 25:4)
>
> Joint plowing with an ox and ass (Deut 22:10)
>
> Centralization of the cult (Deuteronomy 12)

• The differences in layout between the section divisions in Deut 12:1–14:22 in MT and those inserted by a modern edition, such as in *BHS*, illustrate the different points of view involved, summarized in TABLE 7.

TABLE 7: *Section Units in Deut 12:1–14:22*

After Verse	Topic	Section in MT	Section in *BHS*
11:32	Introduction to the laws	none	open
12:3	Centralization formula	none	closed
12:7	Centralization formula	none	closed
12:14	Limitation of the centralization formula	none	closed
12:19	Limitation of the centralization formula	closed	closed
12:28	Introduction to the laws of chapter 13	closed	closed
12:31	Introduction to the laws of chapters 13–26	none	open
13:1	Unlawful prophet inciting to idolatry	open	open
13:6	Other persons inciting to idolatry	closed	closed
13:12	A city inciting to idolatry	closed	closed
13:19	One is forbidden to disfigure oneself in grief	closed	closed (should be open)
14:2	Clean and unclean animals (quadrupeds)	closed	closed

---

[200]Perrot, *"Petuhot et setumot,"* 83; F. Langlamet, "'Le Seigneur dit à Moïse . . .'—Une clé de lecture des divisions massorétiques," *Mélanges bibliques et orientaux en l'honneur de M. Mathias Delcor* (AOAT 215; Neukirchen/Vluyn 1985) 255–74.

14:8	Clean and unclean animals (aquatic creatures)	closed	closed
14:10	Clean and unclean animals (birds and flying insects)	none	closed
14:20	Prohibition to eat dead animals	none	closed
14:21a	Prohibition to boil a kid in its mother's milk	none	closed
14:21b	Tithing	open	open

Since the division of the text is very subjective, almost no 'correct' system exists, but that in *BHS* is often closer to our own understanding. *BHS* records the section units of codex L as פ and ס, while indicating its own sense divisions by spacing without Masoretic letters (see the table above):

The introduction to the laws of Deuteronomy in 11:29-32 is preceded by a closed section in MT (after 11:28), but due to the major distinction between this introduction and the introductory speeches of Moses, an open section would have been in order.

At the point at which ch. 12 starts ('These are the laws ...'), there is no division in MT, while at least a closed section, if not an open section (thus *BHS*), would have been called for.

It is very hard to subdivide ch. 12 because of its multi-layer structure. MT has section divisions only after vv 19 and 28, but a better understanding is obtained by the divisions in *BHS* after vv 3, 7, 14, 19, 28, and 31 (the last verse of the chapter).

The first verse of ch. 13, more specifically introducing the laws that are to follow in chapters 13–26, belongs to the subject matter of that and the following chapters. Yet, the section division of MT links it with the preceding section, 12:29-31.

The different laws in ch. 13 referring to persons inciting unlawful worship are separated by a closed section in both sources (vv 2-6, 7-12, 13-19), and they rightly start after a section division of a higher hierarchy, an open section appearing after v 1.

After the laws dealing with unlawful worship in ch. 13, ch. 14:1-2 turns to a completely different issue, that of forbidding the Israelites to disfigure themselves in passionate grief. In MT and *BHS*, this topic starts with a closed section before v 1, and ends with a closed section after v 2. However, due to the commencement of a completely different area of legislation, this section ought to have started after an open section. It ends with a closed section after 14:2, but could have ended with an open section. The following section, which deals with clean and unclean animals (14:3-20), could have been brought under the same heading as the previous section (cf. the explanation of the law in 14:3 with that of 14:20). If it were conceived of as relating to the same material, the present closed section would be in order, and if it were not, an open section would be in order.

The two different, though related, topics in 14:21a and 21b should probably be separated from the preceding verses by a closed section, as in *BHS*, but in MT they continue as a running text.

After 14:21b, the topic of clean and unclean animals is rightly sealed off with an open section in both sources, since a new topic starts in 14:22 (tithing).

(ι) *Section divisions in the ancient translations and the Samaritan Pentateuch*

The division of the text into section units, together with the verse division in the manuscripts of some early translations (pp. 138–9), reflects the first visible component of context exegesis of the written text, probably initiated by the earliest editors and scribes. This early exegesis must have been extant in the Hebrew manuscripts used by the ancient translators, from where it was transferred to these translations, and is still visible in some early translational witnesses. However, during the course of the transmission of these translations, the evidence was contaminated.

Three typological stages of development (not always evidenced in chronological sequence) with regard to the indication of section divisions are visible in the manuscripts of *Greek* Scripture (until the fifth century CE).[201] In some cases, however, the evidence is too fragmentary to determine whether the space in a manuscript denoted a verse ending or a new section.

Stage 1. Some early witnesses reflect some, most, or all of the section divisions of the Hebrew texts from which the Greek translations were made. Several of these texts reflect early Jewish revisions of the Old Greek (P.Fouad 266a–b of Genesis and Deuteronomy [middle 1 BCE], 8ḤevXIIgr hands A and B [end of 1 BCE]), while others probably reflect more closely the Old Greek translation (4QLXXLev^a [2–1 BCE], 4QpapLXXLev^b [1 BCE]). In P.Oxy. 4.656 of Genesis 14–27 (2 or 3 CE) these sense divisions occur also in the middle of Masoretic verses.

For bibliographical details concerning the papyri listed below, see Aland, *Repertorium* and Van Haelst, *Catalogue*; for a complete listing of the data, see APPENDIX 5.

• 4QLXXLev^a of Leviticus 26 (late 2 or early 1 BCE) has a closed section together with a *paragraphos* sign in frg. 1 21 (after Lev 26:13).

• P.Fouad 266a–b (942 and 848) of Genesis and Deuteronomy (middle of 1 BCE) have open and closed sections, accompanied by a *paragraphos* above the first letter in the following line. While the evidence for the open sections is visible (e.g. after Deut 18:5; 27:26), that for the closed sections is partly reconstructed.

• 4QpapLXXLev^b of Leviticus 2–5 (1 BCE) has closed sections and *paragraphoi* in frgs. 27–31 6 (after Lev 5:19) as well as in frg. 32.

• 8ḤevXIIgr hands A and B (end of 1 BCE) indicated open and closed sections, usually accompanied by *paragraphoi*, and often with *ekthesis* (see below). The system of sense divisions in this scroll is more developed than in MT (40 divisions, partly reconstructed, compared with 21 in MT), and resembles the contemporary Hebrew MurXII (TABLE 12 in E. Tov, *DJD* VIII, 10).

• P.Oxy. 65.4443 of Esther Add. E and ch. 9 (late 1 or early 2 CE) has open sections after 8:12, 13, with *paragraphoi* and *ekthesis*.

• P.Oxy. 4.656 of Genesis 14–27 (2 or 3 CE) has an open section after 19:38, as well as closed sections after 15:7a, 7, 9a; 20:4a, in all cases with high or median dots. The spaces and median dots in 15:7a, 9a precede direct speech.

Stage 2. Several later manuscripts of Greek Scripture, copied by Christian copyists, moved away from the Hebrew manuscript tradition, and consequently reflect fewer content divisions than the original translation, but the spacing systems themselves are more or less identical.

• P.Chester Beatty VI (963) of Numbers and Deuteronomy (end of 2 CE or early 3 CE): some open and closed sections.

• P.Scheide + P.Chester Beatty IX (967) of Ezekiel (early 3 CE): open and closed sections designated by spaces filled with two small oblique strokes or dots (except for the open section in XL 41 at the separation between chapters 39 and 37, in that sequence). The original scribe probably inserted the signs himself (e.g. XXXIX 11 [before Ezek 20:1]; XLIV 24 [Ezek 21:8]; see Johnson, *Scheide*, 13). As a rule, these signs reflect the division of MT, with differences regarding the distinction between open and closed sections. *Ekthesis* is employed at the beginning of some sections (e.g. XLIV 11 [Ezek 21:6]; XLIX 3 [Ezek 22:23]; LV 32 [Ezek 25:1]), but is usually unrelated to these sections.[202]

• P.Oxy. 65.4442 of Exodus 20 (early 3 CE): a closed section after 20:21 with dicolon.

• P.Chester Beatty X (967) of Daniel (early 3 CE): rarely, e.g. a closed section in Dan 4:34 and an open section after 3:24; 7:24.

• P.Oxy. 7.1007 (leather) of Genesis 2–3 (3 CE): a closed section after Gen 1:25.

---

[201] Data concerning the late manuscripts have been provided in the writings of the so-called Kampen school of 'delimitation criticism' as represented by Korpel–de Moor, *Structure* and Korpel–Oesch, *Delimitation Criticism*. See especially W. M. de Bruin, "Interpreting Delimiters—The Complexity of Text Delimitation in Four Major Septuagint Manuscripts," *Studies in Scriptural Unit Division* (ed. M. C. A. Korpel and J. M. Oesch; Pericope 3; Assen 2002) 66–89.

[202] For an analysis, see J. W. Olley, "Paragraphing in the Greek Text of Ezekiel in Pap^967—With Particular Reference to the Cologne Portion," in *Studies in Scriptural Unit Division* (see n. 201) 202–25.

- P.Berlin 17213 of Genesis19 (3 CE): a closed section after 19:18.
- P.Rendel Harris 166 of Exodus 22–23 (3 CE): open and closed sections (after 22:26; 23:14a [?], 15).
- Pap. W (Freer) of the Minor Prophets (3 CE): closed sections with occasional dicola.
- P.Berlin 11778 (BKT 8.17) of Job 33–34 (3 CE): open section + median dot after 33:24.
- P.Chester Beatty V (962) of Genesis (second half of 3 CE): closed sections after Gen 34:60, 61; 35:3.
- P.Alex. 203 of Isaiah 48 (3–4 CE): empty line after 48:11.
- P.Chester Beatty IV (961) of Genesis (4 CE): closed sections with some *paragraphoi*, after Gen 14:24; 18:23; 20:18; 28:22; 34:21; 35:12; 36:10; 41:52.
- P.Genève Gr. 252 of Jeremiah 5–6 (4 CE): an open section after 5:32.

Stage 3. Large sense divisions (as opposed to small units similar to verses and half-verses) were not indicated at all in many sources. For details, see the fourth column in the table in APPENDIX 5.

While the original Greek practices were probably identical to those of the Hebrew manuscripts, there are many differences in details with regard to the indication of specific section units. These details need to be examined in the aforementioned sources as well as the later manuscripts, since the editions of the LXX are imprecise in this regard. These editions reflect a variety of manuscripts, as demonstrated in detail by Barthélemy, *Critique textuelle 1992*, cxvii–cxxiv in his critique of the Göttingen editions.[203]

For a brief description of the systems used in the uncial manuscripts and editions of the LXX, see R. Devreesse, *Introduction à l'étude des manuscrits grecs* (Paris 1954) 139–44. For a description of the internal differences between manuscripts A, B, and S in Isaiah, see J. W. Olley, "Texts Have Paragraphs Too: A Plea for Inclusion in Critical Editions," *Textus* 19 (1998) 111–25; Korpel–de Moor, *Structure*. The latter study denotes in detail the differences among the various ancient witnesses in the paragraph structure of Isaiah 40–55 (including the Qumran material), for the LXX on the basis of the uncials A, B, and S. The textual apparatuses of modern critical editions and critical commentaries neither record these data for the ancient versions, nor for the Qumran scrolls, while the latter are recorded in the HUBP edition.

While the systems used for the indication of sense divisions in the manuscripts of the Greek versions ultimately go back to Hebrew manuscripts, two additional types of indications were indigenously Greek, viz., *paragraphoi* and *ekthesis*.

Several Greek manuscripts indicated new sections with *paragraphoi* in addition to spacing (for details, see column 5 in the table in APPENDIX 5), just like several of the Qumran Hebrew texts. Since these *paragraphoi* were often indicated by users or later scribes, they do not necessarily reflect the practices of the first transcribers.

Some manuscripts denoted new sections with an enlarged initial Greek letter protruding into the margin (*ekthesis*). For a description of the procedure and parallels in secular Greek literature, see Roberts, *Manuscript*, 16–18. The number of sources using *ekthesis* is small, and no pattern, such as frequent occurrence in a certain type of text or period, is detectable:

- 8ḤevXIIgr hands A and B (end of 1 BCE)
- P.Oxy. 65.4443 of Esther Add. E and ch. 9 (late 1 or early 2 CE)
- P.Scheide + P.Chester Beatty IX (967) of Ezekiel (beginning of 3 CE) rarely, and usually not related to the beginning of new sections
- P.Chester Beatty V (962) of Genesis (second half of 3 CE), rarely
- P.Oxy. 11.1351 of Leviticus 27 (4 CE; leather)
- Codex St. Cath. of Genesis 27–28 (4 CE), protruding as much as 3–4 letter-spaces into the margin
- P.Damasc. VII of Canticles 2, 5 (4–5 CE)

It is unclear which system was used in the earliest manuscripts of the *Peshitta* (S), since the oldest known manuscripts did not use any spacing system at all. The break between units was indicated by a combination of 4–5 dots arranged in a diamond shape, without any differentiation between content

---

[203]For a different view of these editions, see P. Harlé and D. Pralon, *La Bible d'Alexandrie, Le Lévitique* (Paris 1988) 16–24.

divisions of a higher or lower rank.[204] At a later stage, probably under the influence of Greek tradition, a single dot (*pasoqah*) was also employed. According to Brock, "Text History," 67 there is a certain degree of agreement in detail between the ancient traditions (MT, 1QIsa[a], and S), but that agreement should not be over-emphasized in view of the differences between these sources. The relations between the three sources are tabulated in Korpel–de Moor, *Structure*, 649–55 for Isaiah 40–55. A more recent study by Jenner illustrates the different paragraphing markers used in Syriac manuscripts and describes the systems used in greater detail than earlier studies.[205] During the course of the transmission of S, the manuscripts drifted away in different directions, and the transmission of the section divisions became imprecise (de Moor, "Unit Division" [n. 204] 246–7). Because of the late date of the witnesses of S, this source is not examined in detail for the present monograph.

11QtgJob has several open sections, e.g. after Job 40:5 (XXXIV 1), before 42:1 (XXXVII 2), but no closed sections at all. It also has completely empty lines (e.g. III 2 before 20:1; X 7 before 27:1).

The system of SP differs again from the practices mentioned above, but the exact nature of the evidence of that version still needs to be examined on the basis of manuscripts and it is unclear which manuscript(s) better reflect(s) the earliest text forms. As with the systems used in the manuscripts of the ancient translations, the SP practice ultimately derived from that used in the Hebrew manuscripts described above.[206] The external form of the system used for sense division resembles system *c* of the Hebrew manuscripts, but the pause is equivalent with both the open and closed sections of the Hebrew and Greek manuscripts. In SP, this sense division takes the form of a completely empty line following a line ending with a graphic sign, a dicolon (:) in *Sefer Abisa*[c] and more elaborate forms in other manuscripts, such as —: , —·: and —:· . This sign always occurs at the end of the inscribed text, even if the text is very short, in which case the words are evenly spread out over the line in order to create a straight left margin.

While most Samaritan manuscripts did not distinguish between open and closed sections, some did. Thus, the fragment described by A. D. Crown, "An Unpublished Fragment of a Samaritan Torah Scroll," *BJRL* 64 (1982) 386–406 (especially 401) distinguished between a *qiṣṣah* representing an open section (leaving a completely empty line after the sign) and a *qiṣṣah* representing a closed section (leaving a half-line after the sign).

With regard to details, there are noticeable differences between SP on the one hand and the proto-Masoretic and medieval Masoretic manuscripts, as well as the non-Masoretic Qumran manuscripts on the other. SP has 20–25 percent more sense divisions than the medieval Masoretic manuscripts according to the statistics of Perrot, "*Petuhot et setumot*," 76–8, while in some individual books the differences are more pervasive (according to Oesch, *Petucha und Setuma*, 313, SP has 20–33 percent more sense divisions). For further details, see J. Bowman, "Samaritan Studies," *BJRL* 40 (1958) 298–327, especially 318–27. Because of the late date of the SP witnesses, this source also is not studied in detail for the present monograph although its proximity to the paragraph system of certain Qumran manuscripts (especially 4QpaleoGen-Exod[l]) has been noticed by Crown, "Samaritan Scribal Habits," 165–6.

(κ) *A common tradition of the sense divisions of the biblical manuscripts?*

The *systems* used for the division of the text into meaningful section units are similar in all ancient and medieval witnesses of Scripture, in Hebrew/Aramaic and in translation.

---

[204]See S. P. Brock, "Text History and Text Division in Peshiṭta Isaiah," in *The Peshitta: its Early Text and History: Papers Read at the Peshiṭta Symposium Held at Leiden 30–31 August 1985* (ed. P. B. Dirksen and M. J. Mulder; Leiden/New York 1988) 49–80; P. B. Dirksen and M. J. Mulder, *The Peshitta: Its Early Text and History* (Leiden 1988) 65–78; K. D. Jenner, "A Review of the Methods by Which Syriac Biblical and Related Manuscripts Have Been Described and Analysed: Some Preliminary Remarks," *Aram* 5 (1993) 255–66; Korpel–de Moor, *Structure*, 6–9; J. C. de Moor, "Unit Division in the Peshitta of Micah," *Journal for the Aramaic Bible* 1 (1999) 225–47.

[205]K. D. Jenner, "The Unit Delimitation in the Syriac Text of Daniel and its Consequences for the Interpretation," in Korpel–Oesch, *Delimitation Criticism*, 105–29.

[206]M. Gaster, "The Biblical Lessons: A Chapter on Biblical Archaeology," *Studies and Texts* I (London 1925–28; reprint: New York 1973) 503–600, especially 515–24, first drew attention to the similarity between the Masoretic and Samaritan traditions. The detailed study by Crown, "Samaritan Scribal Habits" likewise suggests that the system of SP 'arises from the same scribal traditions as produced the MT.

[207]Indirect evidence for the joining of books is further available for Mur 1, probably containing Genesis, Exodus, and Numbers (see *DJD* III, 75–8 and pls. XIX–XXI), 4QExod-Lev[f], and 4QLev-Num[a]. However, in none of these texts has the actual join between the books been preserved.

There is also a large degree of agreement in matters of detail. At the same time, there are many differences among the Hebrew manuscripts, as described above, and also between these manuscripts and the versional evidence. Since the translations were made from Hebrew manuscripts, the assumption of some form of common tradition is possible, but that common tradition would have to be defined with constant reference to the internal differences between the ancient Hebrew manuscripts. The fact that many manuscripts derive from the Middle Ages prevents a sound analysis, but nevertheless Korpel–de Moor, *Structure*, 646–53 assume a 'very ancient common tradition' (p. 646) for all the sources analyzed by them for Isaiah 40–55. Likewise, Oesch, *Petucha und Setuma*, 313 assumes a common tradition for the MT and SP.

(4) *Division between poetical units (Psalms)*

In the analysis of the different types of spacing between poetical units, individual Psalms comprise special entities in that they are smaller than books and larger than verses. Each Psalm forms a separate section-like unit, the beginning and end of which are usually clearly denoted at the content level, not only in biblical Psalms, but also in other poetical units from Qumran, namely 4QNon-Canonical Psalms A–B (4Q380–381), 1–4QHodayot, and 4QBarkhi Nafshi. In the analysis of the layout of the biblical Psalms from Qumran, four different methods for indicating the beginnings are recognized, described as five systems by G. H. Wilson, *The Editing of the Hebrew Psalter* (SBLDS 76; Chico, Calif. 1985) 93–138. The indication of the Psalms and of the individual *Hodayot* basically corresponds with the systems of open and closed sections described in section 3 (for the various manuscripts of 4QBarkhi Nafshi insufficient data are available). Several manuscripts are inconsistent in their indication of new psalms (see below). It is unclear why different systems for the indication of new Psalms are used in the same manuscript by the same scribal hand. Content considerations, stichographic systems, or headers do not seem to have played a part, and in any event it appears that the scribal traditions had not yet been stabilized. It is noteworthy that the two late Psalm scrolls, MasPs[a] and 5/6HevPs, are consistently written in system γ.

α. An open section at the end of a Psalm, while the following text starts at the beginning of a new line.

xxxxxxxxxxxxxxxxxxxxxxxxxxxxxxxxxxxxxxxxxxxxxxxxxx
xxxxxxxxxxxxxxxxxxxxxxxxxxxxxxxxxxxxx
xxxxxxxxxxxxxxxxxxxxxxxxxxxxxxxxxxxxxxxxxxxxxxxxxx

This system is used in many Qumran manuscripts of the book of Psalms and of other hymnic collections: 4QPs[a] (before Psalms 35, 36, 67); 4QPs[c] (before Psalms 51 and 53); 4QPs[d] (before Psalm 104); 4QPs[e] (before Psalms 77, 104, 116, 130, 146); most of the Psalms in 11QPs[a] (before Psalms 103 [frg. C II 11–12], 148 (II 5–6], 123 [III 14–15], 125 [IV 2–3], 127 [IV 15–16], 129 [V 3–4], 119 [VI 10–11], 136 [XV 5–6], 137 [XX 16–17], in this sequence; Psalm 105 (E iii 8); 11QPs[c] (before Psalms 13, 14 [frg. 4–7 6, 11], 18 [frg. 8 8]). See further: 1QH[a] II (Suk. = Puech X) 32; VIII (XVI) 4; 4QH[a] (4Q427) 3 3; 8 ii 10; 4QNon-Canonical Psalms B (4Q381) 24 3; 31 4.

β. An indentation indicates the new Psalm, while the previous one ended either at the end of the previous line or toward the end of that line.

xxxxxxxxxxxxxxxxxxxxxxxxxxxxxxxxxxxxxxxxxxxxxxxxxx
xxxxxxxxxxxxxxxxxxxxxxxxxxxxxxxxxxx
xxxxxxxxxxxxxxxxxxxxxxxxxxxxxxxxxxxxxxxxxxxxxxxxxx

or

```
xxxxxxxxxxxxxxxxxxxxxxxxxxxxxxxxxxxxxxxxxxxxx
xxxxxxxxxxxxxxxxxxxxxxxxxxxxxxxxx
xxxxxxxxxxxxxxxxxxxxxxxxxxxxxxxxxxxxxxxxxxxxx
```

This system is employed in 4QPs^c (before Psalm 28 [6 4]); 4QPs^d (before Psalm 147 [reconstructed]); 4QPs^q (before Psalm 33); 4QPs^s (before Psalm 6 [reconstructed]); 11QPs^a (before Psalms 122 [III 7]; 126 [IV 9]; 145 [XVI 7]; 143 [XXV 6]; 150 [XXVI 4]; 140 [XXVII 12]); 11QPs^b (before Psalm 144 [7 6]); 11QPs^d (before Psalm 37 [5 2]). See further: 1QH^a II (Suk. = Puech X) 20; III (XI) 19; VII (XV) 6; 4QH^b (4Q428) 10 11.

γ. A completely blank line separates the new Psalm from the previous one which terminates at the end of a line or toward the end of that line (illustr. 5a).

```
xxxxxxxxxxxxxxxxxxxxxxxxxxxxxxxxxxxxxxxxxxxxx
xxxxxxxxxxxxxxxxxxxxxxxxxxxxxxxxxxxxx

xxxxxxxxxxxxxxxxxxxxxxxxxxxxxxxxxxxxxxxxxxxxx
```

or

```
xxxxxxxxxxxxxxxxxxxxxxxxxxxxxxxxxxxxxxxxxxxxx
xxxxxxxxxxxxxxxxxxxxxxxxxxxxxxxxxxxxxxxxxxxxx

xxxxxxxxxxxxxxxxxxxxxxxxxxxxxxxxxxxxxxxxxxxxx
```

This system is used in 4QPs^a (before Psalms 6, 35, 54, 63); 4QPs^b (before Psalms 103 [XXII 9] and 118 [XXXIV 6]); 11QPs^a (before Psalms 135 [XIV 7], 145 [XVI 7], 151A [XXVIII 3]); 11QPs^b (before Psalm 78 [1 3]); MasPs^a (before Psalms 82–85; illustr. 5a); 5/6ḤevPs (before Psalms 8, 10, 11, 13, 17, 24). See further: 1QH^a V (Suk. = Puech XIII) 21; IX (XVII) 37; 4QNon-Canonical Psalms A (4Q380) 1 ii 7; 4QNon-Canonical Psalms B (4Q381) 33 6–7 (see the discussion of E. Schuller, *DJD* XI, 88).

δ. A closed section in the middle of the line.

```
xxxxxxxxxxxxxxxx        xxxxxxxxxxxxxxxxxxxxxxx
xxxxxxxxxxxxxxxxxxxxxxxxxxxxxxxxxxxxxxxxxxxxx
```

This system is used only in 4QPs^a (before Psalm 71); 4QPs^c (before Psalm 28); 4QPs^e (before Psalm 126); 4QPs^q (before Psalm 33); 11QPs^a (before Psalm 138 [XXI 1] and the Apostrophe to Zion [XXII 1]). It is not impossible that this system reflects a content division of a lower hierarchy than those preceding.

The above analysis shows that Psalm scrolls often use several systems for separating between Psalms:

4QPs^a	(systems α, γ, δ)
4QPs^c	(systems α, β, δ)
4QPs^d	(systems α, β)
4QPs^e	(systems α, δ)
1QH^a	(systems α, β, γ)
11QPs^a	(systems α, β, γ, δ)
11QPs^b	(systems β, γ)
4QNon-Canonical Psalms B (4Q381; systems α, γ)	

Stanzas are rarely indicated in the Psalters. In Psalm 119, 4QPs^g (illustr. 17a) and 11QPs^a insert a blank line after each eight-line stanza, while 1QPs^a and 5QPs do not leave such extra lines, and in 4QPs^h (illustr. 19) a *paragraphos* sign is used (frgs. 1–2 16, after Ps 119:16).

Probably similar divisions were already indicated in the earliest Psalter scrolls. If these early scrolls contained section divisions (thus § 3η), they probably also somehow separated between individual Psalms.

(5) *Division between books in biblical manuscripts*

In scrolls containing more than one biblical book, spaces were left between successive books.[207]

Torah

In scrolls containing more than one book of the Torah, all but the first books usually started in the middle of a column after several blank lines, as is evident from 4QGen-Exod[a], 4Q[Gen-]Exod[b], 4QpaleoGen-Exod[l], and 4QRP[c] (4Q365). Irrelevant are 4QLev[c], which commences at the top of a column and 11QpaleoLev[a] ending in the middle of a column, and *not* followed by Numbers; both scrolls probably contained a single biblical book only.[208]

4QGen-Exod[a]: In this scroll (MT), Exodus begins more than halfway down the column. Spacing between the books or joined Genesis–Exodus fragments have not been preserved.

4QpaleoGen-Exod[l]: three blank lines were left in the middle of the column between what appears to be the last line of Genesis and the beginning of Exodus in this scroll (MT), preceded by at least one sheet of written text.

4Q[Gen-]Exod[b]: In this scroll (probably independent character), Exodus starts in the middle of a column, preceded by at least two blank lines and probably also by Genesis.

4QRP[c] (4Q365): the first verse of Numbers is preceded by what is probably a paraphrastic version of the last verse of Leviticus (26, a–b), followed by an empty line. This is *not* a biblical manuscript.

Minor Prophets

4QXII[b] 3 5: one line is left between Zephaniah and Haggai.

4QXII[g] 70–75: one-and-a-half lines were left between Amos and Obadiah, and in frgs. 76–81 there is at least one line before Jonah.

MurXII: a space of three lines was left between various books as evidenced by the transition between Jonah and Micah, Micah and Nahum, and Zephaniah and Haggai (*DJD* III, 182, 192, 197, 200, 202, 205 and pls. LXI, LXVI, LXIX, LXXI, LXXII).

Five Scrolls

While most Qumran copies of the Five Scrolls were probably contained in separate scrolls, indirect evidence indicates that 4QLam may have contained all five *Megillot* or at least one additional book beyond Lamentations; see ch. 4, TABLE 10.

Some scrolls are more in agreement with the instructions in rabbinic literature than others, but it should be remembered that most scrolls found in the Judean Desert did not derive from the circles that later were to formulate rabbinic literature. See *b. B. Bat.* 13b:

בין חומש לחומש של תורה ארבעה שיטין וכן בין כל נביא לנביא ובנביא של שנים עשר ג' שיטין

Between each book of the Torah there should be left a space of four lines, and so between one Prophet and the next. In the Twelve Minor Prophets, however, the space should only be three lines.

For similar statements, see *Sof.* 2.4. A slightly different instruction is given in *y. Meg.* 1.71d:

וצריך שיהא גומר באמצע הדף ומתחיל באמצעיתו ובנביא גומר בסופו ומתחיל בראשו ובנביא של שנים עשר אסור

\<In the Torah\> one has to finish in the middle of a page and to commence in the middle of the \<same\> page. In the Prophets one finishes at the end and begins at the top of a page, but in the Dodekapropheton this is forbidden.

---

[208]According to Milik, *Enoch*, 143, the scribes of 4QEn[a] ar (4Q201) and other Qumran texts left half-blank pages in the first column for easy handling. This is not confirmed, however, for 4QEn[a] ar, where such spacing is not evidenced, while the list of the 'other texts' has not been supplied. Examples such as those listed here (books that form part of a multi-book composition) would not be valid examples for this description. See ch. *4g* above.

The following differences between the Judean Desert scrolls and the rabbinic instructions are noticeable: In 4QpaleoGen-Exod[l], three lines are left as opposed to the four lines prescribed by *b. B. Bat.* 13b. Between the books in 4QXII[b] and 4QXII[b] less space is left than prescribed by *b. B. Bat.* 13b for the Minor Prophets (three lines). On the other hand, these instructions are exactly followed in MurXII.

In 8ḤevXIIgr (end of 1 BCE), an early Jewish revision of Greek Scripture, six lines were left in the middle of the column between Jonah and Micah (cf. *DJD* VIII, 33 and pl. IV).

Manuscripts of SP often ended biblical books one-third of the way down a column, leaving two-thirds empty before the start of the next book or at the end of the manuscript. This practice sometimes implied excessive spacing in the first lines of a column in order to reach that point, such as, e.g. in the MS Jew. Nat. and Univ. Libr. Sam. 2°2, Cambr. Add. MS 1846, Topkapi Mus G i 101 (Crown, *Dated Samaritan MSS*).

b. *Special layout and superscriptions of poetical units*

While many of the poetry texts in the Bible are written as running texts in the medieval copies of MT, medieval manuscripts presented the אמ"ת books (Job, Proverbs, and Psalms), some songs of the Torah, the song of Deborah, and the acrostic in Lamentations, as poetry. The manuscripts differ among themselves with regard to the systems of presenting the text, and these differences were multiplied in modern editions. Thus the editions of Letteris (in most of its printings) and Cassuto present the אמ"ת books as poetry, while several of the printings of the Letteris edition present only the book of Psalms as poetry. The layouts of the poems in the medieval manuscripts and printed editions, as well as their relationship to statements in rabbinic literature, were analyzed in detail by M. Breuer, *The Aleppo Codex and the Accepted Text of the Bible* (Heb. with Eng. summ.; Jerusalem 1976) 149–89.

These traditions as well as additional systems of layout of poetical segments were reflected already in some texts from the Judean Desert, while other ancient texts containing poetical segments were written in prose. The practice of a stichographic[209] representation was developed for the books written in a system of strict *parallelismus membrorum*, which therefore could easily be represented stichographically. This pertains also to most Songs in the Torah. Other poetical books, such as the Major Prophets, likewise reflect such *parallelismus*, but not in all chapters, and probably for this reason no stichographic writing tradition has been developed for them. As a result, most poetical books are not represented in stichographic writing.

The stichographic arrangements of poetical texts reflect a certain understanding by their scribes of the poetical structure, while it is unclear to what extent these layouts reflect the original intention of the poets behind the texts. Only in a few instances, and probably at a later period,[210] do these stichographic layouts merely serve a decorative purpose.

The background of the stichographic presentation of some poetical texts is unclear. The special writing of Psalms as poetry could have been related to liturgical chanting, but on the other hand a Psalms scroll such as 11QPs[a] which probably does represent a liturgical collection is not written in this fashion. Furthermore, the stichographic representation of Job, Proverbs, Lamentations, and Ben Sira is not consonant with a

---

[209]The term is used in the discussion by J. Kugel, *The Idea of Biblical Poetry: Parallelism and its History* (New Haven/London 1981) 119–27.

[210]Reference is made to the Samaritan scribal habits and the Masoretic system of writing a 'half-brick over a whole brick and a whole brick over a half-brick' to be mentioned below. For a different view, stressing the decorative function of stichographic writing also for the Qumran documents, see Kugel, *The Idea of Biblical Poetry*, 121.

possible liturgical background (thus also Oesch, *Petucha und Setuma*, 334). Therefore, the stichographic representation of specific texts probably mainly reflects a recognition of the poetical nature of these units. The fact that for almost every occurrence of a stichographic arrangement there are other scrolls displaying the same composition in prose shows that the tradition of stichographic writing was not fixed or that different traditions were in vogue during different periods (see below).

In the Judean Desert texts, a special arrangement of poetical units is known almost exclusively for biblical texts (including Ben Sira [2QSir and MasSir]), but not for any of the nonbiblical poetical compositions from the Judean Desert, such as 4QNon-Canonical Psalms A, B (4Q380, 4Q381), the *Hodayot* from caves 1 (1QH[a,b]) and 4 (4QH[a–f]), 4QBarkhi Nafshi[a–e], 4QShirShabb[a–f], 4QSelf-Glorification Hymn (4Q471b; 4QM[a] [4Q491] 11 [4Q491c]), and the various sapiential compositions (mainly 4Q415–426).[211] The fact that the song in Exodus 15 in 4QRP[c] (4Q365) 6a ii and 6c, a 'rewritten Bible' composition, is written in a special layout may imply that its scribe considered this composition a biblical text. So far, the only known exception is the nonbiblical 4QMessianic Apocalypse (4Q521) 2 ii written in the most simple stichographic layout (system *1b* below). That Ben Sira was included in this group probably implies that this book was considered to be biblical, not necessarily by the Qumran community, but by the scribes of 2QSir and MasSir. Of the medieval Ben Sira scrolls, MS B was written stichographically, while MSS A, C, D, E, and F were not.

Likewise, the poetical segments in the following early *Greek* biblical texts were written stichographically: P.Fouad 266b (848) of Deuteronomy 32 (middle of 1 BCE); P.Antinoopolis 8 of Proverbs 5–20 (3 CE); P.Chester Beatty XI of Sirach (3 CE); as well as most of the manuscripts of Psalms listed in APPENDIX 5.

Within Hebrew Scripture, this stichographic layout is evidenced for the Qumran texts of two poems in the Torah (Exodus 15; Deuteronomy 32), and of Psalms (especially Psalm 119), Proverbs, Lamentations, and Job. All biblical units for which special stichographic arrangements are preserved among the Qumran texts, have also been preserved in Qumran copies which do not display any special arrangement.

No such arrangement is evidenced in any of the Judean Desert texts for the following poetical units in Scripture:

- Genesis 49 as preserved in the fragmentary 4QGen-Exod[a] and 4QGen[e] (nor in MT).
- The poetical portions of Numbers 23–24 in 4QNum[b]. These sections are not arranged stichographically in MT, but they are in SP.
- Deuteronomy 33 in 1QDeut[b], 4QDeut[c], 4QDeut[h], 4QDeut[l], 4QpaleoDeut[r] (Deuteronomy 32 is arranged stichographically in this scroll), and MasDeut. This poem is not arranged stichographically in either MT or in SP.
- The Song of Hannah in 1 Samuel 2 in 4QSam[a]. This poem is not arranged stichographically in MT.
- 2 Samuel 22 in 4QSam[a] (22:11, 13, 17-20, 24-28, 30-51 are preserved), while MT does have a special arrangement (cf. *Sof.* 12.10).

Although two scrolls of Exodus, one of Deuteronomy, many Psalms scrolls, and copies of Lamentations and Job are written *without* any special arrangement (TABLE 9), thirty texts containing poetical units from the Judean Desert are written completely or partially

---

[211]The layout of 1Q38 is unclear: the editors of this 'composition hymnique,' D. Barthélemy and J. T. Milik, presented this fragmentary text as reflecting two columns of hemistichs of a stichographically arranged text, separated by spaces. However, the spaces are large, and it is more likely that the fragment presents remnants of two columns of an otherwise unknown text. Furthermore, our list does not include 4QBeatitudes (4Q525) col. II which appears to be written in a stichographic arrangement, but the scribe of this text left irregular spaces in the lines, at different places, after each אשרי statement.

in one of the forms of stichographic writing. In three cases (Deuteronomy 32, Psalms, and Proverbs) they have different layouts (TABLE 8). These layouts are based on aesthetic or exegetical traditions, which sometimes differ from those of the Masoretes and the early versions. A similar understanding underlies the indication of small spaces after each of the stichs in the running text of Isa 61:10–62:9 in 1QIsa[a] (§ a2 above).

TABLES 8 and 9 include the dates assigned to the scrolls as a possible clue for understanding the differentiation between scrolls written in a special layout and those not written in such a layout (see the discussion below).[212]

TABLE 8: *Manuscripts of Poetical Texts Displaying a Stichographic Layout*

4QRP[c] (4Q365) 6b 1–4 (Exodus 15, including the verse after the Song, Exod 15:19, and also a poetical unit not contained in the biblical text, probably representing the Song of Miriam; 40–10 BCE)

1QDeut[b] (Deuteronomy 32; the other chapters are in prose; no date)

4QDeut[b] (Deuteronomy 32; the other chapters were in prose; 150–100 BCE)

4QDeut[c] (reconstructed layout; only in Deuteronomy 32; 150–100 BCE)

4QDeut[q] (Deuteronomy 32; this scroll probably contained only that poem; 50 BCE–10 CE)

4QpaleoDeut[r] (Deuteronomy 32; the other chapters are in prose; 100–25 BCE)

1QPs[a] (only Psalm 119, the other Psalms are in prose; not dated)

4QPs[b] (Psalms 91–118; 30–68 CE)

4QPs[c] (Psalms 16–53; 50–68 CE)

4QPs[d] (parts of Psalm 104; other parts of that Psalm and of Ps 106 [?] and 147 are in prose; 100–30 BCE)

4QPs[g] (Psalm 119; no other Psalms preserved; *c.* 50 CE)

4QPs[h] (Psalm 119; no other Psalms preserved; 30 BCE–70 CE)

4QPs[l] (only Psalm 104; no other Psalms preserved; 50–1 BCE)

4QPs[w] (Psalm 112; no other Psalms preserved; 125–75 BCE)

5QPs (Psalm 119; no other Psalms preserved; 1–100 CE)

8QPs (Psalms 17–18; no other Psalms preserved; 1–100 CE)

11QPs[a] (Psalm 119; the other Psalms are in prose; 1–50 CE)

11QPs[b] (Psalm 119; the other Psalms are in prose; 30–1 BCE)

5/6HevPs (Psalms 7–16, 18, 22–25, 29–31; 50–68 CE)

MasPs[a] (Psalms 81–85; 30–1 BCE)

MasPs[b] (Psalm 147; 50–25 BCE)

4QJob[a] (chapters 31–37; 100–50 BCE)

4QpaleoJob[c] (probably; chapters 13, 14; 225–150 BCE)

4QProv[a] (chapters 1–2; 50 BCE–30 CE)

4QProv[b] (chapters 9, 13–15; 30 BCE–50 CE)

3QLam (ch. 3; 30 BCE–68 CE)

5QLam[b] (ch. 4; 50 CE)

2QSir (ch. 6; 50–1 BCE)

MasSir (chapters 39–44; 10 BCE–50 CE)

4QMessianic Apocalypse (4Q521) 2 ii (125–75 BCE)

Not all the Qumran biblical scrolls were written in stichographic writing in units which were arranged in a special (poetical) layout in other Qumran scrolls. The greatest amount of information is available for the Psalms scrolls for which more scrolls are known without any such arrangement. TABLE 9 lists twenty-seven texts (twenty Psalms scrolls and seven other texts) written without any stichographic layout as running texts, while four other texts (1QPs[a], 4QPs[d], 11QPs[a], 11QPs[b]) contain both prose and

---

[212]The data are culled from the summary list of Webster, "Chronological Index."

stichographic sections, and eleven Psalms scrolls listed in TABLE 8 present a full stichographic arrangement.

TABLE 9: *Manuscripts of Poetical Texts Not Displaying a Stichographic Layout*[213]

4QExod[c] in Exodus 15 (50–25 BCE)
4QExod[d] in Exodus 15 (225–175 BCE)
4QDeut[j] XII (Deuteronomy 32; see J. A. Duncan, *DJD* XIV, 90; 50 CE)
1QPs[a] (all Psalms excluding Psalm 119 which is written in a special layout; no date)
1QPs[b] (no date)
1QPs[c] (no date)
3QPs (only Psalm 2 is preserved; 1–100 CE)
4QPs[a] (150 BCE)
4QPs[d] (from col. III 5 onwards; 100–30 BCE)
4QPs[e] (30–68 CE)
4QPs[f] (50–68 CE)
4QPs[j] (50 CE)
4QPs[k] (100–30 BCE)
4QPs[m] (30–1 BCE)
4QPs[n] (30–1 BCE)
4QPs[o] (30–1 BCE)
4QPs[p] (probably; 30 BCE–68 CE)
4QPs[q] (30 BCE–30 CE)
4QPs[r] (30 BCE–68 CE)
4QPs[s] (50–68 CE)
4QPs[u] (probably; 50 CE)
4Q522 (Psalm 122) 22–24; see É. Puech, *DJD* XXV and *DJD* XVI, 169–70 (65–30 BCE)
6QpapPs? (probably; 50 CE)
11QPs[a] (all Psalms excluding Psalm 119 which is written in a special layout; 1–50 CE)
11QPs[b] (all Psalms excluding Psalm 119 which is written in a special layout; 30–1 BCE)
11QPs[c] (1–50 CE)
11QPs[d] (30–68 CE)
2QJob (30 BCE–68 CE)
4QJob[b] (50–1 BCE)
4QLam (30–1 BCE)
5QLam[a] (50 CE)

11QapocrPs (11Q11; nonbiblical composition; 50–70 CE)

It is difficult to ascertain whether there is any pattern behind the different ways of presenting the text of poetical units, with or without a stichographic arrangement. The problem is most acute in the Psalms scrolls since they are the largest component in the lists in TABLES 8 and 9. It cannot be determined whether the different background of the biblical texts as reflected in their textual character determined the use or non-use of stichographic systems (see the diffusion of the stichographic systems represented in the chart in APPENDIX 8). There is also no clear chronological distinction between the different types of arrangement (see the dates provided in TABLES 8 and 9), although among the texts presented in TABLE 8 there are more early scrolls than among the texts

---

[213]The graphical arrangement of 4Qapocryphal Psalm and Prayer (4Q448) contains a mixture of layouts. The psalm in col. A is written as prose, while the first column of the prayer, col. B, contains very narrow lines which do not comprise sense units. The small fragment preserves three columns of which col. A is the uppermost writing block preceded by a large indentation, while cols. B and C are written below col. A, although col. B protrudes considerably to the right because of the large indentation of col. A.

recorded in TABLE 9 (see, however, 4QExod[d]). This observation could lead to the view that at the outset a stichographic arrangement was the rule, and that subsequently this layout was often abandoned. This assumption could tally with the general rule in the somewhat later rabbinic literature of presenting only a few units in this way: the lists of the kings of Canaan (Josh 12:9-24) and the sons of Haman (Esth 9:6-9) as well as three Songs (Exod 15:1-18, Deuteronomy 32, and Judg 5:2-30) in the prose books of the Bible, but not the Psalms (see below).

The distinction between the stichographically written poetical units and the poetical units written as prose is unclear, and possibly we need to approach the issue from a different angle. Since the special layout of poetical units among the Judean Desert texts occurs almost exclusively in biblical texts, it would be natural to assume that the texts which do *not* reflect such a layout, especially the Psalms scrolls, are not Scripture in the regular sense of the word. Rather, they served another purpose, such as that of a liturgical collection. This suggestion was raised hesitantly by Oesch, "Textgliederung," 317 who suggested that the parameters of the graphic presentation of the Qumran texts were determined by the purpose for which the compositions were written.

However, it is unclear whether this claim can be made for all the Psalm scrolls mentioned above. If the prose arrangement of the biblical Psalms in Psalms scrolls together with liturgical additions in some collections (especially 11QPs[a]) is an indication of their use in religious gatherings, several such collections are indeed fully or partly arranged stichographically (TABLE 8), but others are not (TABLE 9).

Consequently, it is possible that a reverse logic should be applied. Since Psalm 119 is always arranged stichographically and is part of the later Jewish liturgy, it is possible that stichographic writing was reserved for liturgical use. Indeed, Psalms 119 and 104, either when presented separately (4QPs[g], 4QPs[h], 4QPs[l] [Psalm 104], 5QPs) or together with other Psalms (1QPs[a], 4QPs[d], 11QPs[a], 11QPs[b]) are always written stichographically. The same argument may be used with regard to the two poems in the Torah (Exodus 15; Deuteronomy 32) as well as Lamentations, but not to Proverbs, Job, and Sirach which are also presented stichographically.

In the wake of the above analysis, it is difficult to discern under which circumstances stichographic systems were used. In order to enable further analysis of this issue, the relevant scrolls are indicated in APPENDIX 8 as either representing a stichographic system ('[s]') or not ('[n]').

It is difficult to know to what extent the choice of the presentation system was determined by the personal preference of scribes. Since these texts derived from different circles, possibly the various ways of presenting poetical units do not reflect differences between individual scribes, but rather between the scribal traditions within which scribes operated. In any event, at least for Psalm 119 a special layout was used consistently. That acrostic Psalm was written as poetry with two hemistichs per line separated by spaces (1QPs[a], 5QPs, 11QPs[b]) or without such spaces (4QPs[g], 4QPs[h], 11QPs[a]; illustr. 17a), and all the lines of a stanza started with the same letter. This pertains also to the acrostics in 3QLam (ch. 3) and 5QLam[b] (ch. 4). At the same time, the acrostic Psalm 25 in 5/6XḤevPs XII had two letters of the alphabet per line.[214]

---

[214]Likewise, the acrostic which was reconstructed by Eshel and Strugnell in 4QPs[f] IX–X did not start each line with a new letter of the alphabet: E. Eshel and J. Strugnell, "Alphabetical Acrostics in Pre-Tannaitic Times," *CBQ* 62 (2000) 441–58. For bibliography on acrostics and parallels in other literatures, see K. Seybold, "Akrostichie im Psalter," *ThZ* 57 (2001) 172–83.

Deuteronomy 32 was written once in prose (4QDeut^j) as well as in four or five different stichographic systems: one hemistich per line (most of 4QDeut^q and probably also 4QDeut^c), two hemistichs per line without spaces in the middle (4QDeut^b), two stichs per line separated by spaces between the stichs and hemistichs (1QDeut^b), and two hemistichs per line separated by spaces (4QpaleoDeut^r). The latter system was prescribed by rabbinic literature (see below) and was followed both in Masoretic and Samaritan manuscripts. 4QDeut^q actually presents a fifth system combining lines of single and two hemistichs (see below). As a result, if the first verse of this song is taken as an example, the main part of 4QDeut^q and probably 4QDeut^c were written in short lines such as

האזינו השמים ואדברה
ותשמע הארץ אמרי פי

while 4QDeut^b was written as

האזינו השמים ואדברה ותשמע הארץ אמרי פי

4QpaleoDeut^r as

האזינו השמים ואדברה ותשמע הארץ אמרי פי

and 1QDeut^b as

האזינו השמים ואדברה ותשמע הארץ אמרי פי יערף כמטר לקחי תזל כטל אמרתי

In the texts which are arranged in a special layout, *three main systems* are recognizable.

(1) *One or two hemistichs* (without spaces between them) are written per line, especially in Deuteronomy 32 and Psalm 119. The spaces at the ends of the lines indicate the ends of the poetical units.

(1a) *One hemistich per line* (illustr. 19)

האזינו השמים ואדברה
ותשמע הארץ אמרי פי

4QDeut^c (containing several segments of Deuteronomy), probably, in Deuteronomy 32 (reconstructed layout)

4QDeut^q (Deuteronomy 32 only). This text contains an unusual combination of lines with single hemistichs (I 1–4, 9–10 and all of col. II) and of two hemistichs per line (col. I 5–8, 11); in the latter case, it is unclear whether these hemistichs are separated by spaces. The writing of this text should be considered a variation of system *1a*

4QPs^b (I–XXXIII; illustr. 19); in cols. XXXIV–XXXV, system *1b* is used.

4QPs^d (from III 5 onwards: other sections are in prose; parts of Psalm 104; other parts of that Psalm and of Psalms 106 [?] and 147 are in prose)

4QPs^l (Psalm 104; no other Psalms preserved)

This system is also followed in the early Greek sources P.Fouad 266b (848) of Deuteronomy 32 (middle of 1 BCE; see the reconstruction in Dunand, *Papyrus grecs, Texte et planches*, 144), P.Antinoopolis 7 of Psalms (LXX: 81–82; 2 CE), and P.Antinoopolis 8 of Proverbs 5–20 and Sirach 45 (3 CE).

(1b) *Two hemistichs per line not separated by spaces* (illustr. 17a)

האזינו השמים ואדברה ותשמע הארץ אמרי פי

4QDeut^b (Deuteronomy 32; the remainder is in prose)

4QPs^b XXXIV–XXXV (in the preceding cols. system *1a* is used)

4QPs^g (Psalm 119; no other Psalms preserved; illustr. 17a)

4QPs^h (Psalm 119; no other Psalms preserved)

11QPs^a (Psalm 119; in a few instances a space separates the two hemistichs [VII 4; VIII 6; XI 7; XII 12]; the other Psalms are in prose)

4QJob^a (chapters 31–37)

4QpaleoJob^c (probably; chapters 13, 14)

5QLam^b (or system *1b*; ch. 4; only the beginnings of the lines have been preserved)

4QMessianic Apocalypse (4Q521) 2 ii, the only nonbiblical text in this group.

2QSir (ch. 6; possibly this text was written in system 2)

This group contains three copies of the acrostic Psalm 119 in which each line starts with the determining letter of the alphabet.

(2) *Two hemistichs or stichs per line separated by spacing*

The separation of stichs or hemistichs by spacing creates a layout which resembles the Masoretic system of a 'half-brick (אריח) on top of a half-brick (אריח),' and may well have been the basis for that arrangement (see below). The graphic arrangement more or less reflects the arrangement of parallel hemistichs and stichs; even when the poetical unit consists of three segments, the same graphic arrangement is presented.

(2a) *Two hemistichs per line separated by a space* (illustr. 5a)

The width of the space ranges usually from 0.5 to 1.0 cm, but with very long cola the space is minute; in MasPs^a (illustr. 5a) it varies from 0.5 to 2.2 cm.

------------------   ------------------

האזינו השמים ואדברה   ותשמע הארץ אמרי פי

4QpaleoDeut^r (Deuteronomy 32; the other chapters are in prose)

1QPs^a (Psalm 119; the other Psalms are in prose)

4QPs^c (Psalms 16–53; however, when the lines in the column are too short for the two hemistichs, the second hemistich continues on the next line [col. I 26–29; III 24–25, 26–27])

5QPs (Psalm 119; no other Psalms preserved)

8QPs (Psalms 17–18; no other Psalms preserved)

11QPs^b (Psalm 119; the other Psalms are in prose)

5/6ḤevPs (Psalms 7–16, 18, 22–25, 29–31)

MasPs^a (Psalms 81–85)

4QProv^a (chapters 1–2)

3QLam (ch. 3; three poetical units per line?)

5QLam^b (only the beginnings of the lines have been preserved; or system *1b*)

2QSir (ch. 6; thus the reconstruction in *DJD*. However, possibly this text was written in system *1b*)

MasSir (chapters 39–44)

In this system of presentation, the first hemistichs started from a straight right margin, usually indicated with a vertical dry line, while the second stichs began at a slightly different point on each line, since the first hemistichs were of a different length. Sometimes, however, an attempt was made to start also the second stich with a straight right margin (MasSir II–V). This bi-columnar arrangement is also represented in the Masoretic manuscripts of Deuteronomy 32 (see below) and SP in Exodus 15, the Balaam oracles in Numbers 23 and 24, and Deuteronomy 32.

If the preserved evidence of the scrolls from the Judean Desert does not mislead us, this system of presentation was the most frequently used when these scrolls were written. It is based on the principle of the *parallelismus membrorum*, with the two parallel stichs written next to each other, separated by a space. However, also when three-stich units do not reflect a parallel structure, the three stichs are nevertheless presented in a two-stich system in one-and-a-half lines (thus Ps 81:6, 8, 11 in MasPs^a). One notes that the stichographic arrangement of MasPs^a II 22–24 (Ps 83:9-11) goes against the meaning of the stichs themselves (cf. Talmon, *Masada VI*, 85).

This group contains three copies of the acrostic Psalm 119 in which each line starts with the determining letter of the alphabet.

(2b) *Two stichs per line with spaces between the stichs and hemistichs*

-------------	---------------	------------------	--------------------
חזל כטל אמרתי	יערף כמטר לקחי	ותשמע הארץ אמרי פי	האזינו השמים ואדברה

1QDeut[b] (Deuteronomy 32; the other chapters are in prose)

In the following manuscript, no information regarding the spacing is available:

4QPs[w] (Psalm 112; no other Psalms preserved)

(3) *Hemistichs or clusters of 2–3 words separated by spaces* (illustr. 5a)

Unlike in the first two systems, the spaces occur at different places in the line, in two different patterns.

4QRP[c] (4Q365) 6b 1–4 (Exodus 15)

```
[----------  ------------  ----------  -----------  -----]---
[----------  ----------------  ---]--------------  -----------
[----  ----------------  ----------]-------  -----------------
[----------------------------]  --------------  -----------
```

MasPs[b] II 16–23

```
          -----  -------------
[  ]----  ----------
[    ]  -------------
[     ]---------
[   vacat      ]-----
-----  -------------
[  ]----  ----------
------------  -----
```

4QProv[b] (chapters 9, 13–15; hemistichs)
MasPs[b] (Psalms 147, 150; hemistichs)
4QRP[c] (4Q365) 6b 1–4 (Exodus 15, including the verse after the Song, Exod 15:19 and also a poetical unit not contained in the biblical text, probably the Song of Miriam; illustr. 5a)

The stichographic layout of the writing was probably imbedded in the earliest biblical scrolls (thus already Oesch, *Petucha und Setuma*, 343, 364), as in the case of the division into section units. Supposedly this layout, in different systems, was inserted by the first scribes of these texts, and it reflected the intentions of the original authors. This assumption is partially based on parallels. Thus the scribal tradition of Aramaic texts of the fifth century BCE already shows a division into sense units, though in a different way (cf. § a). The oldest document in Hebrew or Aramaic showing a division into stichs is probably the four-line Carpentras funerary inscription in Aramaic from the fifth-fourth century BCE, containing lines of two hemistichs each without intervening spacing.[215] For much earlier evidence of stichographic notations, see the so-called vertical 'verse-divider' mark or other arrangements in Akkadian texts,[216] the 'verse-points' in Egyptian,[217] and infrequently occurring 'ruled' lines marking the natural divisions of the

---

[215] See *KAI*, 269 and Table XXXIV; J. C. L. Gibson, *Textbook of Syriac Semitic Inscriptions. Aramaic Inscriptions* (Oxford 1975) II.120–22.

[216] See Driver, *Semitic Writing*, 43–5; M. W. Green, "The Construction and Implementation of the Cuneiform Writing System," *Visible Language* 15, 4 (1981) 345–72; A. Robertson, *Word Dividers*.

[217] See H. Grapow, *Sprachliche und schrifliche Formung ägyptischer Texte* (LÄS 7; Glückstadt 1936) I.37–54; G. Möller, *Hieratische Paläographie* (Osnabrück 1965) I.6–8; II.1–6; III.1–5.

text in Ugaritic literature.[218] The oldest Qumran composition reflecting stichographic writing is probably 4QpaleoJob[c] dating to 225–150 BCE.

The texts from the Judean Desert, in common with instructions in rabbinic literature and the evidence of the medieval Masoretic manuscripts, have certain texts written in a special layout, but display several differences in detail as well as in conception. In general terms, the medieval Masoretic manuscripts follow the prescriptions of rabbinic literature, but these prescriptions leave room for several interpretations, and the manuscripts vary accordingly. The layouts described in rabbinic texts are based on the fixed arrangement of inscribed and uninscribed segments, and run parallel to system *2a* of the Qumran scrolls, and possibly also to system *3*. The descriptions in the rabbinic sources refer explicitly to the lists of the kings of Canaan (Josh 12:9-24) and of the sons of Haman (Esth 9:6-9) and three Songs (Exod 15:1-18, Deuteronomy 32, and Judg 5:2-30) in the prose books of the Bible, but not to the Psalms.

One method used in Masoretic manuscripts was 'a half-brick, אריח, over a half-brick and a whole brick, לבנה, over a whole brick,' i.e., an inscribed section above another inscribed part in the following line, with an uninscribed part appearing above an uninscribed section in the following line (our explanation of what constitutes a half-brick and a brick follows Rashi in *b. Meg.* 16b). According to *b. Meg.* 16b and *Sof.* 13.3, the lists of the kings of Canaan (Josh 12:9-24) and of the sons of Haman (Esth 9:6-9) are written in this way, while *Sof.* 1.11 (cf. 12.9) includes Deuteronomy 32 in this layout. Accordingly, Deuteronomy 32,[219] but also 1 Samuel 2 and 22 (see *Sof.* 13.1), Qoh 3:2-8, and several additional texts are thus written in some Masoretic manuscripts. Deuteronomy 32, as well as several other units, are written in this fashion in some Qumran manuscripts (4QpaleoDeut[r]; system *2a* above). The layout of 2 Samuel 22 differs from the more or less identical text of Psalm 18, both in graphic arrangement and in small details (e.g. codex L).

Another system of stichographic arrangement in MT is 'a half-brick over a whole brick and a whole brick over a half-brick,' i.e., an inscribed part placed over an uninscribed section in the following line and vice versa. This system was represented in two different ways for the first verses of the Song at the Sea:

```
      ----            -------------------------         ------
      -------------------------          ---------------------
      -------            ---------------            ------
or
      -------------------------          ---------------------
                   -------------------------
      -------------------------          ---------------------
```

According to *b. Meg.* 16b (see also *b. Menaḥ.* 31b; *b. Shabb.* 103b; *y. Meg.* 3.74b; *Sof.* 1.11), this system was used for 'all the Songs' contained in non-poetical books, e.g. the Song at the Sea (Exod 15:1-18) and the Song of Deborah (Judg 5:2-30). The Talmudic formulation of this system was interpreted in the medieval manuscripts as referring to lines ending at exactly the same point at the end of the column, with three fixed writing blocks separated by two spaces (or two writing blocks separated by one space) in one line and two writing blocks separated by one space (or one writing block in the middle of the line) in the following line, written in such a way that the uninscribed and inscribed sections are always above each other. This system is not known in this exact form from the Qumran texts, but it is not impossible that it reflects a development of system *3* in which the interaction between inscribed and uninscribed sections is more random. It should be stressed that the rabbinic system of a 'half-brick over a whole brick and a whole brick over a half-brick' differs from the aforementioned systems, since it is based on a graphic representation of the elements that does not reflect a certain understanding of the content. That is, the arrangement of the 'Song at the Sea' and the 'Song of Deborah' is based on graphical principles and often runs counter to the division into section units. A similar arrangement is visible at the ends of cols. XIV, XV, XVIII, and most of col. XXII of *Sefer Abisha[c]* of SP (see Pérez Castro, *Séfer Abiša*).

It is unclear what arrangement the Talmudic statements presuppose for the writing of the Songs and Psalms other than those mentioned specifically (Exod 15:1-18; Deuteronomy 32). Kugel, *The Idea of Biblical Poetry*, 123 presupposes that these two texts were singled out, because all other texts were written as

---

[218]See Gordon, *Ugaritic Textbook*, 23–5; W. J. Horowitz, "A Study of Ugaritic Scribal Practices," *UF* 5 (1973) 165–73; idem, *The Ugaritic Scribe* (UF 11; Kevelaer 1979) 389–94.

[219]For the fixed writing of the stichs of this unit and the number of lines according to tradition, see the detailed analysis of codex A by M. H. Goshen-Gottstein, "The Authenticity of the Aleppo Codex," *Textus* 1 (1960) 17–58; Breuer, "Biblical Verses" (n. 188). For an analysis of the different Masoretic writing systems of this Song, see P. Sanders, *The Provenance of Deuteronomy 32* (OTS 37; Leiden 1996) 102–11.

two hemistichs separated by spaces. This assumption is not supported by the Qumran evidence, but that evidence is not necessarily representative for the manuscripts produced by rabbinic circles.

The medieval manuscripts follow the instructions in different degrees; for details on some manuscripts, see Breuer, "Biblical Verses" (n. 188); Oesch, *Petucha und Setuma*, 121–4; and P. Sanders, "The Colometric Layout of Psalms 1 to 14 in the Aleppo Codex," *Studies in Scriptural Unit Division* (ed. M. C. A. Korpel and J. M. Oesch; Pericope 3; Assen 2002) 226–57.

Because of the limited scope of the Qumran manuscripts, in only a few instances can a judgment be pronounced on the relation between these manuscripts and rabbinic regulations.

• Deuteronomy 32 in 4QDeut^q is not written according to either of the two systems mentioned in rabbinic literature since most of its lines are written with one hemistich per line, and some lines with two hemistichs. Interestingly enough, 4QDeut^q does not align with the Masoretic family, but has close affinities to the LXX and also has independent features.

• 4QDeut^b has two hemistichs per line, as prescribed by the rabbinic rule, but they are not separated by spaces, as stipulated there. This text is equally close to MT and SP.

• 1QDeut^b and 4QpaleoDeut^r, following the rabbinic rule for the writing of Deuteronomy 32 in hemistichs separated by spaces, could be proto-Masoretic as they reflect MT and SP equally well.

• The Song at the Sea in the nonbiblical manuscript 4QRP^c (4Q365) 6b (based on a pre-Samaritan biblical text; Qumran scribal practice) is written as a running text with clusters of 2–3 words separated by spaces (illustr. 2a). To some extent, this layout may be presented as an extension of the system which is prescribed by the Talmud ('a half-brick over a whole brick and a whole brick over a half-brick') since the inscribed areas are indeed located above non-inscribed areas, even though the Qumran arrangement is not as fixed as the rabbinic prescription. The arrangement in 4QRP^c (4Q365) also resembles SP since both arrange the Song in groups of words consisting of 2–3 words, in a parallel stichographic layout in SP, and as a running text in 4QRP^c.

• Against the rabbinic instructions, 4QExod^c and 4QExod in Exodus 15 are written as running texts. 4QExod^d (Exod 13:15-16; 15:1) is an unusual text (possibly an abbreviated biblical text), as it lacks a major section (Exod 13:17-22 and all of ch. 14). The unusual character of this scroll may be connected to the fact that it does not reflect the rabbinic regulations for Exodus 15. On the other hand, 4QExod^c is a regular biblical text, but not particularly close to MT, and often with independent features (J. E. Sanderson, *DJD* XII, 103). As in the case of 4QExod^d, the lack of close affinity with MT may be related to the failure to exhibit the features that later became rabbinic prescriptions.

In addition to the relation between the different layout systems, also their place in the history of the transmission of the Bible text is unclear. The writing of the Psalms as either a prose text or in stichs has not been fixed in the manuscripts, even though there are indications of the acceptance at an earlier stage of the writing in hemistichs. Thus the numbers given for the verses (פסוקים) of the book of Psalms (5896) in *b. Qidd.* 30a can only be understood as referring to hemistichs, since the Masoretic version of the book contains 2527 verses. See further the discussion in § a on the division into verses.

The Samaritan writing tradition differs from both the rabbinic tradition and several Qumran texts, although similarities are recognized in details. Although the Samaritan tradition includes the stichographic writing of some poetical sections (see below), Samaritan scribes paid more attention to the technical aspects of the stichographic layout (just like the Masoretic 'half-brick over a whole brick and a whole brick over a half-brick'). In the Samaritan writing tradition, certain sections are written in a fixed way with an identical arrangement of the parts of the line or, sometimes, of the stichs. In such cases, the line is divided into two or three equal parts, especially in some lists of names enumerated by Crown, "Studies. III," 363–70 (see further Robertson, *Catalogue*, xx–xxi). These arrangements resemble the Masoretic lists of the kings of Canaan in Josh 12:9-24 and of the sons of Haman in Esth 9:6-9. In addition, Samaritan scribes often arranged the writing block in such a way that identical letters (especially *lamed* and *waw*) and words were written underneath each other, often by artificially spacing the letters of one or more words in a specific way. Samaritan manuscripts also often leave a blank before the last one or two letters of the line, and accordingly isolated letter(s) at the end of the line stand(s) out prominently (Robertson, *Catalogue*, xx). Although this writing system (colometry) appears to reflect an *ad hoc* arrangement by scribes, Crown stressed the fixed elements of this writing tradition in the main Samaritan centers of manuscript production. According to Crown, "Studies. III," 377, these Samaritan customs reflect Jewish writing traditions from the Second

Temple period. This assumption is likely since certain sections of SP are written in a bi-columnar arrangement, as in the aforementioned Qumran scrolls (system *2a*) and the medieval Masoretic manuscripts. Thus, the Samaritan tradition has the bi-columnar writing of Deuteronomy 32 in common with system *2a* of the Qumran texts and the rabbinic prescriptions, and in addition it arranges Lev 26:3-13 and the poetical sections of Numbers 23–24 (23:7-10, 18-24; 24:3-10, 15-24) in this fashion. The Samaritan writing of the Song at the Sea, in two cols. of clusters of 2–3 words is similar to the writing of that poem in 4QRP^c (4Q365), which therefore reflects a writing tradition embedded in a pre-Samaritan text. The pre-Samaritan 4QNum^b does not share these features with SP in Num 24:3-10.[220] (no further Qumran fragments of the mentioned sections of Leviticus and Numbers have been preserved). The list of the kings of Canaan in Josh 12:9-24 is written stichographically like in MT (see above): M. Gaster, "Das Buch Josua in hebräisch-samaritanischer Rezension, Entdeckt und zum ersten Male herausgegeben," *ZDMG* 62 (1908) 209–79, 494–549 (267).

In a few manuscripts from the Judean Desert, *titles* of the individual Psalms and other poetical units were indicated with a distinctive layout (illustrations 8 and 5a). These titles define the nature of the small unit or mention its author or the person to whom the composition is dedicated. In the Judean Desert texts, these Psalms titles were, as a rule, not indicated with a distinctive layout that identified them as 'titles,' as became the norm in the early Greek Scripture manuscripts and in the Medieval Masoretic manuscripts. Initially, the majority of the Psalms titles in the Judean Desert texts were written as the first element in the running text without any distinctive spacing before or after the superscription. For a well-preserved text, see 4QPs^c II 30 (Ps 51:1), while in other instances the superscription is sometimes reconstructed: 4QPs^a: Psalms 36, 67, 69; 4QPs^c: Psalms 49, 51; 4QPs^j: Psalm 48; 4QPs^r: Psalm 27; 11QPs^a: Psalms 129 (V 4), 151 (XXVIII 3); MasPs^a: Psalm 83. All these titles followed the practice used in most nonbiblical compositions from the Judean Desert whose titles were written as the first elements of the running text, without any special layout (see ch. *4h*).

In the later part of the period covered by the Judean Desert scrolls, a practice developed in which the titles were presented with a special layout.

• One-stich title in texts written in stichographic layouts. The header is centered in the space above the line. [221]

    4QPs^b XXII 10 (Psalm 103): ד[לדו] [30–68 CE]
    5/6ḤevPs VII 8 (Psalm 16): ד[לדו] מכ[תֿֿם [50–68 CE]

• One-stich title in texts written in stichographic layouts. The header is positioned at the beginning of an otherwise empty line exactly above the beginning of the Psalm as the first line of the running text. The position in 4QApocryphal Psalm and Prayer (4Q448) is slightly different.

    5/6ḤevPs V 17 (Psalm 11): למנֿצח ל[ד]וֿ[ד [50–68 CE]
    5/6ḤevPs VI 11 (Psalm 13): למנצח מזמור לדוד [50–68 CE]
    MasPs^a III 5 (Psalm 84): למנצחֿ [על הגתית לבני קרח מזמור] [30–1 CE]
    4QApocryphal Psalm and Prayer (4Q448): הללויה מזמו[ר] שׁיֿרֿ ('Halleluja, a psal[m], a song of . . . '). The word הללויה is written to the right of the first line of col. I, starting in the wide margin preceding the text [100–76 BCE].

• Two-stich title in a text written in stichographic layout. The header is not distinct from the remainder of the Psalm.

    5/6ḤevPs III 17 (Psalm 8) מזמור לדוד *vacat* [למנצח על הגתית]

---

[220]The different Samaritan manuscripts still need to be examined for this purpose. Our observations are based on von Gall's edition.

[221]For an early extra-biblical parallel, see the superscriptions in the fifth century BCE Aramaic letters published by Driver, *Aramaic Documents* mentioning the name of the sender and addressee, as well as the topic of the letter.

• One-stich title in a text written in prose layout. The header is positioned at the end of a line-long indentation.

4QPs^q (Psalm 33) I 2: לדויד שיר מזמור

From this fragmentary evidence it seems that the custom to place headers on a separate line above the Psalms started to develop in the period covered by the Judean Desert scrolls. Some of these were written at the beginnings of the lines above the Psalms, while others were placed in the center. If the fragmentary evidence is to be trusted, it should be noticed that the למנצח headers were positioned at the beginning of the line, while the others were centered. The system of writing the superscription at the beginning of the line was followed in the medieval manuscripts of MT, viz., usually in codex L, and in the שיר המעלות songs ('Songs of Pilgrimage') in codex A.

That this practice developed gradually may be inferred from the fact that three titles were written after the writing was completed, two in 4QPs^e (above the beginning of the Psalms) and one in MasPs^a (centered).

4QPs^e 26 i 6 (Psalm 126): שיר המעלות, in the middle of the line, partly above the space between Psalms 125 and 126. See illustr. 8.

4QPs^e 26 ii 3 (Psalm 130): The superscription (שיר המעלות), also found in MT and 11QPs^a, was added secondarily, partly at the end of line 2, partly above the beginning of line 3: שיר המ[/עול]ות]. Only עול] is visible above the beginning of line 3, but preceding it there is ample room for additional letters. Accordingly, this reconstruction by Skehan-Ulrich-Flint in *DJD* XVI, 84 that assumes the writing of [שיר המ] at the end of line 2, is unusual as it presumes the splitting of a word between two different lines, a practice not known in Judean Desert manuscripts written in the square script (see § *a1* above). Nevertheless no better solution can be seen. שיר] עולות] does not seem likely.

MasPs^a II 3: Ps 82:1 מזמ[ר] לאסף ('A Psalm of Asaph'; illustr. 5a). The irregular spacing between the lines before and after this superscription suggests that these words were written after the writing of the text was completed.

The special layout of these titles, especially in Psalms that were arranged stichographically, was indicated inconsistently, for example, in the aforementioned 4QPs^e, in which titles were placed above the middle and beginning of lines. In another instance, such a title was part of the running text of frg. 18 ii 8 (Psalm 106 [146?]). By the same token, in MasPs^a II 3 a title was added above Psalm 82, while in II 14 (Ps 83:1), III 5 (84:1), and III 24 (85:1) it was part of the running text.

• A few sundry headers:

1QM III 1 (fig. 8.1): The supralinear inscription added at the end of the first line after the completion of the writing possibly served as a superscription to a new section.

4QCant^b 1: Remnants of several letters are visible in the top margin above the beginning of the text on line 1 as well as above the preceding column which appear to be part of two different words, possibly part of a superscription or scribal note (E. Tov, *DJD* XVI, 210).

4QCommGen A (4Q252) IV 3: ברכות יעקוב (header of the blessings of Jacob in Gen 49:1), following a closed section, as part of the running text. This header runs parallel to the one in codex Ambrosianus of S: בורכתא דיעקוב דאתאמר בנביותא.

4QD^e (4Q270) 3 i 19: a superscription to a section of agricultural laws in red ink (see ch. *3e*). See J. Baumgarten, *RevQ* 19 (1999) 217–25.

4QMeditation on Creation C (4Q305): The barely legible first column seems to start one line higher than col. ii. This line may have served as a superscription.

4QRP^c (4Q365) 23 3: An eight-word header of a section on the festivals in the middle of the line, preceded and followed by blank spaces

4QNon-Canonical Psalms A (4Q380) 1 8: תהלה לעבדיה: Unclear circumstances.

4QDibHam^a (4Q504) 1–2 vii 4: הודות ביום השבת, at the beginning of the line, followed by a small space and an apostrophe above the last letter.

MasSir V (above Sir 42:15): זכרה נא מע[ש]י חה חזיתי ואשננה, in the top left margin as well as to the left of line 1, repeating the content of the first line of the text. The superscription, penned in three consecutive lines, was written in a cursive hand, less expert than that of the scribe of the main text. No parallel from the texts in the Judean Desert is known for this type of header, which was often added in similar situations in Greek manuscripts (Turner, *Greek Manuscripts*, 13).

The special layout of superscriptions is comparable to the writing of such titles of Psalms in *red* ink in 2QPs, for which see ch. *3f* above and § c1 below.

c. *Scribal marks and procedures*

The texts from the Judean Desert, especially those from Qumran, contain various scribal markings, some of which recur often in certain texts. A few of these marks may have been simply scribbles, for example, in the bottom margin of 1QIsaᵃ XXXII (fig. 16) and the slightly curved oblique line before the first letter of [וחל]לו below the text of 4QJerᶜ XXII 2 (Jer 31:5; *DJD* XV, pl. XXXV). However, most signs were intentional even if their meaning is often unclear (similarly, McNamee, *Sigla*, 7 notes that a great number of the signs in Greek literary papyri are obscure). There are almost no differences between the scribal practices in this respect between biblical and nonbiblical texts. A few signs are known from Aramaic secular sources preceding the time of the earliest texts from Qumran (the *paragraphos* sign [fig. 1] and the paleo-Hebrew *ʾaleph* [fig. 3]) and from Greek sources concurrent with the earliest Qumran texts (the *paragraphos* sign [fig. 1], cancellation dots [figs. 6.1–4], and the *sigma* and *antisigma* [figs. 8.1–3]). Similar signs were probably also used in Hebrew texts preceding the earliest Qumran texts, but our information regarding Hebrew non-lapidary texts from the period preceding the mid-third century BCE is very fragmentary. Most of the non-lapidary sources are ostraca which may have displayed different scribal practices from those used on papyrus and leather.

Some of these markings were studied by Martin, *Scribal Character*, within the framework of his study of the scribal practices of the cave 1 texts. They are described here in greater detail with regard to all the Judean Desert texts, with attention to their nature, frequency, and background. Although the detailed discussion may create the impression that these scribal markings are widely used in the Qumran texts, their use is almost exclusively limited to the texts written according to the Qumran scribal practice; see the discussion below and ch. 7a.[222] Similarly, the majority of the texts using paleo-Hebrew letters for the divine names (§ d) are written according to the Qumran scribal practice. It should also be noted that the occurrence of these signs is almost exclusively confined to Hebrew, and not Aramaic, texts.

The proportionally largest number of signs is found in 1QIsaᵃ and 1QS–1QSa–1QSb (these three compositions were written by the same scribe who also inserted some corrections in 1QIsaᵃ), 4Q502–511, 4Qpap pIsaᶜ (4Q163), and 4QCantᵇ (illustr. 8a).

When two or more signs show a certain resemblance, the similarity in shape or usage is usually not distinctive enough to posit a certain closeness between individual scribes or users of different texts. At the same time, it appears that a few of the signs in 1QIsaᵃ and 1QS resemble one another closely (c1b, c1g) and that the texts using single letters in the Cryptic A script are of a sectarian nature (§ c3).

---

[222]For comparison, note the various signs used in the Samaritan writing tradition, but it is not known in which period they originated. The various grammatical treatises explaining the use and meaning of these signs were collected by Z. Ben-Hayyim, *The Literary and Oral Tradition of Hebrew and Aramaic amongst the Samaritans*, vol. II (Jerusalem 1957), especially *Qanun Dartha fi l-Maqra*.

The scribal marks were inserted into specific copies of a Qumran composition, and are not indicative to the scribal transmission of the composition in all its copies. Thus, the marks in 1QS are not found in the copies of that composition from cave 4 (e.g. the signs in 1QS V are not found in the parallel 4QSᵇ [4Q256]). For additional examples, see § 1.

We consider any element which is not part of the content of the originally inscribed text, but is additional to it, as a scribal mark. This definition thus excludes guide dots written at the beginnings and ends of sheets guiding the drawing of lines on the leather, since these were inserted before the writing of the text (ch. *4a*). The shapes of these signs are mostly distinct from the letters of the script in which the text was written, although some letters in the square, paleo-Hebrew and Cryptic A scripts are also used as signs. Some markings were inserted by the original scribes, but probably a greater number were inserted by later scribes and generations of users, and usually we are not able to distinguish between these three levels. Sometimes the color of the ink or the shape of the sign show that the sign was written after the text was completed.

Scribal markings identified—in varying degrees of frequency—in nonbiblical as well as biblical manuscripts, may be subdivided into nine categories.[223]

1. Section markers, almost exclusively in the margin, and other scribal systems, pertaining to the division of the text into sections
2. Marks pertaining to scribal intervention, mainly for the correction of errors
3. Single letters in the Cryptic A script primarily written in the margin
4. Single paleo-Hebrew letters written in the margin
5. Marks, including unexplained signs, drawing attention to matters in the text
6. Marks written at the ends of lines as line-fillers
7. Separation dots between words
8. Letters and marks possibly numbering sheets and units
9. Signs for numerals

With regard to the lack of consistency in the use of these signs, McNamee's remarks (*Sigla*, 7) relating to Greek literary papyri are worthy of note:

> While I have tried to present the collected information in as orderly a way as possible, I do not want to overstate its systematic nature. It was human scribes who added signs to papyri, and their work is full of human whim. Conventions existed, but it will be obvious from the start that particular sigla are not used in the same way by every scribe.

(1) *Section markers, almost exclusively in the margin, and other scribal systems, pertaining to the division of the text into sections*

In addition to the indication of new sections by spacing at the ends of the lines, in the middle of the line, and between lines as described above, scribal markings are often used to indicate new sections with an additional type of marking. Thus, the one-column text 4QTest (4Q175) consistently indicates each new section with a section marker. Also in 1QS, the division between sections is indicated rather consistently, referring not only to 'open sections,' but also to some 'closed sections' (see below). However, in the majority of the texts, in which one or more of these section markers appear, they were inserted sporadically and very inconsistently, as far as we can judge, unless the very use of the marking has a special meaning that escapes us. Since the section markers usually appear

---

[223]For an earlier classification, see M. Baillet, *DJD* VII, index: '1. signes de division, 2. séparation des mots, 3. signes de correction, 4. autres signes.'

together with other systems of content division, the very use of a section marker in conjunction with a spacing device *could* indicate a greater content division than mere spacing. However, it is more likely that the section markers were added secondarily by users. In 1QIsa[a], one often has the impression that the section markers had been arranged (by a user?) in pairs, separating the section between two markers (see, e.g. cols. VIII, XXIII, XXIV, XXXIV, XL, XLI, XLVIII).

While occurring between two lines, section markers usually mark the end of the preceding section, and not the beginning of a new one. This is clear when the marks occur at the end of a section before a blank line (e.g. 1QS IX 11) and even at the end of a composition (XI 22 and 1QSa II 22). At the same time, in some compositions the section marker indicates the beginning of a unit, e.g. 4QRitPur A (4Q414) before 7 1; 31 1; 4QSapiential-Hymnic Work A (4Q426) ii 1; 4QpapPrQuot (4Q503) III 1; 4QpapRit-Pur B (4Q512) 13.

It is difficult to determine whether the paragraph signs were inserted by the original scribes, later scribes, or users. The majority of these signs were probably inserted after the writing was completed. In 1QS, for example, the angular paragraph signs neatly denote most open sections as well as several closed sections, but in addition they denote several additional locations in which, according to the later scribe, such a section ought to have been indicated, but presently the *paragraphos* is the only sign indicating a new section: III 19; IX 6, 20; X 7; XI 16, in the latter case used in conjunction with two dots placed as a dicolon in the line itself; see fig. 17 and the analysis in § h below.

The fact that the section markers do not occur at the same place in other copies of these compositions shows that they were specifically inserted by certain scribes and/or users in certain manuscripts, and were not part of the scribal transmission of that manuscript. Thus, the various *paragraphoi* of 1QIsa[a] are not found in the parallel positions in any of the other manuscripts of Isaiah. In another instance, the *paragraphos* in 4QH[b] (4Q428) 10 11 at the beginning of a new hymn was not indicated in the parallel position in 1QH[a] VIII (Suk. = Puech XVI) 4. The signs were probably meant to be *ad hoc* and were not to be transferred to additional copies. Probably only in the case of the transmission of the proto-Masoretic manuscripts were such signs copied to additional manuscripts, and, in that case, could easily be misunderstood (§ c10).

The following section markers are recognized in the Qumran scrolls, almost exclusively between the lines, protruding into the margin, and in a few cases also below the last text unit, and in three instances (4QpapPrQuot [4Q503] 24–25 2; 4QRebukes Reported by the Overseer [4Q477] 2 ii 5, 9; 4QpapSap/Hymn [4Q498] 15) in the middle of the line.

(a) A horizontal or slightly curved line (*paragraphos*). For the different forms, see figs. 1 and 11.2a, 6. Sometimes, this *paragraphos* is formed as a straight line, but it often has a slightly curved downstroke to the left (fig. 1.1) or to the right (fig. 1.2), is shaped like a fish hook, or a more developed downstroke in a 45-degree angle, often gently rounded and with a small stroke on top (figs. 1.3–4, 1.7b), or in a 90-degree angle (MasSir; fig. 1.5). This sign, which resembles the sign for 'ten' in many Hebrew and Aramaic texts (*DJD* II, 98 and below § c9), is used in three biblical (4QDeut[b], 1QIsa[a], 4QPs[h]) and 29 nonbiblical texts from Qumran. For an example of a *paragraphos* together with the surrounding text, see Isa 44:1 in illustr. 21.[224]

---

[224]The paragraph sign in 1QSb V noted in Burrows, *The Dead Sea Scrolls* is not visible on the plate.

a. *Straight line protruding into the margin, with or without ornaments on the right and/or left side*

<u>Biblical Texts</u>

1QIsa^a, scribes A (chapters 1–33) and B (chapters 34–66)

    Straight line below open sections: IV 22; V 21; VIII 4; XI 7; XVI 4; XIX 21; XXIV 2, 6; XXV 12; XXXIV 21; XL 28, 31; XLI 29; XLIII 6; XLIV 5; XLV 18; XLVI 10, 23; XLVIII 5, 13; L 8, 24; LI 27; LIII 17.

    Short descending line to the right in a 45-degree angle, e.g. II 20; IV 7; XXII 17; XXVIII 21; XL 28, 31; LI 26.

    Short descending line to the left, e.g. XLVI 10, 23.

    Short descending lines to the right and left (e.g. L 8). Straight line below closed sections: VIII 9, 19; X 29; XXIII 25; XXXIV 26; XXXVII 7; XXXVIII 1, 17; XLI 1, 25; XLV 18.

    Straight line above indentations: VII 9; VIII 2, 12; X 14; XVI 30; XXII 20; XXIII 22; XXVI 31; XXVII 7; XXXIV 5, 8; XXXVI 26, 31; XL 22, 25; XLI 7; LI 3; LII 13; LIV 2.

1QIsa^a, scribe B

    A developed form of the *paragraphos*, with a semi-circle on top (fig. 1.6 ['Mexican hat']) possibly denotes a larger hierarchy of content division as it occurs mainly at the beginnings of chapters in MT (XXVIII 28 [Isa 36:1] see illustr. 6; XXXII 30 [Isa 40:1]; XXXVIII 6 [Isa 45:1]; XLIX 6 [Isa 60:1]). Like the simple *paragraphos*, it is written between the lines, after a closed or open section (XLIII 29 [Isa 52:7] as well as in the aforementioned examples of beginnings of chapters), or above an indentation (XXXV 23 [Isa 42:13]).[225] The circle on top of the *paragraphos* may reflect the same circular shape as appearing in XVII 1 and XXVIII 18 (fig. 10.4) and described in § *c3* as a letter in the Cryptic A script.

4QDeut^b 2 ii 15 (Deut 31:14-15) evidence unclear

<u>Nonbiblical Texts</u>

1QS IX 3, a developed form of this sign (fig. 11.2a), on which see § c4

4QApocryphal Psalm and Prayer (4Q448; see illustr. 11) I, between lines 2 and 3

4QEnGiants^d ar (4Q532) 1 ii, before line 7

4QTQahat ar (4Q542) 1 ii, before line 9

<u>Greek Texts</u>

4Qpap paraExod gr (4Q127) 17, between lines 2 and 3

4QLXXLev^a 1, between lines 21 and 22 (after Lev 26:14)

b. *Straight or slightly curved line protruding into the margin with angular downstroke to the left* ('fish hook', fig. 1.7b)

1QS I 21; II 12, 19; III 13, 19 (fig. 1.7b); IV 2, 9, 15; V 13, 25; VI 8, 24; VIII 5, 20; IX 6, 12, 20; X 7; XI 16, 22 (under)

1QSa I 6; II 22 (under; fig. 1.3b)

1QH^a XII (Suk. = Puech IV) 5 (very similar to 'horizontal clothespin' shape)

4Qpap pIsa^c (4Q163) 4–7 ii 4, 5, 6, 7, 14, 15, 17, 20 (nature unclear)

4QLevi^b ar (4Q213a) 2 11

4QRitPur A (4Q414) before 1 ii 5; 2 ii 4, 5; 7 1, 10; 12 3; 31 1; 32 ii 3

4QSapiential-Hymnic Work A (4Q426) 1 ii 1: in an empty line, before the beginning of a new unit and with a *pe* on top. This letter is explained as referring to *parashah* by A. Steudel, *DJD* XX, 215.

4QH^b (4Q428) 10 (col. XXXVII) 11 above an indentation

4QRebukes Reported by the Overseer (4Q477) 2 ii 5, 9 (middle of the lines)

4QpapM^f (4Q496) 10 iii 13

4QpapSap/Hymn (4Q498) 15

---

[225]According to Teicher, this sign indicated messianic passages, and it resembles the 'sign of life' in the Egyptian scribal system indicating future eschatological events: "Material Evidence of the Christian Origin of the Dead Sea Scrolls," *JJS* 3 (1952) 128–32.

4QpapRitMar (4Q502) 19 5; 142; 318

4QpapPrQuot (4Q503) III 1, 6, 12, 18, 23; IV 6; VIII 2, 22; XI 1, 6; etc. In the middle of the text: 24–25 2 (probably)

4QpapPrFêtes^c (4Q509) 10 ii–11 8 (according to Baillet); 49, 225, 265

4QpapRitPur B (4Q512) 13; 15 ii (both col. IX); XII 7; 48–50 5; 65, 190

4QpapUnclassified frags. (4Q520) 26

c. *'Horizontal clothespin' shape protruding into the margin* (developed from the shape recorded in § b; fig. 1.3a)

4QPs^h 1–2 16 (after Ps 119:16)

4QTest (4Q175) 9, 14, 20 (separating between the sections in the anthology; for a similar use of the *paragraphos*, see the Greek anthologies P.Tebt. I 1–2 of 100 BCE and P.Petrie 3). See fig. 1.3a.

d. *Two lines at a 90-degree angle* (fig. 1.5)

MasSir II 8 (40:18), 24 (41:1); III 18 (41:14); IV 16 (42:9)

e. *Unique shapes*

4QTanḥ (4Q176) 1–2 i 4 (fig. 1.7a)

4QHistorical Text E (4Q333) 1 2 end of line (fig. 11.6). The inverted *paragraphos* at the end of the line possibly represents a special type of line-filler.

4QNon-Canonical Psalms A (4Q380) 1 7 at the beginning of an empty line before a new psalm (fig. 1.4)

4QpapHodayot-like Text B (4Q433a) 2 2 at the beginning of a large indentation (fig. 18)

4QDibHam^a (4Q504) VII 4 (fig. 2.2) and 11, both at the beginning of new sections

The *paragraphos* sign—the most frequent sign occurring in the Qumran texts—is usually drawn at the right side of the column between the lines of the text, with the greater part of the sign protruding into the right margin, referring to a content division indicated by spacing either in the line above or in the line below. E.g. 1QIsa^a XXXIV 5 (Isa 41:2), at the end of the section, above the indented section:

```
xxxxxxxxxxxxxxxxxxxxxxxxxxxxxxxxxxxxxxxxxxxx ‾‾
xxxxxxxxxxxxxxxxxxxxxxxxxxxxxxxxxxxxxxxxxx
xxxxxxxxxxxxxxxxxxxxxxxxxxxxxxxxxxxxxxxxxxxxx
```

1QS VIII 5 at the end of the section, above a closed section (rare):

```
xxxxxxxxxxxxxxxxxxxxxxxxxxxxxxxxxxxxxxxxxxxxx
xxxxxxxxxxxxxxxxxx        xxxxxxxxxxxxxxxxxxxxxx ‾‾
xxxxxxxxxxxxxxxxxxxxxxxxxxxxxxxxxxxxxxxxxxxxx
```

1QIsa^a XXXIV 27 (Isa 41:21), at the end of the section, below the closed section:

```
xxxxxxxxxxxxxxxxxxxxxxxxxxxxxxxxxxxxxxxxxxxxx
xxxxxxxxxxxxxxxxxxxxxxxxxxxxx          xxxx
xxxxxxxxxxxxxxxxxxxxxxxxxxxxxxxxxxxxxxxxxxxxx ‾‾‾
```

1QIsa^a XLVIII 8 (Isa 58:13), at the end of the section, below the open section:

```
xxxxxxxxxxxxxxxxxxxxxxxxxxxxxxxxxxxxxxxxxxxx
                              xxxxxxxxxx
xxxxxxxxxxxxxxxxxxxxxxxxxxxxxxxxxxxxxxxxxxxxxx ‾‾‾
```

In 1QIsa^a and 4QRitPur A (4Q414) 2 ii 4, 5 the *paragraphos* sign is written almost completely or completely in the margin itself. The different shapes of the *paragraphos* show that the scribes or users developed their own forms, slightly differing from one another.

Not only the shapes of the *paragraphos* signs, but also their usages differ slightly in the various texts. For example, in 1QIsaᵃ the *paragraphos* was usually written below the line ending with an open section or in which a closed section occurs (e.g. V 21 [Isa 6:1]; VIII 9 [Isa 8:16]), and, in the case of an indentation, above the indented space (e.g. VII 10 [Isa 7:21]). Likewise, most of the signs in 1QS were written above an indented space, but in a few cases below lines in which a closed section occurs (above V 14, 26; VI 9; VIII 5). In the latter detail this scroll differed from 1QIsaᵃ.

Since the shapes of the signs differ in the two halves of 1QIsaᵃ, it is not impossible that the scribes of these scrolls inserted these signs and not later users. Thus, the section written by scribe A displays two forms of the *paragraphos*, a straight line and, more frequently, a line with a curve to the left (fig. 1.1), without distinguishable difference in meaning between them. However, the section written by scribe B displays the straight *paragraphos*, the *paragraphos* with a hook to either the left or the right (figs. 1.1–2), and the composite *paragraphos* as described above (fig. 1.6). For a detailed study of the signs in this scroll, see J. W. Olley, "Texts Have Paragraphs Too—A Plea for Inclusion in Critical Editions," *Textus* 19 (1998) 111–25 and idem, "Structure." In the latter study, p. 25, Olley remarks that the *paragraphoi* are irregularly distributed throughout the book. They are clustered especially in Isa 8:9–9:1; 29:13–24; 41:2–20; 48:17–49:7, while they are sparse in 1:1–8:8; 12:1–29:12; 30:1–41:1; 41:21–48:16; 49:8–66:24. Olley suggests (p. 27) that these *paragraphoi* do not denote section divisions, but they may delimit a passage of particular interest, for reading or meditation, or even for skipping in public reading.

Most texts display *paragraphos* forms of similar shapes (see the list above and fig. 1.3). It is not impossible that these signs were inserted by an individual or a group of users in texts of a similar nature. A large percentage of liturgical texts among these texts is noticeable, among them three parallel compositions (4Q414, 4Q503, 4Q512; see E. Eshel's edition of 4QRitPur A (4Q414) in *DJD* XXIX).[226]

By the same token, the curved line in 4QPsʰ marks the end of stanzas in Psalm 119 (this sign is not used in other manuscripts which recognize in some way the existence of different stanzas: 1QPsᵃ, 4QPsᵍ [illustr. 17a], 5QPs, 11QPsᵃ).

The basic form of the *paragraphos* such as found in several Qumran texts is also known from earlier and contemporary sources. The straight *paragraphos*, as well as the curved shapes, occurs already in the Aramaic scribal tradition of the fifth century BCE, from where it could have found its way into the Qumran texts. However, it also occurs in the Greek scribal tradition, which may have influenced the scribal traditions of the Qumran texts. A sign similar to fig.1.2 is used in some manuscripts of SP in the middle of empty lines between sections (see e.g. Anderson, *Studies*, 16).

In Greek secular literature, the straight-line *paragraphos* sign occurs regularly, see Schubart, *Palaeographie*, 173; Turner, *Greek Manuscripts*, 14; Kenyon, *Palaeography*, 27; R. Barbis Lupi, "La *paragraphos*: Analisi di un segno di lettura," in A. Bülow-Jacobsen, *Proceedings of the 20th International Congress of Papyrologists Copenhagen, 23–29 August, 1992* (Copenhagen 1994) 414–7; G. Tanzi Mira, "Paragraphoi ornate in papiri letterari greco-egizi," *Aegyptus* 1 (1920) 224–7. According to Gächter, "Zur Textabteilung," 302–3 the *paragraphos* sign occurs in 140 of the 250 Greek literary papyri analyzed by him. The use of this sign was described and prescribed by Aristotle, *Rhet.* 3.8.1409a.20. The developed shapes of this *paragraphos,* such as found at Qumran (groups *b–e* above), are not evidenced in the Greek tradition. Another difference is evident in the Greek *paragraphoi* which are written more often between the lines, while protruding only slightly into the margin (with the exception of 4QLXXLevᵃ 1 21, written mainly in the margin), while the *paragraphoi* in the Hebrew and Aramaic Qumran manuscripts are mainly written in the margin.

---

[226]The fish-hook sign is probably placed inconsistently in the aforementioned Hebrew and Aramaic texts. On the other hand, according to Pfann, "4Q298," 233–4 the sign occurs only in liturgical texts, in Pfann's words, 'rules of order, hymns, prayers, recited Scriptures, blessings or curses.' Pfann suggests that the sign represents an ʿ*ayin* (for ואמרו ענו or וענה ואמר) in the Cryptic A script referring to an answer expected from the audience. While the label 'liturgical' may indeed be applied to several compositions in this group, the assumption of a response is not applicable to all texts, certainly not in the case of 4QTest (4Q175) in which the second, third, and fourth sections are indicated with this sign. Besides, the resemblance of this sign to other forms of the *paragraphos* signs does not support this hypothesis.

Paragraphoi are found in a number of manuscripts of Greek Scripture, from 1 BCE onwards:

4QLXXLev[a] of Leviticus 26 (late 2 or early 1 BCE) 1 21

4QpapLXXLev[b] of Leviticus 2–5 (1 BCE) 28 6

P.Fouad 266b (848) of Deuteronomy 10–33 (middle of 1 BCE) in Deut 18:6; 19:11; 20:5 etc. (see Oesch, *Petucha und Setuma*, 297–8), above the first letter of the line following each closed and open section

8HevXIIgr hand A, before Nah 3:8, etc. (E. Tov, *DJD* VIII, 10; end of 1 BCE)

P.Oxy. 65.4443 of Esther Add. E and ch. 9 (late 1 or early 2 CE)

P.Chester Beatty VI (963) of Numbers and Deuteronomy (end of 2 CE or beginning of 3 CE)

P.Rendel Harris 166 of Exodus 22–23, after 22:26 (3 CE)

P.Bodmer XXIV of Psalms 17–53, 55–118, hands A and B (3 CE)

P.Berlin 17212 of Jeremiah 2–3 (3 CE)

Pap. W (Freer) of the Minor Prophets, e.g. after Zeph 3:13 (3 CE)

P.Chester Beatty X (967) of Daniel (early 3 CE)

P.Berlin Fol. 66 I/II of Genesis (end 3 BCE), wedge shaped

P.Chester Beatty V (962) of Genesis (end of 3 BCE)

P.Genova P.U.G. 1 of Psalms 21–23 LXX (3–4 CE)

P.Chester Beatty IV (961) of Genesis (4 CE), wedge shaped

P.Oxy. 11.1351 of Leviticus 27 (4 CE; leather)

P.Leipzig 39 of Psalms 30–55 LXX (4 CE)

P.Yale Beinecke 544 of 1 Samuel 24–2 Samuel 1 (4–5 CE)

Horizontal paragraph signs are evidenced also in Aramaic texts from the fifth century BCE onwards, see e.g. Porten–Yardeni, *TAD* 3, C.1.1 (Ahiqar; second half of 5 BCE), at the beginnings of lines 109–124, 142–146, 191, slightly above the text, but mainly in the margin, before lines 197 and 204 in the left margin, in line 137 in the middle of the line, and in line 180 above a closed section in the middle of the line; C.2.1 (Bisitun inscription, 421 BCE), line 51; C3.8 (473–471 BCE), col. 2 14, 19, 32, 37, above empty lines; C3.13 (Record of Memoranda), lines 9, 45, 49, above empty lines; as well as many additional texts in this volume and in *TAD* 2, e.g. B3.3, 3.6, 8.3, 8.4, 8.7; *TAD* 4 D3.16, 17; Saqqara papyri (5–4 BCE)[227] 4, 7, 10, 19, 38, 41, 55; Idumaea ostracon 34 separating between amounts of wheat and barley (4 BCE; see Eph'al–Naveh, *Aramaic Ostraca*, 33). The position of these *paragraphoi* resembles that of the signs in the Qumran texts, which are mainly written in the margin, as well as in many Greek documents from Egypt contemporary with the Qumran texts. The shape of these signs resembles that of the straight lines in 1QIsa[a], while most of the signs in the Qumran texts are of the 'fish-hook' type.

The fish-hook shape (not the gently rounded forms) resembles the διπλῆ sometimes functioning in a similar way in the Greek scribal tradition.[228]

(b) A sloping line in the margin (fig. 2.1) to the right of the text in 1QIsa[a] III 3, 22 (Isa 3:1, 16).

(c) A hyphen written to the right of the first words in the lines: 4QM[a] (4Q491) 1–3 1, 4, 6, 14, 16, 18, 19; 31 1; 32 1–3.

(d) Three signs indicating a minor division, viz. two variations of the apostrophe (fig. 2.2) and a period, listed by M. Baillet, *DJD* VII, 339 for several texts possibly indicate a subdivision of some kind: 4QDibHam[a] (4Q504) 1–2 vii 4 (apostrophe after a superscription); 4QShir[a] (4Q510) 9 2 (period); 4QShir[b] (4Q511) 18 iii 8; 4QOrd[b] (4Q513) 13 2, 4 (apostrophes). For most instances the evidence is unclear. Note further a few additional markings in 4QDibHam[a] (4Q504) for which detailed drawings were presented by M. Baillet in the transcription of the text in *DJD* VII, while these shapes seem to be different on the plates themselves, and on photographs PAM 43.611: 1–2 v 2; VI 2 (parenthesis sign?); vii 4 (fig. 2.2), 11 (both at the beginning of new sections).

---

[227]J. B. Segal, *Aramaic Texts from North Saqqâra* (London 1983).
[228]Cf. Turner, *Greek Manuscripts*, 11; Gardthausen, *Griechische Palaeographie*, II.411–12.

The *paragraphos* and similar paragraphing devices usually occur in conjunction with a system of notation of open or closed sections. The great majority of the Qumran texts listed above (thirty-three) are Hebrew texts written according to the Qumran scribal practice (twenty-two). In addition, they appear in three biblical texts, three Aramaic texts, and five texts that were either not copied according to the Qumran scribal practice, or whose character is unclear. The data are also listed in APPENDIX 1.

(e) *Paleo-Hebrew waw and ʾaleph* (figs. 4–5; 11.3,5; 15)

Paleo-Hebrew waw within the text block. In two scrolls the indication of open and closed sections is accompanied by the writing of a paleo-Hebrew *waw* in the spaces indicating the sections. This *waw* generally appears in an open section when the first word after the space would have started with a (usually conversive) *waw* which is now omitted.

• 4QpaleoExod^m: The *waw* is written in the scroll itself and in the patch in col. VIII. The shape of the *waw* in the patch (fig. 5.1 and illustr. 14) and its position are almost identical to the *waw* in 4QPs^b V 16 (after Ps 93:5; fig. 5.2). For a list of the occurrences in this scroll, see *DJD* IX, 59, 61. In the patch in 4QpaleoExod^m and in 4QNum^b (see below), this *waw* was followed by text written after the space, while in the other instances the space continues until the end of the line.

• 11QpaleoLev^a (fig. 5.3 and illustr. 14a): the *waw* occurs only in some open sections, probably indicating a major division in this scroll.[229] Even though the ends of most lines of 4QpaleoExod^m are missing, an analysis of col. I makes it likely that this *waw* indicates a major division, subdivided into smaller segments indicated by closed sections.

Square waw within the text block. 4QNum^b XXI 28 (Num 27:22): This is the only scroll written in the square script which contains a *waw* in the square script in the space between two sections.

Paleo-Hebrew waw/ʾaleph in the margins. Variations of the paleo-Hebrew *waws* are found in the margins of a few texts written in the square script; see the discussion below, § c4. In 1QIsa^a, 4Qpap pIsa^c (4Q163) 6–7 ii 10, and 1QS V 1 the sign is written in the margin between the columns, indicating the beginning of a new section, and in 4QPs^b V 16 (Ps 93:5) on the last line of col. V before 94:1 in the following column,[230] while in 5QLam^a it was written in the bottom margin, without any context. All these letters probably reflect the paleo-Hebrew *waw*, although the shape of some of them more closely resembles an *ʾaleph* than a *waw*. The shape of this paleo-Hebrew *waw* differs from the paleo-Hebrew *ʾaleph*; the former has a straight line as well as an angular line facing to the right, while in the *waw* these lines are facing to the left. However, rotations of this type are well known in the development of scripts.

Background. The function of the letters described above is close to that of the paleo-Hebrew *ʾaleph* serving as a section marker in the fifth-century Aramaic texts in which a paleo-Hebrew *ʾaleph* was written in the middle of 'closed' or 'open' sections (fig. 3). These signs appear usually in closed sections in the non-proverbial sections of Ahiqar,

---

[229]Thus Freedman–Mathews, *Leviticus*, 11. In this scroll, some sections merely indicate the new paragraph with a space (frg. I 7 [Lev 19:1]; K 6 [Lev 21:10] col. 2 6 [Lev 23:26]), while others display both a space and a *waw* in the middle of that space (frg. J 1 [Lev 20:1]; col. 2 2 [Lev 23:23]; 3 3;8 [Lev 24:10, 13]).

[230]Elsewhere, this scribe left an uninscribed line between Psalms (before Psalms 103 and 118), but in this case only one line was left at the end of the column, which also ends the Psalm, so that the mere leaving open of this line would not have sufficed. The writing of the paleo-Hebrew *waw* made the division more distinctive. Since the bottom margin of this column is larger than that of the surrounding columns (see pl. III), the editors of this text name the sign an 'ornamental space-filler' (*DJD* XVI, 30).

differently from the *ᵓaleph* used in the text itself, see, e.g. lines 88, 90, 105, 139, 140, 168, 171, 172, and in line 135 in an open section (Porten–Yardeni, *TAD* 3). Cowley, *Aramaic Papyri*, 211 tentatively explained this letter as an abbreviated form of אחר ('another matter'), while A. Yardeni, "New Jewish Aramaic Ostraca," *IEJ* 40 (1990) 130–52, especially 132–4 explains the letter as an abbreviated form of אחרן.[231] The shape of this paleo-Hebrew *ᵓaleph,* especially that appearing in the space of a major content division in court record B8.5 (431 BCE) in Porten–Yardeni, *TAD* 2, is very similar to the sign written in the right margin of 4Qpap pIsaᶜ (4Q163) 6–7 ii 10 at the beginning of a new section after a blank line (fig. 4). The shape and function of the sign in 4Qpap pIsaᶜ (4Q163) are thus similar to the scribal tradition in some Aramaic documents (based on the drawing of J. Allegro, *DJD* V, while not visible on the plate itself). Compare also the paleo-Hebrew *ᵓaleph* in 4QInstrᵈ (4Q418) 67 3, without any context, in the inter-columnar margin, close to the end of the line (fig. 5.7).

The use of the paleo-Hebrew *waw* in 11QpaleoLevᵃ and 4QpaleoExodᵐ is paralleled by some Arad ostraca, dating to the end of the First Temple period.[232] In these ostraca, words were split between two lines when there was no space for the remainder of the word at the end of the line, and in such cases sometimes a single *waw* was left in the middle of the space at the end of the line, even when there was room for the whole word (ostraca 2 3, 4; 3 6; 11 4).

It is unclear what the relation is between the paleo-Hebrew *ᵓaleph* of the Aramaic texts (paragraph indicator) and the paleo-Hebrew *waw* of the Arad ostraca (for the shape, not the function, see also several fourth-century ostraca published by Ephᶜal–Naveh, *Aramaic Ostraca*). The scribal traditions of some Qumran texts apparently reflect both traditions. The paleo-Hebrew *waw* written in these texts within the text block probably continues the tradition reflected in the Arad ostraca, while its occurrence in the margin reflects a tradition similar to that of the Aramaic documents.

(f) 4QMessianic Apocalypse (4Q521) 2 ii 4: This scroll contains a sign in the margin adjacent to a new section (fig. 5.6). For some speculations on the meaning of the sign, see É. Puech, "Une Apocalypse Messianique (4Q521)," *RevQ* 60 (1992) 475–519 (482) and idem, *DJD* XXV, 7.

(g) The sign resembling an *epsilon* in the top right margin above the beginning of the column in MasSir V (fig. 15) could represent a numbering device (ch. *5c8*), but it is more likely that it marks a (major?) sense division, indicated also by the superscription in the left margin (ch. *5b*), and paralleled by an empty line in the medieval MS B of Ben Sira. The slant of the sign very much resembles that of an *ancora* (*inferior*) mark (denoting omission or addition) in the Greek scribal tradition (fig. 15.1), although the latter has a longer middle stroke. Cf. also the *epsilon*-like sign in 4QCantᵇ 1 9 (fig. 12.3 and illustr. 8a). Mur 17B (papList of Personal Names) contains a very similar sign which has been explained by its editor (J. T. Milik, *DJD* II, 97) as denoting the measure *seah* occurring in that text together with number signs. Threatte, *Attic Inscriptions*, 92 explains a similar sign in one of the inscriptions as a variation of the *sigma* formed by breaking the semicircle in the middle.

(h) 4Qpap pIsaᶜ (4Q163) 4–7 ii 9–11, 16, 18, 20: In the transcription of these lines, J. Allegro, *DJD* V, 18–19 recorded various shapes in the margin which cannot be

---

[231] For a discussion and further parallels, see also J. M. Lindenberger, *The Aramaic Proverbs of Ahiqar* (Baltimore 1983) 305–7.

[232] See Y. Aharoni, *Judean Desert Studies: Arad Inscriptions* (Jerusalem 1975). The similarity between the Arad ostraca and 11QpaleoLevᵃ was first pointed out by É. Puech, "Notes en marge," 161–83, especially 165.

identified on the plates. Some of these shapes introduce the beginning of a new biblical text in this *pesher*.

(i) 1QM X 9: The scribe indicated a closed section, but upon realizing that there should be no such section he (or a later scribe) canceled it with a thin stroke level with the bottom of the letters.

Several additional signs (§§ 3 and 4 below) likewise occur at the beginning of new sections; however, they probably do not indicate the beginning of a new section, but rather draw attention to a feature connected to the content of that section.

(2) *Marks pertaining to scribal intervention, mainly for the correction of errors*

When a scribe or user corrected or altered the text that he or a previous scribe had written, various systems of denoting these changes were used either in the linear text or in the interlinear space. For a helpful initial analysis on the basis of the texts from cave 1, see Martin, *Scribal Character*, I.144–71, 405. Some data were collected by Kutscher, *Language*, 531–6. Several different systems were employed for deleting letters and words, and most scribes and/or users used these systems interchangeably, although some preferred a specific practice.

The four main systems used for correction are:

i.	cancellation dots/strokes
ii.	crossing out with a line
iii.	parenthesis signs (*antisigma* and *sigma*)
iv.	erasures

The texts that employ cancellation dots/strokes are more frequent than those using lines to cross out letters or words. To some extent, different systems were used under different circumstances, but in the case of deletions, there is no major difference in meaning between these systems. Basically these systems were used under similar circumstances, but one recognizes a preference for the use of parenthesis signs for longer omissions, and of cancellation dots/strokes above and below letters for individual letters. For the deletion of complete words, cancellation dots/strokes and crossing out with a line are more or less equivalent systems. Since much was left to the personal preference of individual scribes, some elected to use cancellation dots/strokes in most circumstances (e.g. 1QIsaᵃ), while others preferred crossing out words (e.g. 4QDᵃ [4Q266]). Others chose to erase the elements with a sharp instrument (e.g. 1QS), while in 1QHᵃ most elements were dotted and afterwards erased. As a parallel for the employment of interchangeable systems see the MT of Num 10:35-36 which is known from the medieval manuscripts as encircled with inverted *nunin* (that is, parenthesis signs) but from rabbinic literature (*Sifre* Numbers § 84) as indicated with cancellation dots.

In the analysis of the correction procedures it needs to be remembered that apparent inconsistency must sometimes be attributed to correction of manuscripts by subsequent scribes and users.

The correction signs occur only in texts written in the square script, and not in texts written in paleo-Hebrew characters. The latter texts were written by a different scribal school (ch. 7*b*), and on the whole they display very little scribal intervention.

All these correction systems were used in a similar way in the Alexandrian Greek scribal tradition (see below). Of the systems listed below, practices *i* (cancellation dots) and *iii* (parenthesis signs) may have been adopted directly from the Alexandrian scribal tradition since they are not known from earlier Hebrew or Aramaic sources. In the scribal tradition of the Alexandrian Greek grammarians, the parenthesis signs play a prominent role in the critical annotation of text editions. The Aramaic papyri from the fifth century BCE, which are rather well documented, use no special notations for canceling letters; the only system used in these documents is that of washing out letters (e.g. Porten–Yardeni, *TAD*, 2, B.2.6 36; B.3.2), recorded below as technique *x*.

In addition to the systems known from the Judean Desert texts, Alexandrian scribes indicated a large omission with an *ancora* (anchor-shaped sign) in the margins of the Greek manuscripts, e.g. Turner, *Greek Manuscripts*, documents 12, 34, and 41 and McNamee, *Sigla*, 11–13. This system was followed in Latin manuscripts.[233] A good example of an *ancora* is found in P.Chester Beatty IV (961) of Gen 29:16 (4 CE), where [ονομα τ]η μειζονι λεια και was omitted by way of homoioteleuton and the corrector wrote an *ancora* in the text and side margin, while the omitted text was added in the top margin of that column (see further P.Chester Beatty VI [963] of Num 5:21). For a possible use of this sign in MasSir V (fig. 15) in the top right margin, though with a different meaning, see § g above. The *ancora* sign was sometimes accompanied by a note κάτω (below) or ἄνω (above) referring to the bottom or top margin where the omitted elements were written. In Greek manuscripts, probably more elements were crossed out with lines than canceled with dots,[234] while in the Qumran texts more elements were dotted. In Greek manuscripts, some *individual* letters were crossed out with lines, while in the Qumran texts mainly words were crossed out. Finally, since most of the Greek texts are on papyrus, the technique of washing out letters with a sponge (technique *x*) was used frequently.

    i. *The marking of the elements to be canceled with cancellation dots/strokes* (figs. 6.1– 6.4). The omission of many elements was indicated by scribes or users with cancellation dots, placed in different positions above or below individual letters and words in texts written in square characters.[235] Cancellation strokes have so far been recognized only in 1QHᵃ X (Suk. = Puech XVIII) 6 אַכְשִׁיל (for אשכיל) and 1QpHab VII 2 עַל כֹּל; VIII 14 (partially preserved also in II 16). Such strokes are also known from the Greek scribal tradition; see Turner, *Greek Manuscripts*, 16; Turner, *Greek Papryri*, pl. VIII; and below, after TABLE 15 for examples. This system was rarely used for papyri from the Judean Desert, in which scribes preferred to use other systems of erasing (sponge?).

    The main systems used may be formulated as follows:

• The cancellation of complete or partial words was usually indicated with dots above (TABLES 10, 11) the letter(s) or both above and below the letters (TABLE 11).

• As a variant of this system: with the addition of dots to the right and left of the linear word.

• Single letters were usually canceled with dots both above and below the letters (TABLE 10), since a single dot could easily be overlooked.

In any event, the different position of the dots vis-à-vis the letters does not carry a special meaning, since all the dots were intended to cancel letters or words. In a few cases, mainly in 1QIsaᵃ, dots were placed on both sides of supralinear words or letters, canceling the addition (technique *e*). In a single case in 1QDM (1Q22) III 10 (technique *f*), a triangular cluster of three dots in the space between the lines indicated the deletion

---

[233]See E. A. Lowe, "The Oldest Omission Signs in Latin Manuscripts: Their Origin and Significance," *Studi e Testi* 126 (Miscellanea Mercati VI; Città del Vaticano 1946) 36–79 = *Palaeographical Papers* 1907–65 (Oxford 1972) II.349–80.

[234]No comparative studies on these different procedures are known to me. For studies on other aspects of correction procedures in Greek manuscripts, see E. G. Turner, "Scribes" (see n. 43 above) 141–6; K. McNamee, "Greek Literary Papyri," 79–91; G. M. Rispoli, "Correzioni, varianti, glosse e scoli nei papiri ercolanesi," *Proceedings of the XVIII Int. Congr. of Papyrology* (Athens 1988) I.309–20.

[235]For other uses of dots in manuscripts, see SUBJECT INDEX, 'dot.'

of a stretch of text appearing after the dots. The same sign appears in P.Oxy. 15.1809 of Plato (Phaedo, 102) of 1 or 2 CE (Turner, *Greek Manuscripts*, 48 and document 19).

Similar dots, mainly above single letters, appear in fifteen instances in the Masoretic manuscripts, and in one instance both above and below the letters (Ps 27:13); see § 10 below.

In all these instances, in the Qumran texts as well as in the Masoretic manuscripts, the dots denote the deletion of the dotted elements, even though Martin, *Scribal Character*, I.166 named them 'alternative or doubtful linear readings.'

a. *Cancellation dots above more than one letter canceling one or more complete words or parts of words* (fig. 6.1)

TABLE 10: *Cancellation Dots Above More Than One Letter*

1QIsaᵃ scribes A and B

XIII 14 (Isa 15:7)	וּפְקֹדֹתִים (corrected text equals MT)
XXVIII 28 (Isa 35:10)	יְשִׂיגוּבֹה (corrected text equals MT שיגו; fig. 6.1)
XXIX 3 (Isa 36:4)	מֶּלֶךְ יְהֹוֹדֹה (lacking in MT and 2 Kgs 18:19)
XXIX 10 (Isa 36:7)	לִפְנֵי הַמִּזְבֵּחַ הַזֶּה תִּשְׁתַּחֲווּ בִּירֹוֹשֹׁלֹיֹם (the longer text is identical to 2 Kgs 18:22 MT and versions; the shorter text agrees with the MT of Isaiah)
XXXV 15 (Isa 42:6)	קֹרֹחִיכה (the purpose of the dots is unclear)
XXXVI 8 (Isa 42:25)	וּתְבַעֵר בֹּוֹ has been canceled, while the nature of the dot on the preceding letter is unclear

4QTanḥ (4Q176) 10 17	בֹֹת (not recognized in the edition)
4QapocrLam A (4Q179) 1 ii 13	הֹיֹקֹרֹיֹם (irregular dots)
4QEnastrᵃ ar (4Q208) 18 2	הֹו
4QTime of Righteousness (4Q215a) 1 ii 9	בא ממשל הֹצֹדֹק הטוב (the second dot is placed between the *dalet* and *qoph*)
4QDᶠ (4Q271) 4 ii 4	כֹּי כי (dittography)
4QHarvesting (4Q284a) 1 4	{וֹאֹת הֹרֹמֹאֹים}
4QCal Doc/Mish C (4Q321a) 7 (col. V) 7	עֹשֹׂרֹ
4QapocrJoshᵇ (4Q379) 22 ii 13	בֹּנֹי יֹעֹקֹֹב וֹשֹׁפֹּ]טֹ דֹם[; these words were written in the wrong place.
4QShirShabbᵃ (4Q400) 2 3	מאלוהימֹיֹם (dittography, possibly there are also dots below the letters)
4QShirShabbᵈ (4Q403) 1 i 34–35	בֹּרֹצֹוֹן דֹּעֹת
1 i 37	דֹּעֹת
1 i 42	הֹו
1 ii 12	נֹשֹׁמֹע
1 ii 21	רֹאֹשֹׁי נשֹׂיֹאֹי כו הֹ]נות (irregular dots)
4QInstrᵈ (4Q418) 81 8	עֹוֹלֹם
107 4	אוֹטֹיֹם
172 8	{וֹבֹ}הֹשדה
174 1	קול}כֹֹה{
4QHᵃ (4Q427) 3 4	שֹׁוֹר
7 ii 16	רחמֹיֹכֹוֹם
7 ii 20a	נפלאותֹיֹכֹה
7 ii 20	להשיב לֹכֹה
4QNarrative H (4Q481e) 3	אֹשֹׁרֹ (eight separate dots above the three letters)
4QMᵃ (4Q491) 1–3 4	לש]מֹחֹת
1–3 8	סביבותֹיֹ הֹמה
11 i 13	יֹדֹמֹ (the scribe forgot to cancel the preceding ולוא)
4QOrdᶜ (4Q514) 1 i 7	חֹעֹוֹד correcting עוד to חד (thus the edition)

11QPs^a XIV 5 (Ps 119:175)   וֹמשפטיכה

      XXVII 1   the last two letters of שׂדוֹף were replaced with a single
                                    pe to read שׂדֿף

     frg. E (*DJD* XXIII) i 2 (Ps 118:26)   {בֹּשֹֿם}
     frg. E (*DJD* XXIII) iii 13 (Ps 105:6)   {עֹבֹֿדֿ}

---

b. *Cancellation dots above single letters*

TABLE 11: *Cancellation Dots Above Single Letters*

4QExod^c V 7 (Exod 12:37)		{אֹ}מאות אלף
4QapocrLam A (4Q179) 1 i 13		נשמֹשעה
	1 i 14	למכאֹבֹם
4QpapJub^h (4Q223–224) unit 2 iv 10		יהיהֿי (unclear dot)
4QD^a (4Q266)	2 i 24	נפשֹמֹה
	5 ii 10	הֿפֿיל
	6 i 11	כֿ (independent unit at the beginning of the line)
	11 16	ושלֹים
4QBer^b (4Q287)	9 13	בעדֹיות
4QMyst^c? (4Q301)	2 1	בשורשֹשי
4QRP^c (4Q365)	12 iii 5	לוֹא
	12 iii 7	זהֹזֿב (*zayin* canceled with three dots)
4QPrayer of Enosh (4Q369) 2 2		וֹחלחם (probably a *he* was to replace the *het*)
4QCommunal Confession (4Q393) 3–7 8		גבורים החיל
4QInstr^a (4Q415)	2 ii 2	בלבבֿך (*waw* above the canceled letter)
4QInstr^d (4Q418)	88 5	יקֹפֿץ
	102 3	ידֹי{מֹ} כה : ידים changed to ידיכה (two added letters)
	126 12	אותֿה
	126 13	חֹשֹ̈ז
	158 5	ב}וֹ{ ניכה
	172 8	וֹבֿ{ הֿשדה
	174 1	קול}כֹֿה{
4QSapiential-Hymnic Work A (4Q426) 1 i 12		מלפניֹו
	1 ii 3	בפעיֿלות
4QH^a (4Q427) 1 3		אתבוננהֿ
4QBarkhi Nafshi^a (4Q434) 1 i 1		מֹעל (parallel text 4Q437 1 1: על)
	1 i 2	אוחניֹו
	1 i 3	שֹׁעֿקֿתם (the scribe first wrote שעתם, canceled the first letter with a dot, remodeled the *waw* to a *zayin*, and added a supralinear *qoph* to read זעקתם)
4QBarkhi Nafshi^e (4Q438) 4 ii 3		רוֹח
4QHodayot-like Text C (4Q440) 3 i 22		ובֿמובכה
4QNarrative C (4Q462) 1 14		ויעמידוֹה
4QText Ment. Descendants of David (4Q479) 2 3		וֹתֿ
11QT^a (11Q19) XLV 18		יטהרוֹ

In two instances, single dots seem to pertain to a complete word:

4QEnastr^a ar (4Q208) 16 4 פלֹג; 17 4 בה בֿה (thus Tigchelaar–García Martínez, *DJD* XXXVI, 119).

c. *Cancellation dots below the letters* (fig. 6.2)

Only rarely were cancellation dots placed solely below the letters:

1QS VII 20 after יגע, dots were written below בטהרת which was subsequently erased. Above the line the scribe wrote משקה.

1QS X 24 אסתר with a *pe* above the *tav* that was canceled.

1QIsaᵃ XXXIII 7 (Isa 40:7) וְדִבְרֵ (fig. 6.2 and illustr. 1: four dots). There was no room in the manuscript for the cancellation dots above the word because of the supralinear addition.

4QInstrᵈ (4Q418) 241 2 לבהפלא

4QapocrLam B (4Q501) 1 הַ (supralinear, with possible line above the letter)

d. *Cancellation dots above and below single letters*

TABLE 12: *Cancellation Dots/Strokes Above and Below Single Letters*[236]

1QIsaᵃ scribes A and B	
X 4 (Isa 10:17)	שׁיתֹ֗ו
XV 9 (Isa 19:5)	יחרֹב (cf. MT יחרב)
XXI 12 (Isa 27:4)	שֹׁ֗מִיר
XXVIII 12 (Isa 34:12)	בָאפֶּס
XXVIII 18 (Isa 34:17)	לֹהֹמֶה with *nun* above the *mem*
XXXI 5 (Isa 37:27)	וֹשֶׁבֹ֗י (cf. MT ובשו)
1QapGen ar XXII 27	אֹחֹזֹתֹֽו
1QHᵃ V (Suk. = Puech XIII) 20	תשׁיב נֹֿפֹֿשֹֿ֗י סערה (strokes; the shorter text agrees with 4QHᶜ [4Q429] 1 ii 5 תשׁב סערה)
X (Suk. = Puech XVIII) 6	אֹכַֹשֹׁיל (for אשכיל)—strokes
1QpHab II 10	כֹ[יא
IV 6	ישׁחֹ֗יֹקֹ (or: ישׁחֹ֗יק)
VIII 14	strokes above and below the *waw* at the beginning of the line
1QM IV 6	ובֹכֹלכתם
1QSa I 16	שֹׁרוֹשׁ
4QDeutᶜ 12–15 4 (Deut 11:10)	ברגלֹ֗יֹךֹ
4QDeutʲ VIII 8 (Deut 11:10)	אתֹֹמֶה
4QSamᶜ II 17 (2 Sam 14:32)	וא[ ]שלחֹ֗כֹה
4QIsaʰ 1–2 10 (Isa 42:11)	מֹבֹדבר
4QJerᵃ IX, part 2 2 (Jer 14:6)	שפאֹ֗יֹם
4QXIIᶜ 34 3 (Zeph 3:1)	אֹֹֿת
4QTanḥ (4Q176) 14 3	שֹׁ֗וֹנאנו
14 4	אֹזֹ֗לֹ'ֿ ס
26 4	אֹֿאֹ֗ ○[
4QCatena A (4Q177) 1–4 15	או[ ]חותֹֿחֹ֗ת
4QJubᵍ (4Q222) 1 1	חֹיֹ֗א
1 4	עֹאֹל (supralinear dot not visible on the plate)
1 5	וֹתֹ֗מֹר (with supralinear *'aleph*)
4QPsJubᵃ (4Q225) 2 i 6	הֹכֹ֗וֹל (with supralinear *ḥet*)
4QCommMal (4Q253a) 4 ii 1	וא'ֹשֹ֗רֹ
4QDᵃ (4Q266) 3 ii 3	למלפֹנֹ]ֹ֗יֹם
4QDᶠ (4Q271) 3 11	מֹֹ֗דבר (with supralinear *bet*)

---

[236] A few spaces in the printed representation of the Hebrew in this table, such as in the first item, are not found in the scrolls.

	5 i 5	יבׄיׄא
4QBerᵃ (4Q286)	1 ii 6	מׄבינה
4QBerᵈ (4Q289)	2 3	וׄבׄאי
4QRPᵇ (4Q364)	17 3	העדוׄתׄ
4QRPᶜ (4Q365)	12 iii 4	חשׄיׄשׄ
	23 5	עשׁׄים (with supralinear ṣadi)
	25c 13	אתכמהׄ
	26a–b 5	מן] אצרׄ
4QTᵃ? (4Q365a)	3 2	גׄיׄרׄע
	2 ii 4	מזרח{הׄ}
4QMMTᶜ (4Q396)	1–2 iii 5	לׄטׄ (the last dot was written in the *tet* itself). The scribe started to write לטהרת, but after writing the first two letters he canceled them, left a space, and continued to write עם טהרת.
	1–2 iii 9	חׄיׄ
4QShirShabbᵃ (4Q400)	1 i 2	ובאלוהותׄןׄ
	22 9	מׄמתחת
	23 i 3	כסאי כׄהׄ
	23 ii 3	כבודוׄהׄ. (the last letter of the word was canceled by four dots)
	27 2	[קׄודׄשׄ
4QVision and Interpretation (4Q410)	1 6	מׄאמת טוב ומה מׄה (in both cases with a *bet* above the *mem*)
4QInstrᵈ (4Q418)	9 18	המשיל} כׄ{ם
	140 4	מׄבׄשרׄ]ים
4QPersonal Prayer (4Q443)	2 6	תעמידׄנׄי
4QMᵃ (4Q491)	1–3 3	ו ׄלׄפׄר]שים
	11 i 17	לׄדׄוׄניא
4QProphecy of Joshua (4Q522)	8 3	בית שׄן[237]

In the following instances, mentioned above, *replacement letters* were placed above the upper cancellation dot:

1QIsaᵃ XXVIII 18 (Isa 34:17) להׄמׄה with *nun* above the *mem* (illustr. 6)
    4QJubᵍ (4Q222) 1 5 ותׄזׄמר (*ʾaleph*)
    4QPsJubᵃ (4Q225) 2 i 6 הכׄול (*het*)
    4QDᶠ (4Q271) 3 11 מׄדבר (*bet*)
    4QRPᶜ (4Q365) 23 5 עשׁׄים (*ṣadi*)
    4QVision and Interpretation (4Q410) 1 6 מׄאמת טוב ומה מׄה (in both cases with a *bet* above the *mem*)

TABLE 13 records instances in which letters were erased after the dots were inserted, leaving spaces in the manuscript.

TABLE 13: *Letters Erased after the Placing of the Cancellation Dots Above and Below Single Letters*

Reference	Corrected Word	Word before Correction
1QS I 16	לפני {ׄ}	ולפני
V 12	שפטים {ׄ}	משפטים
V 14	ובהו{ׄ}ו with supralinear *nun*	ובהושו
V 22	ועלפירׄ{ׄ} ב	ועלפירוב
VI 19	יקרׄ{ׄ}בו	יקריבו
VIII 19	יכח{?}[238]	

---

[237]It is unclear whether the dots are placed on and below the *shin*, and what their function is. É. Puech, *DJD* XXV, 48 suggests that the dots stress the special orthography.

XI 7	אש{?}[239]	
1QHᵃ II (Suk. = Puech X) 17	ותלמד{.}וֹ	ותלמדנו
IV (II) 33	מ{ }פי	מלפני
V (XIII) 14	}ל{ש{ו}ניהם	לשונם
V (XIII) 21	משר{.}תיכה	משרותיכה
V (XIII) 22	{ }	נמה
V (XIII) 38	{text not legible}	
VII (XV) 7	ת{ד}עוٰע	תדזֿעוע (the linear *zayin* and dot were erased)
VI (XVI) 15	הרות{.}אי זٰ ל. A supralinear *nun* was written above the erased letter.	לבזאינהרות[240]
XII (IV) 10	ש{ }קט	
XII (IV) 10	אל ה{ }ד{ }עות	אל הידיעות (both *yods* were marked with dots)
4QTᵃ? (4Q365a) 2 ii 4	מזרחٰ{הٰ}	
2 ii 6	{ומן הٰמשקוף̇}	

In 11QPsᵃ frg. E (*DJD* XXIII) i 2 (Ps 118:26) {בְּשֵׁם}; iii 13 (Ps 105:6) {עֲבֹוד}, complete words were erased after the dots had been inserted.

e. *Cancellation dots/strokes above and below individual letters and words* (fig. 6.3)

TABLE 14: *Cancellation Dots/Strokes Above and Below Individual Letters and Words*

Biblical Texts

1QIsaᵃ X 23 (Isa 11:4)	יֹוֹמֹתֹ רֹשֹׁעֹ (fig. 6.3)
XL 9 (Isa 48:4)	מאשֹׁרֹ ידעתי (cf. MT מדעתי)
4QIsaᵈ 6–10 7 (Isa 49:1)	the first three letters of the Tetragrammaton
6–10 10 (Isa 49:4)	Tetragrammaton
4QXIIᵉ 14–15 2 (Zech 5:9)	ואש[אֹהֹ עֹנֹי
4QPsˣ 4 (Ps 89:22)	שֹמֹוֹ
11QPsᵃ XVI 7 (Ps 145:1)	paleo-Hebrew Tetragrammaton
XXI 2 (Ps 138:1)	paleo-Hebrew Tetragrammaton

Nonbiblical Texts

1QHᵃ I (Suk. = Puech IX) 7	כֹוֹלֹ
II (X) 4	אֹמֹה with supralinear צדק
V (XIII) 20	אֹוֹדֹכֹה with supralinear ברוך אתה
7 6	להֹוֹדֹיֹעֹ גֹבֹוֹרֹה
1QpHab VII 2	על עֹלֹ (strokes)
1QM XI 8	להלחٰםٰ: An original להלחם was changed to להכבד by the supralinear addition of כבד.
4QpIsaᵇ (4Q162) I 4	ואשר אֹאֹשֹרֹ (dittography)
4QCatena A (4Q177) 5–6 12	רֹאٰוٰ: Dots were indicated above and below the first letter and above the third one.
4QInstrᵈ (4Q418) 76 2	{קֹוֹדֹשֹׁ} with supralinear צֹדֹק
81 8	עֹוֹלֹם

[238]The last letter, now erased and probably accompanied by a dot under the letter, can no longer be read. A *bet* is written above the last letter: יכתב.

[239]The last letter, now erased and possibly accompanied by a dot under the letter, can no longer be read. A *resh* is written above the last letter: אשר.

[240]In the first space the scribe forgot to write a *bet*, and strangely enough, instead of the dotted *nun* a supralinear *nun* was written.

4QOrd^b (4Q513) 2 ii 4   בָּמָּה (with supralinear בהם)

The following words were erased after the dots were indicated above and below the letters, leaving spaces in the manuscript.

1QH^a VII (Suk. = Puech XV) 15   {וחיים}

1QS VII 1   {   } after או לכול דבר אשר לו, written by a second hand, a word of some five letters

       VII 20   {רְבְיָם} before ובשגית at the beginning of the line

       VII 20   {בטּהרתי}: above the line the scribe wrote משקה

       XI 9   { } towards the end of the line a two-letter word

---

f. *Cancellation dots below the letters and to the right and left of a linear word,* canceling or replacing the word

This system is frequently used, especially in 1QIsa^a, not only for canceling a word, but also for replacing it with a new one. In these cases, the new word was written in the interlinear space above the word being replaced. The original word was canceled with dots below each letter as well as to the right and left of the word.

1QIsa^a III 24 (Isa 3:17) אֲדֹנָי· (MT אדני) [supralinear יהוה]

1QIsa^a III 25 (Isa 3:18) יָהֹוָה· (MT אדני) [supralinear אדוני]

The latter case resembles XXII 20 (Isa 28:16) in that scroll (יהוה with אדוני added supralinearly), but in that verse no cancellation dots were written. The supralinear word started above the space between the words, and evidently was not intended to replace the original word, but rather was probably meant as an addition.

1QS VII 1, 20; XI 9. See TABLE 14.

1QpHab VII 2 ·לוא· the meaning of the dots is unclear.

In some cases the dots are more or less written around the word to be canceled such as in the case of the box-like shapes around words (§ iii below).

1QM III 4 יכָתֹבֽוֹ·

4QShirShabb^f (4Q405) 3 i 13. The dots were imprecisely placed above, below, and to the left of שבעֹה·.

4QapocrMos^c? (4Q408) 3 6 ·יָהֹוָה· ברוך. The substitute words אתה אדוני were written above the line.

---

g. *Cancellation dots on both sides of supralinear words or letters,* canceling the addition (fig. 6.4)

The scribes of 1QIsa^a and 4QM^a (4Q491) added dots on both sides of supralinear words or letters, thus canceling the added elements. The supralinear letters indicated a correction rather than a variant reading. On the other hand, according to Stegemann, *ΚΥΡΙΟΣ*, A 94, n. 512 the dots to the right and left of the supralinear word indicated variant readings, for which there is hardly any evidence in the Qumran scrolls. It appears that the example from 1QIsa^a VII 2 makes Stegemann's view unlikely.

1QIsa^a VII 2   (Isa 7:16) תעזב [supralinear ·יֹ·]

1QIsa^a XXXIV 25   (Isa 41:20) ויבינו [supralinear ·וישמ·]

1QIsa^a XLI 14   (Isa 49:14) ואדוני (fig. 6.4) [supralinear ·ואלהי·]

4QM^a (4Q491) 11 i 14　אתחשב

h. *A triangular cluster of three cancellation dots*

1QDM (1Q22) III 10　{לחודש שר]ע ביום [ה]　　　{ה} לחודש עש[ור יומ].

The triangular shape preceding a stretch that was to be deleted (and subsequently erased) may have been a mnemonic device inserted by a scribe or user.

i. *A series of cancellation dots around a word*

A series of 12 dots were written around י[הוה in a small unidentified fragment without context (photograph PAM 43.679, frg. 6); see *DJD* XXXIII, pl. XX. Cf. also § iii below.

The mentioned examples show that dots were written above and below individual letters, parts of words, and complete words, and in one instance before a long stretch of text. As a rule, each individual letter was canceled by a single dot, but sometimes there were fewer or more dots than letters, as shown by TABLE 15.

TABLE 15: *Irregular Number of Cancellation Dots*

1QIsa^a XL 9 (Isa 48:4)	מאשֹׁר יֹדעתי: There is no dot on the *ʾaleph*, which was also to be erased (cf. MT מדעתי).
1QM III 4	יֹכֹתוֹבֹו: Three dots above, two below the letters, and one to the left of the word cancel the whole word.
4QCatena A (4Q177) 5–6 12	וֹראֹו: Dots were indicated above and below the first letter and above the third one.
4QapocrLam A (4Q179) 1 ii 11	היקֹרֹיֹם: There is no dot on the *yod* and the other dots are irregularly placed.
4QTime of Righteousness (4Q215a) 1 ii 9	בא ממשל הֹצֹדֹק הטוב: The second dot is placed between the *dalet* and *qoph*.
4QRP^c (4Q365) 12 iii 7	זהֹֹֹב: *zayin* is canceled with three dots
4QShirShabb^f (4Q405) 3 i 13	בֹשבֹעֹהֹ.: The dots were placed carelessly above and below the letters.
23 ii 3	כבודוֹהֹ.: The last letter was canceled by four dots, two above the letter, one below the letter, and one to its left.
4QNarrative H (4Q481e) 3	אשר (eight separate dots above the three letters)
4QOrd^b (4Q513) 13 1	אֹיֹא: Four dots around the first *ʾaleph* and supralinear *bet* above the *yod* (thus M. Baillet, *DJD* VII, 292; not visible on the plate).

Parallels for the use of cancellation dots:
• Alexandrian scribes used cancellation dots in various positions relative to the letters (Turner, *Greek Manuscripts*, 16): above a word (ibid., document 63), on both sides of two letters (document 34), and in a combination of a diagonal line through and a dot above a single letter (documents 16, 67, 72). See further Lieberman, *Hellenism*, 38–46; K. Lehrs, *De Aristarchi studiis homericis* (3rd ed., Leipzig 1882; repr. Hildesheim 1964) 340–41 referring to a Scholion of Aristarchus to Iliad X 398; K. Dziatzko, *Untersuchungen über ausgewählte Kapitel des antiken Buchwesens* (Leipzig 1900) 155. A special case is 4QLXXLev^a 1 5 (Lev 26:5) στοργητον (with a cancellation dot above the

rho and interlinear τρυ producing a correction τρυγητον for the vertical dittography σπορ). The Greek tradition also knows small expunging strokes either above or below, or both above and below the letters (Turner, *Greek Manuscripts*, 16). A special parallel to dots above and below the letters such as described above is found in P.Flor. B.L. 1371 of Psalm 36 LXX (4 CE) ἠ̇ἀ̇ρ̇ανομίας.

• LXX manuscripts of 2–4 CE: P.Bodmer XXIV of Psalms 17–53, 55–118 (3 CE), both above and below letters and complete words (Kasser–Testuz, *Bodmer*, 27–28, e.g. τῆ̇ς̇ θαλάσ̇σῆς̇ in col. LXIX 14 [Ps 68:3 LXX]); P.Chester Beatty VI (963; 2–3 CE) of Num 7:5 (three words), 61; 26:47; 32:12; P.Scheide (early 3 CE) of Ezekiel (LIX 21; LXI 45); P.Chester Beatty X (967) of Dan 3:22 πῦρὸς̇ (early 3 CE); P.Hamb. bil. 1 of Qohelet (3–4 CE) in Qoh 2:4 (XXX 12) μ̇ο̇υ̇.

• Manuscripts of SP: For example, in MS 4 recorded in the edition of Giron Blanc, *Genesis,* cancellation dots were written above the dittography of אלהים in Gen 1:21, subsequently crossed out with two crossing diagonal lines in the shape of an X. A similar procedure was followed in 4:11 for the dittography of ארור. All these instances (see also 7:11; 11:24; 12:2; 17:23; 36:23; 41:4; 41:15 in MS 4) were also crossed out with two lines. See further Crown, *Samaritan Scribes,* 71.

• The medieval MS A of CD I 9 אנשׁׁים with dots above three letters as well as within the final *mem* and the *shin*; V 3 פם dots within the letters; V 8 dot in the final *mem*. See the analysis by Y. Ofer in Charlesworth, *Rule of the Community,* 11.

• Medieval manuscripts of MT: See Birnbaum, "Michigan Codex," 385 referring to dots above and inside letters that were to be disregarded.

• Various Latin documents: See Hermann Hugo, *De prima scribendi origine* (Utrecht 1738) 285 (*non vidi*).

Some of the dots in the Judean Desert texts may have been added to the letters after the copying of the text was completed, but in many cases the dots were inserted during the course of the copying.

The latter procedure is assumed in 4QJubᵍ (4Q222) 1 4 עָׄאׄלׄ. This correction was inserted in the course of the writing process; the scribe started this word with an *ʿayin* of the next word, עליון, but upon recognizing his mistake, he canceled the *ʿayin*, and continued to write the text.

4QExodᶜ V 7 (Exod 12:37) is recorded in *DJD* XII, 114 as אׄלף מאות{א}. The scribe erroneously started the word with an *ʾaleph*, thinking that he was to copy the following word, placed a dot above that letter in order to cancel it, and continued to copy the correct word מאות. Only at a later stage was the *ʾaleph* erased. In actual fact, the erasure was superfluous since the dot denoted the erroneous nature of the *ʾaleph*. At what stage the letter was erased is unknown; it could have occurred during the course of the scribe's copying of these lines, but it could also have been erased at a later stage, by the scribe himself or by a later user. If the scribe had erased the letter upon writing it, there would have been no need to place a dot.[241]

1QIsaᵃX 23 (Isa 11:4; fig. 6.3) יֹׄמָׄתׄ רֹׄשָׄעׄ. Upon realizing that he had written these words too early in the sentence, the scribe canceled them with dots above and below the letters, and wrote them a little later.

The practice of using cancellation dots is evidenced in fifty-two biblical and nonbiblical texts written in the Qumran scribal practice, eight texts not written in that system, six texts of unclear orthographic practice, and three Aramaic texts.[242] These dots are found more frequently in nonbiblical than in biblical texts.

Biblical Texts

1QIsaᵃ scribes A and B: see above and Martin, *Scribal Character,* I.154–71; Kutscher, *Language,* 531–6
4QDeutᶜ 12–15 4 (Deut 11:10)
4QDeutʲ VIII 8 (Deut 11:10)
4QSamᶜ II 17 (2 Sam 14:32)

---

[241]Therefore, it is unlikely that the scribe first erased the *ʾaleph* and then inserted a cancellation dot (thus J. E. Sanderson, *DJD* XII, 103).

[242]The five signs preceding the first letter and above the first three letters of קרחיכה in 1QIsaᵃ XXXV 15 (Isa 42:6) resemble dots, but actually are remnants of an interlinear insertion. Note that the scroll lacks יהוה of MT. See Martin, *Scribal Character,* II.548–50.

4QXII^c 34 3 (Zeph 3:1)
4QXII^e 14–15 2 (Zech 5:9)
11QPs^a: see above and J. A. Sanders, *DJD* IV, 13

Nonbiblical Texts

1QH^a: see above, especially TABLES 13, 14 and Martin, *Scribal Character*, I.148–50
1QS: see above, especially TABLES 13, 14 and Martin, *Scribal Character*, I.144–8
1QSa I 16
1QM III 4; IV 6; XI 8
1QDM (1Q22) III 10
1QpHab II 10, 16; IV 6; VII 2, 2; VIII 14
4QTanḥ (4Q176) 10 17; 14 3, 4; 26 4
4QCatena A (4Q177) 1–4 15 and 5–6 12
4QTime of Righteousness (4Q215a) 1 ii 9
4QJub^g (4Q222) 1 1, 4, 5
4QpapJub^h (4Q223–224) unit 2, IV 10 (unclear dot)
4QPsJub^a (4Q225) 2 i 6
4QD^a (4Q266) 2 i 24; 3 ii 3; 5 ii 10; 6 i 11; 11 16
4QD^f (4Q271) 3 11; 4 ii 4; 5 i 5
4QToh A (4Q274) 3 ii 8 (Qumran orthography unclear)
4QBer^a (4Q286) 1 ii 6
4QBer^b (4Q287) 9 13
4QBer^d (4Q289) 2 3
4QMyst^c? (4Q301) 2 1
4QCal Doc/Mish C (4Q321a) 7 (col. V) 7
4QRP^b (4Q364) 17 3
4QRP^c (4Q365) passim: see above and E. Tov and S. White, *DJD* XIII, 259
4QT^a? (4Q365a) 2 ii 4; 3 2
4QPrayer of Enosh (4Q369) 2 2
4QCommunal Confession (4Q393) 3–7 8
4QMMT^c (4Q396) 1–2 iii 5, 6, 9
4QMMT^d (4Q397) 1–2 3
4QShirShabb^a (4Q400) 1 i 2; 2 3; 22 9; 23 i 3, ii 3; 27 2 (Qumran scribal practice probable)
4QShirShabb^d (4Q403) 1 i 34–35, 37, 42; 1 ii 12, 21
4QShirShabb^f (4Q405) 3 i 13; 20 ii–21–22 9; 23 ii 3; 27 2
4QVision and Interpretation (4Q410) 1 6
4QInstr^a (4Q415) 2 ii 2
4QInstr^d (4Q418) 9 18; 76 2; 81 8; 88 5; 102 3; 107 4; 126 12, 13; 140 4; 158 5; 172 8; 174 1; 241 2
4QSapiential-Hymnic Work A (4Q426) 1 i 12; 1 ii 3
4QH^a (4Q427) 1 3; 3 4; 7 ii 14, 16, 18, 20a, 20
4QBarkhi Nafshi^a (4Q434) 1 i 1, 2, 3
4QBarkhi Nafshi^e (4Q438) 4 ii 3 (Qumran scribal practice probable)
4QHodayot-like Text C (4Q440) 3 i 22
4QPersonal Prayer (4Q443) 2 6
4QNarrative C (4Q462) 1 14
4QM^a (4Q491) e.g. 1–3 8; 11 i 13, 14
4QapocrLam B (4Q501) 1
4QOrd^b (4Q513) 2 ii 4
4QProphecy of Joshua (4Q522) 8 3 (Qumran scribal practice probable)
11QT^a (11Q19) XLV 18

Texts *Not* Written in the Qumran Scribal Practice

4QExod^c V 7 (Exod 12:37)
4QIsa^d 6–10 7, 10 (Isa 49:1, 4)
4QIsa^h 1–2 10 (Isa 42:11)
4QJer^a IX, part 2 2 (Jer 14:6)

4QpIsa^b (4Q162) I 4
4QapocrLam A (4Q179) 1 i 13, 14 and 1 ii 11, 13
4QHarvesting (4Q284a) 1 4
4QapocrJosh^b (4Q379) 22 ii 13

<u>Unclear Orthography System</u>

4QPs^x 4
4QCommMal (4Q253a) 4 ii 1
4QapocrMos^c? (4Q408) 1 6; 3 6
4QText Mentioning Descendants of David (4Q479) 2 3
4QNarrative H (4Q481e) 3
4QOrd^c (4Q514) 1 i 7; 1 ii 7 (sectarian)

<u>Aramaic Texts</u>

1QapGen ar XXII 27
4QEnastr^a ar (4Q208) 16 4; 17 4; 18 2
4QEnGiants^d ar (4Q532) 1 ii 7 (before line 7)

On the firm connection between this practice and the Qumran scribal practice, see ch. *8a2.*

The long discussion in *b. Menaḥ.* 30b concerning the systems used for the correction of the name of God does not mention the possibility of using cancellation dots; it is therefore likely that from a certain point onwards these dots were no longer used for correcting MT copies in rabbinic circles (below, § 10).

Cancellation dots were intended to be *ad hoc* corrections, with no need of perpetuation in subsequent copies of the manuscripts. Nevertheless, in the Masoretic manuscripts a very few such signs were copied and subsequently became part and parcel of the textual transmission of that text (below, § 10). In other cases, the dots may have been disregarded, thus causing the inclusion in the text of superfluous elements. For examples, see L. Gottlieb, "Repetition Due to Homoioteleuton," *Textus* 21 (2002) 21–43.

ii. *Crossing out letters and words with a line* (fig. 7)

In many Qumran manuscripts written on leather, several words and parts of words were crossed out with one or more lines indicating the removal of these elements from the context. Thus, when in 4QCant^b 1 3 the scribe wrongly wrote עת (illustr. 8a) which should have been written later on in the sentence, that word was crossed out (עת), probably by the scribe himself. Indeed, most crossings out of elements were executed by the scribes themselves during the course of the writing. Sometimes, the scribe discontinued the writing in the middle of a word upon realizing his mistake. In such a case, the scribe would cross out the wrong elements and continue with the correct word. Thus, when the scribe of 4QNarrative C (4Q462) 19 recognized his mistake, he crossed out ישרא, the first four letters of 'Israel,' and immediately afterwards wrote the correct word ירושלם (thus: ויזכור את ישרא ירושלם). In 4QM^a (4Q491) 1–3 8, the scribe crossed out one complete and one partial word (partially reconstructed) before continuing with the following word of the running text. In 4QapocrLam B (4Q501) line 7, the scribe imprecisely placed a line through only parts of two words, מבני־ברית, although the cancellation pertained to the complete words. In 4QM^a (4Q491) 1–3 8 להכניע אוי (dittography of להכניע אויב), upon recognizing his mistake, the scribe stopped in the middle of the second word.

The use of this procedure is especially frequent in 4QD^a (4Q266), containing ten such examples in a long, yet very fragmentary, text. The complete composition would have contained more examples.

The placement of the stroke differed from case to case. Sometimes it was neatly placed, almost level with the tops of the letters (4QCant^b 1 3; illustr. 8a); sometimes the line was written through the middle of the word, and sometimes level with the bottom parts of the letters (1QIsa^a XI 10 [Isa 12:6]). With a slightly different procedure, several letters or words were scratched out in a zigzagged fashion with two or three lines:

1QIsa^a XVI 14 (Isa 21:1) בדובקה; XLIX 17 (Isa 59:14) מנאצינך
4QJer^c VII 9 (Jer 20:4). Two letters were crossed out inelegantly, creating a large ink blot.
4QQoh^a 1 ii 2 (Qoh 6:4) שמו
4QNarrative C (4Q462) 1 19 ישראל
4QapocrLam B (4Q501) 7 מבני־ברית

Most of the instances of crossing out pertain to complete words or combinations of words. In other cases, parts of words were crossed out:

4QapocrLam A (4Q179) 1 i 14: An original למכאובנו was changed to מכתינו by adding a cancellation dot to the right of the *lamed*, by crossing out אוב, and by writing תי above the word: למכאובנו

4QMyst^b (4Q300) 10 2: The scribe wrote לא and two illegible letters which were probably crossed out. Above the line he wrote ש, followed by two dots, creating a word לאיש.

4QNarrative C (4Q462) 19 ישראל
4QM^a (4Q491) 10 ii 17 תונף (with כל above the last two letters).
4QDibHam^a (4Q504) 1–2 iii 7 ותל ברנו (corrected to ותרב): ותל בתי

In three cases, single letters were crossed out: 4QLevi^b ar (4Q213a) 3–4 6 עמהא (vertical line); 4QRP^c (4Q365) 38 2 ל'ע; and 4QDibHam^a (4Q504) 1–2 vii 6 מלאכים רקיע.

The crossing out of the word was sometimes combined with the addition of the corrected text above the line, e.g.

1QIsa^a XVI 14 (Isa 21:1) ממדבר בא מארץ בדובקה (cf. MT ממדבר בא מארץ נוראה = LXX T V)
1QIsa^a II 12 (Isa 2:4) בין לעמים

TABLE 16 records words or letters crossed out in thirteen biblical and nonbiblical texts written in the Qumran scribal practice, seven texts not written in that system, and three Aramaic texts:[243]

TABLE 16: *Words or Letters Crossed out with a Line*

Biblical Texts

1QIsa^a scribes A and B	
II 12 (Isa 2:4)	בין לעמים
XI 10 (Isa 12:6)	בה (fig. 7)
XVI 14 (Isa 21:1)	בדובקה with supralinear נוראה
XXXVII 18 (Isa 44:13)[244]	חורש supralinear *waw* crossed out (illustr. 21)
XLIX 17 (Isa 59:14)	מנאצינך
4QDeut^c 32 i–33 10 (Deut 16:11)	בשערכב
4QQoh^a 1 ii 2 (Qoh 6:4)	שמו

---

[243] The segments recorded by D. Barthélemy and J. T. Milik in *DJD* I as having been crossed out in 1QSb I 3, 27 were probably not crossed out (see the plates). It is difficult to accept the editors' assertion, since in both cases a text identical to that written linearly appears above the line. The identical letters (line 3) and letter (line 27) probably were repeated supralinearly because they were not easily visible in the line itself.

[244] See further Kutscher, *Language*, 531–6.

Nonbiblical Texts

1QSb I, 3	יברכבה with רככה written above the line[245]
4QDª (4Q266) 5 ii 13	וחבֹ
6 i	Segment crossed out vertically in margin, parallel to lines 5–9.
6 i c 1	יסגרו
6 i e 2	נגע
6 iii 3	על
6 iv 2	עצי־פרי
8 ii 3	להמשפט
10 ii 11	את
11 16	ד (at the end of the line)
4QRPᶜ (4Q365) 38 2	ע'ל'
4QShirShabbᶠ (4Q405) 3 i 12	אמחנו
19 5	רוקמה (with *he* above the line)
4QHᵇ (4Q428) 3 1	הריה
4QNarrative C (4Q462) 1 19	ישראל
4QMª (4Q491) 1–3 8	להכני[ע] אוני
10 ii 17	תוכד (with כל above the last two letters)
4QapocrLam B (4Q501) 7	מבני־ברית
4QDibHamª (4Q504) 1–2 iii 7	ותֿל בדנו (corrected to ותרב)
1–2 vii 6	מלאכים רקיע
4QOrdᵇ (4Q513) 1–2 3	בֹהמה הטמאה: See also § iii.

Texts Not Written in the Qumran Scribal Practice

4QJerᶜ VII 9 (Jer 20:4)	two letters (which?) crossed out
4QCantᵇ 1 3 (Cant 2:12)	עת; illustr. 8a
4QDanª 14 11 (Dan 8:1)	ד[ב]בר נגלה
4QapocrLam A (4Q179) 1 i 14	למכאובד חי
4QTobᵉ (4Q200) 6 2	ותומהים
4QWork Containing Prayers A (4Q291) 1 5	אל
4QMystᵇ (4Q300) 10 2	לא

Aramaic Texts

4QLeviᵇ ar (4Q213a) 3–4 6	עמהא (vertical line through *aleph*)
4QEnGiantsᵇ ar (4Q530) 2 ii 1	זמא (vertical line through *aleph*)
7 ii 4	כעל
4QEnGiantsᵉ ar (4Q533) 3 2	א כתוב

On the connection between this procedure and the Qumran scribal practice, see ch. *8a2*. Parallels from ancient and medieval sources:

• Egyptian writings from the New Kingdom; see Ashton, *Scribal Habits*, 155.

• Several Greek documents employ horizontal and oblique strokes: See 4QLXXLevª 1 5 (Lev 26:5) σπορ γ[ητον (with a cancellation dot above the *rho* and interlinear τρυ producing a correction τρυγητον) and P.Oxy. 24.2404 (Aeschines, *In Ctesiphontem*; see Turner, *Greek Papyri*, pl. VIII and Dziatzko, *Untersuchungen*, 155). In P.Lit. London 207 of Psalms 11–16 (3–4 CE), a word was crossed out at Ps 13:2 τ]ον αυτω, while the corrected word θυ was written next to it. P.Bodmer XXIV of Psalms 17–53, 55–118 (3 CE) crossed out several letters and words, e.g. XXXIX 23 (Ps 44:10 LXX) βασιλεισσα. In the Greek documentary texts from Masada, some words were crossed out with a diagonal line (Lewis, *Bar Kochba*, document 21 10), with the correction written above the crossed out word (ibid., document 11 3) or next to it (ibid., line 3). See further Turner, *Greek Manuscripts*, 16 and documents 16 (a combination of a diagonal line through a single letter and a dot above that letter) and 24 (diagonal lines through three letters).

---

[245] It is unclear whether the scribe crossed out the letters with a line (thus J. T. Milik, *DJD* I, 120) or whether they were written so close to one another that they became blurred.

• The manuscripts of SP: e.g. MS 5 at Gen 4:11 crosses out אל with two intersecting diagonal lines in the shape of an X (see Giron Blanc, *Genesis*). The same procedure was followed for the dittography of אנכי in Gen 7:4.

• The scribe of the medieval MS B of CD crossed out scribal errors with single or double lines (XIX 11, 12, 16, 25; XX 5, 6, 9).

• Medieval biblical manuscripts, e.g. the Yemenite MS B.M. Or. 2211 (1475 CE) in Zeph 3:11 (dittography of מכל).

This practice is probably not mentioned in rabbinic literature[246] and for this reason, L. Blau, *Papyri*, 16 assumed that this practice would never be found in biblical manuscripts: 'Das *barbarische* <my italics, E.T.> Durchstreichen des fehlerhaften Wortes, das bei ihnen <scil. die antike Schreiber> gleichfalls üblich war, ist jedoch den Bibelschreibern nicht erlaubt gewesen.'

iii. *Parenthesis signs (*antisigma *and* sigma*) or a box-like shape around the element(s) to be canceled* (figs. 8.1–3)

Parenthesis signs in the Qumran texts enclose elements to be omitted and, in one instance, to be added, with an ἀντίσιγμα, antisigma [ )] and σίγμα, sigma [( ]. This practice is known from the Greek scribal tradition as περιγραφή, 'writing around' (cf. figs. 8.1–3 below and Turner, *Greek Manuscripts*, 16 and pls. 15, 25, 63). Zenodotus (b. *c.* 325 BCE) used the *sigma* and *antisigma* in order to indicate two consecutive lines having the same contents and therefore being interchangeable (Pfeiffer, *History*, 178). In the tradition of the Alexandrian grammarians, the *antisigma* denoted erroneous repetition (system of Aristophanes of Byzantium, *c.* 257–180 BCE) or disturbed word-order (system of Aristarchus, *c.* 217–145 BCE). Several examples in the Judean Desert texts do not fit this description, while 4QJer[a] XII 11 as well as the four units in a box-like shape fit the former definition, and 11QpaleoLev[a] I 1–2 fits the latter one. Threatte, *Attic Inscriptions*, 86–7 describes the use of these signs in Attic inscriptions in order to separate elements from the remainder of the text.

It is unclear whether the parenthesis signs in the Qumran texts denoted a different idea from the other deletion systems (cancellation dots, crossing out), but it appears that this system was used mainly for longer stretches than those deleted using the other systems. The section indicated with these signs in the MT of Num 10:35-36 (§ 10 below) is longer than any of the other stretches omitted. Also in the Greek tradition, the elements omitted with parenthesis signs are longer than the elements deleted with alternative practices.

For indicating omissions (and in one instance, an addition), parenthesis signs were used in five texts written in the Qumran scribal practice and three texts not written in that system.

• 1QM III 1 (fig. 8.1)   סדרי המלחמה וחצוצרות
(סדרי המלחמה וחצוצרות)

---

[246]This procedure may be referred to in *Soferim*, depending on one's understanding of the terminology used and the variants listed in Higger, *Mskt swprym*. With regard to the double writing of the divine name, the formulation of *Sof.* 5.1 is מקיים את הראשון ומעכב את האחרון —' . . . he retains the first and *erases* the latter.' The word used for *erases* is מעכב, and the variant readings in the edition of the Gaon from Vilna and in the parallel section in *Massekhet Sefer Torah*, מחשב and מחשיב, are explained by Ben Yehuda's *Thesaurus* as 'to cross out with a line.' The term used for the erasing of the divine name should be contrasted with the erasing of other duplicated words, for which *Soferim* used the term מחק, *erases* (with one of the erasure techniques, such as with a sharp instrument). Because of the uncertainty concerning the readings in *Soferim* and their meaning, the relevance of this detail for the present discussion is unclear.

For some reason (the addition of a header or damage to the leather?), the first three words of col. III were enclosed with parenthesis signs and marked with a line in the middle of the stretch of words above and below the text. These four signs together resemble a box-like shape that is also used for omissions (see below on 4QD^a). The added text is identical to the 'boxed' words.

• 1QS VII 8 שנה אחת

ונענש) שנה חודשים(

The length of the punishment for nursing a grudge against one's fellow-man (six months, also found in 4QS^e [4Q259] 1 i חוד[שים]) was removed from the context through the use of parenthesis signs and replaced by the more stringent punishment of 'one year,' written above the line.

• 4QQoh^a II 1 (Qoh 6:4)) הלך ובחושך שמו(

The *sigma*[247] + text written in the top margin (fig. 8.2), indicates an addition of words which had been omitted by way of homoioteleuton. The writing of the addition in the margin was probably accompanied by a mark in the text itself (such as in 4QpapTob^a ar [4Q196] 6 8 [Tob 3:13]; § iv below and fig. 9) in conjunction with the crossing out of שמו in the text of line 2 (TABLE 14).[248] A direct parallel for this practice is found in the Greek P.Oxy. 4.656 of Genesis 14–27 (2 or 3 CE): before the margin of line 139 a single parenthesis sign) indicated the omission of several words in the text, probably supplied in the top margin. In P.Oxy. 16 (P.Thucydides iii 3 of 1 CE), the *antisigma* in the margin likewise indicates the omitted words which were supplied in the top margin, presumably preceded by the same sign. The combination of the evidence of these two P.Oxy. fragments provides a parallel to 4QQoh^a which is also paralleled by the *ancora* sign (see above and fig. 15.1), even though the shape of the two signs differ.

• 4QM^a (4Q491) 11 i, end of line 15 (probably): see *DJD* VII, pl. VI (not the transcription on p. 27): ישובים .

• 4QDibHam^a (4Q504) 1–2 vi 2 between מכול and צרה (possibly).

The same procedure was also used in three texts not written in the Qumran practice:

• 4QJer^a XII 11 (Jer 18:23)) עֵל עונׂם }{עונׂם}(ע"ל . The second occurrence of על עונם was enclosed within parenthesis signs and subsequently erased. The phrase was written twice, in an identical or almost identical fashion, either by way of dittography or as a correction. The first occurrence included a supralinear word and therefore the second phrase was possibly added as a correction.

• 4QCant^b 2 ii 12 (Cant 4:10))∞ה. The remnants of the first word in this line, best visible on PAM 42.635 and the ABMC photograph, do not reflect כלה of MT (no remnant of a *lamed* is visible). Rather, they probably reflect an incorrectly written word, followed by a *sigma* to the left of the letters, indicating that the scribe wanted to remove the word from the context. The *antisigma*, if ever inscribed, is no longer visible.

• 11QpaleoLev^a I 1–2 (Lev 18:27): The notation of parenthesis signs around ten words from Lev 20:23-24 appearing in the middle of Lev 18:27 indicates that these verses had been inserted in the wrong place. Upon recognizing his mistake, which was triggered by identical words in the two verses, the scribe enclosed the ten words with parenthesis signs (only the *sigma* is preserved) and continued copying the text.

In three texts, the omitted elements were indicated with a *box-like shape* around the letters, in 4QD^a) with a square form, and in 4QOrd^b (4Q513) 1–2 3 with an elliptical form around מהמה הטמאה, partly crossed out. These two texts are halakhical. In 4QJub^f (4Q221) 1 6, the lines around the words are thick and light-colored. See, further, group ii *i* above.

• 4QJub^f (4Q221) 1 6 ומכול תועבתם וש]מור together with the first four words of the following line were crossed out (vertical dittography, cf. line 5 and the beginning of line 6).

• 4QD^a (4Q266) 1a 22 אפר (vertical dittography, cf. line 23).

---

[247]The lack of the right-hand sign is clearly visible in the color photograph in אנציקלופדיה עולם התנ"ך (Ramat Gan 1988) XVI.41.

[248]See photographs PAM 43.092 and 40.967 well reproduced in Cross, *ALQ³*, figure 13 and see also the photograph mentioned in the previous note. The view expressed here agrees with that of E. Ulrich, *DJD* XVI, 225, correcting his earlier view: "Ezra and Qohelet Manuscripts from Qumran (4QEzra, 4QQoh^{a,b})," in *Priests, Prophets, and Scribes: Essays on the Formation and Heritage of Second Temple Judaism in Honour of Joseph Blenkinsopp* (ed. E. Ulrich et al.; JSOTSup 149; 1992) 139–57. A square bracket, used in conjunction with a single round parenthesis sign in 4QEn^a ar (4Q201) II 1 (photograph PAM 41.360, see § iv below and fig. 8.3), indicates either an omission or an insertion (thus Milik, *Enoch*, 150).

• 4QD^a (4Q266) 11 15 והמשתלח (vertical dittography, cf. line 14).

• 4QOrd^b (4Q513) 1–2 3 מֵהֵמָּה הטמאה.

The box-like form of the parenthesis sign is paralleled by P.Berlin 17212 of Jeremiah 2–3 of the LXX (3 CE) around σου which was to be omitted and P.Bodmer XXIV of Psalms 17–53, 55–118, hands A and B (3 CE), e.g. XVIII 10–13. In this case, the text of Ps 24:4-5 was repeated erroneously (dittography), and the first occurrence was encircled by a vertical line together with a long dotted line. For further examples, see Kasser–Testuz, *Bodmer*, 28.

---

iv. *Addition/Omission signs* (figs. 8.3, 9)

Three instances of addition/omission signs are evidenced, with two possible additional instances.

4QpapTob^a ar (4Q196) 6 8 (Tob 3:13): A long vertical line with a short horizontal line at the bottom turning to the right at an angle of 90 degrees written in the space between words on the line (fig. 9) indicated an addition to be inserted in the running text.

4QEn^a ar (4Q201) II 1: Omission or addition (fig. 8.3).

4QapocrJosh^b (4Q379) 22 ii 14: According to Newsom, *DJD* XXII, 279 a high-placed dot indicates the insertion point of a dotted section wrongly placed in line 13. The dots in line 13 denote that the four words so indicated do not belong there.

4QPhyl H 7 and 4QPhyl I 11: According to J. T. Milik, vertical lines possibly denote insertions.

v. *Re-division sign* (fig. 23)

In 1QIsa^a, two dots in the space before the last letter of a word above and below the level of the letters indicate that the following letter needs to be joined to the word after the space. See also the separation dot between words described in § 7 below and illustrated in fig. 17.

1QIsa^a XIII 12 (Isa 15:5) שבר̇י ערו (cf. MT: שבר יעערו).

1QIsa^a XXVI 10 (Isa 32:2) וסתר̇ ם זרם (cf. MT: וסתר זרם; fig. 23).The two dots indicate that the words need to be read as וסתר מזרם (= LXX καὶ κρυβήσεται ὡς ἀφ' ὕδατος).

(3) *Single letters in the Cryptic A script primarily written in the margin* (figs. 10.1–11)

Several individual letters in the Cryptic A script as well as paleo-Hebrew letters (next section, *4*) were used as scribal marks in some Qumran scrolls. These groups of scribal markings probably point to a sectarian background for the copying of these texts or to their use within the Qumran community.

One group of scribal markings consists of single letters in the Cryptic A script used in the following texts, reasonably well preserved as well as very fragmentary, written completely in the Cryptic A script:

> 4Qpap cryptA Midrash Sefer Moshe (4Q249)
> 4QcryptA Words of the Maskil (4Q298)
> 4QcryptA Lunisolar Calendar (4Q317)
>> fragmentary texts:
> 4Qpap cryptA Serekh ha-ʿEdah^{a–i} (4Q249a–i)
> 4Q249j–z: sundry small fragments
> 4Qpap cryptA Text Concerning Cultic Service A (4Q250)
> 4Qpap cryptA Text Concerning Cultic Service B? (4Q250a)
> 4Q250b–j: sundry small fragments
> 4QcryptA Miqṣat Maʿaśe ha-Torah^g? (4Q313)

> 4QcryptA Unidentified Text P (4Q313a)
> 4QcryptA Unidentified Text Q (4Q313b)
> 4QcryptA Cal Doc B (4Q313c)
> 4Q324d–f: sundry small fragments
> 11QcryptA Unidentified Text (11Q23)
> See also:
> 4QHoroscope (4Q186) written in the square, paleo-Hebrew, and Cryptic A scripts

This script is described by S. Pfann, "4Q298" as a development from the Late Phoenician scripts, and is used for several texts of a Qumran sectarian nature as well as for other texts which must have had a special meaning for the Qumran community (see also Pfann's study, "The Writings in Esoteric Script from Qumran," in Schiffman, *Jerusalem Congress*, 177–90). According to Milik, quoted by Pfann, "Writings," 177, and Pfann, this script was used especially by the Maskil.

In the scrolls analyzed here, a few individual letters of the Cryptic A script are written between the lines and, more frequently, in the margins. These letters may well refer to a sectarian coded message. Although the meaning of these letters is not evident, it is clear that they occur irregularly, as is evident from 4Qpap pIsa[c] (4Q163), in which only one column is copiously annotated in the margin (6–7 ii). The scribal markings in this script, consisting of one, two, or three letters, are listed in this section and in figs. 10.1–11 together with their parallels in the Cryptic A script, especially as evidenced in 4QcryptA Words of the Maskil (4Q298), 4QcryptA Lunisolar Calendar (4Q317), and 4QHoroscope (4Q186). In 1QIsa[a], these signs may refer to the sectarian reading of certain passages,[249] or to matters of sectarian interest. At the same time, one of the signs (fig. 10.4) possibly draws attention to elements lacking in the text in comparison with MT; however, if this assumption is correct, this would be the only evidence for the collation of any of the Qumran scrolls with MT.

Since the identification of the Cryptic A script for texts using sectarian terminology is likely (Pfann, "4Q298"), the new evidence shows that at least some biblical Qumran texts were actively used by the Qumran community or copied by sectarian scribes.

The evidence for these signs in the Cryptic A script pertains to six texts written according to the Qumran scribal practice, all sectarian; note in particular 4QMyst[c]? (4Q301) in which an encoded sectarian message is not surprising. The evidence also pertains to one Aramaic and three biblical texts (1QIsa[a], written according to the Qumran scribal practice, and possibly also 4QExod[k] and 4QCant[b]). The use of letters in Cryptic A should be discussed in conjunction with that of individual letters of the paleo-Hebrew script which probably served a similar purpose in 1QIsa[a], 1QS, and 5QLam[a], for which see § 4 below. The appearance of letters in the Cryptic A script has important implications for our understanding of the literature of the Qumran community, in particular of the biblical texts 1QIsa[a] and 4QCant[b], and of works whose sectarian nature is not immediately obvious: 4QInstr[c] (4Q417), 4QDibHam[a] (4Q504), 4QShir[b] (4Q511), and 4QMyst[c]? (4Q301). All these compositions were annotated, although very rarely, with paleo-Hebrew letters and letters of the Cryptic A script. These letters were written by either the original scribes, later scribes, or users.

A relatively large number of *zayin*s are recognizable (figs. 10.6, 10.7 [2x], 10.12, 11, 11.1, 11.2, 12.1).

Several signs appear at the beginning of new sections to which they refer as a whole: figs. 5.5, 10.2, 10.3, 10.5, 10.9, 10.10, 11.1, 11.2. Other signs are written above single words: figs. 10.4, 10.6 (2x), 10.7 (2x).

---

[249]Thus already J. C. Trever in Burrows, *The Dead Sea Scrolls*, xvi and Martin, *Scribal Character*, I.186–7 although they did not recognize the cryptic letters.

On the difficulty concerning the *distinction* between the Cryptic A script and paleo-Hebrew letters, see further below, § 4.

1QIsaᵃ scribes A and B: Several signs in the margin (rarely in the text itself) of this manuscript reflect letters in the Cryptic A script, without any recognizable pattern[250] and, with one exception, not occurring more than once. That the signs described below are probably not related to a paragraphing system is evident from the sign in VIII 9, which occurs in conjunction with a *paragraphos* sign.

VII, between lines 7 and 8 (Isa 7:20; Trever in Burrows, *The Dead Sea Scrolls*, fig. 2), at the beginning of a new section (fig. 10.1a), possibly reflecting a prolonged form of the *resh* in the Cryptic A script (fig. 10.1b).

VIII 9 (Isa 8:16; Trever, fig. 3); cf. the *ḥeth* in the Cryptic A script (fig. 10.2a–b).

XI 4 (Isa 11:15; Trever, fig. 4), at the beginning of a new section (fig. 10.3a); cf. the *qoph* in the Cryptic A script of 4QcryptA Words of the Maskil (4Q298, fig. 10.3b) or a *bet* (*beta*) of 4QHoroscope (4Q186).

XVII 1 (Isa 21:16; Trever, fig. 5) above שלוש. This sign (fig. 10.4a) possibly indicates the lack of שלוש in MT; cf. the *kaph* in the Cryptic A script or an *ʿayin* in the paleo-Hebrew script (fig. 10.4c). A similar sign occurs in XXVIII 18 (Isa 34:17; fig. 10.4b), as well as in 4QInstrᶜ (4Q417) 2 ii 23 (with a different function?; see below), in 4QCantᵇ I 7 (see below), and as part of a paragraph sign in 1QIsaᵃ (fig. 1.6; e.g. XXVIII 29 [illustr. 6]; XXXII 29; XXXV 22). Cf. also XXVIII 18 (Isa 34:17; Trever, fig. 5). The circular sign probably indicates a long missing stretch of text in the original text of the scroll, which was subsequently added by a later hand.

XXI 23 (Isa 27:13; Trever, fig. 6), at the beginning of a new section (fig. 10.5a); cf. the *ṣade* in the Cryptic A script (fig. 10.5b).

XXVII 21 (Isa 33:19; Trever, fig. 8). This sign (fig. 10.6a), written above תראו, differing from תראה of MT, may reflect the notation of a variant reading; cf. the *zayin* in the Cryptic A script (fig. 10.6b) or a paleo-Hebrew *zayin* (fig. 10.6c).

XXXIII 1 (Isa 40:2; Trever, fig. 8),[251] is written above כפלים (fig. 10.7a), cf. the *zayin* in the Cryptic A script or in the paleo-Hebrew script (figs. 10.6b–c). Note also the similar paleo-Hebrew *zayin* in the margin of 4QShirᵇ (4Q511) 18 iii 8 (see below). Cf. also:

XL 19 (Isa 48:14), above בבבל (fig. 10.7b).

4QExodᵏ: For the sign in the upper right corner (fig. 10.11a), above the center of the first word, cf. the *lamed* in the Cryptic A script of 4QcryptA Lunisolar Calendar (4Q317; fig. 10.11b). The positioning of the sign could reflect a numbering system of sheets, on which see below § 8.

4QCantᵇ I 7 (line-filler?; fig. 12.2 and illustr. 8a) at the end of the line; cf. Cryptic A *kaph* (fig. 10.4c) or paleo-Hebrew *ʿayin*.

4QpPsᵇ (4Q173) frg. 5 (which probably does not belong to this manuscript) 4 לאל written in unusual letters. The letters resemble Greek and Latin characters in mirror writing with Hebrew values (α = א and L = ל), and therefore resemble the Cryptic A script of 4QHoroscope (4Q186), which includes a few Greek letters. See fig. 28. J. Allegro named these letters 'some cryptic form' (*DJD* V, 53), while Skehan, "The Divine Name," 27 speaks of 'distorted, unnatural paleohebrew lettering.' For the writing of the divine name in special ways, see § 5d below and ch. 6b2.

4QpapTobᵃ ar (4Q196; fig. 10.8b) 35 (fragmentary; the sign may have been written in the margin between the columns); cf. the Cryptic A letter *kaph* (fig. 10.4c).

4QSᵉ (4Q259) III 3 (frg. 3a): It is not impossible that the ill-defined signs or letters in this line represent cryptic letters (בישראל?), though not in the Cryptic A script. Alexander–Vermes, *DJD* XXVI, 9, 145 do not accept this view, while the views of those who do believe that these are cryptic letters are described in detail on p. 145 of the same publication: S. Metso, "The Primary Results of the Reconstruction of 4QSᵉ," *JJS* 44 (1993) 303–8, especially 307; eadem, *Community Rule*, 53; É. Puech, "L'alphabet cryptique A en 4QSᵉ

---

[250]It is difficult to know whether the paragraphs indicated by the signs are of any specific sectarian importance. Martin, *Scribal Character*, I.184, notes that fig. 10.1, referring to Isa 7:20, pertains to Babylon and Egypt, often mentioned in the Qumran writings, for example, in 1QM. An explanation of this kind is probably behind some of these signs in 1QIsaᵃ, but it is hard to press this point, as the passages which are most central to the Qumran community are not indicated in this way. Another possibility that comes to mind is that some of the signs could be cross-references to the *pesharim* of Isaiah, but this hypothesis cannot be examined as the relevant sections of the *pesharim* have not been preserved.

[251]Trever incorrectly combines his transcription of three similar shapes into one sign.

(4Q259)," *RevQ* 18 (1998) 429–35. Puech, 435, points out that only the sectarians would have been able to fully understand the meaning of the context.

4QMyst^c? (4Q301) 3 2–4 (fig. 10.10a): For the three signs written one above the other, cf. the *samekh*, *ʿayin*, and *sin/shin* in the Cryptic A script (figs. 10.10b–c). These three (lines of?) signs are followed by a blank line before the continuation of the text. The context does not allow us to understand the mystery of these signs, but the existence of a sectarian cryptic message in this text would not be surprising. 4QMyst^c? (4Q301) 3 resembles 4QHoroscope (4Q186), since both compositions are of a physiognomic nature and both contain encoded messages written in the Cryptic A script. If this explanation is correct,[252] the three letters strictly speaking are not scribal signs, since they are part of the composition, as in 4QHoroscope (4Q186).

4QInstr^c (4Q417) 2 ii 23 (fig. 10.8a); cf. the Cryptic A letter *kaph* (fig. 10.4c). It was represented by Strugnell–Harrington in *DJD* XXXIV as a *samekh* in the square script.

4QDibHam^a (4Q504) 1–2 v 3 (not iv 3 as recorded by M. Baillet, *DJD* VII, 143) in the margin to the right of the text, at the beginning of what is probably a new section (fig. 10.9a); cf. the *mem* in the Cryptic A script (fig. 10.9b).[253]

4QShir^b (4Q511) 18 iii 8 (fig. 10.12): The sign could reflect a *zayin* in the Cryptic A or paleo-Hebrew script (figs. 10.6–7).

(4) *Single paleo-Hebrew letters written in the margin* (figs. 10.12–12.2)

Individual letters in the paleo-Hebrew script, written in the margins of several compositions, probably draw attention to certain matters or to passages of special interest. These letters, like all other symbols in the Qumran manuscripts, were probably inserted in the text after the writing was completed.

The decision as to whether a certain letter belongs to the Cryptic A script (§ 3) or the paleo-Hebrew script is sometimes difficult, in particular since some letters are ornamented or stylized. Nevertheless, for the sake of description, a distinction is made here between these two scripts, although letters of both types were used together in the text of 4QHoroscope (4Q186) and in the margin of 1QIsa^a. The use of the paleo-Hebrew letters, with the exception of the use of the paleo-Hebrew *waw* as a paragraph sign, probably reflects the same background as the use of letters of the Cryptic A script.

Although the scribal marks written in the margins of some manuscripts have been known for some time, no satisfactory solution for their occurrence has been suggested, and some of them remain enigmatic. These signs probably direct attention to certain details in the text or to certain pericopes, but they may also refer to the reading by the Qumran covenanters of certain passages, especially in the case of 1QIsa^a. The function of the letters in 4QCant^b differs from that in the other texts. They may have served as a

[252] Three vertically arranged signs are preserved at the left edge of the fragment, while the text to the left of these letters (the continuation of these three words?) has not been preserved. The three preserved letters probably constituted the beginning of a three-line heading or note written in the middle of the text rather than a three-letter note written one above the other. The three signs are preceded by blank spaces, before which one recognizes the remnants of two letters written in the square script, like the remainder of the document. If this explanation is correct, the signs do not constitute a word סמס, but rather the three letters form the beginnings of three words or combinations of words, of which the first one started with a *samekh* (ס[פר ?). A different explanation for these signs was suggested by A. Lange, "Physiognomie oder Gotteslaub? 4Q301 3," *DSD* 4 (1997) 282–96. According to Lange, there is no intrinsic connection between 4QMyst^c? (4Q301) and 4QHoroscope (4Q186), and the third sign serves as a means of identification, such as on Ostracon 100 in I. Ephʿal and J. Naveh, *Aramaic Ostraca of the Fourth Century BC from Idumea* (Jerusalem 1996) 54. Upon comparison of the signs, however, one notes that the ostracon has four and not two semicircles, it lacks the paragraph-like sign under the letter, the bottom line is thicker, and the circles are more rounded than in the case of the letter in 4QMyst^c?, which in all aspects resembles the *samekh* of the Cryptic A script.

[253] The evidence is not clear for a few additional markings in DibHam^a for which detailed drawings were presented by Baillet in *DJD* VII, although these shapes are not visible on the plates themselves, nor on photograph PAM 43.611: 1–2 vi 2 (on the plate this sign has the appearance of a parenthesis sign), 1–2 vii 4, 10 (both at the beginning of new sections).

special type of line-filler (§ *c6* below) or they may have been used for a very specific, as yet undetermined, purpose relating to the content of the manuscript.

The presence of individual letters in the Cryptic A script in the margins of manuscripts has been explained above as pointing to a Qumran sectarian background. It is suggested here that the appearance of individual paleo-Hebrew letters may point in the same direction, although there is no evidence for this suggestion. This assumption is supported mainly by the argumentation concerning the use of paleo-Hebrew letters for the Tetragrammaton, to be discussed in the next section.[254]

1QIsa[a] VI 22 in the margin to the right of Isa 7:8 (Trever, fig. 1; below fig. 5.4) represents a paleo-Hebrew *waw*. This sign should be compared with the similar use of the paleo-Hebrew *waw* in the margins of 1QS V 1 and 4QPs[b] (both: below) as well as in 4QpaleoExod[m] main text and VIII, patch, line 2 (fig. 5.1 and illustr. 14) and 11QpaleoLev[a] J 1 (fig. 5.3 and illustr. 14a). This paleo-Hebrew *waw*, like others (above § 1), sometimes indicates a new section, but there is no indication in the spacing or context of 1QIsa[a] that this is the case in VI 22. In 11QpaleoLev[a], this *waw* occurs only in some open sections, possibly (thus Freedman–Mathews, *Leviticus*, 11) indicating a major sense division (J 1 [Lev 20:1]; II 2 [Lev 23:23]; III 3, 8 [Lev 24:10, 13]), while subdivisions lack this *waw* in the open sections (I 7 [Lev 19:1]; II 6 [Lev 23:26]; K 6 [Lev 21:10]). Frg. K 6 could have included a *waw*, as the next word lacks that conjunction.

1QIsa[a] XXII 10 to the right of Isa 28:9 (new section). This sign (Trever, fig. 7; below fig. 11.1) is an embellished representation of the paleo-Hebrew *zayin* (like 1QS VII below) with an ornamented vertical line on top.

1QS to the right of V 1: This paleo-Hebrew *waw* (fig. 5.5) probably indicates the beginning of a major content division, while almost all other sections in this scroll are indicated with regular paragraph signs.

1QS VII bottom margin and IX 3 (figs. 11 and 11.2): These two signs possibly seal off a text unit. Both are composite signs, and in character, though not in shape, they resemble the *koronis* used in the Greek scribal tradition. The *koronis,* written at the end of literary units, was likewise shaped as a Greek *paragraphos* with ornaments above and below it.[255] The character of the Greek sign thus resembles that of 1QS IX 3 (fig. 11.2) of which the top element likewise is a paragraph sign. The sign in col. VII, bottom margin (fig. 11) is composed of a paleo-Hebrew *zayin* with an ornamental line on top (similar to 1QIsa[a] XXII 10 [above]) and a triangular form below.[256] It could indicate the end of a text unit, since a new one starts at the beginning of the following column. On the other hand, the sign could also be taken to denote a numbering system, for which see below, § *c8*.

1QS IX 3 (fig. 11.2a; with elements in common with the sign in 1QIsa[a] XXII 10; Trever, fig. 7): The sign is composed of the paragraph sign and below it a paleo-Hebrew *zayin* and a *samekh*[257] similar to that found in the Cryptic A letters in 4QHoroscope (4Q186; fig. 11.2b). The paragraph sign indicates a new section, while the letter combination may convey a sectarian message.

4QPs[b] V 16 (Ps 93:5), the last line of col. V before Ps 94:1 in the following column. Cf. the paleo-Hebrew *waw*—see ch. *5c1* (fig. 5.2).

4QCant[b]: The paleo-Hebrew letters at the ends of lines, described in § 6 below as possible line-fillers, could also denote matters of special (sectarian) interest since their use as line-fillers is not consistent.

5QLam[a] II, bottom margin (fig. 11.3): This sign resembles a truncated paleo-Hebrew *waw* or a *waw* in the Aramaic script of the sixth century BCE (oral suggestion by É. Puech). For the writing of this letter in the margin, see 4QPs[b] (above).

4Qpap pIsa[c] (4Q163) 6–7 ii: Two marginal signs resemble either paleo-Hebrew letters or letters in the Cryptic A script. The sign in line 10 (fig. 4) is probably a paleo-Hebrew *waw*. It is written in the margin preceding a new section, after a blank line (a quotation from the biblical text in a *pesher* manuscript, the only instance in this scroll), in the same position as the sign in 1QIsa[a] VI 22 (above) and in 1QS V 1 (fig.

---

[254]On the other hand, the use of paleo-Hebrew letters in several of the Masada ostraca probably has no sectarian background (cf. Y. Yadin and J. Naveh, *Masada I*, 6–7). These paleo-Hebrew letters occur either alone (Ostraca 286–301) or in conjunction with a Greek letter (Ostraca 282–285) or with a Hebrew name together with a Greek letter (Ostraca 302–380).

[255]Cf. Turner, *Greek Manuscripts*, 12 (with bibliography); G. M. Stephen, "The Coronis," *Scriptorium* 13 (1959) 3–14.

[256]Puech, "Une Apocalypse," 482 explains the triangular form as an *ʿayin* and the two signs together as (ד)ע (ה)ז.

[257]Allegro reads the letter as a *waw*, but it is identified as a *samekh* by J. Carmignac, "Les horoscopes de Qumran," *RevQ* 5 (1965) 199–206, and Strugnell, "Notes," 274.

5.5); see the discussion above §§ ii and *c1*. The sign in line 18 (fig. 11.4) probably represents a stylized paleo-Hebrew *sin/shin*, almost of the Samaritan type, introducing a scriptural quotation in the *pesher*.

4QpapMMT[e] (4Q398) 14–17 i 4: paleo-Hebrew *ʾaleph* (fig. 11.5)?

4QInstr[d] (4Q418) 67 3 between cols. i and ii (close to the end of the line in col. i): This sign (fig. 5.7) probably presents a paleo-Hebrew *ʾaleph*; the context is truncated.

(5) *Marks, including unexplained signs, drawing attention to matters in the text*

Some signs, possibly written by users, were meant to draw attention to certain issues or passages, possibly passages of sectarian interest.[258] For parallel signs in Aramaic fourth-century BCE documents, see Ephʿal–Naveh, *Aramaic Ostraca*. Among the Qumran signs, the function of the X-sign is the most evident, while the meaning of some signs (letters?) is unclear. Similarly, McNamee, *Sigla*, 7 notes that a great number of the signs in Greek literary papyri are obscure:

(i) X-sign (fig. 22)

While the X-sign is used in 1QpHab as a line-filler (see below), referring to the text to the right of the sign, in other texts it draws attention to certain words, lines, sections, or issues to the left of the sign. McNamee, *Sigla*, 19 notes that 'there is considerable evidence in secondary sources to support the theory that the sign was a reference mark directing the reader to a commentary.' Epp remarks that the χ sign was used in the Oxyrhynchus papyri 'to indicate something noteworthy in a line.'[259] It is not impossible that this is the case with the examples listed below.

1QIsa[a]: X appearing between columns usually refers to the text to the left, while occasionally it appears to refer to the text to the right (e.g. XLV 23). At the beginning of a new, open, section: XXVI 9 (Isa 32:1; fig. 22.2); XXXIV 15 (Isa 41:11?); XXXV 10 (Isa 42:1); XXXVIII 6 (Isa 45:1) in conjunction with a complex *paragraphos*; XLI 5 (Isa 49:4); XLVI 10 (Isa 56:1); XLVI 13 (Isa 56:3); XLVIII 9 (Isa 58:13); LIII 18 (Isa 66:6?). At the beginning of a new, closed, section: XXXVI 3 (Isa 42:22); XXXVII 5 (Isa 43:26). In XLV 23 (Isa 55:4?), the reason for the X-sign is unclear. That the X-sign does not indicate the division into sense units is clear from XXXVIII 6 (illustr. 21) where it occurs in conjunction with a complex *paragraphos* sign; therefore the X-sign which was probably added secondarily, must have had a different meaning.

4QCatena A (4Q177) 12–13 ii 9 and 29 2, both times in an indented space in the beginning of the line (fig. 22.1); 12–13 i 8 at the beginning of the *pesher*: The X-sign probably indicates the indentation itself, just as it indicates the space in the middle of the line in 8Ḥev Prayer 2 5.

4QInstr[c] (4Q417) 4 1, between cols. i and ii (probably).

A similar use of the X-sign indicating noteworthy passages is evidenced in the Greek scribal tradition, both as the Greek letter X and in the combination of two letters—ρ above X (both denoting χρηστόν) in Greek papyri (cf. Turner, *Greek Manuscripts*, 15 and index; idem, *Greek Papyri*, 116; McNamee, *Sigla*, 19), from where this custom may have been transferred to Semitic sources.[260]

---

[258] No connection was found between the signs found in the texts from the Judean Desert and those mentioned by Epiphanius in his *Treatise on Weights and Measures* referring to certain topics in manuscripts, although some signs have a similar shape. According to Epiphanius, the X-sign denotes the Messiah, another sign marks obscure passages in the Scriptures, and another one (fig. 14) denotes the 'promises to the ancient people.' See J. E. Dean, *Epiphanius' Treatise on Weights and Measures: The Syriac Version* (Chicago 1935) 15. The latter sign (fig. 11.1) most closely resembles the signs and letters analyzed here.

[259] E. Epp, "The New Testament Papyri at Oxyrhynchus in Their Social and Intellectual Context," in: *Sayings of Jesus: Canonocal and Non-canonical—Essays in Honour of Tjitze Baarda* (ed. W. L. Petersen et al.; NTSup 89; Leiden 1997) 47–68 (64).

[260] Teicher linked the X-sign, which according to him was used especially with reference to passages of Messianic content in the Isaiah scroll, with the Greek letter denoting the Christian abbreviation X of Χριστός. See J. L. Teicher, "The Christian Interpretation of the Sign X in the Isaiah Scroll," *VT* 5 (1955) 189–98. However many passages in the Isaiah scroll and elsewhere do not allow for such an interpretation; besides most scrolls were written before the beginning of Christianity. Against Teicher, see I. Sonne, "The X-Sign in the Isaiah Scroll," *VT* 4 (1954) 90–94.

(ii) Other shapes

1QpHab IV 12 straight line in the margin (fig. 20): This is probably not a *paragraphos*, but was meant to indicate a matter of special interest.

4QDeut[b] I 15 end of the line (fig. 25): The meaning of the sign in the shape of a reversed *ḥet* (J. A. Duncan, *DJD* XIV 11: 'three strokes of ink') is unclear.

4Qpap pIsa[c] (4Q163) 4–7 ii 4–7, 14, 15, 17: Horizontal lines in the margin designate the writing of the *pesher*.

4QTime of Righteousness (4Q215a) 1 i, end of line 9 (fig. 5.8): The nature of this sign is unclear.

4QInstr[b] (4Q416) 2 ii 6 (fig. 5.9): The nature of this elliptical shape is unclear. Cf. fig. 10.4.

MasDeut line 5 (Deut 33:20) קָדְקֹד (last word in the verse): The meaning of the wedge-shaped form above the first letter of this word (fig. 20) is unclear.

Note further:

4QIsa[d] 4–5: The marks in the bottom margin are probably remains of letters rather than signs.

4QCal Doc/Mish B (4Q321) V 3: The nature of the sign above the line above the first letter of בחופה in the form of two lines forming a right angle is unclear. The detail could reflect a *nun* without any recognizable contextual meaning (thus S. Talmon, *DJD* XXI, 75).

(6) *Marks written at the ends of lines as line-fillers*

The notion that some signs in the Qumran manuscripts served as special types of line-filler is well established, since such a practice is clearly visible in several of the later texts from Naḥal Ḥever (*DJD* XXVII and Yardeni, *Textbook*). The special purpose of these line-fillers was to point out that the space at the end of the line was not to be taken as a section marker ('open section'), indicated by an X-sign at the point of the left margin, usually flush with the vertical line, or slightly to the right.

5/6Ḥev papLease Contract (5/6Ḥev 42) 2 (Yardeni, *Textbook*, 1.102).

5/6Ḥev papLease of Land (5/6Ḥev 44) 2, 5, 12, 15, 16, 22, 23. The X-signs are written at the ends of the lines, which are somewhat shorter than the other lines. In line 5 it occurs after בעין, while the following line starts with גדי; accordingly the function of the X can only be that of a line-filler, since it is placed between Ein and Gedi. For the data, see *JDS* 3, pl. 77 and Yardeni, *Textbook*, 1.113.

5/6Ḥev papLease of Land (5/6Ḥev 45) 12, 20, 21, 26, 28. Line 12 ends with שמעון בן, and the following line starts with כוסבא. In the relatively large space at the end of line 12, which is too short for כוסבא, an X-sign is indicated. See Yardeni, *Textbook*, 1.115.

5/6Ḥev papLease of Land (5/6Ḥev 46) 5, 10. See Yardeni, *Textbook*, 1.118.

XḤev/Se papDeed of Sale E ar (XḤev/Se 21) a 12: An X-sign is written in the Lower Version, in the middle of a phrase at the end of the line (fig. 22.3).

In three Qumran texts, the X-signs were likewise used for the specific purpose of indicating that a space at the end of a line should not be mistaken for an 'open section,' which has a definite contextual meaning:[261]

1QpHab III 12 (fig. 22.6), 14; IV 11, 14; VI 4, 12; VIII 1; IX 1, 13, 16 (?); X 3; XII 2. This explanation was recognized first by M. H. Lehman, "Materials Concerning the Dating of the Dead Sea Scrolls: I Habakkuk," *PEQ* 83 (1951) 32–54, especially 47.[262] Lehman noted a similar X-sign in an Oxford Genizah fragment MS Heb c. 18, fol. 30. In 1QpHab, these X-signs were always written slightly to the right of, or flush with, the left vertical ruled line (illustr. 3). This also pertains to the single *ʾaleph* in II 5 which

---

[261] According to H. G. Snyder, "Naughts and Crosses: Pesher Manuscripts and Their Significance for Reading Practices at Qumran," *DSD* 7 (2000) 26–48 (especially 42–3) these signs 'are best understood as cues for textual performance.' According to him, these signs were meant to guide the reader who read this text orally to disregard unwanted spaces. Basically Snyder follows our explanation (Snyder quotes my earlier article on this subject), but he connects the writing of the sign with the oral recitation of the text. Doudna, *4Q Pesher Nahum*, 239 follows our explanation.

[262] Other scholars were puzzled by this sign: W. H. Brownlee, "Further Light on Habakkuk," *BASOR* 114 (1949) 10; Martin, *Scribal Character*, I.193; K. Elliger, *Studien zum Habakuk-Kommentar vom Toten Meer* (Tübingen 1953) 75; Horgan, *Pesharim*, 25.

probably reflects a wrongly copied X-sign, implying that 1QpHab was copied from an earlier manuscript.[263] This *ʾaleph* is written in exactly the same position as the X-signs, slightly to the right of the left vertical line.

4QCommGen A (4Q252) I 4 at the end of the line flush left with the vertical line (vague imprint; fig. 22.4).

11QT[b] (11Q20) IV 9 (fig. 22.5); V 9.

Additional shapes:

1QIsa[a]: one or two dots at the end of lines level with the tops of the letters. See III 6 (two dots [Isa 3:4]; fig. 13); IV 8 (two dots [Isa 4:4]); VIII 9 (two dots [Isa 8:17]); XX 10 (two dots [Isa 25:11]; fig. 13); XXI 7, 12 (single dots [Isa 37:1, 4]); XXIII 2 (single dot [Isa 28:25]), 13; XXVI 11, 29 (two dots [Isa 32:3, 18]). The data are recorded by Qimron–Parry, *Isaiah* as 'no V.'

4QCant[b] 1 4, 7, 11, 13; 2 i 4; 3, last line. The markings in this scroll best visible on photograph PAM 40.604 (see illustr. 8a) may be line-fillers, albeit of a different nature.[264] That scroll contains five different scribal marks in frg. 1, at the ends of lines 4 (fig. 12.1; paleo-Hebrew *zayin*?), 7 (fig. 12.2; Cryptic A letter *kaph* or paleo-Hebrew *ʿayin*?), 9 (fig. 12.3, cf. also fig. 15; *epsilon*?), 11 (fig. 12.4; paleo-Hebrew *sin/shin* with a 90 degree rotation or *sigma*?), 13 (fig. 12.5; paleo-Hebrew *bet*?), and probably also in frg. 2 I 4, and at the left edge of the last line of frg. 3 (fig. 12.6; *gamma*? or a sign similar in shape to a *diple obelismene* [a sign used in the Greek scribal tradition for separating different sections in tragedies and comedies]?). These markings probably represent letters in the paleo-Hebrew script or the Cryptic A script (§ 4 above), or a combination of several scripts, including Greek (for the latter, cf. figs. 12.3 and 12.6). Since the Cryptic A script is used for Qumran sectarian writings, the appearance of these letters in 4QCant[b] could point to the use of this scroll within the Qumran community.

4QHistorical Text E (4Q333) 1 2 end of line (fig. 11.6). The inverted *paragraphos* at the end of the line possibly represents a special type of line-filler.

Line-fillers are also known from:

• Egyptian literary texts (Janzen, *Hiërogliefen*, 47).

• Ancient Greek literary texts; for example, see the wedge-formed shapes in Genesis and the Minor Prophets in codex W; P.Chester Beatty VI (963) of Numbers and Deuteronomy of the end of 2 CE or the beginning of 3 CE; see further Gardthausen, *Griechische Palaeographie*, 406–7.

• Greek documentary texts.

• Various manuscripts of T, such as MS Vatican Urbinati 2 (high dots) and Targum Neophyti which filled up the ends of the lines with the beginning letter(s) of the first word on the following line.

• The medieval tradition of MT and SP. For example, codex L of MT used dots as line-fillers before the penultimate words in Exodus 15 in order that the last words would be flush with the left marginal line (see the plates and analysis in Sirat, *Ha-ketav*, 37–9; Beit-Arié, *Hebrew Codicology*, 88; Tov, *TCHB*, pl. 12; Birnbaum, "Michigan Codex," 384). The scribe of L also filled in the ends of several lines in Exodus 14 with parts of letters.

---

[263] A different explanation was voiced by H. Stegemann in a lecture in the Qumran workshop of the Institute for Advanced Studies, Hebrew University, Jerusalem 1994. According to Stegemann, these signs indicated the left sides of the beginnings of new columns, like the *wawei haʿamuddim* in medieval manuscripts. Indeed, in cols. VIII and IX, the X-signs occur on the top lines, while in other columns they occur near the beginning of the columns (VI 4; IX 3; XII 2). According to Stegemann, in these cases in the *Vorlage* of the present copy of the scroll these signs occurred in the top line. Even though the layout had changed in the present copy, these X-signs were copied as such. This pertains also to other instances of an X occurring in the middle or at the end of the column: IV 11, 14; V 12, 14; VI 13; IX 13. The instances of the latter type, however, cast doubts on this explanation. Another explanation was suggested by H. G. Snyder (see n. 261), 40 according to whom this letter 'marks the occurrence of a double pesher.'

[264] They appear in the spaces at the ends of lines that were slightly or much shorter than the surrounding ones. If they were used as line-fillers, their use is not consistent. In three of the five occurrences in frg. 1, they could be line-fillers in spaces left uninscribed (lines 4, 9, 11), but in lines 7 and 13 they occur in 'open sections.' The possible signs in frgs. 2 and 3 are of an unclear nature. It is less likely that the signs somehow referred to the content of the manuscript indicating change of topic or speaker, since they occur in the middle of sentences. At the same time, they may refer to words in the middle of the line, such as the paleo-Hebrew *zayin* in I 4 possibly referring to זמיר and the paleo-Hebrew *shin* (?) in I 9 referring to שמע (Cant 2:14; personal communication, M. Hopf).

(7) *Separation dots between words* (fig. 17)

A dot is occasionally inserted level with the tops of the letters or slightly above them, in order to separate two words lest they be understood as one continuous word or context. This practice is evidenced for seven texts written according to the Qumran scribal practice and one text not written in that practice, 4QMessianic Apocalypse (4Q521). See also the re-division sign described in § 2v above and illustrated in fig. 23.

1QS XI 15 אלי אתה ברוך.תפארתו. A single dicolon-like indication is found in the space between the words above and below the writing surface (fig. 17). Beyond the space between the words no special space was left by the scribe before the beginning of the benediction starting with ברוך אתה אלי, and this oversight was corrected by both the paragraph sign in the margin and by the dicolon in the text itself.

1QS XI 21 מה.ישב

1QHᵃ XII (Suk. = IV) 5 בפנות.גדול; XII 9 והיאה.הווה

4QSᵉ (4Q259) III 3 (frg. 3a) between אלה and the following word, probably starting with a *lamed*

4QMMTᵃ (4Q394) 3–7 i 18 טהורים.להיות; ii 17 מחנה.הוא

4QMᶜ (4Q493) 2 כן.ואחרי

4QOrdᶜ (4Q514) 1 i 2 אים[מ]הט.לכל

4QMessianic Apocalypse (4Q521) 2 iii 3 אדני.ברכת

The separation dot probably is a vestige of an early tradition, such as preserved in texts written in the paleo-Hebrew script, of separating words by dots (§ a1 above).

(8) *Letters and marks possibly numbering sheets and units* (figs. 10.11, 11, 15, 24)

There is some evidence for the numbering of sheets in the Qumran documents. Two examples were provided by J. T. Milik, "Numérotation des feuilles des rouleaux dans le scriptorium de Qumrân," *Semitica* 27 (1977) 75–81 (4QSᵇ [4Q256] 5; 4QDᵃ [4Q266] 1).

• 1QapGen ar V, X, XVII: The clearest evidence for numbering sheets is found in 1QapGen ar where a single Hebrew letter was written in the top right corner of three sheets; see M. Morgenstern, "A New Clue to the Original Length of the Genesis Apocryphon," *JJS* 47 (1996) 345–7: *pe* (col. V), *ṣade* (col. X), and *qoph* (col. XVII). The evidence implies that a very large number of sheets preceded the earliest preserved columns of this composition (dealing with Noah), since presumably each sheet was denoted by a letter of the alphabet.

• 1QS col. VII bottom margin: The composite sign immediately below the right edge of the column is a combination of a paleo-Hebrew *zayin* and a triangular shape (fig. 11). The *zayin* could denote a number, recurring in col. VIII, but more likely it refers to a major subdivision in the text, as suggested in § c1. Note further that cols. V and VIII are not denoted with any signs, while the bottom right margin of the other columns has not been preserved.

• 4QExodᵏ displays a sign (fig. 10.11a) in the upper right corner, above the center of the first word, which resembles the *lamed* in the Cryptic A script: *lamed* of 4QcryptA Lunisolar Calendar (4Q317, fig. 10.11b).

• 4QAges of Creation A (4Q180): Signs in the top margin, above the beginning of the column, and in the bottom margin.

• 4QSᵇ (4Q256) 4 (photographs PAM 42.372 and 43.250): A *gimel* in the upper right margin, above the first letter of the column, probably designates the third sheet of that manuscript (fig. 24.1).

• 4QDᵃ (4Q266) 1a: A letter (*'aleph*?) in the wide margin to the right of the column may indicate that this is the first sheet of that scroll (fig. 24.2).

• 4QEschatological Hymn (4Q457b): E. Chazon surmises that the *'aleph* to the right of 1 10 indicated the first sheet of the scroll (*DJD* XXIX, 409). The position of this letter, two-thirds down the column, is unusual.

• 4QMᶜ (4Q493): The right top corner, very close to the first letter of the first word, contains a somewhat curved line, which M. Baillet, *DJD* VII, 50 describes as a *lamed*. This letter, probably a *waw*, may well reflect a numbering device at the beginning of the sheet (*waw* referring to the sixth sheet; fig. 24.3).

• 4QVisions of Amram[b] ar (4Q544): The slightly curved diagonal line in the top margin above the first word possibly indicates the relative position of the sheet.

• MasSir col. V (fig. 15): The sign resembling an *epsilon* in the top right margin above the beginning of this column could represent a numbering device, but this column does not appear at the beginning of a sheet as with other presumed numbers listed above; besides, the other columns in that scroll have not been numbered. It is more likely that this is a section marker (ch. *5c1*).

As the other sheets of the compositions mentioned above would have had numbers in parallel positions on the other sheets, it is unfortunate that such supporting evidence is unavailable. In the case of 1QapGen ar it is available, while for 1QS negative evidence is available. The evidence for the numbering of quires and pages in codices from later periods cannot be applied to scrolls, since their nature and production were different.

Janzen, *Hiëerogliefen* and Ashton, *Scribal Habits*, 159 mention two examples of numbering in columns in ancient Egyptian papyri (among them P.Ebers from the Middle Kingdom that has numbers above each column); Turner, *Greek Manuscripts*, 16 gives two examples of a similar system in Greek scrolls. In Akkadian clay tablets of multi-column compositions, scribes included in their colophon at the end of each tablet the relative number of the tablet in relation to the complete series of tablets (oral communication, Z. Abusch). Furthermore, folia in Greek codices are usually numbered at the top center or outside corners (Turner, ibid.). See, e.g. the pages of P.Bodmer XXIV of Psalms 17–53, 55–118 (3 CE; codex).

(9) *Signs for Numerals*

Several documentary and non-documentary texts represent numerals with the Aramaic number signs for 1, 10, 20, and 100 (the system is briefly described by A. Yardeni, *DJD* XXXVI, 261 and S. Talmon, *DJD* XXI, 42):[265]

  Copper Scroll (3Q15)
  4QZodiology and Brontology ar (4Q318)
  4QOtot (4Q319)
  4QCal Doc/Mish A (4Q320)
  4QCal Doc C (4Q326)
  4QDeed A ar or heb (4Q345)
  4QDeed B heb? (4Q348)
  4QAccount of Cereal A ar (4Q351)
  4QpapAccount of Cereal B ar or heb (4Q352)
  4QpapAccount A ar or heb (4Q352a)
  4QpapAccount of Cereal or Liquid ar or heb (4Q353)
  4QAccount B ar or heb (4Q354)
  4QAccount C ar or heb (4Q355)
  4QAccount D ar or heb (4Q356)
  4QAccount E ar or heb (4Q357)
  4QpapAccount F? ar or heb (4Q358)
  4QpapUnidentified Fragments B ar (4Q360a)
  4QapocrLevi[a]? ar (4Q540) 1 2
  4QNJ[a] ar (4Q554)
  4QNJ[b] ar (4Q554a) ii 4, 5
  4QpapBibChronology ar (4Q559)
  6QpapCal Doc (6Q17)

---

[265]The signs are listed in Appendix 1 of M. G. Abegg, Jr., with J. E. Bowley and E. M. Cook, in consultation with E. Tov, *The Dead Sea Scrolls Concordance I. The Non-Biblical Texts from Qumran* (Leiden 2003). See further the bibliography provided by S. Talmon, *DJD* XXI, 137, n. 15: S. Gandz, "Hebrew Numerals," *PAAJR* 4 (1933) 53; Y. Yadin, "Ancient Judaean Weights and the Date of the Samaria Ostraca," *Studies in the Bible* (ed. C. Rabin; ScrHier 8; Jerusalem 1961) 9–25; G. B-A. Zarfati, *s. v.* מספר, *EncBib* V, 170–85 (Heb.); A. R. Millard, "Strangers from Egypt and Greece—The Signs for Numbers in Early Hebrew," in *Festschrift E. Lipinski—Immigration and Emigration within the Ancient Near East* (ed. K. van Lerberghe and A. Schoors; OLA 65; Leuven 1995) 189–94.

6QpapAccount or Contract (6Q26)
Sdeir papPromissory Note? ar (Sdeir 2)
All documentary texts from Jericho (*DJD* XXXVIII)

The number signs are always used in documentary texts, and occasionally also in literary texts of a somewhat technical nature mentioning many numbers. In parallel copies of the same text, the individuality of the scribes (or different scribal habits) can easily be seen as some scribes use number signs, while others write the numbers in full. Thus 4QNJ[a,b] ar (4Q554 and 4Q554a) use number signs for numbers larger than 10, while the parallel texts 2QNJ ar (2Q24), 5QNJ ar (5Q15), and 11QNJ ar (11Q18) write the numbers in full. Number signs are also used in three calendrical texts, 4Q320, 4Q326, and 6Q17—albeit not for the same categories—but not in the majority of similar texts (4Q321, 4Q321a, 4Q322, 4Q324a, 4Q325, 4Q328, 4Q329, 4Q329a, 4Q330, 4Q394 1–2).

In documentary texts, the signs are used for all numbers, while in some literary texts they are used selectively, albeit inconsistently, for certain categories only. The data in TABLE 17 show that the Copper Scroll (3Q15) uses the number signs for talents, but not for other monetary units, measures, and quantities. 4QCal Doc/Mish A (4Q320) uses the signs for the days of the week (priestly course) and month, but not for counting months and years. On the other hand, 4QCal Doc C (4Q326) uses the signs for the days of the month, but not for the days of the week nor for counting the months.

The scribe of 4Q326 2 evidently experienced some confusion regarding the use of number signs. He started the numeral of the second line (referring to a day in the month) with regular letters בא, probably intending to write [באחד עשר] ('on the eleventh in it Sabba[th'), but he continued the word with a symbol: באר̇ בו שֹבֹת without erasing the *ʾaleph*. This confusion probably implies that this scribe was used to writing the number signs, but he copied from a text which did not use such signs.

TABLE 17: *Employment of Number Signs in Non-documentary Texts*

Text	Number Signs Used	Number Signs Not Used
Copper Scroll (3Q15)	talents	other monetary units; measures; quantities
4QZodiology and Brontology ar (4Q318)	days of the month	—
4QOtot (4Q319)	signs	days of the week; years and jubilees
4QCal Doc/Mish A (4Q320)	days of the week (priestly course) and month	months and years
4QCal Doc C (4Q326)	days of the month	days of the week; months
4QapocrLevi[a]? ar (4Q540)	?	
4QNJ[a] ar (4Q554)	measures (stadium [*ras*] and cubit [*ʾamah*]) higher than 10	measures (cubit [*ʾamah*]) lower than 10; quantities 2 ii 16; measure (stadium [*ras*]) 1 i 15
4QNJ[b] ar (4Q554a)	measures (cubit [*ʾamah*]) higher than 10	measures (cubit [*ʾamah*]) lower than 10; quantities
4QpapBibChronology ar (4Q559)	years	
6QpapCal Doc (6Q17)	days of the month	—

(10) *Appendix: Paratextual elements in medieval Masoretic manuscripts*

The medieval Masoretic manuscripts contain several groups of paratextual elements, that is, elements indicated by scribes in manuscripts beyond the consonants, vowels, and accents. Almost all of these elements reflect scribal habits also known from antiquity in the biblical and nonbiblical texts from the Judean Desert. Consequently, the presence of these features in the medieval manuscripts proves that at least in the matter of some scribal habits they reflect the period when the Qumran scrolls were copied. At the same time, there is also one major group of paratextual elements in the medieval texts which does not appear in the Qumran texts (*Ketiv/Qere* notes), and likewise some elements in the Qumran texts are *not* shared with the medieval texts. The differences between the two corpora are illuminating, and may assist us in determining the origin of MT that is still unclear.

MT contains several paratextual features that are shared with the biblical and nonbiblical texts from the Judean Desert. Most of these features are concentrated in only a small number of Qumran texts (categories *c–g* below), while some are distributed throughout the Qumran texts (categories *a–b*).

(a) The division of the text into sections (*parashiyyot* or *pisqaʾo t*). See § 3 for a detailed analysis.

(b) *Pisqah bᵉʾemṣaᶜ pasuq.* For an analysis, see § a3 above.

(c) *Inverted nunin.* The printed editions of MT present inverted *nunin* (also named *nunin mᵉnuzarot,* 'separated' or 'isolated' *nunin*) before and after Num 10:35-36, as well as in Ps 107:23-28 (in codex L before vv 21-26 and 40), cf. *Sof.* 6.1. The sign in the manuscripts resembles an inverted *nun*, though tradition also describes it as a *kaph* (Lieberman, *Hellenism*, 40). Actually this sign does not represent a letter, but a misunderstood parenthesis sign (ch. *5c2*), as recognized by Lieberman, *Hellenism*, 38–43 referring to the *antisigma* and *diple*. Indeed, in *b. Shabb.* 115b the *nunin* are called סימניות, 'signs.'

Sifre Numbers § 84 (p. 80) to Num 10:35 (cf. *b. Shabb.* 115b–116a) explains the inverted *nunin* in Num 10:35-36 as signs removing this section from the context:

> When the Ark was to set out . . . There are dots above and below it <this pericope> to indicate that this was not its correct place. Rabbi says, 'It is because the pericope at hand constitutes a scroll unto itself.' . . . R. Simeon says, 'In the written version there are dots above and below it <this pericope> to indicate that this was not its correct place.' And what ought to have been written instead of this pericope? 'And the people complained in the hearing of the Lord' (Num 11:1).

However, when their meaning was no longer understood, these signs came to be denoted by the Masoretes as inverted *nunin*. While the appearance of the inverted *nunin* in Ps 107:23-28 in codex L is unclear, their occurrence in Num 10:35-36 is in accordance with the scribal tradition of the Judean Desert texts, since this section was described by *Sifre* as not having been written in 'its correct place.' The use of parenthesis signs, reflecting the *antisigma* and *sigma* from the Alexandrian scribal tradition, is also documented in Qumran texts; see above, § c2. The section enclosed by parenthesis signs in the Masoretic manuscripts is more extensive than the samples known from the Qumran scrolls, but the principle is the same.

While the Masoretic manuscripts use the inverted *nunin* in Num 10:35-36, according to *Sifre* Numbers § 84 to those verses (cf. *b. Shabb.* 115b–116a) these words were dotted. These two traditions are actually not contradictory. Just as the Qumran manuscripts used different systems for canceling elements (cancellation dots, crossing out with a line, parenthesis, erasure), the rabbinic tradition of cancellation dots and the evidence in the manuscripts of parenthesis signs reflect two alternative systems of deletion.

(d) *The extraordinary points (puncta extraordinaria).* In fifteen places in Scripture, all the medieval manuscripts of MT denote dots above certain letters and words and in one place (Ps 27:13) also below them.[266] Ten of these instances are found in the Torah (*Sof.* 6.3), four in the Prophets, and one in the Hagiographa. The earliest list of these instances is found in *Sifre* Numbers § 69 to Num 9:10 (the ten instances in the Torah) and the full list is in the *Masorah magna* on Num 3:39. In each of these instances, the scribes of the original manuscripts, which later became MT, intended to erase the letters, as in the Qumran manuscripts; for the latter, see § 2 above.

---

[266]The tradition of these dots is rather stable, while a Masoretic list of different dots merely uses this graphic symbol to indicate differences between Tiberian and Babylonian manuscripts. See Y. Ofer, "A Masoretic List of Babylonian Origin of Dotted Words in the Pentateuch," *Proceedings of the Twelfth International Congress of the International Organization for Masoretic Studies* (SBLMasS 8; 1995) 71–85.

Although later tradition explained these dots as indicating doubtful letters (see the detailed discussion by Strack, *Prolegomena*, 88–91; Blau, *Masoretische Untersuchungen*, 6–40; Ginsburg, *Introduction*, 318–34; Butin, *Nequdoth*; Lieberman, *Hellenism*, 43–6; and S. Talmon, 'Prolegomenon,' to Butin, *Nequdoth*, all quoting rabbinic sources), or as reflecting a hidden meaning in the text, the Qumran parallels (ch. *5c2*) leave no doubt that the original intention of these dots was the cancellation of letters. Accordingly, the traditional term ניקוד עליו (dot(s) on it, scil. the letter or word) is more appropriate than the term used in scholarship 'puncta extraordinaria.' Indeed, the wording in *᾿Abot R. Nat.* A, 34 (p. 51 in Schechter's edition; cf. *y. Pes.* 9.36d) shows that the habit of canceling letters and words by means of dots was known to some rabbinic sources. However, the real proof that the dots originally denoted the canceling of letters or words lies in an examination of the biblical text itself. That is, if it can be shown that the word without the dotted letter(s) is contextually possible in the biblical context, or that the context is possible without the dotted word, it is probable that the scribes indeed intended to omit the elements thus marked. The question is not whether the shorter text, without the dotted elements, is preferable to that with these letters, but whether the shorter text presents a viable alternative, which a scribe, for some reason, preferred to the longer text. In this description, there are several possible explanations for the deletion of certain elements. In the forerunner of MT, these elements were possibly considered inappropriate, superfluous, or incorrect and were therefore omitted. It is also not impossible that scribes of an early source of MT omitted these elements upon collation with another, authoritative, manuscript in which these elements were lacking.

In all but one instance, the texts are indeed feasible without the dotted elements: Gen 16:5, 18:9, 19:33, 33:4, 37:12; Num 3:39, 9:10, 21:30, 29:15; Deut 29:28; Isa 44:9; Ezek 41:20, 46:22; Ps 27:13. In these instances, letters or words were dotted in all the medieval Masoretic manuscripts, with occasional variation.

The only instance in which the dotted letters are necessary in the context is 2 Sam 19:20 ביום יצֿאֿ אשר אדני המלך מירושלם. The dotting of יצא is enigmatic (thus already Blau, *Masoretische Untersuchungen*, 35) and reminds us of dots in Cambridge MS Add. 465 (Ginsburg, *Introduction*, 334) in Job 39:15 וחֿיֿת in the *Mᵉdinḥᵃ᾽ê* tradition, where such dots cannot be explained as cancellations.[267]

The assumption that these Masoretic dots were intended to cancel elements is strongly supported by the fact that in seven or eight of the fifteen instances, the shorter text is paralleled by evidence from ancient sources (TABLE 18). This is a very large percentage indeed, if we take into consideration the fragmentary nature of our information, as well as the fact that there need not be any correlation between elements omitted in Masoretic manuscripts and other sources.

TABLE 18: *Dotted Words in MT Supported by External Evidence*

Reference	Dotted Word in MT	Manuscript Support for Short Text
Gen 16:5	וביניך	SP
Gen 33:4	ויחבקהו ויפל על צוארו וֿיֿשֿקֿהֿוֿ ויבכו	LXX?[268]
Num 3:39	וֿאֿהֿרֿן	SP and S[269]
Num 21:30	אשֿר	SP reads אש (= LXX πῦρ and *b. B. Bat.* 79a)
Isa 44:9	הֿמֿה	Supralinear addition in 1QIsaᵃ (ועדיהמה הֿמה)
Ezek 41:20	הֿהֿיֿכֿל (identical to the first word of the next verse)	S V
Ezek 46:22	מהֿקֿצֿעֿוֿת	LXX S V[270]
Ps 27:13	לֿוֿלֿאֿ	LXX. The first two letters (לו) are reflected as ἑαυτῇ at the end of the previous verse (26:12).

In all these instances the shorter readings seem possible and sometimes even preferable in the context. In the other six instances of dotted letters in MT, the context shows that the shorter reading is at least possible.

[267]This situation differs from forty other instances in which, according to a Masoretic list, dots above letters or words denote differences between traditions, such as in section units or *Ketiv/Qere* differences. For the latter, see, e.g. Num 32:7 תֿנֿיֿאֿוֿן. For a detailed analysis, see Y. Ofer, "Masoretic List," 71–85.

[268]It is unclear whether the LXX lacks the dotted word, as that version does not represent וישקד at the same place as MT; on the other hand, the translation of ויהבקד as καὶ περιλαβὼν αὐτὸν ἐφίλησεν may indicate the representation of וישקד at an earlier place in the sentence.

[269]The omission is probably preferable since the census was performed only by Moses (thus already *Sifre* Numbers § 69 on Num 9:10), and the addition of Aaron probably reflects a scribal error influenced by the frequent juxtaposition of both names.

[270]Several commentators delete this *hapax* word as a mistaken repetition of מקצעות in the beginning of the next verse.

Gen 18:9   ויאמרו אֵלָ֗יו איה שרה—the writing of three dots and the lack of a dot above the *lamed* makes little sense in the context.[271] The most likely explanation for the dots is that they were imperfectly placed, as often elsewhere (for parallels, see below), indicating that the scribe intended to cancel אליו as a whole. Indeed, a shorter text without אליו is feasible. Compare Ruth 3:5 תאמרי אלי and 3:17 אמר אלי where אלי is lacking in the *Ketiv* text and added as a *Qere* (*Qere wela Ketiv*). It is also remotely possible that the dot on the *waw* is incorrectly transmitted, and that the scribe intended to cancel two letters only, creating a word לי, for which cf. a frequent interchange between אל and ל-.

Gen 19:33   בשכבה ובקֻמה—defective orthography, probably influenced by בשכבה ובקמה in v 35.

Gen 37:12   לרעות אֹת צאן אביהם—the *nota accusativi* is freely added or omitted in all textual sources. For a Qumran parallel for the cancellation, see below.

Num 9:10   דרך רחוקָה—the masculine and feminine forms of the adjective conform with a different understanding of the gender of דרך. That word usually appears as a masculine noun, but in Exod 18:20 it is used in the feminine. A scribe may have corrected the text in accord with the more frequent usage.

Num 29:15   ועשרֹן עשרון—The same phrase occurs in 28:13 with a defective spelling of the first word (ועשרן עשרון) indicating that a scribe or reader may have adapted the spelling of the second occurrence of the phrase to that of the first by canceling a single letter. Elsewhere, also, scribes seem to have purposely chosen a different spelling for each word in pairs of identical words, e.g. Gen 27:22 הקל קול יעקב; Qoh 1:6 סובב סבב.[272]

Deut 29:28 והנגלת לֹנֹ ולֹבֹנֹֹ עד עולם—the shorter text does have a meaning, but the background of the shortening is as cryptic as the text itself.

That the dotted elements were intended to be deleted is supported not only by the aforementioned textual witnesses of the biblical text and by the general Qumran parallels to the practice of omission by cancellation dots, but also by Qumran parallels in specific details.

• In the Qumran texts, many dots delete small details in spelling and morphology, e.g. 4QJer[a] IX, part 2 2 (Jer 14:6) שפאֹים; 4QRP[c] (4Q365) 12 iii 5 לוֹא; 25c 13 אתחכמֹה.

A few of the Masoretic *puncta extraordinaria* likewise pertain to matters of orthography:

Gen 16:5 בינֹיך. Elsewhere, the defective spelling of this word, בינך, is the rule.

Gen 19:33 ובקֻמה—the same word occurs in v 35 with the defective spelling (according to *Sifre* Numbers § 69 to Num 9:10, however, the whole word was dotted).

Num 29:15 ועשרֹן עשרון.

Num 21:30 אשֹר—the Masoretic dot created the shorter אש as in SP, LXX, and *b. B. Bat.* 79a. For a similar correction, see 4QCommMal (4Q253a) 4 ii 1 וֹאֹשֹׁר, where an original ואשר was corrected to ואיש by scribal dots and a supralinear *yod*.

In the MT of Ezek 41:20, at the end of the verse, the first of the dittography pair of ההיכל, now separated from the second one by the verse division (vv 20-21), is dotted. This phenomenon is paralleled by several cases in the Qumran scrolls in which one of a pair of duplicated letters or words was dotted. Cf. 4QD[f] (4Q271) 4 ii 4 כֹי; for further examples, see ch. 5f δ.

• The cancellation of את in the MT of Gen 37:12 לרעות אֹת צאן אביהם is paralleled by 4QD[a] (4Q266) 10 ii 11 את where the same word was crossed out: יו]צֹא אֹת ידו מחחת בגד]ו.

• In two instances, dots in the Masoretic manuscripts were not placed above or below *all* the letters of a word which was to be omitted.

Gen 18:9 אֵלָ֗יו : Note the lack of a dot above the *lamed*.

Ps 27:13 לֹוּלֵֹאֹ : Dots were written above and below all the letters, except below the *waw*.

Speculations on the background of this irregularity of MT are now superfluous, as the irregularly placed dots are paralleled by several instances in the scrolls: see TABLE 15 above.

• For the deletion of two complete words in the MT of Deut 29:28, cf. several similarly large deletions in the Qumran texts: see TABLES 10, 14, 16 above.

---

[271]The three dotted letters create, as it were, a word איו, similar to the next word איה. The juxtaposition of these two words is explained in the rabbinic tradition, e.g. *b. B. Metsia* 87a; *Sifre* Numbers § 69.

[272]For further examples, see F. I. Andersen and A. D. Forbes, *Spelling in the Hebrew Bible* (BibOr 41; Rome 1986) 218.

(e) *Large and small letters.* MT contains several enlarged letters, which originally were probably unintentional, as there seems to be no intrinsic reason for their emphasis. See ch. *2d* (2). A *smaller* letter is found in the MT of Gen 2:4 בְּהִבָּֽרְאָם ('when they <the heaven and earth> were created'), explained in *b. Menaḥ.* 29b as two words, בה, 'with the letter *he*,' and בראם, 'He created them.' Likewise, the Masorah mentions three instances of a small *nun*: ארן (Isa 44:14); ובשׁובן (Jer 39:13; both *nunin*); נתרן (Prov 16:28). In all these cases, there seems to be no intrinsic reason for the special emphasis of these letters.

The writing of smaller and larger letters in MT is paralleled by the Qumran scrolls, which contain many instances of letters which were larger and smaller than other letters in the context. For examples, see ch. *2d*.

(f) *Unusually shaped letters.* The Masorah based on *b. Qidd.* 66b indicated one instance of an imperfectly written letter, viz., Num 25:12 שׁלום, written with a 'broken *waw*,' that is, a *waw* with a crack in the middle. According to the commentator *Baʿal Haturim*, the *waw* of the *Qere* קרוא in Num 1:16 also is to be written as a broken letter. The origin of these unusually shaped letters probably goes back to antiquity, while in other cases the writing tradition may have started in the Middle Ages.[273]

The number of imperfectly written letters in the Qumran scrolls is very large. Even in well-preserved texts, segments of the ink of many letters were chipped off, for example, when a word was written on a crack in the leather, or when the leather cracked subsequent to the writing, such as the truncated final *mem* of אנשׁים in 4QJer[d] 8 (Jer 43:9), which resembles a *bet*. At a later stage, some such letters were conceived of as 'broken' letters.

(g) *Suspended letters.* In four words in MT, a letter is written as a 'hanging' letter. In retrospect, these letters are now regarded as having been added after the completion of the linear text with the intention of correcting the earlier, shorter, text. In Judg 18:30 מׁשׁה, a suspended *nun* corrected an original מׁשׁה to מְנַשֶּׁה, as indicated by the vocalization of MT. This tendentious addition was apparently meant to correct an earlier reading which ascribed the erecting of the idol in Dan to one of the descendants of Moses (*b. B. Bat.* 109b).

For a similar correction, though not a tendentious one, see the correction in 4QJer[a] XI 7 (Jer 17:16) of פׁיך to פׁניך indicated by the addition of a supralinear *nun* (פׁנׁיך).

In three other verses in MT, guttural letters that had possibly been wrongly omitted by the original scribes were added in the same way: Ps 80:14 מׁיׁער; Job 38:13 רׁשׁעׁים ibid., v 15 מרשׁעׁים). A different explanation for one of the three verses can be found in *b. Qidd.* 30a where it is said that the letter *ʿayin* in Ps 80:14 מׁיׁער 'marks the middle of the Psalms.'

The four suspended letters in MT mentioned above reflect practices which are very well documented in the Qumran scrolls, in which many letters and words were suspended as correcting elements (§ *f* below). In 1QIsa[a] alone, there are many such instances, such as in the second word in that scroll, יׁשׁעׁיׁהו. It is not coincidental that three of the four instances pertain to the letter *ʿayin*, since in many Qumran texts numerous laryngeals and pharyngeals were also added supralinearly as corrections, especially in 1QIsa[a].

Several of the aforementioned paratextual elements that are now part and parcel of the medieval texts, and are also referred to in rabbinic literature, were not meant by their scribes to be transmitted as such to subsequent generations. These elements (categories *c–g* above) were meant to correct the manuscript, just like any other correction in the Judean Desert texts, but when the details of the biblical text were fixed (sanctified), paradoxically these corrections were transmitted. From the point of view of the scribes who inserted the corrections, however, it would have been more appropriate to simply correct the text without leaving traces of the correcting procedure.

The above analysis shows that almost all categories of paratextual elements in the medieval manuscripts were present in the biblical and nonbiblical texts from Qumran. None of these categories is characteristic of the biblical text, as they all reflect scribal practices employed in texts of all kinds. Conversely, most of the scribal features of the Qumran texts also have been perpetuated in the medieval texts, which points to the Qumran texts as being typologically related to the medieval texts, although not necessarily their immediate precursors. At the same time, three practices are *not* reflected in the Masoretic manuscripts.

• *Ketiv/Qere* notes.
• Crossing out elements with a line (ch. *5c2*).
• Scribal signs written in the margin and between the lines (all the categories of sections 5c1, 3–6).

---

[273]Thus the *qoph* of Exod 32:25 and Num 7:2 is described as a '*qoph* joined and without *taggim*,' and several occurrences of the *pe* are described as 'rolled up' letters. For details, see M. M. Kasher, *The Script of the Torah and its Characters, II: Irregular Letters in the Torah* (*Torah Shelemah* 29 [Heb.]; Jerusalem 1978) 183–227.

The fact that the medieval texts reflect no scribal signs or instances of elements crossed out with a line is meaningful with regard to our understanding of these texts, and may be an indication of their careful copying procedures. It is equally significant that the only paratextual feature of the medieval text of MT which is not paralleled in the Qumran texts is that of the *Ketiv–Qere* notations. These notations were not included in Scripture scrolls circulating when the Qumran scrolls were written. However, these notes, based on an early oral tradition, were probably put into writing only at a late stage in the development of MT.[274]

When viewed against the background of the MT corpus as a whole, the 15 instances of dotted letters (mainly in the Torah) and the one (two?) instance(s) of parenthesis should be considered very rare. That is, in the great majority of Qumran manuscripts in which cancellation dots are found, they occur with far greater frequency than in the texts which have been passed down to us as the medieval MT. By the same token, the practice of suspending letters is far more frequent in the Qumran scrolls than the four examples in MT. Likewise, the number of unusual letters (large, small, unusual shapes) was many times greater in the Qumran scrolls than in the medieval texts of MT.

d. *Special writing of divine names*

The divine names were written in a special way in many Hebrew Qumran texts:

(a) Paleo-Hebrew characters in texts written in the square script; for a detailed analysis of this practice used in a large group of manuscripts, see ch. *6b*.

(b) Four dots (named *Tetrapuncta* by Stegemann, *ΚΥΡΙΟΣ*, 152) in texts written in the square script represent the Tetragrammaton in eight nonbiblical and biblical texts written in the Qumran scribal practice, as well as in four additional Qumran texts (in one: strokes) and XḤev/SeEschat Hymn (XḤev/Se 6) 2 7 (four diagonal strokes). These dots and strokes were positioned level with the tops of the letters; see, e.g. 4QTest (4Q175) 1, 19 and 4QT^b (4Q524) 6–13 4. For an example, see fig. 19 and for the evidence, see TABLE 19.

This practice undoubtedly reflects reverence for the divine name, considered so sacred that it was not to be written with regular characters lest an error be made or lest it be erased by mistake. Possibly, the dots or strokes were also meant to alert against pronouncing the divine name. It is unlikely that these dots or strokes were intended to be replaced by paleo-Hebrew characters, since the scribes did not leave sufficient space for this purpose. Usually, the scribe wrote a series of four dots but in 4QTanḥ (4Q176) and 4QNarrative C (4Q462) two clusters of two dots are written. The scribe of 4QHistorical Text A (4Q248) drew five strokes.

TABLE 19: Tetrapuncta *in the Qumran Scrolls*

Eight texts, the first four apparently penned by the same scribe, were probably written in the Qumran scribal practice:

1QS VIII 14 (quotation from Isa 40:3).

1QIsa^a: Supralinear corrections in XXXIII 7 (Isa 40:7; illustr. 1) and XXXV 15 (Isa 42:6). The last mentioned instance seemingly presents five dots, but one of the spots of ink is a remnant of one of the letters of the Tetragrammaton in the square script which was written here initially, and then erased.[275]

4QSam^c 1 3 (1 Sam 25:31); III 7, 7 (2 Sam 15:8).

4QTest (4Q175) lines 1, 19 (biblical quotations, fig. 19).

---

[274]See my study "The *Ketiv-Qere* Variations in Light of the Manuscript Finds in the Judean Desert," *Text, Theology and Translation, Essays in Honour of Jan de Waard* (New York: United Bible Societies, 2004) 183–91, forthcoming.

[275]The transcription with five dots in Burrows, *The Dead Sea Scrolls* is imprecise. As a result, the view of M. Delcor, "Les divers manières d'écrire le tétragramme sacré dans les anciens documents hébraïques," *RHR* 147 (1955) 135–73 (153), according to which these five dots represent the name אדוני is without support.

4QTanḥ (4Q176) 1–2 i 6, 7, 9 (four dots; 1–2 ii 3 (two clusters of two strokes); 8–10 6, 8 (twice), 10 (two clusters of two dots), all biblical quotations. Also once in the square script: 3 1.

4Qpap paraKings et al. (4Q382) 9 5 (quotation of 2 Kgs 2:3-4); 78 2; but not in 11 4 (2 Kgs 2:4) and 53 1.

4QNarrative C (4Q462) 7 (four dots) 12 (two clusters of two dots, probably biblical quotations).

4QTᵇ (4Q524) 6–13 4, 5 (four dots).

Four Qumran texts and one text from Ḥever/Seiyal *not* written in the Qumran scribal practice:

4QpapTobᵃ ar (4Q196) 17 i 5 (Tob 12:22); 18 15 (Tob 14:2).

4QHistorical Text A (4Q248) 5 (five strokes, possibly with a combining stroke between strokes 2 and 3 counted from the right).

4QMen of People Who Err (4Q306) 3 5 (four strokes).

4Qpap psEzekᵉ (4Q391) 36 (3 times), 52, 55, 58, 65 (insufficient data on the orthographic system).

XḤev/SeEschat Hymn (XḤev/Se 6) 2 7 (four strokes).

According to Stegemann, *KYPIOΣ*, 155 the four dots indicating the divine name are also evidenced in an early copy of the LXX, P.Fouad 266b (848) of Deuteronomy (middle of 1 BCE), where they were subsequently overwritten by the Tetragrammaton written in small square characters, leaving much space on both sides.[276] Since, according to Stegemann, the dots in this Greek manuscript were replaced by the Tetragrammaton, he suggested that the scribes of the aforementioned Hebrew texts also intended to replace the dots with actual letters. However, this assumption cannot be examined properly in the Greek text, since it is difficult to recognize any dots behind the writing of the Tetragrammaton in P.Fouad 266b.[277] Besides, in that text the two dots are often indicated above the level of the letters, and accordingly four dots would also have been visible in Hebrew texts. As a result, there is no evidence indicating that the four dots or strokes were ever intended to be replaced by the Tetragrammaton in the Hebrew and Aramaic sources.

Tetrapuncta were indicated in biblical as well as nonbiblical manuscripts. Since the corrector of 1QIsaᵃ (as opposed to the original scribe of that manuscript) employed the *Tetrapuncta* twice in supralinear corrections, he was probably accustomed to representing the divine name in this way. Usually this corrector is identified as the scribe who also copied 1QS, 4QSamᶜ, and 4QTest (4Q175).

While it is difficult to determine the chronological relationship between the different modes of representing the divine name, Stegemann, *KYPIOΣ*, 157 suggested that the *Tetrapuncta* preceded the writing of the divine name in square characters (see above).

Most of the texts displaying *Tetrapuncta* are dated to the Hasmonean era (see the summary list in Webster, "Chronological Index"), possibly pointing to a practice employed in that period.

1QS–4QTest (4Q175)–4QSamᶜ dated in different ways: 100–50 BCE for 1QS, 100–75 BCE for 4QSamᶜ, 125–75 BCE for 4QTest (4Q175)

4QTanḥ (4Q176) hand A: 30 BCE; hand B: 30 BCE–68 CE

4Qpap paraKings et al. (4Q382): *c.*75 BCE

4QNarrative C (4Q462): 50–25 BCE

4QTᵇ (4Q524): 150–125 BCE

4QpapTobᵃ ar (4Q196): *c.*50 BCE

4QHistorical Text A (4Q248): 30–1 BCE

4QMen of People Who Err (4Q306): 150–50 BCE

4Qpap psEzekᵉ (4Q391): 150–100 BCE

XḤev/SeEschat Hymn (XḤev/Se 6): 30 BCE–68 CE

---

[276]Stegemann refers to the photograph provided by W. G. Waddell, "The Tetragrammaton in the LXX," *JTS* 45 (1944) 158–61, even though this photograph does not show more dots than the other photographs.

[277]Thus Dunand, *Papyrus grecs, Introduction*, 13 and Aly–Koenen, *Three Rolls*, 5–6. The view of Dunand and Aly–Koenen is acceptable on the basis of the photographs provided by the latter, with the possible exception of additional dots in frg. 37 (Deut 24:4). See the analysis in ch. *6b2*.

(c) A dicolon (:), followed by a space, is systematically placed before the Tetragrammaton (written in the square script) in 4QRP[b] (4Q364), written in the Qumran practice of orthography and morphology. E.g. 14 3 (Exod 24:17).

(d) 11QpaleoUnidentified Text (11Q22 [*DJD* XXIII, pl. XLVIII]) לאלהיכ was written with a different color of ink (red?), implying either the use of a different pen or the involvement of a different scribe, or both (the fragment itself could not be located, and the photograph remains our only source). If indeed לאלהיכ was written with a different pen, this would be the only recognizable instance of the special treatment of a divine name in a text completely written in paleo-Hebrew characters.

The great majority of the texts in groups *a* and *b* are written in the Qumran orthography and morphology, and this also applies to the great majority of occurrences of paleo-Hebrew characters for the divine names (with the possible exception of 4QS[d] [4Q258]) listed in ch. *6b*.

The picture that emerges from a study of the distribution of the four types of special writing systems for the divine names is that they are closely connected to the Qumran scribal practice. The evidence is not massive for all the texts, but it is clear-cut for the majority of them, while the other texts are too fragmentary for analysis. For one thing, the majority of the texts using the paleo-Hebrew characters for the Tetragrammaton as listed in ch. *6b* are of a sectarian nonbiblical nature. At the same time, the negative evidence must also be taken into consideration. No Hebrew texts of a non-sectarian nature or those clearly not written in the Qumran scribal practice, containing any of the aforementioned scribal systems for the writing of divine names, have been preserved.

Special systems were also used in the manuscripts of Greek Scripture to represent the Tetragrammaton (the use of κύριος, usually without the article, probably represents a later stage in the development of the translation):

1. The writing of the Tetragrammaton in Hebrew characters (for analyses, see Stegemann, *ΚΥΡΙΟΣ*; Skehan, "Divine Name"; G. Mercati, "Sulla scrittura del tetragramma nelle antiche versioni greche del Vecchio Testamento," *Bib* 22 [1941] 339–66; Roberts, *Manuscript*, 26–48; L. W. Hurtado, "The Origin of the *Nomina Sacra*: A Proposal," *JBL* 117 [1998] 655–73):

a. *In the paleo-Hebrew script* (with the exception of the second item, all on leather).

• Scribes A and B of 8ḤevXIIgr (end of 1 BCE); the Tetragrammaton includes a *final* letter *he*.

• P.Oxy. 50.3522 of Job 42 (1 CE); the Tetragrammaton includes a *final* letter *he*.

• P.Oxy. 7.1007 (leather) of Genesis 2–3 (3 CE): Double *yod* with a horizontal stroke through both letters as part of the letters, also known from Jewish coins of the second century CE (at the same time, this text also has the abbreviated θ(εό)ς, which would point to a Christian scribe).

• P.Vindob. Gr 39777 of Psalms 68, 80 in the version of Symmachus (3–4 CE; leather) published, among others, by G. Mercati, "Frammenti di Aquila o di Simmaco," *RB* NS 8 (1911) 266–72.

• The Aquila fragments of Kings and Psalms (5–6 CE) published by F. C. Burkitt, *Fragments of the Books of Kings According to the Translation of Aquila* (Cambridge 1897; the *yod* and *waw* are identical); C. Taylor, *Hebrew-Greek Cairo Genizah Palimpsests from the Taylor-Schechter Collection* (Cambridge 1900).

• An ancient testimony to this custom is preserved in Jerome's *Prologus Galeatus* (*Praef. in Libr. Sam. et Malach.*; Migne, PL XXVIII, cols. 594–5): 'Nomen Domini tetragrammaton in quibusdam Graecis voluminibus usque hodie antiquis expressum litteris invenimus.'

b. *In the square script*

• P.Fouad 266b (848) of Deuteronomy (middle of 1 BCE). The first scribe left spaces indicating where the divine name (either κύριος or the Tetragrammaton) was to be filled in (see the text under TABLE 19). The second scribe wrote these Tetragrammata.

• πιπι: The second column of the Hexapla in the Psalms fragments published by G. Mercati, *Psalterii Hexapli reliquiae* (Vatican 1958).

• πιπι in several Hexaplaric manuscripts (Q, 86, 88, 234[margin], 264).

• פיפי in the Syriac script in the Syro-Hexapla.
For a detailed analysis, see Stegemann, *ΚΥΡΙΟΣ*.

2. 4QpapLXXLev[b] of Leviticus 2–5 (1 BCE) transliterated the Tetragrammaton as ΙΑΩ (preceded and followed by a space) in Lev 3:12; 4:27.[278] This transcription is unique among the witnesses of Greek Scripture.[279]

3. The first scribe of P.Oxy. 4.656 of Genesis 14–27 (2 or 3 CE) left spaces for the divine name (the Tetragrammaton?), as in P.Fouad 266b (848; middle of 1 BCE), filled in by a second hand with the unabbreviated form of κύριος in 15:8; 24:31, 42. According to Van Haelst, *Catalogue*, 17, these occurrences of κύριος were written with a different pen. The scribe of P.Berlin 17213 of Genesis 19 (3 CE) possibly left a space for κύριος, which was not filled in, but more likely the space denotes a closed paragraph after Gen 19:18.

A special practice for the writing of the divine names was also followed in many manuscripts of SP. In those manuscripts, the last one or two letters were always separated from the remainder of the last word in the line, creating an elegant column structure at the beginning and end of the column. However, when the Tetragrammaton was to occur at the end of the line, hence creating a divided Tetragrammaton (יה ה), many scribes retracted the Tetragrammaton slightly from the left margin, in order to avoid the division of its letters. Examples of such 'retractive' manuscripts are provided in Crown, *Dated Samaritan MSS*, e.g. John Rylands MS 1, New York Public Library 11010. This pertains also to the *Sefer Abisha* as described by A. D. Crown, "The Abisha Scroll of the Samaritans," *BJRL* 58 (1975) 36–65, especially 45.

e. *Errors*

Many mistakes were not recognized by the scribes or subsequent users of the ancient scrolls. However, even the recognized errors were not always corrected by either the original or a subsequent scribe, or a user. Some examples of this widespread phenomenon follow:

• Several instances of dittography, see § δ below.

• 1QH[a] VIII (Suk. = Puech XVIII) 15 ל זא֯ינהרות, with a supralinear *nun* of instead of לבזאינהרות (p.m.): In the first space, the scribe forgot to write a *bet* and, strangely enough, instead of the dotted *nun* a supralinear *nun* was written.

• 1QH[a] IX (XVII) 8 תשת שע: The scribe forgot to write an ʿ*ayin* in the space after the *tav*; it is unclear whether the dot above the space is ink.

• 4QNum[b] XV 10 מהלוך: The scribe started writing a *lamed* after the *mem*, but upon recognizing his mistake, he continued writing a *he*. Nevertheless, the upper part of the *lamed* was not erased.

• 4QTob[a] ar (4Q196) 2 2 שביק פ לי: A single letter פ, which was left between spaces, as if it were a separate word, was not erased; possibly a horizontal line was drawn through it.

• 4QJub[a] (4Q216) VII 15 ושים ועשרים for ושנים ועשרים.

• 4QJub[d] (4Q219) II 32: A *he* was left out in ואלויכה (ואלוהיכה).

• 4QCommGen A (4Q252) II 4–5 as recorded in ch. *2h*.

• 4QD[a] (4Q266) 5 i 13 איש ל לפי: A single *lamed*, recognized by the scribe as a mistake, was left untouched in the text.

• 11QT[a] (11Q19): For uncorrected errors, see Yadin, *Temple Scroll (Hebrew)* I.21.

---

[278]See the analysis by F. E. Shaw, *The Earliest Non-Mystical Jewish Use of ΙΑΩ*, unpubl. Ph.D. diss., University of Cincinnati (Cincinnati, Ohio 2002), with much bibliography.

[279]The concordance of Hatch–Redpath misleadingly quotes in the list of the personal names such a marginal reading from codex Marchalianus (Q) in Ezek 1:2 and 11:1. This reading, not mentioned in Ziegler's Göttingen edition, refers in 1:2 to Ιωακειμ and in 11:1 to בניהו represented in this note as οικος ιαω.

f. Correction procedures and the degree of scribal intervention

α. Relation between the correction and the uncorrected text

Upon completing the copying, and often while still in the process, scribes frequently intervened in the text; by the same token, correctors and users often inserted their corrections in the text. Attention to the intricacies of the scribal correction process known from the Qumran scrolls helps us in better understanding scribal transmission as well as the rewriting of ancient literature. This intervention is known in four different forms, or combinations thereof:

• Removal of a written element by erasing or blotting out, crossing out, marking with cancellation dots or a box around the letters or words (§ c2).

• Addition of an element in the interlinear space or, rarely, in the intercolumnar margin (see below).

• Remodeling (reshaping) of an existing letter to another one (see below).

• Changing the spacing between words either by indicating with scribal signs that the last letter of a word belonged to the following word (beyond the space) or by indicating that there should be a space between two words which had been written as one continuous unit (see § c2.7).

The relation between the correction and the uncorrected text differs from case to case:

• Corrections of simple scribal errors (e.g. omission or addition of single letters, words, or whole sentences), recognizable when the text without the addition, omission, or remodeling makes little or no sense. For example

1QSam 4 5 (2 Sam 23:12) ויכה = ויׄכׄה (MT: ויך)
11QPsᵃ XXV 11 (Ps 143:5) בכול = בׄכׄול (MT: בכל)

Partially written words were often dotted or crossed out with a line when the mistake was recognized during the course of the writing (§ 2c).

• Orthographic corrections, mainly additions of *matres lectionis*, for example

2QExodᵃ 1 2 (Exod 1:12) אותם = אׄתם (MT: אתו)
2QExodᵃ 7 3 (Exod 26:12) האוהל = הא[וׄ]הל (MT: האהל)

• Linguistic corrections, especially in gutturals. For example

1QIsaᵃ I 1 (Isa 1:1) ישעיהו = ישׄעׄיהו (= MT)
4QJerᵃ 2 6 (Jer 9:11) ויבין = ויׄבׄין (MT: ויבן)

• Contextual additions, deletions, or changes toward a text that was either the scribe's *Vorlage* or a different text. For example

5QDeut 1 ii 6 (Deut 8:12) וישבת בם = וישׄבׄת בׄם (cf. LXX + ἐν αὐταῖς; MT: וישבת)

• Glosses and variant readings. The evidence for these two categories is either very scanty or non-existent. See § h below.

β. Identity of the correctors

Usually, it cannot be determined whether a given correction was made by the original scribe or a later hand (a later scribe or user), although in some cases certainty can be had. One possible criterion is handwriting, but since most corrections involve very few letters, this criterion often cannot be invoked. Besides, interlinear additions were written under different conditions from those of the base text, without the help of ruling and in a confined area, usually in petite letters.

Nevertheless the different hand of several long additions can be recognized as secondary on the basis of handwriting or scribal habits.

• 1QIsaᵃ XXXIII 7 (Isa 40:7) and XXXV 15 (Isa 42:6): Only in the interlinear additions (illustr. 1) in these places was the Tetragrammaton represented by *Tetrapuncta*, while the main scribe always wrote the Tetragrammaton in the square script.

• 4QJerᵃ III (Jer 7:30–8:3): The handwriting of the long addition in the interlinear space, in the inter-columnar margin, and also below the text reveals a different handwriting from that of the main scribe (note the different shapes of the ʾ*aleph, bet, lamed, mem*, final *mem*, ʿ*ayin*, and *shin*). Likewise, in XI 6, the added לא was written with a different type of *lamed* than that used in the remainder of the scroll. This *lamed* has a streamlined shape, and does not contain a horizontal line.

• 4QpPsᵃ (4Q171) III 5: The supralinear addition ואוהבי יהוה כיקר כורים פשר]ו על בחירו was written after the completion of the text. While in the main text the Tetragrammaton was written with paleo-Hebrew characters, in the addition it was written with square characters.

• Some of the examples in § e above.

In other instances, the type of correction shows that the scribe himself was involved with the correction.

• 1QIsaᵃ XLIX 17 (Isa 60:14) מנאציך מעניך: the first word was crossed out, and since the scribe continued immediately afterwards, he must have crossed the word out himself.

• The writing of the corrected element(s) next to an element deleted with cancellation dots, e.g. 4QJubᵍ (4Q222) 1 4 נאל.

• 4QapocrLam A (4Q179) 1 ii 11: This line started off with בני ציון היקרים ('the precious sons of Zion') in the masculine, but when the scribe realized he should have written בנות ('daughters') he wrote a *tav* above the last letter of the first word and simply left the *yod*, assuming that the reader would accept it in place of the expected *waw*. Furthermore, he canceled the next word, היקרׄׄם, written in the masculine, with dots (see also p. 195) and continued the text with a female form, הרכות ('the sensitive').

• Many examples in ch. *5c2*, especially TABLE 11.

In 4QTQahat ar (4Q542), É. Puech, *DJD* XXXI, 265 distinguishes between the corrections of the original scribe and those of a second scribe using a thinner pen.

γ. *Textual base of corrections*

All the elements imposed on and changed in the base text of the Qumran manuscripts *replace* that base text. No support has been found for the assumption that some of the added elements should be understood as variant readings collated from another manuscript of the same composition (one possible exception: 1QIsaᵃ XXVII 21 [Isa 33:19] analyzed in ch. *5c3*). Furthermore, there is no evidence in the known manuscripts for the marginal notation of so-called 'parallel readings' or 'synonymous readings,' although the techniques of scribal intervention, when understood wrongly by subsequent scribes, could easily give rise to doublets, as demonstrated by Talmon.[280] Likewise, there is no evidence for assuming any glossing in the Qumran texts (§ h below).

Three possibilities come to mind with regard to the textual source from which the visible corrections in the base text derived:

• The manuscript from which the present copy was copied (the *Vorlage* of the scribe), consulted either by the scribe himself or by a subsequent scribe or user.

• External sources from which details could have been added or corrected in the base text, possibly because those sources were considered to be superior to or more authoritative than the base text. This could pertain to an authoritative copy of Hebrew Scripture or to a central copy of one of the sectarian writings, such as possibly implied by some corrections in 1QHᵃ which may have been based on 4QHᶜ (4Q429), see ch. *2g*.

---

[280]S. Talmon, "Aspects of the Textual Transmission of the Bible in the Light of the Qumran Manuscripts," *Textus* 4 (1964) 95–132.

• The internal logic of the first scribe, a later scribe, or a user, without any reference to a written source. Such corrections could reflect the insights or afterthoughts of scribes in matters of content, language, or orthography.

In any given scroll, the origin of the corrections may have derived from more than one source. When trying to decide between the different possible sources mentioned above, some considerations should be kept in mind.

• In no case are we able to identify with certainty the immediate source from which a Qumran scroll was copied. See ch. *2e*.

• Consistency in the presumed correction of a text towards another one should never be assumed because the corrector need not have been consistent.

• If an obvious error in the base text was corrected, such as a similar-looking or erroneously omitted letter, the correction could have been made according to another exemplar of that text, but it is more likely that such a correction would have been caught by the initial scribe or a careful reader, and could thus have been based on the text from which the scroll was copied initially.

• If some or even the majority of the corrections in a given biblical scroll agree with the medieval form of MT, or its proto-Masoretic forerunner, it does not necessarily follow that the corrections were made on the basis of that text. They could still reflect the scribe's own *Vorlage*.

Due to these difficulties, each manuscript must be studied separately. In Tov, "Corrections" these corrections were examined for 4QGen[j], 1QIsa[a,b], 4QDeut[h], 4QJosh[b], 4QSam[c], 4QJer[a], 5QDeut, 11QPs[a], and MurXII. That investigation showed that there is no evidence for any external source for the correction of any of the Qumran scrolls other than the texts used by the original scribes. In a nonbiblical scroll, the strongest case for possible correction on the basis of an external source would be 4QTest (see below), but even in this case the evidence is not sufficiently strong.

• Possible *correction towards a 'standard text' in manuscripts belonging to the Masoretic family*

MurXII: MurXII and the medieval codex L of MT differ in only thirty-seven very small details, a remarkably small number for such a long well-preserved scroll. The great majority of the differences are in matters of orthography. MurXII thus is a typical representative of the proto-Masoretic text, which in eleven instances corrects an earlier text towards the text now named MT. The corrections pertain to small oversights of omitted and incorrectly written details (J. T. Milik, *DJD* II, 183–4).

4QJer[a]: The base text of this scroll is very close to MT. A striking example of their affinity is the unusual spelling תהינה common to MT and 4QJer[a] XII 8 (Jer 18:21), elsewhere always spelled תהיינה in MT (30 times, including three times in Jeremiah, together with fourteen instances of ותהיין). Only in the MT of Jer 18:21 and 48:6 is the defective spelling תהינה found. Beyond this closeness to MT, the scroll contains twenty-eight corrections, mainly towards a text identical to that now named MT. Thus col. XI 7–9 contains as many as eight corrections, erasures, and supralinear additions, or combinations thereof. Consequently, it appears that this scribe was more prone to errors than other scribes. Some of the mistakes are influenced by words in the context, such as the duplication of the previous word and its subsequent correction; others reflect haplography or other types of oversight (E. Tov, *DJD* XV, 153).

1QIsa[b]: This carefully copied text contains eight interlinear corrections, mainly towards a text identical to that now named MT. Otherwise, this text, which presents a relatively large text for comparison with MT (from ch. 38 to the end of the book, with some gaps), is very close to the medieval codex L.

MasEzek: This scroll, which is very close to MT, contains four corrections towards the text which is now named MT (Talmon, *Masada VI*, 68). It appears that these corrections were based on the scribe's *Vorlage*, and not on an external source as suggested by Talmon, ibid.

In all these texts, correction towards an external source is not impossible, in which case one would have to assume that these texts which are already close to what became the medieval MT were corrected towards a central (standard) text, such as the 'corrected copy' (ספר מוגה) mentioned in *b. Pes.* 112a (ch. *2j*). However, most corrections agreeing with MT seem to be corrections of simple mistakes; therefore it is likely that either the first or a later scribe or reader corrected the manuscript towards its base text in the case of an error by the original scribe, and that this base text agreed with the medieval MT.

• *Corrections in texts written in the Qumran scribal practice.* In the biblical and nonbiblical texts which were written in the Qumran scribal practice and which therefore are quite different from MT, several corrections remove that text even further away from MT. Presumably these corrections were not based on an external source, but rather followed an orthographic framework which the scribe had in mind and from which he sometimes deviated. For example

    1QHᵃ IV (Suk. = Puech XIII) 5 כיא = כי^א

    11QTᵃ (11Q19) LX 15 הזואת = הז^ואת

    11QPsᵃ: This manuscript contains twenty-six supralinear corrections (see *DJD* IV, 13 for a list, to which III 8, 15 should be added) and four instances of cancellation dots (see ibid.). That 11QPsᵃ was probably not corrected according to an external manuscript is supported by the fact that the same types of corrections are found in both the canonical and non-canonical sections of that scroll.

    1QIsaᵃ: The 110 orthographic corrections in this manuscript (Kutscher, *Language*, 423) pertain mainly to *matres lectionis* added to the base text, sometimes in agreement with MT, but more often in accordance with the scribe's conventions elsewhere in the scroll; more appear in section written by scribe A (cols. I–XXVII) than in the second part, especially with regard to gutturals (Giese, "Further Evidence"). That these corrections reflect the scribe's personal insights rather than an external source[281] is evident from several faulty corrections. For example

    1QIsaᵃ I 9 (Isa 1:7) כמאפכת = כמ^אפכת (MT: כמהפכת) and thus also 1QIsaᵃ in Isa 13:19)

    1QIsaᵃ XVI 32 (Isa 21:15) הרבות = ה^רבות (MT: חרבות)

    4QTest (4Q175): The Deuteronomy section (Deut 33:8-11) in this scroll was clearly based on a text such as 4QDeutʰ and the LXX, and not MT. This text was corrected three times towards a text now named MT, although in six other details in the same pericope 4QTest was not corrected. For the data, see J. A. Duncan, *DJD* XIV, 69. Since these other details are more significant than the three possible corrections towards MT, the assumption of correction towards MT is less likely.

δ. *Correction procedures*

Most scribes were not consistent in the use of any of the mentioned correction systems.

    Single letters were usually deleted by means of dots being placed above and below them, long stretches were deleted with parenthesis signs, and words written in the wrong place were crossed out with a line. At the same time, some complete words were dotted, crossed out, or erased. Much depended on the personal preference of the scribe, and apparent inconsistency may have been created by the involvement of different scribes and readers in the same manuscript.

    For example, in 1QS, cancellation dots were used often, either by the original scribe or someone else, to delete letters or words that were subsequently erased with a sharp instrument. Therefore, it is unclear why in 1QS VII 8 two words relating to the change of the punishment were deleted from the context by parenthesis (p. 202). It is not impossible that in this document a meaning other than erasure was attached to parenthesis, but it is more likely that the parenthesis signs were inserted by a hand other than that of the main scribe. By the same token, it is unclear why in the same text some words were canceled by cancellation dots while other elements were crossed out with a line. For example, in the same context a word was crossed out in 4QShirShabbᶠ (4Q405) 3 i 12 (p. 200), while cancellation dots were used in the following line. Most elements to be deleted in 4QDᵃ (4Q266) were crossed out with a line (p. 200), but there are also a few cases of dotted letters and erasures in that manuscript.

    Some personal preferences are recognizable in the manuscripts. Thus, 4QDᵃ crossed out more words proportionally than other scribes (p. 200), and the scribe of 1QIsaᵃ added more supralinear additions and used more cancellation dots than other scribes (pp. 189 ff.). In 1QS, most elements to be deleted were physically erased, while in 1QHᵃ most elements were dotted and afterwards erased (p. 193). The same inconsistency is visible in the analysis of a single phenomenon like the correction of dittography.

---

[281]Thus S. Talmon, *The World of Qumran from Within* (Jerusalem/Leiden 1989) 78 with examples.

Some instances of *dittography* were left uncorrected: 4QTob^a ar (4Q196) 2 4 ומ]לך וּמלך; 4QJub^a (4Q216)
VI 4 עשה; VI 12 כ]ל ואת כֹּל ואת. Other instances were treated in different ways:

• *Cancellation dots*: 4QD^f (4Q271) 4 ii 4 כִּי כֹּי; 4QpIsa^b (4Q162) I 4 אֲשֶׁר וֹאשר; 4QCatena A (4Q177) 1–4
15 או]תֹתֹ; 4QEnastr^a ar (4Q208) 18 2 וֹל; 17 4 בֹה or strokes: 1QpHab VII 2 עֵל.

• *Crossing out* with a line: 4QDan^a 14 11 (Dan 8:1) ו־בּר־נּגלה חזון נראה; 4QD^a (4Q266) 5 ii 13 וּהֹבֹוֹ וחב.

• *Erasures*: The erasure of את in 11QpaleoLev^a E 3 and IV 6. 4QInstr^c (4Q417) 2 i 5 {כיא הואה} כיא הואה.
4QInstr^d (4Q418) 9 10 is completely erased (dittography of preceding line). 4QTQahat ar (4Q542) 1 i 2
{ותנדעונה}ותנדעונה. The second occurrence of העם in 11QT^a (11Q19) LVIII 5: {העם} לצאת מעשר העם.

• *Parenthesis* signs: 4QJer^a XII 11 (Jer 18:23) ({עֹל עֹונֹֹם}) עֹל עֹ{ול.

• Instances of vertical dittography were sometimes dotted, and at other times crossed out with a line, or
encircled with a box: 4QTob^e (4Q200) 6 2 ותמהים (cf. following line). 4QTime of Righteousness (4Q215a) 1 ii
9 הצדק בא ממשל הֹצֹדֹק הטוב (הצדק occurs also in the previous line). 4QJub^f (4Q221) 1 6 ומכול תועבתם וֹשׁ]מֹור (box-like
shape around these words, cf. line 5 and the beginning of line 6). 4QD^a (4Q266) 1a 22 אֹפֹר (box-like shape,
cf. line 23). 4QD^a (4Q266) 11 15 והמשתלח (box-like shape, cf. line 14). 4QOrd^b (4Q513) 1–2 3 הטמאה בֹּהֹמה
(box-like shape).

A similar inconsistency characterizes Greek manuscripts. For example, in Turner, *Greek Manuscripts*,
document 50 some elements are crossed out, while others are washed off with a sponge. P.Bodmer XXIV of
Psalms 17–53, 55–118, hands A and B (3 CE) evidences all the possible correction systems: crossing out with
a line, cancellation dots above and below letters, box-like shapes, and remodeling of letters; see
Kasser–Testuz, *Bodmer*, 27–29, 39–40. For a comprehensive analysis of correction procedures in texts from
the ancient Near East, see Ashton, *Scribal Habits*, ch. 9. For the systems used in the manuscripts of SP, see
Crown, *Samaritan Scribes*, 69–73.

When analyzing the correction procedures, we note that several corrections utilize
scribal markings of some sort. These were discussed in § *c2* under the following
headings:

> i. A marking of the elements to be canceled with cancellation dots or strokes
> ii. Crossing out letters and words with a line
> iii. Parenthesis signs (*antisigma* and *sigma*) or a box-like shape around the element(s) to be
> canceled
> iv. Addition/omission signs
> v. Re-division sign

In addition to these five groups, the following systems are presented here (for a good
analysis and many examples, see Martin, *Scribal Character*, II.421–695):

> vi. *Supralinear/infralinear/marginal correcting additions* of letter(s) or word(s)

The system of adding supralinear letters, accepted by *y. Meg.* 1.71c (see below), was
used frequently in most of the texts from Qumran (see illustrations 1, 7, 12, 13, 17,
etc.) and Masada; for a list of such corrections in 1QIsa^a, see Kutscher, *Isaiah*, 522–36;
for 11QT^a (11Q19), see Yadin, *Temple Scroll (Hebrew)* I.18–19; and for 4QExod^c,
see *DJD* XII, 102. For the Masada texts, see MasShirShabb I 13; II 23; MasEzek II 12
(Ezek 36:22), 18 (Ezek 36:25), 26 (Ezek 36:30); III 6 (Ezek 37:4); MasLev^b III 21 (Lev
10:17); V 14 (Lev 11:32), 19 (Lev 11:35). This technique was also used in manuscripts
of SP (Robertson, *Catalogue*, 34).

Usually, the added elements were written directly above the place in which they
needed to be inserted. E.g. 1QIsa^a I 1 (Isa 1:1) יש^עיהו, בימי. By the same token, a
complete word which was to be added between words *a* and *b*, was written exactly
above the space preceding *b*.[282]

E.g. 1QIsa^a VIII 10 (Isa 8:18) המסתיר פניו ^{את}

---

[282]In codices A, B, and S of the LXX, arrows indicated the exact place in the text where the omitted elements,
written in the margin, needed to be inserted (see Milne–Skeat, *Scribes*, 41–3).

Similarly, if a letter was to be inserted before the first letter of a word, it was written above the space preceding that word, e.g. 1QIsaᵃ VII 1 (Isa 7:16) בטרם.

On the other hand, a word or part of a word which was to replace a linear word was written exactly above that word, and not above the space between the words; see technique vii below. This technique was used rather infrequently.

Supralinear additions occasionally continued horizontally into the left intercolumnar margin (illustr. 1) and in rare cases also vertically, alongside the text and even under the column. Other additions were written in the top margin, or to the right of the text in the intercolumnar margin. Some examples follow.

4QSamᵃ X 10 (1 Sam 11:1): The long supralinear addition should be taken as continuing after גלעד.

1QIsaᵃ XXIX 16 (Isa 36:11): The position of the added עמנו in the right intercolumnar margin does not show to which word in the text it referred:

להשחיתה ¹¹ויואמרו אליו אליקים ושׁבנא ויואח דברנא עם עבדיך

עמנו   ארמית כיא שומעים אנחנו ואל תדבר אלינו   את הדברים האלה

This word should be taken as either an addition or correction to עם עבדיך, or as a correction to אלינו. In the latter case, the marginal reading would be identical to MT in the parallel verse, 2 Kgs 18:26.

XXX: Addition between lines 11 and 13 and vertically in the margin of the following sheet.

XXXII 14: Vertical addition in the left intercolumnar margin.

XXXIII 7: Addition at the end of the line and vertically in the margin (illustr. 1).

4QJerᵃ III 6 (Jer 7:30–8:3): A long addition of three lines in small letters between lines 5 and 7 in the original text was continued vertically alongside the text (four lines) and also below the column, in reverse writing (one line).

4QJerᵉ (Jer 50:4): Corrective addition in the right intercolumnar margin before and above the erased first word.

ובעת {הֹהֵֹמֹהֹ} ההיֹא נאם יהוֹה יבאו בני ישראל המה ובני יהודה יחדו הלוך ובכו ילכו]

4QXIIᵉ 18 1: Vertical addition in the left intercolumnar margin alongside lines 1–4.

4QXIIᵍ 1–4 i 18: Vertical addition in the left intercolumnar margin.

4QQohᵃ II 1 (Qoh 6:4) **(הלך ובחושך שמו)**: Addition in the top margin, see § iii above.

4QQohᵃ II 20 (Qoh 7:6): The added הבל is written in the middle of the bottom margin.

4QDᵍ (4Q272) 1 i: Addition above line 6 and in the left intercolumnar margin.

4QMish D (4Q324a) i: Vertical addition in the left intercolumnar margin: ש]וֹא.

4QMish H (4Q329a): Upon realizing that there was no room for an additional line at the end of the sheet, the scribe wrote the last line vertically in the left margin starting from the lower left corner.

4QTQahat ar (4Q542) 3 i: Addition in the left intercolumnar margin.

11QMelch (11Q13) 1 11 (col. I): Supralinear and vertical addition.

4QDᵃ (4Q266) 5 ii 9: The added להור was written in the right intercolumnar margin, just before the first word in the column to which it related (עמו בישוד עם ומם).

Letters were rarely added as corrections *below* the line. In 11QTᵃ (11Q19) XVII 13, the *waw* of the Tetragrammaton, initially omitted, was added below the line. Likewise, the *waw* of ואת was added below the line in 11QTᵃ (11Q19) LX 10. For additional examples, see ch. *4f* ('The written text vis-à-vis horizontal and vertical ruling,' system 6). For economy of space, letters or words were often added below the last word in the line in *tefillin* and *mezuzot* (ch. *7c*). In these texts, scribes had almost no choice since the ragged shape of *tefillin* did not enable the completion of words at the edges.

There was rarely room for words to be added in the line itself. For example, scribe A of 1QHᵃ II (Sukenik = Puech col. X) 23 left out a word in גרו   והמה ם which was filled in by a later scribe with אתכה written in petite letters. As a consequence, the final text reads: והמה מאתכה גרו.

The writing of letters above the line was permitted by *y. Meg.* 1.71c:

חולין בספרים אין חולין לא בתפילין ולא במזוזות

One may hang <the letter above the line> in scrolls, but one may not hang <the letter above the line> in *tefillin* or *mezuzot*.[283]

Likewise, *b. Menaḥ.* 30b (cf. *Sof.* 5.4) approved of the erasure or correction of a word and the writing of the divine name in its stead or above the line:

הטועה בשם גורר את מה שכתב ותולה את מה שגרר וכותב את השם על מקום הגרר. דברי רבי יהודה רבי יוסי אומר אף
תולין את השם. רבי יצחק אומר אף מוחק וכותב. ר"ש שזורי אומר כל השם כולו תולין מקצתו אין תולין ... הלכה
כר"ש שזורי

If <a scribe> omitted the name of God <and had already written the next word>, he should erase the word that was written and insert it above the line, and should write the name upon the erasure. This is the opinion of R. Judah. R. Jose says: 'He may even insert the name above the line.' R. Isaac says: 'He may even wipe away <the word that was written> and write <the name in its place>.' R. Simeon of Shezur says: 'He may write the whole name above the line but not a part of it ...' The *halakha* is in accordance with R. Simeon of Shezur.

Sof. 5.8 restricts the addition of lines in the middle of the text:

הטועה את השיטה אינו תולה מנגד השיטין אלא נגד הטעות. גורר אחת וכותב שתים. שתים וכותב שלש ובלבד שלא יגרור
שלש

If he omits a line in error, he may not suspend it between the lines, but inserts it in close proximity to the place of the error by erasing one <adjacent line> and writing two in its place, or <by erasing> two lines and writing three; provided only that he does not erase three lines.

However, this dictum probably refers to omissions recognized by the original scribe, while in the cases under review the omissions were added by later scribes. In the case of 4QJer[a] (quoted above), the corrector probably had little choice but to act as he did, that is to add lines in small letters between the original lines, in the left margin and in the space under the text.

vii. *Supralinear addition of a word* replacing *a linear word*

Usually, the added elements were meant to correct the linear text by including the addition in the text itself. A few supralinear additions, however, were written above the linear word with the intention of replacing the word in the text, even though that word was not canceled formally by means of one of the cancellation systems.

1QM XI 8 כבד / לְהַלֹּחָם. Through the canceling of three letters and the supralinear addition of three other letters, an original להלחם was changed to להכבד.

1QIsa[a] III 24   (Isa 3:17) יהוה / אֲדֹנָי.

2QapocrDavid (2Q22) II 3   דבריו / בכל דרכיו

4QD[e] (4Q270) 7 i 4 שמיע / להרים [קולו. The supralinear addition was intended to replace להרים with להשמיע, since the correction did not include לה. This correction may have been made on the basis of 1QS VII 14 or a similar manuscript.

Likewise, the Greek papyri from the time of the Second Jewish Revolt added words above the line, without any scribal signs, when these additions were meant to replace the linear text. For the Greek documents, see Lewis, *Bar Kochba*, document 11 3 (pls. 3, 4); 12 4 (pl. 5); 17 6 (pl. 15).

viii. *Reshaping (remodeling) letters*

In an attempt to correct a letter or letters, scribes sometimes reshaped the form of a letter into that of another letter. Over the course of the remodeling, scribes superimposed the new letter on the old one by modifying elements of the old letter. Thus straight lines

---

[283]See, however, the discussion in *b. Menaḥ.* 29b, *y. Shabb.* 16.15b concerning the validity of a relatively large number of such additions.

were rounded, round lines were made straight, and parts of letters were elongated, etc. Not all letters could be modified, and in certain cases scribes turned to partial erasure. Thus the scribe of 1QS II 4 originally wrote ושא, and upon realizing his mistake, he created the new reading וישא by partly erasing the *waw* and by superimposing the *yod* on that letter. He then placed a *waw* before the word, of necessity in the margin, as this was the first word in the line.

• 1QIsa[a] VI 25 (Isa 7:11): The original *aleph* of אאל was changed to a *shin* (שאל = MT); מעם (= MT) was probably changed from מאל.

• 1QpHab III 7: Initially the scribe wrote פשר after the mid-line spacing (closed section) as so often elsewhere in the scroll under similar circumstances. In this case, however, the scribe made a mistake since פשו was required. He created the required word by superimposing a very wide *waw* on the *resh*.

• 4QDeut[n] V 6 (Deut 5:24): היום was remodeled to ביום.

• 4QBarkhi Nafshi[a] (4Q434) 1 i 3 שׁוּעקתם: The scribe initially wrote שועתם, then canceled the first letter with a dot, remodeled the *waw* to a *zayin*, and added a supralinear *qoph* to read זעקתם. א

• 4QD[a] (4Q266) 6 i 3 היא האוחז{ת} ה בעור: *Tav* remodeled to a *he*. Likewise: 6 i 6 ה{ת}חזבא{ו} בזק (ו) ברוש; 6 i 7 והפך מראה{ת} ה לדק.

• 4QD[a] (4Q266) 6 i 9 וגלחו את ה{ב}ר{ש}ר: The scribe corrected הבשר (cf. line 2) to הרוש, while remodeling a *bet* to *resh*.

• 4QD[a] (4Q266) 6 i 10 ספור{ש}י: Correction of phonetic mistake; *sin* remodeled to *samekh*. Likewise: ibid. וה{ש}ס {וח}ק בסכלוֹת 10 ii 12; וראה אם יו{ש} סף מן.

ix. *Erasure*

The technique of erasing letters, words, or a complete line (see below) in leather scrolls (termed גרר or גרד in rabbinic literature) with a sharp instrument is known from many texts. Since the use of the instruments did not completely erase the letters, faint traces can often be discerned. In *DJD* erasures are usually indicated with special brackets: { }.

• 1QS VII–VIII: Some of the manifold erasures in these columns pertain to letters which had been encircled previously by dots (VII 1, 20 bis), while others left spaces, some considerably long, in the middle of lines: VII 6, 10, 11, 22 bis, 23; VIII 10 bis, 19. The erasures of 1QS are clearly recognizable in the facsimile edition by J. H. Charlesworth with H. W. L. Rietz, *The Dead Sea Scrolls: Rule of the Community— Photographic Multi-Language Edition* (Philadelphia 1996). See TABLES 13 and 14 above.

• 1QH[a]: For erasures of words initially indicated with cancellation dots, see TABLES 13 and 14 above.

• 4QTest (4Q175): The end of line 15 and the beginning of line 16 were erased and left empty by the scribe, who at first wrote לוא (line 15) together with an undecipherable word (beginning of line 16) anticipating the phrase that was to be written after ולאמר in line 16.

• 4QInstr[d] (4Q418) 9 10: Complete erasure of line (dittography of preceding line).

• 11QPs[a] XX 13: The erasure of a word in this line (together with the erasure of the cancellation dots) left a large uninscribed space in the middle of the line.

• 11QPs[a] E (*DJD* XXIII) i 2 בשׁם; iii 13 עֲבוֹד: Both words were dotted and subsequently erased.

• 11QpaleoLev[a] E 3 and IV 6: A blank space and remnants of unsuccessfully erased letters testify to the erasure of a dittograph את אֿת.

• 11QT[a] (11Q19): For examples of erasures see Yadin, *Temple Scroll (Hebrew)* I.20–21.

Most erasures were probably executed by the original scribes, and not by later scribes or users. This may be surmised from an analysis of the letters or words surrounding the erasures, especially when the scribe proceeded to write the correct letters or word after the erasure of an erroneous word, either instead of the erased word or after it. For example, the scribe of 4QJer[a] XII 6 (Jer 18:19) who wrote דברי erased the word upon recognizing his mistake, and then wrote the correct word (יריבי) after it on the line itself. The erased area could not easily be inscribed by new text in leather scrolls.

The erased area was sometimes left blank, such as the word-length spaces in the middle of the lines in 1QH[a] VII (Suk. = Puech XV) 15 and 11QPs[a] XX 13. At other times, a word or letters were written in or above the erased area. Some words were erased after they had first been denoted with cancellation dots (TABLE 13 above).

    The technique of erasing is as old as the art of writing. The evidence for erasures in the Ugaritic texts was collected by M. Dietrich and O. Loretz, "Rasuren und Schreibfehler in den keilalphabetischen Texten aus Ugarit: Anmerkungen zur Neuauflage von KTU," *UF* 26 (1994) 23–61.

x. *Washing out letters or words*

The washing out of letters with a damp sponge (σπόγγος, σπογγιά, spongea) was frequently performed in papyri, e.g. in 4QpapPrQuot (4Q503) 11 4 in which three letters repeating part of the previous word were washed off by the scribe who then continued to copy the text: במעמד {במע}. See further 4QpapPrFêtes^c (4Q509) 97–98 I, 2 2; the examples mentioned by Turner, *Greek Manuscripts*, 16; and many of the papyri published by Lewis, *Bar Kokhba*. The two words אשר חטא which were removed from the text of 4QLev^c 4 1 (leather) in Lev 4:23 (where they are not found in the MT, SP, and LXX) were probably washed off with partial success, rather than erased with a sharp instrument.

    This technique presents the easiest solution for correcting mistakes in papyri, but since leather does not lend itself well to this purpose it is not used in most of the Qumran scrolls. This procedure is mentioned in *Sof.* 5.1 (מוחק), and is known from Egyptian sources, as Egyptian scribes had such sponges among their standard equipment. See Ashton, *Scribal Habits*, 154.

    The degree of scribal intervention. Many of the texts from the Judean Desert contain a relatively large number of scribal interventions, some averaging as many as one scribal intervention to every three or four lines of text, e.g. 1QIsa^a, 4QTest (4Q175), and 4QTQahat ar (4Q542); for precise details, see cols. 8–9 in APPENDIX 1. Little scribal intervention is visible in texts written in the paleo-Hebrew script and in the proto-Masoretic texts from sites in the Judean Desert other than Qumran as well as in some Qumran texts (ch. *7b*) and *de luxe* editions (ch. *4j*).

    In none of the Qumran scrolls, biblical or nonbiblical, has any evidence been preserved for substantial corrective activity in matters of *content* after the writing had been completed. Probably such changes were not inserted either in still earlier scrolls because of the technical limitations of writing in scrolls.

g. *Final and nonfinal letters* (illustrations 1, 6, 16, 26)

In the development during the Persian period of the final forms of certain letters in the square script there was a transition period during which certain scribes or scribal centers used the newly developed final forms, while others did not yet do so, or used them inconsistently. Thus, an early text like 4QExod-Lev^f (middle of 3 BCE) did not use final forms, while in the same period 4QSam^b did use such forms and 4QJer^a used most of the final letters except for the final *ṣade*.[284] According to Yardeni, only in the Herodian period did the use of the final letters become established.[285] The differences between the various scribes of the large texts from cave 1, including sections within scrolls, were described by Martin, *Scribal Hands*, I.90–96.

    This as yet unregulated use of final and nonfinal forms is reflected first and foremost in the rather frequent appearance of nonfinal forms in final position, but also in the less frequent use of final forms in nonfinal position. The conditions under which these two groups of letters were used differ, and in the latter case they often reflect mistakes.

---

[284]A. Yardeni, *The Book of Hebrew Script* (Heb.; Jerusalem 1991) 152.
[285]A. Yardeni, "A Deed of Sale from the Judaean Desert: Naḥal Ṣeʾelim 9," *Tarbiz* 53 (1994) 308.

In many Qumran texts as well as in several texts from Masada, nonfinal letters were sometimes also written in final position. Among the Qumran texts, this practice is attested especially in texts written in the Qumran scribal practice (ch. *8a*), and less frequently so in other texts.[286] The data recorded here are not as exhaustive as in the other categories analyzed above; they are based on two lists compiled for this purpose,[287] reverse-order forms in the Qumran texts culled from the database of the Israel Academy of the Hebrew Language referring to all nonbiblical scrolls published until 1975 (list 1), and the final letters in the Qumran texts in nonfinal position and nonfinal letters in final position included in the database of the Accordance computer program (list 2).

The paleographical interpretation of final/nonfinal forms is sometimes subjective. Among other things, one often needs to consider as a final letter not only the shapes that are known as such from most texts, but also elongated nonfinal forms, which were meant to indicate the final position, even in such letters as *bet*, *he*, and *lamed* (not covered by the examples below). As a rule, however, the distinction between final and nonfinal forms is not problematical. The following lists record the texts containing some or many nonfinal forms in final position as well as final forms in nonfinal position.

List *1* almost exclusively contains texts written in the Qumran scribal practice: 1QH[a], 1QS, 1QM, 1QDM (1Q22), 1QApocryphal Prophecy (1Q25), 1QpHab, 1QpZeph (1Q15), 4Qpap pIsa[c] (4Q163), 4QpHos[a] (4Q166), 4QpPs[a] (4Q171), 4QFlor (4Q174), 4QTanḥ (4Q176), 4QCatena A (4Q177), 4QpapS[a] (4Q255). It also contains one text not written in that system, 4QJub[e] (4Q220). Altogether, the list contains fifteen texts, of which eleven are *not* mentioned in list *2*.

List *2* records forty-two texts written in the Qumran scribal practice: 1QH[a], 1QpHab, 1QS, 1QM, 4QTest (4Q175), 4QSapiential Work (4Q185), 4QJub[f] (4Q221), 4QpapJub[h] (4Q223–224), 4QPsJub[a] (4Q225), 4QD[a] (4Q266), 4QD[b] (4Q267), 4QToh A (4Q274), 4QWork Containing Prayers B (4Q292), 4QRP[c] (4Q365), 4QApocryphal Pentateuch B (4Q377), 4Qpap paraKings et al. (4Q382), 4QMMT[a] (4Q394), 4QMMT[d] (4Q397), 4QShirShabb[a] (4Q400), 4QShirShabb[d] (4Q403), 4QShirShabb[f] (4Q405), 4QInstr[c] (4Q417), 4QInstr[d] (4Q418), 4QWays of Righteousness[b] (4Q421), 4QSapiential-Hymnic Work A (4Q426), 4QH[a] (4Q427), 4QH[b] (4Q428), 4QPersonal Prayer (4Q443), 4QNarrative C (4Q462), 4QWar Scroll-like Text B (4Q471), 4QM[a] (4Q491), 4QpapM[f] (4Q496), 4QpapRitMar (4Q502), 4QpapPrQuot (4Q503), 4QDibHam[a] (4Q504), 4QpapDibHam[c] (4Q506), 4QpapPrFêtes[c] (4Q509), 4QpapRitPur B (4Q512), 11QSefer ha-Milḥamah (11Q14), 11QT[a] (11Q19), 11QT[b] (11Q20).

List *2* also contains sixteen texts not written in the Qumran scribal practice or for which insufficient orthographic evidence was available: Copper Scroll (3Q15), 4QText with a Citation of Jubilees (4Q228), 4QHarvesting (4Q284a), 4Q327, 4Q370, 4Q378, 4QapocrJosh[b] (4Q379), 4QpsEzek[a] (4Q385), 4QLiturgical Work A (4Q409), 4QLament by a Leader (4Q439), 4QApocryphal Psalm and Prayer (4Q448), 4QNarrative I (4Q469), 4QText Mentioning Descendants of David (4Q479), 4QpapPrFêtes[b] (4Q508), 4QOrd[c] (4Q514), 4QpapUnclassified frags. (4Q520), 4QMessianic Apocalypse (4Q521).

In the following eleven texts, the present author has noted similar phenomena: 1QIsa[a] (scribes A and B), 4QDeut[j], 4QExod[c], 4QDeut[m], 4QXII[d], 4QPs[o], 4QPs[x], 4QpapD[h] (4Q273), 4QRP[b] (4Q364), 4QParaGen-Exod (4Q422), 4QTQahat ar (4Q542). Seven of these texts are written in the Qumran scribal practice. Single forms are also included in two Masada texts: MasLev[b], MasEzek.

The connection between this procedure and the Qumran scribal practice in these eighty Qumran texts is very likely (75 percent of all the texts), but *further research* is needed especially since these lists are not exhaustive regarding the biblical texts.

---

[286]For comparison, in the Torah scroll from the synagogue of Severus (Gen 27:2 and 36:10; see Tov, *TCHB*, 119–20) as well as in the medieval manuscripts of MT (Neh 2:13, *Ketiv* המפרוצים, 'that-were-breached,' *Qere* הם פרוצים) nonfinal letters were almost never employed in final position. A final *mem* occurs once in the middle of a word in MT Isa 9:6 *Ketiv* לםרבה, 'of the increase of . . ,' *Qere* למרבה. See also the epitaph of Uzzia (late Second Temple period) containing the spellings עצמי (bones) and למפתח (to open) next to מלך.

[287]Thanks are expressed to E. Qimron for compiling the first list in 1990, and to M. G. Abegg for compiling the second list in 1999–2000.

Nonfinal letters in final position (illustrations 1, 6, 26)

Most of the instances in which nonfinal letters were written at the ends of words in these texts appear at the ends of monosyllabic words such as יום, עץ, עם, שם, נאם, אם, גם, indicating that these words were not viewed simply as independent units.[288] According to the statistics provided by Siegel, "Orthographic Convention," and idem, *Scribes of Qumran*, 4–6 in 1QIsa^a יום, עץ, שם, אם, גם were almost always (scribes A and B) written with nonfinal *mem*,[289] while for *neʾum* and *ʿam* there were an equal number of forms with final and nonfinal letters (*ʿam* with final *mem* occurs mainly when preceded by a prefix, a configuration which must have been conceived of as both a monosyllabic and a bisyllabic word). Some examples referring to monosyllabic, bisyllabic, and longer words follow.

Monosyllabic words
4QPs^x 2 (Ps 89:20) עמ
4QPs^x 8 (Ps 89:31) אמ
4QToh A (4Q274) 2 i 2 ביומ
4QToh A (4Q274) 2 i 8 אמ

Bisyllabic words
4QpapS^a (4Q255) 2 5 להלכ תמימ
4QH^a (4Q427) 7 ii 10 ארצ; 7 ii 17 מליצ
4QApocryphal Psalm and Prayer (4Q448) II 2 המלכ; II 3 עמכ; II 9 שממ

Longer words
4QPs^x 1 (Ps 89:20) לֹבֹחֹריכ
4QT^a? (4Q365a) 2 ii 6 המשקומ
4QApocryphal Psalm and Prayer (4Q448) II 8 ממלכתכ; III 1 באהבתכ

None of the texts mentioned in the two lists is consistent with regard to the writing of final forms. For example, in 4QH^a (4Q427) 7 i, probably containing more nonfinal letters in final position than other Qumran texts, final and nonfinal forms alternate constantly.

Final letters in nonfinal position (illustr. 16)

Some final letters were written in nonfinal position because some scribes did not consistently distinguish between the two letters. Such instances can be recognized especially when the final letter does not occur in penultimate position (which usually resulted from an error), e.g. 4QpapS^a (4Q255) 2 4 וֹדה; 4QMMT^a (4Q394) 1–2 ii 4 ושמונה; iii 4 בשמונה; iii 7 וחמשה; v 5 השמן; 3–7 i 4 מקצת, 7 מאים]ומט, 8 מדֹגֹן.

Many, if not most, instances of final letters occur in penultimate position; the scribe must have thought that he had finished the word since most of them represent complete words, such as 1QIsa^a XLIII 27 (Isa 52:11) משמה and 4QInstr^d (4Q418) 81 12 לשמו. A remarkably large number (TABLE 20) pertain to the long pronominal suffixes characteristic of the Qumran scribal practice, such as 4QDeut^j X 2 (Exod 12:48) אתכמה and 4QTest (4Q175) 5 אחיהמה, לאהמה. In particular, scribe B of 1QIsa^a employed such forms; see Siegel, *Scribes of Qumran*, Appendix III (242–4). In all these cases, it appears as if the scribe at first wrote the standard short pronominal suffix, possibly as extant in his *Vorlage*, but subsequently remembered that he should have written the long one. Two different conditions may be distinguished.

---

[288]See Martin, *Scribal Character*, II.631–2; J. P. Siegel, "Final *Mem*," 125–30; idem, "Orthographic Convention"; Qimron, *Grammar*, 126–31.
[289]The exceptions pertain mainly to cases in which these words were preceded by another syllable, such as ה- or ב-.

• *The scribe recognized his mistake while writing.* E.g. 1QH^a II 22 ובבריתכה: Upon completing ובבריתך, the scribe realized that he should have written the long form, with the *he*, which he then added. A space is left between this and the following word. Most instances are of this type.

• *The scribe recognized his mistake upon completing the writing.* Less frequently, when the scribe recognized the mistake only upon completion of the following word, or later, the correction was made by using the space between the words. Thus, in 4QTest (4Q175) line 18 יש'מוקטורה, the singular form of the verb ישם was corrected to a plural one by the addition of *waw* written in the space between the words and the supralinear *yod*. At the same time, the scribe did not change the final form of the *mem* to a nonfinal one. In other cases, the additional letter was added above the line, as in 4QInstr^c (4Q417) 2 i 10 תשם^ה, 11QT^a (11Q19) LVI 13 אשים^ה, and 4QD^a (4Q266) 11 13 מרעיתך^ה, or was smaller than the surrounding letters as in 4QapocrJosh^a (4Q378) 3 i 8 עליך^ה.

TABLE 20 presents the relevant data for the Judean Desert texts (not exhaustive, especially not for the biblical texts).

TABLE 20: *Final Letters in Nonfinal Position*

1QH^a II (Suk. = Puech X) 22 ובבריתכה, VII (XV) 29 מתכדה { ח}

1QIsa^a scribes A and B: I 8 (Isa 1:6) בשמן; XXIII 24 (Isa 29:14) חכמת, 28 (Isa 29:17) והכרמל; XXV 7 (Isa 30:24) האדמה; XXVI 26 (Isa 32:15) לכרמל; XXVII 8 (Isa 34:7) ארצמה ?; XXVIII 10 (Isa 34:10) ויומם; XXXIV 20 (Isa 41:16) אותמה, 23 (Isa 41:18) אשימה; XXXVII 24 (Isa 44:18) לבותמה, 30 (Isa 45:20) פסלמה; XLII 10 (Isa 50:10) בכמה, 14 (Isa 51:2) תחוללכמה; XLIII 14 (Isa 51:23) ותשימי, 17 (Isa 52:3) נמכרתמה, 27 (Isa 52:11) משמה; XLV 22 (Isa 55:3) נפשכמה; XLVI 20 (Isa 56:7) עולותיהמה וזבחיהמה; XLVII 22 (Isa 58:1) כפיכמה, 14 (Isa 59:3) וחטאתיכמה, 13 (Isa 59:2) מקומסמה; XLVIII 7 (Isa 58:12) משכבכמה, 7 (Isa 57:8) פשעיהמה; L 6 (Isa 61:9) רואיהמה; LI 2 (Isa 63:6) ואשכירמה, 17 (Isa 59:6) כמעשיהמה

1QpHab V 3 שמ'; VIII 13 ויקומ'; XII 14 להמה

4QExod^c VI 37 (Exod 15:12) תבלעמו; VI 39 (Exod 15:15) יאחזמו

4QDeut^j X 2 (Exod 12:48) אתכמה

4QPs^o 2 3 (Ps 116:7) גמל

4QTest (4Q175) 5 אליהמה, אחיהמה, לאהמה 6, 18 יש'מוקטורה

4QSapiential Work (4Q185) 1–2 ii 7 ואתמה

4QJub^f (4Q221) 3 4 ההמה

4QpapS^a (4Q255) 2 4 וֹדה

4QD^a (4Q266) 11 13 מרעיתך^ה

4QapocrJosh^a (4Q378) 3 i 8 עליך^ה

4QpsEzek^a (4Q385) 2 5 עצמו

4QMMT^a (4Q394) 3–7 i 2 ושלמה, מאת (?), 4 מקצת, 7 ומט]מאים, 8 סדֹנֹ, 19 הטמה. The editors denote similar forms in 3–7 ii 15–18; 8 iii 9.

4QShirShabb^a (4Q400) 1 ii 4 מרומ'

4QInstr^c (4Q417) 2 i 10 תשם^ה; 2 ii + 23 7 בך^ה

4QInstr^d (4Q418) 81 12 לשמו

4QParaGen-Exod (4Q422) III 8 ב]בתי'המה

4QPersonal Prayer (4Q443) 12 i 3]להֹמה[

4QNarrative C (4Q462) 1 12 יהמה[

4QpapPrQuot (4Q503) 14 2 ש[מ]דה

4QDibHam^a (4Q504) 9 4 ישימו; 18 2 להמה

4QpapPrFêtes^c (4Q509) 9–10 i 3]מ0[; 192 2 עמים

11QPs^a IV 12 (Ps 126:3) עמנו; XVIII 11 (Ps 154:13) אוכלמה; XIX 6 (11QPs^a Plea) מהמה; XXVI 2 (Ps 149:8) ומנחתמה; LIX 10 ונכבדיהמה

11QSefer ha-Milḥamah (11Q14) 1 ii 8 ארצכמה

11QT^a (11Q19) II 6 תיהמה; XLI 13 ולפנימה; מזבחו]; LIX 10 לבבמה; LVI 13 אשים^ה

MasLev^b V 10 (Lev 11:28) המה (MT המה, SP הם)

MasEzek III 12 (Ezek 37:7) ה]עْצֿמות[

Traditions concerning a lack of consistency in the writing of the final forms of letters are also reflected in the Talmud.

In the case of the double letters of the alphabet, one writes the first ones at the beginning and middle of a word, and the second <final forms> at the end. If one did otherwise, the scroll is invalid.[290] In the name of R. Mattiah b. Heresh they have said, '<The letters> *m, n, ṣ, p, k* <that appear in two forms> were revealed to Moses at Sinai.' . . . The men of Jerusalem would write 'Jerusalem' <that is, ירושלים> as 'to Jerusalem' <that is, ירושלים> and <sages> did not scruple in this regard. Along the same lines, צפון, 'north,' was written 'to the north' <that is, צפונ> and חימן, 'south,' was written 'to the south' <that is, חימנ> (*y. Meg.* 1.71d; cf. also *b. Meg.* 2b).

A similar use of nonfinal letters in final position is reflected in the tradition of the three scrolls of the Law found in the temple court (*y. Taʿan.* 4.68a), since one of the books was called the '*maʿon* scroll' after one of its prominent characteristics, namely, the absence of a final *nun* in *maʿon* and apparently also in other words.

h. *Notation of variant readings and glosses?*

It has been suggested by some scholars that some marginal notations in the Qumran scrolls reflect variant readings copied from parallel scrolls of the same composition. Thus Stegemann, *ΚΥΡΙΟΣ*, A 94, n. 512 believed that the cancellation dots to the right and left of the supralinear word in 1QIsaᵃ XLIX 14 (Isa 49:14) mark this word as a variant. According to him, some scribal signs in that scroll (§ c3 above) also indicate such variants. Other scholars suggested that some marginal notations functioned as glosses. However, with one exception, the words written between the lines or in the margins of the scrolls should be viewed as corrections of the linear text.[291] For example, we suggested in ch. *2g* that several corrections in 1QHᵃ may have been based on 4QHᶜ (4Q429) and 4QpapHᶠ (4Q432). There seems to be only one instance of a gloss explaining a word in the text:

Isa 7:25   MT   שמיר ושית (= LXX T S V)
            thornbush and thistle
1QIsaᵃ   ברזל שמיר ושית
            iron thornbush and thistle (the addition is written above שמיר)[292]

An example of a possible (grammatical) interpolation is the following instance:

Isa 44:3   MT   כי אצק מים על צמא ונזלים על יבשה   אצק רוחי על זרעך
            Even as I pour water on thirsty soil, and rain upon dry ground,
            will I will pour my spirit on your offspring.
1QIsaᵃ   כיא אצק מים על צמא ונוזלים על יבשה כֿי אצק רוחי על זרעכה
            Even as I pour water on thirsty soil, and rain upon dry ground,
            ˢᵒ will I pour my spirit on your offspring.

At the same time, the absence or rarity of physically recognizable interpolations does not exclude the possibility that some plus elements of a scroll vis-à-vis parallel manuscripts of that composition are in the nature of interpolations inserted in the body of the text. These assumed interpolations, however, do not necessarily prove the scribal habit of adding interlinear or marginal interpolations at an earlier stage of the textual transmission. Possibly such interpolations were added directly into the running text in the course of its transmission.

---

[290]The non-distinction between the two types of letters was not allowed either in *b. Shabb.* 103b, *Sifre* Deuteronomy § 36 on Deut 6:9, *Sof.* 2.20.

[291]For details, see my study "Glosses, Interpolations, and Other Types of Scribal Additions in the Text of the Hebrew Bible," in *Greek and Hebrew Bible*, 53–74.

[292]In the spoken language of the Second Temple period, שמיר had a secondary meaning of 'iron,' to which the gloss probably referred. See the material collected by S. Lieberman, "Forgotten Meanings," *Leshonenu* 32 (1967–68) 99–102 (Heb.); E. Qimron, "Textual Remarks on 1QIsᵃ," *Textus* 12 (1985) נט-ס (Heb. with Eng. summ.).

One of the difficulties in assuming marginal glosses and interpolations in biblical texts lies in the lack of convincing evidence in the ancient sources. For, while in classical and Mesopotamian texts we can actually point to the physical existence in manuscripts of various types of added elements, only limited evidence is available for biblical texts, for which many glosses and interpolations have been reconstructed.

i. *Abbreviations*

Abbreviations of partial or complete words are not evidenced in the Judean Desert texts. On the other hand, many numbers were represented by number signs in various texts (§ c9 above). See further:

4QpapRitPur B (4Q512) 33–35 (col. IV) 3 א שח[ה שא]ור, translated by the editor as 'and the be[ginning of] the 1st [month]'; cf. also ibid., 51–55 ii 9.

6

SCRIPTS[293]

a. *Square (Jewish) script*

In different periods, Hebrew texts were written in different scripts, at first in the 'early' *Hebrew* script and later in the square script, which developed from the Aramaic script. The late books of Scripture as well as the nonbiblical Qumran texts probably were written directly in this script.

No early fragments of the biblical text written in the Hebrew script have been preserved, unless one considers the silver rolls from Ketef Hinnom (Tov, *TCHB*, 118) as biblical texts, while Qumran yielded various texts written in a later version of this script, now named paleo-Hebrew and evidenced in fragments from the late third century BCE to the middle of the first century CE.

The various changes occurring in the script in which the Hebrew language was written (Naveh, *Alphabet*, 112–24), also occurred in the writing of Scripture. At some stage during the Second Temple period, a gradual transition occurred from the Hebrew to the Aramaic script, from which a script developed which is exclusive to the Jews and which could thus be called the 'Jewish script' (thus many scholars) or the square script (according to the form of the letters); in rabbinic literature (e.g. *b. Sanh.* 21b), it is sometimes called the 'Assyrian script' (כתב אשורית) due to the fact that its ancestor, the Aramaic script, was in use in the Assyrian Empire.

The date attributed by tradition to the use of the square script for the writing of the biblical books (period of Ezra) appears possible but lacks external confirmation. In this context, Naveh, *Alphabet*, 234–5 speaks of a somewhat later date, namely, the third century BCE. One should note that after the introduction of the square script, the ancient Hebrew script did not go out of use. See the material collected by Naveh, *Alphabet*, 119–24. In any event, all texts written in the square script necessarily reflect a relatively late stage of writing.

In the period covered by the Judean Desert texts, scribes wrote in a variety of forms of the Aramaic and square scripts, on the basis of which documents are often dated. In fact, since most documents do not provide their own dates, external sources are often invoked, especially coins and inscriptions which are dated. For example, according to Cross, "Development," the Qumran texts written in the square script can be divided into three main periods, 250–150 BCE ('archaic' script), 150–30 BCE (Hasmonean script), 30 BCE–70 CE (Herodian script). For the relevance of dating based on AMS examinations, see ch. *1c*.

---

[293]Background information: N. Avigad, "The Palaeography of the Dead Sea Scrolls and Related Documents," ScrHier 4 (1958) 56–87; Cross, "Development"; idem, "Palaeography and the Dead Sea Scrolls," in Flint–VanderKam, *Fifty Years*, 379–402; idem, "Paleography," *Encyclopedia DSS*, 2.629–634; J. Naveh, "The Development of the Aramaic Script," *Proceedings of the Israel Academy of Sciences and Humanities*, V, 1 (Jerusalem 1970) 1–69; idem, "Hebrew Texts in the Aramaic Script in the Persian Period?" *BASOR* 203 (1971) 27–32; idem, *Alphabet;* idem, *On Sherd and Papyrus: Aramaic and Hebrew Inscriptions from the Second Temple, Mishnaic and Talmudic Periods* (Heb.; Jerusalem 1992); A. Yardeni, *The Book of Hebrew Script* (Heb.; Jerusalem 1991).

Different writing styles have been recognized, and as a rule, Scripture texts and other authoritative compositions (note the copies of 11QT [11Q19, 11Q20]) were written in formal handwriting, but there are many exceptions. Several authoritative writings have also been written in a cursive script, as noticed, for example, by Alexander, "Literacy," 15: 'Both cursive and formal styles are used for the literary text *par excellence*—the Community Rule.' The relation between content and writing style needs to be investigated further.

b. *Writing in the paleo-Hebrew script and its background*

The finds from Qumran and Masada include several forms of writing in paleo-Hebrew characters:
   • Individual letters used as scribal markings in the margins of texts written in square characters (ch. *5c4*).
   • Divine names in paleo-Hebrew characters in texts written in square characters.
   • Texts written completely in paleo-Hebrew characters.

We suggested in ch. *5c4* that the use of single paleo-Hebrew characters in the margins of Qumran scrolls may reflect sectarian use, while it is suggested here that the texts written completely in paleo-Hebrew script may have been imported to Qumran. The main focus is placed on the Qumran texts written in paleo-Hebrew, while some attention is given to Mas 1o (Mas pap paleoText of Sam. Origin [recto] and Mas pap paleoUnidentified Text [verso]). Several ostraca found at Masada likewise contain single paleo-Hebrew letters (see *Masada I*).

(1) *Individual paleo-Hebrew letters used as scribal markings in the margins of texts written in square characters*

See ch. *5c4*.

(2) *Divine names in paleo-Hebrew characters in texts written in square characters* (figs. 26–28; illustr. 3)

Several Qumran texts, mainly of a nonbiblical, sectarian nature, display a special approach toward the writing of divine names, especially the Tetragrammaton (see 1QpHab in illustr. 3). As in rabbinic literature, most sectarian texts avoided representing the Tetragrammaton and אלהים as much as possible, finding alternative means of expression. This avoidance was described in detail by Stegemann, *ΚΥΡΙΟΣ*[294] and Skehan, "Divine Name" on the basis of the evidence available in 1978 and 1980 respectively, and the assumption of this avoidance is still true for most of the texts known today. For example, 1QS (1QSa, 1QSb) and 1QM do not use the Tetra-

---

[294]See also Stegemann, "Religionsgeschichtliche Erwägungen zu den Gottesbezeichnungen in den Qumran-texten," in *Qumrân*(ed. M. Delcor; see n. 42) 195–217; E. Schuller, *Non-Canonical Psalms from Qumran: A Pseudepigraphic Collection* (HSS 28; Atlanta, Ga. 1986) 40–41. C. Newsom, "'Sectually Explicit' Literature from Qumran," in *The Hebrew Bible and its Interpreters* (ed. W. H. Propp et al.; Winona Lake, Ind. 1990) 167–87, especially p. 177 went one step further when claiming that 'any text containing the tetragrammaton in free and original composition can be presumed to be of non-Qumran authorship.' For much material, see D. W. Parry, "Notes on Divine Name Avoidance in Scriptural Units of the Legal Texts of Qumran," in *Legal Texts and Legal Issues: Proceedings of the Second Meeting of the International Organization for Qumran Studies Cambridge 1995* (ed. M. Bernstein et al.; Leiden/New York/Cologne 1997) 437–49.

grammaton and אל(ו)הים, while אלוהינו occurs four times in 1QS (twice in quotations from Scripture) and twice in 1QM.

The clearest evidence of this avoidance pertains to the *pesharim* which by way of circumlocution often refer to God in the third person. Likewise, the Tetragrammaton is omitted in 1QM X 4, 7 in the quotation of יהוה אלוהיכם from both Deut 20:4 and Num 10:9.

In yet other cases, the Tetragrammaton was replaced by אל; for example, in 4QpPs^b (4Q173) 5 4, לאל replaces ליהוה of MT (fig. 28). Likewise, in 4QHos^b (4Q167) 2 6; 7–9 2; 16 3, אל probably replaces יהוה, in the latter case probably in a biblical quotation (Hos 8:13). In 1QH^a VII (Suk. = Puech XV) 28, אדוני replaces יהוה of Exod 15:11.

Furthermore, the overwhelming preponderance of אל in the sectarian writings (*pesharim, Hodayot*, prayers, blessings, Rules), as opposed to the rare use of the Tetragrammaton in these writings (mainly in biblical quotations), provides ample evidence of this avoidance, especially in 1QS and 1QH^a. Special cases are:

• The circumlocution of the divine name as השם הנכבד in 1QS VI 27 (cf. Deut 28:58 and Sir 47:18). For a discussion, see Schiffman, *Sectarian Law*, 133–6.

• The replacement of the Tetragrammaton with הואהא in 1QS VIII 13 (in a quotation from Isa 40:3). See H. P. Rüger, "הואהא-Er, Zur Deutung von 1QS 8 13–14," *ZNW* 60 (1962) 142–44 and E. Katz, *Die Bedeutung des Hapax Legomenon der Qumraner Handschriften HUAHA* (Bratislava 1966). Katz rather fancifully assumes that the five letters of this word represent five dots which are used once (strokes) for the name of God in 4QHistorical Text A (4Q248) 5 (ch. 5, TABLE 19).

• יוד in 4QShir^b (4Q511) 10 12 (in a quotation from Ps 19:10) probably represents an abbreviation of the divine name by using the letter *yod* (י) which is spelled out here as יוד.

• האמת in 4QS^e (4Q259) III 4 elaborating upon Isa 40:3.

• את הו כול in 4QD^a (4Q266) 11 9 was translated by J. Baumgarten, *DJD* XVIII, as 'Almighty God,' and explained as a parallel to the rabbinic formula אני הו. According to Baumgarten, this phrase is a substitute for the divine name in *m. Sukk.* 4.5 (however, in the Mishna the phrase אני הו was used by R. Judah for אנא יהוה ['we beseech Thee, O Lord'], and therefore it probably reflects a corruption of that phrase). For a discussion, see J. Baumgarten, "A New Qumran Substitute for the Divine Name and Mishna Sukkah 4.5," *JQR* 83 (1992) 1–5.

Reflecting a similar approach to the avoidance of the use of divine names, other scribal solutions were invoked for their safeguarding in the text, especially in biblical quotations. Thus, in addition to the writing of the Tetragrammaton in square characters, which occurs relatively infrequently in the Qumran texts, three scribal systems were employed for the writing of the divine names, especially the Tetragrammaton. The writing in paleo-Hebrew characters probably ensured the non-erasure of the divine names, while the two other systems (dicolon and *Tetrapuncta* [ch. 5, TABLE 19]) indicate a special approach to the Tetragrammaton, possibly alerting against pronouncing it.

The representation of the divine names (mainly the Tetragrammaton) in paleo-Hebrew characters in several Qumran manuscripts has been noticed from the earliest days of the Qumran discoveries, since it is found in several texts from cave 1.

1QpHab (fig. 26 and illustr. 3), especially, has drawn much attention in this regard. For an analysis of the Qumran parallels known until 1980, see Skehan, "Divine Name"; for an earlier, more detailed, analysis, see Stegemann, *KYPIOΣ*, 149–51. A full list of the evidence known in 1983 was provided by Mathews,[295] not yet including three further texts, 4QExod^j, 4QLev^g, and 4QS^d (4Q258), to be mentioned below. In one instance (4QpPs^b [4Q173]), the divine name is written in apparent mirror writing of Greek

---

[295] K. A. Mathews, "The Background of the Paleo-Hebrew Texts at Qumran," in *The Word of the Lord Shall Go Forth, Essays in Honor of David Noel Freedman in Celebration of his Sixtieth Birthday* (ed. C. L. Meyers and M. O'Connor; Winona Lake, Ind. 1983) 549–68.

letters with Hebrew values (fig. 28). The divine name is also written in paleo-Hebrew characters in one Aramaic text, 4QpsDan[a] ar (4Q243) 1 2 (אלהכה). In the latter text, all letters except the *kaph* were written in paleo-Hebrew characters, which may point to the scribe's ignorance of some paleo-Hebrew letters.

It is unclear why certain scribes used paleo-Hebrew characters for the Tetragrammaton, while others wrote the Tetragrammaton in square characters. This question is particularly relevant with regard to the texts written according to the Qumran scribal practice, since most texts using the paleo-Hebrew Tetragrammaton are written in this style. The two different systems are used side by side in the *pesharim*, since in 4QpIsa[b] (4Q162), 4Qpap pIsa[c] (4Q163), 4QpMic? (4Q168), 4QpNah (4Q169), and 4QpZeph (4Q170) the Tetragrammaton is written in square characters, while in other *pesharim* it was written in paleo-Hebrew characters (see TABLE 1). However, as a rule, the two systems do not appear side by side within the same *pesher*. The two different systems are used in different liturgical Psalm collections as well as in different copies of the same nonbiblical and biblical composition. For example, 11QPs[a] and 11QPs[b] represent two copies of the same collection of psalms, both written in the Qumran scribal practice; in the former, the Tetragrammaton is written in paleo-Hebrew characters, while in the latter it is written in the square script (contrast, e.g. 11QPs[a] XXIII 10 with 11QPs[b] 7 5). The scribe of 4QShirShabb[g] (4Q406) wrote אלהים in paleo-Hebrew, while the scribes of the other manuscripts of ShirShabb did not. Some of these texts were written in the same period, indicating different scribal habits rather than a different chronological background. The latter assumption was espoused by P. W. Skehan, "The Qumran Manuscripts and Textual Criticism," *VTSup* 4 (1957) 151 who ascribed the writing of the Tetragrammaton in paleo-Hebrew characters to a late stage of the writing of the Qumran scrolls. Among other things he expressed this view regarding the internal differences within the *pesharim* (Skehan, "Divine Name," 22), assuming that the earlier *pesharim* wrote the Tetragrammaton in square characters, while the later ones used paleo-Hebrew characters, but this is not borne out by the dates now assigned to these manuscripts.[296]

Probably in some manuscripts spaces were left for the paleo-Hebrew words to be filled in later either by the scribe himself or by a special person who was entitled to write the divine name.

• 1QpHab: According to Stegemann, *KYPIOΣ*, A, 91, n. 502, the difference between the somewhat coarse pen of the scribe and the more refined writing of the Tetragrammata written in that text (illustr. 3) shows that the latter were written at a later stage.

• 4QpIsa[e] (4Q165): In this scroll, for which the use of the Tetragrammaton is not evidenced explicitly, a space was left open in 6 4 where MT (32:6) has a Tetragrammaton. This space may have been left for a Tetragrammaton, to be filled in possibly by a different scribe (or was the Tetragrammaton omitted intentionally, indicated by a space in the middle of the line?).

---

[296]The following dates have been assigned to *pesharim* using the square character: 4QpIsa[b] (4Q162; 50–25 BCE), 4Qpap pIsa[c] (4Q163) (4Q163; 85 BCE), 4QpMic? (4Q168; 30 BCE–68 CE), 4QpNah (4Q169; 50–25 BCE). The following dates have been assigned to *pesharim* using the Tetragrammata in paleo-Hebrew characters: 1QpHab (1–50 CE), 4QpIsa[a] (4Q161; 50–25 BCE), 4QpPs[a] (4Q171; 50–25 BCE), 4QpPs[b] (4Q173; 30–1 BCE), 4QpIsa[e] (4Q165; 30–1 BCE). The dates are culled from the summary list of Webster, "Chronological Index." In a similar vein, Stegemann, *KYPIOΣ*, 173–83 suggested that after the beginning of the second century BCE the Tetragrammaton was no longer used freely (that is, not in biblical quotations) in the square script, and therefore texts displaying its free use after this period were not written by the Essenes. This date was pushed down to the middle of the second century by É. Puech, "Les deux derniers psaumes davidiques du rituel d'exorcisme, 11QPsAp[a] IV 4–V 14," in *The Dead Sea Scrolls: Forty Years of Research* (ed. D. Dimant and U. Rappaport; Leiden/New York/Cologne and Jerusalem 1992) 64–89 (80–85) and A. Lange, "Kriterien essenischer Texte," *Qumran kontrovers*, 59–69 (60). If this assumption is correct, all the texts included in TABLE 2b are either early, too fragmentary to be evaluated, or nonsectarian.

• 11QPs^a: The writing of the Tetragrammata shows much variation, both with regard to the size of the letters and the space around them (fig. **27**). It appears that the scribe left irregular spaces, and that at a later stage someone, possibly the original scribe himself, penned in the Tetragrammata, sometimes squeezing them in between the surrounding words. This procedure often created the misleading impression of a ligature (e.g. IV 3, 11; X 9; XIII 8, 12; XIV 4; XVI 11), while in other instances either ample space was left around the Tetragrammaton (XIV 8) or the paleo-Hebrew letters were very large (VIII 5). In one instance, the scribe forgot to write the Tetragrammaton, viz., in the space left in III 4, at which point it is found in MT (Ps 121:5). A. Wolters, "The Tetragrammaton in the Psalms Scroll," *Textus* 18 (1995) 89–98, especially 93, noticed that the shape of the *waw* of the Tetragrammata until VI 11 differs from that of the later occurrences in the scroll. This may imply that two different hands wrote the Tetragrammata.

• 11QpaleoUnidentified Text (11Q22): לאלהיכ was written with a different color of ink.

The above evidence shows that at least in some Qumran texts, the Tetragrammaton was filled in after the writing of the main text, and this was also the case in one manuscript of the LXX. In P.Fouad 266b (848) of Deuteronomy (middle of 1 BCE), ample space was left (equal to 5–6 letters) for the divine names in 31 instances, e.g. Deut 18:5, 20:13, 27:2, 28:61, 29:3. These spaces were large enough for κύριος, although the shorter square Hebrew Tetragrammaton was actually written in them. At some point, two dots were inserted between which the scribe was to write the Tetragrammaton, but these dots were disregarded, as the Hebrew Tetragrammaton required more space (see n. 276). For a good example, see frg. 49 (col. 34). The scribe who wrote the Tetragrammaton in this papyrus was not an expert, as the *yod* and *waw* were penned identically. On the other hand, the Tetragrammata in the Greek 8ḤevXIIgr were probably written by the scribe of the manuscript itself (see the analysis by E. Tov, *DJD* VIII, 12).

The Qumran texts differ internally with regard to the details of the use of paleo-Hebrew characters. Some scribes also wrote the *prefixes* and *suffixes* of the divine names in paleo-Hebrew characters.

4QLev^g 8 (Lev 7:19): prefix
4QIsa^c: prefixes in Isa 26:4; 44:5 and suffixes to *ʾelohim* in Isa 51:15; 52:10 (on the other hand, in 55:5 *ʾelohim* with a suffix was written in square characters).
4QpPs^b (4Q173): prefix

Other scribes wrote the prefixes in square characters and by so doing they concur with the view expressed in *Sof.* 4.3: 'All the letters which are written before or after divine names (as prefixes or suffixes) may be erased …'.

2QExod^b 7 16 (Exod 31:16)
4QpPs^a (4Q171) III 14
6QpapHymn (6Q18) 8 1
11QPs^a: passim, e.g. IV 3 (Ps 125:1); XVI 4, 5, 6 (Ps 118:8, 9, 29); E i 5 (*DJD* XXIII)

4QIsa^c is in agreement with the rules laid down in the Talmud (the main view presented in *y. Meg.* 1.71d and *Sof.* 4.1) since this text alone treated צבאות as a divine name, writing it with paleo-Hebrew characters (24 39 [Isa 44:6]; 50, 62).

TABLE 1 records twenty-eight (twenty-nine?) texts containing the paleo-Hebrew form of the Tetragrammaton and/or of (הים)אל and צבאות. In these texts, paleo-Hebrew characters were used for the Tetragrammaton (not specified below) or *ʾEl(ohim)* (specified). Quotations from the biblical text are so indicated; at the same time, because of the fragmentary character of several texts, it is often unclear whether or not the paleo-Hebrew word occurs in a quotation. All nonbiblical compositions except for those specified as 'not Q' are written according to the Qumran scribal practice.

TABLE 1: *Tetragrammata Written with Paleo-Hebrew Characters*

a. <u>Nonbiblical Compositions</u>[297]

1QpMic (1Q14) 1–5 1, 2 (quotations); 12 3 (*ᵓEl*)

1QpHab VI 14; X 7, 14; XI 10 (all: quotations; fig. 26)

1QpZeph (1Q15) 3, 4 (quotation)

1QMyst (1Q27) II 11 (*ᵓEl*)

1QH^a e.g. I (Suk. = Puech IX) 26; II (X) 34; VII (XV) 5; XV (VII) 25 (all: *ᵓEl*; probably all quotations)
1QH^b (1Q35) 1 5 (*ᵓEl*)

4QpIsa^a (4Q161) 8–10 13 (quotation)

4QpPs^a (4Q171) II 4, 12, 24; III 14, 15; IV 7, 10, 19 (all: quotations); not in the supralinear add. in III 5

4QpPs^b (4Q173) 5 4 (*ᵓEl*, quotation), with לאל instead of ליהוה of MT (ch. *5c3* and fig. 28; too fragmentary for orthographic analysis)

4QAges of Creation A (4Q180) 1 1 (*ᵓEl*)

4QMidrEschat^e? (4Q183) 2 1; 3 1; 1 ii 3 (*ᵓEl*). This text probably is part of the same MS as 4QpPs^a [298] [too small for orthographic analysis]

4QS^d (4Q258; not Q) IX 8 (*ᵓEl*)

4QD^b (4Q267) 9 i 2; iv 4; v 4 (all: *ᵓEl*)

4QD^c (4Q268) 1 9 (*ᵓEl*)

4QShirShabb^g (4Q406) 1 2; 3 2 (both: *ᵓElohim*; Q?)

4QComposition Concerning Divine Providence (4Q413) 1–2 2, 4 (both: *ᵓEl*)

6QD (6Q15) 3 5 (*ᵓEl*; Q?)

6QpapHymn (6Q18) 6 5; 8 5; 10 3; possibly sectarian (all: *ᵓEl*)

11QPs^a II 2 (Ps 146:9), 4 (Ps 146:10), 6 (Ps 148:1), and passim (both in the biblical text and in nonbiblical sections, such as XXVII 4); for a list, see J. A. Sanders, *DJD* IV, 9 (fig. 27).

4QpIsa^e (4Q165) 6 4: The scribe possibly meant to include a paleo-Hebrew Tetragrammaton for which space was left.

Fourteen of the above-listed texts wrote אל(הים) in paleo-Hebrew characters:

1QpMic (1Q14) 1–5 1, 2 (quotations); 12 3

1QMyst (1Q27) II 11 (*ᵓEl*)

1QH^a e.g. I (Suk. = Puech IX) 26; II (X) 34; VII (XV) 5; XV (VII) 25 (all: *ᵓEl*)
1QH^b (1Q35) 1 5 (*ᵓEl*)

4QpPs^b (4Q173) 5 4 (fig. 28)

4QAges of Creation A (4Q180) 1 1

4QMidrEschat^e? (4Q183) 1 ii 3

4QS^d (4Q258; not Q) IX 8

4QD^b (4Q267) 9 i 2; iv 4; v 4

4QD^c (4Q268) 1 9

4QShirShabb^g (4Q406) 1 2; 3 2

4QComposition Concerning Divine Providence (4Q413) 1–2 2, 4

6QD (6Q15) 3 5

6QpapHymn (6Q18) 6 5; 8 5; 10 3

See further 3Q14 18 to be listed below.

Note that 4QD^{a,d,e,f} do not use the paleo-Hebrew characters for אל and that 4QD^b (4Q267) writes אל in both the paleo-Hebrew and square script.

---

[297]"4QPBless" (= 4QpGen49), as published by J. Allegro, *JBL* 75 (1956) 180 has to be deleted from the list of Mathews, "The Background," 561, since the fragment published by Allegro is actually 4QpIsa^a (4Q161). According to J. Baumgarten, a paleo-Hebrew Tetragrammaton is to be reconstructed in 4QMiscellaneous Rules (4Q265) frg. 1 4, but there seems to be no intrinsic reason for this reconstruction.

[298]Thus Strugnell, "Notes," 263. This composition was named 4QmidrEschat^e? by A. Steudel, *Der Midrasch zur Eschatologie aus der Qumrangemeinde (4QmidrEschat^{a.b})* (STDJ 13; Leiden/New York/Cologne 1994).

b. Biblical Manuscripts[299]

4QExod^j 1–2 3 (Exod 8:1; too fragmentary for orthographic analysis)

4QLev^g line 8 (Lev 7:19; too fragmentary for orthographic analysis)

11QLev^b 2 2, 6, 7 (Lev 9:24, 10:1; too fragmentary for orthographic analysis)

4QDeut^k2 5 6 (Deut 26:3; Q)

4QIsa^c יהוה passim, e.g. 6 6 (Isa 11:9); 9 i 25 (Isa 22:12); צבאות, e.g. 24 36 (Isa 44:6); אלוהים + suffixes, e.g. Isa 44:6; אדוני, e.g. 9 i 25 (Isa 22:11; Q)

1QPs^b 2–5 3 (Ps 127:3), not necessarily a biblical text (too fragmentary for orthographic analysis)[300]

3QLam 1 2 (Lam 1:11; too fragmentary for orthographic analysis)

c. A Rewritten Bible Text?

2QExod^b 2 2; 7 1; 8 3 (Exod 12:27; 31:16; 34:10; too fragmentary for orthographic analysis)

d. A Manuscript of Unclear Nature

3QUnclassified fragments (3Q14) 18 2 (*ʾEl*)

The exact relation between the different groups using the Tetragrammaton in paleo-Hebrew letters is unclear. According to Skehan, "Divine Name," this scribal phenomenon was practiced first in nonbiblical manuscripts, from where it spread to some biblical manuscripts. The most developed use is noticeable in 4QIsa^c, where all the divine names, as well as their prefixes and suffixes, were written in the paleo-Hebrew script.

Of the twenty-eight manuscripts using paleo-Hebrew characters for the divine names, nineteen or twenty texts (if 1QPs^b is included) are nonbiblical; six or seven (if 1QPs^b is included) are biblical manuscripts; one is probably a rewritten Bible manuscript (2QExod^b); the nature of one composition (3Q14) is unclear. If the scribe of 4QpIsa^e (4Q165) intended to include a paleo-Hebrew Tetragrammaton, as indicated by the space left in frg. 6 4, this text needs to be added to the list. All texts in this group that are large enough for analysis, with the exception of 4QS^d (4Q258), reflect the orthography and morphology of the Qumran scribal practice. A special link between the writing of the divine names in paleo-Hebrew characters and the Qumran community is therefore highly conceivable.

The connection between the special writing of the Tetragrammaton and the Qumran community is evident also at another level. The name of God was not to be uttered by the covenanters, as becomes clear from 1QS VI 27–VII 1 (א[שר יזכיר דבר בשם הנכבד, 'whoever mentions anything on behalf of the Honored Name . . .'). The penalty for transgressing this ruling (VII 2) was expulsion from the community (Schiffman, *Sectarian Law*, 133–6). In light of this legislation, it is understandable that the divine name was written in ancient characters, which were considered more sacred. See further below, *Background*.

When writing the divine names in paleo-Hebrew characters, the Qumran scribes may have followed the practice of an earlier generation of scribes or, alternatively, each scribe may have initiated this practice in accord with his own beliefs. The latter assumption is supported by the inconsistency of 4QIsa^c: צבאות (following יהוה) was written in square

---

[299]Several manuscripts of the revisions of the LXX similarly presented the Tetragrammaton in paleo-Hebrew characters in the middle of the Greek text, probably reflecting a similar approach to the sacred character of the paleo-Hebrew letters. For details, see § 5d. See further Stegemann, *ΚΥΡΙΟΣ*, 109–33.

[300]According to D. Barthélemy and J. T. Milik, *DJD* I, 71, 1QPs^b does not necessarily reflect a scroll of all the Psalms, and it could have belonged to the same scroll as 1Q30 (1QLiturgical Text A?), written in what may be the same scribe's handwriting.

script in frg. 40 3 (Isa 54:5); likewise, אדוני was written in that script (without the Tetragrammaton) in frg. 9 ii 27 (Isa 24:1); for the writing of these words in the paleo-Hebrew script, see TABLE 1 above.

A reverse examination of the texts written in the Qumran scribal practice reveals that thirty-six texts did *not* use a special system for the writing of the divine names with paleo-Hebrew characters or *Tetrapuncta* (ch. *5d*). The data in TABLE 2 show that within the group of Qumran scribes different practices were employed for writing the divine names; by the same token, the orthographic and morphological features of this group are not evenly spread in all the texts (ch. *8a2*).

TABLE 2: *Divine Names (Tetragrammata and* ʾEl*) Written with* Square *Characters in Texts Written According to the Qumran Scribal Practice*

a. Biblical Texts

1QIsaᵃ (*Tetrapuncta* inserted by the corrector)
2QJer
4QNumᵇ
4QDeutʲ
4QXIIᶜ
4QPsᵒ
11QPsᵇ
11QPsᶜ

b. Nonbiblical Texts

1QSa (*ʾEl*)
1QM (*ʾEl*)
4QRPᵃ (4Q158)
4QpIsaᵇ (4Q162) II 3, 7, 8 (*ʾEl*; quotation)
4Qpap pIsaᶜ (4Q163) I 19; II 6; 15–16 1; 21 9; III 3, 9; 25 7 (all: quotations)
4QHosᵇ (4Q167) 2 6; 7–9 2; 16 3, probably replacing יהוה of such texts as MT with אל (all: *ʾEl*)
4QpNah (4Q169) II 10 (quotation)
4QpPsᵇ (4Q173) 4 2 (quotation)
4QCatena A (4Q177; quotation)
4QTime of Righteousness (4Q215a)
4QJubᵍ (4Q222)
4QPsJubᵃ (4Q225)
4QDᵃ (4Q266; *ʾEl*)
4QDᶠ (4Q271; *ʾEl*)
4QRPᶜ (4Q365)
4QApocryphal Pentateuch B (4Q377) 2 ii 3, 5
4Qpap paraKings et al. (4Q382)
4QShirShabbᶠ (4Q405; *ʾElohim*)
4QSapiential-Hymnic Work A (4Q426; *ʾEl*; Qumran orthography not sufficiently evidenced)
4QMᵃ (4Q491; *ʾEl*)
4QpapMᶠ (4Q496; *ʾEl*)
4QpapRitMar (4Q502; *ʾEl*)
4QDibHamᵃ (4Q504; *ʾEl*)
4QShirᵇ (4Q511; *ʾElohim*)
11QMelch (11Q13; *ʾElohim*, *ʾEl*)
11QTᵃ (11Q19)
11QTᵇ (11Q20)
11QapocrPs (11Q11)

Background. The background of the writing of divine names in paleo-Hebrew characters was analyzed by Siegel, "The Employment" and idem, *Scribes of Qumran*, 29–45. Siegel quoted extensively from *y. Meg.* 1.71d (parallels in *b. Shev.* 35b) providing the rules for the writing of the divine names, in particular stipulating which divine names were not to be erased. These sources also mention the rules governing the erasure of the prefixes and suffixes of the divine names. According to Siegel, this tannaitic text provides the background for the use of paleo-Hebrew characters for the divine names in the Qumran texts. The Qumran scribes apparently devised a system using paleo-Hebrew characters for the divine names; by writing in ancient characters, whose sanctity gave the divine names a special status, they ensured that they would not be erased. While Siegel's explanation is certainly acceptable, it provides only a partial answer to the use of paleo-Hebrew characters. After all, the later rabbinic *halakha* did not prescribe the writing of the divine names in paleo-Hebrew characters, but only prescribed which divine names or parts thereof may not be erased. Even if we assume some genetic relationship between the Qumran custom of using paleo-Hebrew characters and the *halakha*, we still do not know how other scribes reacted to the prescriptions of the rabbis. For example, what was the view of the scribes writing within the Masoretic tradition who closely followed the rabbinic instructions? Since the scribes writing within that tradition did not use paleo-Hebrew characters, how did they carry out the rabbinic prescription that the divine names not be erased? There is no answer to this question, and probably the only possible reply is that these scribes took special care not to err in the writing of the divine names, thereby avoiding the need for erasure.

We cannot examine the question of how the scribes of the Judean Desert texts usually identified with the Masoretic family or other ones related to the rabbinic rules; the only practice which can be examined is the one visible system for insuring that the sacred names were not erased, namely their writing in paleo-Hebrew characters. The use of these characters must have rendered the words more sacred, at least in the eyes of certain religious and/or scribal circles prohibiting their erasure. This assumption of a special status is supported by the practice of 11QPs[a], in which twenty-eight words were erased (for a list, see J. A. Sanders, *DJD* IV, 9), while the Tetragrammaton, written in paleo-Hebrew characters, was not erased, as far as we can see. Instead of being erased, in two instances the Tetragrammaton was marked with cancellation dots, above and below (XVI 7; XXI 2). See, further, 4QIsa[d] which has two sets of cancellation dots, both relating to an incorrectly written Tetragrammaton (6 7, 10). Likewise, in 1QIsa[a], the cancellation dots are used rather infrequently, appearing three times for the Tetragrammaton (III 24, 25 [Isa 3:17, 18]; XLVI 21 [Isa 56:8]) among other occurrences.

In spite of these caveats, it stands to reason that the Qumran scribes who employed paleo-Hebrew characters closely reflected the spirit of the mentioned *halakha*, while finding a practical solution to the same problem. Apparently, some scribes resorted to the use of paleo-Hebrew characters, which were considered so sacred that under no circumstance were they to be erased. When erring, the scribes would never erase a divine name presumably adhering to a traditional norm. This description of the sanctity of the letters is hypothetical, but it is supported by the tradition that the Stone Tablets and the Torah (see *b. Sanh.* 21b to be quoted below) were written in paleo-Hebrew characters. Furthermore, manuscripts written completely in paleo-Hebrew characters reflect a different and far stricter approach to scribal precision than texts written in square characters (§ d below), and it stands to reason that this approach would be reflected in the writing of single words in paleo-Hebrew.

The analysis thus far has been based on three observations to which we now add a fourth:

• The use of the paleo-Hebrew characters for divine names is almost exclusively linked to texts written according to the Qumran scribal practice.

• The use of paleo-Hebrew characters implies the view that these characters require special treatment, and possibly reflect a higher degree of sanctity.

• The use of the paleo-Hebrew characters for the divine names reflects the spirit of the later *halakha*, although this particular practice is not mentioned in rabbinic sources, and actually contradicts the prohibition of the use of the paleo-Hebrew script in *m. Yad.* 4.5 and *b. Sanh.* 21b to be quoted below.

• The combination of these observations leads to an additional supposition, namely that (the) scribes belonging to the Qumran community ascribed a higher degree of sanctity to the use of paleo-Hebrew characters in general (that is, not only with regard to the writing of the divine names) than to the square script. It is not impossible, as surmised by Wolters, "The Tetragrammaton," 98, that the person who filled in the Tetragrammata 'belonged to a higher echelon within the Qumran hierarchy than the original scribe.' This presumed practice is probably reflected by the scribe of 4QpIsa[e] (4Q165) who left a space for a Tetragrammaton to be inserted later. Likewise, the Tetragrammaton in 11QpaleoUnidentified Text

(11Q22) was written in a different ink color implying either the use of a different pen or the involvement of a different scribe. For similar practices in Greek sources, see ch. *5d* and APPENDIX 5C.

In principle, the writing of the divine names in paleo-Hebrew script could somehow be connected to the writing of entire Bible texts in that script, but there is no indication for linking the two types of texts. In fact, from the outset there has been no indication that Scripture texts written in paleo-Hebrew characters were written at Qumran or by Qumran scribes. Thus, while it does not necessarily follow that the scribes who wrote the divine names in paleo-Hebrew characters were those who wrote manuscripts which had been written completely in paleo-Hebrew characters (thus Siegel, "The Employment," 170), the former could still have been influenced by the latter. What the writing of complete texts and of single words in paleo-Hebrew have in common is that both were rejected by the Rabbis (see below). No explicit remarks against the writing of the divine names in paleo-Hebrew characters are found in rabbinic literature, but since the use of paleo-Hebrew script was forbidden for entire biblical texts, individual words written in that script presumably would also have been prohibited.

(3) *Texts written completely in paleo-Hebrew characters* (illustrations 14, 14a)

At Qumran, fragments of twelve biblical texts written in the paleo-Hebrew script were found as well as three nonbiblical paleo-Hebrew texts. One such nonbiblical text was found at Masada:[301]

1QpaleoLev
1QpaleoNum; same scroll as 1QpaleoLev?; frgs. 16–24 possibly derived from yet (a) different scroll(s)
2QpaleoLev
4QpaleoGen-Exod^l
4QpaleoGen^m
4QpaleoExod^m
4QpaleoDeut^r
4QpaleoDeut^s
4QpaleoJob^c
6QpaleoGen
6QpaleoLev
11QpaleoLev^a
4Qpaleo paraJosh (4Q123)
4QpaleoUnidentified Text 1 (4Q124)
11QpaleoUnidentified Text (11Q22)

Mas 1o (Mas pap paleoText of Sam. Origin [recto] and Mas pap paleoUnidentified Text [verso])

Note the following palimpsest in the ancient Hebrew script:
Mur papLetter (Mur 17A)
Mur papList of Personal Names (Mur 17B)

Note further the following text:
4QcryptC Unclassified Religious Text (4Q363a)
This text is written mainly in paleo-Hebrew letters, intermingled with some cryptic signs.

These texts, rather than predating the use of the square script (with the exception of Mur 17A–B), were written at a relatively late period, possibly but not necessarily as a natural continuation of the earlier tradition of writing in the 'early' Hebrew script. They were concurrent with the use of the square script, as can be proved by a

---

[301]Beyond the publications of these texts in *DJD* I, III, IX, XXIII, see: M. D. McLean, *The Use and Development of Palaeo-Hebrew in the Hellenistic and Roman Periods*, unpubl. Ph.D. diss., Harvard University, Cambridge, Mass. 1982, 41–7 (University Microfilms); Freedman–Mathews, *Leviticus*. According to R. L. Edge, *The Use of Palaeo-Hebrew in the Dead Sea Scrolls: Paleography and Historiography*, unpubl. Ph.D. diss., The University of Texas at Austin, 1995, p. 357 (University Microfilms), fifty years separated the writing of entire scrolls in the paleo-Hebrew script in the archaic and Hasmonean periods and the writing of the divine names in paleo-Hebrew characters in the Herodian period.

paleographical examination of the paleo-Hebrew script.[302] Most scholars tacitly assume that with the revival of the paleo-Hebrew script in the Hasmonean period, texts were transformed from the square to the paleo-Hebrew script (thus Mathews, "The Background"), and this is probably correct, although it is not impossible that the practice of writing in the paleo-Hebrew script had never ceased in some circles.

The preserved biblical fragments written in the paleo-Hebrew script contain only texts of the Torah and Job,[303] both of which are traditionally ascribed to Moses (cf. manuscripts and editions of S in which Job follows the Torah).[304] The longest preserved texts written in the paleo-Hebrew script are 4QpaleoExod^m and 11QpaleoLev^a.

All texts written in the paleo-Hebrew script reflect a similar scribal approach, but the scribes of these texts often displayed their individuality in specific features (ch. *7b*).

The only external data regarding the background of the writing in the paleo-Hebrew script is of a negative nature. Various statements in rabbinic literature, e.g. *m. Yad.* 4.5, forbid use of this script for biblical texts:

תרגום שכתבו עברית ועברית שכתבו תרגום וכתב עברי אינו מטמא את הידים. לעולם אינו מטמא עד שיכתבנו אשורית
על העור ובדיו

If an Aramaic <portion of Scripture> was written in Hebrew, or if <Scripture that is in> Hebrew was written in an <Aramaic> version, or in Hebrew script [וכתב עברי], it does not render the hands unclean. <The Holy Scriptures> render the hands unclean only when they are written in Assyrian characters [אשורית], on leather, and with ink (cf. *b. Shabb.* 115b; *Sof.* 1.7).

A more strongly worded statement is found in *b. Sanh.* 21b:

אמר מר זוטרא ואיתימא מר עוקבא בתחלה ניתנה תורה לישראל בכתב עברי ולשון הקודש. חזרה וניתנה להם בימי עזרא
בכתב אשורית ולשון ארמי. ביררו להן לישראל כתב אשורית ולשון הקודש והניחו להדיוטות כתב עברית ולשון ארמי

Mar Zuṭra or, as some say, Mar 'Ukba said: 'Originally the Torah was given to Israel in Hebrew characters [בכתב עברי] and in the sacred <Hebrew> language [לשון הקודש]; later, in the time of Ezra, the Torah was given in the Assyrian script [כתב אשורית] and the Aramaic language <Targum>. <Finally,> Israel selected the Assyrian script and the Hebrew language, leaving the Hebrew characters and Aramaic language for the ordinary people [הדיוטות]' (cf. *b. Meg.* 9a; *y. Meg.* 1.71b–c).

These statements were directed against those who used the paleo-Hebrew script at the time of the Talmud, that is, the Samaritans among others, but also the groups writing and using the paleo-Hebrew scrolls found in the Judean Desert; note that the phrase 'ordinary people' (הדיוטות) in *b. Sanh.* 21b is explained as referring to 'Samaritans' (כותאי) by Rab Ḥisda in the subsequent discussion. Alongside the texts written in the square script, there were paleo-Hebrew texts, such as those found at Qumran, and at a certain point also the Torah scrolls of the Samaritans, who claimed authenticity for their Torah as opposed to the scrolls written in the square script. It is thus understandable that the rabbis rejected the writing in the paleo-Hebrew script, not for any intrinsic religious reason, but due to party politics,[305] since some of their opponents used biblical scrolls written in that script. Hence, they felt impelled to formulate a strong counterclaim, namely that of ascribing the writing in the square script to no less an authority than Ezra (see the quotations from the Talmud mentioned above as well as IV Ezra [2 Esdras] 14:42).

---

[302] See M. D. McLean, *Use and Development*; R. S. Hanson *apud*, Freedman–Mathews, *Leviticus*, 20–23; idem, "Paleo-Hebrew Scripts in the Hasmonean Age," *BASOR* 175 (1964) 26–42 For an earlier discussion, see L. Blau, "Wie lange stand die althebräische Schrift bei den Juden im Gebrauch?" in *Gedenkbuch zur Erinnerung an David Kaufmann* (ed. M. Brann und F. Rosenthal; Breslau 1900) 44–57.

[303] One explanation for the writing of a text of Job in paleo-Hebrew would be to assume that Job was ascribed to patriarchal times. But it is probably more sound to assume that Mosaic authorship was ascribed to that text, cf. *b. B. Bat.* 14b–15a.

[304] Note, however, also 4Qpaleo paraJosh (4Q123). Although this text contains elements from Joshua 21, it is probably not a biblical text in the later sense.

[305] Thus Siegel, *Scribes of Qumran*, 181; M. Bar-Ilan, "Writing in Ancient Israel and Early Judaism, Part Two: Scribes and Books in the Late Second Commonwealth and Rabbinic Period," in Mulder, *Mikra*, 29.

It is not known during which period the negative attitude of the rabbis toward the old script developed.[306] With this in mind it is in order to turn to the background of the writing in paleo-Hebrew characters in the texts found at Qumran. The first issue to be addressed is the textual character of the biblical texts written in paleo-Hebrew characters. Because of the diverse textual nature of these texts (APPENDIX 8), it would not be logical to assume that their common feature, inscription in paleo-Hebrew characters, has anything to do with their textual character.[307]

One specific group of paleo-Hebrew texts seems to defy any explanation. Against the background of the rabbinic prohibition of the use of the paleo-Hebrew script, it is puzzling to see several paleo-Hebrew manuscripts (probably the majority) of proto-Masoretic character among the Qumran texts; see Ulrich, *The Dead Sea Scrolls,* 146–7. After all, the connection between these proto-Masoretic texts and Pharisaic circles with regard to textual developments is demonstrable.[308]

How then should we describe the background of the writing of complete paleo-Hebrew texts or of individual words? Since none of the paleo-Hebrew texts shares the characteristics of the Qumran scribal practice (ch. *8a*), they were probably not written by the Qumran scribes and, more generally, there is no major argument in favor of the assumption that the biblical texts which were completely written in paleo-Hebrew characters were copied by the Qumran scribes.[309] It is unlikely that the paleo-Hebrew texts came from Pharisaic circles, since the use of the paleo-Hebrew script was strictly forbidden in the Talmud (see above). We therefore turn to a third possibility, based on criteria of script, textual character, and scribal approach, namely that the paleo-Hebrew texts found at Qumran came from the circles of the *Sadducees* who ascribed great importance to the authenticity of the ancient characters. This explanation should alleviate the difficulty of the apparent contradiction mentioned above. If this hypothesis holds ground, it is understood that as the rabbis prohibited the use of paleo-Hebrew characters, such texts of proto-Masoretic content were written by others. Likewise, on the basis of Diringer, "Early Hebrew Script," Naveh hesitatingly ascribed the paleo-Hebrew texts from Qumran to the Sadducees, without any arguments.[310] This possibility is discussed extensively elsewhere, but it should be admitted that the nature and status of the nonbiblical paleo-Hebrew fragments from Qumran and Masada remain unclear: E. Tov, "The Socio-Religious Background of the Paleo-Hebrew Biblical Texts Found at Qumran," *Geschichte–Tradition–Reflexion, Festschrift für Martin Hengel zum 70. Geburtstag* (ed. H. Cancik et al.; Tübingen 1996) I.353–74.[311]

---

[306]Diringer, "Early Hebrew Script," especially 48–9, and Mathews, "The Background," 559 suggested that the Hasmonean kings adopted the old script under the influence of priestly Sadducean families.

[307]See the summary statement of Ulrich, *The Dead Sea Scrolls,* 147: 'In sum, except for their script, the palaeo-Hebrew biblical manuscripts from Qumran cave 4 do not appear to form a group distinguishable from the other biblical scrolls in either physical features, date, orthography, or textual character.'

[308]See my paper "The Text of the Hebrew/Aramaic and Greek Bible" (n. 168 above).

[309]Mathews, "The Background," is not consistent in his approach to this issue. On the one hand this scholar speaks of the Essene origin of the paleo-Hebrew texts (551, 558), but at the same time he also considers these texts as having been brought to Qumran (p. 557).

[310]Naveh, *Alphabet,* 122. See also É. Puech, "Notes en marge de 11QpaléoLévitique: Le fragment L, des fragments inédits et une jarre de la grotte 11," *RB* 96 (1989) 161–83, especially 167–8. Little is known about the approach of the Sadducees towards Hebrew Scripture in spite of the analysis of J. le Moyne, *Les Sadducéens* (Paris 1972) 357–9.

[311]For an extensive survey of the different explanations of the background of the Qumran paleo-Hebrew texts, see R. L. Edge, *The Use of Palaeo-Hebrew* (see n. 301), especially 334–69.

7

SPECIAL SCRIBAL CHARACTERISTICS
OF SOME GROUPS OF TEXTS

In this chapter, several groups of texts are examined with the purpose of determining whether or not they reflect special scribal characteristics. Usually an absence of common scribal traits is more expected than their presence as scribal practices had yet to be standardized in the late Second Temple period.

An analysis of the inner scribal coherence involves a study of any of the literary genres present in the Qumran corpus, such as *pesharim*, halakhic writings, biblical texts as a whole as well as Torah scrolls, and especially groups of a technical nature (such as calendrical texts, *tefillin*, *mezuzot*). It also pertains to groups that share common external features, such as texts written on papyrus, texts written in the paleo-Hebrew and Cryptic scripts, and Greek texts.

Within this analysis, attention is paid to all the writing exponents such as described in chapters 3–5. It is recognized that all groups of texts are characterized by an absence of scribal homogeneity, with the exception of the proto-Masoretic biblical scrolls analyzed below in § a3.

When examining, by way of example, the eighteen *calendrical* texts from Qumran (all the texts published in *DJD* XXI as well as 6Q17), a rather well-defined group of texts, we note that in all the above-mentioned categories these texts do *not* reflect a unified tradition:

• Almost all copies are on *leather*, while two copies are inscribed on papyrus (4QpapCal Doc A? [4Q324b] and 6QpapCal Doc [6Q17]). Likewise, elsewhere in the Qumran corpus, in any given literary genre, the great majority of the texts were written on leather (ch. 3, TABLE 5), with one or two copies inscribed on papyrus. These papyrus copies are conceived of as personal copies, in this case belonging to members of the community, while official copies were inscribed on leather.

• *Quality* of writing: Several calendrical texts and *mishmarot* ('Temple Watches') are poorly inscribed with irregular spaces between the lines: 4QMish B (4Q323), 4QMish C (4Q324), 4QMish G (4Q329), 4QMish H (4Q329a), 4QMish I (4Q330), 4QCal Doc D (4Q394 1–2). All other copies were written carefully: 4QCal Doc/Mish A (4Q320), 4QCal Doc/Mish B (4Q321), 4QCal Doc/Mish C (4Q321a), 4Q324a, 4Q326, 4Q328.

• *Size* of letters: Differences in spacing and sizes of letters are visible in four different calendrical texts presented in pl. VII of *DJD* XXI, with letters ranging in size from petite with an interlinear space of 0.4 cm (4Q330), to medium-sized letters with a 0.4 cm (4Q329a) or 0.1–0.2 cm space between the lines (4Q394, 1–2 [illustr. 16]), and medium-sized letters with 0.8 cm between the lines (4Q337).

• Where the *height* of the leather can be examined together with the number of lines per column, it differs from a very small 7.0 cm (including margins) to 14.0 cm. Usually the smaller the height of the scroll, the shorter its length (ch. *4e*). The following data, culled from TABLE 15 in ch. 4, pertain to the number of lines and the height of the leather:

4QCal Doc/Mish D (4Q325)	7 (7.0 cm, slightly reconstructed)
4QCal Doc/Mish B (4Q321)	8, 9 (7.7–8.5 cm)
4QCal Doc/Mish A (4Q320)	14 (14.0 cm, slightly reconstructed)
4QCal Doc D (4Q394 1–2)	16 (9.0 cm; reconstructed)

• Column *width*: The width of the columns varies from a mere 1.7–2.0 cm in 4QMMTᵃ (4Q394) 1–2 i–v (re-edited as 4QCal Doc D by S. Talmon, *DJD* XXI, 157–66) to 7.5–8.0 cm (reconstructed) for the only comparable text, 4QCal Doc C (4Q326). The scribe of 4Q394 1–2 presented the information in a narrow format, in order to record one piece of information per line, either a number or a date. Some exceptions are noted, among other things due to the inclusion of בו ('in it') and because of compound numerals written on either one or two lines. 4QCal Doc/Mish B (4Q321) V is 13.0 cm wide, but that text has a different content. The mentioned columns of 4Q394 and 4QCal Doc/Mish A (4Q320) are the narrowest among all the Qumran documents, together with 4QApocryphal Psalm and Prayer (4Q448) with nine lines of 1–3 words (*c.* 2.7 cm); see ch. *4e*.

• *Size of sheets*: 4QCal Doc/Mish A (4Q320) 4 iii–v is unique: with one sheet of 4.7 cm (col. iii) and one of 9.8 cm (cols. iv–v), this document presents the narrowest sheets in any Qumran document. The fact that a calendrical text contains the narrowest sheets from Qumran is not necessarily connected with the fact that the narrowest columns (see above) are found among these texts as well.

• *Length*: The length of these texts cannot be examined easily. The longest preserved text is 4QCal Doc/Mish A (4Q320), while the shortest is probably 4QMish H (4Q329a). The latter ends with a straight left border without stitching, which is clearly the end of the document, a fact also shown by the vertical addition in the margin (see n. 151).

• Use of *number signs*: Number signs are used in three calendrical texts, 4Q320 4Q326, and 6Q17—albeit not for the same categories of numerals—but not in the majority of similar texts. See ch. *5c9*.

• *Opisthographs*: 4QMish C (4Q324) has on its verso 4QAccount C ar or heb (4Q355). Little is known about this account which includes a few letters and signs for numerals. This is the only opisthograph (ch. 4b) among the calendrical texts. The writing on the back probably implies little with regard to the calendrical texts; it means merely that the verso of this document was used for another purpose.

• *Layout*: A special layout is employed in 4QCal Doc/Mish A (4Q320), with each line beginning with ב followed by a number, signifying the day of the month 'on which' (-ב) a festival occurs. In contrast, other documents with a similar content do not start each unit on a new line, but rather present the details in the list as running prose texts: 4QCal Doc/Mish B (4Q321), 4QCal Doc/Mish C (4Q321a), 4QCal Doc C (4Q326).

• *Final and nonfinal letters*: Within this small corpus, a few final letter forms were used in medial position in 4Q394 1-2 (cf. ch. *2g*).

a. *Biblical texts*

Since no concrete facts are known regarding the background of the Qumran scrolls, these scrolls are assumed to be one corpus. In that corpus, little distinction between biblical and nonbiblical literary manuscripts and, more generally, between sacred and nonsacred literary manuscripts is recognizable in scribal conventions or precision in copying. A few special features of the biblical scrolls are nevertheless mentioned below, but these do not amount to a deliberate overall distinction between the two types of texts.

The analysis shows that the rules for the writing of sacred texts recorded in *Massekhet Soferim* and in earlier rabbinic sources are somewhat misleading when detached from the writing of nonsacred texts, since most details recorded there pertain to writing practices employed in an identical way in nonsacred texts during the Second Temple period. For example, *Sof.* 1.15 states that texts that deviate from the norm regarding the indication of open and closed sections cannot be used as sacred writings. However, this practice, which is basically a paragraphing system, was followed in most compositions written in the Qumran period, biblical and nonbiblical. Thus, the practice itself was not sacred, but rather the tradition of indicating a specific type of paragraphing in a given instance. Likewise, the practice of leaving larger bottom margins than top margins in manuscripts (*Sof.* 2.5; *y. Meg.* 1.71d) was the norm in most texts, and not only in Torah scrolls (ch. *4*, TABLE 19). In other cases, criteria were instituted for regulating precision when copying scrolls, but these criteria were also in vogue for any well-written scroll from the Judean Desert; in the case of sacred scrolls, these criteria were formulated in such a way that the scrolls could not be used if they fell below a certain standard of precision: a scroll of Scripture in which a complete line was erased (*Sof.* 3.9), scrolls containing more than a certain number of mistakes (3.10), scrolls with mixed medial and final letters (2.20), or scrolls displaying letters written beyond the vertical left-hand margin (2.3) could not be used for sacred purposes

Special practices were used for the copying of sacred writings in Pharisaic circles, which at a later stage developed into special rules for the writing of all sacred texts in rabbinic literature. However, these circles probably did not generate any nonsacred literary writings, so that in a way Pharisaic scribes did not distinguish between the writing of sacred and nonsacred manuscripts.

1. THE QUMRAN CORPUS AS A WHOLE. The *lack* of distinction between sacred and nonsacred literary texts is recognizable through an analysis of scribal features and approaches.

Scribal features. The data known regarding the Qumran texts (chapters 3–5) show that sacred and nonsacred literary texts share all the main scribal features relating to handwriting, writing, horizontal and vertical ruling, stitching of sheets, size and shape of columns, correction systems, scribal signs, length of scrolls, number of columns per sheet, height of columns, margins, paragraphing, repair-stitching, patching, initial and final handle sheets, use of guide dots/strokes. Although further research is required, seemingly the leather used for biblical texts was not of superior quality to that used for nonbiblical compositions.

As with the nonbiblical scrolls, the Hebrew biblical scrolls from Qumran show no evidence of verse division (ch. *5a2*).

All the sub-systems used for paragraphing are shared by biblical and nonbiblical manuscripts, relating to small and large spaces within the line and at the end of the line, completely empty lines, and indentations. At the same time, the *paragraphos* signs are rarely used in biblical texts.

Poor tanning, scar tissue, and stitching forced scribes to leave certain areas uninscribed in both types of scrolls (ch. *4i*). Inscribed (4QUnclassified frags. [4Q51a]) and uninscribed papyrus strips were attached in antiquity to the back of the leather of 4QSam^a for support. It is unclear how many words in the Judean Desert texts were re-inked in antiquity when the ink had become faint (ch. *4i*).

Use of scribal marks in biblical scrolls was more limited than in nonbiblical scrolls, but the data do not suffice for drawing a distinction between the two types of texts. Cancellation dots/strokes (above and below single letters, and in the case of 1QIsa^a also for complete words) were found in several biblical scrolls written in the Qumran scribal practice (4QDeut^j [mainly: second part], 4QSam^c, 4QXII^e, 1QIsa^a) as well as in other texts: 4QExod^c, 4QDeut^c, 4QJer^a, 4QIsa^d, 4QIsa^h. Some letters were crossed out with a line in 1QIsa^a and 4QDan^a, written in the Qumran practice, as well as in 4QDeut^c, 4QJer^c and 4QCant^b. Parentheses were used in 4QJer^a, 4QQoh^a, and 4QCant^b, and single paleo-Hebrew letters were written in the margin of 1QIsa^a, 4QCant^b, 4QPs^b, and 5QLam^a. A sign of undetermined nature (numbering?) is found in the top right corner of 4QExod^k. *Tetrapuncta* for the divine name are found in 1QIsa^a and 4QSam^c.

The logical conclusion from this overview would be that the same scribes often copied both sacred and nonsacred texts and this may well be the case for several of the Qumran scrolls. However, this assumption cannot be proven since we only rarely see a scribal hand appearing in more than one Qumran document—an exception is the scribe who wrote 1QS, 1QSa, and 1QSb, as well as the biblical 4QSam^c and some supralinear corrections in 1QIsa^a (ch. 2, TABLE 2). Therefore, although the specific scribes who wrote both types of scrolls cannot be identified, the minimal conclusion should be that all scribes followed similar traditions.

Only a few distinctions between biblical and nonbiblical literary manuscripts are visible:

• A special stichographic layout for the writing of several poetical sections was devised for many biblical scrolls, but only for one nonbiblical scroll. For details, see ch. *5b* and TABLE 8.

• Biblical texts from the Judean Desert were written almost exclusively on leather (thus also the rabbinic prescriptions for the writing of biblical texts in *m. Meg.* 2.2; *y. Meg.* 1.71d). The relatively small number of papyrus fragments of biblical texts (4–6 copies out of a total of 200 biblical manuscripts; see TABLE 9 in ch. *3*) possibly served as personal copies. On the other hand, papyrus was used for almost all documentary texts from the Judean Desert and several literary works from Qumran (APPENDIX 2).

• A single *waw* in the paleo-Hebrew or square script serving as a paragraphing device is found only in three biblical scrolls in the middle of closed or open sections: 4QpaleoExod^m (passim), 11QpaleoLev^a (passim), 4QNum^b XXI 28 (ch. *5c1*).

• Biblical texts were inscribed on only one side of the leather unlike several nonbiblical opisthographs from the Judean Desert; see ch. *4b* and APPENDIX 3.

• A *de luxe* scroll format was used especially for biblical scrolls, and also for a few nonbiblical texts. See ch. *4j* and TABLE 27 there

Scribal approaches. If scribes barely distinguished between the writing of biblical and nonbiblical literary works, and if in at least one instance the same scribe copied both, we should probably not expect a different approach toward the content of manuscripts of both types. The careful copying of sacred texts such as instructed by rabbinic literature should not be invoked as evidence for such a distinction, since this approach pertains to a later period and to specific circles only. However, relevant evidence may be found in other quarters. The Qumran evidence alone shows that, contrary to expectation, the textual development of the Torah was not different from that of the other books of Scripture. Since the Torah contains the most sacred part of Hebrew Scripture, it could have been expected that scribes would have approached that book with special care and with less scribal intervention than the other books of Hebrew Scripture, as instructed by later Jewish tradition. However, this is not the case for the Qumran evidence. There is no indication that the textual transmission of the Torah differed from that of the other Scripture books. Several Torah scrolls are written carelessly and inconsistently in the Qumran scribal practice (e.g. 1QDeut[a], 4Q[Gen-]Exod[b], 4QDeut[j] [mainly: second part], 4QDeut[k1], 4QDeut[k2], 4QDeut[m]), in which several additional biblical scrolls such as 1QIsa[a] and 2QJer were written. Furthermore, the great majority of these texts reflect a free approach to the biblical text which manifests itself in adaptations of unusual forms to the context, in frequent errors, in numerous corrections, and sometimes, also, in careless handwriting. The various witnesses of the Torah (MT, SP, Qumran scrolls, and the *Vorlage* of the LXX) reflect the same degree of editorial intervention as the other books of Hebrew Scripture.

Since the scribal approach to the Torah was not different from the approach to the other books of Hebrew Scripture, it should *not* be expected that scribes copying any book of Scripture had a different approach to these books than to nonbiblical literary compositions. Such an approach would be visible in careful copying, fewer corrections (linear or supralinear), and lack of scribal intervention in general. If the frequency of scribal intervention in general correctly represents the scribal attitude, the approach towards biblical texts is not more careful than that towards nonbiblical texts. Such scribal intervention, pertaining to supralinear corrections, deletions, erasures, reshaping of letters, as well as linear and supralinear scribal signs, can be measured by dividing the number of lines preserved (in full or in part) by the number of instances of scribal intervention. The result of such a calculation yields the average number of lines between each instance of scribal intervention. The lower the number, the higher the rate of scribal intervention (ch. 4, TABLE 27).

It is evident that the majority of the biblical scrolls were not singled out for special care in copying as is shown by the high degree of scribal intervention (an average of one correction in less than 10 lines) especially in 1QIsa[a], and also in other biblical scrolls (4QDeut[m], 5QDeut, 4QJosh[b], 4QJudg[b], 4QIsa[a], 4QJer[a], 4QXII[c], 4QXII[e], 11QPs[a], 4QCant[b], 4QQoh[a]), as tabulated in cols. 12 and 13 of APPENDIX 8. In the nonbiblical texts an equally high degree of scribal intervention is usually an indication that the texts were written according to the Qumran scribal practice (e.g. 1QS, 4QRP[a] [4Q158], 4QTest [4Q175], 4QJub[g] [4Q222], 4QpsJub[a] [4Q225], 4QRP[c] [4Q365], 4QShirShabb[d] [4Q403], 4QBarkhi Nafshi[c] [4Q436], 4QM[a] [4Q491], 4QapocrLam B [4Q501], 4QDibHam[a] [4Q504], 4QOrd[c] [4Q514]). At the same time, other texts written in that scribal practice have a somewhat smaller rate of scribal intervention (APPENDIX 1), while in this group there are no texts with a low degree of scribal intervention.

2. PALEO-HEBREW BIBLICAL SCROLLS. Texts written in the paleo-Hebrew script were copied more carefully than most texts written in the square script, if the criterion of scribal intervention is accepted as a valid criterion. These manuscripts were copied with equal care as the proto-Masoretic scrolls (§ 3). The data presented below (§ b) and in APPENDIX 8 for five manuscripts show that texts written in the paleo-Hebrew script show very little sign of scribal intervention (the other paleo-Hebrew manuscripts are insufficiently preserved for examination). This issue can be examined satisfactorily since several paleo-Hebrew texts have been preserved relatively well. Most of these texts reflect the proto-Masoretic text, but since 4QpaleoExod[m] (close to SP) reflects a different tradition, the lack of scribal intervention should not be connected to the proto-Masoretic character of these scrolls, but rather to the special script which may point to a specific milieu, possibly that of the Sadducees (see the analysis in ch. *6b*).

3. PROTO-MASORETIC TEXTS. The biblical texts found at Qumran were treated in the discussion in § 1 as a uniform corpus. However, these biblical texts are of a differing textual character (proto-Masoretic, pre-Samaritan, and independent texts, as well as texts written according to the Qumran scribal practice [APPENDIX 8]). As scribes developed different approaches to the text, it should be noted that some scribes singled out sacred texts for special care. To some extent this is true of the proto-Masoretic texts from Qumran, and definitely of the biblical texts found at all sites in the Judean Desert except for Qumran.

Almost all biblical scrolls (all: proto-Masoretic) from sites in the Judean Desert other than Qumran were copied carefully, if the criterion of scribal intervention is accepted as being valid. This pertains to the following scrolls: SdeirGen (an average of one correction in every 38 lines), MurXII (75), 5/6HevPs (142), MasLev[b] (30), MasPs[a] (74+). This group overlaps with the *de luxe* editions listed in TABLE 27 in ch. 4, but not completely, since the relevant data about format are not known for all scrolls. Proto-Masoretic manuscripts from Qumran reflecting a low degree of scribal intervention are: 4QGen[e] (an average of one correction in every 49+ lines), 4QLev[b] (136), 4QLev-Num[a] (36), 4QLev[e] (41+), 1QDeut[b] (82+), 4QDeut[g] (43), 4QDeut[o] (46+), 4QSam[b] (50), 4QIsa[e] (58+), 4QIsa[f] (92), 4QPs[c] (52). The full evidence for these and all other scrolls is recorded in APPENDIX 8. However, not all proto-Masoretic scrolls display an equally low level of scribal intervention; note, for example, the well-preserved proto-Masoretic 4QJer[a] reflecting much scribal intervention with an average of one correction per 4 lines (see further 4QExod[c], 4QDeut[f], 4QDeut[h], 4QIsa[d] [all: one correction in every 16–17 lines], 4QIsa[a] [7], 4QIsa[b] [13], MasEzek [18]).

According to Talmudic sources, the sacred character of the text allows for only a minimal number of corrections. The opinions quoted in *b. Menaḥ.* 29b and *y. Meg.* 1.71c allow for two or three corrections per column (but not four), while the opinions in *Sof.* 3.10 allow for one to three corrections. According to these opinions, scrolls containing a greater number of corrections in a single column could not be used by the public, but according to *b. Menaḥ.* 29b there is a certain leniency with regard to superfluous letters which were less disturbing when erased or deleted than were added letters. According to these criteria, many of the Qumran biblical scrolls would not have passed the scrutiny of the rabbis, as is evident from a comparison of the average number of corrections with the number of lines per column (ch. 4, TABLE 15). Thus, with an average of one correction to every four lines, 1QIsa[a] (28–32 lines per column) would not be acceptable, nor would 4QJer[a] (30–32 lines [one correction in every 4 lines]), 4QIsa[a] (35 lines [every 7 lines]), 4QIsa[b] (45 lines [every 13 lines]).

b. *Texts written in the paleo-Hebrew script* (illustr. 14)

Texts written in the square and paleo-Hebrew scripts (for the background, see ch. *6b*) share many scribal features since they reflect the same Hebrew writing tradition.

   • The writing in scrolls, consisting of sheets of leather, and in columns.
   • Most texts were ruled horizontally (indicating lines) and vertically (indicating the beginnings and usually also the ends of columns).
   • The written text is suspended from horizontal lines.
   • Sense units were separated from one another by open and closed sections.
   • A special layout of the text in poetical units pertains to texts written in square characters as well as to 4QpaleoDeut[r] (Deuteronomy 32) and probably 4QpaleoJob[c].
   • Words were separated from one another, albeit in different ways.
   • Biblical texts belonging to the Masoretic family also to the so-called pre-Samaritan group were written in both scripts (APPENDIX 8).

At the same time, the texts written in the two scripts display several different scribal features. Some differences are inherent in the writing traditions of these scripts, and therefore cause no surprise:

• The non-distinction between medial and final letters in the texts written in the paleo-Hebrew script as opposed to their distinction in the square script.

• The splitting of a word in the paleo-Hebrew script at the end of a line with its continuation in the following line was customary in texts written in that script (as well as in ancient Greek texts and some Ugaritic texts),[312] but not in the Samaritan script, that was based on the paleo-Hebrew script.

The two groups also differ from one another in scribal features that are not connected to the writing in these particular scripts:

• While words were separated by spacing in the texts written in the square script, in the Judean Desert texts written in the paleo-Hebrew script most words were separated by dots, or, less frequently, by strokes or triangles. See ch. *5a1*.

• No scribal marks of any kind, such as those inserted either in the margins or between the lines in the texts written in the square script, are known from the texts written in the paleo-Hebrew script. This pertains to the signs indicating new sections, various types of marginal notes indicating remarkable details, and line-fillers (ch. *5c1–4*).

• In 4QpaleoExod[m] and 11QpaleoLev[a], but not in other paleo-Hebrew texts, large *waws* were written in the spaces between the sections, when the first word of the next section would have started with this letter (for an analysis, see ch. *5c1*). This phenomenon is not known from texts written in the square script, but it is paralleled by the single occurrence of such a *waw* in the square script in 4QNum[b] XXI 28 in Num 27:22 (cf. ch. *5c1*).

• The use of cancellation dots/strokes for the correction of mistakes, known from texts written in the square script (ch. *5c2*) and Greek texts (Turner, *Greek Manuscripts*, index), is not known from texts written in the paleo-Hebrew script.

• Whereas all texts written in the square script, including the carefully transmitted texts of the Masoretic family, show *scribal intervention* in differing degrees (see ch. *5f* and col. 11 in APPENDIX 8), the texts written in the paleo-Hebrew script show virtually no scribal intervention, neither by the original scribes nor by subsequent scribes or users, with the exception of a few instances. See § 1a above.

1QpaleoLev: One correction (frg. 3–4 5) in 33 lines.

4QpaleoExod[m]: An average of one correction in every 197 lines (corrections in XVII 30, 33, and a supralinear correction in 10 ii 2).

4QpaleoGen-Exod[l]: An average of one correction in every 105 lines (a linear correction in 24–29 12; a supralinear correction in 10 ii 2).

4QpaleoDeut[r]: No corrections in 114 lines.

11QpaleoLev[a]: An average of one correction in every 66 lines (erasures in E 3 and VI 6).

• No patches inscribed in the square script are known, while the only such patch was attached to a text written in the paleo-Hebrew script (4QpaleoExod[m]). See ch. *4 i*.

• The extant fragments of paleo-Hebrew texts display no indentations, such as found in several texts written in the square script (ch. *5a2*).[313]

---

[312]Cf. i.a., the Mesha inscription, the Lakhish ostraca and see M. Lidzbarski, *Handbuch der Nordsemitischen Epigraphik nebst ausgewählten Inschriften* (Weimar 1898) 126–7. For Greek texts, see Turner, *Greek Manuscripts*, 17. In Ugaritic texts, words usually end at the ends of lines, but in some texts they are spread over two lines; see S. Segert, "Words Spread over Two Lines," *UF* 19 (1987) 283–8.

[313]One such indentation was reconstructed by J. E. Sanderson in 4QpaleoExod[m] IX 30–31 (Exod 12:20-21) but, due to the lack of parallels, this reconstruction is unlikely.

• As a result of the splitting of words between two lines in the paleo-Hebrew texts, almost straight left margins could be obtained (e.g. 4QpaleoExod^m I, VI, IX and all columns of 11QpaleoLev^a). See ch. *4f*.

The various paleo-Hebrew texts reflect a common scribal approach with some idiosyncrasies.

• In only two paleo-Hebrew texts (4QpaleoExod^m and 11QpaleoLev^a) were large paleo-Hebrew *waws* written in the spaces between the sections, when the first word of the following section would have started with this letter.

• 4QpaleoDeut^r is the only paleo-Hebrew text using spacing instead of dots as word-dividers. See above.

• In three paleo-Hebrew texts, little oblique strokes or apostrophes were written at the ends of sheets for the drawing of straight lines (2QpaleoLev; 4QpaleoExod^m; an unidentified fragment on photograph PAM 43.694), but not in 4QpaleoGen-Exod^l and 11QpaleoLev^a. Cf. ch. *4a*.

• Most paleo-Hebrew texts divide the text into sections, separated by spacing at the end of the section after the last word in the line, and subdivided by smaller spaces in the middle of the line. In addition, 4QpaleoGen-Exod^l employed an even larger division with a space extending from the last word to the end of the line and including all the following line. See ch. *5a3*.

• As in texts written in the square script, most paleo-Hebrew texts use spacing in the middle of the line for the indication of closed sections (see 1QpaleoLev, 4QpaleoGen-Exod^l, 4QpaleoExod^m, 4QpaleoDeut^r for clear evidence). On the other hand, the well-preserved 11QpaleoLev^a does not use this device.

• 2QpaleoLev is the only text in which word-dividers were also inserted at the ends of lines.

• The same text is the only source in which both word-dividers and guide dots appear at the ends of lines.

That the writing in two different scripts represents different scribal schools is a likely, but still unproven, assumption. There is no reason to assume that the Qumranites themselves wrote complete texts in paleo-Hebrew characters; it has been suggested cautiously (ch. *6b*) that these texts were written by Sadducees.

c. Tefillin *and* mezuzot (illustr. 9)

Most of the *tefillin* from the Judean Desert derive from Qumran cave 4 (21 copies), with one additional copy from each of caves 1, 5, and 8, as well as from Murabba'at, Naḥal Ḥever, Naḥal Ṣe'elim, and four copies from an undetermined cave, named XQPhyl 1–4.[314] The corpus of these *tefillin* shares several scribal features, most of which pertain also to *mezuzot* (see below regarding the distinction between them).

• Most *tefillin* were written on thin leather of inferior quality with a rough surface and ragged edges, representing scraps of leather left over from hides used for the

---

[314] The main group of *tefillin* was published by J. T. Milik in *DJD* VI; for a preliminary publication of four *tefillin*, see K. G. Kuhn, *Phylakterien aus Höhle 4 von Qumran* (AHAW, Phil.-Hist. Kl. 1957, 1; Heidelberg 1957). A second group was published by Y. Yadin, *Tefillin from Qumran (X Q Phyl 1–4)* (Jerusalem 1969) = *ErIsr* 9 (1969) 60–85. Corrections for the latter are provided by M. Baillet, "Nouveaux phylactères de Qumran (XQ Phyl 1–4) à propos d'une édition récente," *RevQ* 7 (1970) 403–15. See further 1Q13 and 8Q3. XḤev/SePhylactery was published in *DJD* XXXVIII by M. Morgenstern and M. Segal. 5QPhyl (5Q8) has not been opened. Two *tefillin* from Ṣe'elim were published by Y. Aharoni, "Expedition B," *IEJ* 11 (1961) 11–24, especially 22–4. In addition, the editors of *DJD* XXIII described the unidentified text 11Q31 as probably containing a *tefillin* or *mezuzah*.

preparation of scrolls (illustr. 9; cf. 2). The irregular material did not allow for the writing of even lines, and certainly not the forming of columns (a reality which was accepted in *y. Meg.* 1.71c); therefore among the *tefillin* known from antiquity, the rectangular shapes of 4QPhyl K and XQPhyl 1 and the square shapes of 4QPhyl M and XQPhyl 2 constitute exceptions. Note, especially, the elongated shape of MurPhyl. The leather of the *tefillin* published by Yadin was characterized by Y. Frankl in Yadin, *Tefillin,* 43–4 as *qelaph.*

• *Tefillin* were not ruled (the lack of such ruling was allowed by *b. Menaḥ.* 32b; *b. Meg.* 18b). Nevertheless the writing was usually straight.

• For reasons of economy, the text was often inscribed on both sides of the leather, in contrast to that on biblical scrolls. See ch. *4b.*

• No spaces were left between words, while final forms of letters were nevertheless used. The *tefillin* thus employed the same system for separating words as for separating letters. According to Yadin, *Tefillin,* 21 and Rothstein, *From Bible to Murabbaʿat,* 264, the scribes of XQPhyl 1–4 followed the rabbinic rule of leaving minute spaces between letters (*b. Menaḥ.* 30a and *y. Meg.* 1.71d), while the scribes of MurPhyl and 4QPhyl C, in which ligatures are used, followed a different practice.

• As a result of the economy described above, the text was subdivided into fewer units than in regular Scripture texts. For example, the text of the Decalogue in 4QPhyl J is written as a continuous text, with no spaces between the words and commands (illustr. 9). Papyrus Nash follows a middle path, since it has spaces between the words, but no extra spaces between the commands.

• Every cave 4 exemplar used three letter-spaces to separate the sections (see e.g. 4QPhyl C 1 15, 19). In 8QPhyl, sections end in the middle of the line, and are followed by a blank line and an indentation on the subsequent line. Likewise, MurPhyl indicates open sections by leaving the rest of the line blank followed by an empty line. These internal differences are also reflected in rabbinic literature with regard to *mezuzot,* and *b. Menaḥ.* 31b–32a records a long discussion concerning the space between the two pericopes of the *mezuzah.* R. Meir favored an open section ('because they are not adjacent in the Torah'), but by the third generation of Amoraim, a closed section was used (R. Naḥman bar Isaac). The lack of clarity with regard to the use of either open or closed sections is also known to *y. Meg.* 1.71c, but there the verdict (Rav) is in favor of an open section.

• Words were split between lines, as in inscriptions written in the 'early' Hebrew and square scripts, and in Hebrew biblical scrolls written in the paleo-Hebrew script, apparently due to considerations of space. This practice was not used in Scripture texts written in the square or script and was forbidden by *Sof.* 2.1.

• Most *tefillin* written in the Qumran scribal practice allowed for interlinear additions (their absence in some texts may be ascribed to the fragmentary status of their preservation). On the other hand, such additions are not found in the *tefillin* written with MT spelling (ch. *8a2*). The latter group thus reflects the prescription of *y. Meg.* 1.71c: 'One may hang <the letter above the line> in scrolls, but one may not hang <the letter above the line> in *tefillin* or *mezuzot.*'

• Because of the differing shapes of the *tefillin,* the pericopes were laid out differently in each copy.

• For the differences in content between the various preserved samples of *tefillin,* see ch. *8a2.*

• There is no indication that *tefillin* were written by special scribes as was the case in later times. For example, the scribal peculiarities of the *tefillin* written according to the Qumran scribal practice (ch. *8a2*) cannot be distinguished from the other texts written by that group of scribes.

Mezuzot. The scribal features of *mezuzot* are very similar to those of *tefillin,* and indeed in some cases the editors of these texts were uncertain regarding the differentiation between the two (e.g. J. T. Milik, *DJD* VI, 35–7 with regard to 4QPhyl S, U and 4QMez G). The layout of *mezuzot* was discussed in *y. Meg.* 1.71c. *Mezuzot* and *tefillin* contain the same biblical pericopes, but their purpose is different, and they can be distinguished by the following scribal features:

• The leather of *tefillin* was thinner (0.07–0.08 mm according to J. T. Milik, *DJD* VI, 35–7 and 0.04 mm according to Y. Frankl *apud* Yadin, *Tefillin,* 43) than that of *mezuzot* which in most aspects resemble regular manuscripts.

• *Mezuzot* were inscribed only on the recto, while several *tefillin* were additionally inscribed on the verso.

• *Mezuzot* have margins, while *tefillin* usually do not. At the same time, XQPhyl 1 and 2 have minute margins.

• The letters in *mezuzot* are of regular size, while the letters in *tefillin* are minute.

• *Mezuzot* are written on neatly shaped pieces of leather, while *tefillin* were usually inscribed on leather of ragged shapes.

d. *Texts written on papyrus*

See ch. *3a, e.*

e. *Texts written in Greek*

See APPENDIX 4.

f. *Pesharim*

The Qumran *pesharim* were authored by different individuals and were probably copied by yet other scribes, some of whom could have been the authors themselves. These differences in authorship are visible in the distinct focus and tendencies of the *pesher* methods of interpretation, scope of lemmas, etc. Differences in scribal hands are visible primarily in the handwriting, but also in scribal practices. Interestingly enough, none of the scribal hands visible in the *pesharim* appears in a second *pesher*. At the same time, attention should be directed to the following points.

• A change of hands within a manuscript, attested relatively frequently in the Qumran scrolls (ch. *2e*), attests to its status as a copy rather than an autograph. The unusual change of hands toward the end of 1QpHab (XII 13) probably indicates that this manuscript is a copy rather than an autograph.

• The erroneous copying of the scribal sign X as a single *ʾaleph* in 1QpHab II 5, where it serves no purpose, shows that this was a copy of another scroll in which the X served as a line-filler (ch. *5c6*). This *ʾaleph* is written in exactly the same position as the X-signs, slightly to the right of the left vertical line.

• Scribal mistakes which are clearly based on a written *Vorlage* show that the specific *pesher* manuscript was a copy rather than an autograph. Thus, the supralinear addition ואוהבי יהוה כיקר כורים פשר]ו ? על בחירו by the original scribe of 4QpPsª (4Q171) III 5 must have been written after the completion of the text. The writing of this added line (originally omitted by way of homoioteleuton) shows a feature which differs from the writing of the surrounding text. While, in that scroll, the Tetragrammaton was always written in paleo-Hebrew characters, it is inscribed in square characters in the addition in III 5.

The following continuous *pesharim* are known:[315]

1Q14	1QpMic
	1QpHab
1Q15	1QpZeph
1Q16	1QpPs
3Q4	3QpIsa (*pesher?*)
4Q161	4QpIsa^a
4Q162	4QpIsa^b
4Q163	4Qpap pIsa^c
4Q164	4QpIsa^d
4Q165	4QpIsa^e
4Q166	4QpHos^a
4Q167	4QpHos^b
4Q168	4QpMic? (*pesher?*)
4Q169	4QpNah
4Q170	4QpZeph
4Q171	4QpPs^a
4Q172	4QpUnid (*pesher?*)
4Q173	4QpPs^b
5Q10	5QapocrMal (*pesher?*)

Three different scribal practices are recognized among individual *pesharim*, which, however, cannot be combined in order to recognize different subgroups.

α. Paleo-Hebrew characters are used for the Tetragrammaton and sometimes for *'El* in seven or eight *pesharim* (TABLE 1 in ch. *6*), while the Tetragrammaton was written in the square script in quotations from the biblical text in eight other *pesharim* (TABLE 2 in ch. *6*).

β. Differing spacing systems were used to separate the biblical text from its *pesher*; the choice of system was often determined by where in the line the *pesher* started and ended. For the data and analysis see APPENDIX 7.2.

γ. Different scope of lemmas. See ch. *5a2*.

g. *Texts written in Cryptic scripts*

Writing in one of the Cryptic scripts (above § 3e) does *not* involve different scribal habits. The manuscripts written in one of these scripts (Crypt A is the most frequently attested script) share with the other Hebrew texts the use of the same scribal features for writing on papyrus (most Cryptic texts are written on papyrus) and leather and for the preparation of the scrolls. For the leather scrolls this involves: horizontal and vertical ruling, stitching of sheets, size and shape of columns, correction systems (superscript letters in 4Q298 and 4Q317), number of columns per sheet, height of columns, and margins. Open and closed sections have been preserved in 4Q249. Exceedingly large spaces (4.0–4.25 cm) are found between the lines of 4QcryptB Unclassified Text (4Q363). For two texts, the titles have been preserved, in the square script, in 4QcryptA Words of the Maskil (4Q298) as the first words of the running text, and in 4Qpap

---

[315]Thematic *pesharim* are less relevant for the present purpose.

cryptA Midrash Sefer Moshe (4Q249) on the verso of frg. 1. The separation of words with dots is reflected also in the only text written in the Cryptic C script, 4QcryptC Unclassified Religious Text (4Q363a). This text is written mainly in paleo-Hebrew letters, intermingled with some cryptic signs, and the use of dots to separate words is typical of the writing in that script (ch. *5a1*).

8

SCRIBAL TRADITIONS

a. *Common scribal practices*

In the First and Second Temple periods scribal practices or schools are likely to have existed (ch. *2b*), that is, groups of scribes copying scrolls, consistently or not, according to certain conventions. Some evidence for such practices or schools may be detected in the Qumran scrolls. The term 'scribal school' implies an organizational structure that may not have existed in those early days, and therefore 'common scribal practice' may be more appropriate for the description below. Three groups stand out each with their common scribal characteristics.

(1) *Scrolls written in the paleo-Hebrew script*

Scrolls written in the paleo-Hebrew script, although containing material of a diverse textual character, are linked through the very use of the paleo-Hebrew script and several common characteristics. See ch. *7b*.

(2) *The Qumran scribal practice*

Within the Qumran corpus, a group of 167 nonbiblical and biblical texts has been isolated as reflecting an idiosyncratic practice, the characteristics of which are visible in peculiarities in orthography, morphology, and scribal features.[316] Two similar texts were found at Masada (MasShirShabb [Mas 1k] and MasQumran-Type Fragment [Mas 1n]).[317] This group of texts is closely connected with the Qumran community since it includes *virtually all commonly agreed upon sectarian writings* (for seven or eight sectarian texts which do not display these characteristics, see below). The texts found at Qumran can thus be subdivided into texts presumably copied by a sectarian group of scribes, and other texts which were presumably taken there from elsewhere.[318] The

---

[316]Tov, "Orthography"; idem, "Hebrew Biblical Manuscripts"; idem, "Scribal Practices Reflected in the Documents from the Judean Desert and in the Rabbinic Literature: A Comparative Study," in *Texts, Temples, and Traditions: A Tribute to Menahem Haran* (ed. M. V. Fox et al.; Winona Lake, Ind. 1995) 383–403; idem, "*Tefillin* of Different Origin from Qumran?" in *A Light for Jacob, Studies in the Bible and the Dead Sea Scrolls in Memory of Jacob Shalom Licht* (ed. Y. Hoffman and F. H. Polak; Jerusalem/Tel Aviv 1997) 44*–54*; idem, "Further Evidence." See further the linguistic analyses by M. G. Abegg, Jr., "The Hebrew of the Dead Sea Scrolls," in Flint–VanderKam, *Fifty Years*, 325–58 (see notes 1 and 13) and W. M. Schniedewind, "Qumran Hebrew as an Antilanguage," *JBL* 118 (1999) 235–52, especially 247–9.

[317]These texts, as well as other ones, were probably brought to Masada by one of the Qumran covenanters, fleeing from Qumran. See APPENDIX 6.

[318]A basic distinction between two groups of texts reflecting different systems of orthography and correction techniques had been pointed out in 1958 by Martin, *Scribal Character*, I.393–402, II.710–1 on the basis of a detailed study of the texts from cave 1 only. The texts written according to the Qumran scribal practice were named by Martin 'transitional phonetic,' 'phonetic,' and 'official phonetic,' while the other texts were named 'consonantal.' This recognition led Martin to posit a Qumran scribal school, but at the same time he voiced his hesitations:

> ... one can only conclude that if a scribal school existed at Qumran, then all these traits are perfectly reconcilable with such an institution. On the other hand, if no scribal school ever existed there, we can explain most of these facts as arising from the habits of the scribes who transcribed the documents in

combined evidence shows that the great majority of the distinctive scribal features is more or less limited to texts that also display the Qumran orthography and morphology. The texts written in the Qumran scribal practice could have been penned anywhere in Palestine, but they were probably written mainly at Qumran. Early scrolls, such as 4QQoh[a] (175–150 BCE) must have been copied by similarly oriented scribes elsewhere, as this and a few other texts predate the settlement at Qumran; see further below, § υ. The main argument for our view pertains to the fact that within the Qumran corpus a group of 167 biblical and nonbiblical texts (see below) display distinctive features, and that most of them are sectarian. Conversely, virtually all the sectarian texts were written in this special practice.

The main argument in favor of the existence of a Qumran scribal practice is orthographic and morphological, however inconsistent, allowing a distinction between a group of texts displaying a distinctive system and texts which do not display these features.[319] However, the evidence is not clear-cut, and seven or eight sectarian texts do *not* share these features:[320]

> 4QpIsa[b] (4Q162; 50–25 BCE)
> 4QpNah (4Q169; 50–25 BCE)
> 4QCommGen A (4Q252; sporadic 'Qumranic' spellings; 30–1 BCE)
> 4QS[d] (4Q258; 30–1 BCE)
> 4QS[j] (4Q264; 50–25 BCE)
> 4QCal Doc/Mish A (4Q320; insufficient data; 125–100 BCE)
> 4QMMT[b] (4Q395; 30–1 BCE)
> 4QBarkhi Nafshi[a] (4Q434; sporadic 'Qumranic' spellings; 1–30 CE)

In spite of these exceptions, it remains true to say that practically all Qumran sectarian works[321] were penned according to this scribal practice.[322] In the present analysis much stress is placed on scribal features, as these provide more objective criteria for analysis than the analysis of orthography and morphology.

A remark on the statistical picture is in order. The analysis is based on the Qumran corpus containing fragments of 930 texts, from which 150 Aramaic (including 17 Nabatean-Aramaic texts) and 27 Greek texts are excluded, since they display no features comparable to the orthographic and morphological peculiarities recognized for

---

different localities, but who by a natural process shared a technique that had points of resemblance and points of difference (Martin, *Scribal Character*, I.392–3; cf. p. 405 and II.710).

It should be remembered that Martin could not consult many comparative data because the texts from caves 4 and 11 were not yet known to him; furthermore, basing himself on the analogy of the medieval Masoretic tradition, Martin expected too great a unity from a scribal school.

[319]To be precise, there are a few exceptions, but our investigations are based on statistical evidence that is not affected by these exceptions. Beyond these exceptions, it should be stressed that most special forms recorded in APPENDIX 9 such as הואה (col. 1) simply do not appear outside the group of texts written according to the Qumran practice. On the other hand, המה (col. 4) appears elsewhere, and in this case the main argument is statistical. By the same token, cancellation dots (one of the special scribal habits) occur almost exclusively in this group of texts, even though isolated instances also occur elsewhere (TABLES 10–12 in chapter 5).

[320]With the exception of 4Q320 and 4Q434, all texts are dated to the same period which may be significant.

[321]I count 107 sectarian compositions listed in APPENDIX 1b and 85 fragments of possible sectarian compositions (APPENDIX 1c), several of them indicated with question marks.

[322]While the assumption of a Qumran scribal practice based on the evidence of orthography and morphology alone has met with some disagreement, the combined evidence further supports this assumption. For criticisms of our views, limited to the arguments based on orthography, see: Cross, *ALQ³*, 174–7; J. Lübbe, "Certain Implications of the Scribal Process of 4QSam[c]," *RevQ* 14 (1989–90) 255–65; J. Cook, "Orthographical Peculiarities in the Dead Sea Biblical Scrolls," ibid., 293–305; Ulrich, *The Dead Sea Scrolls*, 111; J. Campbell, "Hebrew and its Study at Qumran," in Horbury, *Hebrew Study*, 38–52, especially 41; A. Lange, "Kriterien essenischer Texte," *Qumran kontrovers*, 59–69.

the Hebrew texts.[323] By the same token, at least another 150 items should be excluded due to their fragmentary state. This leaves us with some 600 texts, of which 400–500 are large enough for analysis. Within this group, APPENDIX 1 lists 167 texts (including 25 biblical texts and eight *tefillin*) that in our view reflect the orthographic and morphological features of a Qumran scribal practice (of these 167 texts, some 130 are good candidates, while the remainder are probable candidates).

It cannot be coincidental that the great majority of the sectarian texts were copied, admittedly somewhat inconsistently, in a common orthographic and morphological style and with common scribal features; rather, the only plausible explanation seems to be that the sectarian scribes followed special scribal conventions. This group may represent one third or half of the Qumran corpus if some of the 85 fragmentary sectarian texts included in APPENDIX 1c are also taken into consideration.

Before the full data is presented in favor of our view, the following should be emphasized:

• The content of idiosyncratic Qumran *tefillin* written in the orthography and morphology of the Qumran scribal practice (ch. *7c* and APPENDIX 9) is distinct from the content of the Rabbinic-type *tefillin* written in the MT system. This fact provides an external control supporting our hypothesis.

• Within the Qumran corpus, the writing of the divine names in paleo-Hebrew characters or with four/five dots (*Tetrapuncta*) is documented mainly in texts written in the Qumran orthography and morphology (ch. *6b*). Since this practice is based on a certain conception of the sanctity of the divine names, and since the approach of the Qumran community to this issue is known also from other indicators (ch. *6b2*), this practice provides an independent control supporting our hypothesis.

• The majority (84) of the 131 Hebrew Qumran texts containing scribal markings of some kind as listed in APPENDIX 1 (e.g. the *paragraphos* sign), also reflect the orthographic and morphological features of the Qumran scribal practice. In some groups this percentage is very high, e.g. for cancellation dots (ch. *5c1*).

In the following analysis, the various features of the Qumran scribal practice are reviewed through constant reference to the full discussion in the earlier chapters in this monograph. The logic followed in this description is:

1. A certain group of texts which are characterized with a specific type of orthography and morphology is set apart (§§ o, π below as well as APPENDIX 9 and 1).
2. Independently of the determination of this group, certain scribal phenomena are recognized which occur especially frequently in this group (all other paragraphs below as well as APPENDIX 1).
3. Through a combination of these criteria—some more convincing than others—the texts which were presumably copied in the Qumran scribal practice are determined (APPENDIX 1 and 9).
4. The dates assigned to the texts presumably written in the Qumran scribal practice are listed in the last column in APPENDIX 1, culled from the summary list by Webster, "Chronological Index." These dates are analyzed in § υ ('concluding remarks').

    α. *Paragraphos* signs
    β. Cancellation dots
    γ. Crossing out of letters and words with a line
    δ. Parenthesis signs

---

[323]Nevertheless, the data for individual Aramaic texts are recorded in APPENDIX 1 when they reflect, albeit rarely, one of the scribal features mentioned below.

ε. Writing of the divine names with paleo-Hebrew characters
η. Single letters in the Cryptic A script written mainly in the margin
ζ. Single paleo-Hebrew letters
θ. *Tetrapuncta* designating the Tetragrammaton
ι. The X-sign
κ. Separation dots between words
λ. Nonfinal letters used in final position and final letters used in nonfinal position
μ. Guide dots/strokes
ν. Scribal cooperation?
ο. Orthographic features
π. Morphological features
ρ. *Tefillin*
σ. Ruling with ink
τ. Final handle sheets

α. Paragraphos *signs* (figs. 1.2–1.7 and 11.2,6)

The *paragraphos* and similar paragraphing devices usually occur in conjunction with a system of notation of open or closed sections. The majority of the Qumran texts listed in ch. *5c1* as containing such signs (thirty-three) are Hebrew texts written according to the Qumran scribal practice (twenty-two). In addition, these signs occur in three biblical texts, three Aramaic texts, and five texts that were either not copied by the Qumran group of scribes, or whose character is unclear. The data are also tabulated in APPENDIX 1.

The fact that the majority of the texts containing *paragraphos* signs were written in the Qumran orthography and morphology forms a convincing link between this scribal practice and the Qumran community, especially since most of these texts also contain a sectarian content. The exact number of occurrences of these signs in the Qumran sectarian scrolls cannot be determined due to their fragmentary state of preservation. It is, however, clear that their use was probably limited to certain scribes, users, or periods since less than half of the sectarian texts display these signs.

β. Cancellation dots (figs. 6.1–6.4)

The practice of using cancellation dots is evidenced in fifty-two biblical and nonbiblical texts written in the Qumran scribal practice, eight texts not written in that system, six texts of unclear orthographic practice, and three Aramaic texts (ch. *5c2*). Since only half of the Qumran texts large enough for analysis reflect the features of the Qumran scribal practice, and the majority of the texts using the scribal dots are written in the Qumran orthography and morphology, the use of cancellation dots may be considered characteristic of that scribal practice. Since cancellation dots are used only in half of the texts written in the Qumran scribal practice, the use of this practice was probably limited to certain scribes or periods.

γ. Crossing out of letters and words with a line (fig. 7)

Words or letters were crossed out in thirteen biblical and nonbiblical texts written in the Qumran scribal practice, seven texts not written in that system, and three Aramaic texts. See ch. *5c2* and TABLE 16. Since this scribal practice is used only in a small number of sectarian texts, it was probably limited to certain scribes, users, or periods.

δ. *Parenthesis signs* (figs. 8.1–3)

Parenthesis signs were used in five texts written in the Qumran scribal practice and three texts not written in that system for indicating omissions and, in one instance, an addition. See ch. *5c2.*

ε. *Writing of the divine names with paleo-Hebrew characters* (figs. 26, 27)

Of the twenty-eight manuscripts using paleo-Hebrew characters for the divine names in the middle of a text written in square characters, nineteen or twenty (if 1QPs[b] is included) are nonbiblical; six or seven (if 1QPs[b] is included) are biblical manuscripts; one is probably a rewritten Bible manuscript (2QExod[b]); the nature of 3Q14 is unclear. All texts in this group that are large enough for analysis, with the exception of 4QS[d] (4Q258), reflect the orthography and morphology of the Qumran scribal practice. See ch. *6b2*, TABLE 1, and illustr. 3. We suggested that this practice provides an independent control supporting our hypothesis since the approach of the Qumran community to the divine names is known also from other indicators.

A reverse examination of the texts written in the Qumran scribal practice reveals that thirty-six such texts did *not* use a special system for the writing of the divine names with paleo-Hebrew characters (ch. *6b2* and TABLE 2) or *Tetrapuncta* (below, θ). It therefore seems that within the group of Qumran scribes different practices were employed for writing the divine names, possibly at different times.

η. *Single letters in the Cryptic A script written mainly in the margins* (figs. 10.1–11)

The evidence for single letters in the Cryptic A script designating matters of special interest relates to six texts written according to the Qumran scribal practice, all sectarian. The same phenomenon also is found in one Aramaic and three biblical texts (one of them, 1QIsa[a], is written in the Qumran scribal practice). See ch. *5c3.*

ζ. *Single paleo-Hebrew letters* (figs. 10.12–12.2)

Single paleo-Hebrew letters designating matters of special interest are found in five texts written in the Qumran practice, as well as in three texts not written in that system. For details, see ch. *5c4* and APPENDIX 1. The connection between the paleo-Hebrew letters and the Qumran scribal practice is less strong than in the preceding categories.

θ. Tetrapuncta *designating the Tetragrammaton* (fig. 19)

Tetrapuncta (four dots) denoting the Tetragrammaton occur in eight texts written in the Qumran scribal practice, as well as in five texts not written in this scribal practice. See ch. *5d*, TABLE 1, and illustr. 3. A connection between the *Tetrapuncta* and the Qumran scribal practice is probable.

ι. *The X-sign* (fig. 22)

The X-sign, serving as a line-filler, is used in three Qumran texts written in the Qumran scribal practice: 1QpHab, 4QCommGen A (4Q252)?, 11QT[b] (11Q20). It also designates matters of special interest in three Qumran texts written according to the Qumran scribal practice: 1QIsaᵃ, 4QCatena A (4Q177), 4QInstrᶜ (4Q417). See ch. *5c5*. A connection between this sign and the Qumran scribal practice is likely.

κ. *Separation dots between words* (fig. 17)

Separation dots, written level with the tops of the letters or slightly above them, are evidenced for seven texts written according to the Qumran scribal practice and one text not written in that practice. See ch. *5c7*.

λ. *Nonfinal letters used in final position and final letters used in nonfinal position*

In 83 Qumran texts, nonfinal letters were written in final position. The connection between this procedure and the Qumran scribal practice is very likely (78 percent of the 83 texts), but further research is needed since the data in ch. *5g* are not exhaustive.

Likewise, final forms were sometimes used in medial position, but much less frequently. This lack of distinction is known especially from texts written according to the Qumran scribal practice; see especially ch. 5, TABLE 20.

μ. *Guide dots/strokes*

In fifty-six or fifty-seven Qumran texts written in the square and paleo-Hebrew scripts single guide dots ('points jalons') or, rarely, strokes were drawn as guides for the dry lines. They appear in the space between the right edge of the sheet and the beginning of the first column of the sheet (usually close to the right side of the column) and in the space between the last column and the left edge of the sheet.

The connection between the use of the guide dots/strokes and the Qumran scribal practice is evident in the case of the nonbiblical scrolls, but is inconclusive for the biblical texts. For details, see ch. *4a* and TABLE 3.

ν. *Scribal cooperation?*

Seven of the nine Hebrew manuscripts in which more than one scribal hand is recognized were written in the Qumran scribal practice (ch. 1, TABLE 1). This evidence may point to cooperation within a scribal school with scribes belonging to this group continuing each other's work.

The preceding criteria were meant to isolate a group of texts containing scribal features reflected very frequently, almost exclusively, or exclusively in the texts reflecting the orthographic and morphological features of the Qumran scribal practice. The texts written in the Qumran scribal practice number no more than half of the Qumran texts large enough for analysis, yet the aforementioned features appear exceedingly frequently or almost exclusively in this group of texts. Phrased differently, the texts reflecting the orthographic and morphological features of the Qumran scribal practice are also characterized by further characteristics as analyzed above.

o. *Orthographic features*

One hundred and sixty-seven Qumran texts (of which some forty present a somewhat less convincing case) are characterized by a distinctive orthography and morphology which has no equal among the documents known from other places (see the studies quoted in n. 316). A few features are however reflected in the letters from the period of the Second Jewish Revolt, in Mishna manuscripts (Kutscher, *Language*, 20), and in the oral tradition behind SP, but the evidence known to date does not provide a good parallel to the combined features of the Qumran scribal practice.[324] *Faute de mieux*, we call this practice the 'Qumran' practice, but it could have been in vogue also in other places in Israel; note *Masada I*, inscription 449 השורה הזות (cf. col. 11 in APPENDIX 9), Mur papLetter from Beit-Mashiko to Yeshua b. Galgula (Mur 42) 2 רוש המחניה, and *b. Meg.* 11a where אחשרוש ('Ahasuerus') is explained from ראש ('head').[325] It could therefore be called 'Palestinian' or 'contemporary,' but these terms are too general. The notion that the texts written in this Qumran practice are intimately connected to the Qumran covenanters derives from the fact that virtually *all* the Qumran sectarian writings are written in this system. Note that the person who wrote מדרש ספר מושה in the square script on the back of 4Qpap cryptA Midrash Sefer Moshe (4Q249) written in the Cryptic A script also employed the Qumran orthography (cf. col. 13 in APPENDIX 9).

The internal inconsistency of the Qumran scribal practice (that is, differences between scrolls) should not be taken as an argument against the very assumption of such a scribal school since each individual scribe was inconsistent within his own scroll (note, e.g. 1QIsaᵃ V 26 ... כי נדמיתי כיא [Isa 6:5]). This inconsistency and the free approach to matters of text seemingly contradict the strict approach of the Qumran covenanters to their scriptures, but this contradiction is only apparent, as different aspects of religious life are involved. Apparently within the *Weltanschauung* of the Qumran community there was room for strictness with regard to *halakha* and the interpretation of Scripture, together with the lack of precision in the copying of the biblical text. A telling example of such imprecision is visible in *pesharim* such as 1QpHab in which the biblical text is not well represented (imprecision, mistakes, contextual adaptations), but it is still made the base for sectarian exegesis. Among other things, some of the interpretations in 1QpHab are based on readings differing from the biblical text in the lemma.[326]

The orthography of the Qumran scribal practice has been described in various studies, especially in the detailed description of 1QIsaᵃ by Kutscher, *Language* and in analyses of a number of Qumran texts by Martin, *Scribal Character;* Qimron, *Hebrew*; P. Muchowski, *Hebrajski Qumránski jako język mówiony* (Poznán 2001). Further: Tigchelaar, "The Scribe of 1QS." The statistical aspects outlined by Tov, "Orthography"; idem, "Hebrew Biblical Manuscripts"; and idem, "Further Evidence" are refined in APPENDICES 1 and 9 below.

The Qumran orthography is characterized by the inclusion of many *matres lectionis* whose purpose it is to facilitate the reading. Thus /o/ and /u/ are almost always represented by a *waw*. The *waw* is also used to indicate the short *holem* (e.g. חושך, פוה, מושה), the *qames hatuf* (אצורכה, חוכמה, כול), and the *hatef qames* (אונ יה). Because of scribal inconsistency, many words appear in the same text with different spellings, e.g.

---

[324]The possibility that different spelling systems were used in different localities is strengthened by parallels in Aramaic documents, see M. L. Folmer, *The Aramaic Language in the Achaemenid Period: A Study in Linguistic Variation*, Ph.D. diss., Amsterdam 1995, 691–768.

[325]On the other hand, C. Rabin considered the special orthography of the Qumran writings an innovation of the sectarian scribes: "The Historical Background of Qumran Hebrew," *ScrHier* 4 (Jerusalem 1965) 144–61, especially 160. Cross, *ALQ³*, 174–7 describes the orthography of these texts as a 'baroque style' and he includes the morphological features described below under the heading of orthography.

[326]For details, see my paper "The Biblical Texts from the Judaean Desert—An Overview and Analysis of the Published Texts," in Herbert–Tov, *The Bible as Book*, 139–66 and more in detail T. H. Lim, *Holy Scripture in the Qumran Commentaries and Pauline Texts* (Oxford 1997) chapter IV.

זות/זואת/זאות/ and ראש/רואש/רוש in 1QIsa[a] and in several other texts. *Yod* represents not only /i/ (usually not short i), but also *ṣere*: אבילים (1QIsa[a] 61:2), מית (38:1). Unique for certain lexemes is the representation of /i/ in final position by -יא, especially in כיא (see col. 16 in APPENDIX 9), and sometimes also in מיא (less frequent: נקיא, 49:7; פיא, 40:5), apparently by analogy to הביא, נביא *et sim.*, in which the *ʾaleph* belongs to the root. *He* as a *mater lectionis* for /a/ is very frequent at the end of words, such as in *qtlth* (e.g. שמרתה; see col. 17 in APPENDIX 9), and the second person masculine singular suffix, e.g. מלככה (see col. 18 in APPENDIX 9). *He* in final position for /e/ occurs in an unusual fashion also in חוטה in 1QIsa[a] 1:4 (MT חוטא) and קורה in 6:4 (MT קורא). *ʾAleph* denotes /a/ in final position: עליהא (34:11), בניהא (66:8), and even in medial position: יאתום (1:17), יאכה (30:31). See further below, 'consistency and statistical analysis' and the tabulations in APPENDIX 9.

π. *Morphological features*

The biblical and nonbiblical texts presenting the orthography of the Qumran scribal practice also reflect distinctive morphological features. For a description, see H. Yalon, *Studies in the Dead Sea Scrolls, Philological Essays (1949–1952)* (Heb.; Jerusalem 1967) 11–28; Kutscher, *Language;* M. H. Goshen-Gottstein, *Text and Language in Bible and Qumran* (Jerusalem/Tel Aviv 1960); S. Morag, "Qumran Hebrew: Some Typological Observations," *VT* 38 (1988) 148–64; and Qimron, *Hebrew.*

The following six features characterize this morphology, which has a tendency towards lengthened pronominal, verbal, and in one case, adverbial forms (for statistical details, see APPENDIX 9, cols. 1–10):[327]

> (1) Lengthened independent pronouns: הואה, היאה, אתמה, and המה (the latter form is also found in MT and SP, in MT more in the later than the earlier books): cols. 1–4.
>
> (2) Lengthened pronominal suffixes for the second and third persons plural in nouns and prepositions, e.g. מלכמה, בהמה, במה: cols. 5–6.
>
> (3) Forms of the *Qal* imperfect o *(w)yqtwlw* and *(w)tqtwlw* which serve in MT as pausal forms, but occur in these texts as free forms: col. 7.
>
> (4) Forms of the *Qal* imperfect o with pronominal suffixes construed as *yᵉquṭlenu (et sim.)* instead of *yiqtᵉlenu (et sim.)*: col. 8.
>
> (5) The form *qᵉṭaltemah* for the second person plural in all conjugations: col. 9.
>
> (6) Lengthened forms of מאד, viz., מואדה, מאודה, מודה: col. 10.

Some of these features may have been created by analogy with existing forms, while others may be dialectical. Certain forms are described as archaic by Kutscher, *Language,* 52, 434–40; Qimron, *Hebrew,* 57; F. M. Cross, Jr., "Some Notes on a Generation of Qumran Studies," in Trebolle–Vegas, *The Madrid Qumran Congress,* 1–14. The artificial nature of the lengthened forms was stressed by Fassberg (n. 327).

Consistency and statistical analysis. Scribes writing in the Qumran practice adhered to a general system, but there was much room for variation in individual features as becomes clear from a comparison of overlapping texts written in this scribal system, such as the manuscripts of 4QDibHam, 4QMMT, 4QM[a–f]//1QM, 4QIsa[c]//1QIsa[a], and 4QapocrJosh[b] (4Q379) 22 ii 7–15//4QTest (4Q175) 21–30. Furthermore, these divergences are clearly evident when comparing the segments written by scribes A and B of 1QIsa[a] and scribes A and C of 1QH[a], see ch. 1, TABLE 1 and APPENDIX 9 below.

The shared spellings which are used most consistently in all scrolls in this group are the *plene* writings (ה)זוהת/זואת/זאות (col. 11 in APPENDIX 9), מושה (col. 13), לוא (col. 14), כול (col. 15), and the long spelling of the second person singular suffix כה- in nouns and prepositions (col. 18); the most frequently used forms are the lengthened forms of the verb of the type *(w)tqtwlw* and *(w)yqtwlw* (col. 7) and of מאד (col. 10).

---

[327]See S. E. Fassberg, "The Preference for Lengthened Forms in Qumran Hebrew," in *Meghillot I, Studies in the Dead Sea Scrolls* (ed. M. Bar-Asher and D. Dimant; Heb. with Eng. summ.; Jerusalem 2003) 227–40.

Not all the idiosyncratic spellings and forms recorded in the other columns in APPENDIX 9 appear in all the texts. The combined group of features is probably best visible in the following biblical and nonbiblical texts: 4QNum^b, 1QDeut^a, 4QDeut^k2, 4QDeut^m, 4QSam^c, 1QIsa^a (especially scribe B), 2QJer, 4QXII^c, 4QPhyl A, B, J–K, L–N, 1QS, 1QSa, 1QM, 1QH^a scribe C, 4Qpap pIsa^c (4Q163), 4QFlor (4Q174), 4QM^a (4Q491), 11QMelch (11Q13), and 11QT^a (11Q19).

At the same time, some features are absent from some texts which otherwise display most of the idiosyncrasies of the Qumran scribal practice. Thus כיא used in most texts belonging to this group (col. 16), does not appear in 1QIsa^a (scribe A), 1QpHab, 1QH^a (scribe A, usually), 4QXII^c, the *tefillin*, most copies of D, 4QRP^c (4Q365), 11QPs^a, and 11QT^a (11Q19). By the same token, the following texts lack spellings of the type of מלכם and מלכמה (col. 5): 1QIsa^a (scribe A, usually), 1QS, 1QM, 1QH^a (both scribes), 1QpHab, most copies of D and ShirShabb, 4QRP^c (4Q365), and 11QPs^a. The lengthened forms הואה, היאה, אתמה are not found in 1QIsa^a (scribe A), 4QIsa^c, 1QpHab, 1QH^a scribe A, most copies of D, and 11QT^a (11Q19). There is no recognizable pattern for the distribution of the lack of these features in the various texts, neither regarding their content, scribes, or date, nor when combining these data with the distribution of scribal features such as cancellation dots (indicated in APPENDIX 9 by asterisks after the names of the compositions). These internal differences probably reflect varying personal preferences within a group of scribes, just as the divine names are not represented with paleo-Hebrew letters in all documents written according to the Qumran scribal practice (ch. 6, TABLES 1 and 2).

Orthographic and morphological corrections such as כיא (supralinear *'aleph*) in 1QH^a IV (Suk. = Puech XIII) 5 and הזואת (supralinear *waw*) in 11QT^a (11Q19) LX 15 show that the scribes followed a certain set of conventions which they sometimes forgot in the initial writing. Often, they subsequently corrected these oversights or later readers or scribes did so. For additional examples of this type, see ch. 5, TABLE 20 and the analysis preceding the table.

It is probably relevant to say that MT, in sharp contrast to the mentioned Qumran texts, does not reflect the features described here as characteristic of the Qumran scribal practice. None of the spellings recorded in cols. 11–16 occurs in MT, not even כול (with the exception of Jer 33:8), while לוא occurs only rarely.[328] Also the forms recorded in the other columns do not occur in MT, with the exception of *qtlth* (77 instances as opposed to *qtlt* in 1995 instances, the former not necessarily in the 'late' biblical books) and of המה which occurs with equal frequency to הם. However, eight sporadic 'typical Qumran' forms are encountered in all of MT: אתנה (Gen 31:6; Ezek 13:11, 20; 34:17), אליהמה (Ezek 40:16), זמתכנה (Ezek 23:48, 49), מהנה (Isa 34:17), השלכתהנה (Amos 4:3), ידכה (Exod 13:16), בשמכה (Jer 29:25). In whatever way these exceptions are explained, it cannot be said that MT reflects some of the special forms of the Qumran scribal practice. The fact that very few forms occur in MT or that one or two forms are shared with the oral tradition of SP (see above) does not render our statistics for the Qumran texts less meaningful. A similar argument pertains to the occurrence of 15 instances of cancellation dots in MT (ch. *5c10*).[329]

---

[328] I counted 19 occurrences in Jeremiah (compared with 480 occurrences of לא) as well as 14 cases elsewhere in the Bible. These figures do not include הלוא, which is the usual spelling of that word in MT, and a few instances of בלוא and ללוא.

[329] The fifteen instances of *puncta extraordinaria* in MT constitute a negligible minority in such a long text as MT, as opposed to their relative frequency in some of the Qumran texts.

APPENDIX 9 provides negative and positive data (in this order) concerning the orthographic and morphological features characterizing the Qumran scribal practice. The special forms are named positive, e.g. כיא, presented for each text in the second position, after the negative evidence, that is כי presented in the first position. An analysis of the positive and negative data for the individual features allows us to suggest that the texts included in the APPENDIX are probably written in the Qumran scribal practice. This table thus enables a distinction between these texts and the other Hebrew texts in the Qumran corpus. See also APPENDIX 1.

ρ. *Tefillin* (illustr. 9)

The distinction between the texts written in the Qumran scribal practice and texts imported to Qumran is supported by the data relating to the *tefillin* found in cave 4, already subdivided into two main groups by J. T. Milik in *DJD* VI. When reviewing the complete material, it is now evident that most of the *tefillin* from cave 4 written in the Qumran practice do not reflect the rabbinic instructions regarding their content, while the *tefillin* from cave 4 written in the MT-type orthography and morphology do reflect these instructions. These findings strengthen the views submitted here concerning the distinction between two types of documents presenting a different type of evidence, and they also shed new light on the understanding of the Qumran *tefillin*. It should be noted that in the past the Qumran *tefillin* were often wrongly taken as one homogeneous unit, so that some earlier analyses are necessarily imprecise.[330]

The main criterion for distinguishing between the two types of *tefillin* from cave 4 pertains to their content when compared with the list of sections to be included in the *tefillin* according to rabbinic sources: *b. Menaḥ.* 34a–37b, 42b–43b (especially 34b) and *Massekhet Tefillin* 9 (see Higger, *Minor Treatises*), namely, Exod 13:1-10, 13:11-16; Deut 6:4-9, 11:13-21.

The following *tefillin* from cave 4 reflect the Qumran scribal practice of orthography and morphology: A, B, J, K, L–N, O, P, Q, and probably also G and I. Most of these *tefillin* contain combinations of texts prescribed by the rabbis as well as additional texts, that is, sections from Deut 5:1–6:9 (the Decalogue and its continuation in 6:1-3, preceding the prescribed section, 6:4-9),[331] Deut 10:12–11:12 (the text immediately preceding the prescribed section 11:13-21), a section from the poem in Deuteronomy 32 (in 4QPhyl N only), and Exod 12:43-51 (the text immediately preceding the prescribed sections Exod 13:1-10, 11-16). Four *tefillin* contain only texts that were not prescribed by the rabbis (J–K, L, N). One should also note that while most *tefillin* contain more sections than those prescribed by the rabbis, others lack the prescribed sections. Thus, although the fragmentary status of the *tefillin* does not enable a full discussion of this issue, several *tefillin* lack Deut 6:4-9. Accordingly, the content of these *tefillin* would have made them unfit for use in rabbinic circles; they were probably used by the Qumran community which was not bound by the later rabbinic rules. In this context, it is relevant to quote the general discussion in *y. Ber.* 1.3c on the basis of which the inclusion of the Decalogue in the *tefillin* may, by extension, be ascribed to the *minim* ('sectarians', 'heretics'): 'The Decalogue should be read every day. Why does one not read it <now>? Because of the claim of the *minim*, that they will not say, "These only were given to Moses at Sinai".'

---

[330]J. T. Milik, *DJD* VI, often in pp. 35–8, but not in pp. 39, 47; Kuhn, *Phylakterien*, 24–31; S. Goren, "*Htpylyn mmdbr yhwdh l'wr hhlkh*," *Mḥnym* 62 (1962) 5–14; idem, *Twrt hmwʿdym* (Tel Aviv 1964). Goren attempted to show that the *tefillin* from Murabbaʿat were prepared in accordance with the *halakha*, and those of Qumran were not. It is now clear that some of the Qumran *tefillin* were closer to the *halakha* than others.

[331]According to *m. Tamid* 5.1, the Decalogue was recited daily along with Deut 6:4-9 and 11:13-21. See A. M. Habermann, "The Phylacteries in Antiquity," *ErIsr* 3 (1954) 174–6; H. Schneider, "Der Dekalog in den Phylakterien von Qumrân," *BZ* 3 (1959) 18–31, especially 20–5. According to *y. Ber.* 1.3c these texts were also recited outside the temple. Note further that the Nash papyrus of the 2nd century BCE contains the Decalogue together with Deut 6:4-9.

The great majority of the aforementioned texts bear most of the characteristics of the Qumran practice in spelling and morphology. The data for 4QPhyl A, B, J–K, M, and O seem conclusive, and for L, N, Q, G–I, P likely, although for the latter four insufficient data are available.

An examination of the Qumran *tefillin* of the MT-type supplements the aforementioned analysis with information from a different angle, and thus supports the conclusions reached in this section. Four of the Qumran *tefillin* do not reflect the Qumran practice of orthography and morphology, namely C, F, R, S, reflecting rather the practice found later in MT. Furthermore, although insufficient data are available for D–E, the few available words do not reflect any evidence of the Qumran practice (D, E, and F, however, belonged to the same *tefillin* [cf. J. T. Milik, *DJD* VI, 56], and the evidence of F may therefore be taken as also applying to D and E). All of these texts differ from the first group of *tefillin* in so far as their content is in agreement with the rabbinic prescriptions. Unlike the aforementioned *tefillin,* those not written in the Qumran scribal practice first present the Exodus texts, followed by the texts from Deuteronomy. These *tefillin* reflect the rabbinic prescriptions regarding their content.[332]

The *textual* character of the *tefillin* supports this conclusion. MT is reflected in the texts from cave 4 which are not written in the Qumran scribal practice: 4QPhyl C, F, R, S (the latter three are fragmentary), Mur 4, and Naḥal Ṣeʾelim A, B. On the other hand, the texts from cave 4 written in the Qumran practice often deviate from MT, both in pluses and minuses. Among other things, 4QPhyl A, B, J lack Deut 5:29-30, an issue discussed at length by Rofé.[333] Furthermore, E. Eshel has pointed out the harmonizing readings in 4QPhyl G, J, 8QPhyl, and XQPhyl 3.[334] Since the texts written in the Qumran practice are farther removed from MT than the texts not written in the Qumran practice, and since MT may be closely related to the temple circles (ch. *4j*), the assumed link between the texts not written in the Qumran practice and rabbinic Judaism is further underlined.

The distinction between the two groups of *tefillin* found in cave 4 can be further supported by a few scribal features. *Tefillin* written in the Qumran scribal practice do not conform to the later rabbinic prescriptions, while those not written in the Qumran practice do so rather closely. These prescriptions refer to the breaking up of words at the ends of lines, the squeezing in of letters at the ends of lines, and interlinear additions as a means of correcting (see ch. *7b*). Indeed, such interlinear additions are found in most *tefillin* written in the Qumran practice (their absence in some texts may be ascribed to the fragmentary status of their preservation). On the other hand, similar additions are not found in the other *tefillin*.

Two different systems are thus discernible with regard to the content, textual character, and scribal habits connected to the writing of the *tefillin* found in cave 4. Texts written in the Qumran practice and not reflecting the rabbinic prescriptions probably derived from the Qumranites themselves (thus already Milik).[335] Other texts from cave 4 not written in the Qumran practice do reflect the rabbinic regulations with regard to their content, though not with regard to the writing on only one side of the leather texts of the latter type probably derived from Pharisaic circles. It is not surprising to find *tefillin* of this type in the Bar Kochba caves (Mur 4, and Naḥal Ṣeʾelim A, B), since the biblical texts found there, as the medieval Masoretic texts, reflect the Pharisaic textual traditions, and ultimately those of the temple. If our distinction between the two different types of *tefillin* is correct, it is noteworthy that both types are found in cave 4. At the same time, the background of the *tefillin* from caves 1 and 8, and those of undetermined origin, is unclear.

---

[332]Two sub-systems are allowed in the Talmud (*b. Menaḥ.* 34b). One system, which has become known as 'Rashi's system,' follows the scriptural sequence for the last two sections (that is, Deut 6:4-9; 11:13-21 [thus 4QPhyl C]), while the system now known under the name of Rabbenu Tam reverses the order of these sections (thus Mur 4).

[333]A. Rofé, "Deuteronomy 5:28–6:1: Composition and Text in the Light of the Deuteronomic Style and Three Tefillin from Qumran (4Q128, 129, 137)," *Henoch* 7 (1985) 1–14 = *Tarbiz* 51 (1981–2) 177–84 (Heb.).

[334]E. Eshel, "4QDeutⁿ: A Text That Has Undergone Harmonistic Editing," *HUCA* 72 (1991) 117–54, especially 122–3.

[335]Goren, "*Htpylyn,*" and idem, *Twrt hmwʿdym,* 504, assigned *all* the *tefillin* found in cave 4 to the Essenes or Sadducees on the basis of their not following the rabbinic prescriptions with regard to content. On the other hand, Milik, *DJD* VI, 39, 53, 56, names Phyl C D-F (part of our group *2*) 'Pharisaic type,' but in general he does not consider the others to be sectarian, although on p. 47 he speaks of Essene *tefillin*. He assumes a certain development in the history of the *tefillin,* from *tefillin* containing long stretches of texts, named 'Essene' on p. 47, to a more limited choice of texts in the later ones as prescribed by the Talmud, named 'Pharisaic' on p. 47. In a way, the view proposed here thus further develops the suggestions by Milik.

σ. *Ruling with ink*

A very small number of the texts found at Qumran were ruled with (diluted) ink. The large number of copies of the Damascus Document and the Community Rule as well as other texts written according to the Qumran scribal practice should be noticed. For details, see ch. 4, TABLE 1.

τ. *Final handle sheets*

With one exception (11QpaleoLevᵃ), all of the Qumran texts preserving a final handle sheet (ch. *4g*) are sectarian and were written according to the Qumran scribal practice. Furthermore, the high frequency of texts from cave 11 in this group is striking.

υ. *Concluding remarks*

The data analyzed in this section point to the existence of a Qumran scribal group that copied almost all the works presumably authored by the Qumran community ('sectarian writings') and additional sundry texts, among them twenty-four biblical texts. Col. 6 in APPENDIX 1 lists 167 such texts (of which some forty present less convincing cases) written on leather and papyrus (a minority, eighteen texts).

Turning to the question of which texts have been copied according to the Qumran scribal practice, we find first and foremost sectarian texts (approximately 110 texts, not all with equally convincing evidence). No circular reasoning is involved in this determination, since the decision of whether or not to characterize a text as the Qumran scribal practice was based on the aforementioned criteria, and not on contents. The following non-sectarian texts were included as well: 25 biblical scrolls, eight *tefillin*, as well as some thirty other texts (see APPENDIX 1). These texts include compositions which were of immediate interest for the Qumran community, such as Jubilees and Ps-Jubilees (7 copies), the Temple Scroll (4 copies), and in addition a long list of compositions which have not been designated as sectarian. Some of these texts could be sectarian, but too little is known about them. They belong especially to the genres of rewritten Bible, *halakha*, and prayer: 4QWiles of the Wicked Woman (4Q184), 4QTobᵉ (4Q200), 4QTNaph (4Q215), 4QTime of Righteousness (4Q215a), 4QHalakha A (4Q251), 4QToh A (4Q274), 4QToh B (4Q277), 4QRPᵇ (4Q364), 4QRPᶜ (4Q365), 4QPrayer of Enosh (4Q369), 4QapocrMosᵃ (4Q375), 4QApocryphal Pentateuch B (4Q377), 4Qpap paraKings et al. (4Q382), 4Qpap apocrJer B? (4Q384), 4QRitPur A (4Q414), 4Qpara-Gen-Exod (4Q422), 4QPersonal Prayer (4Q443), 4QNarrative Work and Prayer (4Q460), 4QNarrative C (4Q462), 4QProphecy of Joshua (4Q522), 11QapocrPs (11Q11).

It is noteworthy that the great majority of the identifiable texts from *cave 11* reflects the Qumran scribal practice (11QPsᵃ⁻ᵈ, 11Q11–14, 16, 19, 20, 27; probably also 11QLevᵇ and 11Q30) or are sectarian (the nonbiblical texts included in the previous category as well as 11Q15, 11Q17, 11Q21, 11Q29).[336]

The appreciable number of ten Torah scrolls included among the biblical scrolls, proportionally more than from the other biblical books (for the details, see APPENDIX 1),

---

[336]The collection of texts found in this cave is more homogeneous regarding its contents than that of the other caves. This group was probably subject to better storage conditions than the contents of the other caves, as is suggested by the evidence regarding the final handle sheets (ch. *4g*). Alternatively, the scrolls found in cave 4 reflect a different manufacturing procedure from that of the other scrolls.

implies that the popularizing approach to the writing of biblical scrolls was applied also to the Torah.

The *dates* provided in the last column in APPENDIX 1 reveal that the texts belonging to this group were written in all periods, starting from the middle of the second century BCE. The oldest biblical text is 4QQoh[a] (175–150 BCE); the most recent such texts are 4QDeut[j] (*c.* 50 CE), 4QIsa[c] (30–68 CE), and 11QPs[d] (30–68 CE). Among the oldest nonbiblical texts are 4QDibHam[a] (4Q504; 150 BCE) and 4QT[b] (4Q524; 150–125 BCE). The text which has been assigned the latest date is 11QapocrPs (11Q11) (50–70 CE). Most texts, however, were dated to the period between 50 BCE and 25 CE. The second largest group is texts that were dated to the period between 100–25 BCE. Only a small group is dated to the middle of the first century CE. Since the texts written in this scribal practice also could have been written elsewhere in Palestine, texts predating the settlement at Qumran could still have been written by sectarian scribes.

(3) *A possible scribal school reflected in the proto-Masoretic manuscripts*

Scholars have often remarked on the close relation among the various manuscripts of the proto-Masoretic family.[337] This closeness definitely reflects a tight link among the members of this textual family at the content level of the scrolls, but it is unclear whether the scribal methods can be characterized by any criteria other than precision (usually), minimal scribal intervention (usually), and the appearance of a *de luxe* format, recognized especially in scrolls found at sites other than Qumran (ch. *4j*).

b. *Continuation of scribal traditions in documents inscribed in the square script*

It is natural that the documents found in the Judean Desert would continue scribal practices of earlier periods used for literary and documentary texts on papyrus and leather as well as for inscriptions on various types of material. Several details which the scribal traditions of the documents from the Judean Desert have in common with Aramaic documents of the fifth century BCE lead us to believe that the documents from the Judean Desert continue earlier writing traditions in the square script. Since the documents from the Judean Desert are several centuries more recent than these Aramaic documents, the recognition of common features is the more remarkable. While most of the common features are inherent in the writing itself, the more specific features include:

- Division into units (spacing in the line, at the end of the line, indentation), see ch. *5a*.
- Stichographic arrangement of poetical passages, see ch. *5b*.
- Writing of superscriptions similar to those of the Psalms, see ch. *5b*.
- Use of the *paragraphos*, see ch. *5c1*.
- Use of a specific sign in open and closed sections denoting a sense division, see ch. *5c1*.

c. *Possible influence from Greek scribal practices*

Contemporary Greek papyri, especially from Egypt, share several scribal features with the Hebrew and Aramaic texts found at Qumran (see below and SUBJECT INDEX, 'Greek texts'). Cross-influence is therefore possible in some details, although such influence is

---

[337]For my own analysis, see "The Text of the Hebrew/Aramaic and Greek Bible" (n. 168 above).

less likely if the same procedure is also evidenced in texts written in the square script that precede the earliest documents from the Judean Desert (see § b above).

· The marginal symbol X, explained in ch. *5c5* as drawing attention to a certain feature in the text.

· Several correction procedures in the scrolls from the Judean Desert resemble systems used in Greek sources: crossing out of letters or words with a horizontal line, *antisigma* and *sigma* (parenthesis signs), cancellation dots/strokes (see ch. *5c2* and cf. Turner, *Greek Manuscripts*, 16). The latter two systems are not known from earlier Semitic sources, and may have been transferred from Greek scribal practices.

· The box-like form of the parenthesis sign found in some Qumran texts (ch. *5c2iii*) is paralleled by the LXX manuscripts P.Berlin 17212 of Jeremiah 2–3 (3 CE) and P.Bodmer XXIV of Psalms 17–53, 55–118, hands A and B (3 CE).

On the other hand, the majority of the Alexandrian critical signs used in the editions of earlier literary texts have not been used in the Judean Desert texts: *asteriskos*, *obelos*, *diple* (with the possible exception of the 'fish hook shape *paragraphos*'), *diple obelismene* (with the exception of a doubtful instance in 4QCant[b] at the left edge of the last line of frg. 3 [fig. 12.6]), *keraunion*, *ancora* (with the possible exception of MasSir col. V top right margin above the beginning of the column [fig. 15]). See the analysis in *Paulys Real-Encyclopädie der Classischen Altertumswissenschaft* (ed. G. Wissowa and W. Krohl; Stuttgart 1922) 22.1916–27 ('Kritische Zeichen').

d. *Scribal practices mentioned in rabbinic sources*

Comparative study of the scribal practices reflected in the Judean Desert texts and of descriptions and prescriptions of such practices in rabbinic literature is helpful as long as it is recognized that the latter refer to the writing of religious texts at a later period, and in circles which only partially overlapped with those which produced the texts found in the Judean Desert. Thus, probably only the proto-Masoretic biblical texts and some *tefillin* and *mezuzot* (ch. *7c*) from the Judean Desert derived from the same or similar circles as those issuing the rabbinic prescriptions.

The instructions pertaining to the writing of religious texts are scattered in rabbinic literature, while some are combined in small compilations dealing with topics of various nature, such as *b. Menaḥ.* 29b–32b; *b. Meg.* passim; *b. Shabb.* 103a–105a; *b. B. Bat.* 13b–14b. See below and further SUBJECT INDEX, 'rabbinic literature' and INDEX I.4. The internally best-organized group of such instructions is found in *y. Meg.* 1.71b–72a and in the later compilation *Massekhet Soferim* (see ch. *2a*). The rabbinic instructions are greatly concerned also with various aspects of the sanctity and authority of the religious documents, issues which are not treated here.

The prescriptions in *y. Meg.* 1.71b–72a, which provide a good example of the topics treated in rabbinic literature, are presented in TABLE 1 in the sequence in which they appear in the text. The arrangement in *y. Meg.* follows principles of free association and memorizing of the dicta rather than any internal logic or sequence of scribal activity. The references in parenthesis refer to the page in this monograph where the prescription or analysis of *y. Meg.* is discussed.

TABLE 1: *Scribal Practices and Related Issues Discussed in* y. Meg. *1.71b–72a*

71b The script of the Torah (p. 247).
71c The Greek translation of the Torah.
71c The number of sheets of scrolls, *tefillin*, and *mezuzot* (p. 81).
71c Writing of supralinear letters is permitted in Torah scrolls, but not in *tefillin* and *mezuzot* (pp. 226, 228, 259).
71c Minimum length of lines determined as nine letters (p. 83).

71c Same script to be used for Torah scrolls, *tefillin,* and *mezuzot.*

71c Damaged letters are not permitted in sacred documents (p. 123).

71c Layout of writing in *mezuzot* (pp. 259–60).

71c Paragraphing in *tefillin* (p. 259).

71c Amount of permitted corrections per column (p. 256).

71d Shape of *tefillin.*

71d Space to be left unstitched at the top and bottom of the leather when sheets are stitched together (p. 37).

71d Biblical scrolls need to be written on leather (pp. 32, 254).

71d Ink should be used for writing (p. 53).

71d Ruling is performed with a reed (p. 58).

71d Patching is allowed (p. 124).

71d Stitching is performed with sinews (p. 38).

71d Amount of space to be left between lines, words, letters, and columns (pp. 103, 105, 133, 259).

71d Measurements of top and bottom margins (pp. 99, 253).

71d Amount of space between books (pp. 165).

71d Number of columns per sheet (p. 81).

71d On which side of the leather is the writing to be performed (p. 35)?

71d Use of bars for scrolls of the Torah and the method of rolling and storing scrolls (pp. 42, 118).

71d Medial and final letters (p. 234).

71d Changes made by the Greek translators of the Torah.

71d Writing and correcting of divine names, including prefixes and suffixes (pp. 241, 245).

72a Compound names which are not to be separated (n. 172).

Topics that are *not* covered in this collection are: script to be used, shapes of the letters and their sizes, dipping of ink, nature and use of scribal pens, instruments used for erasure, sizes of the hides, dimensions of the scribal block (size and number of lines), vertical ruling, preparation of the hides, length of scrolls, writing of the text vis-à-vis the lines, application of guide dots, marginal adherence, systems allowed for correcting (erasure, cancellation dots, parenthesis), detailed instructions for paragraphing, and layout of the Songs. Furthermore, there is no reference to details relating to the scroll used as the basis for the copying and the exact presentation of that text (letters, words, layout of the line, shape of the column, paragraphing, etc.), the number of books to be included in a scroll, and copying by more than one scribe. Several of these topics are covered by other instructions appearing elsewhere in rabbinic literature.

Many scribal practices reflected in the Qumran texts are thus covered by instructions or descriptions in the later rabbinic sources and, in these cases, one notices agreements and disagreements between the two corpora. Such a comparison is hampered by the internal variety within both the Qumran literature and the rabbinic sources. The comparison can be applied only to books to which the rabbinic rules could apply, namely Scripture, *tefillin,* and *mezuzot.*

a. *Agreements* with prescriptions of rabbinic literature

   • *Spaces* between the biblical books. See ch. *5a5.*

   • The *stichographic* arrangement of 1QDeut[b] and 4QpaleoDeut[r] follows the rabbinic rule for the writing of Deuteronomy 32. See ch. *5b.*

   • The great majority of the biblical scrolls written on leather are *ruled,* as prescribed by rabbinic sources, but so are the nonbiblical scrolls. See ch. *4a.*

   • *Bottom margins* are usually larger than top margins, as prescribed by *b. Menaḥ.* 30a, *y. Meg.* 1.71d, and *Sof.* 2.5. These conventions were followed in most biblical scrolls. See ch. 4, TABLE 19.

   • *Supralinear* additions were found in most biblical and nonbiblical scrolls, as permitted by *y. Meg.* 1.71c and *b. Menaḥ.* 30b. See ch. *5f.*

   • The *division* of the text into section units reflects in general terms the system prescribed by *b. Shabb.* 103b. See ch. *5a3.*

• Unstitched areas at the tops and bottoms of sheets (prescribed by *b. Meg.* 19b, *Sof.* 2.18) are found in a few texts: 4QNum[b] XV, 4QSapiential Work (4Q185), 11QT[a] (11Q19) (further research is needed in this area). See ch. *3c.*

b. *Disagreement* with rules prescribed by rabbinic literature, or rules not mentioned in that literature (rabbinic instructions pertain only to the writing of sacred texts):

• *Crossing out a word with a horizontal line.* This practice, also known from Greek sources and not mentioned in rabbinic literature, has been identified in six biblical texts, mainly non-Masoretic. See ch. 5, TABLE 16.

• *Stichographic* arrangement. Several Songs in the Torah are not written according to the rabbinic regulations, and various types of stichographic arrangement of the Psalms are not mentioned in rabbinic literature. See ch. *5b.*

• *Guide dots,* not mentioned in rabbinic literature, are found in many biblical texts. See ch. 4, TABLES 3 and 4.

• *Cancellation dots* are mentioned in rabbinic sources, but not as a correction procedure. This procedure was used in several biblical scrolls. See cf. *5f.*

• *Parenthesis signs,* not mentioned in rabbinic literature as a correction procedure, are found in some biblical texts. See ch. *5c2.*

• The writing of biblical texts on *papyrus* is forbidden according to *m. Meg.* 2.2 and *y. Meg.* 1.71d, while a few such papyri are known. See ch. *3a.*

• Against the prescription in *b. Menaḥ.* 31b, several *tears* in 1QIsa[a] were stitched up after the leather had been inscribed. See ch. *4i.*

• *Writing on attached patches,* disallowed by *Sof.* 2.17, but allowed by *y. Meg.* 1.71d, is found in 4QpaleoExod[m] col. VIII. See ch. *4i.*

• *Scribal markings* of several types are found in the margins of biblical and nonbiblical texts of different types (ch. *5c2*). Rabbinic literature does not explicitly forbid scribal marks, but probably they would be disallowed by the stringent copying laws. At the same time, a *small* number of such notations are found in MT (ch. 5c10).

• *Section markers* of different types found in several biblical scrolls are not mentioned in rabbinic literature. See ch. *5c1.*

• The writing of the Tetragrammaton and other divine names in the *paleo-Hebrew* script as recorded in ch. 6, TABLE 1 is not explicitly forbidden in rabbinic literature. Since the use of that script was forbidden for complete biblical texts, it can also be assumed that individual words written in that script would probably be disallowed. At the same time, the concept of the sanctity of the divine names, which is behind the writing in paleo-Hebrew characters, is in agreement with *y. Meg.* 1.71d (cf. *Sof.* 4.1–8).

• The *remodeling* of letters in 1QIsa[a] and in several sectarian texts is not mentioned in *Soferim* as a legitimate correcting procedure. See ch. *5f.*

• The writing of *nonfinal* letters in final position and final letters in nonfinal position, was not allowed according to *y. Meg.* 1.71d and other texts. See ch. *5g* and TABLE 20.

In the great majority of instances in the Qumran biblical texts in which a scribal custom can be identified as disagreeing with the rabbinic instructions, it reflects a text that for other reasons has been labeled non-Masoretic. It should be remembered that the largest identifiable group of biblical manuscripts from Qumran is proto-Masoretic (some 52% in the Torah and 44% in the rest of Scripture), so that discrepancies between rabbinic sources and specific scribal practices in the Qumran texts are to be expected.

APPENDIX 1

CHARACTERISTIC FEATURES
OF THE QUMRAN SCRIBAL PRACTICE

Positive and negative evidence pertaining to the documents found at Qumran and Masada

The appendix records all the relevant evidence regarding the scribal, orthographic, and morphological criteria, both positive and negative, which are mentioned elsewhere in this monograph as possible criteria for the recognition of the Qumran scribal practice. These criteria point to differences between the texts supposedly written in this scribal system and the other texts within the Qumran corpus. For each text for which a single criterion of this type is recognized, for example a scribal mark recorded in col. 3, all other criteria are recorded as well, with relevant positive and negative information.[338]

This appendix aims at exhaustiveness in three areas for which positive and negative evidence is recorded: specific scribal practices, certain orthographic and morphological features (listed in detail in APPENDIX 9), and the probability of authorship by the Qumran community ('sectarian character'). In other words, even if a given scribal practice occurs in a text that was probably not copied according to the assumed Qumran scribal practice, for example, an Aramaic text, it is nevertheless recorded. This is to enable the objective listing of all the available evidence for that scribal practice. By the same token, additional compositions, often very fragmentary, that are presumed to be sectarian, but which do not reflect positive evidence for a Qumran scribal practice are listed in § c below, in order to present as complete a picture as possible.

The absence of a remark in a column indicates that the composition does not evidence that feature, although it is recognized that the fragmentary condition of the texts enables only partial analysis. Thus the absence of scribal marks in a fragmentary text does not preclude their presence in the parts of the text that have not been preserved. For example, a notation of the presence ('gd') or absence ('no-gd') of guide dots/strokes is only relevant if the beginning or end of a sheet has been preserved.

The above description implies that the data which follow do not pertain to all the texts found at Qumran; e.g. 1QIsa^a is included, while 1QIsa^b is excluded, since it does not contain any positive information in cols. 1–6. Other information relating to that scroll is included in APPENDIX 8 ('Scribal features of biblical manuscripts').

This first appendix records the following types of data in seven columns for the biblical texts and nine columns for the nonbiblical texts:

1. *Section markers*	section markers except for spacing denoted as 'y[es]', including hyphens and apostrophe signs besides the *paragraphos* (ch. *5c1*)
2. *Correction systems*	
dots	cancellation dots/strokes (ch. 5, TABLES 10–14)
cross	crossing out of letters or words with a line (ch. 5, TABLE 16)

---

[338]The appendix does not record the data concerning the writing of final letters in nonfinal position and nonfinal letters in final position (see ch. *5g*) since they have not been recorded exhaustively.

| par | parenthesis sign(s) (ch. *5c2*) |
| par (box) | box-like parenthesis signs (ch. *5c2*) |

3. *Scribal markings*

gd	guide dots/strokes (ch. *4a*, TABLES 2 and 3)
no-gd	lack of guide dots/strokes (ch. *4a*, TABLE 6)
cr	single cryptic A letters written in the margin (ch. *5c3*)
pHeb	single paleo-Hebrew letters written in the margin (ch. *5c4*)
waw	paleo-Hebrew or square *waw* indicated in closed and open paragraphs (ch. *5c1*)
X	X-sign (ch. *5c5*)

4. *Divine names*

pal-Tetragr	paleo-Hebrew Tetragrammaton (ch. *6b*, TABLE 1)
pal-*el*	*ʾEl* in paleo-Hebrew characters (ch. *6b*, TABLE 1)
:	Tetragrammaton preceded by dicolon (ch. *5d*)
puncta	*Tetrapuncta* (dots/strokes; ch. *5d*, TABLE 19)

5. *Sectarian nature*   data on the presumed authorship by the Qumran community, recorded as 'y[es]', 'n[o]', or '—' (irrelevant in the case of biblical and Aramaic texts).[339] In several cases, this column has been left empty.

6. *Qumran scribal practice* (ch. *8a*). The data in this column (mainly referring to orthographic and morphological features) are based on the data recorded in APPENDIX 9. Texts like 1QPs[b], 1QpZeph (1Q15), 3QUnclassied frags. (3Q14), and 11QLev[b], that lack convincing data regarding their orthographic and morphological features but probably were copied according to the Qumran scribal practice (note the paleo-Hebrew Tetragrammata) are nevertheless not indicated as such. This procedure is followed in order to avoid circular reasoning.

7. *Scribal intervention*   number of scribal interventions (ch. *4j* and TABLE 27; ch. *7a*), listed only for the nonbiblical texts. Similar information for the biblical scrolls is provided in APPENDIX 8. The data listed are imprecise for papyrus texts as the scribes of those texts could correct the text by erasing letters with a sponge without leaving any trace.

8. *Average number of lines between scribal interventions*, listed only for the nonbiblical texts (ch. *4j* and TABLE 27; ch. *7a*). Similar information for the biblical scrolls is provided in APPENDIX 8.

9. (7.) *Assumed date*   paleographical date of the composition assigned in the official publication, usually *DJD*. The dates are culled from the

---

[339]This column records whether or not the composition is assumed to be sectarian (reflecting the terminology and ideas of the Qumran community) on the basis of its contents. This admittedly subjective judgment draws much on Dimant, "Qumran Manuscripts." The discussion was advanced much by the analyses of C. A. Newsom, "'Sectually Explicit' Literature from Qumran," in *The Hebrew Bible and its Interpreters* (ed. W. H. Propp et al.; Winona Lake, Ind. 1990) 167–87; A. Lange, "Kriterien essenischer Texte," *Qumran kontrovers*, 59–69; C. Hempel, "Kriterien zur Bestimmung 'essenischer Verfassenschaft'," ibid., 71–85. Additional presumed sectarian texts are included in § b and § c.

summary list by Webster, "Chronological Index." In this list the dates assigned in the editions are recorded as the middle point in the range suggested (e.g. a date like '*c*.10 BCE–30 CE' is recorded as 10 = 10 CE). Dates BCE are recorded as 'b' (e.g. 'b 112'), while dates CE are recorded without any prefix.

The data recorded in cols. 1–4, 7–8 of the nonbiblical texts (cols. 1–4, 7 of the biblical texts) are largely objective, while the information in cols. 5–6, 9 (cols. 5–7 of the biblical texts) is subjective. Names of compositions printed in boldface in the very first column were probably copied according to the Qumran scribal practice. Less certain examples are indicated with a question mark in col. 6. See further the above description of that column.

Name	Sect. Mar- kers	Correction Systems	Scribal Markings	Divine Names	Sectarian Nature	Qumran Scribal Practice	Date Assigned

a. BIBLICAL TEXTS AND *TEFILLIN*

Name	Sect. Markers	Correction Systems	Scribal Markings	Divine Names	Sectarian Nature	Qumran Scribal Practice	Date Assigned
1QDeut^a			gd		—	y	
1QIsa^a scribes A, B	y	dots cross	cr pHeb X *waw* no-gd	puncta (correc tor of MS)	—	y	b 112
1QPs^b				pal-Tetragr	—	no data	
2QExod^b				pal-Tetragr	—	y?	20
2QpaleoLev			gd		—	no data	
2QNum^b					—	y?	b 15
2QDeut^c			gd		—	y?	35
2QJer			no-gd		—	y	
3QLam				pal-Tetragr	—	no data	20
4QGen-Exod^a			gd		—	n	b 112
4QGen^k			gd?		—	n	15
4Q[Gen-]Exod^b					—	y	b 5
4QExod^c		dots			—	n	
4QExod^j				pal-Tetragr	—	y?	15
4QExod^k			cr		—		82
4QpaleoExod^m			gd *waw*		—	n?	b 62
4QLev^g				pal-Tetragr	—	no data	
4QLev-Num^a			gd		—	n	b 125
4QNum^b			gd *waw*		—	y	b 25
4QDeut^c		dots cross			—	n	b 125
4QDeut^j V–XII[340]		dots	no-gd		—	y	50
4QDeut^{k1}					—	y	b 15
4QDeut^{k2}				pal-Tetragr	—	y	b 15
4QDeut^m					—	y	b 25
4QDeutⁿ			gd		—	n?	b 15
4QDeut^o			gd		—	n	b 62

[340]The fragments of 4QDeut^j, published as a single scroll, should probably be separated into two entities since only cols. V–XII reflect the orthographic and morphological features of the Qumran scribal practice. Scribal dots are found only in that section (VIII 8 [Deut 11:10]). Since the script and column size are identical in both segments, possibly they were copied from different *Vorlagen*.

Appendix 1

Name	Sect. Markers	Correction Systems	Scribal Markings	Divine Names	Sectarian Nature	Qumran Scribal Practice	Date Assigned
4QSam^c		dots		puncta	—	y	b 87
4QIsa^a			gd		—	n	b 37
4QIsa^c			no-gd	pal-Tetragr	—	y	50
4QIsa^d		dots (Tetragr)			—	n	50
4QIsa^g			gd		—	n	b 25
4QIsa^h		dots			—	n	b 75
4QJer^a		dots par			—	n	b 200
4QJer^c		cross			—	n	b 15
4QJer^d			gd		—	n	b 175
4QXII^c		dots	gd		—	y	b 75
4QXII^e		dots			—	y	b 62
4QXII^g					—	y?	b 18
4QPs^b			*waw* gd		—	n	50
4QPs^f			gd		—	n	b 50
4QPs^h	y				—	n	20
4QPs^o					—	y?	b 15
4QPs^x		dots			—	no data	b 15
4QCant^b		par cross	cr pHeb		—	n	b 15
4QLam			no-gd		—	y	b 15
4QQoh^a		par			—	y	b 162
4QDan^a		cross			—	n	b 50
5QLam^a			*waw?*		—	no data	50
11QpaleoLev^a		par	*waw*		—	n	25
11QLev^b				pal-Tetragr	—	no data	
11QPs^a		dots (Tetragr)	no-gd	pal-Tetragr	y?	y	25
11QPs^b					—	y	b 15
11QPs^c					—	y?	25
11QPs^d					—	y?	50
4Q128 4QPhyl A					y?	y	
4Q129 4QPhyl B					y?	y	
4Q137 4QPhyl G–I					y?	y?	
4Q138 4QPhyl J–K					y?	y	
4Q139 4QPhyl L–N					y?	y	
4Q142 4QPhyl O					y?	y	
4Q143 4QPhyl P					y?	y	
4Q144 4QPhyl Q					y?	y	

b. NONBIBLICAL TEXTS

Name	Sect. Markers	Correction Systems	Scribal Markings	Divine Names	Sectarian Nature	Qumr. Scribal Practice	Scrib. Interventions	Aver. No. Ll. between Scr. Int.	Date Assigned
1Q14 1QpMic				pal-Tetragr	y	y			
1QpHab		dots	X no-gd	pal-Tetragr	y	y	16	11	25
1Q15 1QpZeph				pal-Tetragr	y	no data			
1Q20 1QapGen ar		dots	no-gd		—	n	8	17	20
1Q22 1QDM		dots				y?			b 62
1Q26 1QInstr					y?	y?			b 1
1Q27 1QMyst			gd	pal-Tetragr	y?	y			
1Q28 1QS	y	dots par	pHeb cr X *waw* no-gd	puncta	y	y	49	6	b 75
1Q28a 1QSa	y	dots	no-gd			y	y	5	10	b 75
1Q28b 1QSb		cross	no-gd			y	y	3	27	b 100
1Q33 1QM		dots par	no-gd			y	y	25	17	b 15
1Q34 1QH^a scribes A and B	y	dots	no-gd	pal-*el*	y	y	92	11	b 15
1Q35 1QH^b			no-gd	pal-Tetragr	y	y?			b 15
1Q36 1QHymns			gd		y	y			
2Q18 2QSir			gd		—	no data			b 25
3Q14 3QUnclassified Fragments				pal-Tetragr		no data			
4Q158 4QRP^a			gd			y	8	8	b 20
4Q159 4QOrdin					y	y	2	18	b 15
4Q160 4QVisSam						y	0	24	b 112
4Q161 4QpIsa^a				pal-Tetragr	y	y	0	54+	b 37
4Q163 4Qpap pIsa^c	y		cr? pHeb? *waw*	341	y	y	1	220	b 85
4Q165 4QpIsa^e					y	y?	0	33+	b 15
4Q166 4QpHos^a			gd		y	y?	0	33+	20
4Q171 4QpPs^a				pal-Tetragr	y	y	2	42	b 37
4Q173 4QpPs^{b}5			cr? pHeb?	pal-*el*	y	no data			b 15
4Q174 4QFlor					y	y	1	75	b 15
4Q175 4QTest	y		no-gd	puncta	y	y	9	3	b 100
4Q176 4QTanḥ	y	dots		puncta	y	y	10	16	b 90
4Q177 4QCatena A		dots	X no-gd		y	y	6	22	b 15
4Q179 apocrLam^a		dots cross				n	4	11	b 37
4Q180 AgesCreat A				pal-*el*	y	y			50
4Q181 AgesCreat B					y	y?			b 15
4Q183 4QMidr Eschat^e? = 4QpPs^a?				pal-*el* pal-Tetragr	y	no data			
4Q184 4QWiles						y?	0	17	b 37
4Q186 4QHorosc			pHeb no-gd		y	y			b 1
4Q196 4QpapTob^a ar			cr	puncta	—	—	7	20	b 50
4Q200 4QTobit^e		cross			—	y	4	16	b 5
4Q213 4QLevi^a ar			gd		—	—			b 37
4Q213a 4QLevi^b ar	y	cross	gd		—	—			b 62
4Q214 4QLevi^d ar			gd		—	—			b 62
4Q215 4QTestNapht			gd		—	y			b 5

[341]A large number of signs were written in the margin, either by the scribe or a subsequent user of the manuscript.

Name	Sect. Markers	Correction Systems	Scribal Markings	Divine Names	Sectarian Nature	Qumr. Scribal Practice	Scrib. Interventions	Aver. No. Ll. between Scr. Int.	Date Assigned
4Q215a 4QTimes		dots			y?	y			5
4Q219 4QJub^d						?	0	37	b 80
4Q221 4QJub^f		box	no-gd			y	2	35	b 37
4Q222 4QJub^g		dots box				y?	3	6	b 62
4Q223–224 papJub^h		dots?				y?	5	30	b 62
4Q225 4QpsJub^a		dots				y	5	9	b 5
4Q227 4QpsJub^c			gd			y			b 15
4Q248 4QHistText A				puncta		n			b 15
4Q251 4QHalakha A						y?	1	90	b 15
4Q252 ComGen A			X no-gd		y	n	4	15	b 15
4Q253a 4QComMal		dots				no data			b 37
4Q254 ComGen C					y	y		40	b 13
4Q256 4QS^b					y	y	3	20	b 15
4Q257 4QpapS^c					y	y	1	40	b 87
4Q258 4QS^d			no-gd	pal-Tetragr	y	n	3	28	b 15
4Q259 4QS^e		cr?			y	y	3	18	b 37
4Q260 4QS^f					y	y?	0	27+	b 15
4Q265 Misc Rules					y	y?	0	90+	
4Q266 4QD^a		dots cross par (box)	no-gd		y	y	52	10	b 75
4Q267 4QD^b			no-gd	pal-*el*	y	y	2	65	b 15
4Q268 4QD^c				pal-*el*	y	y	0	20+	15
4Q269 4QD^d			no-gd		y	y?	2	41	b 15
4Q271 4QD^f		dots	gd		y	y	3	21	b 40
4Q273 4QpapD^h					y	y?			b 15
4Q274 4QToh A		dots				y?	3	16	b 15
4Q277 4QToh B						y			b 15
4Q280 4QCurses					y	y?			b 50
4Q284a 4QHarvest		dots				no data			
4Q285 Sefer ha-Mil					y	y			b 15
4Q286 4QBer^a		dots	gd		y	y	5	22	50
4Q287 4QBer^b		dots	gd		y	y	1	50	50
4Q289 4QBer^d		dots			y	y?	1	13	35
4Q291 4QWork Cont. Prayers A		cross			y	no data			b 50
4Q292 4QWork Cont. Prayers B			gd		y	y			b 30
4Q298 4QcrA Words			cr no-gd		y	no data			b 25
4Q299 4QMyst^a					y?	y	5	84	35
4Q300 4QMyst^b		cross			y?	n	1	70	50
4Q301 4QMyst^c?		dots	cr		y	y	0	50+	50
4Q303 MedCrea A					y?	y?			b 25
4Q321a 4QCal Doc/Mish C		dots	gd		y	no data	2	17	b 75
4Q326 4QCal Doc C			gd		y	no data			b 37
4Q333 HistText E	y					no data			b 15
4Q364 4QRP^b		dots	gd	':'		y	6	53	b 26
4Q365 4QRP^c		dots cross	gd			y	31	9	b 26
4Q365a 4QT^a?		dots	gd		y?	y	7	9	b 26

4Q366 4QRP[d]			gd			n	0	49+	b 26
4Q367 4QRP[e]			gd			n	1	45	b 87
4Q369 Prayer Enosh		dots			y?	y			20
4Q375 apocrMos[a]					y?	y			b 37
4Q377 4QapocPent B						y	2	20	b 75
4Q379 4QapocJosh[b]		dots				n	7	25	b 100
4Q380 nonCan Ps A	y					n	2	16	b 87
4Q382 pap paraKings				puncta		y			b 75
4Q383 apocrJer A			gd			no data			
4Q384 pap apocrJer B?					y?				35
4Q391 pap psEzek[e]				puncta		no data			b 125
4Q393 4QCommConf		dots	no-gd		y	y			b 5
4Q394 4QMMT[a]			no-gd		y	y?	3	21	b 15
4Q396 4QMMT[c]		dots			y	y?	2	22	b 1
4Q397 4QMMT[d]		dots			y	y			b 5
4Q398 papMMT[e]				pHeb?	y	y?			b 25
4Q400 4QShirShabb[a]		dots			y	y?	2	45	b 62
4Q401 4QShirShabb[b]			no-gd		y	y	1	115	b 25
4Q402 4QShirShabb[c]					y	y	1	70	b 25
4Q403 4QShirShabb[d]		dots	no-gd		y	y	14	7	b 15
4Q405 4QShirShabb[f]		dots cross	gd		y	y	13	23	b 62
4Q406 4QShirShabb[g]				pal-*elohim*	y	no data			
4Q408 4QapocMos[c]?		dots			y?	n?			b 100
4Q410 4QVision Int		dots			y	y?			b 15
4Q413 4QDivProv				pal-*el*	y?	no data			20
4Q414 4QRitPur A	y		no-gd			y	0	105+	20
4Q415 4QInstr[a]		dots	no-gd		y?	y	4	30	b 15
4Q416 4QInstr[b]			no-gd		y?	y	4	34	b 37
4Q417 4QInstr[c]			X cr no-gd		y?	y	11	17	b 15
4Q418 4QInstr[d]		dots	pHeb gd		y?	y	30	30	b 30
4Q418a 4QInstr[e]					y?	y			b 25
4Q419 4QInstr-like Composition A					y?	y?			b 60
4Q420 4QWays[a]					y	y?			10
4Q421 4QWays[b]					y	y			25
4Q422 4QPara-Gen-Ex			gd			y			b 100
4Q423 4QInstr[g]					y?	y	3	28	20
4Q426 4QSap-Hym Work A	y	dots			y?	y?			112 b
4Q427 4QH[a]		dots			y	y	5	24	b 37
4Q428 4QH[b]	y	cross	no-gd		y	y	2	91	b 87
4Q429 4QH[c]					y	y?	0	52+	b 40
4Q432 4QpapH[f]					y	y?	1	65	b 15
4Q433a 4QpapH-like	y				y	no data			b 75
4Q434 4QBN[a]		dots	no-gd		y	n?	3	20	15
4Q435 4QBN[b]			no-gd		y	y?	0	25+	20
4Q436 4QBN[c]					y	y	3	6	10
4Q437 4QBN[d]					y	y	0	46+	20
4Q438 4QBN[e]		dots			y	y?			b 37
4Q440 4QH-like C		dots	no-gd		y	y			b 15

Name	Sect. Markers	Correction Systems	Scribal Markings	Divine Names	Sectarian Nature	Qumr. Scribal Practice	Scrib. Interventions	Aver. No. Ll. between Scr. Int.	Date Assigned
4Q440a 4QH-like D			no-gd		y?	no data			b 50
4Q441 4QInd Th A			gd		y?	no data			b 75
4Q443 4QPers Prayer		dots				y			b 87
4Q448 4QApocr Ps	y		no-gd			n			b 87
4Q458 4QNarr A			gd			no data			b 62
4Q460 4QNarr Work						y			b 37
4Q462 4QNarr C		dots cross	no-gd	puncta		y			b 37
4Q464 4QExpos Patr					y	y?			20
4Q468c 4QUnid Frgs.C, c			gd			no data			
4Q471 4QWarText B					y	y			20
4Q473 4QTwo Ways					y	y			b 15
4Q474 4QRachJos					y?	y			b 15
4Q477 4QRebukes	y		no-gd		y	y?			20
4Q479 4QDescDavid		dots				no data			b 62
4Q481e 4QNarr H		dots				no data			
4Q491 4QMᵃ	y	dots cross par			y	y	25	5	b 15
4Q496 4QpapMᶠ	y				y	y	3	35	b 55
4Q497 4QpapWar Scroll-like Text A					y	no data			b 50
4Q498 papSap/Hymns	y					no data			b 1
4Q500 4QpapBened					y?	no data			b 75
4Q501 4QapocrLam B		dots cross	no-gd		y	y	2	5	b 37
4Q502 4QpapRitMar	y				y	y	4	95	b 85
4Q503 4QpapPrQuot	y	cross			y	y	11	81	b 85
4Q504 4QpapDMᵃ	y	par cross	cr no-gd		y	y	34 [342]	9	b 150
4Q505 4QpapDMᵇ					y	y?			b 65
4Q506 4QpapDMᶜ					y	y			50
4Q509 4QpapPrFêtᶜ	y				y	y			b 65
4Q511 4QShirᵇ	y		cr? no-gd		y	y	4	125	b 1
4Q512 4QpapRitPur B	y				y	y	11	32	b 85
4Q513 4QOrdᵇ	y	dots cross par (b ox)			y	y	7	17	b 55
4Q514 4QOrdinancesᶜ		dots			y	no data	4 [343]	4	b 50
4Q520 4QpapUncl. frags.	y					no data			
4Q522 Proph Josh		dots				y?	1	78	b 47
4Q524 4QTᵇ				puncta	y?	y			b 137
4Q525 4QBeatitudes			no-gd		y?	y	4	66	b 25
4Q530 EnGiantsᵇ ar		cross			—	—	4	16	b 95
4Q532 EnGiantsᵈ ar	y				—	—	1	35	b 75
4Q533 EnGiantsᵉ ar		cross			—	—	1	20	b 75
4Q542 4QTQahat ar	y				—	—	15	2.5	b 112
4Q546 VisionAmᵈ ar			gd		—	—	0	92+	b 50

[342]Not all the signs indicated in the transcriptions are visible on the plates.
[343]Not all the signs indicated in the transcriptions are visible on the plates.

4Q547 VisionAm^e ar		gd	—	—	6	9	b 125
5Q13 5QRule			y	y?			50
6Q15 6QD		pal-*el*	y	no data			50
6Q18 6QpapHymn		pal-*el*	y	y			20
11Q11 11QapocPs		no-gd		y	0	86+	60
11Q12 11QJub + XQText A			y?	y			50
11Q13 11QMelch			y	y	0	70+	b 50
11Q14 11QSefer ha-Milhamah			y	y			40
11Q16 11QHymns^b			y	y[344]			
11Q19 11QT^a	dots	no-gd	y?	y	60	16	b 95
11Q20 11QT^b		X no-gd	y?	y	8	27	35
11Q27 11QUnid C				y?			
Mas 1h MasSir		gd	—	n	10	13	20
Mas 1k ShirShabb			y	y	2	20	50
Mas 1n MasUnid. Qumran-Type Frg.				y			b 138

c. ADDITIONAL SECTARIAN COMPOSITIONS

While the following sectarian compositions (recognized, along with others, by Dimant, "Qumran Manuscripts") reflect some of the criteria of the Qumran scribal practice, they are not included in § *b* due to lack of sufficient information on their system of orthography and morphology. The recording of the scribal, orthographic, and morphological features of these texts follows the pattern of APPENDIX 9. The details of the notation are explained in the introduction to that appendix.

	1 הוא / הואה	2 היא / היאה	3 אתם / אתמה	4 הם / המה	5 suff. 2d and 3rd p. pl. in nouns and verbs	6 suff. 2d and 3rd p. plur. in preps.	7 *yiqt*^{e}-*lu* / *tiqt*^{e}-*lu* / *yiqtolu* / *tiqtolu*	8 *yiqt*^{e}-*lenu* / *y*^{e}*qut-lenu*	9 *qetaltem* / *qetaltemah*	10 מאד / מאודה מאורה	11 זאת / הזאת / זואת / זות הזות מוארה מורה	12 כה / כוה	13 משה / מושה	14 לא / לוא	15 כל / כול	16 כי / כיא	17 *qatalta* / *qataltah*	18 suffix ך/כה- in nouns and prepositions	Sect. Nature
1Q16 1QpPs																			y
1Q29 Tongues Fire					0/1									0/3				0/2	y?
1Q30 Lit Text? A					1/0									0/1	1/0	0/1	1/0		y
1Q31 Lit Text? B						1/0								0/1					y
3Q4 3QpIsa																			y
3Q5 3QJub																0/1			y?
3Q6 3QHymn																			y
3Q9 Sectarian Text																0/1			y
4Q162 4QpIsa^b		1/0		2/0	2/0		1/0				1/0			3/0					y
4Q164 4QpIsa^d																			y
4Q167 4QpHos^b														0/1		0/1		0/1	y
4Q168 4QpMic?														1/0		1/0		0/1	y
4Q169 4QpNah	1/0	2/0		all/0	all/0	3/0	0/3							all/0	2/3	3/0		0/all	y

---

[344] See especially XQText B identified as part of the same manuscript in *DJD* XXXVI.

	1 הוא / הואה	2 היא / היאה	3 אתם / אתמה	4 הם / המה	5 suff. 2d and 3rd p. pl. in nouns and verbs	6 suff. 2d and 3rd p. plur. in preps.	7 yiqtᵉ-lu / tiqtᵉ-lu / yiq-tolu tiqtolu	8 yiqtᵉ-lenu / yᵉqut-lenu	9 qetal tem/ qetal temah	10 מאד / מאודה / מאורה מודה	11 זאת / הזאת / הזאות / הזואת זות הזות	12 כה / כוה	13 משה / מושה	14 לא / לוא	15 כל / כול	16 כי / כיא	17 qatal ta / qatal tah	18 suffix -כה/סה in nouns and prepositions	Sect. Nature
4Q172 4QpUnid		0/1			1/0										0/1				y
4Q182 4QCatena B																		0/1	y
4Q185 Sap Work	1/0		0/1		5/0	1/0								10/1	5/0	4/0			y
4Q255 4QpapSᵃ = v													0/1		0/3				y
4Q261 4QSᵍ	1/0						1/0						1/0						y
4Q262 4QSʰ														1/0	0/1				y
4Q263 4QSⁱ																			y
4Q264 4QSʲ	1/0						1/0								all/0	1/0	1/0	all/0	y
4Q270 4QDᵉ	4/0	2/0					4/0							all/0	7/1	all/0			y
4Q272 4QDᵍ	1/0	1/0												0/2	0/1				y
4Q290 4QBerᵉ															0/1	0/1			y
4Q304 4QMedCrea B																			y
4Q305 4QMedCrea C																			y?
4Q306 4QMen of People					1/0	1/0	1/0							1/0	2/0	1/0			y?
4Q317 4QcryptA Lunisolar Cal																			y
4Q320 4QCal Doc/Mish A																			y
4Q321 4QCal Doc/Mish B	0/2																		y
4Q322 4QMish A	1/0																		y?
4Q323 4QMish B																			y
4Q324 4QMish C	1/0																		y
4Q324a 4QMish D	1/0																		y
4Q324b 4QpapCal Doc A?																			y
4Q324c 4QMish E																			y
4Q325 4QCal Doc/Mish D																			y
4Q328 4QMish F																			y
4Q329 4QMish G																			y
4Q329a 4QMish H																			y
4Q330 4QMish I																			y
4Q337 4QCal Doc E?																			y
4Q371 4QNarr and Poet Comp						0/1									0/1				y
4Q390 4QapcrJer Cᵉ	2/0			1/0	4/0	6/3	0/2							4/0	2/2	1/0			y?
4Q392 4QWorks	1/0				1/0	1/0								0/1	3/0	1/1			y?
4Q399 4QMMTᶠ																		3/0	y
4Q404 4QShirShabbᵉ															0/all				y
4Q407 4QShirShabbʰ																			y
4Q409 4QLiturgical Work A															0/2				y

Manuscript																		
4Q412 4QSap-Didactic Work A						0/1								0/1			0/4	y
4Q418c 4QInstr[f]															1/0			y?
4Q424 4QInstruct-like Comp B	2/0												6/1	4/2	all/0		all/0	y?
4Q425 4QSap-Didactic Work B														0/3				y?
4Q430 4QH[d]					1/0										1/0			y
4Q431 4QH[e]													0/1					y
4Q434 4QBN[a]	1/0				all/0		all/0						all/0	2/2	3/1	0/2	all/1	y
4Q439 4QLament						1/0								0/3				y
4Q442 4QIndiv Thanksgiving B											0/1			0/1				y
4Q444 4QIncant													0/1					y
4Q457b Eschat H					1/1									0/2				y?
4Q461 4QNarr B					0/1	0/1												y
4Q463 4QNarr D					0/2	0/1												?
4Q464a 4QNarr E						0/1												?
4Q471a 4QPol Text			1/0						2/0				0/1			0/2		y
4Q471b 4QSelf-Glorifying Hymn													0/1		1/0			y?
4Q475 4QRenewEarth					0/1			0/1					0/3	0/4	0/1			y
4Q487 4QpapSapB?														0/1				y
4Q492 4QM[b]																	4/2	y
4Q493 4QM[c]					3/0	0/1							0/1	0/2				y
4Q494 4QM[d]																		y
4Q495 4QM[e]														0/1		0/3	0/1	y
4Q498 4QpapSap/Hy															1/2			?
4Q499 4QpapHy/Pra															0/2	0/2		y?
4Q500 4QpapBened																	0/all	y?
4Q507 4QPrFêtes[b]																		y
4Q508 4QpapPr Fêtes[b]													0/1	0/1	2/0	0/2	0/2	y
4Q510 4QShir[a]													0/1	0/5				y
5Q10 5QapocrMal (5QpMal?)															0/1			y?
5Q11 5QS																	0/3	y
5Q12 5QD													0/1	0/1				y
6Q9 6Qpap apocrSamKgs			1/0		1/0		1/0							3/0				y?
6Q12 6Qapocr Proph	0/1																	y
11Q15 11QHymns[a]														0/1		0/1	0/2	?
11Q17 11QShir Shabb						1/0							0/1	0/12				y?
11Q29 11QFrg Related to S																		y?

d. ADDITIONAL INFORMATION ABOUT SCRIBAL INTERVENTION

The following list contains data concerning scribal intervention not included in the above charts (see ch. *4j* and *7a*).

Name	Scribal Interventions	Average No. of Lines
4Q185 4QSapiential Work	2	27
4Q197 4QTob[b] ar	2	37
4Q368 4QapocrPent. A	1	62
4Q370 4QAdmonition Based on the Flood	2	14
4Q372 4QNarrative and Poetic Composition	0	125+
4Q378 4QapocrJosh[a]	0	145+
4Q381 4QNon-Canonical Psalms B	10	33
4Q385 4QpsEzek[a]	1	48
4Q385a 4QapocrJer C[a]	1	141
4Q387 4QapocrJer C[f]	2	39
4Q389 4QapocrJer C[d]	0	48+
4Q390 4QapocrJer C[e]	1	46
4Q521 4QMessianic Apocalypse	3	90
4Q531 4QEnGiants[c] ar	5	34
4Q534 4QBirth of Noah[a] ar	1	47
4Q537 4QTJacob? ar	0	52+
4Q541 4QapocrLevi[b]? ar	3	35
11Q10 11QtgJob	23	13

APPENDIX 2

PAPYRUS TEXTS FROM THE JUDEAN DESERT

This appendix lists all the papyrus texts in Hebrew, Aramaic, Greek, and Latin found in the Judean Desert.[345] They are arranged according to find-site, beginning with the most northerly location. (Due to the fragmentary state of the material, several inventory numbers, such as 1Q69, refer to an undetermined number of texts.

boldface (e.g. 4Q163) = sectarian text, as recorded in APPENDIX 1, including cases in which the sectarian nature is questionable. The determining of the sectarian character usually follows Dimant, "Qumran Manuscripts."

a. *Non-documentary Papyrus Texts*

Text No.	Name	Reverse Side of Opistho-graph	Secta-rian Work	Qumran Scribal Practice
1Q69	1QpapUnclassified frags.			no data
1Q70	1QpapUnclassified frags.	r + v		no data
1Q70bis	1QpapUnclassified frags.			no data
4Q51a	4QpapUnclassified frags.			no data
4Q69	4QpapIsa^p		—	no data
4Q120	4QpapLXXLev^b		—	—
4Q127	4Qpap paraExod gr		—	—
4Q163	4Qpap pIsa^c (cf. also 4Q515)		y	y
4Q196	4QpapTob^a ar		—	—
4Q217	4QpapJub^b?			no data
4Q223–224	4QpapJub^h		y?	y?
4Q249	4Qpap cryptA Midrash Sefer Moshe		y	no data
4Q249a	4Qpap cryptA Serekh ha-ʿEdah^a		y	no data
4Q249b	4Qpap cryptA Serekh ha-ʿEdah^b		y	no data
4Q249c	4Qpap cryptA Serekh ha-ʿEdah^c		y	no data
4Q249d	4Qpap cryptA Serekh ha-ʿEdah^d		y	no data
4Q249e	4Qpap cryptA Serekh ha-ʿEdah^e		y	no data
4Q249f	4Qpap cryptA Serekh ha-ʿEdah^f		y	no data
4Q249g	4Qpap cryptA Serekh ha-ʿEdah^g		y	no data
4Q249h	4Qpap cryptA Serekh ha-ʿEdah^h		y	no data
4Q249i	4Qpap cryptA Serekh ha-ʿEdah^i		y	no data
4Q249j	4Qpap cryptA Lev^h?		y?	no data
4Q249k	4Qpap cryptA Text Quoting Leviticus A		y?	no data
4Q249l	4Qpap cryptA Text Quoting Leviticus B		y?	no data
4Q249m	4Qpap cryptA Hodayot-like Text E		y?	no data
4Q249n	4Qpap cryptA Liturgical Work E?		y?	no data
4Q249o	4Qpap cryptA Liturgical Work F?		y?	no data

---

[345]The list includes papyri found at Wadi Daliyeh. A similar list is presented in E. Tov, *DJD* XXXIX, 203–11.

Text No.	Name	Reverse Side of Opistho- graph	Secta- rian Work	Qumran Scribal Practice
4Q249p	4Qpap cryptA Prophecy?		y?	no data
4Q249q	4Qpap cryptA Fragment Ment. Planting		y?	no data
4Q249r	4Qpap cryptA Unidentified Text A		y?	no data
4Q249s	4Qpap cryptA Unidentified Text B		y?	no data
4Q249t	4Qpap cryptA Unidentified Text C		y?	no data
4Q249u	4Qpap cryptA Unidentified Text D		y?	no data
4Q249v	4Qpap cryptA Unidentified Text E		y?	no data
4Q249w	4Qpap cryptA Unidentified Text F		y?	no data
4Q249x	4Qpap cryptA Unidentified Text G		y?	no data
4Q249y	4Qpap cryptA Unidentified Text H		y?	no data
4Q249z	4Qpap cryptA Miscellaneous Texts A		y?	no data
4Q250	4Qpap cryptA Text Conc. Cultic Service A		y?	no data
4Q250a	4Qpap cryptA Text Conc. Cultic Service B?	r + v	y?	no data
4Q250b	4Qpap cryptA Text Related to Isaiah 11	r + v	y?	no data
4Q250c	4Qpap cryptA Unidentified Text I = r	4Q250d	y?	no data
4Q250d	4Qpap cryptA Unidentified Text J = v	4Q250c	y?	no data
4Q250e	4Qpap cryptA Unidentified Text K = r	4Q250f	y?	no data
4Q250f	4Qpap cryptA Unidentified Text L = v	4Q250e	y?	no data
4Q250g	4Qpap cryptA Unidentified Text M	r + v	y?	no data
4Q250h	4Qpap cryptA Unidentified Text N	r + v	y?	no data
4Q250i	4Qpap cryptA Unidentified Text O	r + v	y?	no data
4Q250j	4Qpap cryptA Miscellaneous Texts B	r + v	y?	no data
4Q255	4QpapS^a = v	4Q433a	y	no data
4Q257	4QpapS^c		y	y
4Q273	4QpapD^h		y	y?
4Q302	4QpapAdmonitory Parable		y	no data
4Q324b	4QpapCal Doc A?		y	no data
4Q331	4QpapHistorical Text C			no data
4Q362	4QcryptB papUnidentified Text A			no data
4Q363	4QcryptB papUnidentified Text B			no data
4Q382	4Qpap paraKings et al.			y
4Q384	4Qpap apocrJer B?			y?
4Q391	4Qpap psEzek^e			no data
4Q398	4QpapMMT^e		y	y?
4Q432	4QpapH^f		y	y?
4Q433a	4QpapHodayot-like Text B = r	4Q255	y	no data
4Q465	4QpapText Mentioning Samson?			no data
4Q468j	4QpapUnclassified frags.			no data
4Q478	4QpapFragment Mentioning Festivals			no data
4Q482	4QpapJub^i?			no data
4Q483	4QpapGen^o or papJub^j		—	no data
4Q484	4QpapTJud? (4QpapJub^k?)			no data
4Q485	4QpapProphetical/Sapiential Text			no data
4Q486	4QpapSap A?			no data
4Q487	4QpapSap B?			no data
4Q488	4QpapApocryphon ar		—	—
4Q489	4QpapApocalypse? ar		—	—
4Q490	4QpapFragments ar		—	—

4Q496	4QpapMᶠ = v	4Q505, 4Q509	y	y
4Q497	4QpapWar Scroll-like Text A = v	4Q499	y	no data
4Q498	4QpapSap/Hymn			no data
4Q499	4QpapHymns/Prayers = r	4Q497	y?	no data
4Q500	4QpapBened		y?	no data
4Q502	4QpapRitMar		y	y
4Q503	4QpapPrQuot = r	4Q512	y	y
4Q505	4QpapDibHamᵇ = r	4Q496, 4Q506	y	y?
4Q506	4QpapDibHamᶜ = v	4Q496, 4Q505	y	y
4Q509	4QpapPrFêtesᶜ = r	4Q496	y	y
4Q512	4QpapRitPur B = v	4Q503	y	y
4Q515	4QpapUnclassified frags. (cf. 4Q163)			no data
4Q516	4QpapUnclassified frags.			no data
4Q517	4QpapUnclassified frags.			no data
4Q518	4QpapUnclassified frags. = r	4Q519		no data
4Q519	4QpapUnclassified frags. = v	4Q518		no data
4Q520	4QpapUnclassified frags. = v			no data
4Q558	4QpapVisionᵇ ar		—	—
4Q559	4QpapBibChronology ar		—	—
6Q3	6QpapDeut?		—	no data
6Q4	6QpapKgs		—	no
6Q5	6QpapPs?		—	no data
6Q7	6QpapDan		—	no
6Q8	6QpapGiants ar		—	—
6Q9	6Qpap apocrSam-Kgs			no data
6Q10	6QpapProphecy			no
6Q16	6QpapBened		y?	no data
6Q17	6QpapCal Doc		y?	no data
6Q18	6QpapHymn		y	y
6Q22	6QpapUnclassified frags.		y?	no data
6Q23	6QpapUnclassified frags. ar (Words of Michael?)		—	—
6Q24	6QpapUnclassified frags.			no data
6Q25	6QpapUnclassified frags.			no data
6Q27	6QpapCursive Unclassified frags.			no data
6Q28	6QpapCursive Unclassified frags.			no data
6Q30	6QpapCursive Unclassified frags.			no data
6Q31	6QpapUnclassified frags.			no data
6QX1	6QpapUnclassified frags.			no data
7Q1	7QpapLXXExod		—	—
7Q2	7QpapEpJer gr		—	—
7Q3	7QpapBiblical text? gr		—	—
7Q4	7QpapBiblical text? gr		—	—
7Q5	7QpapBiblical text? gr		—	—
7Q6	7QpapUnclassified frags. gr		—	—
7Q7	7QpapUnclassified frags. gr		—	—
7Q8	7QpapUnclassified frags. gr (papEn gr?)		—	—
7Q9	7QpapUnclassified frags. gr		—	—
7Q10	7QpapUnclassified frags. gr		—	—
7Q11	7QpapUnclassified frags. gr (papEn gr?)		—	—
7Q12	7QpapUnclassified frags. gr (papEn gr?)		—	—
7Q13	7QpapUnclassified frags. gr (papEn gr?)		—	—

Text No.	Name	Reverse Side of Opistho-graph	Secta-rian Work	Qumran Scribal Practice
7Q14	7QpapUnclassified frags. gr (papEn gr?)		—	—
7Q15	7QpapUnclassified frags. gr		—	—
7Q16	7QpapUnclassified frags. gr		—	—
7Q17	7QpapUnclassified frags. gr		—	—
7Q18	7QpapUnclassified frags. gr		—	—
7Q19	7QpapImprint gr		—	—
9Q1	9QpapUnclassified frag.		—	—
11Q28	11QpapUnidentified Text D			no data

Text No.	Name			
Mur 108	Mur papPhilosophical Text gr		—	—
Mur 109	Mur papLiterary Text gr		—	—
Mur 110	Mur papLiterary Text gr		—	—
Mur 111	Mur papLiterary Text gr		—	—
Mur 112	Mur papLiterary Text gr		—	—

Text No.	Name	Reverse Side		
Mas 1o r	pap paleoText of Sam. Origin = r	Mas 1o v		no data
Mas 1o v	pap paleoUnidentified Text = v	Mas 1o r		no data
Mas 721 r	Mas papVirgil lat	Mas 721 r	—	—
Mas 721 v	Mas papUnidentified Poetic Text lat	Mas 721 v	—	—
Mas 739	Mas papLiterary Text? gr		—	—

b. *Documentary Papyrus Texts*

Text No.	Name
WDSP 1–36	*See DJD* XXVIII

Text No.	Name
Jer 1	Jer papList of Loans ar
Jer 2	Jer papDeed of Sale or Lease ar
Jer 3	Jer papDeed of Sale ar
Jer 4	Jer papDeed of Sale or Lease? gr
Jer 5a–d	Jer papUnidentified Text(s) gr
Jer 5e	Jer papTransaction Concerning Seeds gr
Jer 6	Jer papUnidentified Text
Jer 7	Jer papSale of Date Crop ar
Jer 8	Jer papDeed A ar
Jer 9	Jer papDeed A heb?
Jer 10	Jer papDeed B heb?
Jer 11	Jer papDeed or Letter
Jer 12	Jer papDeed B ar
Jer 13	Jer papUnclassified Text ar
Jer 14	Jer papUnclassified Text heb?
Jer 15	Jer papUnclassified Fragments B ar/heb
Jer 16	Jer papText Mentioning the Emperor Hadrian gr
Jer 17	Jer papDeed? gr
Jer 18	Jer papFiscal Acknowledgement gr
Jer 19	Jer papWritten Order? gr
Jer 19a	Jer papUnidentified Text A gr

Jer 19b	Jer papList of Witnesses? gr
Jer 19c–h	Jer papUnidentified Texts B gr

4Q344	4QDebt Acknowledgement ar
4Q345	4QDeed A ar or heb (r + v)
4Q346	4QDeed of Sale ar
4Q347	4QpapDeed F ar (part of XHev/Se 32)
4Q348	4QDeed B heb? (r + v)
4Q351	4QAccount of Cereal A ar
4Q352	4QpapAccount of Cereal B ar or heb
4Q352a	4QpapAccount A ar or heb
4Q353	4QpapAccount of Cereal or Liquid ar or heb
4Q354	4QAccount B ar or heb
4Q355	4QAccount C ar or heb (= verso of 4Q324)
4Q356	4QAccount D ar or heb
4Q357	4QAccount E ar or heb
4Q358	4QpapAccount F? ar or heb
4Q359	4QpapDeed C? ar or heb
4Q360a	4QpapUnidentified Fragments B ar
4Q361	4QpapUnidentified Fragment gr
6Q26	6QpapAccount or Contract
6Q29	6QpapCursive Unclassified frag.

Nar 1	Nar papUnidentified Text A gr
Nar 2	Nar papUnidentified Text heb/ar
Nar 3	NarUnidentified Text B gr
Nar 4	Nar papUnclassified Fragments

Ghweir? 1	Ghweir? papCursive Fragment gr

Mur 17A–B	*See DJD* II and XXXIX, section B
Mur 18–71	*See DJD* II and XXXIX, B
Mur 113–155	*See DJD* II and XXXIX, B

Sdeir 2	Sdeir papPromissory Note? ar

5/6Hev 1–32a	*See DJD* XXXIX, B
5/6Hev 34–39	*See DJD* XXXIX, B
5/6Hev 42–47a,b	*See DJD* XXXIX, B
5/6Hev 49–53	*See DJD* XXXIX, B
5/6Hev 55–64	*See DJD* XXXIX, B
8Hev 3	8Hev papFragments
8Hev 4	8Hev papUnidentified Text gr
6Hev/Se 8–19	*See DJD* XXXIX, B
6Hev/Se 21–48	*See DJD* XXXIX, B
6Hev/Se 50–51	*See DJD* XXXIX, B
6Hev/Se 60–169	*See DJD* XXXIX, B
6Hev/Se Nab. 2–6	*See DJD* XXXIX, B
X6Hev/Se? 1–57	*See DJD* XXXIX, B

34Se 3	34Se papDeed ar
34Se 4	34Se papCensus List from Judaea or Arabia gr

Text No.	Name
34Ṣe 5	34Ṣe papAccount gr

1Mish 1	1Mish papOfficial Document
1Mish 2	1Mish papList of Names and Account gr = r
1Mish 3	1Mish papPromissory Note?

Mas 721–737	Latin texts: *see Masada II*
Mas 740	Mas papUnidentified Text gr
Mas 741	Mas papLetter of Abakantos to Judas gr
Mas 742	Mas papByzantine Document gr
Mas 744	Mas papList of Names? gr
Mas 745	Mas papLetter gr
Mas 746	Mas papLetter(s) gr
Mas 747	Mas papUnidentified Text gr
Mas 748	Mas papBilingual List of Names lat + gr
Mas 749	Mas papUnidentified Frags. lat and gr

APPENDIX 3

OPISTHOGRAPHS FROM THE JUDEAN DESERT

The following documents (mainly non-literary papyri) in Hebrew, Aramaic, Greek, Latin, (and Nabatean-Aramaic from Wadi Daliyeh, Qumran, Naḥal Ḥever/Seiyal, and Masada (listed from north to south) are inscribed on both sides (see the analysis in ch. 4b).

	Text No.	Title	Sectarian Nature	Qumran Practice
recto	WDSP 11	WDSP papDeed of Slave Sale J? ar	—	—
verso	WDSP 11	WDSP papDeed of Cession? ar	—	—
recto	WDSP 13	WDSP papPledge of Slave C? ar	—	—
verso	WDSP 13	WDSP papRelease of Pledged Slave? ar	—	—
recto	WDSP 23	WDSP papDeed A? ar	—	—
verso	WDSP 23	WDSP papDeed B? ar	—	—
recto	WDSP 28	WDSP papMiscellaneous Fragments A ar	—	—
verso	WDSP 28	WDSP papMiscellaneous Fragments B ar	—	—
recto	WDSP 29	WDSP papMiscellaneous Fragments C ar	—	—
verso	WDSP 29	WDSP papMiscellaneous Fragments D ar	—	—
recto	WDSP 30	WDSP papMiscellaneous Fragments E ar	—	—
verso	WDSP 30	WDSP papMiscellaneous Fragments F ar	—	—
recto	WDSP 33	WDSP papMiscellaneous Fragments I ar	—	—
recto	WDSP 33	WDSP papMiscellaneous Fragments I ar	—	—
recto	WDSP 34	WDSP papMiscellaneous Fragments K ar	—	—
recto	WDSP 34	WDSP papMiscellaneous Fragments K ar	—	—
recto	WDSP 35	WDSP papMiscellaneous Fragments H ar	—	—
verso	WDSP 35	WDSP papMiscellaneous Fragments I ar	—	—
recto	1Q70	1QpapUnclassified frags.		no data
verso	1Q70	1QpapUnclassified frags.		no data
recto	4Q201	4QEnᵃ ar	—	
verso	4Q338	4QGenealogical List?		no data
recto	4Q250a	4Qpap cryptA Text Conc. Cultic Service B?	y?	no data
verso	4Q250a	4Qpap cryptA Text Conc. Cultic Service B?	y?	no data
recto	4Q250b	4Qpap cryptA Text Related to Isa 11	y?	no data
verso	4Q250b	4Qpap cryptA Text Related to Isa 11	y?	no data
recto	4Q250c	4Qpap cryptA Unidentified Text I	y?	no data
verso	4Q250d	4Qpap cryptA Unidentified Text J	y?	no data

	Text No.	Title	Sectarian Nature	Qumran Practice
recto	4Q250e	4Qpap cryptA Unidentified Text K	y?	no data
verso	4Q250f	4Qpap cryptA Unidentified Text L	y?	no data
recto	4Q250g	4Qpap cryptA Unidentified Text M	y?	no data
verso	4Q250g	4Qpap cryptA Unidentified Text M	y?	no data
recto	4Q250h	4Qpap cryptA Unidentified Text N	y?	no data
verso	4Q250h	4Qpap cryptA Unidentified Text N	y?	no data
recto	4Q250i	4Qpap cryptA Unidentified Text O	y?	no data
verso	4Q250i	4Qpap cryptA Unidentified Text O	y?	no data
recto	4Q250j	4Qpap cryptA Miscellaneous Texts B	y?	no data
verso	4Q250j	4Qpap cryptA Miscellaneous Texts B	y?	no data
recto	4Q324	4QMish C	y	no data
verso	4Q355	4QAccount C ar or heb	—	—
recto	4Q342	4QLetter? ar	—	—
verso	4Q342	4QLetter? ar	—	—
recto	4Q343	4QLetter nab	—	—
verso	4Q343	4QLetter nab	—	—
recto	4Q415	4QInstr[a]	y?	y
verso	4Q414	4QRitPur A	no data	y
recto	4Q433a	4QpapHodayot-like Text B	y?	no data
verso	4Q255	4QpapS[a]	y	no data
recto	4Q460 frg. 9	4QNarrative Work and Prayer [*in Hebrew*]		y
verso	4Q350	4QAccount gr	—	—
recto	4Q499	4QpapHyms/Prayers	y	y?
verso	4Q497	4QpapWar Scroll-like Text A	y	no data
recto	4Q503	4QpapPrQuot	y	y
verso	4Q512	4QpapRitPur B	y	y
recto	4Q505	4QpapDibHam[b]	y	y?
verso	4Q496	4QpapM[f]	y	y
	4Q506	4QpapDibHam[c]	y	y
recto	4Q509	4QpapPrFêtes[c]		y
verso	4Q496	4QpapM[f]	y	y
	4Q506	4QpapDibHam[c]	y	y
recto	4Q518	4QpapUnclassified frags.		—
verso	4Q519	4QpapUnclassified frags.		—
recto	XḤev/Se 7	XḤev/SeDeed of Sale A ar	—	—
verso	XḤev/Se 7	XḤev/SeDeed of Sale A ar	—	—
recto	Mas 1o	Mas pap paleoText of Sam. Origin		—
verso	Mas 1o	Mas pap paleoUnid. Text		—
recto	Mas 721	Mas papVirgil lat	—	—
verso	Mas 721	Mas papUnidentified Poetic Text lat	—	—

	Text No.	Title	Sectarian Nature	Qumran Practice
recto	Mas 724	Mas papLetter to Iulius Lupus lat	—	—
verso	Mas 724	Mas papLetter to Iulius Lupus lat	—	—
recto	Mas 731	Mas papMilitary Document? lat	—	—
verso	Mas 731	Mas papMilitary Document? lat	—	—

APPENDIX 4

THE GREEK TEXTS FROM THE JUDEAN DESERT[346]

The Greek texts from the Judean Desert constitute merely a small percentage of the texts found in the area; the best known are Hebrew and Aramaic texts, especially those found at Qumran. However, the Greek texts are by no means negligible, since at several sites their number equals that of the Hebrew/Aramaic texts, and at one site they even constitute the majority. Thus, while the overall number of Greek texts found at Qumran may be negligible, this is not the case for cave 7 where all 19 items constitute Greek papyri. This cave thus witnesses activity in the Greek language; it is all of a literary nature, since probably all the fragments found in this cave are non-documentary.

Turning now to absolute numbers of texts, a word of caution is in order. While acknowledging that we can only refer to the numbers of texts that have survived, it should be recognized that there is no reason to assume that a larger or smaller percentage of Greek texts perished than documents in other languages. Comparative statistics of the various extant texts should therefore be considered legitimate. The majority of the texts found in the Judean Desert are Semitic, with Hebrew being the predominant language, but with the presence also of Aramaic. The Qumran corpus consists of remnants of some 930 compositions. Of these, some 150 are in Aramaic (including 17 Nabatean-Aramaic texts), 27 in Greek, and the remainder are in Hebrew (including texts written in one of the Cryptic scripts and in paleo-Hebrew). The Greek texts in the Qumran corpus thus comprise a very small segment of the complete corpus, namely 3%. This small percentage is matched only by the finds in Wadi Daliyeh, beyond the Judean Desert, while Greek texts were found in much larger proportions at all other sites in the Judean Desert. Because of the fragmentary state of many texts, especially papyri, statistics for these sites can only be approximate:[347]

TABLE 1: *Greek Texts from the Judean Desert*

Sites (Listed from North to South)	Total Number of Texts (Leather, Papyrus)	Greek Texts	Percentage of Total Texts
Wadi Daliyeh	29	1+	3
Jericho	30	17+	56+
Qumran	930	27	3
Wadi Nar	4	2	50
Wadi Ghweir	2	1	50
Wadi Murabbaʿat	158	71	45
Wadi Sdeir	4	2	50
Naḥal Ḥever[348]	157+	55+	35+

---

[346]See: A. R. C. Leaney, "Greek Manuscripts from the Judaean Desert," in *Studies in New Testament Language and Text. Essays in Honour of George D. Kilpatrick on the Occasion of his Sixty-Fifth Birthday* (ed. J. K. Elliott; NTSup 44; Leiden 1976) 283–300; L. Greenspoon, "The Dead Sea Scrolls and the Greek Bible," in Flint–VanderKam, *Fifty Years*, 101–27; Ulrich, *The Dead Sea Scrolls*, 165–83. For an analysis and images, see Kraft, *Jewishpap*.

[347]The precarious nature of statistics may be illustrated by the following: The numerous Greek fragments from what is named XḤev/Se and which are grouped on two different plates (*DJD* XXVII, pls. XLVIII and XLIX, are numbered XḤev/Se 74–169 for the sake of convenience, and likewise Ḥev/Se? 1–57 are grouped on pls. L–LIII in the same volume. It is hard to know how these collections should be accounted for in a statistical analysis. The author responsible for these items (H. Cotton) did not want to imply that these items have to be counted as 96 and 57 different compositions, and hence they should probably be counted as seven different ones, although both types of accounting are very imprecise. Many of the fragments in these collections will have belonged to documents from Naḥal Ḥever published in *DJD* XXVII, while other fragments must have belonged to different texts, not published in the volume. The collections of fragments known as 1Q69 and 1Q70 are treated similarly.

[348]Including Ḥever/Seiyal.

Naḥal Mishmar	3	1	3 3
Naḥal Ṣeʾelim	6	2	3 3
Masada	48	11+	23+

We now turn to some detailed remarks regarding the Greek leather and papyrus texts from the Judean Desert, excluding ostraca. First, attention will be directed to sites other than Qumran, with the exclusion of the approximately fifty texts from Ḥirbet Mird because of their Byzantine date.

Greek texts, most of them documentary, were found in various places in the Judean Desert (listed from north to south): Wadi Daliyeh (1+ [undeciphered]), Jericho (17 and several fragments), Wadi Nar (2), Wadi Ghweir (1), Wadi Murabbaʿat (71), Wadi Sdeir (2), Naḥal Ḥever (32 from cave 5/6; 2 from cave 8; 21, and many unidentified fragments from 'XḤev/Se' and 'Ḥev/Se?'),[349] Naḥal Mishmar (1), Naḥal Ṣeʾelim (2), and Masada (remains of probably 11 texts [a few in either Greek or Latin] and several fragments).[350] The largest groups of Greek texts thus derive from Murabbaʿat and Naḥal Ḥever, originally denoted incorrectly as 'Seiyal,'[351] and involving two archives in Greek and Aramaic from Naḥal Ḥever (the archive of Salome Komaïse daughter of Levi, and that of Babatha [R. Katzoff, *Encyclopedia DSS*, 2.73–4]). The documentary texts found at these sites relate to such matters as marriage contracts (e.g. 5/6Ḥev 18, 37), receipts (5/6Ḥev 27; XḤev/Se 12), deeds of gift (5/6Ḥev papDeed of gift gr [5/6Ḥev 19]), registration of land (5/6Ḥev papRegistration of Land gr [5/6Ḥev 16]), summons (5/6Ḥev 23, 25, 35), letters (5/6Ḥev 52), etc. The nature of the documents found at locations other than Qumran thus shows that Greek was in active use among the persons who left these documents behind. That Greek was in active use beyond Qumran can also be seen from the percentage of documentary texts among the Greek texts found at the individual sites. At all sites other than Qumran, this percentage is relatively high.

TABLE 2: *Documentary and Non-documentary Greek Texts from the Judean Desert*

Sites (Listed from North to South)	Total Number	Documen-tary Texts	Percentage of Total Number	Non-docu-mentary Texts	Percentage of Total No.
Wadi Daliyeh[352]	1+		—		—
Jericho	17+	17+	100	0	0
Qumran	27	1	3	26	9 7
Wadi Nar	2	2	100	0	0
Wadi Ghweir	1	1	100	0	0
Wadi Murabbaʿat	71	66	93	5	7
Wadi Sdeir	2	2	100	0	0
Naḥal Ḥever	55+	54	98+	1	2
Naḥal Mishmar	1	1	100	0	0
Naḥal Ṣeʾelim	2	2	100	0	0
Masada	11+	9+	82+	2	18

Beyond the documentary texts, a few, sometimes ill-defined *literary* Greek texts, were found at various sites other than Qumran, and are included among the statistics in TABLE 2: five papyri from Wadi Murabbaʿat, mostly of undetermined nature (*DJD* II, 108–12), probably two from Masada (Mas woodTablet gr [Mas 743] from 73 or 74 CE; Mas papLiterary Text? gr [Mas 739]),[353] and one from Naḥal Ḥever (8HevXIIgr [end of 1 BCE]), but none from the other sites of Wadi Ghweir, Wadi Nar, Wadi Sdeir, Naḥal Mishmar, and Naḥal Ṣeʾelim. 8HevXIIgr (publication: *DJD* VIII), the best preserved of these literary texts, was found at Naḥal Ḥever.

In striking contrast to the texts found beyond Qumran, all but one of the twenty-seven Greek texts found at Qumran are literary, although admittedly it is difficult to be certain in the case of small papyrus

---

[349]See N. Lewis, *The Documents from the Bar Kochba Period in the Cave of Letters: Greek Papyri* (Jerusalem 1989).

[350]See H. M. Cotton and A. Yardeni, *DJD* XXVII, 134–5; *Masada II*; Tov–Pfann, *Companion Volume*.

[351]See Cotton and Yardeni, *DJD* XXVII, 1–6.

[352]These papyrus fragments (photograph PAM 43.962; Rockefeller Inv. 550) have not been deciphered. They are published in *DJD* XXVIII, pl. XL.

[353]See Cotton and Geiger, *Masada II*, 90.

fragments, viz., 4Q119–122, 126–127; 7Q1–19 (all the preserved texts of cave 7 are Greek papyri); altogether, there are five texts on leather and three on papyrus from cave 4, and 19 papyri from cave 7. Almost all of these contain Greek Scripture texts in the wide sense of the word (including 7QpapEpJer gr). This characterization includes the literary papyri 7Q4–18, which are too fragmentary for a precise identification of their contents. The one non-literary item among the Qumran Greek texts is the documentary text 4QAccount gr (4Q350), written on the verso of frg. 9 of a Hebrew text, 4QNarrative Work and Prayer [4Q460]), the nature and date of which cannot be determined easily (see below). Likewise, the nature of 4QpapUnidentified Fragment gr (4Q361) remains unclear (*DJD* XXVII, pl. LXI, without transcription).

The picture emerging from an analysis of the Greek texts from the Judean Desert is that the situation at Qumran differs totally from that of the other sites. At most sites, all the Greek texts (and in Wadi Murabbaʿat and Masada, the great majority) are documentary, showing that Greek was actively used among the persons who deposited the texts. These texts include documents showing that administrative affairs were conducted in Greek in the Roman provinces of Syria, Arabia, and Judaea, evidenced by letters written in that language (see, i.a., Greek letters written by Bar Kokhba's followers, found in the Cave of Letters in Naḥal Ḥever). On the other hand, there is no proof that the Greek language was in active use among the inhabitants of Qumran. It is possible that at least some of them knew Greek, since fragments of Greek Scripture were found in caves 4 and 7. However, cave 4 probably served as a depository of some kind (not a library) in which the Qumranites placed all their written texts (mainly Hebrew and Aramaic literary works, but also a number of *tefillin* and *mezuzot* as well as brief notes and scribal exercises). This depository in cave 4 contained eight Greek texts, which may signify that the person(s) who brought them to Qumran had used them prior to their arrival, thus implying a knowledge of Greek. However, it is not impossible that these texts came directly from an archive. Furthermore, the small number of Greek texts found at Qumran is also in striking contrast to the large number from the other sites in the Judean Desert. The difference is partly chronological (most of the sites in the Judean Desert are from a later period than Qumran), but more so a matter of content since the Qumran Greek corpus is mainly religious.

The evidence does not suggest that the Greek texts from cave 4 were written, read or consulted at Qumran. Cave 7, probably used for lodging (thus R. de Vaux, *DJD* III, 30) or as a workplace, is a different issue. The contents of that cave consisted solely of Greek literary papyri, probably all Greek Scripture, that possibly were deposited there directly from an archive outside Qumran or from a specific site within the Qumran compound. No relation between the Greek texts of cave 4 and cave 7 need to be assumed, and there is no reason to believe that any of these texts was penned at Qumran.

Since the documentary texts found at Naḥal Ḥever show that Greek was used actively by the persons who deposited the texts at that site, the Minor Prophets Scroll was probably also used by these persons. Indeed, that scroll contains a Jewish revision of the first Greek translation, and as such a version would be consonant with what is known of the freedom fighters of Bar Kochba, it was probably used by them. See further Tov, "Greek Biblical Texts."

The situation was completely different for the Scripture finds at Qumran, which attest to an earlier period, until 70 CE. In the period attested by the settlement at Qumran, the *kaige*-Th revision of the Old Greek, such as reflected in 8ḤevXIIgr (end of 1 BCE) already existed. However, neither this revision nor those similar, found their way to Qumran; this was probably not due to any disagreement on the part of the Qumran covenanters with the concept behind these revisions, but rather because they did not turn to Scripture in Greek. For them, Scripture existed mainly in the source languages, and among the 220 biblical texts found at Qumran, Greek and Aramaic translations (4QtgLev, 4QtgJob, and 11QtgJob) form a small minority.

In light of the preceding, special attention should be paid to an opisthograph, the recto of which formed fragment 9 of a Hebrew text named 4QNarrative Work and Prayer, while the verso contained a Greek documentary text, 4QAccount gr (4Q350 [H. Cotton, *DJD* XXXVI]). It is difficult to characterize that Hebrew composition, which was described by its editor, E. Larson, as 'somewhat akin to the *Hodayot*.'[354]

---

[354] E. Larson, *DJD* XXXVI, 372: 'It is difficult to discern the overall character of the work in its present state of preservation. The major part of the extant fragments is given over to prayer, exhortation, and admonition. It is possible, therefore, that 4Q460 is a collection of psalms somewhat akin to the *Hodayot*. This may be suggested by the paragraphing of material which is clear on frg. 9 and is supported by the fact that the material before the *vacat* is addressed to God while that occurring after the *vacat* is addressed to Israel with little or no intervening narrative to explain the change. If this understanding of the nature of the manuscript is correct, then the person speaking in the first singular in frg. 9 i 2 is some unknown psalmist.'

Its orthography and morphology suggest that it was copied, though not necessarily authored, by a sectarian scribe, while the verso contains a documentary Greek text. For an analysis, see n. 124.

With regard to the first possibility that Greek was in use at Qumran, and that there was once a small corpus of administrative documentary texts in Greek, attention should be directed to the documentary texts 4Q342–360 in Aramaic and Hebrew, the idea being that if documentary texts were written at Qumran in Hebrew and Aramaic, they could also have been written in Greek. However, serious doubts regarding the Qumranic origin of 4Q342–360 were raised by A. Yardeni, *DJD* XXVII, 283–317 (see n. 124).

We therefore resort to the assumption that 4Q350 was written on the verso of frg. 9 of the Hebrew text 4Q460 after the occupation of the site by the Qumranites, when documents that were still laying around were reused due to the scarcity of writing material: (1) Only the verso of frg. 9 of 4Q460 was inscribed, which necessarily points to a period in which that manuscript had already been torn into pieces or had partially disintegrated. (2) The writing of a documentary text on the back of a literary text is paralleled by many Greek papyri from Hellenistic Egypt (see the analysis by Gallo),[355] by Elephantine papyri,[356] and by 4QMish C (4Q324)—a documentary/literary text—that has 4QAccount C ar or heb (4Q355) on its verso. Likewise, Mur papLiterary Text gr (Mur 112) has on its verso Mur pap Proceedings of Lawsuit gr (Mur 113). See APPENDIX 3. (3) As a rule, writing on the flesh side (the verso) of the leather (4Q350 in this case), occurs subsequent to that on the recto (4Q460). At the same time, it remains difficult to understand the realia of the writing on 4Q350 and 4Q460: if frg. 9 was indeed hidden in cave 4 by the Qumran community, it could have been reused by those who occupied the site after the Qumran community only if they had access to the hidden treasures of that cave and did not burn its contents.

The writing of the Greek text 4Q350 on the verso of frg. 9 of the Hebrew text 4Q460 must have occurred later than the writing of the recto (4Q460), but it is conceivable that the Greek writing performed within the period of the occupation of Qumran by the Qumran covenanters themselves. However, E. Larson argues that the Qumran sectarians would not have reused a scroll that contained the Tetragrammaton on the recto (4Q460 9 i 10) for such a profane use as recording a list of cereals in Greek (*DJD* XXXVI, 369). See ch. *5d*. Larson adds: 'If not, then this list could become evidence of a later occupation of the Qumran caves in the wake of the destruction of the settlement in 68 CE.' If this explanation is accepted, it may imply that this text is irrelevant to our analysis of the use of Greek within the Qumran community. The views expressed on this text in my paper "Greek Biblical Texts" are based largely on those of Cotton–Larson, who strengthened their position on the secondary nature of the Greek text on the verso of 4Q460 9 with additional arguments in their paper "4Q460/4Q350 and Tampering with Qumran Texts in Antiquity," in Paul, *Emanuel*, 113–25.

Beyond the enigmatic Greek 4Q350, the Qumran corpus bears a clearly religious character with regard to both the Hebrew/Aramaic texts and the Greek documents. Alongside the Hebrew biblical texts, several Greek literary texts were found which contain mainly Greek Scripture. One such text was also found at Naḥal Ḥever.

---

[355]Gallo, *Papyrology*, 10 i; Manfredi, "Opistografo," 44–54. Among other things, P.Rylands Greek 458 of Deuteronomy (2 BCE) has an account of expenditures on its verso, see C. H. Roberts, *Two Biblical Papyri in the John Rylands Library Manchester* (Manchester 1936) 16–17, 21–22.

[356]See Porten–Yardeni, *TAD* 3. Occasionally even a biblical text was reused, as the Greek P.Leipzig 39 of Psalms (4 CE) has a list on the reverse.

APPENDIX 5

SCRIBAL FEATURES OF EARLY WITNESSES
OF GREEK SCRIPTURE

This appendix analyzes several scribal features displayed in early witnesses of Greek Scripture with an eye toward discovering links with early Jewish scribal traditions such as those known from the Hebrew scrolls from the Judean Desert. Special attention is paid to the indication of verses, sections, *paragraphoi*, *ekthesis*, and the writing of the divine names. The parameters of this investigation are as follows:

• The coverage of the Greek texts is intentionally vague ('Greek Scripture'), since the dividing line between the so-called Old Greek translation and other early translations and revisions is often unclear, as are the exact limits of what may be considered Scripture.

• All early papyri that could be located in the libraries of Tübingen and Macquarie University (especially in the Ancient History Documentary Research Centre [AHDRC]) were examined, with the exclusion of very fragmentary texts. The table, which is rather exhaustive, lists in presumed chronological sequence, all the texts that were given dates up to and including the fourth century CE in their publications. Most texts examined were dated to the third and fourth centuries CE (see the statistics in Van Haelst, *Catalogue*, 419). The large codices A, B, S, and G are excluded from the analysis.

• The distinction between Jewish and Christian copies is relevant in as far as the former are more likely to preserve ancient Jewish scribal practices. Although this distinction is often very difficult, all texts antedating the middle of the first century CE are Jewish. According to K. Treu, "Die Bedeutung des Griechischen für die Juden im römischen Reich," *Kairos* NF 15 (1973) 123–44, it is possible that several texts written after that period might also be recognized as Jewish; they are indicated in the first column of the table as '*Jewish* (Treu).' A major though not exclusive criterion for the Jewish nature of a text is the writing in scrolls, indicated as 'S' in the second column of the table (see already C. H. Roberts, "The Christian Book and the Greek Papyri," *JTS* 50 [1949] 155–68, especially 157–8). The Christian nature of Scripture texts can usually be detected by their inscription in codex form (indicated as 'C' in the second column), and their use of abbreviated forms of the divine names (indicated in the seventh column). See further Kraft, "Textual Mechanics."

• Texts and plates were examined in their *editio princeps* or in a central edition, located with the aid of Aland, *Repertorium*; Van Haelst, *Catalogue* (both until 1976); and the index of the AHDRC. Bibliographical details concerning the papyri listed below are either found or are otherwise apparent for the user of these sources (such as volumes of P.Oxy. subsequent to 1976). In the fifth and sixth columns, the data is indicated as '**x**' (= extant), '—' (= not extant), and '**no evidence**.'

The table lists information on the following items:

• Name and suggested date, together with a possible reference to the Jewish nature of the source.

• Scroll (**S**) or Codex (**C**). This information is based on the plates provided and on the indications in the various sources: Aland, *Repertorium*; Van Haelst, *Catalogue*; and especially the AHDRC index. Items listed by AHDRC as 'sheet' are listed below as '—'.

• Indication of biblical verses or parts of verses through spacing or other systems, or the lack of such indications. The notation 'spaces' or sim. refers to spaces after verses, sometimes also indicated after groups of words or hemistichs.

• Indication of section divisions through spacing or additional systems, or the lack of such indications.

• Indication of *paragraphoi* (straight line, unless indicated as 'wedge-shaped').

• *Ekthesis* (enlarged letters protruding into the margin at the beginning of new sections).

• Special features used in the writing of the **divine names**. The notation 'κ(ύριο)ς' implies that the abbreviated form of this word is included in the text, usually together with other abbreviated *nomina sacra*. The notation 'θ(εό)ς' implies that κ(ύριο)ς has not been preserved, but other abbreviated *nomina sacra*, mainly θ(εό)ς, do appear in the text.

• Writing of poetical texts in **stichographic** layout (yes/no and irrelevant, indicated as '—').

Scribal Features of Early Greek Sources

Name and Suggested Date	S / C	Indication of Verses	Indication of Section Units	*Paragraphos*	Ekthesis	Divine Names	Sticho-graphic Layout
P.Rylands Greek 458 of Deuteronomy (2 BCE) *Jewish*	S	spaces (in one case + high dot), also after groups of words	no evidence	—	—	no evidence	—
4QLXXDeut of Deut 11 (middle 2 BCE) *Jewish*	S	no evidence	no evidence	no evidence	no evidence	no evidence	—
4QLXXLev^a of Leviticus 26 (late 2 or early 1 BCE) *Jewish*	S	—	closed	x	—	no evidence	—
P.Fouad 266a (942) of Gen 3–38 (middle 1 BCE) *Jewish* (Treu)	S	spaces, also after groups of words	open and closed	—	—	no evidence	—
P.Fouad 266b (848) of Deuteronomy 10–33 (middle 1 BCE) *Jewish* (Treu)	S	spaces, also after groups of words	open and closed	x	—	first scribe left spaces and two dots; the 2nd scribe wrote the Tetragr. in square chars.	*stichoi* (Deuteronomy 32)
P.Fouad 266c (847) of Deut 10–11, 31–33 (50–1 BCE) *Jewish* (Treu)	S	spaces, also after groups of words	no evidence	—	—	no evidence	—
7QpapLXX-Exod of Exod 28 (1 BCE) *Jewish*	S	no evidence	no evidence	—	no evidence	no evidence	—
4QpapLXX-Lev^b of Lev 2–5 (1 BCE) *Jewish*	S	spaces	closed	x	no evidence	ΙΑΩ	—
4QLXXNum of Numbers 3–4 (1 BCE) *Jewish*	S	spaces, also after groups of words	no evidence	—	—	no evidence	—
8ḤevXIIgr hand A (end of 1 BCE) *Jewish*	S	spaces, also after groups of words	open and closed	x	x	paleo-Hebrew Tetra, including final *he*	—
8ḤevXIIgr hand B (end of 1 BCE) *Jewish*	S	spaces	open and closed	no	x	paleo-Hebrew Tetra	—
P.Oxy. 50.3522 of Job 42 (1 CE) *Jewish*	S	spaces, also after groups of words	—	—	—	paleo-Hebrew Tetra, including final *he*	—

P.Yale 1 of Genesis 14 (end of 1 CE)[357] *Jewish* (Treu)	C	spaces + median dots	—	—	—	no evidence	—
P.Bodl. MS. bibl. Gr. 5 of Ps 48–49 (late 1 or early 2 CE)	C	—	—	—	—	no evidence	*stichoi*
P.Oxy. 65.4443 of Esther E and ch. 9 (late 1 or early 2 CE) *Jew.?*	S	—	open	x	x	θεός	—
P.Baden 56b = P.Heid. Gr. 8 of Exod 8 (2 CE)	C	some spaces	closed section after 8:11	—	—	κ(ύριο)ς	—
P.Antinoopolis 7 of Psalms (2 CE)	C	—	—	—	—	κ(ύριο)ς	*stichoi*
P.Coll. Horsley (Deissmann) of Exodus 4 (2–3 CE)[358]	C	—	—	—	—	κ(ύριο)ς	—
P.Chester Beatty VI (963) of Num and Deut (end of 2 CE or early 3 CE)	C	—	some open and closed sections	x (rarely)	—	κ(ύριο)ς	—
P.Chester Beatty VIII of Jeremiah 4–5 (2–3 CE)	C	spaces + high and median dots, also after groups of words; dicolon before speech in 4:31	—	—	—	κ(ύριο)ς	—
P.Leipzig 170 of Psalm 118 LXX (2–3 CE)	C	—	—	—	—	κ(ύριο)ς	*stichoi*
P.Oxy. 4.656 of Genesis 14–27 (2 or 3 CE) *Jewish* (Treu)	C	—	open and closed, with dots in different positions	—	—	spaces left by original scribe, filled in by a second scribe with κύριος	—
P.Oxy. 65.4442 of Exodus 20 (early 3 CE)	C	—	closed section + dicolon	—	—	κ(ύριο)ς	—
P.Schøyen 2648 of Joshua 9–11 (early 3 CE)	C	—	no			κ(ύριο)ς	—
P.Scheide + P.Chester Beatty IX (967) of Ezek (early 3 CE) *same codex as next*	C	high and median dots, dots on the line, also after groups of words	open and closed, filled with two diagonal dots or strokes	—	rarely, and usually not related to beginning of new sections	κ(ύριο)ς	—
P.Chester Beatty X (967) of Daniel and Esth (early 3 CE)	C	oblique strokes in spaces, also when no space was left	rarely closed and open sections	x	—	κ(ύριο)ς	—

---

[357]This date, given in the *editio princeps*, is contested by several scholars, who date this text to the second or third century CE. See R. A. Kraft in http://ccat.sas.upenn.edu/rs/rak/jewishpap.html#jewishmss and idem, "Textual Mechanics," 60.

[358]G. Horsley, *Archiv für Papyrusforschung* 30 (1993) 35–8.

Name and Suggested Date	S / C	Indication of Verses	Indication of Section Units	*Paragraphos*	Ekthesis	Divine Names	Sticho-graphic Layout
P.Oxy. 7.1007 of Genesis 2–3 (3 CE) *Jewish* (Treu) *leather*	C	—	closed (once)	—	—	two paleo-Hebrew *yod*s; θ(εό)ς	—
P.Oxy. 9.1166 of Genesis 16 (3 CE) *Jewish* (Treu)	S	spaces + median dots, also after groups of words	no	—	—	κ(ύριο)ς	—
P.Berlin 17213 of Gen 19 (3 CE) *Jewish* (Treu)	C	space + high dot (once)	closed (once)	—	—	possibly space left for divine name	—
P.Rendel Harris 166 of Exodus 22–23 (3 CE)	S	no	open and closed	x	—	no evidence	—
P.Oxy. 8.1075 of Exodus 40 (3 CE) *Jewish* (Treu)	S	space + high dot after 40:28; otherwise continuous	—	—	—	κ(ύριο)ς	—
P.Heid. 290 of Lev 19 (3 CE)	C	—	—	—	—	θ(εό)ς	—
P.Merton 2 = P.Chester Beatty VII of Isa 8–60 and Ezekiel 11–17 (3 CE)	C	high dots and dicola, sometimes in spaces	—	—	—	κ(ύριο)ς	—
P.Fir. 8 of Isa 19 (3 CE)		spaces + high dots	—	—	—	no evidence	—
P.Berlin 17212 of Jer 2–3 (3 CE)	C	spaces + high dots	—	x	—	κ(ύριο)ς	—
Pap. W (Freer) of the Minor Prophets (3 CE) *Jewish* (Treu)	C	high dots, also after groups of words (no spaces)	closed sections with occasional dicola	x	—	κ(ύριο)ς	—
P.Lit. London 204 of Psalm 2 (3 CE)	C	no	—	—	—	κ(ύριο)ς	—
P.Mich. 22 of Psalms 8–9 (3 CE)	C	spaces after each hemistich	—	—	—	κ(ύριο)ς	—
P.Bodmer XXIV of Psalms17–53, 55–118, hand A (3 CE)	C	spaces + high dots and some dicola, also after hemistichs	—	x	—	κ(ύριο)ς	—
P.Bodmer XXIV of Psalms17–53, 55–118, hand B (3 CE)	C	spaces + dicola and some high dots, also after hemistichs	—	x	—	κ(ύριο)ς	—

P.Vindob. Gr. 26035B of Psalms 68–69 LXX (3 CE)	C	—	—	—	—	θ(εό)ς	*stichoi*
P.Alex. 240 (PSI 921) of Psalm 77 LXX (3 CE)	C	—	—	—	—	θ(εό)ς	*stichoi*
P.Berlin Inv. 21265 of Ps 144 LXX (3 CE)	C	—	—	—	—	κ(ύριο)ς	*stichoi*
P.Antinoopolis 9 of Proverbs 2–3 (3 CE)	C	spaces + dicola or high dots, also after groups of words	—	—	—	no evidence	—
P.Antinoopolis 8 of Proverbs 5–20 (3 CE) *Jewish* (Treu)	C	—	—	—	—	κ(ύριο)ς	*stichoi*
P.Berlin 11778 (BKT 8.17) of Job 33–34 (3 CE)	S	spaces + median dots, also after parts of verses	open section + median dot after 33:24	—	—	κ(ύριο)ς	—
P.Mil. 13 of Qoh 3 + (?) P.Mich. 135 of Qohelet 6 (3 CE)	C	spaces + some dicola after hemistichs	—	—	—	θ(εό)ς	*stichoi*
P.Egerton 4 (B.M.) of 2 Chr 24 (3 CE)	C	high dots, usually in spaces	—	—	—	κ(ύριο)ς	—
P.Chester Beatty V (962) of Genesis (second half of 3 CE)	C	—	closed	x (rare)	rarely	κ(ύριο)ς	—
P.Berlin Fol. 66 I/II of Genesis (end of 3 CE)	C	—	—	x	—	κ(ύριο)ς	—
P.Lit. London 202 of Gen 46–47 (300 CE) *Jewish* (Treu)	C	spaces + high dots	no evidence	—	—	no evidence	—
P.Berlin 14039 of Exodus 34–35 (3–4 CE) *leather*	C	spaces + high dots, also after groups of words	—	—	—	κ(ύριο)ς	—
P.Alex. 203 of Isa 48 (3–4 CE)	S	no evidence	empty line after 48:11	—	—	κ(ύριο)ς	—
P.Laur. Inv. 140 (34) of Psalm 1 (3–4 CE)	S?	no evidence	no evidence	—	—	κ(ύριο)ς	*stichoi*
P.Oxy. 10.1226 of Psalms 7–8 (3–4 CE)	C	—	—	—	—	κ(ύριο)ς	*stichoi*
P.Lit. London 207 of Psalms 11–16 (3–4 CE)	S/C	—	—	—	—	κ(ύριο)ς	*stichoi*

Name and Suggested Date	S/C	Indication of Verses	Indication of Section Units	*Paragraphos*	Ekthesis	Divine Names	Stichographic Layout
P.Genova P.U.G. 1 of Psalms 21–23 LXX (3–4 CE)	C	spaces + dicola after hemistichs	—	x	—	κ(ύριο)ς	—
P.Bonn Coll. P147v of Ps 30 LXX (3–4 CE)	S?	—	—	—	—	no evidence	*stichoi*
P.Vindob. Gr. 39777 of Psalms 68, 80 LXX (3–4 CE) *leather* (*Symmachus*)	S	—	—	—	—	paleo-Hebrew Tetra; θεός	—
P.Flor. B.L. 980 (PSI 980) of Psalms 143–48 LXX (3–4 CE)	C	dicola mostly in spaces	—	—	—	κ(ύριο)ς	—
P.Hamb. bil. 1 of Qohelet (3–4 CE)	C	spaces + 2 oblique strokes or *obelus* after hemistichs	—	—	—	θ(εό)ς	—
P.Vindob. Gr. 39786 of Psalm 9 (early 4 CE)	S/C	spaces + oblique strokes after hemistichs	—	—	—	κ(ύριο)ς	—
P.Oxy. 11.1352 of Psalms 82–83 LXX (early 4 CE) *leather*	C	spaces + dicola after groups of words	—	—	—	κ(ύριο)ς	—
Louvre MND 552 H–L of Psalm 146 LXX (early 4 CE)	—	spaces + 2 oblique strokes after hemistichs	—	—	—	κ(ύριο)ς	—
P.Lit. London 209 of Canticles 5–6 (early 4 CE)	C	high dots mostly in spaces	—	—	—	no evidence	—
P.Chester Beatty IV (961) of Gen (4 CE)	C	no	closed	x (wedge-shaped)	—	κ(ύριο)ς	—
P.Amherst 1 (*Aquila*) of Gen 1 (4 CE)	—	—	—	—	—	θ(εό)ς	—
codex St. Cath. of Genesis 27–28 (4 CE)[359]	C	spaces + high dots, also after groups of words	open	—	x (distance of 3–4 letters in margin)	κ(ύριο)ς	—
P.Oxy. 9.1167 of Gen 31 (4 CE)	C	no	—	—	—	θ(εό)ς	—

[359]J. H. Charlesworth, *The New Discoveries in St. Catherine's Monastery: A Preliminary Report of the Manuscripts* (ASOR Monograph Series 3; Winona Lake, Ind. 1981).

P.Hamb. Ibscher 5 of Genesis 41 (4 CE)	C	rarely spaces + high dots, also after groups of words	—	—	—	no evidence	—
P.Berlin 11766 of Exodus 5–7 (4 CE)	C	space after 6:24a; + dicolon after 6:24; otherwise continuous text	—?	—	—	κ(ύριο)ς	—
P.Bodl. Ms. Gr. Bibl. f. 4 of Exodus 9–10 (4 CE) *leather*[360]	C	spaces + high and low dots	—	—	—	κ(ύριο)ς	—
P.Oxy. 1225 of Lev 16 (4 CE) *Jewish* (Treu)	S	spaces + high and low dots	—	—	—	no evidence	—
P.Oxy.11.1351 of Leviticus 27 (4 CE) *leather*	C	no	open	x	x	no evidence	—
P.Rylands 1 of Deut 23 (4 CE)	C	spaces + median dots	—	—	—	κ(ύριο)ς	—
P.Oxy. 9.1168 of Josh 4–5 (4 CE)	C	spaces + high dots	—	—	—	κ(ύριο)ς	—
P.Oslo 11, frg. 1 of Isaiah 42, 52, 53 (4 CE)	C	spaces + high dots	—	—	—	κ(ύριο)ς	—
P.Genève Gr. 252 of Jeremiah 5–6 (4 CE)	C	spaces + high dots	open section (once)	—	—	κ(ύριο)ς	—
P.Grenfell 5 of Ezek 5–6 (4 CE)	C	—	—	—	—	κ(ύριο)ς	—
P.Antinoopolis 10 of Ezekiel 33–34 (4 CE) *Jewish* (Treu)	C	high dots, in spaces, also when no space was left	—	—	—	κ(ύριο)ς	—
P.Oxy. 15.1779 of Psalm 1 (4 CE)	C	spaces + high dots, also after groups of words	—	—	—	κ(ύριο)ς	—
P.Chester Beatty XIV of Psalms 31, 26, 2 LXX (4 CE)	C	spaces + dicola, also after groups of words	—	—	—	κ(ύριο)ς	—
P.Vindob. Gr. 26205 of Psalm 34 LXX (4 CE)	—	spaces + apostrophes in middle of the line	—	—	—	no evidence	—
P.Flor. B.L. 1371 of Psalm 36 LXX (4 CE)	C	no	—	—	—	κ(ύριο)ς	*stichoi*

---

[360]See V. Pottorno and N. Fernández Marcos, "Nuevos fragmentos del Exodo griego (Ms. Gr. Bibl. f. 4 [P])," *Emerita* 44 (1976) 385–95.

Name and Suggested Date	S/C	Indication of Verses	Indication of Section Units	*Paragraphos*	Ekthesis	Divine Names	Sticho-graphic Layout
P.Chester Beatty XIII of Psalms 72–88 LXX (4 CE)	C	spaces, also after hemistichs; dicolon in 82:9	—	—	—	κ(ύριο)ς	—
P.Vindob. Gr. 35781 of Psalm 77 LXX (4 CE)	C	—	—	—	—	no evidence	*stichoi*
P.Berlin 18196 Cant 5–6 (4 CE)	C	—	—	—	—	no evidence	*stichoi*
P.Flor. B.L. 1163 of Job 1–2 (4 CE)	C	—	—	—	—	κ(ύριο)ς	—
P.Leipzig 39 of Psalms 30–55 LXX (4 CE)	S	—	—	x	—	κ(ύριο)ς	—
P.Vindob. Gr. 26205 (MPER 4,9) of Psalm 34 LXX (4 CE)	—	spaces + commas after hemistichs	—	—	—	κ(ύριο)ς	—
P.Erlangen 2 of Genesis 41 (4–5 CE)	C	spaces + high and low dots	no evidence	—	—	θ(εό)ς	—
P.Yale Beinecke 544 of 1 Samuel 24–2 Samuel 1 (4–5 CE)[361]	C	minute spaces + high dots and dicola, also after groups of words	—	x	—	κ(ύριο)ς	—
P.Vindob. Gr. 29274 of Psalm 32LXX (4–5 CE)	C	spaces + low dots with an apostrophe	—	—	—	κ(ύριο)ς	—
P.Oxy. 6.845 of Psalms 68–70 LXX (4–5 CE)	C	—	—	—	—	no evidence	*stichoi*
P.Oxy. 24.2386 of Psalms 83–84 LXX (4–5 CE)	S	spaces + two oblique strokes	—	—	—	κ(ύριο)ς	*stichoi*
P.Damasc. VII of Canticles 2, 5 (4–5 CE)	C	—	—	—	x	no evidence	*stichoi*
Cod. Cambridge of 2 Kings 21–23 (*Aquila*; 5 CE)	C	some spaces + high dots, also after groups of words	open (rare)	—	—	paleo-Hebrew Tetragrammaton with identical *yod* and *waw*	—

[361]B. G. Wright, "A Greek Fragment of the Books of Samuel: Beinecke Library MS 544 (Ra 846)," *Textus* 17 (1994) 79–100.

A. *Indication of small sense units (verses)*

a. *Small spaces without additional indications*

The earliest sound evidence from the second century BCE onwards for the indication of small sense units in Scripture texts (verses) pertains not to Hebrew manuscripts, but to the *Targumim* and several early Greek sources. See ch. 5a2.

The use of spacing for the indication of small sense units (verses) was a natural development in the tradition of Scripture-writing, both in Hebrew and in the translations, as larger units (sections) were likewise indicated with spacing. The size of the space indicating new sections was always larger than that indicating verses, which usually equaled a single letter-space, and sometimes slightly more.

A small group of early Greek texts indicated the ends of verses, and sometimes also groups of words, with small spaces without additional notations. In all these texts, with the exception of hand B of 8HevXIIgr in Zechariah (end of 1 BCE), word-division was not indicated with spaces. Since almost all these texts are early, they undoubtedly reflect early Jewish traditions. Some of these texts reflect early Jewish revisions (P.Fouad 266a–c, 8HevXIIgr), while others probably reflect the tradition of the Old Greek translation (4QpapLXXLev[b], 4QLXXNum), different from the text contained in other witnesses. The nature of P.Oxy. 3522 is unclear.

P.Rylands Greek 458 of Deuteronomy (2 BCE): after Deut 24:1 (+ high dot); 25:2; 26:17, 18; as well as after groups of words.[362]

P.Fouad 266a–c of Genesis and Deuteronomy (1 BCE) consisting of three different scrolls (Aly–Koenen, *Three Rolls*): after verses, and sometimes also after groups of words: P.Fouad 266a of Genesis (942; middle of 1 BCE); P.Fouad 266b of Deuteronomy (848 [middle of 1 BCE]), in the latter case, e.g. after Deut 22:8; 28:67; 32:19, 25, as well as after 28:9a, 65a, but not after Deut 28:65; 31:25; 32:46; P.Fouad 266c of Deuteronomy 10–11, 31–33 (847 [second half of 1 BCE]). See Dunand, *Papyrus grecs, Texte et planches*; Aly–Koenen, *Three Rolls*, p. 5, n. 24 and p. 7, n. 32; Oesch, *Petucha und Setuma*, 297–8.

4QpapLXXLev[b] of Leviticus 2–5 (1 BCE): after Lev 3:11; 4:26.

4QLXXNum of Numbers 3–4 (1 BCE): after 3:41 and 4:6, as well as after groups of words.

8HevXIIgr hand A (end of 1 BCE) containing substantial segments of the Minor Prophets: after almost all verses (E. Tov, *DJD* VIII, 11–12), as well as after some groups of words.

8HevXIIgr hand B (end of 1 BCE): after Zech 9:5, but not after 9:1. This scribe also indicated divisions between words with small spaces.

P.Oxy. 50.3522 of Job 42 (1 CE): after 42:11, as well as after groups of words (42:11a, 12a).

P.Baden 56b = P.Heidelberg gr. 8 of Exodus 8 (2 CE): some spaces, e.g. after 8:8, 9.

P.Mich. 22 of Psalms 8–9 (3 CE): spaces in different positions in the line after each hemistich.

P.Chester Beatty XIII of Psalms 72–88 LXX (4 CE): after hemistichs, including a dicolon in 82:9.

This group may be extended by the following group of texts that likewise indicated spaces.

b. *Graphic indicators (usually high dots or dicola) added in spaces left by the original scribes*

Graphic indicators (usually high dots or dicola, rarely oblique strokes or *obelus* signs [P.Hamb. bil. 1 of Qohelet]) were often added in texts that already had spaces marking the ends of verses. With two exceptions, all these texts are from the third century CE onwards, which shows that the ancient tradition of marking verse-endings with spacing was supplemented with a Greek system of indicating small sense units with dots. Sometimes these dots were inserted by the original scribes, but often they were added after the completion of the writing (§ c below). In those instances, extant spaces could not be erased, and if no spaces had been left, new markings were inserted between existing letters. The use of either a dot or dicolon depended on the preference of the scribe.

P.Rylands Greek 458 of Deuteronomy (2 BCE): a space after Deut 24:1 (+ high dot).

P.Yale 1 of Genesis 14 (end of 1 CE?): spaces with median dots.

P.Chester Beatty VIII of Jeremiah 4–5 (2–3 CE): high and median dots, also after groups of words; dicolon before speech in 4:31.

P.Chester Beatty X (967) of Daniel and Esther (early 3 CE): oblique strokes both in spaces and when no space was left (see group *c* below).

---

[362]Roberts, *Two Biblical Papyri* (see n. 355) with plates. A more complete photograph is found in E. Würthwein, *The Text of the Old Testament* (Grand Rapids, Mich. 1979) 177.

P.Scheide + P.Chester Beatty IX (967) of Ezekiel (early 3 CE): spaces with high dots, median dots, and dots on the line (no spaces left), also after groups of words.

P.Oxy. 9.1166 of Genesis 16 (3 CE): spaces with median dots, also after some groups of words.

P.Berlin 17213 of Genesis 19 (3 CE): a space with a high dot after 19:17.

P.Oxy. 8.1075 of Exodus 40 (3 CE): a space with a high dot after 40:28; otherwise the text is continuous.

P.Fir. 8 of Isaiah (3 CE): high dots, mainly in spaces.

P.Merton 2 of Isaiah 8–60 = P.Chester Beatty VII (965) (3 CE): high dots + dicola, sometimes in spaces.

P.Berlin 17212 of Jeremiah 2–3 (3 CE): spaces with high dots.

P.Bodmer XXIV of Psalms 17–53, 55–118, hand A: (3 CE) spaces + high dots and some dicola, also after hemistichs.

P.Bodmer XXIV of Psalms 17–53, 55–118, hand B: (3 CE) spaces + dicola and some high dots, also after hemistichs.

P.Antinoopolis 9 of Proverbs 2–3 (3 CE): spaces with a dicolon or high dot.

P.Berlin 11778 (BKT 8.17) of Job 33–34 (3 CE): spaces + median dot, also after parts of verses.

P.Mil. 13 of Qohelet 3 + (?) P.Mich. 135 of Qohelet 6 (3 CE): spaces with some dicola after hemistichs.

P.Egerton 4 (B.M.) of 2 Chronicles 24 (3 CE): high dots, usually in spaces.

P.Berlin 14039 of Exodus 34–35 (3–4 CE): spaces with high dots, also after groups of words.

P.Genova P.U.G. 1 of Psalms 21–23 LXX (3–4 CE): spaces with dicola after hemistichs.

P.Flor. B.L. 980 of Psalms 143–48 LXX (3–4 CE): dicola, mainly in spaces.

P.Hamb. bil. 1 of Qohelet (3–4 CE): spaces + 2 oblique strokes or *obelus* signs after hemistichs.

P.Lit. London 202 of Genesis 46–47 (*c.* 300 CE): spaces with high dots.

P.Lit. London 209 of Canticles 5–6 (early 4 CE): spaces, sometimes with high dots.

P.Vindob. Gr. 39786 of Psalm 9 (early 4 CE): spaces with oblique strokes after hemistichs.

Louvre MND 552 H–L of Psalm 146 LXX (early 4 CE): spaces with 2 oblique strokes after hemistichs.

P.Oxy. 11.1352 (leather) of Psalms 82–83 LXX (early 4 CE): spaces with dicola after groups of words.

Codex St. Cath. of Genesis 27–28 (4 CE): spaces with high dots, also after groups of words.

P.Hamb. Ibscher 5 of Genesis 41 (4 CE): some spaces with high dots, also after groups of words.

P.Berlin 11766 of Exodus 5–7 (4 CE): a space with dicolon after 6:24 and a space in the middle of 6:24; otherwise the text is continuous.

P.Bodl. Ms. Gr. Bibl. f. 4 of Exodus 9–10 (4 CE): spaces with low and high dots.

P.Oxy. 10.1225 of Leviticus 16 (4 CE): spaces with high and low dots.

P.Rylands 1 of Deuteronomy 23 (4 CE): spaces with median dots.

P.Oxy. 9.1168 of Joshua 4–5 (4 CE): spaces with high dots.

P.Oslo 11, frg. 1 of Isaiah 42, 52, 53 (4 CE): spaces with high dots.

P.Genève Gr. 252 of Jeremiah 5–6 (4 CE): spaces with high dots.

P.Antinoopolis 10 of Ezekiel 33–34 (4 CE): inconsistently placed high dots, sometimes in spaces, but also when no space was left.

P.Oxy. 15.1779 of Psalm 1 (4 CE): spaces with high dots, also after groups of words.

P.Chester Beatty XIV of Psalms 31, 26, 2 LXX (4 CE): spaces with dicola, also after groups of words.

P.Vindob. Gr. 26205 of Psalm 34 LXX (4 CE): hemistichs with commas.

P.Erlangen 2 of Genesis 41 (4–5 CE): spaces with high and low dots.

P.Yale Beinecke 544 of 1 Samuel 24–2 Samuel 1 (4–5 CE): minute spaces with high dots and dicola, also after groups of words.

P.Vindob. Gr. 29274 of Psalm 32 LXX (4–5 CE): spaces + low dots with an apostrophe.

P.Oxy. 24.2386 of Psalms 83–84 LXX (4–5 CE): spaces with two oblique strokes after each stich.

Cod. Cambridge of 2 Kings 21–23 (*Aquila*; 5 CE): spaces with high dots, also after groups of words.

c. *High dots and/or dicola superimposed on texts written without spaces*

Many of the high dots and dicola were superimposed, often inelegantly, on texts that were initially written continuously. The secondary status of these interpunction signs is evident from the lack of space left and often also from the color of ink of the dots.

P.Scheide and P.Chester Beatty IX (967) of Ezekiel (early 3 CE), which originally formed one scroll, systematically indicated the end of each verse, as well as segments of verses, with dots in different positions (high dots, median dots, and dots on the line), apparently without assigning a different meaning to each one (Johnson, *Scheide*, 16–17).

P.Chester Beatty VII of Ezekiel 11–17 (3 CE): high dots and strokes superimposed on a running text without spaces.

P.Merton 2 = P.Chester Beatty VII (965) of Isaiah 8–60 (3 CE): usually high dots and dicola super-imposed on a running text.

Pap. W (Freer) of the Minor Prophets (3 CE) indicates dots at the ends of verses as well as after groups of words. All of them were probably inserted after the completion of the writing.

Dots or dicola appear in many of the texts listed in the previous section, sometimes in existing spaces, and often when no space had been left (see the table). In this regard, Psalms manuscripts form a special group since the graphic indicators are found only at the ends of the lines when the texts are arranged stichographically, and the secondary nature of such indicators cannot be determined easily.

A special case are a few papyri in which high dots were superimposed on the text after each syllable as scribal exercises: P.Rendel Harris 166 of Exodus 22–23 (3 CE); P.Laur. Inv. 140 (34) of Psalm 1 (3–4 CE); P.Lit. London 207 of Psalms 11–16 (3–4 CE). Similar exercises are also known for literary texts.

d. *Continuous writing involving no notation for the indication of verse endings*

The scribes of some texts did not indicate verse endings. Although in principle such texts could reflect the first stage of the Greek translation, it appears that they reflect a secondary development since the earliest available evidence (group *a* above) reflects spacing between the verses.

> P.Oxy. 4.656 of Genesis 14–27 (2 or 3 CE)
> P.Coll. Horsley (Deissmann) of Exodus 4 (2 or 3 CE)
> P.Chester Beatty VI (963) of Numbers and Deuteronomy (2 or 3 CE)
> P.Oxy. 7.1007 of Genesis 2–3 (3 CE) (leather)
> P.Heidelberg 290 of Leviticus 19 (3 CE)
> P.Lit. London 204 of Psalm 2 (3 CE)
> P.Schøyen 2648 of Joshua 9–11 (early 3 CE)
> P.Chester Beatty V (962) of Genesis (second half of 3 CE)
> P.Vindob. Gr. 39777 of Psalms 68, 80 LXX (3–4 CE; *Symmachus*)
> P.Chester Beatty IV (961) of Genesis (4 CE)
> P.Amherst 1 of Genesis 1 (4 CE) (*Aquila*)
> P.Oxy. 9.1167 of Genesis 31 (4 CE)
> P.Grenfell 5 of Ezekiel 5–6 (4 CE)
> P.Oxy. 15.1779 of Psalm 1 (4 CE)
> P.Flor. B.L. 1163 of Job 1–2 (4 CE)
> P.Vindob. Gr 26205 of Psalm 34 LXX (4 CE)
> P.Oxy. 6.845 of Psalms 68–70 LXX (4 CE)

When the text is laid out in *stichoi*, the layout renders the need for explicit verse-indications superfluous:

> P.Bodl. MS. bibl. Gr. 5 of Psalms 48–49 (late 1 or early 2 CE)
> P.Antinoopolis 7 of Psalms LXX (2 CE)
> P.Leipzig 170 of Psalm 118 LXX (2–3 CE)
> P.Vindob. Gr. 26035B of Psalms 68–69 LXX (3 CE)
> P.Alex. 240 (PSI 921) of Psalm 77 LXX (3 CE)
> P.Berlin Inv. 21265 of Psalm 144 LXX (3 CE)
> P.Antinoopolis 8 of Proverbs 5–20 (3 CE)
> P.Laur. Inv. 140 (34) of Psalm 1 (3–4 CE)
> P.Oxy. 10.1226 of Psalms 7–8 LXX (3–4 CE)
> P.Lit. London 207 of Psalms 11–16 (3–4 CE)
> P.Bonn Coll. P147v of Psalm 30 LXX (3–4 CE)
> P.Flor. B.L. 1371 of Psalm 36 LXX (4 CE)
> P.Leipzig 39 of Psalms 30–55 LXX (4 CE)
> P.Vindob. Gr. 35781 of Psalm 77 LXX (4 CE)
> P.Berlin 18196 of Canticles 5–6 (4 CE)
> P.Oxy. 24.2386 of Psalms 83–84 LXX (4–5 CE)

e. *Presumed development*

As the earliest available Greek sources reflect spaces between verses (group *a*), this practice probably reflects the oldest form of the Greek translation in which verse division was indicated, possibly in the original translation itself. See ch. *5a2*. According to this assumption, the continuous writing of the Greek texts as recorded in group *d* is secondary. Over the course of time, graphic signs were added in these spaces in accord with the Greek manuscript writing tradition (groups *b* and *c*). *See further* the summary of Greek scribal traditions in ch. *5a2*.

According to Revell, the spacing and high dots in the middle of a verse in early Greek manuscripts reflected, though not consistently, the Hebrew accent system known from the later Masoretic sources regarding disjunctive accents.[363] A similar claim was made throughout the study of Korpel–de Moor, *Structure*. However, while this claim can be made for such probable Jewish sources as:

> P.Rylands Greek 458 of Deuteronomy (2 BCE)
> P.Fouad 266a–c of Genesis and Deuteronomy (middle 1 BCE)
> 4QLXXNum of Numbers 3–4 (1 BCE)
> 8HevXIIgr hand A (end of 1 BCE)
> P.Oxy. 50.3522 of Job 42 (1 CE),

it is unlikely for such non-Jewish sources as:

> P.Scheide + P.Chester Beatty IX (967) of Ezekiel (early 3 CE)
> Pap. W (Freer) of the Minor Prophets (3 CE)
> P.Antinoopolis 9 of Proverbs 2–3 (3 CE)
> P.Berlin 14039 of Exodus 34–35 (3–4 CE)
> P.Oxy. 11.1352 of Psalms 82–83 LXX (early 4 CE) (leather)
> P.Hamb. Ibscher 5 of Genesis 41 (4 CE)
> Codex St. Cath. of Genesis 27–28 (4 CE)
> P.Oxy. 15.1779 of Psalm 1 (4 CE)
> P.Chester Beatty XIV of Psalms 31, 26, 2 LXX (4 CE)
> P.Yale Beinecke 544 of 1 Samuel 24–2 Samuel 1 (4–5 CE).

In the case of the later manuscripts A, B, S, and Q, which form the basis of the study of Korpel–de Moor, *Structure*, it is even more difficult to invoke the antiquity of the Greek tradition, as the Christian scribes of these late manuscripts probably would not have had access to the earlier Hebrew traditions.

In Greek inscriptions, the high dot (˙), dicolon (:), *tricolon* (three vertical dots), as well as various additional graphic signs (see especially Threatte, *Attic Inscriptions*, 73–94), were used regularly from the seventh century BCE onwards to indicate small or large sense divisions, while in papyri this system was developed further. Thus in the punctuation system devised by Aristophanes of Byzantium (*c.* 257–180 BCE), and recorded by Aristotle, *Rhet.* 3.8.1409a.20, different values were assigned to the dot as it stood above the line (a full stop), in the middle of the line (a comma), or on the line (a semicolon). See Hall, *Companion*, 13; Gardthausen, *Griechische Palaeographie*, II.400; Schubart, *Palaeography*, 173; Kenyon, *Palaeography*, 28; Pfeiffer, *History*, 180; Turner, *Greek Manuscripts*, documents 20, 21, and index, with examples from manuscripts from the second century CE onwards; D. C. Parker, *Codex Bezae: An Early Christian Manuscript and its Text* (Cambridge 1992) 31–4. The high dots were often inserted by a later hand, as illustrated by a papyrus of Homer's Iliad presented in Turner, *Greek Papyri*, pl. IV.

B. *Indication of sections*

See ch. *5a*.

C. *Special writing of the divine names*

The limited evidence for special writing of the divine names points to differences between Jewish and Christian texts.

---

[363] E. J. Revell, "The Oldest Evidence for the Hebrew Accent System," *BJRL* 54 (1971–2) 214–22; idem, "Biblical Punctuation and Chant in the Second Temple Period," *JSJ* 7 (1976) 181–98.

• Jewish texts display the Tetragrammaton in various ways, see ch. *5d*.

• Christian scribes employed κ(ύριο)ς, together with other abbreviated *nomina sacra*.[364] See the penultimate column in the table.

As expected, early Jewish copies of Greek Scripture reflect some scribal phenomena of the Hebrew manuscripts from which the Greek translation was made. However, with the transmission of this translation by Christian scribes, these features were contaminated and in many cases can no longer be recognized. This pertains to the following features: indication of small sense units (verses) and sections with spacing, and the writing of the divine names in Hebrew characters. Several new features were introduced that reflected the Greek writing tradition (graphic indicators for the indication of verses; *paragraphos* signs; *ekthesis*) or early Christian practices (abbreviated *nomina sacra*).

---

[364]The isolated case of the unabbreviated κύριος in P.Oxy. 4.656 of Genesis 14–27 (2 or 3 CE) is unclear. In this manuscript the spaces left by the original scribe were filled in by a second scribe with κύριος.

APPENDIX 6

THE HEBREW TEXTS FROM MASADA

In this appendix, an attempt is made to demonstrate that the Masada nonbiblical texts may be considered an extension of the Qumran corpus. The Masada corpus comprises fifteen literary texts in Hebrew (and one in either Hebrew or Aramaic), found in various loci at Masada. The analysis excludes the 720 ostraca in Hebrew and Aramaic and the thirty ostraca and papyrus texts in Latin and Greek. They are less relevant to the topic under investigation since they derived from the Roman soldiers, while the literary texts were probably taken to Masada by the Zealots and possibly also by Essene fugitives.

An analysis of the find-sites of the Masada texts shed little light on their nature. The facts known regarding the finding of the texts in each locus are described in detail in Netzer, *Masada III* and Tov, "Masada." All texts are in Hebrew, while the language of Mas Unidentified Text heb or ar (Mas 1p)[365] is unclear.

Since the literary remains were found in various loci at Masada, it is unlikely that they were once kept in a central place as were the writings at Qumran (viz., caves 1, 4, and 11), at least not at the final stage of the siege. The Zealots who spent their final turbulent days on Masada probably kept their literary possessions in their respective dwelling places up to the very last moments of the siege.

The Masada biblical texts are identical to the medieval Masoretic texts, and may be considered members of the same textual family, within which a small number of differences may be allowed for, just as differences exist among the medieval manuscripts themselves (see my paper "The Text of the Hebrew/ Aramaic and Greek Bible," mentioned in n. 168). Most of these texts were luxury editions, as defined in ch. *4j*, written in accordance with the rabbinic instructions for the copying of biblical books.

A case can be made that some, most, or all of the nonbiblical texts were taken to Masada by fugitives from the Qumran community.[366] There is no reason to believe that any of the Masada texts were actually

---

[365]Originally this text was classified by Talmon as an Aramaic text, and in the final publication as 'Aramaic?' (Talmon, *Masada VI*, 18, 136), but no certainty can be had regarding the language of this document. The few preserved words allow us to conceive of this text as either Aramaic or Hebrew, and since no other Aramaic texts were found at Masada, the pendulum probably swings in the direction of Hebrew. The reading אלכן in line 2 is certain, but no such form is known from either Hebrew or Aramaic (it is described as an 'apparently Aramaic vocable' by Talmon, *Masada VI*, 137). The same reading may be included also in line 1 of a small scrap of this text: א]לכן. In our view, this reading represents a phonetic spelling of על כן written as one word as occasionally in the Qumran scrolls: 4QAdmonition Based on the Flood (4Q370), line 6. While Aramaic usually has בכן, על כן is also documented (11QtgJob 42:6; Ahiqar lines 122, 165; see Porten–Yardeni, *TAD* 3). By the same token למקרה in line 3 could represent a Hebrew infinitive למקרא or an Aramaic infinitive (for which, cf. 1QapGen ar XIX 22 למפנה, to turn towards). Cf. למקרא in Dan 5:8, 16. On the other hand, this word is taken by Talmon as the Hebrew word 'incident.' וכן אמר in line 4 could be either Hebrew or Aramaic (for the latter see Dan 2:24). The fine handwriting and the relatively large right margin (1.4 cm) lead to the suggestion that this is a fragment of a literary text. The main fragment was preceded by another column or a handle sheet, as suggested by the remains of stitching on the right side of the fragment.

[366]It is of interest to note Netzer's concluding remarks, in which he adduces archeological evidence for the assumption that the western palace was inhabited by a community such as the Essenes, that made relatively few architectural changes to the internal structure of the building, unlike those carried out by the Zealots elsewhere at Masada (*Masada III*, 634). The Qumran sectarian nature of some texts found at Masada is a major indication of their Qumran origin and induces some further thoughts regarding the Qumran corpus. The fact that most texts found at Masada are not sectarian does not militate against this view, since most texts found at Qumran are likewise not sectarian. However, the situation is complex; since most of the texts found at *Qumran* do not carry any distinctive signs of the Qumran community and were presumably imported. In principle, these or similar texts could have been taken to Masada from Qumran. Thus Talmon, *Masada VI*, 104, with regard to Mas apocrGen: 'The work was presumably carried to Masada by a member of the Covenanters' community, who fled to the wilderness fortress when the Romans overran their settlement at Qumran.' For a similar view, see D. Seely, "The Masada Fragments, the Qumran Scrolls, and the New Testament," in *Masada and the World of the New Testament* (ed. J. F. Hall and J. W. Welch; Provo, Utah 1997) 287–301, especially 298. Likewise, Newsom and Yadin, *Masada VI*, 120, with regard to MasShirShabb, which they published as 'The Masada Fragment of the *Qumran* <my italics, E. T.> Songs of the Sabbath Sacrifice': . . . it suggests the participation of members of the Qumran community, almost certainly to be identified with the Essenes, in the revolt against Rome.' These two scholars further add that

penned at Masada itself; see further ch. *1c*. The only scribal activity probably carried out on the spot pertains to the writing of the Hebrew, Aramaic, and Greek ostraca prior to the destruction of Masada, and of Latin ostraca and probably some Greek papyri under the Roman occupation, while other papyrus and leather texts may have been imported to Masada, such as the fragment of Virgil in Mas 721.[367] This fragment contains one or possibly two lines from Virgil, *Aeneas* 4.9 on the recto and an Unidentified Poetical Text on the verso. The extensive spacing on both sides of the inscribed text shows that the papyrus probably contained just this limited text.

Beyond these considerations, the only solid piece of evidence concerning the Masada fragments is that two scrolls of Deuteronomy and Ezekiel were buried under the floor of the synagogue. Why these specific scrolls, and not others, were buried there remains unknown since only fragments of the scrolls have been preserved. These scrolls, or segments of them, may have been damaged at an earlier stage or were otherwise deemed unfit for public reading, rendering mandatory their disposal in a special religious burial place (*genizah*). These scrolls were probably buried by the Zealots during their sojourn at Masada (thus providing us with a *terminus ante quem* for the copying and storage, namely 73 CE). The burial in separate pits probably shows that the scrolls were discarded at different times.[368] Note that the two scrolls probably represented two individual biblical books, and were not segments of larger scrolls. That is, the Deuteronomy scroll probably was not part of a larger Torah scroll, and the Ezekiel scroll did not contain all of the Later Prophets. If the scrolls had been larger, it is probable that some additional fragments would have been preserved. The Deuteronomy scroll contains the very end of the book (Deut 32:46-47; 33:17-24; 34:2-6), as well as the attached uninscribed handle sheet, and it is not impossible that the final sheet or sheets had become damaged due to excessive use (cf. the re-inking of the final column of 1QIsaᵃ), and hence was/were placed in storage without the remainder of the book.

1. *The nature of the corpora found in the Judean Desert*

The approximately 200 biblical texts found at *Qumran* form 21.5% of the 930 texts found there.[369] Furthermore, a large number of the 730 nonbiblical texts were inspired by Scripture or represent biblical exegesis.[370]

Among the Masada fragments, the biblical texts are proportionally better represented than those at Qumran, since among the fifteen/sixteen literary texts there are seven biblical texts, four of the Torah, two of Psalms, and one of Ezekiel. The statistical analysis of the Masada texts is based either on a total of fifteen texts (assuming that Mas pap paleoUnidentified Text (r) and Mas pap paleoText of Sam. Origin (v) reflect the same text; thus Talmon, *Masada VI*, passim) or on a calculation of sixteen texts based on the assumption that the two mentioned texts reflect different compositions (the scribal features of the two sides of the papyrus are different, and the contents are not necessarily related). According to these calculations, the biblical component in the Masada corpus is either 46.6 or 43.75%, double the percentage of biblical scrolls in the Qumran corpus, viz., 22%. For a list of the Masada fragments, see Tov, "Masada," and idem, *DJD* XXXIX, 27–114.

'the participation of Essenes in the revolt is attested by Josephus in *War* II 20 4; III 2 1.' However, Josephus merely mentions an Essene (Ἰωάννης) as a general in the rebellion against Rome in *Bell. Jud.* III 2 1 and II 567.

[367]This is probably the oldest surviving papyrus fragment of the Aeneid. For an analysis, see Cotton and Geiger, *Masada II*, 1–2; E. Ulrich, "Aeneid," *Encyclopedia DSS*, 1.10–11; C. P. Thiede, *The Dead Sea Scrolls and the Jewish Origins of Christianity* (Oxford 2000) 75-7.

[368]On the other hand, according to C. P. Thiede, *The Dead Sea Scrolls and the Jewish Origins of Christianity* (Oxford 2000) 74, this was not a *genizah*. Thiede suggest that the scrolls were first located in a room behind the *aron hakodesh* and he assumes that 'when the Romans approached, the scrolls were hastily buried under the floor, and when the Romans arrived and found the synagogue, they burnt furniture and other objects and threw them into that room. The scrolls survived underneath the rubble.' Although the details in the description may be hypothetical, it is not impossible that the burial does not point to a *genizah*, and that the scrolls were indeed buried for safeguarding against burning by the Romans. See further the description of the archeological evidence by Netzer, *Masada III*, 407 ff., especially the discussion on pp. 411–13 regarding the nature of the synagogue building at an earlier stage. In any event, according to Netzer, p. 410, the pits were dug at a later stage of the occupation by the Zealots.

[369]Some texts which are conceived of as 'biblical' are probably nonbiblical (e.g. liturgical), while some texts which are now recorded as 'parabiblical' may in fact be biblical. Accordingly, there is imprecision in both cases.

[370]The central place of the Bible within the Qumran collection is thus larger than represented by the 200 biblical manuscripts, but this fact does not change the numerical relation between the two groups of texts.

2. *A Qumran origin for the Masada Nonbiblical Hebrew texts?*

It has been suggested by Yadin and Talmon that two or three individual Masada texts were brought to Masada by fugitives from Qumran.[371] This suggestion is expanded here for the collection of nonbiblical texts as a whole. Our suggestion is based on the similarity in content and structure of the corpora of Masada and Qumran. First, the texts which could have originated at Qumran are listed:

• MasQumran-Type Fragment (Mas 1n) is similar in nature to many of the Qumran compositions with regard to morphology and orthography. Little can be said regarding the content of this tiny fragment of nine lines, except that it contains the typical Qumran form הואה (line 3) as well as two further words, קודשו (line 2) and לנבואתה (line 4). The form הואה is not known in Jewish literature outside Qumran.[372]

• MasShirShabb (Mas 1k) represents a composition that is well documented at Qumran (for the eight copies from cave 4 and the one from cave 11, see *DJD* XI and XXIII), and which has a distinct Qumran sectarian content.

• The two texts on biblical themes, named by S. Talmon 'apocryphon of Joshua' and 'apocryphon of Genesis,' resemble Qumran documents reworking biblical texts or motifs. Moreover, I suggested that the Masada apocryphon of Joshua may reflect a manuscript copy of the same composition as that contained in 4QapocrJosh[a,b] (4Q378, 379), 4QProphecy of Joshua (4QapocrJosh[c]?; 4Q522), and 5QapocrJosh (5Q9, published as 'Ouvrage avec toponymes').[373]

• Mas apocrJosh (Mas 1l) reflects some MT-type spellings and linguistic forms (כי line 4, יהם- lines 5–7), but also some Qumran-type spellings. In one detail, it contains a typical Qumran form not known beyond that corpus,[374] viz., מאדה in line 8,[375] and also two additional *plene* spellings, אדוני in line 8, and לוא in lines 5 and 7.

---

[371]See n. 366 above and S. G. F. Brandon, 'Zealots,' *Encyclopaedia Judaica* (Jerusalem 1971) 16.949–50.

[372]This statement is based on the data contained in the electronic Historical Dictionary of the Academy of the Hebrew Language, Jerusalem.

[373]"The Rewritten Book of Joshua as Found at Qumran and Masada," in *Biblical Perspectives: Early Use and Interpretation of the Bible in Light of the Dead Sea Scrolls: Proceedings of the First International Symposium of the Orion Center for the Study of the Dead Sea Scrolls and Associated Literature, May 12–14 1996* (ed. M. E. Stone and E. G. Chazon; Leiden/Boston/Cologne 1998) 233–56.

[374]This statement is based on the following sources: The Historical Dictionary of the Academy of the Hebrew Language covering Qumran texts published until 1975; *The Dead Sea Scrolls Database (Non-Biblical Texts), The Dead Sea Scrolls Electronic Reference Library, Vol. 2; Prepared by the Foundation for Ancient Research and Mormon Studies [FARMS]* (ed. E. Tov; Leiden 1999); J. H. Charlesworth, *Graphic Concordance to the Dead Sea Scrolls* (Tübingen/Louisville 1991). Within the Qumran corpus, with one possible exception, this form occurs only in texts written in the Qumran orthography.

מדה
  1QS X 17
  1QH[a] XI 3
  4QTime of Righteousness (4Q215a) frg. 1 ii 11
  4QMyst[a] (4Q299) 6 ii 15
  4QInstr[d] (4Q418) 81 17; 137 4
מאדה
  1QH[a] 10 10
  1QM XII 12
  4QS[f] (4Q260) IV 2
מאודה
  4QInstr[b] (4Q416) 2 ii 16
  4Q474 1 5
  11QT[a] (11Q19) LXII 12
מואדה
  1QM XIX 5
  1QIsa[a] hand B 5 times, also מואד (56:12), מאודה (36:2; 38:17); in the first part: מואד (16:6).
  4QInstr[a] (4Q415) 11 12
  4QInstr[c] (4Q417) 3 3
  4QInstr[d] (4Q418) 81 5
  4QWisdom Text with Beatitudes (4Q525) 14 ii 24, 26
  4QDibHam[a] (4Q504) 25 3
  11QT[a] LXI 19
  11QapocrPs (11Q11) IV 9

[375]The Qumran sectarian nature of this spelling was recognized by Yadin, *IEJ* 15 (1965) 105.

• MasJub/psJub (Mas 1j) reflects a composition that was especially close to the views of the Qumran covenanters and that is represented at Qumran in a relatively large number of copies in caves 1 (2), 4 (11), and 11 (1). The Masada fragment contains seven lines of two columns in a very fragmentary form. The spelling system is unclear (the occurrences of לכה in I 7 and II 5 slightly tip the balance in favor of a Qumran spelling system). The main clue regarding the background of this fragment is the phrase ושרהמשטמה, written as one word, which in the Jewish literature of this period is known only from Jubilees and some additional compositions found at Qumran: 4QpsJubª (4Q225) 2 i 9, 2 ii 13, 14; 11QapocrPs (11Q11) II 5 (ש[ר המשט]מה); 1QM XIII 11 (מלאך משטמה); and without שר also in 1QM XIII 4; 1QS III 23; 4QpsJubª (4Q225) 2 ii 6; 4QBerª (4Q286) 7a ii 2; 6QpapHymn (6Q18) 9.

On the basis of these criteria, it may be argued that the aforementioned four Masada texts derived from Qumran. Content as well as Qumran orthography and morphology are our guides, but it should be admitted that in the latter case some circular reasoning is involved.

An alternative explanation stressing the universal nature of the finds of Qumran and Masada, and hence disproving any special link between the two sites, was offered by Schiffman in his discussion of the copy of MasShirShabb (Mas 1k) at Masada: ' . . . study of the remaining Masada texts makes it clear that the Masada corpus contained a number of texts parallel to those found in the Qumran collection. Apparently, these were commonly known works that circulated widely in Palestine during this period, at least in the case of the apocryphal texts.'[376]

The implications of the finding of a text now named Mas pap paleoText of Sam. Origin (Mas 1o recto) at Masada are unclear. For a detailed discussion, see Tov, "Masada."

3. *Similarity between the corpora of Masada and Qumran*

Assuming that the Masada nonbiblical texts were brought to Masada by fugitives from Qumran, we note that the corpora of Masada and Qumran resemble one another in the following aspects:

• The biblical texts found at Masada, like those from Qumran, derive from all three segments of the Hebrew canon (Torah, Ezekiel, Psalms). In addition, individual texts belonging to the so-called Apocrypha (Ben Sira) as well as hitherto unknown works were found at both places.

• The two collections resemble one another with regard to the inclusion of writings of sectarian content among the nonbiblical texts. The Qumran corpus contains a large group of sectarian writings, probably between 100 and 140[377] of a total of 930 texts (10.75–15%). A similar percentage is apparent among the Masada texts (two among fifteen/sixteen texts, 12.5–13.5%), viz., MasShirShabb (Mas 1k) and MasQumran-type Fragment (Mas 1n). This calculation does not include the Jubilees text. If the Masada Jubilees text were to be included in this calculation, the percentage of Qumran sectarian texts would be even higher than that at Qumran itself. At the same time, we should remember that no fragments of the central sectarian texts from Qumran were found at Masada.

• The two collections resemble one another with regard to the inclusion of paleo-Hebrew texts. Among the fifteen/sixteen Hebrew Masada texts, one is written in the paleo-Hebrew script (6.2–6.6%). Similarly, among the 930 Qumran texts there are 15 or 16 such texts (1.61–1.72%). [378]

• One of the fifteen/sixteen Masada texts is written on papyrus (inscribed on both sides; 6.5%). Likewise, 131 of the 930 Qumran texts are written on papyrus (14%).

• Parallels in content between the nonbiblical texts from Masada and Qumran were noted above. Five Masada texts are matched by similar or identical texts from Qumran:

> Mas apocrJosh (Mas 1l)
> MasShirShabb (Mas 1k)
> MasSir (Mas 1h)
> MasJub/psJub (Mas 1j)
> Mas apocrGen (Mas 1m)

At the same time, differences, in proportion as well as in character, are visible between the two corpora.

---

[376]L. Schiffman, *Reclaiming the Dead Sea Scrolls* (Philadelphia/Jerusalem 1994) 355.

[377]Not to be confused with the larger group of texts written in the Qumran scribal practice (see APPENDIX 1).

[378]It is unclear whether the paleo-Hebrew text found at Masada differs from its counterparts at Qumran. The great majority of the Qumran paleo-Hebrew texts are biblical, while the character of four texts is unclear: two unidentified texts (4Q124, 125), 4Qpaleo paraJosh (4Q123), and 11QpaleoUnidentified Text (11Q22). But even if the character of the latter four texts is unclear, none is as unbiblical as the Masada text.

(1) Although the Masada fragments are often small, there is nevertheless enough evidence available to realize that the biblical texts constitute a higher percentage of the Masada corpus than of the Qumran corpus. The biblical component in the Masada corpus is either 46.6 or 43.75%, far more than the percentage of biblical scrolls in the Qumran corpus, viz., 21.5% (not counting the *tefillin* and *mezuzot*). These data probably imply that the Zealots, the inhabitants of Masada, were more Bible-oriented than the Qumran covenanters. It should also be noted that among the texts discovered in the Judean Desert, those from Masada, Murabbaʿat, and Naḥal Ḥever are the closest to the medieval Masoretic texts (see the Appendix in Tov, "Masada"). Statistics are always misleading because of the fragmentary status of the evidence but, for the sake of the argument, we should probably surmise that the same percentage of biblical and nonbiblical texts perished. When stating that 21.5% of the Qumran corpus consists of biblical manuscripts (not counting *tefillin* and *mezuzot*), one should remember that the percentages vary for the different caves:

> cave 1: 12 biblical texts out of a total of 80 texts (15%)
> cave 2: 17 biblical texts out of a total of 33 texts (51%)
> cave 3: 3 biblical texts out of a total of 15 texts (20%)
> cave 4: 136 Hebrew/Aramaic biblical texts out of a total of 683 texts (20%)
> cave 5: 8 biblical texts out of a total of 25 texts (32%)
> cave 6: 7 biblical texts out of a total of 33 texts (21%)
> cave 8: 2 biblical texts out of a total of 5 texts (40%)
> cave 11: 10 biblical texts out of a total of 31 texts (32%)

Caves 2 and 8 contain a substantially higher percentage of biblical texts than the other caves, and if they are counted as individual sites they resemble the evidence for the sites other than Qumran in the Judean Desert.

(2) It cannot be coincidental that the number of Torah scrolls among the Masada finds is relatively large. Of the seven biblical texts, four contain portions from the Torah, and the other texts contain parts of Psalms (2) and Ezekiel (1). Thus, of fifteen or sixteen literary texts found at Masada, 26.5% or 25% represent the Torah, as compared with merely 8.4% (78 texts) of the 930 Qumran texts (counting scrolls containing two books, such as 4QGen-Exod[a], only once, and not including *tefillin* and *mezuzot*). A similar percentage pertains to the Psalms scrolls, two scrolls at Masada (13.5% or 12.5%) as opposed to 36 scrolls at Qumran (4%). This situation resembles that of the biblical scrolls left behind by the Bar Kochba fighters, that consisted mainly of texts from the Torah and Psalms in Murabbaʿat (MurGen, MurExod, MurNum, MurDeut, MurIsa, MurXII), Naḥal Ḥever (5/6ḤevNum[a]; 5/6ḤevPs; XḤev/SeNum[b]; XḤev/SeDeut), Naḥal Ṣeʾelim (34ṢeNum), and Sdeir (SdeirGen). The only literary texts beyond the Torah and Psalms from these sites are single copies of Isaiah and the Minor Prophets found in Murabbaʿat and of the Greek Minor Prophets from Naḥal Ḥever, that are similar in this connection to the Ezekiel scroll from Masada.

(3) The identifying of the Masada biblical texts with the textual tradition that was to become the central text of Judaism (MT), as reflected in rabbinic literature and in the medieval manuscripts, points to a community which must have been closely connected to the Jerusalem spiritual center where the proto-rabbinic texts were at home. This assumption is corroborated by the large proportion of biblical texts found at Masada. On the other hand, Qumran reflects biblical texts of a different textual nature, and the Qumran proto-Masoretic texts are less similar to the medieval tradition than those found at Masada and at the sites dating to the time of the Second Jewish Revolt. See my paper "The Text of the Hebrew/Aramaic and Greek Bible" (n. 168).

(4) If our understanding is correct that MasUnidentified Text heb or ar (Mas 1p) is Hebrew, no Aramaic literary texts were found at Masada, while some 130 such texts were found at Qumran.

Two further points should be noticed with regard to the non-Hebrew texts.

(5) Statistically, the number of Greek texts at Masada (at least 11 texts together with fragments of several additional texts; the total number is similar to the fifteen/sixteen Hebrew texts from Masada) greatly exceeds the Greek texts found at Qumran (probably 27 of an overall number of 930 texts).

(6) No Latin texts were found at Qumran, while some were found at Masada.

The similarities between the corpora of Qumran and Masada are not expected as these features are absent from the collections of texts found in Murabbaʿat, Naḥal Ḥever, Ṣeʾelim, Sdeir, Wadi Daliyeh, and Jericho. The latter sites contained mainly documentary texts written on papyrus, while the Qumran and Masada corpora are mostly literary and on leather, leaving aside the Masada ostraca. These data further support the assumption that all the texts found at Masada were imported from Qumran, as suggested above, or at least that this was the case for the nonbiblical texts.[379]

As a rule, the Masada documents were penned at a later period than the majority of the Qumran texts. The former were ascribed to Herodian times, with the exception of the Ben Sira scroll written in the Hasmonean period (Talmon, *Masada VI*, 20), while the Qumran scrolls derived from all periods between 250 BCE and 70 CE.

---

[379]The similarity in content between the corpora of Masada and Qumran is matched by similarity in scribal habits, as suggested by Talmon, *Masada VI*, 21–3. Beyond such similarities as were probably found in all texts written in this period, several scribal practices link the two corpora: guide dots and ruling; differences in the ruling of adjacent sheets; special layout of the poetical texts, etc.

APPENDIX 7

SCOPE AND SPACING OF THE UNITS IN THE BIBLICAL TEXT QUOTED IN THE *PESHARIM*

1. *Scope*

The following list provides the full evidence for the Scriptural units quoted as lemmas in the *pesharim*, excluding fragments in which the beginning of the quotation has not been preserved. These lemmas comprise anywhere between half a verse and five continuous verses of the MT tradition. This list does not refer to the repeated quotation of part of the lemma within the exposition itself. For an analysis, see ch. *5a2*.

Biblical Verse(s)	Reference in *Pesher*
Hab 1:1-2a	1QpHab I 1–2
Hab 1:3a	1QpHab I 5
Hab 1:3b	1QpHab I 7
Hab 1:4a	1QpHab I 10–11
Hab 1:4bα	1QpHab I 12
Hab 1:4bβ	1QpHab I 14–15
Hab 1:5	1QpHab I 16–17, II 1
Hab 1:6a	1QpHab I 10–11
Hab 1:6b	1QpHab II 16–17
Hab 1:6bβ-7	1QpHab III 1–3
Hab 1:8-9a	1QpHab III 6–9
Hab 1:9aβ-9b	1QpHab III 14
Hab 1:10a	1QpHab III 14–IV 1
Hab 1:10b	1QpHab IV 3–4
Hab 1:11	1QpHab IV 9
Hab 1:12	1QpHab IV 16–17
Hab 1:12b-13a	1QpHab V 1–2
Hab 1:13aα	1QpHab V 6–7
Hab 1:13b	1QpHab V 8–9
Hab 1:14-16	1QpHab V 12–16
Hab 1:17	1QpHab VI 8–9
Hab 2:1-2	1QpHab VI 12–16
Hab 2:3a	1QpHab VII 5–6
Hab 2:3b	1QpHab VII 9–10
Hab 2:4a	1QpHab VII 14–15
Hab 2:4b	1QpHab VII 17
Hab 2:5-6	1QpHab VIII 3–8
Hab 2:7-8a	1QpHab VIII 13–15
Hab 2:8b	1QpHab IX 8
Hab 2:9-11	1QpHab IX 12–15
Hab 2:12-13	1QpHab X 6–8
Hab 2:14	1QpHab X 14–15
Hab 2:15	1QpHab XI 2–3
Hab 2:16	1QpHab XI 9–11
Hab 2:17a	1QpHab XI 17–XII 1
Hab 2:17b	1QpHab XII 7
Hab 2:18	1QpHab XII 10–12
Hab 2:19-20	1QpHab XII 15–XIII 1

Biblical Verse(s)	Reference in *Pesher*
Mic 1:2b-5a	1QpMic (1Q14) 1–5 1
Mic 1:5b	1QpMic (1Q14) 10 2
Mic 1:5c	1QpMic (1Q14) 10 3–4
Mic 1:6a	1QpMic (1Q14) 10 8
Mic 1:9b	1QpMic (1Q14) 11 3
Mic 1:16-17	1QpMic (1Q14) 17–18 2–5
Ps 68:31	1QpPs (1Q16) 9 2–3
Isa 10:22-23	4QpIsa^a (4Q161) 2–6 ii 1–3
Isa 10:24-27	4QpIsa^a (4Q161) 2–6 ii 10–15
Isa 10:28-32	4QpIsa^a (4Q161) 2–6 ii 21–25
Isa 10:33-34	4QpIsa^a (4Q161) 7 1–3
Isa 11:1-5	4QpIsa^a (4Q161) 7 15–20
Isa 5:11-14	4QpIsa^a (4Q162) ii 2–6
Isa 5:24c-25	4QpIsa^a (4Q162) ii 7–10
Isa 8:7-8	4Qpap pIsa^c (4Q163) 2 2–4
Isa 9:11	4Qpap pIsa^c (4Q163) 2 6–7
Isa 9:13-16	4Qpap pIsa^c (4Q163) 2 8–13
Isa 9:17-20	4Qpap pIsa^c (4Q163) 2 16–21
Isa 10:19	4Qpap pIsa^c (4Q163) 6–7 ii 3–7
Isa 10:20-22bα	4Qpap pIsa^c (4Q163) 6–7 ii 10–16
Isa 10:22-22bβ-23	4Qpap pIsa^c (4Q163) 6–7 ii 18–19
Isa 10:24	4Qpap pIsa^c (4Q163) 6–7 ii 21
Isa 14:8	4Qpap pIsa^c (4Q163) 8–10 1–3
Isa 14:26-27	4Qpap pIsa^c (4Q163) 8–10 4–7
Isa 14:28-30	4Qpap pIsa^c (4Q163) 8–10 11–14
Isa 29:18-23	4Qpap pIsa^c (4Q163) 18–19 1–6
Zech 11:11	4Qpap pIsa^c (4Q163) 21 7–8
Isa 30:1-5	4Qpap pIsa^c (4Q163) 21 9–15
Isa 30:15-18	4Qpap pIsa^c (4Q163) 23 3–9
Isa 30:19-21	4Qpap pIsa^c (4Q163) 23 15–19
Isa 31:1	4Qpap pIsa^c (4Q163) 25 5–7
Isa 54:11c	4QpIsa^d (4Q164) 1 1
Isa 54:12a	4QpIsa^d (4Q164) 1 3
Isa 54:12b	4QpIsa^d (4Q164) 1 6
Isa 40:12	4QpIsa^e (4Q165) 1 3–4
Isa 21:11-15	4QpIsa^e (4Q165) 5 3–5
Isa 32:6-7	4QpIsa^e (4Q165) 6 3–6
Hos 2:8a,c	4QpHos^a (4Q166) 1 7–8
Hos 2:9b,c	4QpHos^a (4Q166) 1 15–16
Hos 2:11-12	4QpHos^a (4Q166) 2 8–11
Hos 2:13	4QpHos^a (4Q166) 2 14–15
Hos 2:14	4QpHos^a (4Q166) 2 17–19
Hos 5:15	4QpHos^b (4Q167) 2 5–6
Hos 8:6	4QpHos^b (4Q167) 11–13 3
Hos 8:7-8	4QpHos^b (4Q167) 11–13 6–8
Nah 1:4aα	4QpNah (4Q169) 1–2 ii 3
Nah 1:4aβ	4QpNah (4Q169) 1–2 ii 4
Nah 1:4b	4QpNah (4Q169) 1–2 ii 5

Nah 1:5-6	4QpNah (4Q169) 1–2 ii 9–11
Nah 2:12b	4QpNah (4Q169) 3–4 i 1–2
Nah 2:13a	4QpNah (4Q169) 3–4 i 4
Nah 2:13b	4QpNah (4Q169) 3–4 i 6
Nah 2:14	4QpNah (4Q169) 3–4 i 8–10
Nah 3:1a-baα	4QpNah (4Q169) 3–4 ii 1
Nah 3:1a-bβ-3	4QpNah (4Q169) 3–4 ii 3–4
Nah 3:4	4QpNah (4Q169) 3–4 ii 7
Nah 3:5	4QpNah (4Q169) 3–4 ii 10–11
Nah 3:6-7a	4QpNah (4Q169) 3–4 iii 1–2
Nah 3:7b-c	4QpNah (4Q169) 3–4 iii 5–6
Nah 3:8a	4QpNah (4Q169) 3–4 iii 8
Nah 3:8b	4QpNah (4Q169) 3–4 iii 10
Nah 3:9a	4QpNah (4Q169) 3–4 iii 11
Nah 3:10	4QpNah (4Q169) 3–4 iv 1–2
Nah 3:11a	4QpNah (4Q169) 3–4 iv 4–5
Nah 3:11b	4QpNah (4Q169) 3–4 iv 6–7
Nah 3:12a	4QpNah (4Q169) 3–4 iv 8
Ps 37:7	4QpPs^a (4Q171) 1–10 i 25–26
Ps 37:8-9a	4QpPs^a (4Q171) 1–10 ii 1–2
Ps 37:9b	4QpPs^a (4Q171) 1–10 ii 4
Ps 37:10	4QpPs^a (4Q171) 1–10 ii 5–7
Ps 37:11	4QpPs^a (4Q171) 1–10 ii 9
Ps 37:12-13	4QpPs^a (4Q171) 1–10 ii 13–14
Ps 37:14-15	4QpPs^a (4Q171) 1–10 ii 16–17
Ps 37:16	4QpPs^a (4Q171) 1–10 ii 22
Ps 37:17	4QpPs^a (4Q171) 1–10 ii 24
Ps 37:18-19a	4QpPs^a (4Q171) 1–10 ii 26–27
Ps 37:19b-20	4QpPs^a (4Q171) 1–10 iii 2–3
Ps 37:20b-c	4QpPs^a (4Q171) 1–10 iii 5a
Ps 37:20d	4QpPs^a (4Q171) 1–10 iii 7
Ps 37:21-22	4QpPs^a (4Q171) 1–10 iii 8–9
Ps 37:23-24	4QpPs^a (4Q171) 1–10 iii 14–15
Ps 37:25-26	4QpPs^a (4Q171) 1–10 iii 17–18
Ps 37:29	4QpPs^a (4Q171) 1–10 iv 2
Ps 37:30-31	4QpPs^a (4Q171) 1–10 iv 3–4
Ps 37:32-33	4QpPs^a (4Q171) 1–10 iv 7
Ps 37:34	4QpPs^a (4Q171) 1–10 iv 10–11
Ps 37:35-36	4QpPs^a (4Q171) 1–10 iv 13–14
Ps 37:37	4QpPs^a (4Q171) 1–10 iv 16
Ps 37:38	4QpPs^a (4Q171) 1–10 iv 17–18
Ps 37:39	4QpPs^a (4Q171) 1–10 iv 19–20
Ps 45:1	4QpPs^a (4Q171) 1–10 iv 23
Ps 45:2a	4QpPs^a (4Q171) 1–10 iv 24–25
Ps 45:2b	4QpPs^a (4Q171) 1–10 iv 26–27
Ps 60:8-9	4QpPs^a (4Q171) 13 4

2. *Spacing*

Differing spacing systems were used to separate the biblical text from its *pesher*; the choice of system was often determined by where in the line the *pesher* started and ended. Reconstructed evidence appears in square brackets.[380] See the analysis below.

---

[380]For a different type of recording these data, see the listing in Doudna, *4Q Pesher Nahum*, 233–52 ('Vacats').

Spacing Systems in the Pesharim

1QpHab

Before the *Pesher* (between the Lemma and the *Pesher*)

Closed Section	Open Section	No Indication
	[1 7 <2nd half>]	
II 1 <1st half>		
II 5 before second interpretation <1st half>		
	II 11 <2nd half>	
	III 3 <2nd half>	
III 9 <1st half>		
		III 14 end of line (2d quotation)
IV 1 <middle>		
		IV 4 end of line
IV 10 <1st half>		
		IV 13 end of line
	V 2 <2nd half>	
V 7 <1st half>		
V 9 <1st half>		
VI 3 <1st half>		
		VI 5 end of line
	VI 9 <2nd half>	
	VII 6 <2nd half>	
VII 10 <1st half>		
VII 15 <1st half>		
VIII 8 <1st half>		
	VIII 16 (indentation)	
IX 4 <1st half>		
IX 7 part of a *pesher* <1st half>		
		IX 8
	X 2 <2nd half>	
	X 8 <2nd half>	
X 15 <1st half>		
	XI 4 (indentation)	
	XI 11 <1st half>	
		XII 1 end of line
		XII 12

After the *Pesher*

Closed Section	Open Section	No Indication
		III 6
		IV 3, 9
		V 6, 8, 12
		VI 5, 8, 12
		VII 5, 7, 14
		VIII 13
		IX 8, 12
		X 5, 13
		XI 8
		XII 14

1QpMic (1Q14)

Before the *Pesher* (between the Lemma and the *Pesher*)

Closed Section	Open Section	No Indication
10 3		

1QpZeph (1Q15)

Before the *Pesher* (between the Lemma and the *Pesher*)

Closed Section	Open Section	No Indication
line 4		

1QpPs (1Q16)

Before the *Pesher* (between the Lemma and the *Pesher*)

Closed Section	Open Section	No Indication
9 1		
9 3?		

After the *Pesher*

Closed Section	Open Section	No Indication
9 2		

4QpIsa^a (4Q161)[381]

Before the *Pesher* (between the Lemma and the *Pesher*)

Closed Section	Open Section	No Indication
	[2–6 ii 16] + blank line	
	2–6 ii 25 <2nd half>	
		7–10 iii 9 (quote within quote)
	7–10 iii 14 (blank line?)	
		7–10 iii 27

After the *Pesher*

Closed Section	Open Section	No Indication
	2–6 ii 10 (indentation?)	
	2–6 ii 20 (+ blank line)	
	7–10 iii 21 (blank line?)	
7–10 iii 26 (quote within quote)		

4QpIsa^b (4Q162)

Before the *Pesher* (between the Lemma and the *Pesher*)

Closed Section	Open Section	No Indication
		I 2
II 6		

After the *Pesher*

Closed Section	Open Section	No Indication
		II 2
		II 7

[381]In the *pesharim* from cave 4, the numbering follows Horgan, *Pesharim*.

Appendix 7

4Qpap pIsa^c (4Q163)

Before the *Pesher* (between the Lemma and the *Pesher*)

Closed Section	Open Section	No Indication
	[6–7 ii 3] <1st half>	
8–10 3 <1st half>		
8–10 7 <1st half>		
		23 ii 10 end of line

After the *Pesher*

Closed Section	Open Section	No Indication
	6–7 ii 9 (+ blank line)	
	25 4 (+ blank line)	

4QpIsa^e (4Q165)

Before the *Pesher* (between the Lemma and the *Pesher*)

Closed Section	Open Section	No Indication
5 2		
6 6		

4QHos^a (4Q166)

Before the *Pesher* (between the Lemma and the *Pesher*)

Closed Section	Open Section	No Indication
	i 6	
		ii 15

After the *Pesher*

Closed Section	Open Section	No Indication
	i 13 (+ blank line)	
	ii 6 (+ blank line)	
	ii 11	
		ii 14

4QHos^b (4Q167)

Before the *Pesher* (between the Lemma and the *Pesher*)

Closed Section	Open Section	No Indication
2 1		
7–8 2		
10 2		
	11–13 8	

After the *Pesher*

Closed Section	Open Section	No Indication
		2 2

4QpNah (4Q169)

Before the *Pesher* (between the Lemma and the *Pesher*)

Closed Section	Open Section	No Indication
1–2 ii 5 <middle>		
3–4 i 6 <2nd half>		
		3–4 ii 1 end of line
3–4 ii 4 <2nd half>		
	3–4 ii 7 <2nd half>	

3–4 ii 11 <2nd half>		
	3–4 iii 2 <1st half>	
3–4 iii 6 <2nd half>		
	3–4 iii 10 <2nd half>	
3–4 iv 3 <1st half>		
3–4 iv 5 <1st half>		

After the *Pesher*

Closed Section	Open Section	No Indication
1–2 ii 9 <1st half>		
3–4 i 1 <1st half>		
3–4 i 4 <middle>		
3–4 ii 1 <2nd half>		
	3–4 ii 2 <2nd half>	
		3–4 ii 6 end of line
3–4 ii 10 <1st half>		
		3–4 iii 1 <middle>
		3–4 iii 5 <middle>
3–4 iii 8 <1st half>		
		3–4 iii 9 end of line
3–4 iv 1 <2nd half>		

4QpPsᵃ (4Q171)

Before the *Pesher* (between the Lemma and the *Pesher*)

Closed Section	Open Section	No Indication
		1–10 i 26
		1–10 ii 2? poss. closed section
		1–10 ii 4
		1–10 ii 7
		1–10 ii 9
		1–10 ii 14
		1–10 iii 3
		1–10 iii 7
		1–10 iii 10 end of line
		1–10 iii 12

After the *Pesher*

Closed Section	Open Section	No Indication
	1–10 i 24 <2nd half>	
1–10 ii 1 <1st half>		
1–10 ii 4? (possibly no closed section) <1st half>		
	1–10 ii 5 <2nd half> (+ blank line)	
		1–10 ii 8 end of line
		1–10 ii 16
		1–10 ii 17 end of line
		1–10 ii 24
		1–10 iii 2
		1–10 iv 2
1–10 iv 19 <1st half>		
	1–10 ii 12 <1st half>	
	1–10 ii 20 <2nd half> (+ blank line)	

	1–10 iii 6 <1st half>	
	1–10 iii 13 <1st half>	
	1–10 iv 5 <2nd half> (+ blank line)	
	1–10 iv 12 <2nd half>	
	1–10 iv 21 <2nd half> (+ blank line)	

Spacing, used to mark off different sections within most known texts, is used in all *pesharim* (apart from thematic *pesharim*). Three systems are used.

Spacing before but not after the pesher

1QpHab is the only surviving *pesher* that separated the biblical text from the *incipit* of the *pesher*, but inserted no space between the *pesher* and the next biblical lemma. In this system, the biblical text was considered to be one continuous text together with its *pesher*, which was preceded by a space. The length of this space was determined by whether the lemma ended in the first half of the line, in which case it was usually followed by a closed section (II 1, 5; III 9; IV 1, 10; V 7, 9; VI 3; VII 10, 15; VIII 8; IX 4; X 15). On the other hand, if the biblical text ended in the second half of the line, the scribe left the remainder of that line open (II 11; III 3; V 2; VII 6; X 2, 8; differently in XI 11 where the open line started in the first part of the line). If the scribe wished to indicate the beginning of the *pesher* at the very end of the line, where there was no room for such an indication, he either indented the following line (VIII 16; XI 4) or left no space at all (IV 4, 13; VI 5; IX 8; XII 1). At the same time, this scribe did not separate the end of the *pesher* from the next biblical quotation.

No spacing before but with spacing after the pesher

4QpPs^a (4Q171) is the only surviving *pesher* which did not indicate the *incipit* of the *pesher* with any spacing system, while it often indicated its end with a closed section (usually in the first half of the line) or an open section (usually in the second half of the line); in other cases no space was left. Likewise, no spacing was left before the individual *pesher* of Num 24:7 in 4QD^a (4Q266) 3 iii 21, but after the *pesher* such a space was left in line 22. The *pesher* in 4QOrdinances (4Q159) frg. 5 did not start with a space in line 1, but ended with a closed section in line 2.

Spacing both before and after the pesher

This system is the most frequently used, although fragmentary evidence precludes any certainty. With some exceptions, 4QpNah (4Q169), the best preserved text in this group, left spaces both before and after the *pesher*. The width of these spaces differed from case to case but, unlike in 1QpHab, the position of the spacing in the line (first or second half) is irrelevant for the type of spacing used. After the *pesher*, some closed sections are of average size (3–4 i 6), some are very small (3–4 i 1), while others are very large, covering as much as half a line (1–2 ii 9; 3–4 ii 10; 3–4 iii 8). 1QpPs (1Q16), 4QpIsa^a (4Q161), 4Qpap pIsa^c (4Q163), and 4QpHos^a (4Q166) probably followed the same system. Likewise, the single *pesher* of Isa 40:3 in 1QS VIII 13–16 was preceded and followed by a closed section. Similarly, an open section was indicated before the *pesher* of Num 21:18 in 4QD^b (4Q267) 2 10 (the end of the *pesher* has not been preserved). An individual *pesher* within 4QCommGen A (4Q252) 4 5 is set apart by spacing before the *incipit* of the *pesher* (the end has not been preserved). In addition, 4Qpap pIsa^c (4Q163) indicated the beginning of a *pesher* with marginal signs (6–7 ii 4, 8, 14, 17).

The marking of the beginning and end of the commentary by spacing is known also in the Greek scribal tradition; see P.Oxy. 31.2536 of 2 CE (*Hypomnema* of Theon on Pindar, *Pythians*). In other cases, however, the spacing was used in conjunction with additional ways of separating the text from its commentary. Thus P.Oxy. 24.2390 of 2 CE (Commentary on Alcman) has spacing before the lemma and a *diple* protruding into the margin, while P.Oxy. 25.2429 of 175–200 CE (Commentary on Epicharmus, Ὀδυσσεὺς αὐτόμολος) has a colon before the lemma, a space after the lemma, and *paragraphoi* in the margins. Further systems are analyzed by M. Del Fabbro, "Il commentario nella tradizione papiracea," *Studia Papyrologica* 18 (1979) 69–123, especially 87–9. For example, in P.Oxy. 20.2262 of 150–200 CE (Commentary on Callimachus, Αἴτια), the lemmas are made to project into the left margin (*ekthesis*) by 1.5 cm.

APPENDIX 8

SCRIBAL FEATURES OF BIBLICAL MANUSCRIPTS

This appendix records the scribal features of the biblical manuscripts from the Judean Desert. This is not an exhaustive list of all the biblical manuscripts, as texts with no special scribal features are not included.

Columns 1–4 repeat the data in APPENDIX 1 enabling a separate analysis in this appendix of the scribal features of the biblical texts. Further, while in APPENDIX 1 the scrolls are arranged sequentially by inventory number, in this appendix they appear according to biblical book.

Stichographic arrangement (in the 'name' column)

[s]	employment of a s(tichographic) system for some or all poetical sections in manuscripts containing such sections, see ch. *5b*
[n]	lack of such a layout[382]

1. Section markers

2. *Correction systems*

dots	cancellation dots/strokes (ch. 5, TABLES 10–14)
cross	crossing out of letters or words with a line (ch. 5, TABLE 16)
par	parenthesis sign(s) (ch. *5c2*)

3. *Scribal markings*

gd	guide dots/strokes (ch. *4a*, TABLES 2 and 3)
no-gd	lack of guide dots/strokes (ch. *4a*, TABLE 6)
cr	single cryptic A letters written in the margin (ch. *5c3*)
pHeb	single paleo-Hebrew letters written in the margin (ch. *5c4*)
waw	paleo-Hebrew or square *waw* indicated in closed and open paragraphs (ch. *5c1*)
X	X-sign (ch. *5c5*)

4. *Divine names*

pal-Tetragr	paleo-Hebrew Tetragrammaton (ch. *6b*, TABLE 1)
puncta	*Tetrapuncta* (dots/strokes; ch. *5d*, TABLE 19)

5–9. *Textual character*

These columns record the textual character of most scrolls, by approximation only:[383]

5. Qumran scrib. pract.   scrolls of various textual backgrounds, displaying the Qumran scribal practice; see ch. *8a*

---

[382]For example, when '[s]' is written next to the name of an Exodus scroll, reference is made to the stichographic writing of the Song at the Sea (chapter 15) as described in ch. *5b*. A similar system is used for Deuteronomy 32. In all other cases, complete books are presented in this fashion (Psalms, Job, Proverbs, Lamentations).

[383]These data are provided mainly as background information for the analysis of individual scribal phenomena: it is not impossible that certain scribal features occur predominantly in scrolls of a specific background.

6. MT   scrolls belonging to the MT family
7. SP   scrolls related to SP
8. LXX   scrolls related to the *Vorlage* of the LXX
9. Independent scrolls   scrolls unrelated exclusively to any of the above, often named
                          'independent' or non-aligned

10–11. *Scribal activity*

10. Scribal intervention This column records the number of scribal interventions in the
                          scroll (supralinear corrections, deletions, erasures, reshaping of
                          letters, linear and supralinear scribal signs).

11. Average number   This column records the *average* number of lines in a
                          manuscript between two scribal interventions.

Name	1 Section Markers	2 Correction Systems	3 Scribal Markings	4 Divine Names	5 Qumran Scrib. Pract.	6 MT	7 SP	8 G	9 Independent	10 Scribal Intervention	11 Aver. No. of Lines
4QGen-Exod[a]			gd			y				6	30
4QGen[b]						y				1	62
4QGen[c]						y	y			1	20
4QGen[d]						y	y			1	11
4QGen[e]						y	y			0	49+
4QGen[f]						y	y			0	17+
4QGen[g]						y	y			2	13
4QGen[j]						y	y			2	30
4QGen[k]			gd?						y	1	13
4QpaleoGen-Exod[l]						y				2	105
1QExod						y	y				
2QExod[b]				pal-Tetra	y?				y?		
4Q[Gen-]Exod[b]						y		y	y	2	35
4QExod[c] [n]		dots				y				8	17
4QExod[d] [n]									y!		
4QExod[e]									y?		
4QExod-Lev[f]							y		y	1	57
4QExod[j]				pal-Tetra	y?						
4QpaleoExod[m]			gd *waw*				y			3	197
1QpaleoLev						y	y			1	33
2QpaleoLev			gd								
4QLev[b]			gd			y	y			0	136
4QLev[c]						y	y			1	36
4QLev[d]							y	y		0	31+
4QLev[e]						y	y			0	41+
4QLev[g]				pal-Tetra							
4QLev-Num[a]			gd			y	y			7	36
11QpaleoLev[a]		par	*waw*						y	2	66
11QLev[b]				pal-Tetra					y?	0	20+
2QNum[b]					y?						
4QNum[b]			gd *waw*			y		y	y	10	38

1QDeut^a			gd		y						
1QDeut^b [s]						y	y			0	82+
2QDeut^c			gd		y?						
4QDeut^b [s]	y								y	2	14
4QDeut^c [s]		dots cross							y	6	27
4QDeut^d						y	y			0	35+
4QDeut^e						y	y				
4QDeut^f						y	y			6	17
4QDeut^g						y	y			1	43
4QDeut^h									y	3	16
4QDeut^i						y	y				
4QDeut^j [n]		dots	no-gd		y				y!	3	30
4QDeut^k1					y				y	2	12
4QDeut^k2				pal-Tetra	y				y	1	45
4QDeut^m					y				y	2	8
4QDeut^n			gd				y?		y!	2	33
4QDeut^o			gd			y	y			0	46+
4QDeut^q [s]								y			
4QpaleoDeut^r [s]						y	y			0	114+
5QDeut									y	4	4
4QJosh^a									y!	3	19
4QJosh^b						y				3	9
4QJudg^a									y!		
4QJudg^b						y				2	8
1QSam					y						
4QSam^a								y	y!	8	110
4QSam^b						y				1	50
4QSam^c		dots		puncta	y			384	y	6	10
4QKgs						y				0	38+
6QpapKgs									y		
1QIsa^a	y	dots cross	cr pHeb X *waw* no-gd	puncta (corrector)	y				y	398	4
1QIsa^b						y				8	55
4QIsa^a			gd			y	y			10	7
4QIsa^b						y	y			17	13
4QIsa^c			no-gd	pal-Tetra	y				y	8	28
4QIsa^d		dots(Tetra)				y	y			6	17
4QIsa^e						y	y			0	58+
4QIsa^f			gd			y	y			1	92
4QIsa^g			gd			y	y			1	26
4QIsa^h		dots				y	y				
4QIsa^i			gd								
4QIsa^k									y?		
4QIsa^m						y	y				
4QIsa^o						y	y				
2QJer			no-gd		y				y	0	60+

---

[384] This scroll is equally close to MT and the Lucianic manuscripts of 2 Samuel 14–15, which in that section probably reflects the Old Greek translation.

Name	Section Markers	Correction Systems	Scribal Markings	Divine Names	Qumran Scrib. Pract.	MT	SP	G	Independent	Scribal Intervention	Aver. No. of Lines
4QJer[a]		dots par				y				32	4
4QJer[b]								y			
4QJer[c]		cross				y				7	25
4QJer[d]			gd						y		
4QEzek[a]			gd						y	1	50
4QEzek[b]						y?					
11QEzek						y					
4QXII[a]									y	2	46
4QXII[b]						y?					
4QXII[c]		dots	gd		y				y	13	8
4QXII[d]									y?		
4QXII[e]		dots			y				y	8	8
4QXII[f]						y?					
4QXII[g]					y?				y	9	38
1QPs[a] **[s]/[n]**											
1QPs[b] **[n]**				pal-Tetra							
1QPs[c] **[n]**											
3QPs **[n]**											
4QPs[a] **[n]**									y	1	87
4QPs[b] **[s]**			*waw* gd						y	4	43
4QPs[c] **[s]**						y				2	52
4QPs[d] **[s]/[n]**									y	1	41
4QPs[e] **[n]**									y	6	12
4QPs[f] **[n]**			gd						y	2	61
4QPs[g] **[s]**						y				1	23
4QPs[h] **[s]**	y										
4QPs[j] **[n]**											
4QPs[k] **[n]**									y		
4QPs[l] **[s]**									y?		
4QPs[m] **[n]**						y?					
4QPs[n] **[n]**									y		
4QPs[o] **[n]**					y?						
4QPs[p] **[n]**											
4QPs[q] **[n]**									y	0	22+
4QPs[r] **[n]**									y		
4QPs[s] **[n]**											
4QPs[u] **[n]**											
4QPs[w] **[s]**											
4QPs[x]		dots							y		
5QPs **[s]**											
8QPs **[s]**											
11QPs[a] **[s]/[n]**		dots Tetra	no-gd	pal-Tetra	y				y	55 + 1	9
11QPs[b] **[s]/[n]**					y				y	0	36+
11QPs[c] **[n]**					y?				y	0	56+
11QPs[d] **[n]**					y?				y	0	64+
2QJob **[n]**											

4QJoba **[s]**					y?				2	23
4QJobb **[n]**										
4QpaleoJobc **[s]**					y?					
4QProva **[s]**					y					
4QProvb **[s]**					y				0	37+
2QRutha					y		y		1	37
2QRuthb					y		y			
4QRutha					y		y		1	14
4QRuthb					y		y			
4QCanta								y!	0	28+
4QCantb	par cross	cr pHeb						y!	6	8
6QCant								y		
4QQoha	par			y				y	7	5
3QLam **[s]**			pal-Tetra							
4QLam **[n]**		no-gd		y				y	1	33
5QLama **[n]**		*waw?*								
5QLamb **[s]**										
1QDan					y					
4QDana	cross							y	5	22
4QDanb								y?	2	39
4QDanc								y?	2	20
4QDand								y?	2	22
6QpapDan								y		
4QEzra					y				0	19+
4QChron								y?		
MurGen (a)					y				0	23+
SdeirGen					y				1	38
MurExod					y					
MasLeva					y					
MasLevb					y				3	30
MurNum					y					
XHev/SeNumb					y				0	28+
MasDeut					y				0	17
XJosh					y					
MurIsa					y					
MasEzek					y				6	18
MurXII					y				8	75
5/6HevPs **[s]**					y				0	142
MasPsa **[s]**					y				0	74+
MasPsb **[s]**					y					

APPENDIX 9

ORTHOGRAPHIC AND MORPHOLOGICAL FEATURES OF TEXTS WRITTEN IN THE QUMRAN SCRIBAL PRACTICE

This appendix provides the statistical evidence regarding several significant features of the texts written in the Qumran scribal practice, thus enabling a distinction between these texts and the other Hebrew texts in the Qumran corpus. The individual features are tabulated in eighteen columns presenting both negative and positive evidence (in this sequence) for the characteristic features of the Qumran scribal practice separated by a diagonal line. Thus in the case of the spelling כיא, its frequency in 1QpHab is recorded as 3/18, referring to 3 instances of כי (negative evidence) and 18 instances of כיא (positive evidence). Evidence of more than four occurrences is usually recorded as 'all,' while in rare cases it is spelled out.

The features of some texts listed below should be viewed in conjunction with scribal features such as cancellation dots and paragraph signs (see APPENDIX 1) that occur almost exclusively in the texts displaying the Qumran features. For example, in some texts in which the orthographic and morphological evidence is limited, these scribal features ought to be consulted: Thus, the cancellation dots in 4QJub[g] (4Q222), 4QBer[d] (4Q289), 4QMMT[c] (4Q396) and the paleo-Hebrew Tetragrammata in 1QpMic (1Q14), 2QExod[b], and 4QExod[j] should be taken into consideration together with the scanty orthographic/morphological evidence for these texts. Lengthened forms of the types ʾeqtᵉlah and ʾeqtolah instead of ʾeqtol have not been recorded because of the complex conditions of their occurrence, but they probably also serve as a good criterion for the Qumran scribal practice. The same pertains to imperatives of the types qᵉṭoli and qᵉṭolu for qiṭli and qiṭlu.

The Qumran texts recorded below are also documented in APPENDIX 1a–b although that appendix includes information for a number of additional texts which display evidence of scribal features, but not of a special morphology and morphology. For each text listed here the recording is meant to be precise, but reversely in each column one should not expect to find all the relevant references to a certain feature, such as הואה (col. 1). Although the information below is almost exhaustive, some additional occurrences of that particular feature are listed in APPENDIX 1c. That appendix lists fragmentary texts displaying insufficient evidence for the Qumran scribal practice, such as a single occurrence of כיא. The combination of these two listings (the list below and APPENDIX 1c) should provide an exhaustive list of the evidence in the Qumran corpus in columns 1–3, 5–6, 8–10, 16, but not in the other ones. The distinction between texts written in the Qumran scribal practice and other texts is based on the assumption that texts which otherwise reflect an orthography and morphology similar to that of MT do not contain a single occurrence of כיא, הואה, or מלכמה, etc.

The data (including linguistic data) for the nonbiblical texts were culled from the Qumran module (June 2003) within the Accordance computer program (I used version 5.6, Gramcord 2002). These texts have been recorded and analyzed by M. G. Abegg on the basis of the DJD editions and, in the absence of such editions, of other ones—full bibliographical references are provided in the 'readme' file for the Qumran module in the Accordance program. The biblical texts are recorded on the basis of the official editions, mainly in *DJD*.

Completely reconstructed words in these editions are not included in the statistics. Partial reconstructions are included only when the significant elements have been preserved. Thus for כי/כיא, כ[ן] and כי[א] are not recorded, while כ[יא], כי[א], and כ[י] are included pending on the context. מלכם] is not included as evidence for מלכם since forms like מלכם]ה are evidenced as well.

The recording of both negative and positive evidence allows for a balanced judgment, since the positive evidence alone does not suffice for this purpose. For the sake of convenience, when the positive evidence for a certain feature prevails (e.g. הואה instead of הוא), the data are presented in **boldface**. Although even a single occurrence of הואה against two occurrences of הוא is meaningful (as in 4QInstr^b [4Q416]),[385] for the sake of objectivity, such cases are nevertheless *not* presented in boldface. In important categories such information should thus be taken into consideration. For example, the information in col. 5 regarding the noncanonical segments of 11QPs^a (4/4) corroborates the assumption that this scroll was written according to the Qumran scribal practice.

See further the analysis in ch. *8a2*. A star next to the name of a composition indicates the presence of cancellation dots (see the data in APPENDIX 1).

The table refers to the following categories:

α. Morphology

(1) Regular/lengthened independent pronoun: הואה/הוא.

(2) Regular/lengthened independent pronoun: היאה/היא.

(3) Regular/lengthened independent pronoun: אתמה/אתם.

(4) Regular/lengthened independent pronoun: המה/הם.

(5) Regular/lengthened pronominal suffixes of the second and third persons plural in nouns, e.g. מלכמה/מלכם.

(6) Regular/lengthened pronominal suffixes of the second and third persons plural in prepositions, e.g. בהמה/בהם.[386]

(7) Forms of the *Qal* imperfect *o* (*w*)*yqtwlw* and (*w*)*tqtwlw* (without suffixes) which serve in MT as pausal forms, but occur in these texts as free forms.

(8) Forms of the *Qal* imperfect *o* with pronominal suffixes (in all persons) construed as *yiqt̠elenu* (*et sim.*)/*y^equt̠lenu* (*et sim.*).

(9) The form *q^etaltem*/*q^et̠altemah* for the second person plural in all conjugations.

(10) Regular[387]/lengthened forms of מודה, מאודה, מואדה/מאד.

β. Orthography

(11) (ה)זאת as opposed to (ה)זות/זואת/זאות.

(12) כוה/כה.

(13) מושה/משה.

(14) לא (rarely לו[388])/לוא.

(15) כול/כל (without suffixes).

(16) כיא/כי.

(17) The verbal form *qtlt*/*qtlth*.[389]

---

[385]הואה and similar forms are not found in texts not written according to the Qumran scribal practice.

[386]Among the texts using at least some long forms, there is a tendency to always write להמה instead of להם. On the other hand, in virtually all texts, the short form בם is not lengthened to במה except for 4QMiscellaneous Rules (4Q265) 4 i 10 and several times in 11QT^a (11Q19). In other texts, בהמה is used instead.

[387]Including in rare cases מואד (Isa 16:6 and 56:12 in 1QIsa^a).

[388]Thus often or sometimes in 4QJub^d (4Q219), 4QD^a (4Q266), 4QNarrative and Poetic Composition^a (4Q371), 4QH^c (4Q429).

(18) Suffix ך–/כה– in nouns and prepositions.

The *asterisk* sign after the name of the composition indicates the occurrence of cancellation dots.

	1 הוא / הואה	2 היא / היאה	3 אתם / אתמה	4 הם / המה	5 suff. 2d and 3rd p. plur in nouns and verbs	6 suff. 2d and 3rd p. plur in preps	7 *yiqtᵉlu tiqtᵉlu / yiqtolu tiqtolu*	8 *yiqtᵉlenu / yᵉqutlenu*	9 *qetal tem / qetal temah*	10 מאד / מאודה מאורה מואדה מודה	11 זאת / הזואת / ז(א)ות זו(א)ת	12 כה / כוה	13 משה / מושה	14 לא / לוא	15 כל / כול	16 כי / כיא	17 *qatal ta / qatal tah*	18 suffix –כה/ך in nouns and prepositions	Sect. Nature
1QDeut[a]	0/2	1/0			0/1	0/1								0/1		0/3	0/1	0/5	y
1QIsa[a] scribe A[390]*	all/0	all/0	0/2	1/1	80%/20%	80%/20%	1/all	2/2	13/4	1/1	0/all	13/1		0/all	1/all	80%/20%	7/21	90%/10%	y
1QIsa[a] scribe B*	1/all	3/all	0/all	0/6	30%/70%	30%/70%	1/all	4/11	0/10	1/all	0/all	0/all	0/2	0/all	0/all	5%/95%	11/41	20%/80%	y
2QExod[b]													0/1		0/2			0/1	y?
2QNum[b]						0/1							0/1		1/0				y?
2QDeut[c]		0/1																	y?
2QJer	0/1	0/1				0/1						0/1		0/1	0/2	0/2		0/3	y
4Q[Gen-]Exod[b]	1/0			3/0	all/0	3/1				0/1		1/0	0/all	2/0	1/0	3/0	0/2	3/0	y?
4QExod[j]													0/1		1/0				y?
4QNum[b]	2/all	0/1	1/1		2/all	3/all			4/3	0/2			0/all	0/all	0/all	0/all	0/1	0/all	y
4QDeut[j] cols. I–IV*[391]		1/0			4/0	5/0			2/0		1/0			0/1	1/3	0/6	3/0	6/1	y?
4QDeut[j] cols. V–XII*		0/1			2/0	0/1			0/1				0/1	0/1	0/2	1/0	0/4	0/6	y
4QDeut[k1]		0/1	0/1		1/0	3/0			2/1					0/1	0/4	0/1	0/1	0/3	y
4QDeut[k2]						0/2								0/2	0/3	0/3	0/2	0/8	y
4QDeut[m]		0/1		0/1	0/5	0/1								0/1	0/2		0/1	0/4	y
4QSam[c]	0/1	0/1								0/1	0/1			0/all	0/2	0/1		0/all	y
4QIsa[c]	all/0				all/0	1/1	0/2		0/1		0/2	0/3		0/all	0/all	0/all	0/1	50%/50%	y
4QXII[c]*					0/all	0/2			0/2	0/1		0/2		0/all	0/all	all/0		0/all	y
4QXII[e]*	1/0	1/0				1/0			0/1			0/1		0/4	0/2				y
4QXII[g]	3/0	1/0			all/0	4/0			2/0			2/0		4/7	0/all	all/0	0/1	3/3	y?
4QPs[o]							.							0/1		0/2			y?
4QLam	1/0	0/1			0/1									0/4	1/4	0/3			y
4QQoh[a]														0/all	0/4	1/1			y
11QPs[a] canon. (includ. Frg. E)*	2/0				11/4	6/1	0/3	0/2		0/all	0/1			0/all	0/all	all/0	0/all	0/all	y
11QPs[a] noncanon.*	1/2				4/4	1/3		1/1		0/1				0/all	0/all	all/0	0/1	33/34 [392]	y

[389] Scribes who normally wrote *qtlth* sometimes used the defective forms in היה and חיה (see 4QBarkhi Nafshi[d] [4Q437]).

[390] See Kutscher, *Isaiah*, passim for some statistical data (often incomplete) and an analysis. In col. 3, only interchanges of MT *hem/hemah* 1QIsa[a] were calculated, disregarding two instances of *hemah* MT = 1QIsa[a] in the section of scribe A and ten such cases in the segment of scribe B. By the same token, in col. 7 defective pausal forms in MT were disregarded for the statistics.

[391] See n. 340 above.

	1	2	3	4	5	6	7	8	9	10	11	12	13	14	15	16	17	18	Sect. Nat.
11QPs^b canon.					0/1								0/1					0/2	y
11QPs^b noncanon.						2/0									0/1	1/0		0/all	y
11QPs^c															0/1		0/2	0/all	y?
11QPs^d					1/0					0/1				1/1		1/0		0/1	y?
4Q128 Phyl A	0/4				0/all	0/all			0/4	0/1	0/1		0/1	0/all	0/all	all/0	0/2	0/all	y
4Q129 Phyl B			0/1		0/all	0/4		0/1	0/2		0/2			0/all	0/all	4/0	0/all	0/all	y
4Q137 Phyl G–I			1/0		all/0	all/0			3/0				0/3	1/all	0/all	all/1	2/0	80%/20%	y?
4Q138 Phyl J–K	0/3	0/2	0/1		0/all	0/all	0/1		0/all	0/1	0/1			0/all	0/all	all/0	0/4	0/all	y
4Q139 Phyl L–N	0/1		0/1		0/all	0/4			0/2	0/1	0/3		0/1	3/all	0/3	2/0	0/all	0/all	y
4Q142 Phyl O					0/1				0/3				0/1		0/1			0/all	y
4Q143 Phyl P					2/0				1/0						0/1		0/1	0/3	y
4Q144 Phyl Q			0/1		0/2				0/1									0/1	y
1Q14 1QpMic	0/1				1/0									1/0	0/all	0/1			y
1QpHab*	all/0	1/1		0/all	all/0	all/1	0/2	1/1						0/all		3/18	0/all	1/8	y
1Q22 1QDM*	1/0			0/1	3/0	all/0				0/2			0/all	0/all	0/all	4/0	0/all	5/2	y?
1Q26 1QInstr														0/all	1/0		0/1	0/all	y?
1Q27 1QMyst	3/0				0/2	1/1		0/1						0/all	0/all	all/0			y
1Q28 1QS*	0/14	0/5			all/0	all/1	1/5	0/3		0/1	0/4		0/4	0/all	0/all	1/34	0/1	0/all	y
1Q28a 1QSa*	1/0			0/1	9/2		0/1							0/all	0/all	0/3			y
1Q28b 1QSb					1/0	2/0		0/1						0/all		0/4	0/all	0/all	y
1Q33 1QM	1/4	0/4	2/2	1/7	all/0	19/4	1/39 393		2/1	0/2			0/1	0/all	0/all	0/all	0/all	4/96	y
1Q34 1QH^a scribe A*	13/0	1/1		4/7	all/0	all/0	2/7	1/4		0/3	2/0		0/1	most/few	0/all	91/25	0/all	95%/5%	y
1Q34 1QH^a scribe C	0/1	0/1		1/0	all/0		1/2				0/4			few/most	0/all	5/26	0/all	0/all	y
1Q35 1QH^b														0/2				0/all	y?
1Q36 1QHymns																	0/2	0/all	y
4Q158 4QRP^a	1/2			0/1	0/2	2/6			0/1		0/1		0/3	0/all	0/all	3/4		0/all	y
4Q159 4QOrdin		1/0					0/1						0/3	0/all	0/all	1/1			y
4Q160 4QVisSam	0/2					0/2					0/1			0/1	0/all	0/all	0/2	0/all	y
4Q161 4QpIsa^a		0/1		0/1				0/1						0/2	0/all	0/1			y
4Q163 4Qpap pIsa^c	2/8	1/1		0/3	0/1	1/2			0/2		1/3	0/2		1/all	0/all	3/10		1/all	y
4Q165 4QpIsa^e														1/0		1/0			y?
4Q166 4QpHos^a				2/1	all/0	4/0								0/3	0/all	0/2			y?
4Q171 4QpPs^a				0/5	all/0	2/0		1/0						0/all	0/all	0/12		0/1	y
4Q174 4QFlor	1/4	0/4		0/4	0/3	0/all							0/1	0/all	0/all	0/all		0/all	y
4Q175 4QTest					2/1	0/2				0/2			0/1	0/all	0/all	1/0		5/4	y
4Q176 4QTanḥ*	1/1				2/0	1/1			1/0		0/1			0/all	0/all	2/13	0/2	4/10	y
4Q177 Catena A*	0/3	1/0		0/all	2/2	8/3				0/1			0/1	0/all	0/all			0/all	y
4Q180 AgesCreat A	2/0			0/1	1/1	1/0								2/1	0/1				y
4Q181 AgesCreat B					2/0	0/1								0/2					y?

---

[392] In this feature, the whole scroll is written *plene* with the exception of the 'Apostrophe to Zion' (col. XXII) written defectively. Immediately after this hymn, in the same column, the scribe continued to write the second person singular suffixes defectively (XX 16 = Ps 93:2).

[393] Mainly יכתובו and יעמדו.

4Q184 4QWiles		1/1			1/0					0/1	0/all	0/1			0/all		y?
4Q186 4QHorosc	1/1	0/1			0/2						0/3			0/1			y
4Q200 4QTobit^e	4/3	0/1	0/1	0/1	0/2					0/2	0/all	2/1			5/9		y
4Q215 4QTNaph		0/1								0/1			1/0				y
4Q215a 4QTimes*	0/1				all/0	1/0	0/1		0/1		0/all	0/3					y
4Q219 4QJub^d	0/1				1/2	2/0				all/0	0/all	1/0			1/9		y?
4Q221 4QJub^f	0/1			0/2	all/0	2/0				0/all	0/all	2/1		0/1	all/0		y
4Q222 4QJub^g*	0/1										2/1		1/0				y?
4Q223–224 4QpapJub^h*	2/0			2/0	2/2		1/2			0/all	0/all	2/1		0/all	0/all		y?
4Q225 4QpsJub^a*	0/2	1/0			2/0		0/1			0/1	2/0		1/0	0/1	0/all		y
4Q227 4QpsJub^c					2/0					0/1	0/1	0/all					y
4Q251 Halakha A	4/2	2/0		1/0	1/0						3/0	5/2	all/0		0/all		y?
4Q254 ComGen C	1/0	0/1			1/0								0/4		0/all		y
4Q256 4QS^b	0/1				5/2		0/1		0/1	0/1	0/all	0/all	1/0		0/all		y
4Q257 4QpapS^c										0/all	0/all	0/1					y
4Q259 4QS^e	0/1	0/2			2/1	1/0				0/1	0/all	0/all					y
4Q260 4QS^f					1/0		0/1				0/all	0/all					y?
4Q265 Misc Rules	1/1	2/0			2/1						all/0	0/all	1/0				y?
4Q266 4QD^a*	6/4	2/3		3/3	all/1	all/0	1/1			0/all	all/0	0/all	all/0	0/all		2/4	y
4Q267 4QD^b	1/0	0/1		0/2	all/0						0/all	0/all	6/1	0/2	0/all		y
4Q268 4QD^c	1/0				0/2	0/2					0/2	0/all	2/0				y
4Q269 4QD^d	2/0	1/0		0/1	all/0						0/1		0/2		0/1		y?
4Q271 4QD^f*	3/0	3/0			1/0					0/2	0/all	1/10	all/0			2/1	y
4Q273 4QpapD^h	1/1	2/0		0/1	1/0						3/0		1/0				y?
4Q274 4QToh A*	2/0	1/0			2/2	0/1		0/1	0/1		0/all	0/all	4/0				y?
4Q277 4QToh B	1/0				3/0							1/2	0/2				y
4Q280 4QCurses					1/0						0/2	0/all			0/all		y?
4Q285 Sefer ha-Mil		0/1			2/0		1/0				0/3	0/all	0/1		0/1		y
4Q286 4QBer^a*	1/0			0/3	0/all						0/3	0/all	0/2		0/all		y
4Q287 4QBer^b*				0/3	0/all						0/all	0/1		0/1	0/all		y
4Q289 4QBer^d*					0/2							2/0		0/1			y?
4Q292 4QWork Cont. Prayers B					2/0							0/1	0/1				y
4Q299 4QMyst^a	15/2	1/1	1/0		all/0	all/0		1/0	0/2	1/0	1/all	4/38	5/7		0/1	2/1	y
4Q301 4QMyst^c?*	2/8				3/1	2/1					0/all	1/2	0/2				y
4Q303 MedCrea A					2/0	1/0						0/2	0/2				y?
4Q364 4QRP^b*	1/1		1/0		7/4	3/6		1/2		0/1	0/all	0/all		8/2	0/all	0/all	y
4Q365 4QRP^c*	1/all	1/2	0/1	0/2	13/5	3/6		5/1		0/1	0/all	1/all	0/all	8/2	0/all	0/all	y
4Q365a 4QT^a?*					0/3	1/1		0/1				0/2		0/1			y
4Q369 4QPrayer Enosh*		0/1			3/0	3/0						0/all	3/0	0/all	0/all		y
4Q375 apocrMos^a	0/4										0/1	0/all	0/2	0/3	0/all		y
4Q377 apocPent B										0/3	0/2	0/all	0/4		0/1		y

	1	2	3	4	5	6	7	8	9	10	11	12	13	14	15	16	17	18	Sect. Nat.
4Q382 pap para Kgs	0/1			1/0	2/0	3/0		1/0					0/1	0/all	0/all	all/0	0/all	1/all	y
4Q384 4Qpap apocr Jer B?			0/2		2/0	1/0									0/1				y?
4Q393 ComConf*	2/0				1/0	0/1							0/1	1/0	0/1	0/1	1/2	all/2	y
4Q394 4QMMTᵃ	1/0	4/1	2/0	4/1	all/0	all/0								1/all	1/1	6/0			y? 394
4Q396 4QMMTᶜ*	3/1	1/0	2/0	4/2	2/0	3/1								1/all	2/1	3/0			y?
4Q397 4QMMT*	0/1	1/2	1/1			1/0							0/2	0/1	0/all	3/0		0/all	y
4Q398 papMMTᵉ	1/0			1/0	0/1	1/0							0/1	0/1	1/0	1/0		all/0	y?
4Q400 ShirShabbᵃ*				0/2	all/0	3/0								0/1	0/all	0/1		0/2	y?
4Q401 ShirShabbᵇ				0/1	2/0									0/1	0/all			0/3	y
4Q402 ShirShabbᶜ				0/1	1/0									0/3	0/all	0/2			y
4Q403 ShirShabbᵈ*					all/0	1/0									0/all	1/2			y
4Q405 ShirShabbᶠ*					all/0		0/2							0/all	0/all	0/1			y
4Q410 Vision Int*						0/1								0/3	0/2			0/all	y?
4Q414 RitPur A	0/1													0/3	2/1		0/2	0/all	y
4Q415 4QInstrᵃ*		0/1			1/1					0/1				0/all	0/all	1/3		2/all	y
4Q416 4QInstrᵇ	2/1	1/0		0/1	3/3	0/1				0/1				7/3	all/0	all/0	1/3	0/all	y
4Q417 4QInstrᶜ	1/7	0/1			6/4					0/1				5/6	0/all	5/12	1/0	0/all	y
4Q418 4QInstrᵈ*	6/1	2/0	1/0	2/2	19/9	4/0	4/0		4/1	1/3	1/1		1/0	5/44	0/all	18/21	0/all	0/all	y
4Q418a 4QInstrᵉ	0/1				1/1										0/all	1/4		0/all	y
4Q419 4QInstr-like Composition A	3/0			0/2	3/0	2/0							1/0	1/2	0/all	0/1			y?
4Q420 4QWaysᵃ					2/0						0/1			0/all	0/2				y?
4Q421 4QWaysᵇ		0/1												0/2	1/0	0/2			y
4Q422 4QParaGen-Exod	0/1				6/3	1/1							0/1	0/1	0/all	0/1			y
4Q423 4QInstrᵍ	3/0				0/2	0/1				0/1			1/0	5/1	16/5	4/1	0/1	0/all	y
4Q426 4QSap-Hymn Work A*					0/1									0/all	0/all				y?
4Q427 4QHᵃ*					1/6									2/all	0/all	0/7	0/all	0/all	y
4Q428 4QHᵇ					all/0		0/1				0/1			0/all	0/all	1/5	0/all	0/all	y
4Q429 4QHᶜ					1/2									2/0	2/0	2/0	0/1	0/all	y?
4Q432 4QpapHᶠ					1/1		0/1							0/all	1/0	0/1	0/all	y?	
4Q433a papH-like														0/1	0/2				
4Q435 4QBNᵇ														0/1		1/3	0/1		y?
4Q436 4QBNᶜ					0/1										0/all	0/all			y
4Q437 4QBNᵈ					2/0			0/1						0/2	0/all		3/4	all/1	y
4Q438 4QBNᵉ*					1/0									0/1	0/1			6/3	y?
4Q440 H-like C*														0/2	0/all		0/2	0/all	y
4Q443 Pers Pray.*						0/1								0/1	1/0		1/0	2/all	y
4Q460 Narr Work	1/0				3/0									0/3	0/3	0/all	0/3	0/all	y
4Q462 4QNarr C*						1/0	0/1								0/1	2/0			y
4Q464 4QExp Patr	1/1													1/1		1/2		0/1	y?
4Q471 WarText B					2/0										0/all	0/1			y

394 The statistical evidence does not allow for the inclusion of 4QMMTᵃ (4Q394) and 4QMMTᶜ (4Q396) in this group, although these two texts contain a few 'Qumran spellings' as minority readings. Nevertheless, the whole system of orthography of these two texts, with their 'vulgarisms and other oddities' (Qimron–Strugnell, *DJD* X, 6), is very similar to 1QIsaᵃ, and these texts may, by extension, be included here.

4Q473 Two Ways	0/1												0/2		0/1	0/4			y
4Q474 4QRachJos				2/1			0/1							0/all	0/1		0/1			y
4Q477 4QRebukes	0/3			1/1																y?
4Q491 4QMa*	0/3		0/1	1/all	1/6	1/0		1/0		0/2				0/all	0/all	0/all	0/2	0/all		y
4Q496 4QpapMf		0/1				0/4								0/1	0/2					y
4Q501 apocrLamB*				0/3	0/3									0/1		0/1		0/all		y
4Q502 papRitMar	0/2			4/0	1/0									0/all				0/all		y
4Q503 papPrQuot	0/1													0/1	0/all	0/2	0/1	0/all		y
4Q504 papDMa	0/1	0/2		11/2	3/2			0/1	0/1				0/all	0/all	0/all	1/20	0/all	0/all		y
4Q505 4QpapDMb												0/1	0/1	0/1			0/all	0/all		y?
4Q506 4QpapDMc														0/all	0/1		0/all	0/all		y
4Q509 4QpapPrFêtc				3/0				1/0	0/1		0/1		0/all	0/all		7/1	0/all	0/all		y
4Q511 4QShirb	0/2		0/1	all/0	all/0	0/1								0/all	0/all	1/21	0/all	0/all		y
4Q512 papRitPurB				2/0	1/0									0/3	0/all	1/3	0/1	0/all		y
4Q513 4QOrdb*			0/all	2/0	0/1					1/0				0/3	0/all	1/2				y
4Q522 Proph Josh*	1/1			1/0	1/0									0/all	1/1	1/0				y?
4Q524 4QTb	0/1	0/1	0/1	3/1	1/1			0/1						0/all	0/all		0/2			y
4Q525 Beatitudes				3/2	1/0	0/1	0/1		0/2					0/all	0/all	4/0	0/all	4/all		y
5Q13 5QRule				1/2										0/all	0/3		0/all	0/3		y?
6Q18 papHymn						1/0								0/3	1/1	0/2		0/3		y
11Q11 11QapocPs			1/0		1/0			0/1	0/2					0/all	0/all		0/2	all/1		y
11Q12 11QJub + XQText A	1/1			3/0										0/all	0/3		0/2			y
11Q13 11QMelch	0/all		0/2	1/1	0/all	0/1		0/1		0/1				0/all	0/1	3/0				y
11Q14 11QSefer ha-Milhamah				4/1	all/0								0/1	0/2	0/1					y
11Q16 11QHymnsb														0/1	0/1	0/1	0/1			y[395]
11Q19 11QTa*	34/1	12/1	0/2	0/all	1/all	1/74	0/all	0/4	1/18	0/2	1/all			0/all	0/all	67/2	0/all	0/all		y
11Q20 11QTb	0/1	1/0		0/all	0/all	0/1		0/1		0/all				0/all	0/all	3/1		0/all		y
11Q27 11QUnid C														0/1		0/1				y?
Mas 1k ShirShabb				2/0									1/0	0/all	0/1					y?
Mas 1n MasUnid. Qumran-Type Frg	0/1																			y?

395 See especially XQText B identified as part of the same manuscript by H. Eshel, 'Three New Fragments from Cave 11,' *Tarbiz* 68 (1999) 273–8 (Hebr.).

BIBLIOGRAPHY

1. *DISCOVERIES IN THE JUDAEAN DESERT (OF JORDAN)*

D. Barthélemy and J. T. Milik, *Qumran Cave 1* (DJD **I**; Oxford 1955)

P. Benoit et al., *Les grottes de Murabbaʿat* (DJD **II, IIa**; Oxford 1961)

M. Baillet et al., *Les 'petites grottes' de Qumrân* (DJD **III, IIIa**; Oxford 1962)

J. A. Sanders, *The Psalms Scroll of Qumrân Cave 11 (11QPsᵃ)* (DJD **IV**; Oxford 1965)

J. M. Allegro with A. A. Anderson, *Qumrân Cave 4.I* (DJD **V**; Oxford 1968)

R. de Vaux and J. T. Milik, *Qumrân grotte 4.II: I. Archéologie, II. Tefillin, Mezuzot et Targums (4Q128–4Q157)* (DJD **VI**; Oxford 1977)

M. Baillet, *Qumrân grotte 4.III (4Q482–4Q520)* (DJD **VII**; Oxford 1982)

E. Tov, *The Greek Minor Prophets Scroll from Naḥal Ḥever (8ḤevXIIgr)* (DJD **VIII**; Oxford 1990; 2nd rev. ed., Oxford 1995)

P. W. Skehan, E. Ulrich, and J. E. Sanderson, *Qumran Cave 4.IV: Palaeo-Hebrew and Greek Biblical Manuscripts* (DJD **IX**; Oxford 1992)

E. Qimron and J. Strugnell, *Qumran Cave 4.V: Miqṣat Maʿaśe ha-Torah* (DJD **X**; Oxford 1994)

E. Eshel et al., in consultation with J. VanderKam, *Qumran Cave 4.VI: Poetical and Liturgical Texts, Part 1* (DJD **XI**; Oxford 1998)

E. Ulrich, F. M. Cross, et al., *Qumran Cave 4.VII: Genesis to Numbers* (DJD **XII**; Oxford 1994 [repr. 1999])

H. Attridge et al., in consultation with J. VanderKam, *Qumran Cave 4.VIII: Parabiblical Texts, Part 1* (DJD **XIII**; Oxford 1994)

E. Ulrich, F. M. Cross, et al., *Qumran Cave 4.IX: Deuteronomy, Joshua, Judges, Kings* (DJD **XIV**; Oxford 1995 [repr. 1999])

E. Ulrich et al., *Qumran Cave 4.X: The Prophets* (DJD **XV**; Oxford 1997)

E. Ulrich et al., *Qumran Cave 4.XI: Psalms to Chronicles* (DJD **XVI**; Oxford 2000)

J. M. Baumgarten, *Qumran Cave 4.XVII: The Damascus Document (4Q266–273)* (DJD **XVIII**; Oxford 1996)

M. Broshi et al., in consultation with J. VanderKam, *Qumran Cave 4.XII, Parabiblical Texts, Part 2* (DJD **XIX**; Oxford 1995)

T. Elgvin et al., in consultation with J. A. Fitzmyer, S.J., *Qumran Cave 4.XV: Sapiential Texts, Part 1* (DJD **XX**; Oxford 1997)

S. Talmon, J. Ben Dov; U. Glessmer, *Qumran Cave 4.XVI: Calendrical Texts* (DJD **XXI**; Oxford: 2001)

G. Brooke et al., in consultation with J. VanderKam, *Qumran Cave 4.XVII: Parabiblical Texts, Part 3* (DJD **XXII**; Oxford 1996)

F. García Martínez, E. Tigchelaar, and A. S. van der Woude, *Qumran Cave 11.II: 11Q2–18, 11Q20–31* (DJD **XXIII**; Oxford 1998)

M. J. W. Leith, *Wadi Daliyeh Seal Impressions* (DJD **XXIV**; Oxford 1997)

É. Puech, *Qumran Cave 4.XVIII: Textes hébreux (4Q521–4Q528, 4Q576–4Q579)* (DJD **XXV**; Oxford 1998)

P. Alexander and G. Vermes, *Qumran Cave 4.XIX: 4QSerekh Ha-Yaḥad and Two Related Texts* (DJD **XXVI**; Oxford 1998)

H. M. Cotton and A. Yardeni, *Aramaic, Hebrew and Greek Documentary Texts from Naḥal Ḥever and Other Sites, with an Appendix Containing Alleged Qumran Texts (The Seiyal Collection II)* (DJD **XXVII**; Oxford 1997)

D. M. Gropp, *Wadi Daliyeh II: The Samaria Papyri from Wadi Daliyeh*; E. Schuller et al., in consultation with J. VanderKam and M. Brady, *Qumran Cave 4.XXVIII: Miscellanea*, Part 2 (DJD **XXVIII**; Oxford 2001)

E. Chazon et al., in consultation with J. VanderKam and M. Brady, *Qumran Cave 4.XX: Poetical and Liturgical Texts, Part 2* (DJD **XXIX**; Oxford 1999)

D. Dimant, *Qumran Cave 4.XXI: Parabiblical Texts, Part 4: Pseudo-Prophetic Texts* (DJD **XXX**; Oxford 2001)

É. Puech, *Qumran Cave 4.XXII: Textes araméens, première partie: 4Q529–549* (DJD **XXXI**; Oxford 2001)

D. Pike and A. Skinner, in consultation with J. VanderKam and M. Brady, *Qumran Cave 4.XXIII: Unidentified Fragments* (DJD **XXXIII**; Oxford 2001)

J. Strugnell, D. J. Harrington, S.J., and T. Elgvin, in consultation with J. A. Fitzmyer, S.J., *Qumran Cave 4.XXIV: 4QInstruction (Mûsār lᵉMēvîn): 4Q415 ff.* (DJD **XXXIV**; Oxford 1999)

J. Baumgarten et al., *Qumran Cave 4.XXV: Halakhic Texts* (DJD **XXXV**; Oxford 1999)

S. J. Pfann, *Cryptic Texts*; P. Alexander et al., in consultation with J. VanderKam and M. Brady, *Miscellanea, Part 1: Qumran Cave 4.XXVI* (DJD **XXXVI**; Oxford 2000)

J. Charlesworth et al., in consultation with J. VanderKam and M. Brady, *Miscellaneous Texts from the Judaean Desert* (DJD **XXXVIII**; Oxford 2000)

E. Tov (ed.), *The Texts from the Judaean Desert: Indices and an Introduction to the* Discoveries in the Judaean Desert *Series* (DJD **XXXIX**; Oxford 2002)

2. FREQUENTLY QUOTED STUDIES AND SOURCES

ABMC

Ancient Biblical Manuscripts Center

Aland, *Repertorium*

K. Aland, *Repertorium der griechischen christlichen Papyri, I Biblische Papyri, Altes Testament, Neues Testament, Varia, Apokryphen* (PTS 18; Berlin/New York, 1976)

Alexander, "Literacy"

P. Alexander, "Literacy among Jews in Second Temple Palestine: Reflections on the Evidence from Qumran," *Hamlet on a Hill. Semitic and Greek Studies Presented to Professor T. Muraoka on the Occasion of his Sixty-Fifth Birthday* (ed. M. F. J. Baasten and W. Th. van Peursen; Leuven 2003) 3–24

Aly–Koenen, *Three Rolls*

Z. Aly and L. Koenen, *Three Rolls of the Early Septuagint: Genesis and Deuteronomy* (Papyrologische Texte und Abhandlungen 27; Bonn 1980)

Anderson, *Studies*

T. Anderson, *Studies in Samaritan Manuscripts and Artifacts: The Chamberlain–Warren Collection* (ASOR Mon 1; Cambridge, Mass. 1978)

Ashton, *Scribal Habits*

J. Ashton, *The Persistence, Diffusion and Interchangeability of Scribal Habits in the Ancient Near East before the Codex*, unpubl. Ph.D. diss., University of Sydney, 1999

Avigad–Yadin, *Genesis Apocryphon*

N. Avigad and Y. Yadin, *A Genesis Apocryphon* (Jerusalem 1956)

Bardke, "Die Parascheneinteilung"

H. Bardke, "Die Parascheneinteilung der Jesajarolle I," in *Festschrift Franz Dornseiff zum 65. Geburtstag* (ed. H. Kusch; Leipzig 1953) 33–75

Barthélemy, *Critique textuelle 1992*

D. Barthélemy, *Critique textuelle de l'Ancien Testament* (OBO 50/3; Fribourg/Göttingen 1992)

Beit-Arié, *Hebrew Codicology*

M. Beit-Arié, *Hebrew Codicology: Tentative Typology of Technical Practices Employed in Hebrew Dated Medieval Manuscripts* (Jerusalem 1981)

Beyer, *Ergänzungsband*

K. Beyer, *Die aramäischen Texte vom Toten Meer, Ergänzungsband* (Göttingen 1994)

Bierbrier, *Papyrus*

M. L. Bierbrier, *Papyrus: Structure and Usage* (Occasional Paper 60; British Museum, 1986)

Birnbaum, "Michigan Codex"

E. Birnbaum, "The Michigan Codex: An Important Hebrew Bible Manuscript Discovered in the University of Michigan Library," *VT* 17 (1967) 373–415

Birt, *Buchwesen*

Th. Birt, *Das antike Buchwesen in seinem Verhältniss zur Litteratur* (Berlin 1882)

Blau, *Masoretische Untersuchungen*
> L. Blau, *Masoretische Untersuchungen* (Strasbourg i. E. 1891) 6–40

—, "Massoretic Studies"
> —, "Massoretic Studies, III. The Division into Verses," *JQR* 9 (1897) 122–44. IV, ibid., 471–90

—, *Studien*
> —, *Studien zum althebräischen Buchwesen und zur biblischen Literatur- und Textgeschichte* (Strasbourg i. E. 1902)

Bonani et al., "Radio-carbon Dating"
> G. Bonani, M. Broshi, I. Carmi, S. Ivy, J. Strugnell, and W. Wölfli, "Radio-carbon Dating of the Dead Sea Scrolls," *ʿAtiqot* 20 (1991) 27–32 = *Radiocarbon* 34 (1992) 843–9

Burrows, *The Dead Sea Scrolls*
> M. Burrows with the assistance of J. C. Trever and W. H. Brownlee, *The Dead Sea Scrolls of St. Mark's Monastery, I, The Isaiah Manuscript and the Habakkuk Commentary* (New Haven: ASOR, 1950)

Butin, *Nequdoth*
> R. Butin, *The Ten Nequdoth of the Torah* (Baltimore 1906; repr. New York 1969)

Caminos, "Reuse of Papyrus"
> R. A. Caminos, "Some Comments on the Reuse of Papyrus," in Bierbrier, *Papyrus*, 43–61

Černy, *Paper*
> J. Černy, *Paper & Books in Ancient Egypt* (Inaugural Lecture 29 May 1947; London 1952)

Charlesworth, *Rule of the Community*
> J. H. Charlesworth (editor, with F. M. Cross et al.), *The Dead Sea Scrolls: Hebrew, Aramaic, and Greek Texts with English Translations, I, Rule of the Community and Related Documents* (Tübingen/Louisville 1994)

Cross, "Development"
> F. M. Cross, Jr., "The Development of the Jewish Scripts," in *The Bible and the Ancient Near East, Essays in Honor of W. F. Albright* (ed. G. E. Wright; Garden City, N. Y. 1965) 133–202

—, *ALQ³*
> —, *The Ancient Library of Qumran* (3rd ed.; Sheffield 1995)

Cross–Talmon, *QHBT*
> *Qumran and the History of the Biblical Text* (ed. F. M. Cross and S. Talmon; Cambridge, Mass./London 1976)

Crown, "Studies. III"
> A. D. Crown, "Studies in Samaritan Scribal Practices and Manuscript History: III. Columnar Writing and the Samaritan Massorah," *BJRL* 67 (1984) 349–81, *reprinted* in Crown, *Samaritan Scribes*, 488–516

—, *Dated Samaritan MSS*
> —, *Dated Samaritan MSS. Some Codicological Implications* (Sydney 1986)

—, *Samaritan Scribes*
> —, *Samaritan Scribes and Manuscripts* (TSAJ 80; Tübingen 2001)

—, *Samaritan Scribal Habits*

    —, "Samaritan Scribal Habits with Reference to the Masorah and the Dead Sea Scrolls," in Paul, *Emanuel*, 159–77

Dimant, "Qumran Manuscripts"

    D. Dimant, "The Qumran Manuscripts: Contents and Significance," in Dimant–Schiffman, *Time to Prepare*, 23–58

Dimant–Schiffman, *Time to Prepare*

    A Time to Prepare the Way in the Wilderness. Papers on the Qumran Scrolls by Fellows of the Institute for Advanced Studies of the Hebrew University, Jerusalem, 1989–1990 (ed. D. Dimant and L. H. Schiffman; STDJ 16; Leiden 1995)

Diringer, "Early Hebrew Script"

    D. Diringer, "Early Hebrew Script *versus* Square Script," in *Essays and Studies Presented to Stanley Arthur Cook* (ed. D. W. Thomas; London 1950) 35–49

—, *The Book*

    —, *The Book before Printing–Ancient, Medieval and Oriental* (New York 1982 [1953])

Doudna, "Dating"

    G. Doudna, "Dating the Scrolls on the Basis of Radiocarbon Analysis," in Flint–VanderKam, *Fifty Years*, 430–65

—, *4Q Pesher Nahum*

    —, *4Q Pesher Nahum, A Critical Edition* (JSPSup 35; Copenhagen International Series 8; Sheffield 2001)

Driver, *Semitic Writing*

    G. R. Driver, *Semitic Writing from Pictograph to Alphabet, The Schweich Lectures of the British Academy 1944* (3rd ed.; London 1976)

—, *Aramaic Documents*

    —, *Aramaic Documents of the Fifth Century B.C.* (Oxford 1954)

Dunand, *Papyrus grecs, Texte et planches*

    F. Dunand, *Papyrus grecs bibliques (Papyrus F. Inv. 266): Volumina de la Genèse et du Deutéronome, Texte et planches* (Extrait des études de papyrologie IX; Cairo 1966)

—, *Papyrus grecs, Introduction*

    —, *Papyrus grecs bibliques (Papyrus F. Inv. 266): Volumina de la Genèse et du Deutéronome, Introduction* (Recherches d'archéologie, de philologie et d'histoire XXVII; Cairo 1966)

Elgvin, *Analysis*

    T. Elgvin, *An Analysis of Admonition Writings from Qumran*, unpubl. Ph.D. diss., Hebrew University, Jerusalem 1998

Encyclopedia DSS

    Encyclopedia of the Dead Sea Scrolls, vols. 1–2 (ed. L. H. Schiffman and J. C. VanderKam; New York 2000)

Eph'al–Naveh, *Aramaic Ostraca*

    I. Eph'al and J. Naveh, *Aramaic Ostraca of the Fourth Century BC from Idumaea* (Jerusalem 1996)

Flint, *Psalms Scrolls*

    P. W. Flint, *The Dead Sea Psalms Scrolls and the Book of Psalms* (STDJ 17; Leiden/New York/ Cologne 1997)

Flint–VanderKam, *Fifty Years*

    The Dead Sea Scrolls After Fifty Years: A Comprehensive Assessment, vol. I (ed. P. W. Flint and J. C. VanderKam; Leiden/Boston/Cologne 1998)

Freedman–Mathews, *Leviticus*

    D. N. Freedman and K. A. Mathews, *The Paleo-Hebrew Leviticus Scroll (11QpaleoLev)* (Winona Lake, Ind. 1985)

Gächter, "Zur Textabteilung"

    P. Gächter, "Zur Textabteilung der Evangelienhandschriften," *Bib* 15 (1934) 301–20

Gallo, *Papyrology*

    I. Gallo, *Greek and Latin Papyrology* (Classical Handbook 1; London: Institute of Classical Studies, University of London 1986)

Gamble, *Books and Readers*

    H. Y. Gamble, *Books and Readers in the Early Church: A History of Early Christian Texts* (New Haven, Conn. and London 1995)

Gardthausen, *Griechische Palaeographie*

    V. Gardthausen, *Griechische Palaeographie* (2nd ed.; Leipzig 1913)

Giese, "Further Evidence"

    R. L. Giese, "Further Evidence for the Bisection of 1QIs^a," *Textus* 14 (1988) 61–70

Ginsburg, *Introduction*

    C. D. Ginsburg, *Introduction to the Massoretico-Critical Edition of the Hebrew Bible* (London 1897; repr. New York 1966)

Giron Blanc, *Genesis*

    L. F. Giron Blanc, *Pentateuco Hebreo-Samaritano, Genesis* (Textos y Estudios "Cardenal Cisneros" 15; Madrid 1976)

Golb, *The DSS*

    N. Golb, *Who Wrote the Dead Sea Scrolls: The Search for the Secret of Qumran* (New York 1994)

Gordon, *Ugaritic Textbook*

    C. H. Gordon, *Ugaritic Textbook* (AnOr 38; Rome 1965)

Hall, *Companion*

    F. W. Hall, *A Companion to Classical Studies* (Oxford 1913)

Haran, "Workmanship"

    M. Haran, "Scribal Workmanship in Biblical Times: The Scrolls and the Writing Implements," *Tarbiz* 50 (1981) 65–87 (Heb.)

—, "Book-Scrolls"

    —, "Book-Scrolls in Israel in Pre-Exilic Times," *JJS* 33 (1982) 161–73

Herbert, *A New Method*
> E. D. Herbert, *Reconstructing Biblical Dead Sea Scrolls. A New Method Applied to the Reconstruction of 4QSam*ᵃ (STDJ 22; Leiden/New York/Cologne 1997)

Herbert–Tov, *The Bible as Book*
> *The Bible as Book—The Hebrew Bible and the Judaean Desert Discoveries* (ed. E. D. Herbert and E. Tov; London 2002)

Higger, *Mskt swprym*
> M. Higger, *Mskt swprym wnlww 'lyh mdrš mskt swprym b'* (New York 1937; repr. Jerusalem 1970)

—, *Minor Treatises*
> —, *Seven Minor Treatises, Sefer Torah; Mezuzah; Tefillin; Zizith; 'Abadim; Kutim; Gerim* (New York 1930)

Horbury, *Hebrew Study*
> *Hebrew Study from Ezra to Ben-Yehuda* (ed. W. Horbury; Edinburgh 1999)

Horgan, *Pesharim*
> M. Horgan, *Pesharim: Qumran Interpretations of Biblical Books* (Washington, D.C. 1979)

Humbert–Chambon, *Fouilles de Khirbet Qumrân*
> J.-B. Humbert and A. Chambon, *Fouilles de Khirbet Qumrân et de Aïn Feshkha*, I (NTOA, Series Archaeologica 1; Fribourg/Göttingen 1994)

HUBP
> Hebrew University Bible Project: M. H. Goshen-Gottstein, *The Hebrew University Bible, The Book of Isaiah* (Jerusalem 1995); C. Rabin, S. Talmon, E. Tov, *The Book of Jeremiah* (Jerusalem 1997)

Janzen, *Hiërogliefen*
> J. M. A. Janssen, *Hiërogliefen: Over lezen en schrijven in Oud-Egypte* (Leiden 1952)

JDS 3
> Y. Yadin, J. C. Greenfield, A. Yardeni, and B. A. Levine, *The Documents from the Bar Kokhba Period in the Cave of Letters: Hebrew, Aramaic and Nabatean-Aramaic Papyri* (JDS 3; Jerusalem 2002)

Johnson, *Scheide*
> A. C. Johnson et al., *The John H. Scheide Biblical Papyri: Ezekiel* (Princeton 1938)

W. A. Johnson, *The Literary Papyrus Roll*
> W. A. Johnson, *The Literary Papyrus Roll: Formats and Conventions. An Analysis of the Evidence from Oxyrhynchus*, unpubl. Ph.D. diss., Yale University 1992

Jull et al., "Radiocarbon Dating"
> A. J. T. Jull, D. J. Donahue, M. Broshi, and E. Tov, "Radiocarbon Dating of Scrolls and Linen Fragments from the Judean Desert," *Radiocarbon* 37 (1995) 11–19 = *ʿAtiqot* 28 (1996) 85–91

KAI
> H. Donner and W. Röllig, *Kanaanäische und Aramäische Inschriften* (2nd ed.; Wiesbaden 1968)

Kasser–Testuz, *Bodmer*
> R. Kasser and M. Testuz, *Papyrus Bodmer XXIV: Psaumes XVII–CXVIII* (Cologne/Geneva: Bibliothèque Bodmer, 1967)

Kenyon, *Palaeography*
> F. G. Kenyon, *The Palaeography of Greek Papyri* (Oxford 1899)

—, *Books and Readers*

    —, *Books and Readers in Ancient Greece and Rome* (Oxford 1951)

Korpel–de Moor, *Structure*

    M. C. A. Korpel and J. C. de Moor, *The Structure of Classical Hebrew Poetry: Isaiah 40–55* (OTS 41; Leiden/Boston/Cologne 1998)

Korpel–Oesch, *Delimitation Criticism*

    M. C. A. Korpel and J. M. Oesch, *Delimitation Criticism: A New Tool in Biblical Scholarship* (Pericope I; Assen 2000)

Kraeling, *Aramaic Papyri*

    E. G. Kraeling, *The Brooklyn Museum Aramaic Papyri* (New Haven, Conn. 1953)

Kraft, jewishpap

    R. A. Kraft, http://ccat.sas.upenn.edu/rs/rak/jewishpap.html

—, "Textual Mechanics"

    —, "The 'Textual Mechanics' of Early Jewish LXX/OG Papyri and Fragments," in *The Bible as Book: The Transmission of the Greek Text* (ed. S. McKendrick and O. A. O'Sullivan; London 2003) 51–72

Krauss, *Talmudische Archäologie*

    S. Krauss, *Talmudische Archäologie*, III (Leipzig 1912; repr. Hildesheim 1966)

Kuhl, "Schreibereigentümlichkeiten"

    C. Kuhl, "Schreibereigentümlichkeiten: Bemerkungen zur Jesajarolle (DSIa)," *VT* 2 (1952) 307–33

Kutscher, *Language*

    E. Y. Kutscher, *The Language and Linguistic Background of the Isaiah Scroll (1Q Is^a)* (STDJ 6; Leiden 1974)

Langlamet, "Samuel"

    F. Langlamet, "Les divisions massorétiques du livre de Samuel: À propos de la publication du codex du Caïre," *RB* 91 (1984) 481–519

Lefkovits, *Copper Scroll*

    J. K. Lefkovits, *The Copper Scroll: 3Q15: A Reevaluation. A New Reading, Translation, and Commentary* (STDJ 25; Leiden/Boston/Cologne 2000)

Lemaire, *Les écoles*

    A. Lemaire, *Les écoles et la formation de la Bible dans l'ancien Israël* (OBO 39; Fribourg/Göttingen 1981)

—, "L'enseignement"

    —, "L'enseignement essénien et l'école de Qumrân," in *Hellenica et Judaica, Hommage à Valentin Nikiprowetzky* (ed. A. Caquot et al.; Leuven/Paris 1986) 191–203

—, "Writing and Writing Materials"

    —, "Writing and Writing Materials," *ABD* 6 (New York 1992) 999–1008

Lewis, *Papyrus*

    N. Lewis, *Papyrus in Classical Antiquity* (Oxford 1974)

—, *Bar Kochba*

     —, *The Documents from the Bar Kochba Period in the Cave of Letters: Greek Papyri* (JDS 2; Jerusalem 1989)

Lieberman, *Hellenism*

     S. Lieberman, *Hellenism in Jewish Palestine* (2nd ed.; New York 1962)

Martin, *Scribal Character*

     M. Martin, *The Scribal Character of the Dead Sea Scrolls*, I–II (Bibliothèque du Muséon 44, 45; Louvain 1958)

Masada I

     Y. Yadin and J. Naveh, *Masada I, The Yigael Yadin Excavations 1963–1965, Final Reports, The Aramaic and Hebrew Ostraca and Jar Inscriptions* (Jerusalem 1989)

Masada II

     H. M. Cotton and J. Geiger, *Masada II, The Yigael Yadin Excavations 1963–1965, Final Reports, The Latin and Greek Documents* (Jerusalem 1989)

Masada III

     E. Netzer, *Masada III, The Yigael Yadin Excavations 1963–1965, Final Reports, The Buildings: Stratigraphy and Architecture* (Jerusalem 1991)

Masada VI

     S. Talmon and Y. Yadin, *Masada VI, The Yigael Yadin Excavations 1963–1965, Final Reports, Hebrew Fragments from Masada* (Jerusalem 1999) 1–149

McNamee, *Sigla*

     K. McNamee, *Sigla and Select Marginalia in Greek Literary Papyri Bruxelles*: (Papyrologica Bruxellensia 26: Brussels: Fondation Égyptologique Reine Élisabeth, 1992)

Metso, *Community Rule*

     S. Metso, *The Textual Development of the Qumran Community Rule* (STDJ 21; Leiden/New York/Cologne 1997)

Milik, *Enoch*

     J. T. Milik, *The Books of Enoch: Aramaic Fragments of Qumrân Cave 4* (Oxford 1976)

Millard, *Reading and Writing*

     A. Millard, *Reading and Writing in the Time of Jesus* (Sheffield 2000)

Milne–Skeat, *Scribes*

     H. J. M. Milne and T. C. Skeat, *Scribes and Correctors of the Codex Sinaiticus* (London 1938)

Mulder, *Mikra*

     Mikra, Compendia Rerum Iudaicarum ad Novum Testamentum, Section Two, I (ed. M. J. Mulder; Assen–Maastricht/Philadelphia 1988)

Naveh, *Alphabet*

     J. Naveh, *Early History of the Alphabet: An Introduction to West Semitic Epigraphy and Palaeography* (2nd ed.; Jerusalem 1987)

Nir-El–Broshi, "Black Ink"

     Y. Nir-El and M. Broshi, "The Black Ink of the Qumran Scrolls," *DSD* 3 (1996) 157–67

Oesch, *Petucha und Setuma*

> J. M. Oesch, *Petucha und Setuma, Untersuchungen zu einer überlieferten Gliederung im hebräischen Text des Alten Testament* (OBO 27; Freiburg/Göttingen 1979)

—, "Textgliederung"

> —, "Textgliederung im Alten Testament und in den Qumranhandschriften," *Henoch* 5 (1983) 289–321

Olley, "Structure"

> J. W. Olley, "'Hear the Word of YHWH': The Structure of the Book of Isaiah in 1QIsaᵃ," *VT* 43 (1993) 19–49

Parry–Qimron, *Isaiah*

> D. W. Parry and E. Qimron, *The Great Isaiah Scroll (1QIsaᵃ): A New Edition* (STDJ 32; Leiden/Boston/Cologne 1999)

Parry–Ricks, *Current Research*

> D. W. Parry and S. D. Ricks, *Current Research and Technological Developments on the Dead Sea Scrolls* (STDJ 20; Leiden/New York/Cologne 1996)

Paul, *Emanuel*

> *Emanuel, Studies in Hebrew Bible, Septuagint, and Dead Sea Scrolls in Honor of Emanuel Tov* (ed. S. M. Paul, R. A. Kraft, L. H. Schiffman, and W. W. Fields, with the assistance of E. Ben-David; VTSup 94; Leiden/Boston 2003)

Pérez Castro, *Séfer Abiša‵*

> F. Pérez Castro, *Séfer Abiša‵* (Textos y Estudios del Seminario Filologico Cardenal Cisneros 2; Madrid 1959)

Perrot, "*Petuhot et setumot*"

> C. Perrot, "*Petuhot et setumot*. Étude sur les alinéas du Pentateuque," *RB* 76 (1969) 50–91

Peters, *Nash*

> N. Peters, *Die älteste Abschrift der zehn Gebote der Papyrus Nash* (Freiburg im Breisgau 1905)

Pfann, "4Q298"

> S. J. Pfann, "4Q298: The Maskîl's Address to All Sons of Dawn," *JQR* 85 (1994) 203–35

—, "*Kelei Demaᶜ*"

> —, "*Kelei Demaᶜ*: Tithe Jars, Scrolls and Cookie Jars," in *Copper Scroll Studies* (ed. G. J. Brooke and Ph. R. Davies; JSPSup 40; Sheffield 2002) 163–79

Pfeiffer, *History*

> R. Pfeiffer, *History of Classical Scholarship from the Beginnings to the End of the Hellenistic Age* (Oxford 1968)

Porten–Yardeni, *TAD*

> B. Porten and A. Yardeni, *Textbook of Aramaic Documents from Ancient Egypt*, vol. 2 (Jerusalem 1989); 3 (Jerusalem 1993); 4 (Jerusalem 1999)

Posener-Kriéger, "Old Kingdom Papyri"

> P. Posener-Kriéger, "Old Kingdom Papyri: External Features," in Bierbrier, *Papyrus,* 25–41

Preliminary Concordance

R. E. Brown, J. A. Fitzmyer, W. G. Oxtoby, J. Teixidor, *A Preliminary Concordance to the Hebrew and Aramaic Fragments from Qumran Caves II–X, Including Especially the Unpublished Material from Cave IV* (Göttingen: privately printed, 1988)

Puech, "Quelques aspects"

É. Puech, "Quelques aspects de la restauration du Rouleau des Hymnes (1QH)," *JJS* 39 (1988) 38–55

Pulikottil, *Transmission*

P. Pulikottil, *Transmission of Biblical Texts in Qumran—The Case of the Large Isaiah Scroll 1QIsaᵃ* (JSOTSup 34; Sheffield 2001)

Qimron, *Grammar*

E. Qimron, *A Grammar of the Hebrew Language of the Dead Sea Scrolls* (Heb.; unpubl. Ph.D. diss., Hebrew University, Jerusalem 1976)

—, *Hebrew*

—, *The Hebrew of the Dead Sea Scrolls* (HSS 29; Atlanta, Ga. 1986)

—, *Temple Scroll*

—, *The Temple Scroll, A Critical Edition with Extensive Reconstructions* (Beer Sheva/Jerusalem 1996)

Qumran kontrovers

Qumran kontrovers–Beiträge zu den Textfunden vom Toten Meer (ed. J. Frey and H. Stegemann; Einblicke–Ergebnisse–Berichte–Reflexionen aus Tagungen der Katholischen Akademie Schwerte 6; Paderborn 2003)

Roberts, *Manuscript*

C. H. Roberts, *Manuscript, Society and Belief in Early Christian Egypt* (London 1979)

A. F. Robertson, *Word Dividers*

A. F. Robertson, *Word Dividers, Spot Markers and Clause Markers in Old Assyrian, Ugaritic, and Egyptian Texts: Sources for Understanding the Use of Red Ink Points in the Two Akkadian Literary Texts, Adapa and Ereshkigal, Found in Egypt*, unpubl. Ph.D. diss., New York University, 1993

Robertson, *Catalogue*

E. Robertson, *Catalogue of the Samaritan Manuscripts in the John Rylands Library Manchester*, vol. 1 (Manchester 1938)

Rothstein, *From Bible to Murabbaᶜat*

D. Rothstein, *From Bible to Murabbaᶜat*, unpubl. Ph.D. diss., University of California, Los Angeles 1992

Safrai, *Jewish People*

S. Safrai, *The Jewish People in the First Century—Historical Geography, Political History, Social, Cultural and Religious Life and Institutions* (ed. S. Safrai and M. Stern; CRINT, Section One, Volume Two; Assen–Amsterdam: 1976)

Sanders, *Freer*

H. A. Sanders, *The Minor Prophets in the Freer Collection and the Berlin Fragment of Genesis* (New York 1927)

Schams, *Jewish Scribes*

C. Schams, *Jewish Scribes in the Second Temple Period* (JSOTSup 291; Sheffield 1998)

Schiffman, *Sectarian Law*

    L. H. Schiffman, *Sectarian Law in the Dead Sea Scrolls: Courts, Testimony and the Penal Code* (BJS 33; Chico, Calif. 1983)

—, *Jerusalem Congress*

    The Dead Sea Scrolls: Fifty Years After Their Discovery: Proceedings of the Jerusalem Congress, July 20–25, 1997 (ed. L. Schiffman et al.; Jerusalem 2000)

Schubart, *Das Buch*

    W. Schubart, *Das Buch bei den Griechen und Römern* (2nd ed.; Berlin/Leipzig 1921)

—, *Palaeographie*

    —, *Griechische Palaeographie* (Munich 1966)

Siegel, *Scribes of Qumran*

    J. P. Siegel, *The Scribes of Qumran. Studies in the Early History of Jewish Scribal Customs, with Special Reference to the Qumran Biblical Scrolls and to the Tannaitic Traditions of Massekheth Soferim*, unpubl. Ph.D. diss., Brandeis University 1971 (University Microfilms, 1972)

—, "The Employment"

    —, "The Employment of Palaeo-Hebrew Characters for the Divine Names at Qumran in the Light of Tannaitic Sources," *HUCA* 42 (1971) 159–72

—, "Orthographic Convention"

    —, "An Orthographic Convention of 1QIs[a] and the Origin of Two Masoretic Anomalies," in *1972 and 1973 Proceedings IOMS* (ed. H. M. Orlinsky; Masoretic Studies 1; Missoula, Mont. 1974) 99–110

Sirat, *Ha-ketav*

    C. Sirat, *Min Ha-ketav ʾel Ha-sepher* (Jerusalem 1992)

Skehan, "The Divine Name"

    P. W. Skehan, "The Divine Name at Qumran, in the Masada Scroll, and in the Septuagint," *BIOSCS* 13 (1980) 16–44

Sperber, *Grammar*

    A. Sperber, *A Historical Grammar of Biblical Hebrew—A Presentation of Problems with Suggestions to Their Solution* (Leiden 1966)

Steck, *Jesajarolle*

    O. H. Steck, *Die erste Jesajarolle von Qumran (1QIsa): Schreibweise als Leseanleitung für ein Prophetenbuch* (SBS 173/1; Stuttgart 1998)

—, "Bemerkungen"

    —, "Bemerkungen zur Abschnittgliederung der ersten Jesajarollen von Qumran (1QIs[a]) im Vergleich mit redaktionsgeschichtlichen Beobachtungen im Jesajabuch," in *Antikes Judentum und Frühes Christentum, Festschrift für Hartmut Stegemann zum 65. Geburtstag* (ed. B. Kolbmann et al.; BZNW 97; Berlin/New York 1999) 12–28

—, "Abschnittgliederung"

    —, "Bemerkungen zur Abschnittgliederung in den Jesaja-Handschriften aus der Wüste Juda," in *Die Textfunde vom Toten Meer und der Text der Hebräischen Bibel* (ed. U. Dahmen et al.; Neukirchen-Vluyn 2000) 51–88

—, "Sachliche Akzente"

—, "Sachliche Akzente in der Paragraphos-Gliederung des Jesajatextes von 1QIsᵃ," in *Qumran kontrovers*, 147–56

Stegemann, *ΚΥΡΙΟΣ*

H. Stegemann, *ΚΥΡΙΟΣ Ο ΘΕΟΣ und ΚΥΡΙΟΣ ΙΗΣΟΥΣ: Aufkommen und Ausbreitung des religiösen Gebrauchs von ΚΥΡΙΟΣ und seine Verwendung im Neuen Testament* (Habilitationsschrift, Bonn 1969)

—, "Reconstruction"

—, "Methods for the Reconstruction of Scrolls from Scattered Fragments," in L. H. Schiffman, *Archaeology and History in the Dead Sea Scrolls: The New York University Conference in Memory of Yigael Yadin* (JSOT/ASOR Monograph Series 2; Sheffield 1990) 189–220

—, *Die Essener*

—, *Die Essener, Qumran, Johannes der Täufer und Jesus—Ein Sachbuch* (9th ed.; Freiburg/Basel/Vienna 1993)

—, *Library of Qumran*

—, *The Library of Qumran: On the Essenes, Qumran, John the Baptist, and Jesus* (Grand Rapids/ Cambridge and Leiden/New York/Cologne 1998)

Steudel, "Assembling"

A. Steudel, "Assembling and Reconstructing Manuscripts," in Flint–VanderKam, *Fifty Years*, 516–34

Strack, *Prolegomena*

H. L. Strack, *Prolegomena critica in Vetus Testamentum hebraicum* (Leipzig 1873)

Strugnell, "Notes"

J. Strugnell, "Notes en marge du Volume V des 'Discoveries in the Judaean Desert of Jordan'", *RevQ* 7 (1970) 163–276

Sukenik, *Mgylwt gnwzwt*

E. L. Sukenik, *ʾwṣr hmgylwt hgnwzwt šbydy hʾwnybrsyṭh hʿbryt* (Jerusalem 1954)

—, *Dead Sea Scrolls*

—, *The Dead Sea Scrolls of the Hebrew University* (Jerusalem 1955)

Sussmann–Peled, *Scrolls*

A. Sussmann and R. Peled, *Scrolls from the Dead Sea: An Exhibition of Scrolls and Archeological Artifacts from the Collections of the Israel Antiquities Authority* (Washington 1993)

Talmon, *Masada VI* see: *Masada VI*

Tait, "Guidelines"

W. J. Tait, "Guidelines and Borders in Demotic Papyri," in Bierbrier, *Papyrus*, 63–89

Taylor, *IX Congress*

IX Congress of the International Organization for Septuagint and Cognate Studies, Cambridge, 1995 (ed. B. A. Taylor; SCS 45; Atlanta, Ga. 1995)

Threatte, *Attic Inscriptions*

L. Threatte, *The Grammar of Attic Inscriptions I, Phonology* (Berlin/New York 1980)

Tigchelaar, "The Scribe of 1QS"

E. J. C. Tigchelaar, "In Search of the Scribe of 1QS," in Paul, *Emanuel*, 439–52

Tov, "Orthography"
> E. Tov, "The Orthography and Language of the Hebrew Scrolls Found at Qumran and the Origin of These Scrolls," *Textus* 13 (1986) 31–57

—, "Hebrew Biblical Manuscripts"
> —, "Hebrew Biblical Manuscripts from the Judaean Desert: Their Contribution to Textual Criticism," *JJS* 39 (1988) 5–37

—, "Corrections"
> —, "The Textual Base of the Corrections in the Biblical Texts Found at Qumran," *The Dead Sea Scrolls: Forty Years of Research* (ed. D. Dimant and U. Rappaport; Leiden/Jerusalem 1992) 299–314

—, *Greek and Hebrew Bible*
> —, *The Greek and Hebrew Bible: Collected Essays on the Septuagint* (VTSup 72; Leiden 1999)

—, "Further Evidence"
> "Further Evidence for the Existence of a Qumran Scribal School," in Schiffman, *Jerusalem Congress*, 199–216

—, *TCHB*
> —, *Textual Criticism of the Hebrew Bible* (2nd rev. ed.; Minneapolis and Assen/Maastricht 2001)

—, "Greek Biblical Texts"
> —, "The Greek Biblical Texts from the Judean Desert," in *The Bible as Book: The Transmission of the Greek Text* (ed. S. McKendrick and O. A. O'Sullivan; London 2003) 97–122

—, "Masada"
> "A Qumran Origin for the Masada Nonbiblical Texts?," *DSD* 7 (2000) 57–73

—, "Greek Texts"
> "The Nature of the Greek Texts from the Judean Desert," *NovT* 43 (2001) 1–11

Tov–Pfann, *Companion Volume*
> E. Tov with the collaboration of S. J. Pfann, *Companion Volume to the Dead Sea Scrolls Microfiche Edition* (2nd rev. ed.; Leiden 1995)

Trebolle–Vegas, *The Madrid Qumran Congress*
> *The Madrid Qumran Congress: Proceedings of the International Congress on the Dead Sea Scrolls: Madrid, 18–21 March, 1991* (ed. J. Trebolle Barrera and L. Vegas Montaner; STDJ 11; Leiden/Madrid 1992)

Turner, *Greek Papyri*
> E. G. Turner, *Greek Papyri: An Introduction* (Princeton 1968)

—, *Greek Manuscripts*
> —, *Greek Manuscripts of the Ancient World* (2nd ed., revised and enlarged by P. J. Parsons; Institute of Classical Studies, Bulletin Supplement 46; London 1987)

Ulrich, "4QSam^c"
> E. Ulrich, "4QSam^c: A Fragmentary Manuscript of 2 Samuel 14–15 from the Scribe of the *Serek Hayyaḥad* (1QS)," *BASOR* 235 (1979) 1–25

—, *The Dead Sea Scrolls*
—, *The Dead Sea Scrolls and the Origins of the Bible* (Grand Rapids/Leiden 1999)

VanderKam–Flint, *Meaning DSS*
J. VanderKam and P. Flint, *The Meaning of the Dead Sea Scrolls—Their Significance for Understanding the Bible, Judaism, Jesus, and Christianity* (San Francisco 2002)

Van der Ploeg–Van der Woude, *Targum Job*
J. P. M. van der Ploeg–A. S. van der Woude, *Le Targum de Job* (Leiden 1971)

Van Haelst, *Catalogue*
J. Van Haelst, *Catalogue des papyrus littéraires juifs et chrétiens* (Paris 1976)

Webster, "Chronological Index"
B. Webster, "Chronological Index of the Texts from the Judaean Desert," *DJD* XXXIX, 351–446

Wenke, "Ancient Egypt"
E. F. Wenke, "The Scribes of Ancient Egypt," in *CANE* (ed. M. Sasson; New York 1995) IV.2211–21

Wise, *Thunder in Gemini*
M. O. Wise, *Thunder in Gemini, and Other Essays on the History, Language and Literature of Second Temple Palestine* (JSPSup 15; Sheffield 1994)

Yadin, *War Scroll*
Y. Yadin, *The Scroll of the War of the Sons of Light* (Heb.; Jerusalem 1955)

—, *Ben Sira*
—, *The Ben Sira Scroll from Masada, With Introduction, Emendations and Commentary* (Jerusalem 1965) = *ErIsr* 8 (1965) 1–45; rev. ed.: Yadin, *Ben Sira* 1999 (see below)

—, *Tefillin*
—, *Tefillin from Qumran (X Q Phyl 1–4)* (Jerusalem 1969) = *ErIsr* 9 (1969) 60–85

—, *Temple Scroll (Hebrew)*
—, *The Temple Scroll*, vols. 1–3 (Heb.; Jerusalem 1977)

—, *Temple Scroll*
—, *The Temple Scroll*, vols. 1–3 (Jerusalem 1983)

—, *Ben Sira* 1999
Y. Yadin, *The Ben Sira Scroll from Masada* in *Masada VI*, 151–252

Yardeni, *Textbook*
A. Yardeni, *Textbook of Aramaic, Hebrew and Nabatean Documentary Texts from the Judaean Desert and Related Material*, vols. I–II (Jerusalem 2000)

FIGURES

For the sake of clarity, some of the signs have been enlarged

Fig. **1.1** 1QIsa^a XXIII 26 (Isa 29:12) *paragraphos*	Fig. **1.2** 1QIsa^a LI 27 (Isa 65:1) *paragraphos*	Fig. **1.3** **a.** 4QTest (4Q175) 14 **b.** 1QSa II 22 **c.** 4QpapPrQuot (4Q503) 1 ii 6 *paragraphos*	Fig. **1.4** 4QNon-Canonical Psalms A (4Q380) 1 7 *paragraphos*
Fig. **1.5** MasSir II 8 *paragraphos*	Fig. **1.6** **a.** 1QIsa^a XXVIII 23 (Isa 36:1) **b.** 1QIsa^a XXXII 29 (Isa 40:1) **c.** 1QIsa^a XXXV 23 (Isa 42:13) *composite paragraphos*	Fig. **1.7** **a.** 4QTanḥ (4Q176) 1–2 i 4 *paragraphos* **b.** 1QS III 19 *paragraphos* ('fish hook')	Fig. **2.1** 1QIsa^a III 3, 22 (Isa 3:1, 16) *section marker*
Fig. **2.2** **a.** 4QOrd^b (4Q513) 13 2, 4 **b.** 4QDibHam^a (4Q504) 1–2 vii 4 *section markers*	Fig. **3** **a.** Court record *TAD* 2, B8.5 **b.** Ahiqar VI 1, 88 (*TAD* 3) *section markers in Aramaic texts*	Fig. **4** 4QpIsa^c (4Q163) 4–7 ii 10 *paleo-Heb. ʾaleph*	Fig. **5.1** 4QpaleoExod^m round patch, col. VIII 2 See illustr. 21. *paleo-Hebrew waw*
Fig. **5.2** 4QPs^b V 16 (Ps 93:5) *paleo-Hebrew waw*	Fig. **5.3** 11QpaleoLev^a frg. J 1 (Lev 20:1) See illustr. 27. *paleo-Hebrew waw*	Fig. **5.4** 1QIsa^a VI 22 (Isa 7:8) *paleo-Hebrew waw*	Fig. **5.5** 1QS V 1 *paleo-Hebrew waw*

Fig. 5.6 4QMess. Apoc. (4Q521) 2 ii 4 *section marker?*	**Fig. 5.7** 4QInstr^d (4Q418) 67 3 between cols. i and ii *paleo-Hebrew ʾaleph?*	**Fig. 5.8** 4QTime of Righteousness (4Q215a) 1 i, end of line 9 *nature of sign unclear*	**Fig. 5.9** 4QInstr^b (4Q416) 2 ii 6 See fig. 10.4. *nature of sign unclear*
Fig. 6.1 1QIsa^a XXVIII 28 (Isa 35:10) See illustr. 6. *cancellation dots above letters*	**Fig. 6.2** 1QIsa^a XXXIII 7 (Isa 40:7) See illustr. 1. *cancellation dots below letters*	**Fig. 6.3** 1QIsa^a X 23 (Isa 11:4) *cancellation dots above and below letters*	
Fig. 6.4 1QIsa^a XLI 14 (Isa 49:14) *cancellation dots to the right and left of a supralinear addition*	**Fig. 7** 1QIsa^a XI 10 (Isa 12:6) *crossing out of* בת *with supralinear addition of* יושבת	**Fig. 8.1** 1QM III 1 *parenthesis signs used for omission*	**Fig. 8.2** 4QQoh^a II 1 top margin (Qoh 6:4) *parenthesis signs used for marginal insertion (cf. fig. 9)*
Fig. 8.3 4QEn^a (4Q201) II 1 *omission or insertion*	**Fig. 9** 4QTob^a 6 8 (Tob 3:13) *insertion*	**Fig. 10.1** **a.** 1QIsa^a VII 7–8 (Isa 7:20) **b.** 4QcryptA Words of the Maskil (4Q298) 3–4 ii 5 *Cryptic A resh*	**Fig. 10.2** **a.** 1QIsa^a VIII 9 (Isa 8:16) **b.** 4Q298 1–2 i 4 *Cryptic A ḥeth*

Fig. **10.3**
a. 1QIsaᵃ XI 4
(Isa 11:15)
b. 4Q298 1–2 i 4

Cryptic A qoph

Fig. **10.4**
a. 1QIsaᵃ XVII 1
(Isa 21:16)
b. 1QIsaᵃ XXVIII 18
(Isa 34:17) cf. illustr. 6
c. 4Q298 3–4 ii 6
Cryptic A kaph

Fig. **10.5**
a. 1QIsaᵃ XXI 23
(Isa 27:13)
b. 4Q298 3–4 ii 6

Cryptic A ṣade

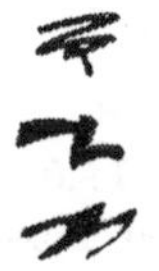

Fig. **10.6**
a. 1QIsaᵃ XXVII 21
(Isa 33:19)
b. 4Q298 3–4 ii 4
Cryptic A zayin
c. 1QpaleoLev frg. 2 5
paleo-Hebrew zayin

Fig. **10.7**
a. 1QIsaᵃ XXXIII 1
(Isa 40:2)
See illustr. 1.
b. 1QIsaᵃ XL 19 (Isa 48:14)

See figs. 10.6b, c.

Fig. **10.8**
a. 4QInstrᶜ (4Q417) 1
i 23
b. 4QpapTobᵃ ar
(4Q196) 35

See fig. 10.4c.

Fig. **10.9**
a. 4QDibHamᵃ
(4Q504) 1–2 v 3
b. 4Q298 frgs. 3–4 ii 7

Cryptic A mem

Fig. **10.10**
a. 4QMystᶜ? (4Q301) 3
2–4
b. 4QcryptA Lunisolar
Calendar (4Q317) 5 4
Cryptic A samekh
c. 4Q317 5 10
Cryptic A ʿayin

Fig. **10.11**
a. 4QExodᵏ top margin
b. 4QcryptA Phases of
the Moon (4Q317)
2 i 10
Cryptic A lamed

Fig. **10.12**
4QShirᵇ (4Q511) 18 iii
8
See figs. 10.6, 10.7.
Cryptic A or paleo-Hebrew zayin

Fig. **11**
1QS VII bottom
margin

paleo-Hebrew zayin + undetermined sign

Fig. **11.1**
1QIsaᵃ XXII 10
(Isa 28:9)

paleo-Hebrew zayin

Fig. **11.2**
a. 1QS IX 3
paragraphos + paleo-Hebrew zayin + paleo-Hebrew samekh
b. 4QHoroscope
(4Q186) 1 i 5
paleo-Hebrew samekh

Fig. **11.3**
5QLamᵃ II bottom
margin

paleo-Hebrew waw?

Fig. **11.4**
4Qpap pIsaᶜ (4Q163)
4–7 ii 18

paleo-Hebrew sin/shin

Fig. **11.5**
4QpapMMTᵉ (4Q398)
14–17 i 4

paleo-Hebrew ʾaleph?

Fig. 11.6 4QHistorical Text E (4Q333) 1 2, end of line *line-filler or section marker?*	**Fig.12.1** 4QCant^b 1 4 See illustr. 28. *paleo-Hebrew zayin?*	**Fig. 12.2** 4QCant^b 1 7 See illustr. 28. *paleo-Hebrew ʿayin or Cryptic A kaph (fig. 10.4c)?*	**Fig. 12.3** 4QCant^b 1 9 See illustr. 28. *epsilon denoting omission/addition?* See fig. 15.1.
Fig. 12.4 4QCant^b 1 11 See illustr. 28. *paleo-Hebrew sin/shin or sigma?*	**Fig. 12.5** 4QCant^b 1 13 See illustr. 28. *paleo-Hebrew bet?*	**Fig. 12.6** 4QCant^b 3, last line See illustr. 28. *gamma or diple obelismene?*	**Fig. 13** **a.** 1QIsa^a III 6 (Isa 3:4) **b.** 1QIsa^a XX 10 (Isa 25:11) *line-fillers*
Fig. 14 Epiphanius, *On Weights and Measures*, p. 47b of the Syriac ms. (see n. 258)	**Fig. 15** MasSir V, top margin *section marker? numbering device?*	**Fig. 15.1** *ancora (inferior) omission/addition sign in the Greek scribal tradition*	**Fig. 16** 1QIsa^a XXXII (under Isa 40:1-2), bottom margin *scribble?*
Fig. 17 1QS XI 15 See fig. 23. *separation dot between words*	**Fig. 18** 4QpapHodayot-like Text B (4Q433a) 2 2 *section marker*	**Fig. 19** 4QTest (4Q175) 1 *Tetrapuncta*	**Fig. 20** MasDeut, line 5 above the first letter of קדקד (Deut 33:20) *nature of sign unclear*
Fig. 21 1QpHab IV 12 before the line *matter of special interest*	**Fig. 22.1** 4QCatena A (4Q177) 13 ii 9 *marks indentation?*	**Fig. 22.2** 1QIsa^a XXVI 9 (Isa 32:1) *matter of special interest*	**Fig. 22.3** XHev/Se papDeed of Sale E ar (XHev/Se 21) a 12 *cancels open section*

ϟ	✗	✗	יֹחתֹּרְֵדִיוֹתֹ
Fig. 22.4	**Fig. 22.5**	**Fig. 22.6**	**Fig. 23**
4QCommGen A (4Q252) I 4	11QT^b (11Q20) IV 9	1QpHab III 12 See illustr. **3**.	1QIsa^a XXVI 10 See fig. 17.
indicates that space is not an 'open section'	*indicates that space is not an 'open section'*	*indicates that space is not an 'open section'*	*re-divison of words*
⋏	⋏	ⸯ	н
Fig. 24.1	**Fig. 24.2**	**Fig. 24.3**	**Fig. 25**
4QS^b (4Q256) frg. 4, upper right margin (*gimel*)	4QD^a (4Q266) frg. 1a right margin (*ᵓaleph?*)	4QM^c (4Q493), right top corner (*waw?*)	4QDeut^b I 15, end of the line
numbering device	*numbering device?*	*numbering device?*	*nature of sign unclear*
𐤉𐤄𐤅𐤄	𐤉𐤄𐤅𐤄	لىل	
Fig. 26	**Fig. 27**	**Fig. 28**	
1QpHab X 14 See illustr. **3**.	11QPs^a II 4	4QpPs^b (4Q173) 5 4	
paleo-Hebrew Tetragrammaton	*paleo-Hebrew Tetragrammaton*	*Greek and Latin letters in mirror writing:* לאל	

INDEX I: ANCIENT SOURCES

2. JUDEAN DESERT TEXTS

The texts are arranged by site and cave, and within each cave alphabetically with the inventory number provided in parenthesis

See also Index II, 'Qumran,' 'Masada,' etc.

Hebrew/Aramaic Scripture

Nonbiblical Texts

3. ANCIENT BIBLICAL TRANSLATIONS

Greek

Targumim

4. RABBINIC AND MEDIEVAL JEWISH LITERATURE

5. OTHER SOURCES

Inscriptions and Ostraca

Classical Literature

Apocrypha and Pseudepigrapha

New Testament

Josephus

Additional Sources

INDEX II: SUBJECTS

ILLUSTRATIONS

Photographs are 1:1, unless indicated otherwise

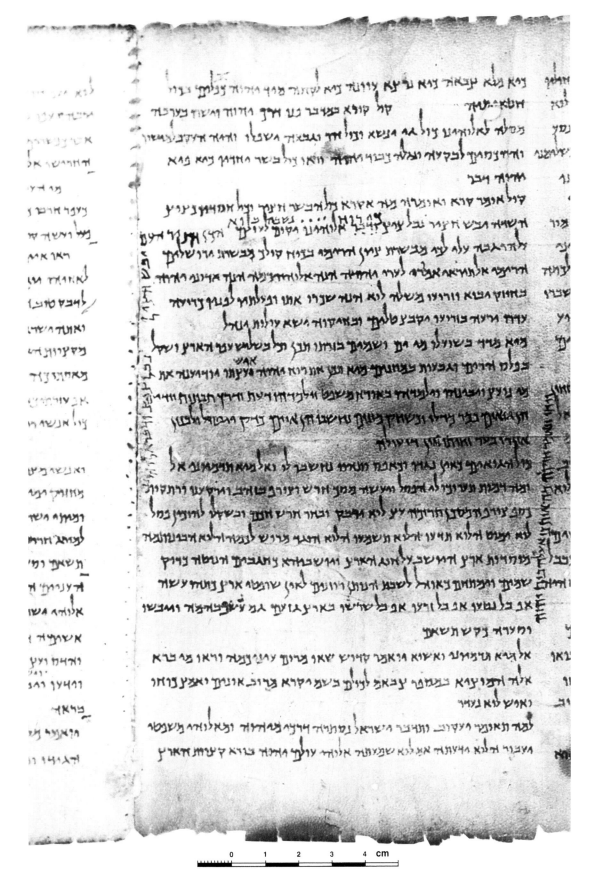

1. 1QIsaᵃ col. XXXIII (Isa 40:2-28), publication: Parry–Qimron, *Isaiah*. Open sections (ch. *5a2*) are indicated in lines 5, 11, 16, 24, 27 and there is a closed section in line 2. A segment of the text which was omitted mistakenly by the first scribe in line 7 (Isa 40:7b-8a) was added by a second scribe above the line and vertically in the left margin. In this added section, cancellation dots (ch. *5c2* and fig. 6.2) appear under one word and the Tetragrammaton is indicated by four dots (*Tetrapuncta*, see fig. 19 and ch. *5d*). The text in lines 14–16 (Isa 40:14b-16) was likewise added by a second hand. For the scribal sign above line 1, see fig. 10.7 and ch. *5c3*. Several non-final letters are used in final position (see especially the *pe, sadi,* and *mem* in line 23). The remains of threads and the stitches show how this sheet was combined with that following. Photograph Israel Museum.

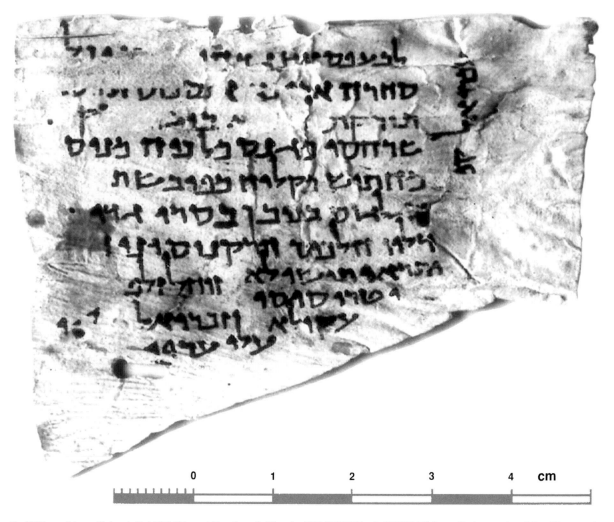

2. 4QExercitium Calami C (4Q341), publication: J. Naveh, *DJD* XXXVI, pl. XVIII. This scribal exercise (ch. *2b*) contains a sequence of proper names starting with the letter *mem*, a series of words, mainly proper names, in alphabetical order from *bet* to *zayin*, and sequences of single letters. The last lines of this document were shortened in accordance with the slanting bottom margin. The irregular shape of this fragment (ch. *3b,c*) shows that it was probably no more than a scrap of leather, a remnant left after a large rectangular sheet had been cut from a hide for a regular scroll (see illustr. 9). Photograph PAM 43.407.

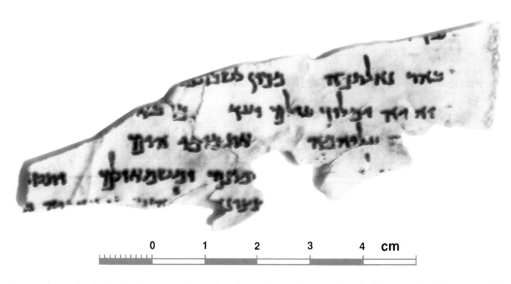

2a. 4QRP^c (4Q365) frg. 6b 1–4 (Exod 15:16-19), publication: Tov–White, *DJD* XIII, pl. XXIII. In this poem, clusters of 2–3 words are separated by spaces (ch. *5b*). The purpose of the guide dots to the right of the column was to guide the drawing of the dry lines (ch. *4a* and illustrations 10a and 15). Photograph PAM 43.373.

3. 1QpHab cols. XI–XII, publication: Burrows, *The Dead Sea Scrolls*, pl. LX. Horizontal and vertical lines are neatly drawn (ch. *4a*). Scribe A wrote the major part of this scroll up to col. XII 13, and scribe B took over in the middle of that line. Scribe B, writing with larger characters, completed the composition by finishing that column and inscribing only four lines of col. XIII. The X-sign in col. XII 2, written flush with the left vertical ruled line (ch. *5c6* and fig. 22.6), indicates that the space at the end of the line should not be mistaken as an 'open section.' Every column in the second sheet of 1QpHab (cols. VIII–XIII) has a top margin with three ruled lines, a rather unusual feature among the Judean Desert texts. The manufacturer of this scroll must have used an existing ruled sheet of larger size than needed for the second sheet of this scroll. When preparing this scroll, he cut the sheet to the size required for the present purpose, cutting off the unruled top margin of that sheet, and using the ruled area as the top margin for the new scroll (ch. *3b*). A similar procedure was followed for the first sheet of 4QDeut^n (see illustr. 15) which was cut to the size of the second sheet. The Tetragrammaton in col. XI 10 is written in the paleo-Hebrew script, as was the custom in several nonbiblical and a few biblical scrolls (ch. *6b2*). For the spacing before each *pesher*, see APPENDIX 7. Photograph J. C. Trever in Burrows, *The Dead Sea Scrolls*, pl. LX with the permission of the Israel Museum.

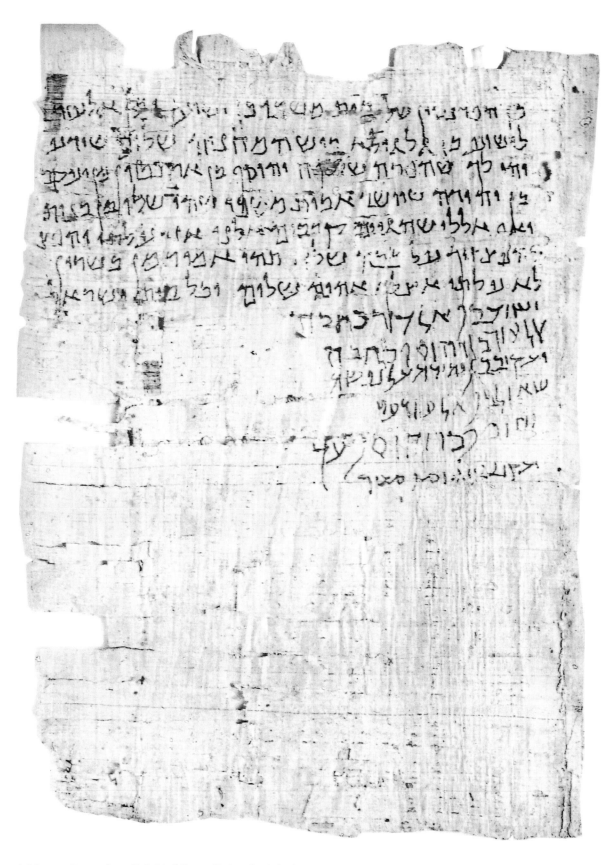

4. Mur papLetter from Beit-Mashiko to Yeshua b. Galgula (Mur 42), publication: J. T. Milik, *DJD* II, pl. XLV. A letter written by the administrators of Beth Mashiko to Yeshuaᶜ ben Galgula. The letter itself is well written by a skilled hand, while the signatures are irregular. The word written partially at the end of line 5 was repeated in full on the following line (ch. *4f*). Photograph PAM 42.553.

5. Ostracon 3 from Khirbet Qumran, publication: E. Eshel, *DJD* XXXVI, pl. XXXIV. This abecedary represents a scribal exercise probably pointing to a learning process for scribes at Qumran (ch. *2b*). Photograph PAM 40.405.

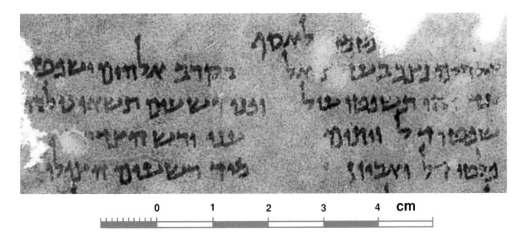

5a. MasPs[a], col. II 3–7 (Ps 82:1-4), publication: S. Talmon, *Masada VI*, p. 80 and illustr. 9. This manuscript presents one of the best examples of *de luxe* scrolls written beautifully in large characters and with large margins around the text (ch. *4j*). The twenty-nine lines of the text are written in a bi-columnar stichographic arrangement extending to the space between the two columns (ch. *5b*). The scribe wrote several superscriptions above the Psalms (see ch. *5a4*, *5b* and illustr. 8). In Ps 82:1, the superscription לאסף [ר]מזמו ('A Psalm of Asaph') was written on a separate, indented, line above the left side of the first column. The irregular spacing between the lines before and after this superscription suggests that these words were added after the writing of the text was completed. Photograph Israel Exploration Society.

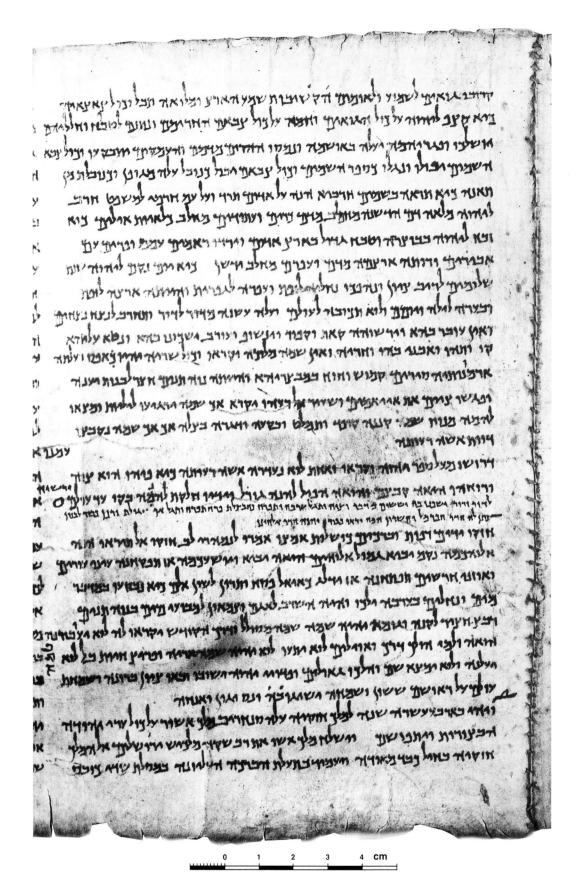

6. 1QIsaᵃ col. XXVIII (Isa 34:1–36:2), publication: Parry–Qimron, *Isaiah*. Open sections (ch. *5a2*) are indicated in lines 16 and 28 and closed sections in lines 8 and 30. This column is the first on a new sheet (ch. *3c*), marking the beginning of the segment copied by scribe B (ch. *2e*). A scribal mark is written to the left of the column, level with line 18 (ch. *5c5* and fig. 10.4). The text of Isa 34:17b–35:2 was omitted by the first scribe and added by a second scribe in smaller characters in lines 19–20. Cancellation dots (ch. *5c2* and fig. 6.1) in line 28 (Isa 35:10) remove two letters which had been written wrongly according to the corrector. In the margin of line 29 (Isa 36:1), a special sign indicates the beginning of a large unit (ch. *5c1* and fig. 1.6). Several non-final letters are used in final position. The stitching reaches until the end of the leather (ch. *2c*). Photograph Israel Museum.

7. 1QH[a] col. XI according to Sukenik (= col. XIX in the arrangement of Puech, "Quelques aspects"), publication: Sukenik, *Mgylwt gnwzwt*, pl. 45. Scribe A of this scroll probably copied the text from col. I to the middle of col. XI (XIX) 22. From that point, scribe B took over for a very short stretch of text (lines 23–26), while scribe C copied col. XI (XIX) 27–35 and the remainder of the scroll (ch. 2 TABLE 1). Photograph Sukenik, *Mgylwt gnwzwt*, pl. 45 with the permission of the Israel Museum.

8. 4QPs^e frg. 26 col. i (Ps 125:2–126:5), publication: Skehan–Ulrich–Flint, *DJD* XVI, pl. XII. In line 6, representing the beginning of Psalm 126, שור המעלות was added secondarily between the lines as a superscription above the first line of the Psalm, partly above the space separating Psalms 125 and 126. See ch. *5a4*, *5b* and illustr. 5a. Photograph PAM 43.026.

8a. 4QCant^b frg. 1 (Cant 2:9–3:2), publication: E. Tov, *DJD* XVI, pl. XXV. The proportionally largest number of signs in the Qumran texts is found in this text, involving paleo-Hebrew, Greek, and Cryptic A letters in lines 4, 7, 9, 11, 13 (ch. *5c5*). See also figs. 12.1–6. Stitches in the bottom margins with remains of thread show repair (ch. *4i*). Stitches to the left of the column indicate where the sheet was attached to that following. Photograph PAM 41.277.

9. 4QPhyl J verso (4Q137), publication: J. T. Milik, *DJD* VI, pl. XIX. In this and other *tefillin*, in order to economize on space, no gaps were left between the words, although final letters were employed at the ends of words (ch. *7c*). The irregular shape of this fragment indicates that this *tefillin* was inscribed on a scrap of leather, a remnant left after a large rectangular sheet had been cut from a hide for a regular scroll (see ch. *3b* and illustr. 2). The unusual shape of the leather necessitated the writing of long lines at the beginning of the text and very short lines at the end. The space in the middle separates two segments of the *tefillin*. The sequence of the text is as follows: after the space in the middle of the text, the fragment presents Deut 5:24-[28], continued at the top of the fragment by Deut 5:29-32 (five lines upside down) and Deut 6:2-3 (4 lines of regular writing). Photograph PAM 43.453.

10. 4QIncantation (4Q444), publication: E. Chazon, *DJD* XXIX, pl. XXVI. In this document, three tiny fragments of leather of four lines each were stitched together one above the other, rather than horizontally, as in all other Qumran scrolls (ch. *3c*). Photograph PAM 43.539.

10a. 4QShirShabb^f (4Q405) frgs. 17, 19a, publication: E. Schuller, *DJD* XI, pl. XXIV. The purpose of the guide dots to the right and left of the column was to guide the drawing of dry lines (ch. *4a* and illustrations 2a and 15). In very few instances, such as in the present scroll, these guide dots were indicated in the intercolumnar margin in the middle of a sheet. Photographs PAM 43.497 (frg. 17), 43.498 (frg. 19a).

11. 4Qapocryphal Psalm and Prayer (4Q448), publication: Eshel–Eshel–Yardeni, *DJD* XI, pl. XXXII. The preserved segment of this scroll was written by two different hands (scribe A wrote col. I [upper section] and scribe B wrote cols. II and III [lower section]), see ch. *2e*. When rolled, this scroll was fastened with a thong (ch. *2d*) connected to the reinforcing tab stuck to the scroll itself, at its beginning (shown on the photograph). The layout of the columns was arranged in the present way in order to enable the attachment of the tab. The title הללויה was written in the margin. A *paragraphos* sign was written in col. I between lines 2 and 3. Photograph PAM 43.545.

11a. 4QDibHam^a (4Q504) frg. 8 verso, publication: M. Baillet, *DJD* VII, pl. XLIX. The title of this composition, דברי המאורות, was written on the verso perpendicular to the writing of the first inscribed sheet, towards the right edge of frg. 8, probably containing the beginning of that composition (ch. *4g*). Photograph PAM 43.613.

12. 4QD[e] (4Q270) frg. 7, publication: J. Baumgarten, *DJD* XVIII, pl. XXXV. This fragment displays the end of this composition. The last column that is ruled after the end of the composition, is followed by an uninscribed ruled area (ch. *4g*). This shows that the manufacturer or scribe prepared the scroll without knowing the exact length of the text to be inscribed (ch. *3d*). Photograph PAM 43.298.

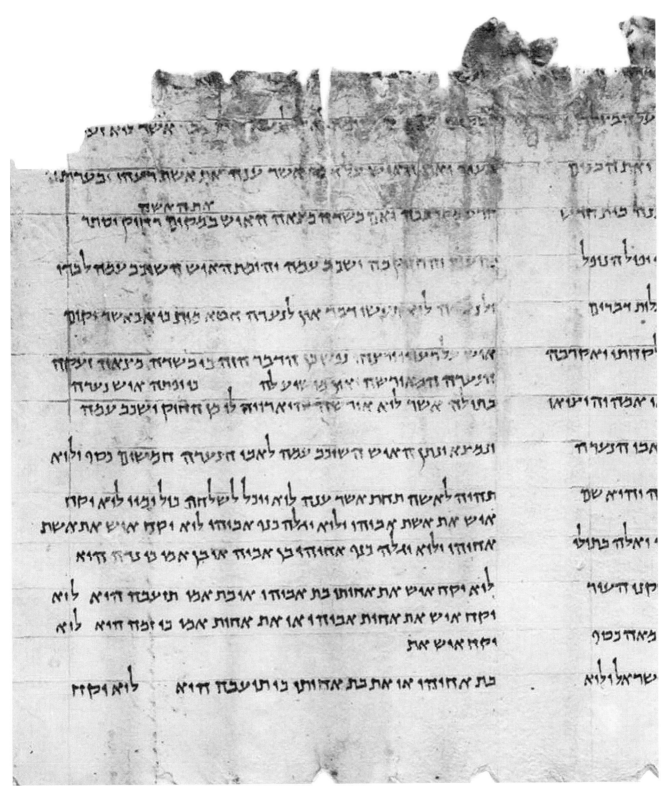

13. 11QT[a] col. LXVI, publication: Yadin, *Temple Scroll*, pl. 81. Horizontal and vertical lines are neatly drawn in each column (ch. *4a*). In this column the scribe of 11QT[a] sometimes wrote two lines (lines 7–8, 11–12, 14–15) instead of one between the ruled lines with the intent of finishing the writing at the bottom of that column. However, upon reaching the penultimate line, he realized that he had erred in his calculation and had surplus space left. He therefore left most of line 16 open and added some space towards the end of line 17. The top part of the last column (LXVII) has not been preserved. The imprint of the stitching of the previous sheet is clearly visible towards the ends of the lines (ch. *3d*). Photograph Israel Museum.

14. 4QpaleoExod^m col. VIII, patch (Exod 11:8–12:2), publication: Skehan–Ulrich–Sanderson, *DJD* IX, pl. XI. The patch was sewn on from the back of the manuscript, as is clear from the partially written words on the patch written within the stitching and blank rims of the patch (ch. *4i*), continued in the main text of the manuscript which has not been preserved. The patch shares with the main manuscript the length of lines and the distinctive use of the *waw* in closed sections (fig. 5.1) when the next word would have started with a conversive *waw*. See ch. *5c1* and illustr. 14a. The results of AMS analysis (Jull and others, "Radiocarbon Dating") may point to a slightly later date for the patch (between 98 BCE and 13 CE) than for the scroll itself (between 159 BCE and 16 CE). Photograph PAM 42.648.

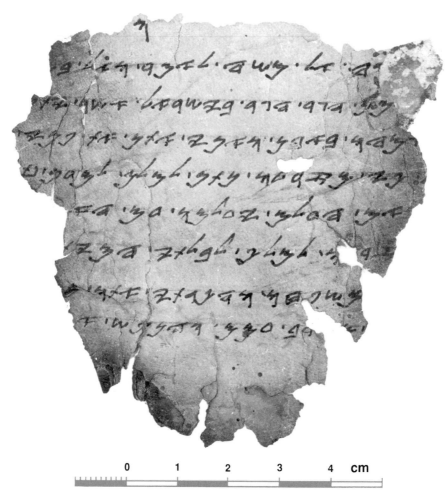

14a. 11QpaleoLev^a frg. J (Lev 20:1-6), publication: Freedman–Mathews, *Leviticus*, pl. 13. Line 1 displays a single *waw* in the middle of an open section (to be combined with the first word after the space in the next line) probably indicating a major division. See ch. *5c1*, illustr. 14, and fig. 5.3. Photograph PAM 42.174 (top right).

0   1   2   3   4   cm

15. 4QDeut^n, sheets 1 (col. I) and 2 (cols. II–VI), publication: S. Crawford, *DJD* XIV, pls. XXVIII–XXIX. Col. I contains fifteen ruled lines but only a block of eight are inscribed. Line 5 is empty and there is one empty ruled line above and six below the text. Thus this sheet was prepared originally for a larger scroll, and was subsequently adapted to the needs of 4QDeut^n (see ch. 3–d and illustr. 3). Likewise, the first column of the second sheet (col. II), but not those following, has fourteen ruled but only twelve inscribed lines; the two uninscribed lines appear in what is now the bottom margin. Sheet 1 contains Deut 8:5-10, while sheet 2 contains the earlier Deut 5:1–6:1. The unusual spaces in the middle of the lines in col. III probably reflect the scribe's avoidance of surface problems on the leather (ch. 4i). The guide dots and strokes to the right of col. II, to the bottom of the sheet, were used for the purpose of guiding the drawing of the dry lines (ch. 4a and illustrations 2a and 10a). Photograph reproduced from *DJD* XIV, pls. XXVIII–XXIX (PAM 42.642?).

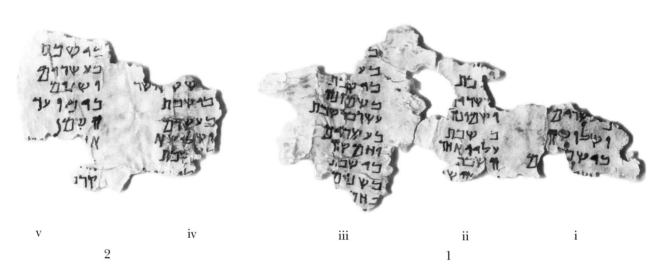

v   iv   iii   ii   i

2   1

16. 4QCal. Doc. D (4Q394) 1–2 i–v, publication: Strugnell–Qimron, *DJD* X, pl. I (as 4QMMTᵃ); republication as 4QCal. Doc. D: S. Talmon, *DJD* XXI, pl. VIII. With a width of 1.7–2.0 cm per column, this text contains the narrowest columns among the Qumran texts (ch. *4e*). Note the use of final *mem* in non-final position (col. iii 4 בשמונה, iii 7 וחמשה, v 6 השמן; see ch. *5f*). Photograph PAM 43.521.

17. 4QProphecy of Joshua (4Q522) 9–10 i-ii, publication: É. Puech, *DJD* XXV, pl. V. In these fragments, as well as in frgs. 22–24, the letters were written irregularly between, on and below the lines, and often also through them (ch. *4f*). Among other things, the scribe squeezed two lines of writing between two ruled lines (9–10 i 13–14). On the other hand, in the great majority of the Qumran texts, the letters (except for the *lamed*) were suspended from below horizontal lines in such a way that the text was written flush with these lines. Photograph PAM 43.606.

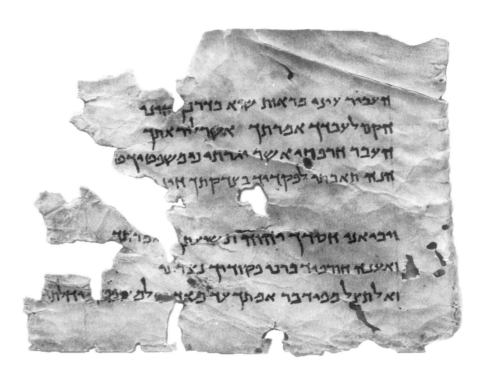

17a. 4QPs^g frg. 1 (Ps 119:39-43), publication: Skehan–Ulrich–Flint, *DJD* XVI, pl. XV. The column in this scroll of very small dimensions (8 lines) preserves four lines of the *he* stanza and three of the *waw* stanza (ch. *4e* and *5b*). The stanzas in this scroll are separated by an empty line. In most other Qumran texts, stanzas are not indicated in the Psalters. Photograph PAM 43.026.

18. 4QGen[b] (Gen 1:1-25), publication: J. Davila, *DJD* XII, pl. VII. A large handling area is found before the first column of this scroll, the beginning of Genesis (ch. *4g*). Photograph B. and K. Zuckerman.

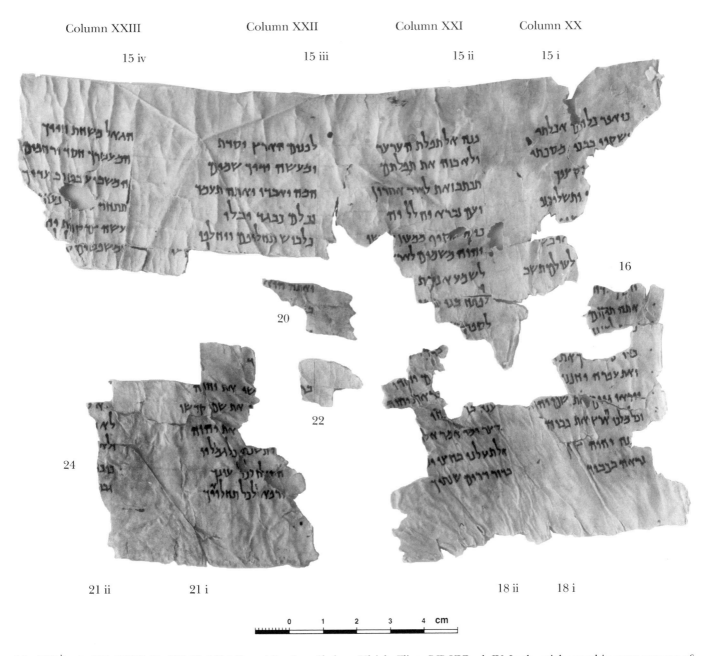

Column XXIII   Column XXII   Column XXI   Column XX

15 iv   15 iii   15 ii   15 i

16

20

22

24

21 ii   21 i   18 ii   18 i

19. 4QPs[b] cols. XX–XXIII (Ps 102:10–103:11), publication: Skehan–Ulrich–Flint, *DJD* XVI, pl. IV. In the stichographic arrangement of this text, each line contains a hemistich (system *1a* in ch. *5b*). Photograph PAM 43.032.

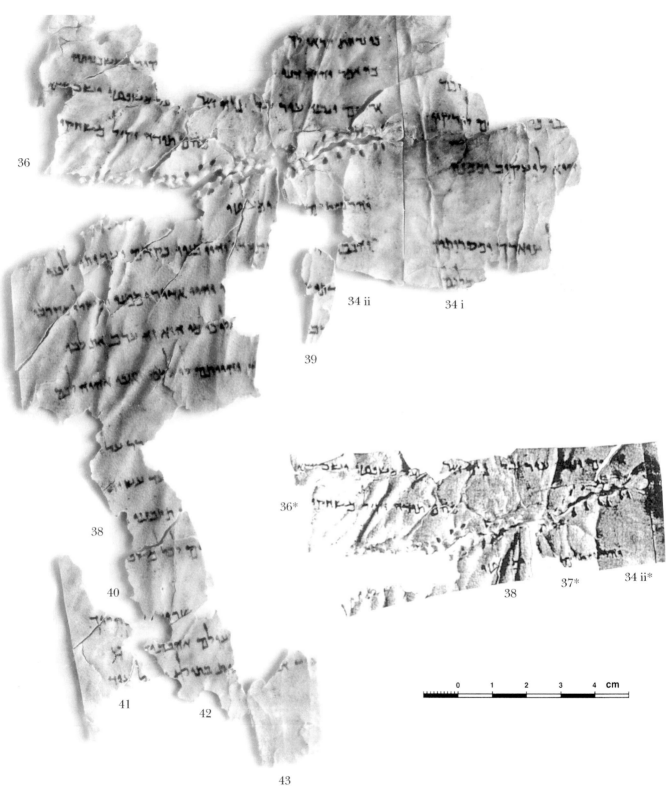

34 ii   34 i

39

36*

37*   34 ii*

38

36

38

40

41   42

43

20. 4QJer^c col. XXI (Jer 30:17–31:4), publication: Tov, *DJD* XV, pl. XXXIV. Tears in this column were stitched prior to the writing, making it necessary for the scribe to leave spaces in lines 4 and 5 in the middle of the sentence (ch. *4i*). Photographs PAM 43.103 and 43.155 (bottom right, enlargement of lines 3–5).

21. 1QIsaᵃ col. XXXVII (Isa 43:20–44:23), publication: Parry–Qimron, *Isaiah*. Open sections (ch. *5a2*) are apparent in lines 7, 11, 28 and there are many closed sections in the first lines. In addition, the beginning of line 2 is indented. A *paragraphos* sign between lines 7 and 8 indicates the open section at the end of line 7 (ch. *5c1*). The X-sign to the left of line 5 and the *paragraphos* sign with a semicircle on top at the end of line 6 indicate new sections in the next column (XXXVIII). Several non-final letters are used in final position. See ch. *5c1* and fig. 1.6. Photograph Israel Museum.